Production / Operations Management

The Irwin Series in Quantitative Analysis for Business
Consulting Editor **Robert B. Fetter** *Yale University*

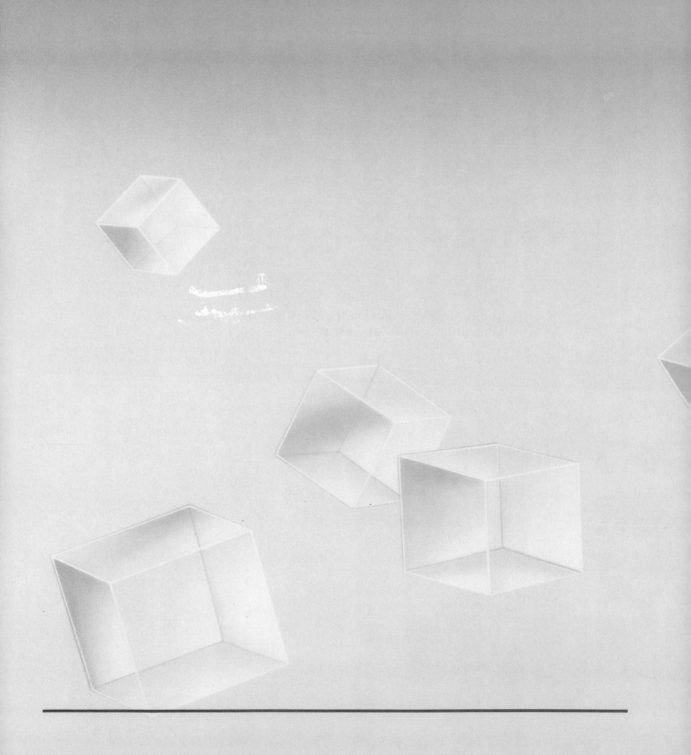

Production / Operations Management

WILLIAM J. STEVENSON

College of Business
Rochester Institute of Technology

Second Edition   1986

IRWIN

Homewood, Illinois   60430

© RICHARD D. IRWIN, INC., 1982 and 1986

All rights reserved. No part of this publication may be
reproduced, stored in a retrieval system, or transmitted,
in any form or by any means, electronic, mechanical,
photocopying, recording, or otherwise, without the prior
written permission of the publisher.

ISBN   0-256-03379-X

Library of Congress Catalog Card No. 85–82003

Printed in the United States of America

3 4 5 6 7 8 9 0 K 3 2 1 0 9 8 7 6

This book is dedicated to you.

Preface

The material in this book is intended as an introduction to the field of production and operations management. It is suitable for both undergraduate and graduate students.

The subject matter is somewhat technical in parts. It represents a blend of concepts from industrial engineering, cost accounting, general management, quantitative methods, and statistics. Even so, readers should find the material interesting and informative. Production and operations activities, such as forecasting, choosing a location for an office or plant, allocating resources, designing products and services, scheduling activities, and assuring quality are core activities of most business organizations. Very often, the majority of employees and assets of an organization are controlled by the production/operations function. Some of you are—or will be—employed directly in a production/operations capacity, while others will have jobs that are indirectly related to this area. So whether this is your field of study or not, this field will probably have an impact on your work.

Historically, production and operations management (POM) techniques developed in manufacturing organizations. However, as time went on, it became more and more apparent that nonmanufacturing organizations have to contend with problems similar to those encountered in manufacturing settings. Consequently, the scope of POM has been expanded to cover both manufacturing and service organizations. Moreover, many of the techniques can be directly applied to both areas without modification.

Since the first edition was published, new techniques and technological advances have emerged, necessitating this revised edition. Among the new or updated material are the following topics:

1. Japanese manufacturing methods.
2. Just-in-time production.
3. Cellular manufacturing.

4. Group technology.
5. Flexible manufacturing systems.
6. Robotics.
7. Computer-aided design and manufacturing.
8. MRP II.
9. Quality circles.

In addition, there are some new examples and solved problems, and approximately 40 percent of the problems are new or revised. Also, there are several new cases and readings, and several chapters have undergone major revision.

This second edition continues with many of the features of the first edition, such as:

1. Each chapter begins with an outline of topics covered and a set of learning objectives.
2. Concepts and techniques are presented in such a way that they are both interesting and fairly easy to grasp.
3. This book offers more examples, solved problems, and end-of-chapter problems than most other books. Students seem to benefit greatly from being able to review the solved problems.
4. The answers to most problems are given—but not solutions.
5. Materials and problems have been thoroughly class-tested and revised accordingly.
6. Many chapters have a short reading or a case suitable either for class discussion or for homework assignments.
7. There is a great deal of flexibility permitted in terms of depth and order of coverage of topics.
8. Manufacturing and service are integrated rather than separated.
9. Forecasting is covered early in the text (Chapter 3).
10. Productivity and quality assurance are emphasized.

The text contains more material than one could normally hope to cover in a one-semester course. Rather than relying on the author's personal bias, each instructor can choose those topics most suited to his or her own proclivities. Those who prefer quantitative emphasis, for example, will be quite comfortable with the abundance of student problems. Those who prefer a more qualitative approach will welcome the fact that some of the more quantitative material is placed in chapter supplements. Moreover, some of the chapter problems are less quantitative than others, and the cases and readings tend to be qualitative. Obviously, there are many possibilities between these two extremes.

I have gained a great deal in revising this book. I was fortunate again to have an excellent panel of reviewers who contributed significantly to the final product.

I want to thank these reviewers of this second edition for their help: Patrick Spagon, formerly of San Francisco State University, now at Frac Corporation; Ralph D. Badinelli, Virginia Polytechnic Institute and State University; Paul G. Marlin, University of Missouri–St. Louis; J. Donald Phillips, University of Alabama; Mildred Golden Pryor, Stephen F. Austin State University; Herbert Blake, California State University of Sacramento; Jack Wimer, Baylor University; Mitchell O. Locks, Oklahoma State University; and Stan Stockton, Indiana University. In addition, several of my colleagues at Rochester Institute of Technology offered suggestions for improvement, and I want to thank them: George Johnson, Erhan Mergen, Paul Van Ness, and Bob Wilferth.

I also want to mention the original set of reviewers of the first edition, and all the helpful suggestions they offered. They helped build the foundation: Suresh Chand, Purdue University; Stephen Goodman, Florida State University; Chan Hahn, Bowling Green State University; Dennis McLeavey, University of Rhode Island; Jugoslav Milutinovich, Temple University; Richard Newman, Indiana University Northwest; Hilbert Schultz, University of Wisconsin, Oshkosh; Edward Thode, New Mexico State University; Mathew Tuite, Northwestern University; Walter Warrick, Drake University; Paul Van Ness, Rochester Institute of Technology; and Eitan Zemel, Northwestern University. I also want to thank Professor Robert Fetter for his comments and encouragement. Many students also offered comments and suggestions, and many others are to be commended for suffering through revisions of problems and solutions and text material. Derek deSa of the University of Alabama did a great job in checking the accuracy of all the examples and problems.

William J. Stevenson

Note to the Student

The material in this text is part of the core knowledge in your education. Consequently, you will derive considerable benefit from your study of operations management, *regardless of your major.* Practically speaking, production and operations is a course in *management.*

After reading each chapter or supplement in the text, attending related classroom lectures, and completing assigned questions and problems, you should be able to do each of the following:

1. *Identify the key features* of that material.
2. *Define and use terminology.*
3. *Solve typical problems.*
4. *Recognize applications* of the concepts and techniques covered.
5. *Discuss the assumptions and limitations* which underlie each model or technique covered.

You will encounter a number of chapter supplements. Check with your instructor to determine whether or not to study them.

This book places an emphasis on problem solving. There are many examples throughout the text illustrating solutions. In addition, at the end of most chapters and supplements you will find a group of solved problems. The examples within the chapter itself serve to illustrate concepts and techniques. Too much detail at those points would be detrimental to learning. However, later on, when you begin to solve the end-of-chapter problems, you will find the *solved problems* quite helpful. Moreover, those solved problems usually illustrate more and different details than the problems within the chapter.

I suggest the following approach for studying and problem solving:

1. Look over the chapter outline and learning objectives.
2. Read the chapter summary.
3. Read the chapter and reread the summary.
4. Look over and try to answer the discussion and review questions.
5. Solve the problems, referring to the solved problems and chapter examples as needed.

Note that the answers to many problems are given at the end of the book. Try to solve each problem before turning to the answer. Remember—tests don't usually come with answers.

A study guide is now available. If your bookstore does not stock it, you can ask them to order it for you.

Good luck!

W. J. S.

Contents

Part I
Introduction 2

  1. **Production and Operations Management** 4
Introduction. Functions within Business Organizations: *Operations. Finance. Marketing. Other Functions.* The Operations Management Function: *Designing and Operating Production Systems. The Operations Manager and the Management Process. Productivity.* Classifying Production Systems: *Degree of Standardization. Type of Operation. Manufacturing Operations versus Service Operations. Implications for Production Systems.* Contemporary Issues and Developments.
Reading: Report from the Assembly Line: My Turn, 28

  2. **Decision Making** 32
The Decision Process: *Reasons for Poor Decisions.* Characteristics of Operations Decisions: *The Use of Models. Quantitiative Approaches. Analysis of Trade-Offs. Sensitivity Analysis. The Systems Approach. Priority Recognition. Decision Environments.* Decision Theory: *Decision Making under Certainty. Decision Making under Uncertainty. Decision Making under Risk. Decision Trees. Expected Value of Perfect Information. Sensitivity Analysis.*

Supplement to Chapter 2: Linear Programming 63
Graphical Linear Programming: *Outline of Graphical Procedure. Plotting Constraints. Identifying the Feasible Solution Space. Plotting the Objective Function Line. Solutions and Corner Points. Minimization.* The

Simplex Method: *Setting up the Initial Tableau. The Test for Optimality. Developing the Second Tableau. Developing the Third Tableau. Handling $\geq$ and $=$ Constraints. Summary of Maximization Procedure. Minimization Problems. Sensitivity Analysis.*

Part II
Forecasting   **102**

3. Forecasting   **104**
Introduction. Features Common to All Forecasts. Steps in the Forecasting Process. Approaches to Forecasting: *Forecasts Based on Judgment and Opinion. Forecasts Based on Historical Data. Associative Forecasts.* Forecasts Based on Judgment and Opinion: *Executive Opinions. Salesforce Composite. Consumer Surveys. Outside Opinion. Opinions of Managers and Staff.* Analysis of Time Series Data: *The Naive Approach. Moving Averages. Exponential Smoothing. Exponential Smoothing Adjusted for Trend. Decomposition of a Time Series. Other Techniques for Time Series.* Associative Forecasting Techniques: *Simple Linear Regression. Comments on the Use of Linear Regression Analysis. Curvilinear and Multiple Regression Analysis.* Accuracy and Control of Forecasts: *Measuring the Accuracy of Forecasts. Controlling the Forecast.* Choosing a Forecasting Technique: *Elements of a Good Forecast.* Using Forecast Information.
Case: Watch Our Forecasts Grow, 168

Part III
Design of Production Systems   **170**

4. Capacity Planning: Facilities and Equipment   **172**
Introduction. Product/Service Choices. Importance of Capacity Decisions. Defining and Measuring Capacity. Determinants of Effective Capacity. Determining Capacity Requirements: *Long-Term Considerations. Short-Term Considerations.* Developing Capacity Alternatives. Evaluating Alternatives: *Cost-Volume Analysis. Financial Analysis. Decision Theory. Queuing Theory.*

Supplement to Chapter 4: Financial Analysis 197

Terminology: *Economic Life. Net Cash Flow. Salvage Value. Depreciation. Time Value of Money.* Tax Considerations. Methods of Evaluation: *Payback Period. Net Present Value. Internal Rate of Return.*

5. **Location Planning** 214

The Need for Location Decisions. The Nature of Location Decisions: *Importance of Location Decisions. Objectives of Location Decisions. Location Options.* General Procedure for Making Location Decisions. Factors That Affect Location Decisions: *Regional Factors. Community Considerations. Site-Related Factors.* Evaluating Location Alternatives: *Locational Break-Even Analysis. The Transportation Model. Factor Rating.*

Supplement to Chapter 5: The Transportation Model 237

Introduction. Obtaining an Initial Solution: *The Northwest-Corner Method. The Vogel Approximation Method. The Intuitive Approach.* Testing for Optimality: *Evaluating Empty Cells: The Stepping-Stone Method. Evaluating Empty Cells: The MODI Method.* Obtaining an Improved Solution. Special Problems: *Unequal Supply and Demand. Degeneracy.* Summary of Procedure. Location Decisions. Other Applications.

6. **Product and Service Design** 276

The Need for Product/Service Design: *Product Life Cycles.* Research and Development. Standardization: *Modular Design. Metric Conversion.* Computer-Aided Design (CAD). Reliability: *Measuring Reliability. Improving Reliability.*
Reading: Toying with High-Tech, 305

7. **Facilities Layout** 308

Introduction: *The Need for Layout Decisions.* Types of Processing: *Continuous Processing. Intermittent Processing. Projects.* Basic Layout Types: *Product Layouts. Process Layouts. Fixed-Position Layouts. Combination Layouts.* New Approaches to Production: *Computer-Aided Manufacturing (CAM). Cellular Manufacturing. Group Technology. Flexible Manufacturing Systems.* Line Balancing: *Other Factors.* Designing Process Layouts: *Measures of Effectiveness. Information Require-*

ments. *Minimizing Transportation Costs or Distances. Closeness Ratings. Computer Analysis.*
Reading: The Technocratic Hamburger, 353

8. **Design of Work Systems**   358
    Job Design: *Specialization. Behavioral Approaches to Job Design. Automation. Sociotechnical Systems. Methods Analysis. Motion Study. Working Conditions.* Work Measurement: *Stopwatch Time Study. Standard Elemental Times. Predetermined Time Standards. Work Sampling.* Compensation: *Individual Incentive Plans. Group Incentive Plans.*
    Case: Making Hotplates, 410
    Case: Allstate Automotive Analyzers, Inc., 411

Supplement to Chapter 8: Learning Curves   415
    The Concept of Learning Curves. Applications of Learning Curves. Cautions and Criticisms.
    Case: Product Recall, 429

**Part IV
Operating and Controlling the System**   430

9. **Aggregate Planning**   432
    Introduction: *The Concept of Aggregation.* Aggregate Planning in Perspective. An Overview of Aggregate Planning. The Purpose and Scope of Aggregate Planning: *Demand and Capacity. The Purpose of Aggregate Planning. Inputs to Aggregate Planning. Decision Variables and Costs.* Basic Strategies for Meeting Uneven Demand: *Choosing a Strategy.* Techniques for Aggregate Planning: *Informal Techniques. Mathematical Techniques.* Disaggregating the Aggregate Plan.

10. **Inventory Management**   464
    Introduction: *Independent and Dependent Demand. Types of Inventories. Functions of Inventory. Objectives of Inventory Control.* Requirements for Effective Inventory Management: *Inventory Accounting Systems. Demand Forecasts and Lead-Time Information. Cost Information. Classification System.* How Much to Order: Economic-Order-Quantity Models: *Basic Economic-Order-Quantity (EOQ) Model. Economic Production Run Size. Quantity Discounts.* When to Reorder: *Constant Demand Rate and Constant Lead Time.*

Variable Demand Rates and/or Variable Lead Times. Shortages and Service Levels. How Much to Order: Fixed-Order-Interval Model: *Reasons for Using. Determining the Amount to Order. Benefits and Disadvantages.* How Much to Order: Single-Period Model: *Continuous Stocking Levels. Discrete Stocking Levels.*
Case: The Dewey Stapler Company, 527

Supplement to Chapter 10   **531**
Purchasing Interfaces. Purchasing Objectives. The Purchasing Cycle. Value Analysis. Evaluating Sources of Supply (Vendor Analysis). Centralized versus Decentralized Purchasing. Vendor Relations.

11.   **Material Requirements Planning**   **540**
Dependent versus Independent Demand. An Overview of MRP. MRP Inputs: *The Master Schedule. The Bill-of-Materials File. The Inventory-Records File.* MRP Processing: *Updating the System.* MRP Outputs. Other Considerations: *Safety Stock. Lot Sizing.* Capacity Requirements Planning. Benefits and Limitations of MRP. MRP II. The Japanese Approach: *Will It Work Here?* MRP II versus Kanban.

12.   **Scheduling**   **590**
Scheduling in High-Volume Systems. Scheduling in Intermediate-Volume Systems. Scheduling in Job Shops: *Loading. Sequencing. Sequencing Jobs through Two Work Centers. Optimized Production Technology.* Scheduling in Service Systems: *Appointment Systems. Reservation Systems. Scheduling Multiple Resources.*

13.   **Project Management**   **624**
Behavioral Aspects of Project Management: *The Nature of Projects. The Project Manager. The Pros and Cons of Working on Projects.* Planning and Scheduling with Gantt Charts. PERT and CPM: *The Network Diagram. Network Conventions.* Deterministic Time Estimates. A Computing Algorithm: *Computing ES and EF Times. Computing LS and LF Times. Computing Activity Slack Times.* Probabilistic Time Estimates. Activities on Nodes Diagrams. Simulation. Time-Cost Trade-Offs—Crashing. Advantages and Limitations of PERT.
Case: The Case of the Mexican Crazy Quilt, 668

14.   **Queuing**   672
      Why Is There Waiting? Goal of Queuing Analysis. Sys-
      tem Characteristics: *Population Source. Number of
      Servers (Channels). Arrival and Service Patterns.
      Queue Discipline.* Measures of System Performance.
      Queuing Models: Infinite–Source: *Basic Relationships.
      Model 1: Single Channel, Exponential Service Time.
      Model 2: Single Channel, Constant Service Time. Model
      3: Multiple Channel.* Queuing Model: Finite Source.
      Other Approaches.

Supplement to Chapter 14: Simulation   707
      Steps in the Simulation Process. Monte Carlo Simula-
      tion: *Simulating Theoretical Distributions.* Simulation
      Applications. Computer Simulation. Advantages and
      Limitations of Using Simulation.

15.   **Quality Assurance**   732
      Introduction: *Defining Quality.* The Importance of
      Quality. Determinants of Quality. The Evolution of
      Quality Control. Improving Quality. Quality of Confor-
      mance. Inspection: *How Much to Inspect and How Of-
      ten. Where in the Process to Inspect. Centralized versus
      On-Site Inspection. Attributes versus Variables Inspec-
      tion.* Acceptance Sampling: *Sampling Plans. Operating
      Characteristic Curve. Average Quality of Inspected
      Lots.* Process Control: *The Control Process. Variations
      and Control. Control Charts. Control Charts for Varia-
      bles. Control Charts for Attributes. Tolerances, Control
      Limits, and Process Variability. Run Tests.*
      Case: Marion Camp Memorial Hospital, 793
      Case: Anyone for Sushi? 794

Answers to Selected Problems   797

Appendix Tables   811

Index   821

Production / Operations Management

Part I

Introduction

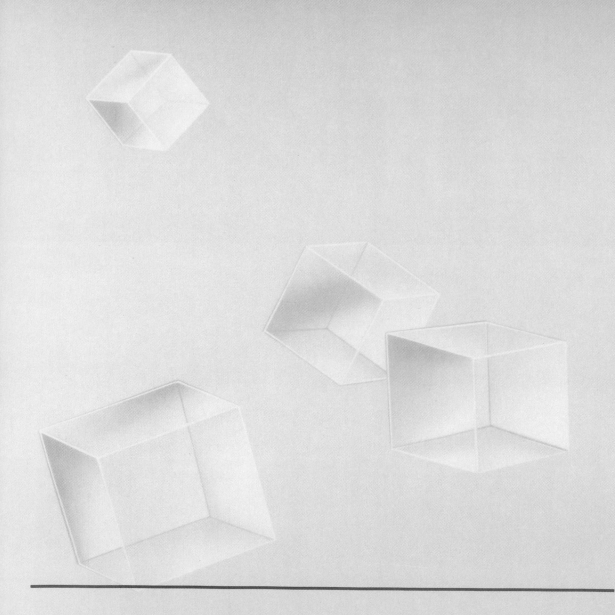

Chapter 1 outlines the nature and scope of operations management. In that chapter you will learn that operations is one of the three main functions of most organizations, along with marketing and finance; what the function of operations involves; some of the different ways operations systems are classified; and what some of the current issues in operations management are. You will also read about a topic that is causing great concern throughout the world: *productivity*.

Chapter 2 focuses on decision making, with emphasis on operations decisions. The use of linear programming as a decision tool is described in the supplement to Chapter 2.

Chapter 1

Production and Operations Management

After completing this chapter, you should be able to:

1. Define the term *operations management* and give examples.
2. Identify the three major functional areas of organizations and briefly describe how they interrelate.
3. Describe the operations function and the nature of the operations manager's job.
4. Differentiate between design and operation of production systems.
5. Discuss productivity in terms of what it is, why it is important, who is primarily responsible for it, and ways of increasing it.
6. Compare and contrast service and manufacturing.
7. Identify some of the current issues in operations management.
8. Describe the hierarchy of operations management decisions.

INTRODUCTION, 6

FUNCTIONS WITHIN BUSINESS ORGANIZATIONS, 7

Operations, 8
Finance 9
Marketing, 10
Other Functions, 11

THE OPERATIONS MANAGEMENT FUNCTION, 13

Designing and Operating Production Systems, 13
The Operations Manager and the Management Process, 15
Productivity, 16

CLASSIFYING PRODUCTION SYSTEMS, 19

Degree of Standardization, 20
Type of Operation, 20
Manufacturing Operations versus Service Operations, 21
Implications for Production Systems, 23

CONTEMPORARY ISSUES AND DEVELOPMENTS, 24

SUMMARY, 26

DISCUSSION AND REVIEW QUESTIONS, 26

SELECTED BIBLIOGRAPHY, 28

READING: REPORT FROM THE ASSEMBLY LINE, 28

This book is about production and operations management (POM). The subject matter is fascinating and very timely: productivity, quality, foreign competition, and the use of robots in manufacturing are very much in the news. These are all a part of production and operations management. This first chapter presents an introduction and overview of POM. Among the issues it addresses are: What is operations management? Why is it important? What does an operations manager do? What is productivity and why is it important? In addition to these issues, this first chapter also presents a glimpse of the remainder of the book.

The goal of the book is to present a broad conceptual framework for the management of the operations function in organizations. This first chapter lays the groundwork for the book. It begins with a brief description of the various functions of business organizations and their relationships to each other. Then the operations function is described in more detail, including a description of methods of classifying production systems and a comparison of manufacturing and service systems. The chapter concludes with a brief discussion of the major issues that are confronting POM managers today.

INTRODUCTION

To many people, the term *production* conjures up images of factories, machines, and assembly lines. Interestingly enough, the field of production management in the past focused almost exclusively on manufacturing management. Heavy emphasis was placed on methods and techniques that dealt with operating a factory. In recent years the scope of production management has broadened considerably. Currently, production concepts and techniques are being applied to a wide range of activities and situations *outside* of manufacturing (i.e., in *services*) as well as in manufacturing. Among the services are health care, food service, recreation, banking, hotel management, retail sales, education, transportation, and government. Because of this broadened scope, the field has taken on the name *operations management,* which more closely reflects the diverse nature of activities to which its concepts and techniques are applied.

Operations management is responsible for the management of productive systems; that is, it is responsible for systems that either *create goods* or *provide services* (or both). As an example of an operations management system, consider a luxury cruise ship. Most of the activities performed by the captain and crew during a cruise or in preparation for the cruise fall within the realm of operations management.

Among those activities are running the ship, managing food service, providing medical services, supervision and training of the crew, overseeing activities of passengers, and housekeeping. Navigation, maintenance, and general repairs are required to keep the ship on course and in good operating condition. Food and beverages must be ordered, meals must be prepared and served in an appetizing manner, and eating areas must be kept clean. Medical supplies must be on hand and personnel sufficiently prepared to handle a wide range of illnesses and emergencies. Motivation, training, productivity, job assignments, and personal appearance of crew members are important. Passengers must be assigned to cabins, activities must be scheduled, trips ashore at ports-of-call must be arranged, and other needs must be attended to in order to maintain satisfactory customer relations. Of course, there are other activities involved in operating a luxury ship, but this gives you some idea of the nature and scope of operations management in that regard.

Now consider managing a factory. Decisions have to be made on what raw materials to order, how much to order, and when to order; what products to make and when and how much to make; work assignments have to be set; workers may have to be hired and trained; quality levels must be established and achieved; inventories of parts and supplies, raw materials, and finished goods must be maintained; worker grievences must be dealt with; workers must be motivated; production bottlenecks and equipment breakdowns must not be allowed to disrupt output; new equipment and production methods must be integrated with existing equipment and methods; and products must be periodically redesigned to incorporate new features and to meet the competition. Moreover, in some cases, locations for new facilities must be found, new factories must be designed and built, and decisions must be made on the layout (arrangement) of departments and equipment.

While on the surface it may appear that the managing of a cruise ship and the managing of a manufacturing facility are quite different, in reality both involve many of the same elements: facilities, work force, inventories, scheduling, and quality assurance. Hence, as diverse as these two examples are, they both reflect activities that fall within the realm of production and operations management.

FUNCTIONS WITHIN BUSINESS ORGANIZATIONS

There are three primary functions that exist in most business organizations: operations, finance, and marketing, as depicted in Figure 1–1. The fact that the three circles overlap suggests that these three functions *overlap:* they do not exist or function independently of

FIGURE 1–1

The Three Major Functions of Business Organizations Overlap

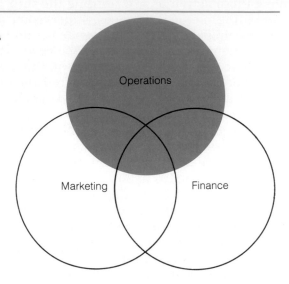

each other. Rather, they interact to achieve the goals and objectives of the organization; they are dependent on each other, and each has an important contribution to make. Often the success of an organization depends not only on how well each area performs but also on how well they *interface* with each other. For instance, in manufacturing, it is essential that production and marketing work together. Otherwise, marketing may attempt to promote products that production cannot profitably produce, and production may turn out products for which there is no demand. Similarly, unless finance and production people work closely, funds for expansion or new equipment may not be available when needed.

Aside from these three primary functions, there are a number of supporting functions that exist in many organizations, such as personnel, accounting, and engineering. Obviously, the presence of these functions and the emphasis placed on each one depend on the type of business a firm is engaged in. Thus, nonmanufacturing firms would be less apt to have an engineering department than manufacturing firms.

Let's take a closer look at these functions, beginning with the three primary ones.

Operations   The operations function consists of all activities that are *directly related to producing goods or providing services*. The production function exists not only in manufacturing and assembly operations, which are *product-oriented,* but also in such areas as health care, transportation, food handling, and retailing, which are primarily

TABLE 1–1

	Type of operation	Examples
Examples of Types of Operations	Physical	Farming, mining, construction, manufacturing, power generation
	Storage/transportation.	Warehousing, trucking, mail service, moving, taxis, buses
	Exchange.	Retailing, wholesaling, banking, renting or leasing, library loans
	Entertainment	Films, radio and television, plays, concerts, recording
	Communication	Newspapers, radio and TV newscasts, telephone, satellites

service-oriented. Table 1–1 provides some examples that illustrate the diversity of operations management settings. As you can see, there is quite a range in the types of operations.

The operations function is the core of most business organizations; operations is responsible for the creation of an organization's products or services. Inputs of labor, materials, energy, and time are used to obtain finished goods or services using one or more *transformation processes* (e.g., storing, transporting, cutting), thereby *adding value.* In order to assure that the desired outputs are obtained, measurements are taken and collected at various points in the transformation process (feedback), and then compared to previously established standards to determine if corrective action is needed (control). Figure 1–2 shows the conversion process.

Table 1–2 provides some examples of inputs, transformation processes, and outputs.

Finance

The finance function is comprised of activities related to securing monetary resources at favorable prices and allocating those resources throughout the organization. Finance and operations man-

FIGURE 1–2

Operations Management Manages the Conversion of Inputs to Outputs

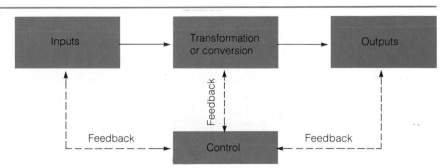

TABLE 1–2

	Inputs	*Transformation*	*Outputs*
Examples of Inputs, Transformation, and Outputs	Human	Processes	Goods
	Physical	Cutting, drilling	Houses
	Intellectual	Storing	Automobiles
	Raw materials	Transporting	Textbooks
	Energy	Extracting	Clothing
	Water	Farming	Typewriters
	Chemicals	Teaching	Machines
	Metals	Assembling	Televisions
	Lumber	Equipment	Food
	Fibers	Machines	Energy
	Other	Computers	Furniture
	Technology	Typewriters	Services
	Information	Trucks	Health care
	Time	Buses	Entertainment
		Facilities	Car repair
		Factories	Car wash
		Schools	Transportation
		Hospitals	Delivery
		Service garages	Gift wrapping
		Offices	Banking
		Retail stores	Education
		Warehouses	

agement personnel cooperate in exchange of information and expertise in such activities as:

1. *Budgeting.* Budgets must be periodically prepared in order to plan financial requirements. Budgets must sometimes be adjusted, and performance relative to budget must be evaluated.
2. Economic *analysis of investment proposals.* Evaluation of alternative investments in plant and equipment requires inputs from both operations and finance people.
3. *Provision of funds.* The necessary funding of operations and the amounts and timings of funding can be important and even critical when funds are tight. Careful planning can help avoid cash flow problems.

Marketing

The marketing function's main concern is with selling the organization's products or services. Primary marketing activities in addition to selling include advertising and promotion, and generally developing and maintaining a market, and sales forecasting. Because of the direct contact between marketing people and consumers, marketing can be a valuable source of information relating to ideas for product or service improvement as well as for ideas for new products or services. One important bit of information marketing people need from operations are manufacturing and service *lead*

FIGURE 1–3

**Operations Interfaces
with a Number of
Supporting Functions**

times so that customers can be given realistic estimates of how
long it will take to fill their orders.

Other Functions In addition to the three major functions in organizations, there are
a host of other supporting functions that interface with the main
three. Among them are accounting and purchasing. In addition,
depending on the nature of the organization, there may be personnel, product design and development, industrial engineering, and
maintenance (see Figure 1–3).

Accounting has responsibility for preparing the financial statements including the income statement and balance sheet. It also
supplies cost data on labor, materials, and overhead and may provide reports on such items as scrap, downtime, and inventories. It
must keep track of receivables, payables, and insurance costs and
prepare tax statements for the firm.

Purchasing is charged with procurement of materials, supplies, and equipment. Close contact with operations is necessary to insure correct quantities and timing of purchases. Also, the purchasing department is often called upon to evaluate vendors for quality, reliability, service, price, and ability to adjust to changing demand. Purchasing also involves shipping and receiving and material inspections.

The *personnel* department is concerned with recruitment and training of personnel, labor relations, contract negotiations, wage and salary administration, assisting in manpower projections, and assuring the health and safety of employees.

Public relations has the responsibility for building and maintaining a positive image of the organization in the eye of the general public. This might involve sponsoring a little league team, donating to cultural events, giving public tours of facilities, sponsoring community affairs (e.g., marathons, bike races), and so on. Donating the use of facilities and providing public service messages and information about the organization, its employees, its products, and its services all fall under the heading of public relations. There are many potential benefits of good public relations. An obvious one is in the marketplace. Other potential benefits might be being regarded as a good place to work (labor supply), improving chances of getting zoning change requests approved, getting community acceptance of expansion plans, generating a positive attitude among employees, and so on.

Industrial engineering is often concerned with scheduling, performance standards, work methods, quality control, and material handling. This function is typically found in manufacturing installations in medium and large firms.

Maintenance, or building and grounds, as it is sometimes referred to, is responsible for general maintenance and upkeep, heating and air conditioning, removing toxic wastes, parking, and perhaps security.

Many of these interfaces are elaborated upon in later chapters.

The importance of production and operations management, both for organizations and for society, should be fairly obvious: The consumption of goods and services is an integral aspect of society as we know it. Production and operations management is responsible for creating those goods and services. Organizations exist primarily for the purpose of providing services or creating goods. Hence, production is the *core function* of an organization. Without this core, there would be no need for any of the other functions—the organization would simply have no purpose. Given the central nature of its function in our society, it is not surprising that more than half of all employed people in this country have jobs within the production/operations area. Furthermore, the operations function controls a major portion of the assets in most organizations.

THE OPERATIONS MANAGEMENT FUNCTION

We have already noted that the operations manager is responsible for the creation of goods and services. This encompasses acquisition of resources and the conversion of their inputs into outputs using one or more transformation processes. This involves planning, coordinating, and controlling the elements that comprise the process, including workers, equipment, facilities, allocation of resources, and work methods. It also includes *product and/or service design*. This is a vital, ongoing process that most organizations must do. It is an activity that operations performs in conjunction with marketing. As previously noted, marketing people can be a source of ideas concerning new products and services as well as improvements to existing products and services. Operations people can also be a source of new ideas that include improvements related to the production aspect of the organization. These can include ideas on new procedures for fabrication and assembly as well as improved designs, handling and storage procedures, and so on. From a practical standpoint, product and service design can be the lifeblood of a competitive organization.

The main function of the operations manager is to guide the system through decision making. Generally speaking, there is a major emphasis on productive use of resources.

There are various ways of classifying the decisions that an operations manager must make, such as qualitative versus quantitative, according to the management process (planning, staffing, etc.) and according to whether the decisions relate to system design or system operation. Each of these approaches has its merits. The approach used in this text—indeed, the framework of the entire book—is this last approach: the material is arranged according to topics that relate primarily to *design* and according to topics that relate primarily to system *operation*. The following section examines this approach in more detail.

Designing and Operating Production Systems

Systems *design* involves decisions that relate to system capacity, the geographic location of facilities, arrangement of departments and placement of equipment within physical structures, product and service planning, and acquisition of equipment. These are usually, but not always, decisions that require long-term commitments. System *operation* involves management of personnel, inventory planning and control, scheduling, project management, and quality assurance. In many instances, the operations manager is more involved in day-to-day operating decisions than with decisions relating to system design. In fact, much of systems design lies in the province of top management. However, the operations manager has a vital stake in system design because *system design essentially*

TABLE 1–3

Design and Operating Decisions

Decision area	Basic questions	Chapter
Forecasting	How much will be demanded? When, and what products and services?	3
Design		
Product and service selection	What products and services should the organization offer?	4, 6
Capacity (long range)	How much capacity will be needed? How can the organization best meet capacity requirements?	4
Location	What is a satisfactory location for a facility (factory, store, etc.)?	5
Layout	What is the best arrangement for departments, equipment, work flow, and storage in terms of cost, productivity?	7
Product and service design	How can products and services be improved?	6
Design of work systems	What is the best way to motivate employees? How can productivity be improved? How to measure work? How to improve work methods?	8
Operation		
Aggregate planning	How much capacity will be needed over the intermediate range? How can capacity needs best be met?	9
Inventory management	How much to order? When to reorder? Which items should get the most attention?	10
Materials requirements planning	What materials, parts, and subassemblies will be needed, and when?	11
Scheduling	How can jobs best be scheduled? Who will do which job? Which equipment to use?	12
Project management	Which activities are the most critical to the success of a project? What are the goals of a project? What resources will be needed and when will they be needed?	13
Queuing	How can bottlenecks be reduced? What is effective capacity?	14
Quality assurance	How can quality be improved? Are processes performing adequately? What standards should be used? Are standards being met?	15

determines many of the parameters of system operation. For example, costs, space, capacities, and quality are all directly affected by design decisions. Even though the operations manager is not responsible for making certain design decisions, he or she can provide a wide range of information to decision makers, which will have a bearing on those decisions.

A brief description of design and operating decisions is given in Table 1–3.

These decisions are generally *hierarchical* in nature; plans and designs are usually sequential, and those at the lower levels are constrained to a certain extent by higher-level plans and decisions. At the highest level are *strategic* decisions. These are broad in scope and involve choice of products and services, new facilities and locations, and general policies of the organization. For the most part, strategic decisions have long-term implications for the organization. At the next level are *tactical* decisions. These are narrower in scope than the strategic decisions. Tactical decisions often involve allocating financial resources, equipment selection and use, and planning work force levels, output rates, and inventory levels. Tactical decisions are made within the framework established by strategic decisions. At the lowest level are *operating* decisions. These involve such activities as scheduling of equipment and personnel, adjusting production rates, and handling equipment breakdowns, absenteeism, shortages, inventory replenishment, and quality control. Operating decisions are made within the framework established by tactical decisions. The decision hierarchy is illustrated in Figure 1–4.

The Operations Manager and the Management Process

The operations manager is the key figure in the system: he or she has the ultimate responsibility for the creation of goods or services.

As you might imagine, the kinds of jobs that operations managers oversee vary tremendously from organization to organization, largely because of the differences in products or services different organizations are involved with. Thus, managing a banking operation obviously requires a different kind of expertise than managing a steel-making operation. However, in one very important respect, the jobs of the managers are the same: they are both essentially *managerial.* In fact, the same thing can be said for the job of any operations manager, regardless of the kinds of goods or services being created. In every case, the operations manager must coordi-

FIGURE 1–4

Hierarchy of Operations Management Decisions

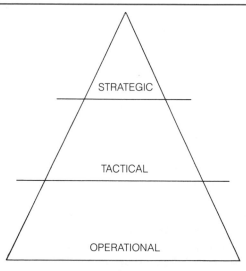

Broad scope

Examples include:
  Product selection
  New facility construction
  Choice of location
  Choice of technology

Moderate scope

Examples include:
  Employment levels
  Output levels
  Equipment selection
  Allocating financial resources

Narrow scope

Examples include:
  Scheduling personnel
  Adjusting output rates
  Controlling quality
  Inventory replenishment

TABLE 1–4

Responsibilities of Operations Managers

Planning	Organizing
Capacity	Degree of centralization
Location	Make or buy
Products and services	Subcontracting
Layout	Staffing
Projects	Use of overtime
Scheduling	Hiring/laying off
Controlling	Directing
Inventory control	Incentive plans
Quality control	Issuance of work orders
	Job assignments

nate the use of resources through the management process, which involves planning, organizing, staffing, directing, and controlling.

Planning involves determining a future course of action. The planning process begins by deciding what is desired, and then designing a way for accomplishing that objective.

Organizing refers to the administrative structure of the organization. It involves putting the pieces of the system together in such a way that desired results can be achieved. It requires decisions regarding who, what, where, when and how.

Staffing involves selection and training of the personnel who will operate the system.

Directing refers to the issuance of commands or orders, making suggestions, or otherwise motivating subordinates to perform their assigned duties in a timely and efficient manner.

Controlling involves measuring the results of operations, deciding if they are acceptable, and instituting corrective action if need be.

Examples of some of the responsibilities of operations managers according to these classifications are given in Table 1–4.

Productivity

One of the primary responsibilities of operations managers is the productive use of resources. *Productivity* is a measure of the relative amount of input used in achieving a given amount of output. In fact, it is commonly expressed as the ratio of quantity of output to quantity of input:

$$\text{Productivity} = \frac{\text{Output}}{\text{Input}}$$

Thus, if a manager is able to obtain an increase in the amount of output without increasing input, productivity has increased. By the same token, if a given output can be realized with a decrease in the amount of input needed, productivity has also increased.

Business and government leaders in virtually every industrialized country are very much concerned about productivity. Moreover, the United States is especially concerned, even though its productivity is among the highest in the world. Much of the concern relates to the fact that U.S. productivity *increases* are not keeping pace with certain other nations—most notably Japan. In addition, Japanese productivity in some industries (e.g., steel making, automobile manufacturing) currently exceeds U.S. productivity.

The interest in productivity is not merely academic; productivity increases are largely responsible for the high standards of living enjoyed by industrial nations. Moreover, wage and price increases not supported by productivity increases create inflationary pressures on the economy.

The obvious question is: How are certain nations or industries able to achieve productivity gains while others are not? Before examining that complex issue, it would be wise to pause for a moment to reflect on the meaning of productivity and some of the ways that productivity can be increased.

Consider the student who plans to type a lengthy term paper. The student is an average typist and can turn out about three pages per hour. How could the student increase productivity (i.e., turn out more pages per hour)? One way would be to enroll in a short course offered by the college to improve typing skills (method). Another possibility might be to replace a manual typewriter with a more expensive electric typewriter (capital) to gain the speed of automatic features. If quality (e.g., typing errors) is a problem, an even more expensive word processor (capital) that will allow errors to be corrected before they appear on the page could help. Still other productivity improvements might be achieved through improving organization and preparation for the actual typing (management). The incentive of receiving a good grade and the personal pride of doing a good job might also be important. The point is that all of these factors are potential sources of productivity, not only for typing papers but for any kind of work, and it is generally up to the manager to see to it that they are fully exploited.

A commonly held misconception is that workers are the main determinant of productivity. According to that theory, the route to productivity gains involves getting employees to work harder. However, the fact is that many productivity gains in the past have come from *technological* improvements. Familiar examples include:

Paint rollers	Long-distance direct dialing, pay-by-phone
Power lawn mowers	
Electric typewriters	Computerized billing and inventories
Duplicating/copying machines	
Microwave ovens	Automation
Automatic washers, dryers, dishwashers, electric blenders	Electronic calculators
	Computers and computer terminals

The current view of productivity is that technology, work methods, choice of equipment, and *management* are the primary factors that determine productivity of a work force, rather than employees themselves.

The nature of productivity sometimes makes it more complex than it appears to be. For example, in some instances, productivity can be difficult to measure. This is often the case with service activities such as legal matters, health care, and repair work. In addition, the *cost* of the resources, especially energy, must be taken into consideration, and not simply the rate of output. *Quality* is another factor that is often related to productivity; usually the rate of output can be increased if quality (e.g., typing errors) is de-emphasized.

Some of the reasons commonly cited for the recent low productivity gains in this country are:

1. Increasing government regulations have added to the administrative (and nonproductive) burden of many companies.
2. Increased legal staffs are needed to handle product liability claims.
3. There has been an increasing demand for services, which are generally less efficient than manufacturing operations.
4. There is often emphasis on *short-run* performance (e.g., annual profits and sales), and this reduces the incentive to develop long-term solutions to problems. In addition, in periods of inflation and increased costs of borrowed money, managers are perhaps understandably hesitant to commit funds for long periods of time because it reduces their flexibility to take advantage of other opportunities that might arise in the meantime.

In searching for ways to improve productivity and to regain some of the competitive edge that they have lost to foreign companies, some American managers have begun to examine how those foreign companies operate. Japanese companies are often pointed to in terms of what can be accomplished in both productivity and quality.

The Japanese are particularly well noted for quality, reliability, and productivity in the automotive, steel, and electronic industries. This has not always been the case. After World War II, Japan was best known for the inferior goods—mostly junk by today's standards. However, in the intervening years, many Japanese companies have been able to overcome that reputation and are now established leaders in their fields. Moreover, while numerous U.S. companies are laying off workers, their Japanese counterparts are running at full steam.

While this about-face for Japanese companies seems remarkable, it appears even more so in view of the fact that—unlike the United States—Japan has been blessed with little in the way of natural resources. Consequently, most of Japan's raw material and energy needs must be satisfied through imports. Some of the reasons often cited for the success of Japanese firms are the following:

1. Japanese firms rely more heavily on debt financing (i.e., borrowing from banks and other lenders) rather than equity financing (i.e., issuing stocks). Banks are less apt to press for short-term gains than stockholders.
2. Banks have the money to lend because the Japanese have a greater propensity to save than do Americans.
3. Japanese firms plow back more of their earnings into research and development; they devote more of their resources to improving product and process design, reliability, and quality.
4. Many consumers perceive Japanese products to be more reliable and of a higher quality than American products.
5. One possible reason for the higher quality is the extent of automation used in Japan. Industrial robots handle many tasks that are repetitive, boring, dirty, or dangerous, freeing people for more interesting jobs and yielding quality that cannot be matched by human workers.
6. The Japanese are also known for their use of *quality circles*— groups of workers who meet periodically to discuss ways of improving productivity and quality in their plants.
7. Workers are encouraged to offer suggestions for improvement, even if they result in eliminating jobs, through a system of job security that guarantees that workers will not be laid off. Instead, they are transferred to other jobs. In fact, many Japanese workers remain with the same company throughout their careers. Consequently, they tend to be more loyal to the company and derive a certain degree of satisfaction and pride in contributing to productivity and quality improvements.

Our discussion of productivity would be incomplete without pointing out that productivity and efficiency are not the only goals that society values. Americans in particular are concerned with the human aspects of their jobs and would probably resist changes that tended to increase productivity at the expense of job satisfaction.

CLASSIFYING PRODUCTION SYSTEMS

There are a number of schemes used to classify production systems. A brief discussion of some of these schemes will help you to develop a better picture of the nature and scope of operations management.

The three schemes described below are: degree of standardization, type of operation, and manufacturing versus service operations.

Degree of Standardization

Production systems produce output that ranges from highly standardized to highly customized. *Standardized* output means that there is a high degree of uniformity in products or services. Examples of products include radios, televisions, typewriters, newspapers, canned foods, automobile tires, pens, and pencils. Examples of services include automatic car washes, televised newscasts, taped lectures, and commercial airline service. *Customized* output means that the product or service is designed for a specific case or individual. Examples of products include eye glasses, custom-fitted clothing, window glass (cut to order), and customized drapery. Examples of services include tailoring, taxi rides, and surgery.

Systems with standardized output can generally take advantage of standardized methods, materials, and mechanization, all of which contribute to higher volumes and lower unit costs than specialized systems in which each job is different enough that workers must be more skilled, the work moves slower, and the work is less susceptible to mechanization.

Type of Operation

The degree of standardization of a product or service and the volume of output influence the way that production is organized. On one end of the scale we have a single, large-scale product or service such as the launching of a space shuttle (service) or the construction of a sky scraper (product). On the other end we have a continuous process, such as oil refining. In between these extremes we have small batches or individual units of output, such as custom-made furniture, lamps, special-purpose machines, and auto repair, all the way to mass production (high volume of output), such as automobiles, typewriters, and appliances.

Let's take a closer look at these different types of operations.

A *project* is a set of activities directed toward a unique goal. Usually, projects are relatively large-scale. Examples of situations in which a project approach would be used include development of a new product, installation of a computerized production line, transfer of equipment to a new facility from a current one, and construction of a hospital. Sometimes the situations are of a more personal nature, such as planning for the visit of foreign dignitaries, planning an extended vacation that involves travel, and organizing a walk-for-water or other charitable activity. A key feature of all of these projects is their limited time frame. That is, they do not continue indefinitely; they have specific starting and ending points.

Unit or *batch* production is typically performed by a *job shop*. A job shop maintains the ability to render certain types of production but generally does not have specific products that it produces.

Instead, it performs to customer specifications; jobs tend to vary according to the needs of customers. Examples of job shops include organizations that do repair work (appliances, televisions, stereos, automobiles), health care, printing, and so on. Some of these are highly customized while others offer a list of services or products of a more standardized nature from which customers can select.

On the other extreme of the scale of volume of output is *mass production.* Organizations using this type of operation generally confine output to one or a relatively small number of similar products or services and organize in such a way as to accomplish production as efficiently as possible. Both the work and the output tend to be highly standardized. Mass production systems are examples of *repetitive* production. This type of production lends itself to automation or other specialized equipment.

Continuous processing is employed when a homogeneous product or service is produced or rendered. Processing of chemicals, photographic film, newsprint, and oil products are all examples of this type of operation. Machines often provide continuous services, such as air conditioning, heating, continuous cleaning, and monitoring systems.

Manufacturing Operations versus Service Operations

Manufacturing implies production of a *tangible output,* such as an automobile, a clock radio, a golf ball, a refrigerator, or something similar that we can see or touch. Service, on the other hand, generally implies an *act* rather than a physical product. A doctor's examination, TV and auto repair, lawn care, and showing a film are examples of services.

Manufacturing and service are often similar in terms of *what* is done but different in terms of *how* it is done. For example, both involve design and operating decisions. Manufacturers must decide how large a factory is needed, and service organizations (e.g., hospitals) must decide how large a building they need. Both must make location decisions, and both become involved in scheduling and controlling operations and allocating scarce resources.

Most of the differences between manufacturing and service organizations relate to manufacturing being product-oriented and service being act-oriented. The differences involve the following:

1. The nature and consumption of output.
2. Uniformity of input.
3. Labor content of jobs.
4. Uniformity of output.
5. Measurement of productivity.

Let us briefly consider each of these differences.

1. By its very nature, service involves a much higher degree of customer contact than manufacturing does. The performance of a service typically occurs at the point of consumption. That is, the two often occur simultaneously. For example, repairing a leaky roof must take place where the roof is, and surgery requires the presence of the surgeon and the patient. On the other hand, manufacturing allows a separation of production and consumption, so that manufacturing often occurs in an isolated environment, away from the consumer. This permits a fair degree of latitude in selecting work methods, assigning jobs, scheduling work, and exercising control over operations. Service operations, because of their contact with customers, can sometimes be much more limited in their range of options in these areas. Moreover, customers are sometimes a part of the system (e.g., self-service operations such as gas stations, shopping), so tight control is not possible. Then, too, product-oriented operations can build up inventories of finished goods, which enables them to absorb some of the shocks caused by varying demand. However, service operations cannot build up inventories of *time,* so service capacity is much more sensitive to demand variability. Thus, banks and supermarkets alternate between lines of customers waiting for service and idle tellers or cashiers waiting for customers.

2. Service operations are subject to more variability of inputs than typical manufacturing operations are. Each patient, each lawn, and each TV presents a somewhat unique problem that often must be diagnosed before it can be remedied. There is often the ability in manufacturing to carefully control the amount of variability of inputs, so it is often possible to achieve low variability. Consequently, job requirements in manufacturing are generally more uniform than for services.

3. Because of the on-site consumption of services and because of the high degree of variation of inputs, services require a higher labor content, while manufacturing can be more capital-intensive (i.e., mechanized), although there are exceptions.

4. High mechanization generates products with low variability, so manufacturing tends to be smooth and efficient, while service activities sometimes appear to be slow and awkward, and output more variable.

5. Measurement of productivity is relatively straightforward in manufacturing due to the high degree of uniformity of most manufactured items. However, in many cases, variations in demand intensity, as well as variations in service requirements from job to job, make productivity measurement considerably more difficult. For example, the workload of two doctors might be compared. One may have had a large number of routine cases while the other did not, so their productivity would appear to be different unless a very careful analysis was made.

Table 1–5 gives an overview of the comparison of manufacturing and service operation differences.

TABLE 1–5

Differences between Manufacturing and Service

Characteristic	Manufacturing	Service
Output	Tangible	Intangible
Customer contact	Low	High
Labor content	Low	High
Uniformity of output	High	Low
Measurement of productivity	Easy	Difficult

Although at times it may be convenient to think in terms of systems that are exclusively devoted to products or services, most real systems are a blend of the two. For instance, maintenance and repair of equipment are two services performed by virtually every manufacturing firm. Similarly, most so-called service organizations typically sell products that complement their services. Thus, a lawn care firm usually sells such products as weed killers, fertilizers, and grass seed. Hospitals dispense medical and surgical supplies along with health services. Restaurants sell food. Movie theaters sell popcorn, candy, and beverages.

Obviously, then, operations managers must be familiar with both types of systems if they are to be effective.

Implications for Production Systems

These different ways of classifying production systems have important implications for designing and operating them. The degree of standardization of output, the type of operation, and whether the system involves mainly products, mainly service, or some combination of products and services have a bearing on capital requirements, choice of equipment, capacity planning, location planning, layout, inventory management, work force requirements, scheduling, and quality assurance.

Management of a project is quite different than managing an assembly line, and managing a job shop operation is different than managing a project or a high-volume operation. Forecasting requirements are different for the three types of systems. A high-volume operation requires a steady rate of output, and it can be costly as well as difficult to vary that rate. Hence, a good forecast is necessary in order to adequately design the system. Conversely, a job shop has a great deal more flexibility, so forecasting is less crucial at the design stage. Inventory requirements for a job shop are different than for a system making standard products. Job shops typically make products to order. Thus, they would have little or no finished goods inventories. They may carry raw materials and supplies for frequently used operations. In repetitive manufacturing systems an inventory of both raw materials and finished goods generally exists. However, purchasing is standardized, as are most of the activities associated with the operation. Projects tend to be very unique, and their requirements vary considerably. Most do not involve "products" in the sense of the other two types of systems, so a comparison among all three would be difficult.

In terms of actual operation, repetitive systems exhibit the highest degree of certainty, job shops the next highest, and projects the lowest. Consequently, repetitive systems involve a more routine set of activities than job shops, which involve a more routine set of activities than projects. The differences among the systems and their implications for operations management will be elaborated on in the remainder of the book.

CONTEMPORARY ISSUES AND DEVELOPMENTS

A number of important issues and recent developments in the practice of operations management are currently influencing managerial decisions. This section presents a brief overview of the major ones, which are:

1. Productivity.
2. Inflation.
3. Increasing scarcity of certain resources.
4. Government regulation.
5. The international scope of operations.
6. Foreign competition.
7. Technological change.
8. The increasing importance of service operations.
9. Managerial attention to employee's viewpoints.

A key issue in all organizations is *productivity.* In many cases, it has become a key measure of the effectiveness of management. Moreover, as noted earlier in the chapter, a major objective of operations management is to improve productivity. Management has always been concerned with productivity. However, factors such as inflation and the scarcity of certain resources have generated an increased emphasis on achieving productivity gains.

Uncertainty in *financial markets* has created problems. Inflation, high interest rates, fears of recession, and speculative buying have had an effect on the vast majority of business organizations and will continue to do so. Furthermore, inflation increases the costs of inputs as well as the costs of transformation. In many instances, organizations are being squeezed by the rising costs.

The *scarcity of resources,* particularly *energy,* can have a profound effect on operations. This is often reflected by efforts to upgrade existing facilities to make them more energy efficient and to incorporate energy efficiency in the design of new facilities. Similarly, emphasis in product design is on energy-efficient products. Research is continuing on ways to improve gasoline mileage in the automotive industry. Efforts are being made to design efficient appliances. And home heating, air conditioning, and insulation are coming under closer scrutiny by homeowners and by law makers in an effort to conserve energy. Already the impact of fuel shortages has been felt by airlines, motels, restaurants, tourist attractions, and service stations, and it must be regarded as a serious factor in both the design and operation of production systems.

Pollution control has also had a tremendous impact on some industries in terms of design and operation, and the government continues to strengthen standards on waste disposal and emission controls. When local or state government regulations differ from national standards, business organizations face the burden of designing for both. For instance, California emission-control requirements are more stringent than most other states', and automotive firms have been forced to create special designs and pricing policies to compensate for them.

Increasing *consumer awareness,* particularly in the area of *product safety,* has emerged as a new force that must be reckoned with. Between the government and concerned consumers, major manufacturer recalls have been made on TVs, hairdryers, tires, bicycles, medicines, canned foods, coffee pots, and other items. Designers and quality inspectors have had to reconsider their activities.

Government regulations related to *worker safety* (OSHA) and *hiring practices* (EEO) have had an impact on the design of work systems.

The *international scope of operations* has resulted in increased opportunities to develop foreign markets, created additional sources for raw material and labor inputs, and forced numerous organizations to reassess their strategies. It has also brought an increase in multinational companies. It is becoming increasingly common to encounter firms that obtain their raw materials in one country, fabricate parts in another, and assemble the final products in still another country. Managing such far-flung operations poses new challenges for managers as well as new opportunities.

Foreign competition has made serious inroads in areas that have been traditionally dominated by U.S. firms. West Germany, Japan, Taiwan, and Korea are notable examples of major foreign competitors. Some U.S. firms have suffered substantial losses in market share to these competitors. This is a continuing problem that must be dealt with in order to avoid even more serious consequences.

Technological changes are an increasingly important factor in operations management. New products and services are being developed as firms attempt to maintain competitiveness, and new production technologies are appearing that must be integrated into production systems. Robotics is an important example of this, particularly in the automotive industry (but also in other industries). Robots offer certain advantages in automation and have some of the benefits of flexibility not generally associated with automation. The increased use of computers has enlarged the decision-making capabilities of managers, enabling them to use more quantitative techniques in analyzing decisions, and its use has greatly enlarged information storage and handling capabilities. A major impact has been in the area of inventory control where much interest centers on a technique called material requirements planning (MRP).

As previously noted, *service systems* are becoming increasingly important in operations due to the growth in the number of such systems and because of the challenges that they present to the operations manager.

In an effort to improve quality and productivity, managers are encouraging *employee inputs* in the form of suggestions, quality circles, and other vehicles. Although this input is quite small, some feel that it will become more important in the years ahead.

SUMMARY

The goal of this book is to present a broad conceptual framework for operations management. Operations, finance, and marketing are seen as the three primary functions of most business organizations. Although traditionally regarded as primarily manufacturing oriented, in recent years the scope of operations management has expanded greatly, and it is currently applied to both manufacturing and service activities. Operations management oversees all activities that are directly related to making a product or providing a service. Operations management is charged with transforming inputs of people, materials, energy, money, and information into useful goods and services. There are two main decision areas within operations, system design and system operation. System design is concerned with decisions related to capacity, location, layout, and product and process design. System operation is concerned with human resources, scheduling, project management, inventory management, and quality assurance.

One of the major responsibilities of the operations manager is productivity; much effort is typically devoted to maintaining and improving productivity.

Current issues in operations management include an increased emphasis on service systems, dealing with the scarcity of resources, contending with high costs of funds and energy, operating under increasing and changing government regulations, foreign competition, and integrating technological changes into production systems.

DISCUSSION AND REVIEW QUESTIONS

1. Briefly describe the three primary functions that exist within most business organizations.

2. What are the categories used to describe each of these: Inputs? Transformation? Outputs?

3. Along what lines is the text organized?
4. Contrast system design and system operation. Give four examples of topics for each.
5. What are five important differences between manufacturing and service operations?
6. What is productivity and why is it important? Who in the organization is primarily responsible for productivity?
7. What are some of the possible reasons offered in this chapter for the recent slump in productivity in some U.S. companies?
8. From time to time, various groups clamor for import restrictions on automobiles to help American manufacturers. In what ways might those restrictions be helpful? What disadvantages do you feel such restrictions might entail?
9. Much of the quality and productivity gain accomplished by the Japanese can be traced to their use of industrial robots. Assuming this is true, why do you feel that U.S. companies have not made more extensive use of robots?
10. The United States has the highest productivity in agriculture of any country in the world and also ranks among the highest in textiles. What are some of the reasons for this high productivity?
11. Most experts agree that American workers are not primarily responsible for productivity problems. Nonetheless, workers sometimes contribute to the problem. Outline some of the ways this can happen.
12. Why study operations management?
13. Comment on the drawing on this page. What are its implications?

"If only people would work a little harder, we could increase productivity."

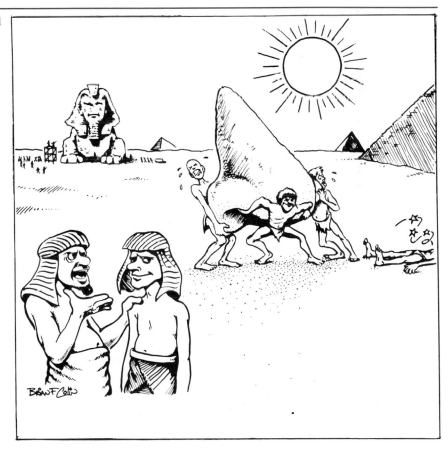

SELECTED BIBLIOGRAPHY

Chase, Richard, and Nicholas Aquilano. *Production and Operations Management.* 4th ed. Homewood, Ill.: Richard D. Irwin, 1985.

Huse, Edgar F. *The Modern Manager.* St. Paul, Minn.: West Publishing, 1979.

Malkiel, Burton G. "Productivity—The Problem behind the Headlines." *Harvard Business Review,* May–June 1979, pp. 81–85.

Moore, Franklin G., and Thomas E. Hendrick. *Production/Operations Management.* 8th ed. Homewood, Ill.: Richard D. Irwin, 1980.

NBC White Paper: "If Japan Can . . . Why Can't We?" (Film available from Films, Inc.)

"The Productivity Crisis." *Newsweek,* September 8, 1980.

Reeser, Clayton. *Management: Functions and Modern Concepts.* Glenview, Ill.: Scott, Foresman, 1973.

Sasser, W. Earl; R. Paul Olsen; and D. Daryl Wyckoff. *Management of Service Operations: Text, Cases, and Readings.* Boston: Allyn & Bacon, 1978.

Striner, H. "Regaining the Lead in Productivity Growth." *National Productivity Review* 1, no. 1, 1982.

Wheelwright, Steven C. "Japan—Where Operations Really are Strategic." *Harvard Business Review,* July–August, 1981.

Winter, Ralph. "Many Culprits Named in National Slowdown of Productivity Gains." *The Wall Street Journal,* October 21, 1980, p. 1.

Reading

Report from the Assembly Line: My Turn

John Hilton

I work in an auto plant in Michigan. A lot of people, when I tell them that, ask me why I make such lousy cars. Few of them wait for an answer to the question. It's just a fashionable complaint, casually made, and among strangers I rarely try to argue. I already have enough arguments about my job with my friends.

My friends from work, for their part, won't believe that I finished college. Mostly high-school graduates themselves, they accept as an article of faith that a college degree would qualify them for better-paid, more respected work. If I tell them that many degrees don't, that my own in the liberal arts didn't, they look away. I never even mention Phi Beta Kappa.

My friends from college, on the other hand, don't believe that I actually work hard for my living. They uniformly assume that I spend the night counting parts or pushing buttons. Their misconception reflect what I call "the myth of automation." It credits American industry with a degree of sophistication more appropriate to science fiction, or perhaps Japan.

Outdated. In fact, the average American factory—my factory—is a functioning antique. Body styles have changed and pneumatic tools have accelerated the pace, but little else has altered since the days of Henry Ford. From the primary body assembly to hoisting on the wheels, virtually everything is still done by hand. Though technically outdated, my factory is still a fascinating human complex, but I can seldom interest my educated friends in its intricate workings. On a much simpler level, they even seem reluctant to believe that my co-workers and I do what we are told to do and would be fired if we didn't.

I realize that people with "good, general educations" often know nothing useful about business. But it angers me to hear them question the very existence of corporate discipline. Do they think these leviathans run on trust?

Of course, discipline has its drawbacks. Following instructions sometimes means throwing trash in the trunk of an outbound car or concealing water leaks with putty. More often, though, corporate discipline means a worker's struggle to fit an additional task into an already difficult job.

Bear in mind that the moving assembly line is itself a triumph of management. It requires a person to master a sequence of brief tasks, and then demands that the sequence be repeated at high speed for hours on end. Knowing their schedule will be enforced automatically by the movement of the line, "process engineers" can schedule each task in the sequence down to the hundredth of a minute.

The revolution in productivity that the assembly line made possible is now taken for granted, but that does not mean the pace has slowed. On the contrary, every one of the ten jobs I know has been added to in some way in the last three years. Such speed-ups are part of a continuing, and successful, effort to improve productivity: for the years 1967–1977, Department of Commerce figures show a 47 percent increase in output per hour for production workers in motor-vehicle manufacturing.

These gradual improvements are not revolutions, however, and each carries a hidden price. Assembly-line work depends on a steady, scarcely conscious flow of movement, swift yet unhurried, which I think of as a kind of Zen. Each time the engineers alter a job sequence, that flow is disrupted and must be regained. Until that adjustment is achieved, the worker is harried and clumsy, and errors are inevitable.

Yet every gain in productivity is now more vital than ever. With the collapse of the big-car market, the U.S. auto industry is competing head-on with the Japanese producers. And the Japanese are already well into a new productivity revolution, one that makes traditional factories like mine virtually obsolete. Serious automation remains largely a myth here, but in Japan it is quickly becoming reality.

The resulting productivity, as described earlier this year by The Washington Post News Service, is almost unbelievable. The Post's reporter toured a number of Japanese factories, including a Nissan (Datsun) plant at Zama, south of Tokyo. The Zama factory, 97 percent automated, builds cars almost without human participation, thanks to the large-scale use of programmable robots. Its daily output of 1,300 cars requires a per-shift work force of only 67. My own plant has a comparable output—and about 20 times as many workers.

Zama is outstanding even in Japan, but it gives some idea of the challenge facing the U.S. auto industry. It must restructure not only product lines, but production methods as well. The only alternative, protective trade legislation, would be unfair both to comsumers and to the Japanese, who, after all, have earned their success.

Hope. There is reason to doubt that all the U.S. car makers will rise to the challenge (Ford and Chrysler just threw away enormous sums redesigning their *largest* cars), but there are some signs of hope. My own plant will soon be overhauled and partially automated to begin production of a small, front-wheel-drive car. It will still be less than a match for Zama, but the rumors suggest that management is aiming for a respectable jump in productivity.

The increased automation will not mean the immediate loss of jobs. Instead of being laid off, the extra workers will be reassigned to assist and monitor small groups of assemblers. This new arrangement is designed so that every stage of production can be scrutinized as it is actually performed—a radical departure from the old system of spot-checks and on-the-run repairs.

But the handwriting is on the wall. Japan's productivity is expected to double in the next five years, and we will have little choice but to keep pace. That inevitably means that some workers will be permanently laid off and, given my own low seniority, I could well be among them. In effect, I may soon be replaced by a machine. But I'd rather be replaced by a machine than compete with one. I can't see much future for myself, or the domestic industry, if we continue to play John Henry to Japan's steam drill.

Questions

1. Explain the "myth of automation."

2. Why are productivity gains vital to the U.S. auto industry?

3. Why would protective trade legislation be unfair to consumers? Why would it be unfair to Japan?

4. What is meant by the phrase "continue to play John Henry to Japan's steam drill"?

Chapter 2

Decision Making

After completing this chapter, you should be able to:

1. Explain the importance of decision making.
2. Outline the steps in the decision making process.
3. Discuss the characteristics of operations decisions.
4. Describe the different environments under which operations decisions are made.
5. Describe and use techniques that apply to decision making under uncertainty.
6. Describe and use the expected value approach.
7. Construct a decision tree and use it to solve a problem.
8. Compute the expected value of perfect information.
9. Conduct sensitivity analysis on a simple decision problem.

THE DECISION PROCESS, 34

    Reasons for Poor Decisions, 36

CHARACTERISTICS OF OPERATIONS DECISIONS, 37

    The Use of Models, 37
    Quantitative Approaches, 39
    Analysis of Trade-Offs, 40
    Sensitivity Analysis, 41
    The Systems Approach, 42
    Priority Recognition, 43
    Decision Environments, 44

DECISION THEORY, 44

    Decision Making under Certainty, 46
    Decision Making under Uncertainty, 46
    Decision Making under Risk, 49
    Decision Trees, 50
    Expected Value of Perfect Information, 52
    Sensitivity Analysis, 54

SUMMARY, 56

SOLVED PROBLEMS, 57

DISCUSSION AND REVIEW QUESTIONS, 58

PROBLEMS, 59

SELECTED BIBLIOGRAPHY, 62

SUPPLEMENT: LINEAR PROGRAMMING, 63

The chief role of the operations manager is that of decision maker. In this capacity, the operations manager has considerable influence over the degree to which the goals and objectives of the organization are achieved.

Throughout this book you will be exposed to a broad range of decision areas that are encountered in operations management and to the tools necessary to handle those decisions. In this chapter the process of decision making is examined, as well as typical reasons for poor decisions, the characteristics of operations decisions, and the classification of decision problems according to degree of certainty. The chapter concludes with a discussion of decision theory, which is a general approach to decision making that has applications in many areas of operations management.

THE DECISION PROCESS

Decision making is a fundamental process of management, and most of the efforts of managers are related to this process. Unfortunately, decisions do not always turn out as planned. Most successful decision making follows a process that consists of these steps:

1. Identify the problem.
2. Specify objectives and the decision criteria for choosing a solution.
3. Develop alternatives.
4. Analyze and compare alternatives.
5. Select the best alternative.
6. Implement the chosen alternative.
7. Monitor the results to assure desired results are achieved.

Success or failure in decision making often depends on how well each of these steps is handled.

Identifying the problem can be the most crucial element in the decision making process. One danger is that problem-solving efforts will be directed toward removing the *symptoms* of the problem rather than the actual problem itself, leaving the problem to resurface at a later time. For instance, athletic injuries are sometimes treated with pain-killing drugs that can effectively mask the symptoms. However, the drugs do not heal the actual injury. Even worse, the person may feel so much better that he or she returns to action and risks aggravating the injury. Or, consider the young driver who became so annoyed at the strange noises coming from his car's engine that he was forced to turn up the volume on the car's radio to drown them out. *Solutions must attack the basic problem.*

The decision maker must *identify the criteria* by which proposed solutions will be judged. Common criteria often relate to costs, profits, return on investment, increased productivity, risk, company image, impact on demand, and similar variables.

The ability to satisfactorily handle problems often depends on the degree of success one has in *developing suitable alternatives.* There is always the danger that one or more potentially superior alternatives will be overlooked in the search for alternatives. Consequently, when it comes to choosing an alternative, the selection of the "optimum" may actually turn out to be something less than optimum. Obviously, there is a limit to the number of possible alternatives that can be identified. Much depends on the experience and creativity of the decision maker as well as the nature of the situation. However, as a general rule, efforts expended in carefully identifying alternatives can yield substantial dividends in terms of the overall decision. One alternative that is frequently overlooked, possibly because it seems too simple, is to do nothing. The beauty of doing nothing lies not only in the fact that no time or effort is needed, but also that it may cost nothing and requires no implementation.

Analyzing and comparing alternatives often benefits from the use of mathematical or statistical techniques. Many of these are described and demonstrated throughout this book.

Selection of the best alternative will depend upon the objectives of the decision maker and the criteria that are being used to evaluate alternatives.

Implementing a solution simply means to carry out the actions indicated by the chosen alternative. Examples include buy the machine, refuse the loan application, begin development of a new product, and authorize the use of overtime. Of course, if the alternative selected is to do nothing, no action will be required to implement it. Note that many decision makers use this by default: By the time they get around to making a decision it is too late!

Effective decision making requires that the results of the decision be *monitored* to make certain that the desired consequences have been achieved. If they have not, the decision maker may have to repeat the entire process, or perhaps a review of the situation may reveal an error in the actual implementation, an error in calculations, a wrong assumption, or some similar point that will allow the situation to be remedied fairly quickly.

It should be noted that the decision process is not always completed in a sequential manner. Instead, there is usually a certain amount of backtracking and feedback involved, especially in terms of developing and analyzing alternatives. For example, if none of the alternatives being analyzed can achieve the desired results, additional alternatives must be developed. Or perhaps the problem has not been clearly identified, and so additional work must be done there as well as on the other steps in the process.

Reasons for Poor Decisions

Occasionally, despite the best efforts of a manager, a decision turns out rather poorly due to unforeseeable circumstances. However, such occurrences are not all that common. More often, failures can be traced to some combination of the following reasons: mistakes made in the decision process, bounded rationality, or suboptimization.

In many cases, managers fail to appreciate the importance of each step in the decision process that was just outlined. They may skip a step or not devote enough effort to completing it before jumping to the next step. Sometimes this is due to a manager's style of making quick decisions or because of a failure to recognize the consequences of a poor decision. The manager's ego can be a factor. This sometimes happens after a period in which the manager has experienced a series of successes—important decisions that all turned out right. Under these circumstances, some managers begin to get the impression that they can do no wrong, and soon the trouble begins. This is enough to bring some managers back down to earth, but others seem oblivious to the negative results and continue the process they associate with their previous successes, not recognizing that perhaps some of that success was due more to luck than to any special abilities of their own. A part of the problem may be related to the manager's ego—and the unwillingness to admit a mistake. Then too, some managers demonstrate an inability to make a decision—they hem and haw, stalling long past the time when the decision should have been rendered.

Now, of course, all managers do not fall into these traps. In fact, it would seem safe to say that the majority do not. Even so, this does not necessarily mean that every decision works out as expected. Another factor with which managers must contend is *bounded rationality,* a term that refers to the limits imposed on decision making because of costs, human abilities, time, technology, and the availability of information. Because of these limitations, managers cannot always expect to reach decisions that are optimal in the sense of providing the best possible outcome (e.g., highest profit, least cost). Instead, they must often resort to achieving a *satisfactory* solution.

Still another source of poor decisions arises because organizations typically departmentalize decisions. Naturally, there is a great deal of justification in departments in terms of overcoming span-of-control problems and human limitations. However, one problem that can arise is *suboptimization.* This occurs as a result of different departments each attempting to reach a solution that is optimum for that department. Unfortunately, what is optimum for a specific department may not be optimum for the organization as a whole. For example, the quality control department of a wire manufacturer may want to introduce a program that will guarantee that every nail that is produced is perfect. However, the cost of doing so may be so great that to cover costs, a price so ridiculously high would have to be charged that it would be unlikely that anyone would be willing to buy the product!

CHARACTERISTICS OF OPERATIONS DECISIONS

Operations decisions are often characterized by the use of models, by quantitative methods, by analysis of trade-offs, by sensitivity analysis, and by a systems approach. These characteristics are discussed in this section.

The Use of Models

A *model* is an abstraction of reality. That is to say, a model presents a simplified, incomplete version of something. For example, a child's toy car is a model of a real automobile—it has many of the same visual features (shape, relative proportions, wheels), which make it quite suitable for its intended purpose in terms of the child's learning and playing. However, it does not have a real engine, it cannot transport people, and it does not weigh 2,000 pounds. Similarly, an instructor commonly uses chalk markings on a blackboard to represent just about anything under the sun. Again, these are models, for although they often communicate a point rather effectively, they are merely bits of chalk dust arranged on the blackboard.

Some common examples of models include wind tunnels, which are designed to model the effects of air turbulence on the outer surfaces of airplanes, formulas, graphs and charts, balance sheets and income statements, and financial ratios. Common statistical models include descriptive statistics such as the mean, median, mode, range, and standard deviation as well as random sampling, the normal distribution, and regression equations.

Models are sometimes classified as physical, schematic, and mathematical:

Physical models look like their real-life counterparts. Examples include miniature cars, trucks, airplanes, toy animals and trains, and scale-model buildings. The advantage of these models is their visual correspondence with reality.

Schematic models are more abstract than their physical counterparts. That is, they have less of the physical features of reality. Examples include graphs and charts, blueprints, pictures, and drawings. The advantage of these models is that they are often relatively simple to construct and to change. Moreover, they have some degree of visual correspondence.

Mathematical models are the height of abstraction; they do not look at all like their real-life counterparts. Examples include numbers, formulas, and certain symbols. These models are usually the easiest to manipulate, and they are essential forms of inputs for computers and calculators.

The variety of models in use is enormous. Those models range from the simple to the exotic; some are very crude while others are extremely elegant. Nonetheless, they all have certain common features: They are all considered as decision-making aids, and they are all abstractions (simplifications) of some more complex real-life phenomenon. The extensive use of models stems from the fact that real life involves an overwhelming amount of detail, much of which is irrelevant for any particular problem. Models strip away these unimportant details so that attention can be concentrated on the relatively few important aspects of the situation, thus increasing the opportunity for effective understanding of a problem and its solution.

The underlying goal in modeling is to develop a model that adequately portrays some real-life phenomenon. Once a model has been developed, a great deal can be learned about it by manipulating its variables and observing the results. Moreover, if the model is a good one, a great deal can be learned about its real-life counterpart.

Since models play a significant role in operations-management decision making, they are heavily integrated into the subject matter of this text. As you progress through the text, you will encounter a fair number of these models. For each model, try to learn *(a)* the purpose of the model, *(b)* how to use the model to generate results, *(c)* how results are interpreted and used, and *(d)* what assumptions and limitations apply.

The last point is particularly important because virtually every model has an associated set of requirements that indicate the conditions under which the model is valid. Failure to satisfy all of the assumptions (i.e., to try and use a model where it isn't meant to be used) will make the results suspect. Attempts to apply the results to a problem under such circumstances can sometimes lead to disastrous consequences. Hence, it is extremely important to be aware of the assumptions and limitations of each model.

Managers use models in a variety of ways and for a variety of reasons. Among them are the following:

1. They are generally easy to use and less expensive than dealing directly with the actual situation.

2. They require users to organize and quantify information and, in the process, often indicate areas where additional information is needed.
3. They provide a systematic approach to problem solving.
4. They increase understanding of the problem.
5. They enable managers to ask "what if . . .?" questions.
6. They require users to be very specific about objectives.
7. They serve as a consistent tool for evaluation.
8. They enable users to bring the power of mathematics to bear on a problem.
9. They provide a standardized format for analyzing a problem.

This impressive list of benefits not withstanding, there are certain limitations of models that you should also be aware of. Some of the more important limitations are:

1. Quantitative information may be emphasized at the expense of qualitative information.
2. Models may be incorrectly applied and/or results can be misinterpreted. The widespread use of computerized models adds to this risk because highly sophisticated models may be placed in the hands of users who are not sufficiently grounded in mathematics to appreciate the subtleties of a particular model; they generally cannot fully comprehend the circumstances under which the model can be successfully employed.
3. Model building can become an end in itself.

Quantitative Approaches

Quantitative approaches to problem solving often embody an attempt to obtain mathematically optimum solutions to managerial problems. Although quantitative techniques have traditionally been associated with production and operations management, it was not until World War II that major efforts were made to develop these techniques. In order to handle complex logistics problems associated with military activity, interdisciplinary teams were assembled (e.g., psychologists, mathematicians, economists) that combined efforts in search of workable solutions. These efforts continued and expanded after the war, and many of the resulting techniques found applications in operations management. *Linear programming* and related mathematical techniques are widely used for optimum allocation of scarce resources. *Queuing techniques,* originating around 1920 in telephone work but remaining dormant until work was greatly expanded in the 50s and 60s, are useful for analyzing situations in which waiting lines form. *Inventory models,* again after some early work and then a long period of low interest, are now widely used to control inventories. *Project models* such as PERT (program evaluation and review technique) and CPM (critical path method) are useful for planning, coordinating, and controlling large-scale projects. *Forecasting techniques* are increasingly being used as a basis for planning and scheduling. *Statistical models* are currently used in all areas of decision making where elements of risk are present.

In large measure, quantitative approaches to decision making in operations management (as well as in other areas of decision making) have been accepted because of the introduction of calculators and the availability of high-speed computers that are capable of handling the required calculations. Computers have had an enormous influence on the practice of operations management, particularly in the areas of scheduling and inventory control. Because of their capability for rapid, error-free computations and the ability to keep track of thousands of bits of information with instantaneous retrieval, computers have made significant inroads in handling some very difficult problem areas. Moreover, the growing availability of software packages covering virtually every quantitative technique in use has greatly enhanced management's use of the computer for problem solving. Many heretofore impractical techniques, such as multiple regression analysis and linear programming, can now be handled with virtual ease, thanks to computer packages and the widespread availability of computers.

Computers have proven invaluable in simulation studies where analysts explore real-life problems that do not lend themselves to solution using formulas, by varying parameters in repeated computer trials and analyzing the results in order to better understand a problem and to generate alternative solutions.

Because of the emphasis on quantitative approaches in operations-management decision making, it is important that you not lose sight of the fact that *managers typically use a combination of qualitative and quantitative approaches and that many important decisions are based on qualitative approaches.* The reason for the emphasis on quantitative methods lies in the fact that quantitative analysis is typically more difficult to understand without a fair amount of explanation and demonstration problems.

Analysis of Trade-Offs

The decisions encountered by operations managers can easily be described as *trade-off* decisions. For example, in deciding on the amount of inventory to stock, the manager's eventual decision must take into account the trade-off between the increased level of customer service that increasing the amount stocked would yield and the increase in costs required to stock that amount. Similarly, in choosing a level of quality inspection, a manager must evaluate the merits of fewer defectives slipping through by increasing inspection efforts versus the increase in costs that would require. In allocating funds, the manager may have to weigh the potential for increased profits from a certain action against the higher risk of loss relative to what another proposal might entail. Use of overtime to increase output is another example. In that case, the manager must weigh the value of the increased output against the increased costs of overtime (e.g., lower productivity, higher labor costs, lower quality, and increased risk of accidents).

Throughout this book you will be presented with decision models that reflect these kinds of trade-offs. Managers often deal with decisions of this nature by listing the advantages and disadvantages of opposing courses of action in an effort to obtain a better understanding of the consequences of potential decisions.

Sensitivity Analysis

A key feature of many quantitive techniques is the ability of the user to perform *sensitivity analysis* on a solution. That is, the user is able to test how sensitive a given solution is to a change in one or more of the parameters (i.e., the "numbers") taken as givens in a problem. For instance, suppose a manager has these two models:

$$\text{Profit A} = 2x + 4{,}000 \text{ and Profit B} = 2x + 4.$$

Suppose also that the variable x typically takes on a value of approximately 5.0. The manager may have estimated the coefficient of x (i.e., 2) in both models, and he now wants to know how sensitive the profit computed with the equation is to that value. Suppose that the manager feels the true value may be closer to 1 than to 2. For profit A, substituting a 1 into the equation with $x = 5$ yields a profit of 4,005; substituting a 2 into the equation with $x = 5$ yields a profit of 4,010. There is little difference between the profit of A with these two different values of the coefficient.

Now let's see what happens in the case of profit B, again with $x = 5$. For a coefficient of 1, profit B is 9; for a coefficient of 2, profit B is 14. Comparing these two cases, we see that the model for profit B is quite sensitive to a possible estimation error of the magnitude given, whereas the model for profit A is rather insensitive.

The knowledge provided by sensitivity analysis can be useful in a variety of ways. One is for a manager to learn whether additional effort is needed to pin down an estimate of a parameter. If the solution is not particularly sensitive to a change of a reasonable magnitude, the manager can use the solution with a certain degree of confidence. Conversely, if a solution is sensitive to a change, the manager will probably want to devote more attention to obtaining a reasonably accurate estimate of the parameter.

Another use of sensitivity analysis is to enable managers to explore how certain *changes* might affect a solution. For instance, the availability of a resource (e.g., raw material) very often constrains a solution. A manager might have the opportunity to obtain an additional amount of the resource for a given cost. In order to decide whether or not to buy an additional amount of the resource, the manager will want to know how much improvement in profit the resource will generate and then compare that to the added cost.

The Systems Approach

A systems viewpoint is almost always beneficial in decision making. A *system* can be defined as a set of interrelated parts that must work *together.* In the case of a business organization, the organization is viewed as a system comprised of subsystems (e.g., marketing subsystem, operations subsystem, finance subsystem), which in turn are composed of lower subsystems. The systems approach emphasizes interrelationships among subsystems, but its main theme is that *the whole is greater than the sum of its individual parts.* Hence, from a systems viewpoint, the output and objectives of the organization as a whole take precedence over those of any one subsystem, and should be optimized even if this requires a less than optimum output in one or more subsystems. In contrast to this, an alternative approach would be to concentrate on efficiency within subsystems and thereby achieve overall efficiency. That view tends to overlook the fact that organizations must operate in an environment of scarce resources and that subsystems are often in direct competition for those scarce resources, so that an orderly approach to the allocation of resources is called for.

One important implication relative to quantitative techniques is that many of the techniques tend to produce solutions that are optimal in a narrow sense but that may not be optimal in a broader sense (e.g., a department, plant, division, overall organization). Consequently, managers must evaluate "optimal" solutions produced by quantitative techniques in terms of the larger framework and perhaps modify decisions accordingly.

An interesting problem that has system connotations involves world hunger. We read in the newspapers about how people in some parts of the world are starving, while in other parts of the world, there is an overabundance of food or even that food is rotting and being destroyed. The solution seems simple enough: Why not send the surplus food to those who need it? Unfortunately, that "solution" does not deal with the realities of the *system.* There are other key aspects of this problem that must be overcome. One is transporting the surplus food from current locations to those other areas where it is needed. This is a fairly demanding task. The locations with surplus food have to be identified; the food has to be temporarily stored; arrangements for shipping have to be made (schedules, timing, who will pay for shipping, finding available shipping capacity, and so on). An even more formidable task is distributing the food once it reaches the country in which it is needed. Not only must the political system of that country be dealt with, as well as possible graft and corruption, but also the transportation system of the region. More often than not, the region will have poor roads and very limited capacity for moving goods from ports to inland areas. Suitable landing fields are usually nonexistent in these areas. And even if all these problems could be overcome, the "solution" would only be a temporary one in that the broader problem that must be addressed is how to permanently solve the hunger problem in the region. Thus, taking a systems perspective enables us to achieve a truer picture of a problem and increases the chances that a meaningful resolution to the overall problem will be realized.

Priority Recognition

In virtually every situation a manager must deal with, certain aspects are more important than others. Recognizing this fact of life will enable the manager to direct his or her efforts to where they will do the most good and to avoid wasting time and energy on insignificant aspects of the situation.

Consider an automobile. It has many parts and systems that can malfunction. Some of these are *critical* to the operation of the automobile: it will not function without them or would be dangerous to operate without them. The list of critical items would include the engine and drive train, steering, brakes, tires, electrical system, cooling system, and so on. In terms of maintaining and repairing the car, these items should receive the highest priority if the goal is to have reliable transportation.

There are other items that are of much less importance, such as scratches in the paint, minor dents, a missing piece of chrome, and worn seatcovers. In terms of transportation, these should receive attention only if other more important items have been attended to.

Between these two extremes lie a range of items with priorities between the lowest and the highest. These would be given attention corresponding to their importance to the overall goal. The list might include soft tires, weak battery, wheel alignment, noisy muffler, body rust, inoperative radio, headlights that need adjustment, and so on.

It is fairly obvious that certain parts of an automobile are more critical to its operation than others. The same concept applies to *management.* By recognizing this and setting priorities, a manager will be in a position to more effectively deal with problems as they arise and to prevent many problems from arising at all.

Decision Environments

The environments in which operations-management decisions are made can be classified according to the degree of certainty present. There are three basic categories: certainty, risk, and uncertainty:

> *Certainty* implies that relevant parameters such as costs, capacity, demand, and so on have *known values.*
> *Risk* implies that certain parameters have *probabilistic outcomes.*
> *Uncertainty* implies that it is impossible to assess the likelihood of various possible future events.

Consider these situations:

> **a.** Profit per unit is $5. We have an order for 200 units. How much profit will we make? (This is an example of *certainty* since unit profits and total demand are known.)
> **b.** Profit is $5 per unit. Based on previous experience, there is a 50 percent chance of an order for 100 units and a 50 percent chance of an order for 200 units. What is expected profit? (This is an example of *risk* since demand outcomes are *probabilistic.*)
> **c.** Profit per unit is $5. The probabilities of potential demands are unknown. (This is an example of *uncertainty.*)

The importance of these three decision environments is that they require different techniques of analysis. Thus, some techniques are better suited for one category than for others. One thing you should make note of is the environment for which each technique is appropriate.

DECISION THEORY

Decision theory represents a general approach to decision making. It is suitable for a wide range of operations-management decisions. Among them are capacity planning, product and service design, equipment selection, location planning, and so on. Decisions that lend themselves to a decision theory approach tend to be characterized by these elements:

> 1. A set of possible future conditions exists that will have a bearing on the results of the decision.

2. The manager has a list of alternatives to choose from.
3. There is a known payoff for each alternative under each possible future condition.

In order to use this approach, a decision maker would employ this process.

1. Identify the possible future conditions (e.g., demand will be low, medium, or high; the number of contracts awarded will be one, two, or three; the competitor will introduce a new product, or the competitor will not introduce a new product). These are called *states of nature.*
2. Develop a list of possible *alternatives,* one of which may be to do nothing.
3. Determine or estimate the *payoff* associated with each alternative for every possible future condition.
4. If possible, estimate *how likely* each possible future condition is.
5. Evaluate alternatives according to some *decision criterion* (e.g. maximize expected profit) and select the best alternative.

The information for a decision is often summarized in a decision matrix. A *decision matrix* is a tabular presentation that shows the *expected* payoffs for each alternative under the various possible states of nature. These matrixes can be extremely helpful in choosing among alternatives because they can facilitate comparison of alternatives. Consider the matrix below, which illustrates a capacity planning problem.

	Possible future demand		
Alternatives	*Low*	*Moderate*	*High*
Small facility.	$10*	$10	$10
Medium facility.	7	12	12
Large facility.	(4)	2	16

* Present value in $ millions.

The payoffs are shown in the body of the table. In this instance the payoffs are in terms of present values, which represent an equivalent current dollar value of expected future income minus cost. This is a convenient measure because it places all alternatives on a comparable basis. We can see in the table that if a small facility is built the payoff will be the same for all three possible states of nature. For a medium facility, low demand will have a present value of $7 million, while both moderate and high demand will have present values of $12 million. A large facility will have a loss of $4 million if demand is low, a present value of $2 million if demand is moderate, and a present value of $16 million if demand is high.

The problem for the decision maker is to select one of the alternatives, taking the present values into account.

Evaluation of the alternatives differs, depending on the degree of certainty associated with the possible future conditions. There are three possibilities to consider: complete certainty, risk, and uncertainty.

Decision Making under Certainty

When it is known for certain which of the possible future conditions will actually happen, the decision is usually relatively straightforward: simply choose the alternative that has the highest payoff under that state of nature.

EXAMPLE 1

Determine the best alternative in the preceding decision matrix, if it is known with certainty that demand will be: *(a)* low, *(b)* moderate, *(c)* high.

Solution

Choose the alternative with the highest payoff. Thus, if we know demand will be low, we would elect to build the small facility and realize a payoff of $10 million. If we know demand will be moderate, a medium facility would yield the highest payoff (12 versus either 10 or 2), while for high demand, a large facility will provide the highest payoff.

Although complete certainty is rare in such situations, exercises like the preceding one do provide some perspective on the analysis. Moreover, in some instances there may be an opportunity to consider allocation of funds to research efforts, which may be able to reduce or remove some of the uncertainty surrounding the states of nature.

Decision Making under Uncertainty

At the opposite extreme, there is complete uncertainty: no information is available on how likely the various states of nature are. Under those conditions, four possible decision criteria are *maximin, maximax, Laplace* and *minimax regret.* These approaches can be defined as follows:

> *Maximin*—Determine the worst possible payoff for each alternative, and then choose the alternative that has the best "worst."
>
> *Maximax*—Determine the highest possible payoff, and choose the alternative with that payoff.
>
> *Laplace*—Determine the average payoff for each alternative, and choose the alternative with the highest average.
>
> *Minimax regret*—Determine the worst regret for each alternative, and choose the alternative with the best "worst."

The next two examples illustrate these decision criteria.

EXAMPLE 2

Referring to the above decision matrix, determine which alternative would be chosen under each of these strategies:

a. Maximin
b. Maximax
c. Laplace

Solution

a. The worst payoffs for the alternatives are:

Small facility:	$10 million
Medium facility:	$7 million
Large facility:	−$4 million

Hence, since $10 million is the best, choose to build the small facility using the maximin strategy.

b. The best overall payoff is the $16 million in the third row. Hence, the maximax criterion leads to building a large facility.

c. For the Laplace criterion, first find the row *totals* and then divide each of those amounts by the number of states of nature (three, in this case). Thus we have:

	Row total	Row average
Small facility	30	10.00
Medium facility	31	10.33
Large facility	14	4.67

Since the medium facility has the highest average, it would be chosen under the Laplace criterion.

The maximin approach is essentially a *pessimistic* one in that it takes into account only the worst possible outcome for each alternative. The actual outcome may not be as bad as that, but this approach establishes a "guaranteed minimum."

The maximax approach is an *optimistic*, "go for it" strategy; it does not take into account any payoff other than the best.

The Laplace approach treats the states of nature as equally likely.

EXAMPLE 3

Determine which alternative would be chosen using a minimax regret approach to the capacity planning problem.

Solution

The first step in this approach is to prepare a table of opportunity losses, or regrets. To do this, subtract every payoff *in each column* from the largest positive payoff in that column. For instance, in the first column the largest positive payoff is 10, so each of the three numbers in that column must be subtracted from 10. Going down the column, the regrets will be $10-10=0$, $10-7=3$, and $10-(-4)=14$. In the second column the largest positive payoff is 12. Subtracting each payoff from 12 yields 2, 0, and 10. In the third column, 16 is the largest payoff. The regrets are 6, 4, and 0. These results are summarized in a regret table:

Regrets

Alternatives	Low	Moderate	High
Small facility	0	2	6
Medium facility	3	0	4
Large facility	14	10	0

The second step is to identify the worst regret for each alternative. For the first alternative, the worst is 6; for the second, the worst is 4; and for the third, the worst is 14.

The best of these "worsts" would be chosen using minimax regret. The lowest regret is 4, which is for a medium facility. Hence, that alternative would be chosen.

The main weakness of these approaches (except for Laplace) is that they do not take into account *all* of the payoffs. Instead, they focus on the worst or best, and so they lose some information. The weakness of Laplace is that it treats all states of nature as equally likely. Still, for a given set of circumstances, each has certain merits that can be helpful to a decision maker.

Decision Making under Risk

Between the two extremes of certainty and uncertainty lies the case of risk; the probability of occurrence for each state of nature can be estimated. (Note that because the states are mutually exclusive and collectively exhaustive, these probabilities must add to 1.00.) A widely used approach under such circumstances is the *expected monetary value criterion.* The expected value is computed for each alternative, and the one with the highest expected value is selected. The expected value is the sum of the payoffs for an alternative where each payoff is *weighted* by the probability for the relevant state of nature. Thus, the approach is:

> *Expected monetary value criterion* (EMV)—Determine the expected payoff of each alternative, and choose the one that has the highest expected payoff.

EXAMPLE 4

Using the expected monetary value criterion, identify the best alternative for the previous payoff matrix for these probabilities: low = .30, moderate = .50, and high = .20.

Solution

Find the expected value of each alternative by multiplying the probability of occurrence for each state of nature and the payoff for that state of nature and summing them:

$$EV_{small} = .30(\$10) + .50(\$10) + .20(\$10) = \$10$$
$$EV_{medium} = .30(\$7) + .50(\$12) + .20(\$12) = \$10.5$$
$$EV_{large} = .30(-\$4) + .50(\$2) + .20(\$16) = \$ 3$$

Hence, choose the medium-size facility because it has the highest expected value.

The expected monetary value approach is most appropriate when a decision maker is neither risk adverse nor risk seeking, but instead is risk neutral. Typically, well-established organizations with numerous decisions of this nature tend to use expected value since it provides an indication of the long-run, average payoff. That is, the expected value amount (e.g., $10.5 in the last example) is not an actual payoff, but an expected or average amount that would be approximated if a large number of identical decisions were to be made. Hence, if a decision maker applies this criterion to a large number of similar decisions, the expected payoff for the total will equal the sum of the individual expected payoffs.

Decision Trees

A *decision tree* is a schematic representation of the alternatives available to a decision maker and their possible consequences. The term gets its name from the tree-like appearance of the diagram (see Figure 2–1). While tree diagrams can be used in place of a decision matrix, they are particularly useful for analyzing situations that involve *sequential* decisions. For instance, a manager may initially decide to build a small facility only to discover that demand is much higher than anticipated. In this case, the manager may then be called upon to make a second decision on whether to expand or perhaps build an additional facility.

A decision tree is composed of a number of *nodes* that have *branches* emanating from them (see Figure 2–1). A square node is used to denote a decision point, and circular nodes are used to denote chance events. The tree is read from left to right. Branches leaving square nodes represent alternatives; branches leaving circular nodes represent chance events (i.e., the possible states of nature).

After the tree has been drawn, it is analyzed from *right to left* (i.e., starting with the last decision that might be made). For each decision, choose the alternative that will yield the greatest return. If chance events follow a decision, choose the alternative that has the highest expected monetary value (or lowest expected loss).

FIGURE 2–1

**Format of a
Decision Tree**

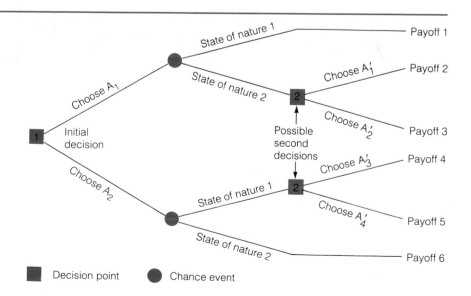

■ Decision point   ● Chance event

EXAMPLE 5

Analyze the decision tree below and determine which initial alternative (build small or build large) should be chosen in order to maximize expected monetary value.

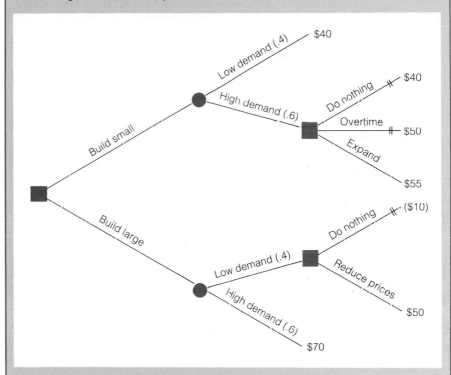

Solution

The dollar amounts at the branch ends indicate the estimated payoffs (usually in terms of present value) if the sequence of chance events and decisions that is traced back to the initial decision occurs. For example, if the initial decision is to build a small facility and it turns out demand is low, the expected value will be $40 (thousand). Similarly, if a small facility is built, demand turns out high, and a later decision is made to expand, the expected value will be $55. The figures in parentheses on branches leaving the chance nodes indicate the probabilities of those states of nature. Hence, the probability of low demand is .4 and the probability of high demand is .6.

Analyze the decisions from right to left:

1. Determine which alternative would be selected for each possible second decision. For a small facility with high demand, there are three choices: do nothing, work overtime, and expand. Since expand has the highest payoff, it would be chosen. Indicate this by placing a double slash through each of the other alternatives. Similarly, for a large facility with low demand, there would be two choices:

EXAMPLE 5 *(concluded)*

do nothing and reduce prices. Reduce prices would be chosen because it has the higher expected value, so a double slash is placed on the other branch.

2. Determine the product of the chance probabilities and their respective payoffs for the remaining branches:

Build small
Low demand   .4($40) = $16
High demand   .6($55) = 33
Build large
Low demand   .4($50) = 20
High demand   .6($70) = 42

3. Determine the expected value of each initial alternative:

Build small: $16 + $33 = $49
Build large: $20 + $42 = $62

Hence, the choice should be the large facility because it has a larger expected value than the small facility.

Expected Value of Perfect Information

In certain situations it is possible to ascertain which state of nature will actually occur in the future. For instance, the choice of location for a restaurant may weigh heavily on whether a new highway will be constructed or whether a zoning permit will be issued. A decision maker may have probabilities of these states of nature. However, it may be possible to delay a decision until it is clear which state of nature will exist. This might involve taking an option to buy the land. If the state of nature is favorable, the option can be exercised; if the state is unfavorable, the option can be allowed to expire. The question to consider is whether the cost of the option will be less than the expected gain due to delaying the decision (i.e., the expected payoff *above* the expected value). This is known as the *expected value of perfect information,* or EVPI.

> *Expected value of perfect information*—the difference between the expected payoff under certainty and the expected payoff under conditions of risk.

Other possible ways of obtaining perfect information depend somewhat on the nature of the decision being made. For example, information about consumer preferences might come from market research; additional information about a product could come from product testing; legal experts might be called on, and so on.

There are two ways to determine the EVPI. One is to compute the expected payoff under certainty and subtract out the expected payoff under risk. Thus,

$$\text{Expected value of perfect information} = \text{Expected payoff under certainty} - \text{Expected payoff under risk} \quad [2\text{--}1]$$

EXAMPLE 6

Using the information contained in Example 4, determine the expected value of perfect information using the formula above.

Solution

First, compute the expected payoff under certainty. To do this, identify the best payoff under each state of nature. Then, combine these by weighting each payoff by the probability of that state of nature and adding the amounts. Thus, the best payoff under low demand is $10, the best under moderate demand is $12, and the best under high demand is $16. The expected payoff under certainty is then:

$$.30(\$10) + .50(\$12) + .20(\$16) = \$12.2$$

The expected payoff under risk, as computed in Example 4, is $10.5. The EVPI is the difference between these:

$$\text{EVPI} = \$12.2 - \$10.5 = \$1.7$$

This figure indicates the upper limit on the amount the decision maker should be willing to spend to obtain perfect information in this case. Thus, if the cost equals or exceeds this amount, the decision maker would be better off not spending additional money and simply going with the alternative that has the highest expected payoff.

A second approach is to use the regret table to compute the EVPI. To do this, find the expected regret for each alternative. The minimum expected regret is equal to the EVPI.

EXAMPLE 7

Determine the expected value of perfect information for the capacity planning problem using the expected regret approach.

Solution

Using information from Examples 2, 3 and 4, we can compute the expected regret for each alternative. Thus:

Small facility	.30(0) + .50(2) + .20(6) = 2.2	
Medium facility	.30(3) + .50(0) + .20(4) = 1.7 [minimum]	
Large facility	.30(14) + .50(10) + .20(0) = 9.2	

The lowest expected regret is 1.70, which is associated with the second alternative. Hence, the EVPI is $1.7 million, which agrees with the previous example using the other approach.

Sensitivity Analysis

Generally speaking, in a decision problem such as the kind being discussed here, both the payoffs and the probabilities are estimated values. Consequently, it can be useful for the decision maker to have some indication of how sensitive the choice of an alternative is to changes in one or more of these values. Unfortunately, it is impossible to consider all possible combinations of every variable in a typical problem. Nevertheless, there are certain things a decision maker can do to judge the sensitivity.

One thing that can be done is to compare the expected values of the alternatives. If one or more of the expected values of other alternatives is close to the best one, it would seem reasonable to conclude that a modest change in a payoff or a probability could result in another alternative having the best expected value. Moreover, very often one or a few values are suspect: the decision maker usually has certain estimates that are less firm than others, and these are the ones he or she would focus on. Hence, an intuitive approach to the problem can be useful.

A more formal approach that can be useful when there are two states of nature involves constructing a graph and then using algebra to determine a range of probabilities for which a given solution is best. In effect, the graph provides a visual indication of the range of probability over which the various alternatives are optimal, while the algebra provides exact values of the end points of the ranges. The following example illustrates the procedure.

EXAMPLE 8

Given the following table, determine the range of probability for state of nature #2 (P)(2) for which each alternative is optimal under the expected value approach.

		State of nature #1	#2
	A	4	12
Alternative	B	16	2
	C	12	8

Solution

First, plot each alternative relative to P(2). To do this, plot the #1 value on the left side of the graph and the #2 value on the right side. For instance, for alternative A, plot 4 on the left side of the graph and 12 on the right side. Then connect these two points. The three alternatives are plotted on the graph as shown.

EXAMPLE 8 *(continued)*

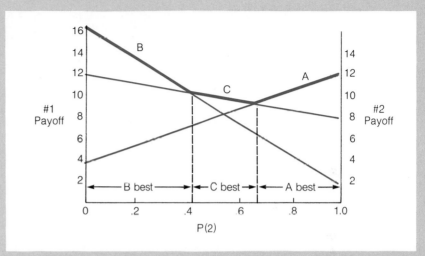

The graph shows us the range of values of P(2) over which each alternative is optimal. Thus, we see that for low values of P(2), (and thus high values of P(1), since P(1) + P(2) = 1.0) alternative B will have the highest expected value; for intermediate values of P(2), alternative C is best, and for higher values of P(2), alternative A is best.

For exact values of the ranges, we need to determine where the upper parts of the lines intersect. Note that at the intersections, the two alternatives represented by the lines would be equivalent in terms of expected value. Hence, the decision maker would be indifferent between the two at that point. To determine the intersections, we must obtain the equation of each line. This is relatively simple to do. Since these are straight lines, they have the form $y = a + bx$ where a is the value at the left axis, b is the slope of the line, and x is P(2). Slope is defined as the change in y for a one-unit change in x. In this type of problem, the distance between the two vertical axes is 1.0. Consequently, the slope of each line is equal to the left-hand value minus the right-hand value. The slopes and equations are:

	#1	#2	Slope	Equation
A	4	12	12 − 4 = +8	4 + 8P(2)
B	16	2	2 − 16 = −14	16 − 14P(2)
C	12	8	8 − 12 = −4	12 − 4P(2)

From the graph we can see that alternative B is best from P(2) = 0 to the point where that straight line intersects with the straight line of alternative C, and that begins the region where C is better. To find that point, we can solve for the value of P(2) at their intersection. This requires setting the two equations equal to each other and

EXAMPLE 8 (concluded)
solving for P(2). Thus,

$$16 - 14P(2) = 12 - 4P(2).$$

Rearranging terms gives us

$$4 = 10P(2).$$

Solving, we obtain P(2) = .40. Thus, alternative B is best from P(2) = 0 up to P(2) = .40. B and C are equivalent at P(2) = .40.

Then alternative C is best from that point until its line intersects with alternative A's line. To find that intersection, we set those two equations equal and solve for P(2). Thus,

$$4 + 8P(2) = 12 - 4P(2)$$

Rearranging terms, we have

$$12P(2) = 8.$$

Solving, we obtain P(2) = .67. Thus, alternative C is best from P(2) > .40 up to P(2) = .67, where A and C are equivalent. For values of P(2) greater than .67 up to P(2) = 1.0, A is best.

SUMMARY

Decision making is an integral part of operations management. Successful decision making tends to be comprised of a number of steps. The most important of these steps is the first one, which is to carefully define the problem.

Operations decision making frequently involves the use of quantitative models, a systems approach, and sensitivity analysis of solutions.

The chapter concludes with a description of decision theory, which is a general approach to decision making that is useful in many different aspects of operations management. Decision theory provides a framework for analysis of decisions. It includes a number of different techniques that can be classified according to the degree of uncertainty associated with a particular decision problem.

The solved problems in this chapter refer to this payoff table:

		New bridge built	No new bridge
Alternative locations	A	(4)	14
for new	B	2	10
warehouse	C	4	6

1. Determine the alternative that would be chosen under each of these decision criteria:
   a. Maximin.
   b. Maximax.
   c. Laplace.

Solution

	New bridge	No new bridge	Maximin (worst)	Maximax (best)	Laplace (average)
A	(4)	14	(4)	14	$10 \div 2 = 5$
B	2	10	2 [best]		$12 \div 2 = 6$ [best]
C	4	6	4 ↙		$10 \div 2 = 5$

Thus, the alternatives chosen would be B under maximin, A under maximax, and B under Laplace.

2. Using the information in the payoff table, develop a table of regrets, and then:
   a. Determine the alternative that would be chosen under minimax regret.
   b. Determine the expected value of perfect information using the regret table, assuming that the probability of a new bridge being built is .60.

Solution

To obtain the regrets, subtract all payoffs in each column from the best payoff in the column. The regrets are:

	New bridge	No new bridge
A	8	0
B	2	4
C	0	8

a. Minimax regret involves finding the worst regret for each alternative and then choosing the alternative that has the "best" worst. Thus, B would be chosen:

	Worst
A	8
B	4 [best]
C	8

b. Once the minimax regret alternative has been determined, the EVPI can be computed as the expected regret for that alternative. Since the probability of a new bridge is given as .60, we can deduce that the probability of no new bridge is $1.00 - .60 = .40$. The expected regret is then:

$$.60(2) + .40(4) = 2.80.$$

Hence, the EVPI is 2.80.

3. Using the probabilities of .60 for a new bridge and .40 for no new bridge, compute the expected value for each alternative in the payoff table, and identify the alternative that would be selected under the maximum expected value approach.

Solution

$$A: .60(-4) + .40(14) = 3.20$$
$$B: .60(2)\ \ + .40(10) = 5.20 \text{ [best]}$$
$$C: .60(4)\ \ + .40(6)\ = 4.80$$

4. Compute the EVPI using the information from the previous problem.

Solution

Using formula 2–1, the EVPI is the expected payoff under certainty minus the maximum expected value. The expected payoff under certainty involves multiplying the best payoff in each column by the column probability and then summing those amounts. The best payoff in the first column is 4, and the best in the second is 14. Thus,

$$\frac{\text{Expected payoff}}{\text{under certainty}} = .60(4) + .40(14) = 8.00$$

The expected value of perfect information is then

$$\text{EVPI} = 8.00 - 5.20 = 2.80.$$

DISCUSSION AND REVIEW QUESTIONS

1. What is the chief role of the operations manager?
2. Outline the steps in the decision-making process.
3. What are the main characteristics of operations decisions?
4. What is a model? What are the primary advantages and limitations of models?
5. How would you respond to this criticism of models: "Because all models are incomplete—they leave out one or more variables—they are misleading."
6. What are some of the reasons given in the chapter for poor decisions?
7. What is sensitivity analysis and how can it be useful to a decision maker?

8. Contrast maximax and maximin decision strategies. Under what circumstances would one rather than the other be appropriate?

9. Under what circumstances is expected monetary value appropriate as a decision criterion? When isn't it appropriate?

10. What is a systems approach and how can failure to use this approach lead to poor decisions?

11. Explain or define each of these terms:
    a. Laplace criterion.
    b. Minimax regret.
    c. Expected value.

d. Expected value of perfect information.

12. What information does a decision maker need to do an expected value analysis of a problem? What options are available to the decision maker if the probabilities of the states of nature are unknown? Can you think of a way sensitivity analysis might be useful in such a case?

13. Explain why a systems approach to productivity improvements would be beneficial, and why without that perspective, actual improvements might end up being less than anticipated.

PROBLEMS

1. A small building contractor has recently experienced two successive years in which work opportunities exceeded the firm's capacity. The contractor must now make a decision on capacity for next year. He has estimated profits under each of the two states of nature he believes might occur, as shown in the matrix below. Which alternative should be selected if the decision criterion is:
   a. Maximax?
   b. Maximin?
   c. Laplace?
   d. Minimax regret?

| | Next year's demand | |
Alternative	Low	High
Do nothing.	$50*	$60
Expand	20	80
Subcontract	40	70

* Profit in $ 000s.

2. (Refer to the previous problem.) Suppose after a certain amount of discussion, it turns out that the contractor is able to subjectively assess the probabilities of low and high demand: $P(\text{low}) = .3$ and $P(\text{high}) = .7$.
   a. Determine the expected profit of each alternative. Which alternative is best? Why?
   b. Analyze the problem using a decision tree. Show the expected profit of each alternative on the tree.
   c. Compute the expected value of perfect information. How could the manager use this knowledge?

3. (Refer to the previous two problems.) Construct a graph that will enable you to perform sensitivity analysis on the problem. Over what range of $P(\text{High})$ would the "Do nothing" alternative be best? Expand? Subcontract?

4. A firm that plans to expand its product line must decide whether to build a small or a large facility to produce the new products. If it builds a small facility and demand turns out to be low, the net present value after deducting for building costs will be $400,000. If demand turns out to be high, the firm can either maintain the small facility or expand it. Expansion would have a net present value of $300,000, and maintaining the small facility would have a net present value of $50,000.

   If a large facility is built and demand is high, the estimated net present value is $800,000. If demand turns out to be low, the net present value will be −$10,000.

   The probability that demand will be high is estimated to be .60, and the probability of low demand is estimated to be .40.

a. Analyze using a tree diagram.
b. Compute the EVPI. How could this information be used?

5. (Refer to the previous problem.) Perform sensitivity analysis on P(demand low). Determine the range over which each alternative would be best in terms of the value of P(demand low).

6. Theme Park, Incorporated's lease is about to expire, and management must decide whether to renew the lease for another 10 years or to relocate near the site of a proposed motel. The town planning board is currently debating the merits of granting approval to the motel. A consultant has estimated the net present values of Theme Park's two alternatives under each state of nature as shown below. What course of action would you recommend using:
a. Maximax?
b. Maximin?
c. Laplace?
d. Minimax regret?

Options:	Motel approved	Motel rejected
Renew . . .	$ 500,000	$4,000,000
Relocate . .	5,000,000	100,000

7. (Refer to the previous problem.) Suppose that after some thought, the manager has decided that there is a .35 probability that the motel's application will be approved.
a. If the manager uses maximum expected monetary value as the decision criterion, which alternative should be chosen?
b. Represent this problem in the form of a decision tree.
c. If the manager has been offered the option of a temporary lease while the town planning board considers the motel's application, would you advise the manager to sign the lease? The lease will cost $24,000.

8. Construct a graph that can be used for sensitivity analysis for the preceding problem.
a. How sensitive is the solution to the problem in terms of the probability estimate of .35?
b. Suppose that after consulting with a member of the town planning board, management decides that an estimate of approval is approximately .45. How sensitive is the solution to this revised estimate? Explain.

9. A firm must decide whether to construct a small, medium, or large stamping plant. A consultant's report indicates a .20 probability that demand will be low and an .80 probability that demand will be high.

If the firm builds a small facility and demand turns out to be low, the net present value will be $42 million. If demand turns out to be high, the firm can either subcontract and realize a net present value of $42 million or expand greatly for a net present value of $48 million.

A medium-size facility could be built as a hedge: if demand turns out to be low, its net present value is estimated at $22 million, while if demand turns out to be high, the firm could do nothing and realize a net present value of $46 million or expand and realize a net present value of $50 million.

If the firm builds the large facility and demand is low, the net present value will be −$20 million, while high demand will result in a net present value of $72 million.
a. Analyze this problem using a decision tree.
b. What would the maximin alternative be?
c. Compute the EVPI and interpret it.
d. Perform sensitivity analysis on P(high).

10. A manager must decide how many machines of a certain type to buy. The machines will be used to fill demand for a new gear. The manager has narrowed the decision down to two alternatives: buy one machine or buy two. If only one machine is purchased and demand is more than it can handle, a second machine can be purchased at a later time. However, the cost per machine would be lower if the two machines were to be purchased at the same time.

The estimated probability of low demand is .30, and the estimated probability of high demand is .70.

The net present value associated with

the purchase of two machines initially is $75,000 if demand is low and $130,000 if demand is high.

The net present value for one machine and low demand is $90,000. If demand is high, there are three options. One option would be to do nothing, and it would have a net present value of $90,000. A second option would be to subcontract; it would have a net present value of

$110,000. The third option would be to purchase a second machine. This option would have a net present value of $100,000.

How many machines should the manager purchase initially? Use a decision tree to analyze this problem.

11. Determine the course of action that has the highest EMV for the accompanying tree diagram.

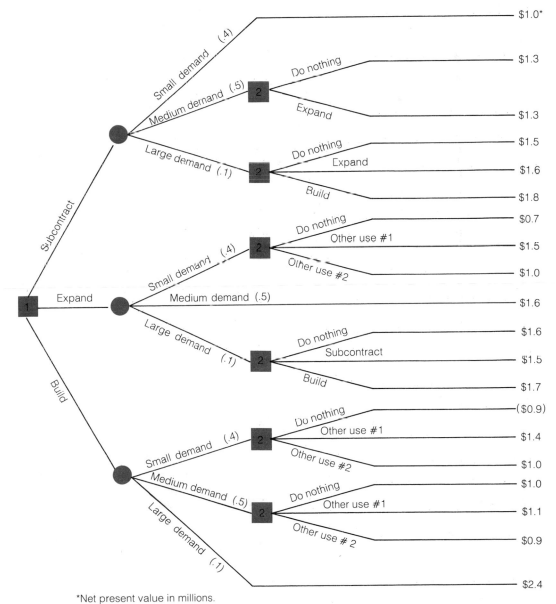

*Net present value in millions.

12. Space engineers have three alternative designs from which to choose the configuration of a component for an unmanned space shot. The space vehicle is likely to encounter one of four different conditions, which have probabilities of occurrence as listed in the decision matrix shown along with the payoffs for each combination of design and state of nature. Additional data from previous flights are available but will require additional expenditures to analyze. However, the project director is quite confident that analysis of the data will clearly indicate which state of nature will be encountered. What amount would be justified for the data analysis?

	States of nature			
	A	*B*	*C*	*D*
Probability	.3	.4	.2	.1
Designs				
001	20*	10	10	0
002	15	10	0	40
003	10	20	30	30

* ($000).

SELECTED BIBLIOGRAPHY

Bierman, Harold; Charles P. Bonini; and Warren H. Hausman. *Quantitative Analysis for Business Decisions.* 6th ed. Homewood, Ill.: Richard D. Irwin, 1981.

Eppen, G. D. and F. J. Gould. *Introductory Management Science.* Englewood Cliffs, N.J.: Prentice-Hall, 1984.

Levin, Richard I.; Charles A. Kirkpatrick; and David S. Rubin. *Quantitative Approaches to Management.* 5th ed. New York: McGraw-Hill, 1982.

Stevenson, William J. *Business Statistics: Concepts and Applications.* 2d ed. New York: Harper & Row, 1985.

Taylor, Bernard W. *Introduction to Management Science.* Dubuque, Iowa: Wm. C. Brown, 1982.

Ulvila, J. W. and R. V. Brown. "Decision Analysis Comes of Age." *Harvard Business Review,* September–October 1982, p. 130.

Linear Programming

GRAPHICAL LINEAR PROGRAMMING, 66

    Outline of Graphical Procedure, 66
    Plotting Constraints, 67
    Identifying the Feasible Solution Space, 69
    Plotting the Objective Function Line, 69
    Solutions and Corner Points, 72
    Minimization, 73

THE SIMPLEX METHOD, 75

    Setting up the Initial Tableau, 77
    The Test for Optimality, 79
    Developing the Second Tableau, 79
    Developing the Third Tableau, 81
    Handling $\geq$ and $=$ Constraints, 83
    Summary of Maximization Procedure, 84
    Minimization Problems, 85
    Sensitivity Analysis, 88

SOLVED PROBLEMS, 93

DISCUSSION AND REVIEW QUESTIONS, 97

PROBLEMS, 98

SELECTED BIBLIOGRAPHY, 100

The term *linear programming* refers to a quantitative approach to problem solving that consists of a sequence of steps that will lead to an optimal solution to a class of problems in cases where an optimum exists. There are a number of different linear programming techniques, some of which are special purpose (i.e., used to find solutions for specific types of problems) and others that are more general in scope. This supplement describes the two general-purpose models: graphical linear programming and the simplex method. Graphical linear programming is presented because it provides a visual portrayal of many of the important concepts of linear programming. However, it is limited to problems that involve only two variables. Simplex is a mathematical approach, which lacks the visual features of the graphical approach, but it can handle more than two variables, making it much more useful for solving real problems which often involve a large number of variables.

Linear programming models are used to help operations managers make decisions in many different areas. These include allocation of scarce resources, assignment problems (assigning workers to jobs, jobs to machines, and so on), transportation problems (determining distribution plans when shipping goods from multiple origins to multiple destinations, such as from 4 warehouses to 10 retail outlets), blending problems (petroleum products, diets), and other problems. As you can see, linear programming has a broad range of application. Moreover, in all applications the use of linear programming guarantees an optimal solution to the mathematical model.

Situations that lend themselves to modeling using linear programming techniques are characterized by:

1. Decision making in an environment of certainty.
2. A single goal or objective.
3. Decision variables.
4. Constraints.
5. Linear relationships among variables.
6. Nonnegativity.

Linear programming algorithms require that a *single goal* or objective, such as the maximization of profits, be specified. There are two general types of goals, maximization and minimization. For example, a manager might wish to maximize profits, revenues, efficiency, or rate of return. Conversely, a manager might want to minimize cost, time, distance traveled, or scrap. The profit, cost (etc.) per unit of output or input is summarized by an *objective function*.

Decision variables represent choices available to the decision maker either in terms of amounts of inputs or outputs. For example, some problems involve choosing a combination of inputs that will minimize total costs, while others involve selecting a combination of outputs that will maximize profits or revenues.

Constraints are limitations that restrict the alternatives available to decision makers. There are three types of constraints: less than or equal to ($\leq$), greater than or equal to ($\geq$) and simply equal to ($=$). A less than or equal to constraint implies an upper limit on the amount of some scarce resource (e.g., machine hours, labor hours, materials) available for use. A greater than or equal to constraint specifies a lower bound that must be achieved in the final solution (must contain at least 10 percent real fruit juice; must get at least 30 MPG on the highway). The equal to constraint is more restrictive in the sense that it specifies *exactly* what a decision variable should equal (make 200 units of product A). A linear programming model can consist of one or more constraints. In cases where there are multiple constraints, they may all be of the same type (e.g., all "less than or equal to" constraints), or they might be a mixture of types (e.g., three "less than or equal to" constraints and one "greater than or equal to" constraint). Many possibilities exist. Taken as a whole, the constraints related to a given problem define the set of all feasible combinations of decision variables, which is referred to as the *feasible solution space.* Linear programming algorithms are designed to search the feasible solution space for the combination of decision variables that will yield an optimum in terms of the objective function.

Use of a linear programming model requires *linear* constraints and a *linear* objective function. This means that no variable can have an exponent other than 1 and that there are no *combinations* of variables (e.g., $x \times y$). For example, a maximization problem might have as its objective function:

$$\text{Maximize:} \quad Z = \$3x + \$5y$$

This would mean that there are two products involved, x and y, and that each unit of x that is produced or sold will contribute $3 while each unit of y will contribute $5 to profit or revenue, depending on the problem. Linearity is reflected by the fact that the total contribution of x is a linear function of the number of units of x involved: 3 units of x will yield $3(3) = $9, 4 units will yield $3(4) = $12, and 10 units will yield $3(10) = $30. Similarly, 1 unit of y will yield $5(1) = $5, 10 units will yield 10 times that amount, and so on. A similar situation also occurs in minimization. For instance, if each unit of x costs $2 and each unit of y costs $4, we have:

$$\text{Minimize:} \quad Z = \$2x + \$4y$$

The total cost will be the number of units of x used times its cost per unit plus the number of units of y used times its cost per unit.

Hence, 10 units of x and 20 units of y will result in a total cost of $2(10) + $4(20) = $100.

A similar interpretation applies to constraints. For example, a constraint might be $15x + 10y \leq 200$ labor-hours. This indicates that there are 200 labor-hours available (say, in a week) and that each unit of x that is produced will consume 15 labor-hours and each unit of y will consume 10 labor-hours. The total number of hours consumed is a linear function of x and y: 15 times the number of x units plus 10 times the number of y units.

The *nonnegativity* aspect of linear programming means that negative values of decision variables are not permitted; decision variables can only take on positive values or be equal to zero. This has intuitive appeal: in a problem involving a question of how much of product A to produce, an answer of A = −9 would not make sense.

In some situations only *integer* solutions are acceptable. For example, in a situation where a few units of a large item such as oil-carrying supertankers are to be produced, an answer that requires, say, 2.5 tankers would not be acceptable. Conversely, if we are producing an item daily, such as a two-cycle engine and the optimal linear programming solution is to produce 2.5 per day, this will result in 5 units every other day. Or, if the output is measured on a *continuous* scale, such as gallons, pounds, or feet, noninteger solutions would be acceptable. For problems that require integer optimal solutions, a technique known as *integer programming* would be used. However, that technique is somewhat more complicated than necessary for our purposes and, consequently, will not be covered in this text.

Let's now turn our attention to the basic concepts of linear programming as illustrated by the graphical method.

GRAPHICAL LINEAR PROGRAMMING

Graphical linear programming is a method for finding optimal solutions to two-variable problems. This section describes that approach.

Outline of Graphical Procedure

The graphical method of linear programming involves plotting the constraints on a graph and identifying an area or region that satisfies all of the constraints. This is known as the *feasible solution space.* Next, the objective function is plotted and used to identify the optimal point in the feasible solution space. The coordinates of the point can sometimes be read directly from the graph, although generally, an algebraic determination of the coordinates of the point is necessary.

The general procedure followed in the graphical approach is:

1. Set up the objective function and the constraints in mathematical format.
2. Plot the constraints.
3. Determine the feasible solution space.
4. Plot the objective function.
5. Determine the optimum solution.

The technique can best be illustrated through solution of a typical problem. Consider the following:

Two products, x and y, can be produced on a certain machine. There are 12 hours of machine time available to produce these products. Product x requires one hour per unit, and product y requires three hours per unit. Both products require one raw material: product x uses 4 pounds of raw material per unit, and product y uses 3 pounds. There are 24 pounds of this raw material available for these two products. If the goal is to maximize the profit from these two products and product x contributes \$4 per unit to profit and product y \$5 per unit, what quantity of each should be produced?

To solve this problem, we must first set it up in mathematical format. This involves the following:

1. Identify the decision variables. In this case they are product x and product y.
2. Formulate the objective function. It is:

$$\text{Maximize:} \quad Z = \$4x + \$5y.$$

3. Identify and formulate the constraints. There are two constraints: machine time and raw material. The constraints are:

$$\text{Machine time:} \quad x + 3y \leq 12$$

$$\text{Raw material:} \quad 4x + 3y \leq 24$$

4. Add the nonnegativity constraints. They are $x, y, \geq 0$.

Thus the problem is:

$$\text{Maximize:} \quad Z = \$4x + \$5y$$

Subject to:
Machine time: $\quad x + 3y \leq 12$
Raw material: $\quad 4x + 3y \leq 24$
$$x, y \geq 0$$

The next step is to plot the constraints.

Plotting Constraints

The procedure for plotting constraints is quite simple:

1. Replace the inequality sign with an equal sign. This transforms the constraint into an equation of a *straight line*.

2. Determine where the line intersects each axis.
   a. To find where it crosses the y-axis, set x equal to zero and solve the equation for the value of y.
   b. To find where it crosses the x-axis, set y equal to zero and solve the equation for the value of x.
3. Mark these intersections on the axes and connect them with a straight line.
4. Indicate by shading (or by arrows at the ends of the constraint line) whether the inequality is greater than or less than. (A general rule to determine which side of the line satisfies the inequality is to pick the point 0,0 and see whether it is greater than or less than the constraint amount.)
5. Repeat steps 1–4 for each constraint.

First, let's plot the machine hours constraint, which is $x + 3y = 12$.

1. Make it an equality: $x + 3y = 12$.
2. Set $x = 0$ and solve for y: $(0) + 3y = 12$, so $y = 4$.
   Set $y = 0$ and solve for x: $x + 3(0) = 12$, so $x = 12$.
3. Mark the points on the graph and connect with a straight line.
4. Shade the area that satisfies the constraint. (Inserting $x = 0$, $y = 0$ into the equation yields a value of 0, which is less than 12. Hence, all points on that side of the line are less than 12.) See Figure 2S–1. Note that only the area in the first quadrant is shaded due to the nonnegativity constraints.

FIGURE 2S–1

The Machine Constraint

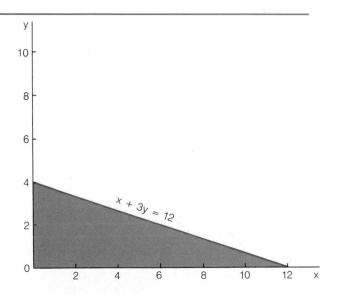

FIGURE 2S–2

The Raw Material Constraint Is Added to the Graph

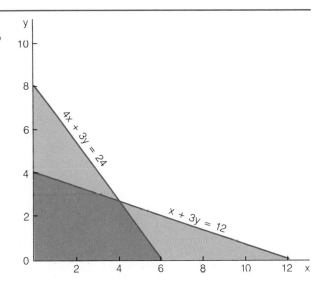

The second constraint can be plotted similarly.

1. Make it an equality: $4x + 3y = 24$.
2. Set $x = 0$ and solve for y: $4(0) + 3y = 24$, so $y = 8$.
   Set $y = 0$ and solve for x: $4x + 3(0) = 24$, so $x = 6$.
3. Mark the points on the graph and connect them with a straight line.
4. Shade in the area that satisfies this constraint (see Figure 2S–2). Notice that some of the points satisfy only one of the constraints while other points satisfy both.

Identifying the Feasible Solution Space

The feasible solution space is the set of all points (i.e., the *area*) that satisfies all constraints. (Recall that the x and y axes form nonnegativity constraints.) The heavily shaded area shown in Figure 2S–2 is the feasible solution space for our problem.

Plotting the Objective Function Line

The objective function is actually a *family* of lines; the lines are parallel, but each represents a different amount. For example, one line could be $\$4x + \$5y = 20$; another $\$4x + \$5y = 40$; and another $\$4x + \$5y = 60$. These lines are illustrated in Figure 2S–3. Note that the lines are *parallel* and that the farther away from the origin the line is, the greater the value of the objective function. In addition, each line is an *isoprofit* line: every combination of x and y on the line will yield the same profit (e.g., $\$40$).

These are but a few of the many different lines that could be drawn. Some of these lines would cross the feasible solution space and others would not. This is important since points that do not

FIGURE 2S–3

Three Isoprofit Lines

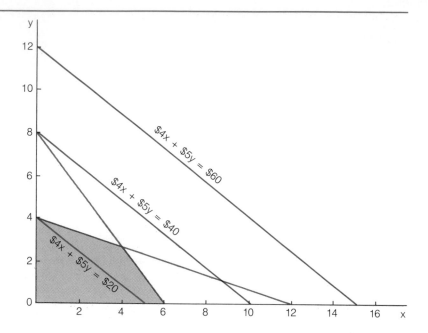

lie within the feasible solution space cannot possibly be feasible solutions. Given the three lines in Figure 2S–3, only the line $4x + $5y = 20 has points within the feasible solution space. However, it is not difficult to see that other lines parallel to this, but farther from the origin, could be drawn. What we want is the farthest line that *touches* the feasible solution space because it will yield the greatest *feasible* value for the objective function.

Instead of using trial-and-error, we can easily identify the line that will yield the maximum profit for an *x–y* combination that is in the feasible solution space, in another way. All we need is an isoprofit line that crosses the feasible solution space.[1]

To plot the objective function, select a value to set it equal to. One easy-to-use value would be the product of the *x* and *y* coefficients (in this case 4 and 5: $4 \times 5 = 20). This is one of the lines plotted in Figure 2S–3. Note that it does cross the feasible solution space. However, that will not always happen. When a line is outside of the feasible solution space, divide the selected value of the objective function (e.g., $60) by a constant so that it does cross the feasible solution space (e.g., $60/3 = $20, and the $20 crosses the space). Conversely, if the line crosses the feasible solution space but is too close to the origin to be useful, multiply the value by a constant— 1.5, 2, 10, 100, or other number—to obtain a more useful line.)

---

[1] Strictly speaking, the line need not cross the feasible solution space. However, it is convenient to work with such a line.

FIGURE 2S–4

The Optimum Point

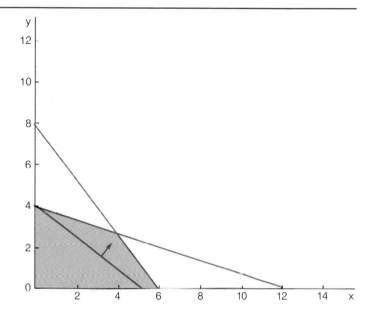

Plot the line as you would a constraint line: set $x = 0$ and solve for y and then set $y = 0$ and solve for x.

Since the profit increases as the line moves away from the origin, "slide" the line—parallel to itself—away from the origin (imagine a series of parallel lines being drawn). The objective is to identify the last point in the feasible solution space touched by one of the parallel lines. The x and y coordinates of that point indicate the quantities of x and y that will maximize the objective function. (See Figure 2S–4.) In this example, the point is where the two constraints intersect. While we can read this directly from the graph in some cases, it is usually best to use algebra to determine the exact coordinates of the intersection. We can do this by solving the equations of the two lines *simultaneously* (i.e., find the one value of x and one value of y that satisfy both equations). To do this, we make both constraints equalities:

$$x + 3y = 12$$
$$4x + 3y = 24$$

We have two equations and two unknowns. What we would like to have is one equation with one unknown since this would enable us to readily determine the value of one of the two variables. Then by substituting that value into one of the two constraints, the value of the other variable can be determined.

When solving equations simultaneously we usually have to modify one or both of the equations to obtain one set of coefficients that are equal, so that when we subtract one equation from the other, one of the terms will drop out, leaving us with the one variable in a single equation. In this instance, the y coefficients are equal, so modifying is not necessary. (The first solved problem at the end of this section illustrates the more general case.) Hence, merely subtracting one from the other will produce the desired result. Thus,

$$\begin{array}{r} 4x + 3y = 24 \\ -(\ x + 3y = 12) \\ \hline 3x \qquad = 12 \end{array}$$

Solving, we find that $x = 4$. Next, we can substitute this value into one of the equations to find the value of y. Either equation will do. For example, the second equation yields:

$$4 + 3y = 12.$$

Solving for y we find $y = 8/3$, or 2.67.

Thus, the solution to the problem that will maximize profit is to produce 4 units of x and 2.67 units of y. Substituting these values into the objective function will indicate the optimal profit. Thus,

$$\$4(4) + \$5(2.67) = \$29.35.$$

Solutions and Corner Points

The feasible solution space in graphical linear programming is a polygon. Moreover, the solution to all problems will be at one of

The Solution Is Always at a Corner Point

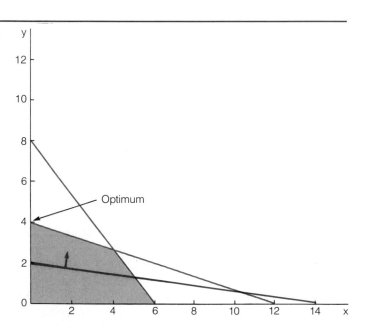

FIGURE 2S–6

The Objective Function Is Parallel to One of the Constraint Lines

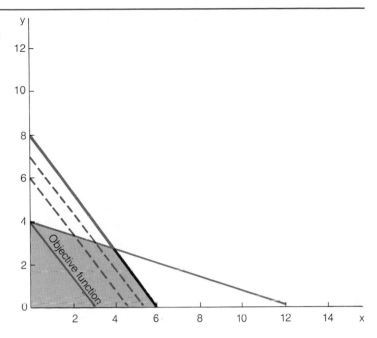

the corner points of the polygon. In a few rare instances, the objective function may be *parallel* to one of the constraint lines. In such a case, *every* combination of x and y on the segment of the constraint that touches the feasible solution space is equally optimal. Hence, there are *multiple* optimal solutions to the problem. Even in such a case, the solution will also be at a corner point. In fact, the solution will be at *two* corner points: those at the ends of the segment that touches the feasible solution space. Figures 2S–5 and 2S–6 illustrate solutions at corner points and an objective function line that is parallel to a constraint line. Figure 2S–5 shows the same problem that was solved in this section with a different objective function: $Z = \$2x + \$14y$.

Minimization

Graphical minimization problems are quite similar to maximization problems. There are, however, two important differences. One is that the constraints are usually of the "greater than or equal to" type instead of "less than or equal to." This causes the feasible solution space to be outside of the polygon instead of inside. The other difference is that the objective is to *minimize* (e.g., minimize cost, distance, scrap). The optimum corner point is found by sliding the objective function (which is an *isocost* line) *toward* the origin instead of away from it.

EXAMPLE S–1

Solve the following problem using graphical linear programming.

$$\text{Minimize:} \quad Z = \$8x + \$12y$$
$$\text{Subject to:} \quad 5x + 2y \geq 20$$
$$4x + 3y \geq 24$$
$$y \geq 2$$

Solution

1. Plot the constraints (shown in Figure 2S–7).
   a. Change constraints to equalities.
   b. For each constraint, set $x = 0$ and solve for y, then set $y = 0$ and solve for x.
   c. Graph each constraint. Note that $y = 2$ is a horizontal line parallel to the x-axis and 2 units above it.

FIGURE 2S–7

The Constraints Define the Feasible Solution Space

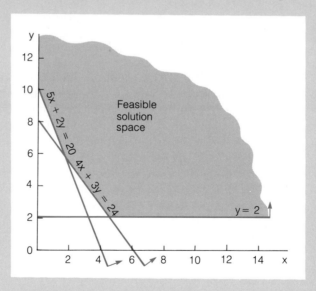

2. Shade in the feasible solution space (see Figure 2S–7).
3. Plot the objective function.
   a. Select a value for the objective function which causes it to cross the feasible solution space. Try $8 \times 12 = 96$: $\$8x + \$12y = \$96$ (acceptable).
   b. Graph the line (see Figure 2S–8).
4. Slide the objective function *toward* the origin, being careful to keep it parallel to the original line.
5. The optimum (last feasible point) is shown in Figure 2S–8. The

---

EXAMPLE S–1 (concluded)
FIGURE 2S–8

The Optimum Is the Last Point the Objective Function Touches As It Is Moved Toward the Origin

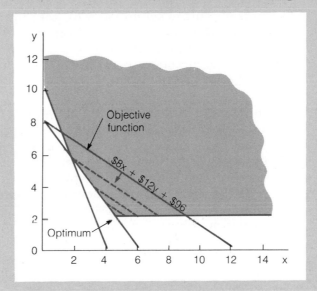

y coordinate ($y = 2$) can be determined by inspection from the graph. Note that the optimum point is at the intersection of the line $y = 2$ and the line $4x + 3y = 24$. Substituting the value of y into the latter equation will yield the value of x at the intersection:

$$4x + 3(2) = 24; \quad \text{so } x = 4.5$$

Thus, the optimum is $x = 4.5$ units and $y = 2$.

6. Compute the minimum cost:

$$\$8x + \$12y = \$8(4.5) + \$12(2) = \$60$$

THE SIMPLEX METHOD

The *simplex method* is a general-purpose linear programming algorithm that is widely used to solve large-scale problems. Although it lacks the intuitive appeal of the graphical approach discussed in this chapter, its ability to handle problems with more than two decision variables makes it extremely valuable for solving problems often encountered in operations management.

The simplex technique involves a series of iterations; successive improvements are made until an optimum solution is achieved. The technique requires simple mathematical operations (addition, subtraction, multiplication, and division), but the computations are lengthy as well as tedious, and the slightest error can lead to a good deal of frustration. For these reasons, most users of the technique rely on computers to handle the computations, while they concentrate on the solutions. Still, some familiarity with manual computations is helpful in understanding the simplex process. You will discover that it is better to *not* use your calculator in working through these problems because the rounding involved can easily distort the results. Instead, it is best to work with numbers in fractional form.

Even though simplex can readily handle three or more decision variables, you will gain considerable insight on the technique if we use a two-variable problem to illustrate it, because you will be able to compare what is happening in the simplex calculations with a graphical solution to the problem.

It will be instructive to consider the simplex solution of the same problem that was used to illustrate a graphical solution. That problem is repeated here:

$$\text{Maximize:} \quad Z = \$4x + \$5y$$
$$\text{Subject to:} \quad x + 3y \leq 12$$
$$4x + 3y \leq 24$$
$$x,\ y \geq 0$$

The solution is shown graphically in Figure 2S–9. Now let's see how the simplex technique can be used to obtain the solution.

The simplex technique involves generating a series of solutions that are in tabular form, called *tableaus*. By inspecting the bottom row of each tableau, one can immediately tell if it represents the optimum solution. Each tableau corresponds to a corner point of the feasible solution space. The first tableau corresponds to the origin. Subsequent tableaus are developed by shifting to an adjacent

FIGURE 2S–9

Graphical Solution

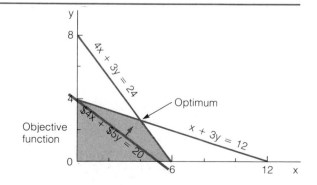

corner point in the direction that yields the highest rate of return. This process continues as long as a positive rate of return exists. Thus, the process encompasses the following steps:

1. Set up the initial tableau.
2. Develop a revised tableau using the information contained in the first tableau.
3. Inspect to see if it is optimum.
4. Repeat steps 2 and 3 until no further improvement is possible.

Let's see how it works.

Setting up the Initial Tableau

Obtaining the first tableau is a two-step process. First, we must rewrite the constraints and objective function so that they are in the necessary form. Then we put this information into tabular form and supply a few computations that are needed to complete the table.

Rewriting the objective function and constraints involves the addition of *slack variables,* one for each constraint. These variables represent the amount of each resource that will not be used if the solution is implemented. In the initial solution, with each of the real variables equal to zero, the solution consists solely of slack. The constraints with slack added become equalities:

$$(1) \quad x + 3y + 1s_1 \qquad = 12$$
$$(2) \quad 4x + 3y \qquad + 1s_2 = 24$$

It is useful in setting up the table to represent each slack variable in every equation. Hence, we can write these equations in an equivalent form:

$$(1) \quad x + 3y + 1s_1 + 0s_2 = 12$$
$$(2) \quad 4x + 3y + 0s_1 + 1s_2 = 24$$

The objective function can be written in similar form:

$$Z = \$4x + \$5y + \$0s_1 + \$0s_2$$

The slack variables are given coefficients of zero in the objective function because they do not produce any contribution to profits. Thus, the information above can be summarized as:

Maximize:　$Z = \$4x + \$5y + \$0s_1 + \$0s_2$
Subject to:
$$(1) \quad x + 3y + 1s_1 + 0s_2 = 12$$
$$(2) \quad 4x + 3y + 0s_1 + 1s_2 = 24$$

This forms the basis for our initial tableau, which is shown in Table 2S–1.

TABLE 2S–1

Partial Initial Tableau

Profit per unit for variables in solution			Decision variables				
C_j			$4	$5	$0	$0	Objective row
	Variables in solution		x	y	s_1	s_2	Solution quantity
$0	s_1		1	3	1	0	12
$0	s_2		4	3	0	1	24

In order to complete the first tableau, we will need two additional rows, a Z row and a $C - Z$ row. The Z row values indicate the reduction in profits that would occur if one unit of the variable in that column were added to the solution. The $C - Z$ row shows the potential for increasing profits if one unit of the variable in that column were to be added to the solution.

To compute the Z values, multiply the coefficients in each column by their respective row profit per unit amounts and sum within columns. To begin with, all values are zero:

C_j	x	y	s_1	s_2	Quantity
$0	(1)0	(3)0	(1)0	(0)0	(12)0
$0	(4)0	(3)0	(0)0	(1)0	(24)0
Z	0	0	0	0	0

The last value in the Z row indicates the total profit associated with a given solution (tableau). Since the initial solution has $x = 0$ and $y = 0$, it is not surprising that profit is 0.

Values in the $C - Z$ row are computed by subtracting the Z value in each column from the value of the objective row for that column. Thus:

Variable row:	x	y	s_1	s_2
Objective row (C):	$4	$5	$0	$0
Z	0	0	0	0
$C - Z$	4	5	0	0

The completed tableau is shown in Table 2S–2.

TABLE 2S–2

The Initial Tableau

$C \rightarrow$			$4	$5	$0	$0	
$\downarrow$	Variables in solution		x	y	s_1	s_2	Solution quantity
$0	s_1		1	3	1	0	12
$0	s_2		4	3	0	1	24
	Z		0	0	0	0	0
	$C - Z$		4	5	0	0	

The Test for Optimality

If all the values in the $C - Z$ row of any tableau are zero or negative, the optimum solution has been obtained. In this case you can see that the $C - Z$ row contains two positive values, 4 and 5, indicating that improvement is possible.

Developing the Second Tableau

Values in the $C - Z$ row reflect the profit potential for each unit of the variable in a given column. For instance, the 4 indicates that each unit of variable x added to the solution will increase profits by $4. Similarly, the 5 indicates that each unit of y can contribute $5 to profits. Given a choice between $4 per unit and $5 per unit, we shall select the larger and focus on that column, which means that y will come into the solution. Now we must determine which variable will leave the solution. (At each tableau, one variable will come into solution and one will go out of solution, keeping the number of variables in solution constant. Note that the number of variables in solution must always equal the number of constraints. Thus, since in this problem there are three constraints, all solutions will have three variables.)

To determine which variable will leave the solution, we will use the numbers in the body of the table in the column of the entering variable (i.e., 3 and 3). These are called *row pivot values*. Divide each one into the corresponding solution quantity amount, as shown in Table 2S–3. The smaller of these two ratios indicates the variable that will leave the solution. Thus, variable s_1 will leave and be replaced with y. In graphical terms, we have moved up the y axis to the next corner point. By determining the smallest ratio, we have found which constraint is the limiting factor. Turn back to Figure 2S–2. Note that the two constraints intersect the y axis at 4 and 8, the two row ratios we have just computed. The second tableau will describe this corner point; it will indicate the profits and quanti-

TABLE 2S–3

The Leaving and Entering Variables

C		$4	$5	$0	$0	
	Variables in solution	x	y	s_1	s_2	Solution quantity
$0	s_1	1	3	1	0	$12/3 = 4$ ← Leaving variable
$0	s_2	4	3	0	1	$24/3 = 8$
	Z	0	0	0	0	0
	$C - Z$	4	5	0	0	

↑
Entering variable

ties associated with that corner point. It will also reveal if the corner point is an optimum, or if we must develop another tableau.

At this point we can begin to develop the second tableau. The row of the leaving variable will be transformed into the *new main row* of the second tableau. This will serve as a foundation on which to develop the other rows. To obtain this new main row we simply divide each element in the s_1 row by the row pivot (intersection of the entering column and leaving row), which is 3. The resulting numbers are:

Column:	x	y	s_1	s_2	Solution quantity
Main row value:	1/3	1	1/3	0	4

These numbers become the new y row of the second tableau.

The main row numbers are used to compute the values for the other constraint rows (in this instance, the only other constraint row is the s_2 row). The procedure is:

1. Determine the value in the constraint row (i.e., the s_2 row), which is in the entering variable column. It is 3.
2. Multiply each value in the new main row by this value.
3. Subtract the resulting values, column by column, from the current row values.

Thus,

Column:	x	y	s_1	s_2	Quantity
Current value:	4	3	0	1	24
$-3 \times$ (Main row):	$-3(1/3)$	$-3(1)$	$-3(1/3)$	$-3(0)$	$-3(4)$
New row value:	3	0	-1	1	12

The two new rows are shown in Table 2S–4.

TABLE 2S–4

Partially Completed Second Tableau

C		$4	$5	$0	$0	
	Variables in solution	x	y	s_1	s_2	Solution quantity
$5	y	1/3	1	1/3	0	4
$0	s_2	3	0	-1	1	12

The new Z row can now be computed. Multiply the row unit profits and the coefficients in each column for each row. Sum the results within each column. Thus:

Row	Profit	Column x	y	s_1	s_2	Quantity
y	$5	5(1/3)	5(1)	5(1/3)	5(0)	5(4)
s_1	$0	0(3)	0(0)	0(−1)	0(1)	0(12)
New Z row:		5/3	5	5/3	0	$20

TABLE 2S–5

Completed Second Tableau	C		$4	$5	$0	$0	
		Variables in solution	x	y	s_1	s_2	*Solution quantity*
	$5	y	1/3	1	1/3	0	4
	$0	s_2	3	0	−1	1	12
		Z	5/3	5	5/3	0	$20
		$C - Z$	7/3	0	−5/3	0	

Next, we can compute the $C - Z$ row:

Column:	x	y	s_1	s_2
C	4	5	0	0
Z	5/3	5	5/3	0
$C - Z$	7/3	0	−5/3	0

The completed second tableau is shown in Table 2S–5. It tells us that at this point, 4 units of variable y are the most we can make (see column *Variables in solution* and column *Solution quantity*, row y) and that the profit associated with $y = 4$, $x = 0$ is $20 (see row Z, Solution quantity column).

The fact that there is a positive value in the $C - Z$ row tells us that this is not the optimum solution. Consequently, we must develop another tableau.

Developing the Third Tableau

The third tableau will be developed in the same manner as the previous one:

1. Determine the entering variable: find the column with the largest positive value in the $C - Z$ row (7/3 in the x column).
2. Determine the leaving variable: Divide the solution quantity in each row by the row pivot. Hence,

$$\frac{4}{1/3} = 12 \qquad 12/3 = 4.$$

The smallest ratio indicates the leaving variable is s_2. See Table 2S–6.
3. Divide each value in the row of the leaving variable by the row pivot (3) to obtain the new main row values:

Column:	x	y	s_1	s_2	*Quantity*
Current value:	3	0	−1	1	12
New main row value:	1	0/3	−1/3	1/3	12/3 = 4

TABLE 2S–6

The Leaving and
Entering Variables

C		$4	$5	$0	$0	
	Variables in solution	x	y	s_1	s_2	Solution quantity
$5	y	1/3	1	1/3	0	$\dfrac{4}{1/3} = 12$
$0	s_2	3	0	−1	1	$12/3 = 4$ ← Leaving variable
	Z	5/3	5	5/3	0	20
	C − Z	7/3	0	−5/3	0	

↑
Entering
variable

4. Compute values for y row: Multiply each new main row value by the y row pivot value (i.e., 1/3) and subtract from corresponding current values. Thus,

Column:	x	y	s_1	s_2	Quantity
Current value:	1/3	1	1/3	0	4
−1/3 × (Main row):	−1/3(1)	−1/3(0)	−1/3(−1/3)	−1/3(1/3)	−1/3(4)
New row value:	0	1	4/9	−1/9	8/3

5. Compute new Z row values. Note that now variable x has been added to the solution mix; that row's unit profit is $4.

				Column		
Row	Profit	x	y	s_1	s_2	Quantity
y	$5	5(0)	5(1)	5(4/9)	5(−1/9)	5(8/3)
x	$4	4(1)	4(0)	4(1 − 1/3)	4(1/3)	4(4)
New Z row:		4	5	8/9	7/9	88/3

6. Compute the $C − Z$ row values:

	x	y	s_1	s_2
C	4	5	0	0
Z	4	5	8/9	7/9
C − Z	0	0	−8/9	−7/9

The resulting values of the third tableau are shown in Table 2S–7. Notice that each of the $C − Z$ values is either 0 or negative,

TABLE 2S–7

The Third Tableau
Contains the Optimum
Solution

C		$4	$5	$0	$0	
	Variables in solution	x	y	s_1	s_2	Solution quantity
$5	y	0	1	4/9	−1/9	8/3
$4	x	1	0	−1/3	1/3	4
	Z	4	5	8/9	7/9	88/3
	C − Z	0	0	−8/9	−7/9	

indicating that this is the final solution. The optimum values of x and y are indicated in the Quantity column: $y = 8/3$ or $2\frac{2}{3}$ and $x = 4$. (The y quantity is in the y row and the x quantity in the x row. Total profit is 88/3 or $29.33 (Quantity column, Z row).

At this point, it can be useful to consider the tableaus in relation to a graph of the feasible solution space. This is shown in Figure 2S–10.

Handling ≥ and = Constraints

Up to this point, we have experienced constraints that are ≤. Constraints that involve equalities and ≥ are handled in a slightly different way.

When an equality constraint is present, use of the simplex method requires addition of an *artificial* variable. The purpose of such variables is merely to permit development of an initial solution. For example, the equalities

$$(1) \quad 7x + 4y = 65$$
$$(2) \quad 5x + 3y = 40$$

FIGURE 2S–10

Graphical Analogies to
Simplex Tableau

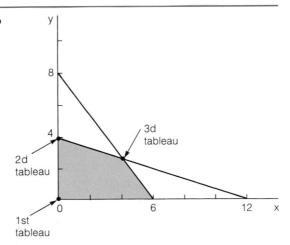

would be rewritten in the following manner:

$$(1) \quad 7x + 3y + 1a_1 + 0a_2 = 65$$
$$(2) \quad 5x + 3y + 0a_1 + 1a_2 = 40.$$

Slack variables would not be added. The objective function, say $Z = \$2x + \$3y$, would be rewritten as:

$$Z = \$2x + \$3y + Ma_1 + Ma_2$$

where

$$M = \text{A large number (e.g., 999).}$$

Since the artificial variables are not desired in the final solution, selecting a large value of M (much larger than the other objective coefficients) will insure their deletion during the solution process.

For a $\geq$ constraint, surplus variables must be *subtracted* instead of added to each constraint. For example, the constraints

$$(1) \quad 3x + 2y + 4z \geq 80$$
$$(2) \quad 5x + 4y + z \geq 70$$
$$(3) \quad 2x + 8y + 2z \geq 68$$

would be rewritten as equalities:

$$(1) \quad 3x + 2y + 4z - 1s_1 - 0s_2 - 0s_3 = 80$$
$$(2) \quad 5x + 4y + z - 0s_1 - 1s_2 - 0s_3 = 70$$
$$(3) \quad 2x + 8y + 2z - 0s_1 - 0s_2 + 1s_3 = 68.$$

As equalities, each constraint must then be adjusted by inclusion of an artificial variable. The final result looks like this:

$$(1) \quad 3x + 2y + 4z - 1s_1 - 0s_2 - 0s_3 + 1a_1 + 0a_2 + 0a_3 = 80$$
$$(2) \quad 5x + 4y + z - 0s_1 - 1s_2 - 0s_3 + 0a_1 + 1a_2 + 0a_3 = 70$$
$$(3) \quad 2x + 8y + 2z - 0s_1 - 0s_2 - 1s_3 + 0a_1 + 0a_2 + 1a_3 = 68$$

If the objective function happened to be

$$\$5x + \$2y + \$7z$$

it would become

$$\$5x + \$2y + \$7z + \$0s_1 + \$0s_2 + \$0s_3 + \$Ma_1 + \$Ma_2 + \$Ma_3.$$

Summary of Maximization Procedure

The main steps in solving a maximization problem using the simplex algorithm are:

1. Set up the initial tableau.
   a. Rewrite the constraints so that they become equalities; add a slack variable to each constraint.

      b. Rewrite the objective function to include the slack variables. Give slack variables coefficients of 0.

      c. Put the objective coefficients and constraint coefficients into tableau form.

      d. Compute values for the Z row: Multiply the values in each constraint row by the row's C value. Add the results within each column.

      e. Compute values for the $C - Z$ row.

2. Set up subsequent tableaus.

      a. Determine the entering variable (the largest positive value in the $C - Z$ row). If a tie exists, choose one column arbitrarily.

      b. Determine the leaving variable: divide each constraint row's solution quantity by the row's pivot value; the smallest ratio indicates the leaving variable. If a tie occurs, divide the values in each row by the row pivot value, beginning with slack columns and then other columns, moving from left to right. The leaving variable is indicated by the lowest ratio in the first column with unequal ratios.

      c. Form the new main row of the next tableau: Divide each number in the leaving row by the row's pivot value. Enter these values in the next tableau in the same row positions.

      d. Compute new values for remaining constraint rows: For each row, multiply the values in the new main row by the constraint row's pivot value and subtract the resulting values, column by column, from the original row values. Enter these in the new tableau in the same row positions as the original row.

      e. Compute values for Z and $C - Z$ rows.

      f. Check to see if any values in the $C - Z$ row are positive; if they are, repeat $2a$–$2f$. Otherwise, the optimum solution has been obtained.

Minimization Problems

The simplex method handles minimization problems in essentially the same way it handles maximization problems. However, there are a few differences. One is the need to adjust for ≥ constraints, which requires both artificial variables and negative slack variables. This tends to make manual solution more involved. A second major difference is the test for the optimum: A solution is optimum if there are no *negative* values in the $C - Z$ row.

EXAMPLE S–2

Solve the following problem for the quantities of x and y that will minimize cost.

$$\text{Minimize:} \quad Z = \$12x + \$10y$$
$$\text{Subject to:} \quad x + 4y \geq 8$$
$$3x + 2y \geq 6$$

Solution

1. Rewrite the constraints so that they are in the proper form:

$$x + 4y = 8 \quad \text{becomes} \quad x + 4y - 1s_1 - 0s_2 + 1a_1 + 0a_2 = 8,$$
$$\text{and } 3x + 2y = 6 \quad \text{becomes} \quad 3x + 2y - 0s_1 - 1s_2 + 0a_1 + 1a_2 = 6.$$

2. Rewrite the objective function (coefficients of C row):

$$\$12x + 10y + \$0s_1 + \$0s_2 + \$999a_1 + \$999a_2$$

3. Compute values for rows Z and $C - Z$:

C_j	x	y	s_1	s_2	a_1	a_2	Q
$999	1(999)	4(999)	−1(999)	0(999)	1(999)	0(999)	8(999)
$999	3(999)	2(999)	0(999)	−1(999)	0(999)	1(999)	6(999)
Z	3,996	5,994	−999	−999	999	999	13,986
$C - Z$	−3,984	−5,984	999	999	0	0	

4. Set up the initial tableau:

C		$12	$10	$0	$0	$999	$999	
	Var. in sol.	x	y	s_1	s_2	a_1	a_2	Sol. qty.
$999	a_1	1	4	−1	0	1	0	8
$999	a_2	3	2	0	−1	0	1	6
	Z	3,996	5,994	−999	−999	999	999	13,986
	$C - Z$	−3,984	−5,984	999	999	0	0	

5. Find the entering variable (largest negative $C - Z$ value: y column) and leaving variable (smallest of $8/4 = 2$ and $6/2 = 3$; hence, row a_1).

6. Divide each number in the leaving row by the pivot value (4, in this case) to obtain values for the main row of the second tableau:

$$1/4 \quad 4/4 = 1 \quad -1/4 \quad 0/4 \quad 1/4 \quad 0/4 \quad 8/4 = 2$$

7. Compute values for other rows:

a_2 is

Column:	x	y	s_1	s_2	a_1	a_2	Quantity
Current value:	3	2	0	−1	0	1	6
$-2 \times$ (Main row value):	−2/4	−2	2/4	−0/4	−2/4	−0/4	−4
New row value:	10/4	0	+2/4	−1	−2/4	1	2

EXAMPLE S–2 (continued)

8. Compute a new Z row:

Row	Cost	x	y	s_1	s_2	a_1	a_2	Quantity
y	$10	10(¼)	10(1)	10(−¼)	10(0)	10(¼)	10(0)	10(2)
a_2	999	999(¹⁰⁄₄)	999(0)	999(²⁄₄)	999(−1)	999(−²⁄₄)	999(1)	999(2)
Z:		2,500	10	497	−999	−497	999	2018

9. Compute the $C - Z$ row:

	x	y	s_1	s_2	a_1	a_2	Quantity
C	12	10	0	0	999	999	
Z	2,500	10	497	−999	−497	999	
$C - Z$	−2,488	0	−497	999	1496	0	

10. Set up the second tableau:

C		12	10	0	0	999	999	
	Var. in sol.	x	y	s_1	s_2	a_1	a_2	Quant.
10	y	1/4	1	−1/4	0	1/4	0	2
999	a_2	10/4	0	2/4	−1	2/4	1	2
	Z	2,500	10	497	−999	−497	999	2,018
	$C - Z$	−2,488	0	497	999	1496	0	

11. Repeat the process.
   a. Check for optimality: it is not optimum because of negatives in $C - Z$ row.
   b. Determine the entering variable: the largest negative is in column x.
   c. Determine the leaving variable: $2/(1/4) = 8$, $2/(10/4) = .8$. Therefore, it is row a_2.
   d. Find new main row value using the pivot value of 10/4:

$$1 \quad 0 \quad .2 \quad -.4 \quad -.2 \quad .4 \quad .8$$

   e. Determine values for new y row:

$$0 \quad 1 \quad -.3 \quad .1 \quad .3 \quad -.1 \quad 1.8$$

   f. Determine new values for row Z:

Row	Cost	x	y	s_1	s_2	a_1	a_2	Quantity
y	$10	10(0)	10(1)	10(−.3)	10(.1)	10(.3)	10(−.1)	10(1.8)
x	$12	12(1)	12(0)	12(.2)	12(−.4)	12(−.2)	12(.4)	12(.8)
Z:		12	10	−.6	−3.8	.6	3.8	27.6

EXAMPLE S–2 *(concluded)*

g. Determine values for the $C - Z$ row:

	x	y	s_1	s_2	a_1	a_2	Quantity
C	12	10	0	0	999	999	
Z	12	10	−.6	−3.8	.6	3.8	27.6
$C - Z$	0	0	.6	3.8	998.4	995.2	

h. Set up the next tableau. Since no $C - Z$ values are negative, the solution is optimum. Hence, $x = .8$, $y = 1.8$, and the minimum cost is $27.60.

C		12	10	0	0	999	999	
	Variables in solution	x	y	s_1	s_2	a_1	a_2	Quantity
	y	0	1	−.3	.1	.3	−.1	1.8
	x	1	0	.2	−.4	−.2	.4	.8
Z		12	10	−.6	−3.8	.6	3.8	27.6
$C - Z$		0	0	.6	3.8	998.4	995.2	

Sensitivity Analysis

A decision maker is often interested in more than the immediate solution to a problem. The decision maker can benefit from *sensitivity analysis* of the solution in several ways. In preparing the problem for a linear programming solution, the decision maker may have used subjective estimates for certain parameters (e.g., the coefficients of the constraints, the coefficients of the objective function, and the right-hand side values of the constraints). Understandably, the decision maker would want to know how sensitive the optimal solution would be to changes in the value of one or more of those parameters. If the solution is relatively insensitive to reasonable changes, the decision maker can feel more confident in implementing the solution. Conversely, if the solution is sensitive to such changes, the decision maker will undoubtedly want to obtain more precise estimates of the suspect parameters.

A related issue involves a specific change in a parameter. For instance, there may be a price change that would alter a coefficient in the objective function. Similarly, a change in a production process could require a change in a coefficient of one or more constraints. Again, sensitivity analysis could provide the decision maker with the necessary insight.

A third possibility other than changes of this sort is the question of whether it might be beneficial to obtain larger amounts of certain resources. This question often arises when large amounts of some resources are unused by the optimal solution; by adding more of the other resources, it may be possible to realize a disproportionate increase in the value of the objective function.

Thus, we see that there are a number of reasons that a decision maker might want to pursue sensitivity analysis. We will explore two of these possibilities: a change in an objective function coefficient and a change in the right-hand side value of a constraint. We will not consider a change in a coefficient of a constraint. Also, the discussion pertains to *one* change with all other parameters remaining unchanged. In a situation where more than one change is of interest, the problem must be reworked with the changed values.

Much of the information needed to do sensitivity analysis is contained in the final simplex tableau. That plus the original problem statement will suffice to perform the analysis. Let's see how sensitivity analysis could be applied to the maximization problem that was solved using simplex earlier in this section. That problem and its final tableau are reproduced in Table 2S–8 for easy reference.

First, let us consider changes to one of the objective function coefficients. Sensitivity analysis will answer this question for a variable that is in solution: for what range of values will the solution quantities of all the decision variables remain the same? This is known as the *range of optimality.* Of course, if one of the coefficients of the objective function is changed, the total profit (e.g., 88/3) will change even if the optimal quantities of x and y do not change.

The analysis involves computing a series of ratios using the $C - Z$ row of the final tableau and the row corresponding to the variable whose range of optimality is to be determined. The elements of the bottom row are divided by the corresponding elements of the variable's row. For instance, for variable x, the ratios are:

TABLE 2S–8

Maximize: $Z = \$4x + \$5y$
Subject to:
$$x + 3y \le 12$$
$$4x + 3y \le 24$$

C		$\$4$	$\$5$	$\$0$	$\$0$	
	Variables in solution	x	y	s_1	s_2	*Solution quantity*
$\$5$	y	0	1	4/9	−1/9	8/3
$\$4$	x	1	0	−1/3	1/3	4
	Z	4	5	8/9	7/9	88/3
	$C - Z$	0	0	−8/9	−7/9	

$$C - Z: \qquad \frac{0}{1} = 0 \qquad \frac{5}{0} = \text{und.*} \qquad \frac{-8/9}{-1/3} = 8/3 \qquad \frac{-7/9}{1/3} = -7/3.$$
$$x:$$

* undefined.

The positive ratio closest to zero indicates the amount by which the original coefficient of x in the objective function could be increased without changing the optimal solution quantities. Thus, the \$4 could be increased by $8/3 = \$2.67$ (i.e., to \$6.67) and not change the solution. Similarly, the \$4 could be decreased by the amount of the negative closest to zero (i.e., $-7/3 = \$2.33$) and not change the solution quantities. Hence, the range of optimality for the x coefficient is:

$$\$4 - \$2.33 \leq x \leq \$4 + \$2.67.$$

If x remains at \$4, the range of optimality for y is:

$$C - Z: \qquad \frac{0}{0} = \text{und.*} \qquad \frac{0}{1} = 0 \qquad \frac{-8/9}{4/9} = -2 \qquad \frac{-7/9}{-1/9} = 7.$$
$$x:$$

* undefined.

The smallest positive ratio is 7, hence the original coefficient of \$5 can be increased by \$7, or up to $\$5 + \$7 = \$12$. The negative ratio closest to zero is -2. Hence, the original y coefficient can be decreased by that amount. Therefore, its lower bound is $\$5 - \$2 = \$3$. Thus, the range of optimality for y is \$3 to \$12.

In this example there are two decision variables, and both are in solution. In some cases one or more of the decision variables will not be in solution. In those situations we talk about the *range of insignificance,* which refers to the range over which that variable will remain out of the solution. In order for that variable to come into the solution, its objective function coefficient would have to increase by an amount greater than the value that appears in row $C - Z$ in this variable's column. For instance, if -4 appeared, the variable's objective function coefficient would have to increase by more than \$4 for it to come into solution. Its range of insignificance would be 0 to \$4.

Now let's consider changes to the right-hand side of a constraint. Again, remember that only one constraint is assumed to change; all others remain fixed at their original amounts. First, it should be noted that some constraints are not candidates for change; nothing beneficial would be accomplished by increasing their amounts (assuming a $\geq$ constraint). This is the case for constraints that are slack in the final solution, since such constraints are not limiting factors on the problem. Hence, the *range of feasibility* for a slack constraint on the *down* side is equal to its value in the final solution. Thus, if $s_1 = 250$ in the final solution of a problem, the first constraint's right-hand side original amount can be decreased by that amount and not change the solution. On the *up* side, the right-hand side value can be increased forever and not change the solution; increasing it will merely increase the amount of slack. Note that a constraint that is slack will have a 0 in the $C - Z$ row for the column that corresponds to that slack variable.

If a constraint is a limiting factor, its slack variable will not appear in the final solution. (In some rare instances, a slack variable will appear but have a solution quantity equal to zero. In effect, there is no slack for that constraint even though it appears in the solution.) For slack variables not in solution, there will be a negative value under its column in the $C - Z$ row. These negative amounts are known as *shadow prices.* They indicate how much a *one-unit* decrease in the original amount of a constraint would *decrease* the final value of the objective function. Thus, we can see in Table 2S–8 that a one-unit decrease in the first constraint of that problem would lead to a decrease in the final value of the objective function of $8/9 = \$.89$. Similarly, a decrease of one unit in the second constraint would lead to a decrease in the objective function of $7/9 = \$.78$. Conversely, a one-unit *increase* in *one* of these values would have the opposite effect: a one-unit increase in the first constraint would increase the optimal value of the objective function by $\$.89$, and a one-unit increase in the second would lead to an increase of $\$.78$. The question that can be answered by sensitivity analysis is this: over what range of right-hand side values of a constraint will these shadow prices remain valid?

To determine the range of feasibility for a constraint, first identify the values in the body of the final tableau under the column for that constraint's slack variable. For instance, for s_1 in Table 2S–8, the values are $4/9$ and $-1/3$. Next, divide these values into the corresponding values in the *Solution quantity* column. For s_1 the results are:

$$\frac{8/3}{4/9} = +6$$

$$\frac{4}{-1/3} = -12.$$

The positive ratio closest to zero indicates the amount by which the original constraints can be *decreased,* and the negative ratio closest to zero indicates the amount by which the original value of the constraint can be *increased.* Hence, in this instance the original first constraint's right-hand side value was 12. It could be decreased by as much as 6 units or increased by as much as 12 units and have an impact of $8/9 = \$.89$ per unit on the optimum value of the objective function. Similarly, the ratios for s_2 are:

$$\frac{8/3}{-1/9} = -24$$

$$\frac{4}{1/3} = +12.$$

Hence, if the first constraint remained unchanged, the second could be increased by as much as 24 units or decreased by as much as 12 units and have an impact of $7/9 = \$.78$ per unit on the optimum value of the objective function.

1. A small construction firm specializes in building and selling single-family homes. The firm offers two basic types of houses, model A and model B. Model A houses require 4,000 labor-hours, 2 tons of stone, and 2,000 board-feet of lumber. Model B houses require 10,000 labor-hours, 3 tons of stone and 2,000 board-feet of lumber. Due to long lead times for ordering supplies and the scarcity of skilled and semi-skilled workers in the area, the firm will be forced to rely on its present resources for the upcoming building season. It has 400,000 hours of labor, 150 tons of stone, and 200,000 board-feet of lumber. What mix of model A and B houses should the firm construct if model As yield a profit of $1,000 per unit and model Bs yield $2,000 per unit? Assume that the firm will be able to sell all the units it builds.

   Solution

   a. Formulate the objective function and constraints.[2]

   Maximize: $Z = \$1,000A + \$2,000B$
   Subject to:

Labor:	$4,000A + 10,000B =$	400,000 labor-hours
Stone:	$2A + 3B =$	150 tons
Lumber:	$2,000A + 2,000B =$	200,000 board-feet

   b. Graph the constraints and objective function and identify the optimum corner point (see graph). Note that the lumber constraint is *redundant:* it does not form a boundary of the feasible solution space.

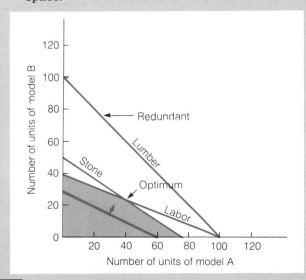

---

[2] For the sake of consistency, let's agree to assign to the horizontal axis the first decision variable mentioned in the problem. Hence, in this case variable A will be represented on the horizontal axis and variable B on the vertical axis.

c. Determine the optimum quantities of model A and B and compute the resulting profit. Since the optimum point is at the intersection of the stone and labor constraints, we solve those two equations for their common point.

$$\begin{aligned} \text{Labor } 4{,}000A + 10{,}000B &= 400{,}000 \\ \underline{-2{,}000 \times (\text{Stone} \qquad 2A + \qquad 3B} &= \underline{\quad 150)} \\ 4{,}000B &= 100{,}000 \\ B &= 25 \end{aligned}$$

Substitute $B = 25$ in one of the equations and solve for A:

$$2A + 3(25) = 150, \qquad \text{so } A = 37.5$$

If we decide that it would be unreasonable to make 37.5 model A houses, we could simply round *down,* and make 37. Profits would be: $1,000(37) + $2,000(25) = $87,000.

2. Solve the following problem using graphical linear programming:

$$\begin{aligned} \text{Maximize:} \quad & Z = \$12x + \$6y \\ \text{Subject to:} \quad & (1) \quad 2x + 4y \le 16 \\ & (2) \quad 5x + 3y \ge 15 \\ & (3) \qquad\quad x \le 5 \end{aligned}$$

Solution

a. Plot constraints, shade in the feasible solution space, and plot the objective function (see graph).

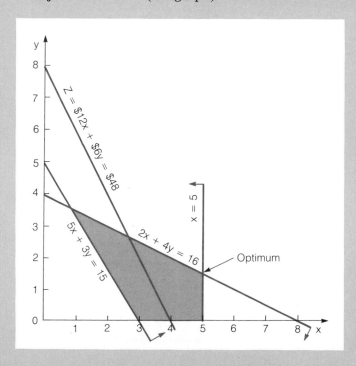

b. It is apparent from the graph that $x = 5$ at the optimum. To determine the value of y, substitute $x = 5$ in the equation $2x + 4y = 16$ and solve for y:

$$2(5) + 4y = 16, \quad \text{so } y = 1.5$$

c. Compute the value of the objective function at $x = 5$, $y = 1.5$.

$$Z_{max} = \$12(5) + \$6(1.5) = \$69$$

3. Solve the following problem for the quantities of x, y, and w that will maximize the objective function.

Maximize: $Z = 20x + 16y + 10w$
Subject to:

$$
\begin{array}{ll}
(1) & 4x + 2y + 3w \leq 120 \\
(2) & 5x + 4y + 2w \leq 100 \\
(3) & 2x + 3y + 3w \leq 90
\end{array}
$$

Solution

a. Start by rewriting the constraints as equalities using slack variables:

$$
\begin{array}{ll}
(1) & 4x + 2y + 3w + 1s_1 + 0s_2 + 0s_3 = 120 \\
(2) & 5x + 4y + 2w + 0s_1 + 1s_2 + 0s_3 = 100 \\
(3) & 2x + 3y + 3w + 0s_1 + 0s_2 + 1s_3 = 90
\end{array}
$$

b. Next, develop the initial tableau:

TABLEAU 1

C		20	16	10	0	0	0	
	Variable	x	y	w	s_1	s_2	s_3	*Quantity*
0	s_1	4	2	3	1	0	0	120
0	s_2	5	4	2	0	1	0	100
0	s_3	2	3	3	0	0	1	90
	Z	0	0	0	0	0	0	0
	$C - Z$	20	16	10	0	0	0	

c. Identify the entering variable (column with largest *positive* $C - Z$ value). Divide the numbers in that column (i.e., 4, 5, and 2) into their respective row quantities. The smallest resultant indicates the leaving variable. Hence, x is the entering variable and s_2 is the leaving variable.

d. Divide all numbers in the s_2 row by the pivot number (i.e., 5) to obtain the main row of the next tableau. To compute new s_1 and s_3 rows, use the pivot number for that row (e.g., 4 for s_1 row) to multiply each main row value and subtract the resulting values from the corresponding values of the previous tableau.

e. Compute values for the Z and $C - Z$ rows. If the $C - Z$ row values are all negative or zero, the optimum solution has been found. If any positive values appear, repeat steps 3–5.

f. The second and third tableaus are shown below. The optimum quantities are: $x = 10.91$, $y = 0$, $w = 22.73$. The corresponding value of the objective function with those quantities is 445.46. In addition, note that constraints 2 and 3 have been fully used, but 8.18 of constraint 1 remains.

TABLEAU 2

C		20	16	10	0	0	0	
	Variable	x	y	w	s_1	s_2	s_3	Quantity
0	s_1	0.0	−1.2	1.4	1.0	−0.8	0.0	40.0
20	x	1.0	0.8	0.4	0.0	0.2	0.0	20.0
0	s_3	0.0	1.4	2.2	0.0	−0.4	1.0	50.0
	Z	20.0	16.0	8.0	0.0	4.0	0.0	400.0
	$C - Z$	0.0	0.0	2.0	0.0	−4.0	0.0	

TABLEAU 3

C		20	16	10	0	0	0	
	Variable	x	y	w	s_1	s_2	s_3	Quantity
0	s_1	0.0	−2.1	0.0	1.0	−0.5	−0.6	8.18
20	x	1.0	0.5	0.0	0.0	0.3	−0.2	10.91
10	w	0.0	0.6	1.0	0.0	−0.2	−0.5	22.73
	Z	20.0	17.3	10.0	0.0	3.6	0.9	445.46
	$C - Z$	0.0	−1.3	0.0	0.0	−3.6	−0.9	

4. Given the third tableau of the preceding problem, perform sensitivity analysis. Specifically, do the following:

a. Determine the range of insignificance of variable y.
b. Determine the range of optimality for the coefficient of variable x.
c. Determine the range of feasibility for the third constraint.
d. If the third constraint can be increased at a cost of $.20 per unit and 200 units are available, how many should the firm purchase?

Solution

a. The value of −1.3 for the y column in row $C - Z$ indicates that the unit contribution of y in the objective function would have to increase by more than $1.30 in order for it to come into solution. Its range of insignificance is $0 to $17.30.

b. Dividing the values in row $C - Z$ by the values in row x produces these ratios:

Column:	x	y	w	s_1	s_2	s_3
	$\dfrac{0.0}{1.0}=0$	$\dfrac{-1.3}{0.5}=-2.6$	$\dfrac{0.0}{0.0}=$ und.	$\dfrac{0.0}{0.0}=$ und.	$\dfrac{-3.6}{0.3}=-12$	$\dfrac{-0.9}{-0.2}=+4.5$

The smallest positive ratio is 4.5, and the negative ratio closest to zero is -2.6. Hence, the coefficient of x of $20 can be decreased by as much as $2.60 and increased by as much as $4.50 and not affect the optimal solution quantities. Hence, its range of optimality is $17.40 to $24.50.

c. First, divide the values in the *Quantity* column by the corresponding values in the s_3 column since we are interested in the third constraint. The ratios are:

$$\frac{8.18}{-0.6} = -13.63$$

$$\frac{10.91}{-0.2} = -54.55$$

$$\frac{22.73}{0.5} = 45.46$$

The smallest positive ratio indicates the amount by which the right-hand side can be decreased, and the negative ratio closest to zero (i.e., -13.63) indicates the maximum amount of increase. Hence, the range of feasibility for the third constraint is (using the original right-hand side value of 90):

$$90 - 45.46 = 54.54 \text{ to } 90 + 13.63 = 103.63.$$

d. The shadow price of the third slack variable is -0.9, which means an increase of $.90 in the value of the objective function for each unit of increase in the third constraint's right-hand side value *up to the upper end of the range of feasibility*. Since the cost to acquire additional units is $.20 each, the net increase will be +$.70 per unit. Thus, acquire as many units as possible. In part c we found an increase of 13.63 units was possible. Thus, acquire that amount. Note that beyond that point, the shadow price will change, so additional units of this constraint might just add to slack; another constraint would become binding (limiting) on the solution.

DISCUSSION AND REVIEW QUESTIONS

1. For which decision environment is linear programming most suited?.
2. What is meant by the term *feasible solution space*? What determines this region?
3. In graphical linear programming problems, what is the upper limit on the number of:
   a. Variables in a problem?
   b. Constraints in a problem?
4. What is an isocost line? An isoprofit line?

5. What does sliding an objective function line toward the origin represent? Away?

6. In the simplex technique, how is the entering variable determined for a maximization problem? How is the leaving variable determined?

7. With what aspect of a graphical solution does a simplex tableau correspond? To what does the initial tableau correspond?

8. In what direction does the second solution move away from the initial solution in a two-variable problem?

9. After the optimum solution has been obtained, it is possible to consider acquisition of additional scarce resources in a maximization problem. How does one determine:
   a. If it is worthwhile to add a given resource?

   b. The change in the value of the objective function for a change within the feasible range?

10. Explain what is meant by the terms *slack variable* and *artificial variable*.

11. What mix of surplus, slack, and artificial variables are used in each of these constraints:
    a. ≤?   b. =?   c. ≥?

12. Is there any theoretical limit to the number of decision variables that can be handled by the simplex method?

13. How are the numbers in the $C - Z$ row in slack columns interpreted?

14. At what point does it become apparent that a tableau contains the optimum solution?

PROBLEMS

1. Solve for the optimum quantities using graphical linear programming:
   a. Maximize: $Z = \$10x + \$20y$ (profit)
      Subject to:
      Cutting $5x + 2y \leq 40$ manhours
      Sewing $4x + 4y \leq 48$ manhours
   b. Maximize: $Z = \$6A + \$3B$ (revenue)
      Subject to:
      Material $20A + 5B \leq 600$ lb.
      Machinery $25A + 20B \leq 1,000$ hr.
      Labor $20A + 30B \leq 1,200$ hr.

2. Use graphical linear programming to determine the quantities that will minimize cost:
   a. Minimize: $Z = \$1.80S + \$2.20T$
      Subject to:
      Potassium $5S + 8T \geq 200$ gr.
      Carbohydrate $15S + 6T \geq 240$ gr.
      Protein $4S + 12T \geq 180$ gr.
                                   $T \geq 10$ gr.
   b. Minimize: $Z = \$1.50C + \$1.20D$
      Subject to: (1) $-8C + 4D \leq 104$
                         (2) $30C + 5D \geq 210$
                         (3) $7C + 7D \geq 133$

3. An appliance manufacturer produces two models of microwave ovens, H and W. Both models require fabrication and assembly work: each H uses four hours of fabrication and two hours of assembly, while each W uses two hours of fabrication and six hours of assembly. There are 600 fabrication hours available this week and 480 hours of assembly. Each H contributes \$40 to profits and each W contributes \$30 to profits. What mix of H and W will maximize profits?

4. A small candy shop is preparing for the holiday season. The owner must decide how many bags of deluxe mix and how many bags of standard mix of peanut/raisin delite to put up. The deluxe mix has ⅔ pounds of raisins and ⅓ pounds of peanuts, and the standard mix has a half pound of raisins and a half pound of peanuts per bag. The shop has 90 pounds of raisins and 60 pounds of peanuts to work with.

   Peanuts cost \$.60 per pound and raisins

cost $1.50 per pound. The deluxe mix will sell for $2.90 per pound, and the standard mix will sell for $2.55 per pound. The owner estimates that no more than 110 bags of one type can be sold.

If the goal is to maximize *profits,* how many bags of each type should be prepared? What is the expected profit?

5. A firm produces cast-iron parts that require three basic operations: casting, grinding, and drilling. Available time for casting is 36,000 minutes; for grinding, 2,250 minutes; and for drilling, 3,600 minutes per week. Two products, x and y, require these operations. Product x requires 80 minutes for casting, 2.5 minutes for grinding, and 9 minutes for drilling per unit. Product y requires 60 minutes for casting, 4.5 minutes for grinding, and 4 minutes for drilling per unit. Each unit of x contributes $4 to profits, and each unit of y contributes $2. What combination of x and y will maximize profits on a weekly basis?

6. A retired couple supplement their income by making fruit pies, which they sell to a local grocery store. During the month of September they produce apple and grape pies. The apple pies are sold for $1.50 to the grocer, and the grape pies are sold for $1.20. The couple is able to sell all of the pies they produce due to the high quality they maintain. They follow a policy, for instance, of always using fresh ingredients. Flour and sugar are purchased once each month. For the month of September they have 1,200 cups of sugar and 2,100 cups of flour. Each apple pie requires one and one-half cups of sugar and three cups of flour, while each grape pie requires two cups of sugar and three cups of flour. Determine the number of grape and number of apple pies that will maximize revenues if the couple working together can make an apple pie in six minutes and a grape pie in three minutes. They plan to work no more than 60 hours. In addition, determine the amounts of sugar and/or flour that will be unused.

7. Solve Problem 1a using simplex.

8. Solve Problem 1b using the simplex and then determine the following:
   a. The range of feasibility for each constraint.
   b. The range of optimality or significance, whichever is appropriate, for the coefficients of the objective function.

9. Solve Problem 3 using simplex and interpret your answer. Then:
   a. Find the range of feasibility for each constraint and interpret your answers.
   b. Determine the range of feasibility or optimality, whichever is appropriate, for each coefficient of the objective function. Interpret your results.

10. Repeat the previous question for Problem 5.

11. Solve Problem 6 using simplex.

12. Given this information:

   Maximize:
   $$Z = \$10.50x + \$11.75y + 10.80z$$
   Subject to:
   Cutting: $5x + 12y + 8z \leq 1,400$ minutes
   Stapling: $7x + 9y + 9z \leq 1,250$ minutes
   Wrapping: $4x + 3y + 6z \leq 720$ minutes

   a. Solve for the quantities of products x, y, and z that will maximize revenue.
   b. Answer the questions posed in parts a and b of Problem 9 in terms of this problem.

13. A small firm makes three similar products, which all follow the same three-step process, which consists of milling, inspection, and drilling. Product a requires 12 minutes of milling, 5 minutes for inspection, and 10 minutes for drilling per unit; product b requires 10 minutes of milling, 4 minutes for inspection, and 8 minutes of drilling per unit; and product c requires 8 minutes of milling, 4 minutes for inspection, and 16 minutes of drilling. The department has 20 hours available during the next period for milling, 15 hours for inspection, and 24 hours for drilling. Product a contributes $2.40 per unit to profit, b contributes $2.50 per unit, and c contributes $3.00 per unit. Use the simplex method to determine the optimum mix of

products in terms of maximizing contribution to profits for the period. Then, find the range of optimality or insignificance, whichever is appropriate, for the profit coefficient of each variable.

14. Use the simplex method to solve these problems:

    a. Minimize: $Z = 21x + 18y$
        Subject to:

            (1) $5x + 10y \geq 100$
            (2) $2x + 1y \geq 20$

    b. Minimize: $Z = \$5x + \$2y + \$3z$
        Subject to:

            (1) $16x + 10y + 18z \geq 340$
            (2) $11x + 12y + 13z \geq 300$
            (3) $2x + 6y + 5z \geq 120$

(The remaining problems are best handled using a computer program.)

15. Determine the combination of variables x_1, x_2, x_2 that will maximize profits given the information below:

Maximize:
$$Z = \$34x_1 + \$18x_2 + \$27x_3 + \$40x_4$$
Subject to:

    (1) $x_1 + x_2 + x_3 + x_4 \leq 4{,}000$
    (2) $x_4 \geq 500$
    (3) $2x_1 + x_2 + 3x_3 + \leq 4{,}200$
    (4) $4x_2 + 3x_4 \leq 2{,}000$
    (5) $x_1 + x_2 + 2x_4 \leq 2{,}300$

16. Find the combination of A, B, C, D, and E that will maximize revenues given the information below:

Maximize: $Z = \$1.50A + \$2.10B + \$3.00C$
$$+ \$1.40D + \$1.80E$$
Subject to:

    (1) $2A + 8B + D \leq 220$
    (2) $A + 3C + E \leq 140$
    (3) $+ 4B + 3D + 2E \leq 150$
    (4) $5A + 2B + C + 3E \leq 185$
    (5) $A + B + C + D + E \leq 50$
    (6) $C \leq 10$

SELECTED BIBLIOGRAPHY

Anderson, David R.; Dennis J. Sweeney; and Thomas A. Williams. *An Introduction to Management Science: Quantitative Approaches to Decision Making.* 4th ed. St. Paul, Minn.: West Publishing, 1985.

Bierman, Harold; Charles P. Bonini; and Warren H. Hausman. *Quantitative Analysis for Business Decisions.* 6th ed. Homewood, Ill.: Richard D. Irwin, 1981.

Eppen, G. D. and F. J. Gould. *Introductory Management Science.* Englewood Cliffs, N.J.: Prentice-Hall, 1984.

Heinze, David. *Management Science: Introductory Concepts and Applications.* Cincinnati: South-Western Publishing, 1978.

Levin, Richard; Charles A. Kirkpatrick; and David S. Rubin. *Quantitative Approaches to Management.* 5th ed. New York: McGraw-Hill, 1982.

Part II

Forecasting

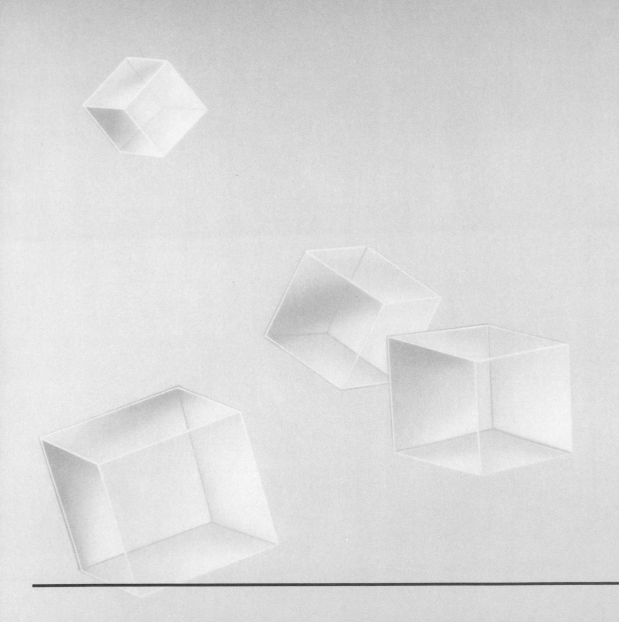

This part deals solely with forecasting (Chapter 3). It is presented early in the book because forecasts are the basis for a wide range of design and operating decisions. Consequently, this chapter serves as a basis for many of the remaining chapters.

Although forecasts are frequently developed as part of the marketing function, operations people are often called upon to assist in forecast development. More important, though, is the fact that *operations is a major user of forecasts.* Hence, the subject of forecasting is exceedingly important for operations management.

Chapter 3

Forecasting

After completing this chapter, you should be able to:

1. Describe at least four qualitative forecasting techniques with advantages and disadvantages for each.
2. Compare and contrast qualitative and quantitative approaches to forecasting.
3. Briefly describe averaging techniques, decomposition of time series data and regression analysis, and solve typical problems.
4. Describe two measures of forecast accuracy.
5. Describe two ways of evaluating and controlling forecasts.
6. Identify the major factors to consider when choosing a forecasting technique.
7. List the elements of a good forecast.
8. Outline the steps in the forecasting process.

INTRODUCTION, 106

FEATURES COMMON TO ALL FORECASTS, 107

STEPS IN THE FORECASTING PROCESS, 108

APPROACHES TO FORECASTING, 108

Forecasts Based on Judgment and Opinion, 109
Forecasts Based on Historical Data, 109
Associative Forecasts, 109

FORECASTS BASED ON JUDGMENT AND OPINION, 109

Executive Opinions, 109
Salesforce Composite, 110
Consumer Surveys, 110
Outside Opinion, 111
Opinions of Managers and Staff, 111

ANALYSIS OF TIME SERIES DATA, 113

The Naive Approach, 115
Moving Averages, 115
Exponential Smoothing, 118
Exponential Smoothing Adjusted for Trend, 122
Decomposition of a Time Series, 124
Other Techniques for Time Series, 135

ASSOCIATIVE FORECASTING TECHNIQUES, 135

Simple Linear Regression, 135
Comments on the Use of Linear Regression Analysis, 143
Curvilinear and Multiple Regression Analysis, 144

ACCURACY AND CONTROL OF FORECASTS, 144

Measuring the Accuracy of Forecasts, 144
Controlling the Forecast, 146

CHOOSING A FORECASTING TECHNIQUE, 150

Elements of a Good Forecast, 151

USING FORECAST INFORMATION, 152

SUMMARY, 152

SOLVED PROBLEMS, 154

DISCUSSION AND REVIEW QUESTIONS, 160

PROBLEMS, 161

SELECTED BIBLIOGRAPHY, 167

CASE: WATCH OUR FORECASTS GROW, 168

Planning is an integral part of a manager's job. If uncertainties cloud the planning horizon, it can be quite difficult for a manager to effectively plan. Forecasts can help managers by reducing some of the uncertainty, thereby enabling them to develop more meaningful plans than they might otherwise.

This chapter discusses business forecasting. Its purpose is to provide a survey of business forecasting. It covers basic forecasting techniques, how to monitor a forecast, the necessary steps in preparing a forecast, and elements that are common to forecasts.

INTRODUCTION

At one time or another, most of us have witnessed weather forecasts that were flops, even though most of the time the forecasters are close in predicting what the weather will be like. Forecasting demand is a lot like forecasting the weather. In both instances, there is no such thing as a sure bet: predictions usually turn out to be in the ballpark, but occasionally they can miss the mark completely. Moreover, in both instances, the forecasts serve as a *basis for planning.* Weather forecasts influence travel and recreation plans, choice of clothing each day, and whether to walk or ride to work. Farmers rely on weather forecasts to determine when to plant and harvest and when to take precautionary steps (e.g., protect against frost). In business, forecasts are the basis for capacity planning, budgeting, sales planning, production and inventory planning, manpower planning, purchasing planning, and more. Forecasts play such an important role in the planning process because they enable managers to *anticipate the future* and to *plan* accordingly.

In a sense, there are two uses of forecasts. One is to help managers *plan the system,* and the other is to *plan the use of the system.* Planning the system generally involves making long-range plans concerning the types of products and services to offer, what facilities and equipment to have, where to locate, and so on. Planning the use of the system refers to short- and intermediate-range planning, which involve such tasks as planning inventory and work force levels, planning purchasing and production, budgeting, and scheduling.

It should be noted that business forecasting pertains to more than predicting demand. Forecasts are also used to predict profits, revenues, costs, productivity changes, prices and availability of energy and raw materials, interest rates, movements of key economic indicators (GNP, inflation, government borrowing), and prices of stocks and bonds as well as other variables. However, for the sake of simplicity, the focus of the chapter will be on forecasting demand.

Nevertheless, the concepts and techniques apply equally well to these other variables.

In spite of the use of computers and sophisticated mathematical models in forecasting, it is not an exact science. Instead, successful forecasting often requires a skillful blending of art and science. Experience, judgment, and technical expertise all play a role in developing useful forecasts. Even so, a certain amount of luck and a dash of humility can be helpful, since the worst of forecasters occasionally produce a very good forecast, while even the best forecasters sometimes miss completely. Forecasting techniques currently in use range from the mundane to the exotic. Some work better than others, but no one technique works all of the time.

Generally speaking, the responsibility for preparing demand forecasts lies with marketing or sales rather than operations. Nonetheless, operations people are called on to make certain forecasts as well as to help others to prepare forecasts. In addition, since forecasts are major inputs for many operations decisions, it is essential for operations managers and staff to be knowledgeable about the kinds of forecasting techniques that are available, the assumptions that underlie their use, and their limitations. In other words, forecasting is an integral part of operations management.

FEATURES COMMON TO ALL FORECASTS

There is a wide variety of forecasting techniques in use. In many respects they are quite different from each other, as you shall soon discover. Nonetheless, there are certain features that are common to all, and it is important to recognize them.

1. Forecasting techniques generally assume that the same underlying causal system that existed in the past will continue to exist in the future.
2. Forecasts are rarely perfect; actual results will usually differ from predicted values. The inability to precisely predict how an often-large number of related factors will impinge upon the variable being forecast and the presence of randomness preclude a perfect forecast. Allowances should be made for inaccuracies.
3. Forecasts for groups of items tend to be more accurate than forecasts for individual items because forecasting errors among items in a group usually have a canceling effect. Opportunities for grouping may arise if parts or raw materials are used for multiple products or when a service is demanded by a number of independent sources.
4. Forecast accuracy decreases as the time period covered by

the forecast (i.e., the time *horizon*) increases. Generally speaking, short-range forecasts must contend with fewer uncertainties than longer-range forecasts, so they tend to be more accurate.

STEPS IN THE FORECASTING PROCESS

There are five basic steps in the forecasting process:

1. *Determine the purpose* of the forecast and when it will be needed. This will provide an indication of the level of detail required in the forecast, the amount of resources (manpower, computer, dollars) that can be justified, and the level of accuracy necessary.
2. *Establish a time horizon* that the forecast must cover, keeping in mind that accuracy decreases as the length of the forecast period increases.
3. *Select a forecasting technique.*
4. *Gather and analyze the appropriate data,* and then *prepare the forecast. Identify any assumptions* that are made in conjunction with preparing and using the forecast.
5. *Monitor the forecast* to see if it is performing in a satisfactory manner. If it is not, reexamine the method, assumptions, validity of data, and so on, modify as needed, and prepare a revised forecast.

APPROACHES TO FORECASTING

There are two general approaches to forecasting, qualitative and quantitative. Qualitative methods consist mainly of subjective inputs, which often defy precise numerical description. Quantitative methods involve either the extension of historical data or development of associative models that attempt to utilize *causal variables* to make a forecast.

Subjective techniques permit inclusion of soft information (human factors, personal opinions, hunches) in the forecasting process. These factors are often omitted or downplayed when quantitative techniques are used because they are difficult or impossible to quantify. Quantitative techniques consist mainly of analyzing objective or hard data. They usually avoid personal biases that sometimes contaminate qualitative methods. In practice either or both approaches might be used to develop a given forecast. Sometimes the two approaches can serve as a check on each other.

Forecasts Based on Judgment and Opinion

Judgmental forecasts rely on analysis of subjective inputs obtained from various sources, such as consumer surveys, the sales staff, managers and executives, and panels of experts. Quite frequently these sources provide insights that are not otherwise available.

Forecasts Based on Historical Data

Some forecasting techniques depend on uncovering relationships between variables that can be used to predict future values of one of them, while others simply attempt to project past experience into the future. The second of these approaches exemplifies forecasts that use historical, or time series, data. The theme of that approach is that the future will be like the past. Some of the models merely attempt to smooth out random variations in historical data while others attempt to identify specific patterns in the data. In effect, approaches based on historical data treat the data as a mirror that reflects the combination of all forces that influence the variable of interest (e.g., demand), without trying to identify or measure those forces directly.

Associative Forecasts

Associative models involve identification of one or more variables that can be used to predict future demand. For example, demand for paint might be related to such variables as the price per gallon and the amount spent on advertising as well as specific characteristics of the paint (e.g., drying time, ease of cleanup). The analysis in such cases yields a mathematical equation that enables the manager to predict volume of sales, for example, on the basis of given values of the causal or "explaining" variable(s).

The discussion of forecasting techniques begins with techniques that are based on judgment and opinion.

FORECASTS BASED ON JUDGMENT AND OPINION

When a forecast must be prepared quickly, there is usually not enough time to gather and analyze quantitative data. At other times, especially when political and economic conditions are changing, available data may be obsolete, and more up-to-date information might not yet be available. Similarly, the introduction of new products, as well as the redesign of existing products or packaging, all suffer from the absence of historical data that would be useful in forecasting. In such instances, forecasts based on judgment and experience are commonly used. Among those techniques are forecasts that use executive opinions, consumer surveys, opinions of the sales staff, and opinions of experts.

Executive Opinions

A small group of upper-level managers (e.g., marketing, product, engineering, manufacturing, and financial managers) may meet and collectively develop a forecast. This approach is often used as a part of long-range planning and new product development. It has the advantage of bringing together the considerable knowledge and talents of these top management people. However, there is the risk that the view of one person will prevail as well as the possibility that diffusing responsibility for the forecast over the entire group may result in less pressure to produce a good forecast.

Salesforce Composite

The sales staff is often a good source of information because of its direct contact with consumers. Thus, these people are often aware of any plans the customers may be considering for the future. There are, however, several drawbacks to this approach. One is that salespeople may be unable to distinguish between what customers would *like* to do and what they actually *will* do. Another is that salespeople are sometimes overly influenced by recent experiences. Thus, after several periods of low sales, their estimates may tend to become pessimistic, while after several periods of good sales, they may tend to be too optimistic. In addition, if forecasts are to be used to establish sales quotas, there will be a conflict of interest because it would be to the salesperson's advantage to provide low sales estimates.

Consumer Surveys

Since the consumer is the one who will ultimately determine demand, it would seem natural to solicit input from consumers. In some instances, every customer or potential customer can be contacted. In most cases, however, there are either too many customers or no way to identify all potential customers. Because of these and similar factors, organizations that seek consumer input usually resort to the use of consumer surveys, which enable them to *sample* consumer opinions. The obvious advantage of such surveys is that they can tap information that might not be available elsewhere. On the other hand, surveys require a considerable amount of skill to handle correctly. A great deal of care is necessary to construct a survey, administer it, and correctly interpret the results in order to obtain valid information. In addition, even under the best of conditions, surveys involving the general public must contend with the possibility of irrational behavior patterns. For example, much thoughtful information gathering done by consumers before purchasing a new car is often washed out by the glitter of a new car showroom or a high-pressure sales pitch. Along the same lines, low response rates to a mail survey should (but often don't) make the results suspect.

If these and similar pitfalls can be avoided, surveys can produce useful information both for forecasting and for product design and promotion.

Outside Opinion

Occasionally, outside opinions are needed in order to make a forecast. This may concern advice on political or economic conditions in the United States or in a foreign country or some other aspect of interest with which an organization lacks familiarity.

Opinions of Managers and Staff

A manager may use a staff to generate a forecast or to provide several forecasting alternatives from which to choose. At other times, a manager may solicit opinions from a number of other managers and/or staff people. The *Delphi method* is sometimes useful in this regard. It involves circulating a series of questionnaires among those individuals who possess the knowledge and ability to contribute meaningfully. Responses are kept anonymous, which tends to encourage honest responses. Each new questionnaire is developed using any information extracted from the previous one, thus enlarging the scope of information on which participants can base their judgments. The goal is to achieve a consensus forecast.

The Delphi technique originated in the RAND Corporation in 1948, where it was used to assess the potential impact of an atomic bomb attack on the United States. Since that time it has been applied to a variety of situations, not all of which involve forecasting. However, the discussion here will be limited to its use as a forecasting tool.

As a forecasting tool, the Delphi technique is useful for *technological* forecasting. That is, the technique is a method for assessing changes in technology and their impact on an organization. Often the goal is to predict *when* a certain event will occur. For instance, the goal of a Delphi forecast might be to predict when video telephones might be installed in at least 50 percent of residential homes or when a vaccine for a disease might be developed and ready for mass distribution. For the most part, these are long-term, single-time forecasts. In these situations there is usually very little hard information to go on, or data are costly to obtain, so the problem does not lend itself to analytical techniques. Rather, judgments of experts or others who possess sufficient knowledge to make predictions are used.

The first step in the Delphi process is the establishment of a small group of individuals who will design the study. This group is the Delphi committee. They will first decide the channel of communication (e.g., mail, hand delivery, computer), the size of the group to be queried, and the participants. Next, the initial questionnaire must be developed. It must be constructed in such a way that it elicits opinions unambiguously. This is essential in order to achieve a true consensus from the group. The initial questionnaire must introduce the desired purpose and scope and focus on the desired points, factors, and opinions. Pretesting of the questionnaire to ensure its validity is very important. Next, the questionnaire is distributed to the participants for their initial inputs and returned to the Delphi committee, which then compiles the results. Using this information, the committee develops and distributes a second questionnaire. This second questionnaire usually asks respondents to expand on key factors or place priorities on key items. This questionnaire receives cursory pretesting to eliminate ambiguities along with the results of the initial questionnaire. The intent of including the initial results is to exert pressure to conform; since it is human nature to conform, the feedback these results provide helps the process. The process is repeated with a third questionnaire. If there is to be a consensus, it will usually be achieved by this point. Hence, the process usually terminates after the third questionnaire. At that point the forecast can be made, assuming consensus has been reached. Otherwise, the process may be started all over, perhaps with some new participants, a revised questionnaire, or a completely different approach to the problem (e.g., a face-to-face meeting of a few key experts).

There are a number of reasons for considering a Delphi approach. Among them are the following:

1. A group of experts can provide needed judgmental input.
2. More individuals are needed than can effectively interact in a face-to-face situation, and/or the individuals cannot be conveniently assembled in one place. Time and cost can also be factors.
3. It is important to avoid a "bandwagon effect."
4. It is desirable to preserve the anonymity of the participants.
5. There is controlled feedback between rounds and a statistical summary of group responses.
6. It is highly useful for situations that involve the creation of event scenarios ("what if . . . ?").

There are a number of weaknesses of the Delphi approach, some of them fairly serious. Among them are the following:

1. The questions may contain ambiguous phrasing so that panel members reach a false consensus.
2. Panel membership may change, especially if the process requires a long time (some may take a year or more).
3. The "experts" may not be experts.
4. Studies have failed to prove that Delphi forecasts generally achieve a high degree of accuracy.
5. The process (questionnaire development, administration, and evaluation) in many instances does not meet the criteria of the American Psychological Association.[1]

---

[1] Harold Sackman, *Delphi Critique* (Lexington, Mass.: Lexington Books, 1975), p. 27.

6. Preserving anonymity removes accountability and responsibility.
7. Results are difficult or impossible to replicate.

ANALYSIS OF TIME SERIES DATA

A *time series* is a time-ordered sequence of observations that have been taken at regular intervals over a period of time (hourly, daily, weekly, monthly, quarterly, annually, and so on). Common examples include measurements of demand, earnings, profits, shipments, accidents, output, precipitation, productivity, and the consumer price index. Forecasting techniques that are based on time series data are predicated on the assumption that future values of the series can be estimated from past values of the series. In spite of the fact that no attempt is made to identify variables that influence the series, these methods are widely used, often with very satisfactory results.

Analysis of time series data requires the analyst to identify the underlying behavior of the series. This can often be accomplished by merely *plotting* the data and visually examining the plot. One or more of the following behaviors might appear: trend, seasonal variations, cycles, and variations around an average. In addition there can be random and irregular variations. These behaviors can be described as follows:

1. *Trend* refers to a gradual, long-term movement in the data. Population shifts, changing incomes, and cultural changes often account for such movements.
2. *Seasonality* refers to short-term, fairly regular, periodic variations that are generally related to weather factors or to manmade factors such as holidays and vacations. Restaurants, supermarkets, and theaters experience weekly and even daily "seasonal" variations.
3. *Cycles* are wave-like variations of more than one year's duration. These are often related to a variety of economic and political factors and even to severe weather conditions.
4. *Irregular* variations are due to unusual circumstances such as severe weather conditions, strikes, or a major change in a product or service. They do not reflect typical behavior, and inclusion in the series can distort the overall picture. Whenever possible, these should be identified and removed from the data.
5. *Random* variations are the residual variations that remain after all of the other behaviors have been accounted for. These behaviors are illustrated in Figure 3–1. The small "bumps" in the plots represent random variability.

FIGURE 3–1

Trend, Seasonal, Cyclical, Random, and Irregular Variations

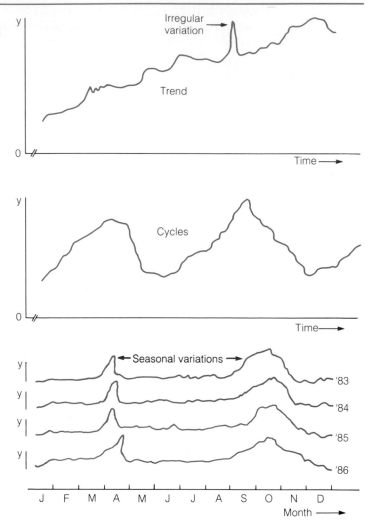

In the remainder of this section, four approaches to the analysis of time series data are described:

1. The naive approach.
2. Moving averages.
3. Exponential smoothing.
4. Decomposition of a time series.

Before turning to those discussions, one point should be emphasized: A demand forecast should be based on a time series of past *demand* rather than sales. Sales would not truly reflect demand unless demand was less than the amount of a good or service available for sale. Conversely, sales quantities are acceptable if it can be confirmed that sales were consistently below available supplies. Similarly, *shipments* would not truly reflect demand if there are backlogs of orders; the timing of shipments would then not correspond to the *timing* of demand.

The Naive Approach

The *naive* approach to forecasting is wonderfully simplistic: The latest observation in a sequence is used as the forecast for the next period. Thus, if October *demand* is 310 units, the November *forecast* is 310 units. In effect, users of this method are saying that the immediate future is expected to be pretty much like the recent past. While on the surface such an approach might appear to be just a little *too* simplistic, it does have its merits. For instance, the approach is easy to understand and use, and there is little or no cost involved in preparing the forecast. Moreover, at times naive forecasts can be amazingly accurate. For instance, forecasting tomorrow's weather by saying it will be like today's weather will usually produce forecasts that are correct about 70 percent of the time. In comparison, weather forecasts issued by the U.S. Weather Bureau tend to be right about 90 percent of the time. The catch with the naive approach is that it only works if there is little variation in actual values from period to period.

The naive method can also be extended to seasonal and trend variations. For instance, if seasonality is the primary factor, the forecast for the upcoming season would equal demand in the preceding season (e.g., predicted demand for this December equals last December's actual demand). If trend is the primary behavior, the predicted *change* in demand for the next period equals the previous change in demand (e.g., if demand for last period was 120, which was an increase of 10 units from the previous period, the forecast for the next period would be 130 units).

Obviously, there will be many cases in which a naive approach will not work very well. Even in such cases, however, the naive approach can serve a useful purpose by providing a standard against which other forecasting alternatives can be measured. In other words, the manager can decide if the higher degree of accuracy a more sophisticated forecasting approach could provide would be worth the cost of using that approach, relative to the accuracy that would be provided by "free" naive forecasts.

Moving Averages

Historical data typically contain a certain amount of random variation or *noise* that tends to obscure systematic movements in the data. This randomness arises from the combined influence of many—perhaps a great many—relatively unimportant factors, and it cannot be reliably predicted. Ideally, it would be desirable to be able to completely remove any randomness from the data and leave only "real" variations, such as changes in the *level* of demand (e.g., a step or a ramp change). However, as a practical matter, it is usually impossible to distinguish between these two kinds of variations, so the best one can hope for is to be able to smooth out the randomness but leave the nonrandom variations intact. In effect, small variations are treated as random—they are smoothed out. Averaging techniques are often used for this purpose.

Averaging techniques smooth out some of the fluctuations in a time series, because the individual highs and lows in the data offset each other when they are combined into an average. A *moving average* is an average that is repeatedly updated: as new observations become available, the oldest values in the series are deleted, thereby keeping the average current. Two common types of moving averages are the simple moving average and the weighted moving average.

Using a *simple average* approach involves computing the average value of a time series for a certain number of the most recent periods and treating that average as the forecast for the upcoming period. Thus, a 3-period moving average would require determining the average of the three previous values, while a 5-period moving average would involve the average of the last five values of a series.

EXAMPLE 1

Compute a 4-period simple moving average for demand for tires given the figures (demand in 000s of tires) below:

Month	Demand
May	20
Jun.	24
Jul.	22
Aug.	26
Sept.	25

Solution

Predicted sales for October are computed as:

$$MA_4 = \frac{24 + 22 + 26 + 25}{4} = \frac{97}{4} = 24.25, \text{ or } 24,250 \text{ tires}$$

A second kind of moving average is the *weighted average*. This is similar in many respects to a simple moving average. For example, both reflect only the most recent values of the series. However, unlike the simple moving average, which assigns an *equal* weight to each observation (e.g., in a 4-period moving average, each value has a weight of ¼), a weighted average generally weights the most recent observations more heavily than older ones. For instance, a weighted scheme might have these weights: .1, .2, .3, and .4. (Note that the sum of the weights is 1.00 and that the .1 would be assigned to the oldest value and the .4 to the newest value in the series.)

EXAMPLE 2

Sales of electric coffee makers at a discount department store over the last five months are shown below. Using weights of .1, .2, .3, and .4, prepare a forecast for next month.

Month	Unit sales
Jan.	90
Feb.	70
Mar.	80
Apr.	85
May	82

Solution

$$Forecast_{June} = .1(70) + .2(80) + .3(85) + .4(82) = 81.3$$

Hence, the expected demand is approximately 81 coffee makers.

The advantage of weighted averages over simple moving averages is that older values are given less importance than more recent values of a series and that the number of values included in the average can be large while still achieving a responsiveness to change through judicious selection of weights. However, the choice of weights is somewhat arbitrary and is often left to trial and error judgments.

Comment. Averaging techniques have two fundamental characteristics that users should be aware of. One is that they smooth variations in the data, and the other is that they do not react immediately to changing patterns in the data. These characteristics are illustrated in Figure 3–2. The extent of smoothing and lagging are a function of the number of periods included in the average: the more periods, the greater the smoothing and lagging, and vice versa. Hence, a 9-period moving average will smooth and lag much more than, say, a 3-period moving average. The choice of number of periods to include in a moving average will depend on such things as the degree to which random variations are present as well as the cost of not reacting quickly to changes relative to the cost of reacting when no real changes are present.

FIGURE 3–2

Moving Averages Smooth Out Some of the Variations in Data and Lag Changes

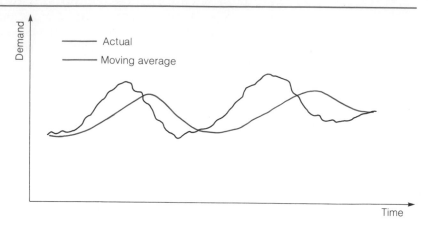

Exponential Smoothing

Exponential smoothing is a widely used method of forecasting. In actuality, it is a form of weighted moving average, although somewhat superior to the methods discussed in the preceding section. Its superiority stems from the ease with which weighting patterns can be altered to meet the needs of a particular situation and from its minimal data storage requirements. The latter makes exponential smoothing attractive for computerization, especially when many items require forecasts. In contrast, moving average methods like those mentioned previously require retaining all the values that comprise the average. For a large number of items, the data storage requirements can be enormous.

The name *exponential smoothing* is derived from the way weights are assigned to historical data: the most recent values receive most of the weight and weights fall off *exponentially* as the age of the data increases.

Simple exponential smoothing is appropriate for data that vary around an average. It can also handle changes in the average level.

The method is relatively easy to use and understand. Each new forecast is based on the previous forecast plus a percentage of the difference between that forecast and the actual value of the series at that point. That is:

$$\text{New forecast} = \text{Old forecast} + \alpha(\text{Actual} - \text{Old forecast}) \quad \textbf{(3–1)}$$

where α is a percentage and (Actual $-$ Old forecast) represents the forecast error. More concisely, we have

$$F_t = F_{t-1} + \alpha(A_{t-1} - F_{t-1}) \quad \textbf{(3–2)}$$

where

$\alpha = $ Smoothing constant
$t = $ Current period

A_{t-1} = Previous (actual) value of the time series
F_{t-1} = Previous forecast

EXAMPLE 3

Annual sales of air conditioners are forecast by exponential smoothing using a smoothing constant of $\alpha = .30$. Suppose that the previous forecast for the latest period was 20,000 units and that actual sales were 21,000 units. What is the forecast for the next period?

Solution

$$\alpha = .30, F_{old} = 20,000 \text{ units}$$
$$\text{Actual} = 21,000 \text{ units}$$
$$F_{new} = F_{old} + \alpha(\text{Actual} - F_{old})$$
$$F_{new} = 20,000 + .30(21,000 - 20,000) = 20,300 \text{ units}$$

If exponential smoothing is to be done where no previous forecasts have been made, a starting forecast can be made using an average of the data over the last n periods, where n is: $n = 2/\alpha - 1$. Round n to the nearest integer. Hence, if alpha = .1, $n = 2/.1 - 1 = 19$, and if alpha = .3, $n = 2/.3 - 1 = 5.7$, which would be rounded to 6. One drawback to this approach is that small values of alpha produce large values of n, which requires a considerable amount of historical data that might not be available. In such cases, some users simply take an average of the first four or five values as a starting point.

EXAMPLE 4

Using exponential smoothing with a smoothing constant of .5, develop a predictive model for weekly sales of color televisions, given the data below:

Period	Demand (units)
1	10
2	14
3	9
4	13
5	15
6	10
7	

Solution

1. Determine the starting forecast: $n = 2/.5 - 1 = 3$-period average. Hence, use the average of the first three values for the initial forecast (i.e., for period 4):

EXAMPLE 4 (concluded)

$$F_4 = \frac{10 + 14 + 9}{3} = 11$$

2. Compute the updated forecasts for each period using the formula

$$F_t = F_{t-1} + \alpha(A_{t-1} - F_{t-1}):$$

$F_5 = F_4 + .5(A_4 - F_4):$ $11 + .5(13 - 11) = 12,$
$F_6 = F_5 + .5(A_5 - F_5):$ $12 + .5(15 - 12) = 13.5,$
$F_7 = F_6 + .5(A_6 - F_6):$ $13.5 + .5(10 - 13.5) = 11.75.$

The weighting pattern of exponential smoothing can be seen more readily by rewriting the equation:

$$F_t = F_{t-1} + \alpha(A_{t-1} - F_{t-1})$$

by grouping the F_{t-1} terms:

$$F_t = \alpha A_{t-1} + (1 - \alpha)F_{t-1}$$

and then expanding this:

$$F_t = \alpha A_{t-1} + (1 - \alpha)[\alpha A_{t-2} + (1 - \alpha)F_{t-2}] \text{ and so on.}$$

This produces an equation of the form:

$$F_t = \alpha A_{t-1} + \alpha(1 - \alpha)A_{t-2} + \alpha(1 - \alpha)^2 A_{t-3} + \alpha(1 - \alpha)^3 A_{t-4}.$$

For $\alpha = .2$, this becomes:

$$F_t = .2A_{t-1} + .16A_{t-2} + .128A_{t-3} + .1024A_{t-4} + \cdots \text{ and}$$

for $\alpha = .5$, this becomes:

$$F_t = .5A_{t-1} + .25A_{t-2} + .125A_{t-3} + .0625A_{t-4} + \cdots$$

The responsiveness of an exponential forecast to changes in a time series is totally dependent on the value of the smoothing constant. Typical values range from .01 to .50. Small values of the smoothing constant cause a slow response to discrepancies between actual and forecast values, while values closer to .50 cause a more rapid response to any discrepancies. A comparison of the response rates of a small and a large value of alpha to a large change in a time series is illustrated in Figure 3–3.

The choice of a smoothing constant depends on the extent to which the forecaster feels future changes will reflect mainly random variations versus the extent to which "real" changes (e.g., shift to a different average) might occur. Practically speaking, it boils down to the relative cost of failing to respond to real changes in the data compared to the cost of reacting to chance fluctuations in the data.

FIGURE 3–3

A Smoothing Constant of $\alpha = .4$ Will Cause the Forecast to React More Quickly to a Sudden Change than an $\alpha = .1$ Will

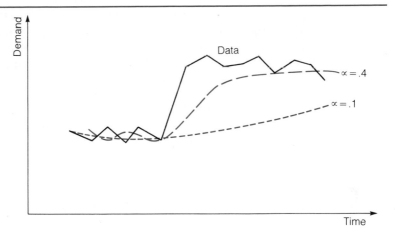

One important limitation of simple exponential smoothing is that it is ill-suited for data that include long-term upward or downward movements (i.e., trend). Use of simple exponential smoothing in such instances would produce forecasts that were too low for upward movements and too high for downward movements. This tendency is illustrated in Figure 3–4. Therefore, *when trend is present in time series data, simple exponential smoothing should not be used.* Instead, exponential smoothing adjusted for trend should be used.

FIGURE 3–4

Simple Exponential Smoothing Will Lag a Trend

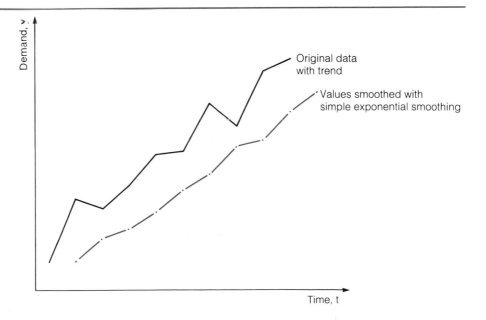

Exponential Smoothing Adjusted for Trend

Trend-adjusted smoothing is relatively simple. It involves two smoothings. First, the original data are smoothed as in single smoothing. Then the resulting values are smoothed as if they are original values. These double-smoothed values have two useful properties. One is that they are smoother than the single-smoothed values, which means they will provide a clearer indication of the trend. The other property is that the double-smoothed values lag the single-smoothed values by about as much as the single-smoothed values lag the original data. Consequently, by adding the difference between single- and double-smoothed values to the single-smoothed values, the resulting series will approximate the original series. Finally, by including an allowance for trend in the forecast, the forecasts will give a fairly good indication of future values. The smoothing and double lagging can be seen in the graph in Figure 3–5.

The exponentially smoothed forecast adjusted for trend is:

$$F_{t+1} = \begin{array}{c} \text{Single} \\ \text{smoothed} \end{array} + \left(\begin{array}{c} \text{Single} \\ \text{smoothed} \end{array} - \begin{array}{c} \text{Double} \\ \text{smoothed} \end{array} \right) + \begin{array}{c} \text{Trend} \\ \text{adjustment} \end{array} \quad (3\text{–}3)$$

$$= \quad S_t' \quad + (\quad S_t' \quad - \quad S_t'' \quad) + \quad b_t$$

The trend adjustment, b_t, can be approximated by the amount of change each period in S''. That is:

$$b_t = S_t'' - S_{t-1}''. \quad (3\text{–}4)$$

FIGURE 3–5

The Double-Smoothed Values (*S"*) Are Much Smoother than the Single-Smoothed Values (*S'*), and They Lag the Single Values by about as Much as the Single Lag the Original Data (*A_t*). Compensating for the Lagging and Adjusting for Trend Yields a Forecast That Approximates the Original Series.

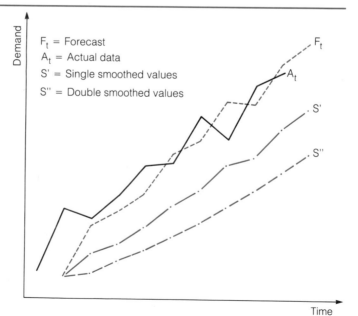

F_t = Forecast
A_t = Actual data
S' = Single smoothed values
S'' = Double smoothed values

EXAMPLE 5

Calculator sales for a California-based firm over the past 10 years are shown below. Using trend-adjusted exponential smoothing with a single smoothing constant of $\alpha_1 = .4$ and a double smoothing constant of $\alpha_2 = .3$, prepare a forecast for period 11.

Period	Unit sales
1	700
2	724
3	720
4	728
5	740
6	742
7	758
8	750
9	770
10	775

Solution

1. Smooth the data using the equation $S_t' = S_{t-1}' + .4(A_t - S_{t-1}')$. Use the first data point, 700, as the beginning forecast. The results are shown in Table 3–1 under the S_t' column.

TABLE 3–1

Calculations for Trend-Adjusted Forecast

t	A_t (data)	S_t' (single)	S_t'' (double)	$S_t'' - S_{t-1}''$ (b_t)	Forecast
1	700.00	700.00	700.00		
2	724.00	709.60	702.88	2.88	700.00
3	720.00	713.76	706.14	3.26	719.20
4	728.00	719.46	710.14	3.99	724.64
5	740.00	727.67	715.40	5.26	732.77
6	742.00	733.40	720.80	5.40	745.21
7	758.00	743.24	727.53	6.73	751.41
8	750.00	745.95	733.06	5.52	765.68
9	770.00	755.57	739.81	6.75	764.36
10	775.00	763.34	746.87	7.06	778.08
11					786.87

2. Smooth the S_t' values using the equation $S_t'' = S_{t-1}'' + .3(S_t' - S_{t-1}'')$, with 700 as the first value. The results are shown in Table 3–1 under the S'' column.
3. Compute the trend adjustment, b_t, using the equation $b_t = S_t'' - S_{t-1}''$. The results are shown under column b_t.
4. Determine the forecast for each period using the equation $F_{t+1} = S_t' + (S_t' - S_t'') + b_t$. The forecasts are shown in the last column of Table 3–1.
5. The data, forecasts, and smoothed values are plotted in Figure 3–6.

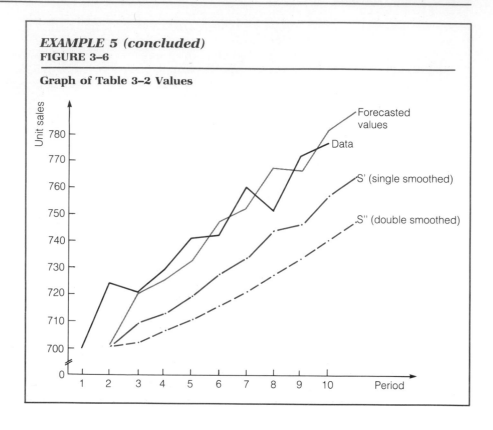

EXAMPLE 5 (concluded)
FIGURE 3–6

Graph of Table 3–2 Values

Decomposition of a Time Series

In this classical approach to the analysis of historical data, a time series is viewed as being made up of four possible components: trend, seasonality, cycles, and random plus irregular variations.

The essence of the decomposition approach is to attempt to isolate various components (except random and irregular variations) so their effects can be considered separately. In some cases, interest may focus on only one of these components rather than all of them. For example, a buyer for a department store may be more concerned with seasonal variations in demand than with long-term projections. Financial planning and capacity planning, on the other hand, usually must take into account both cyclical variations and long-term expectations.

There are two models for describing how these components are combined in a series. The *additive model* treats the series as the *sum* of components:

$$Y = T + S + C + r \tag{3–5}$$

where

T = Trend component
S = Seasonal
C = Cyclical
r = Residual

The *multiplicative* model treats the series as the *product* of the components:

$$Y = T \times S \times C \times r \qquad (3\text{--}6)$$

In the additive model, each factor is an actual amount (e.g., trend may be 200 units, seasonality may be 15 units, and so on), while in the multiplicative model only trend is in actual units; the others are stated as percentages of trend (e.g., seasonality might be 120 percent of trend, or 1.20). In practice, the multiplicative model enjoys wider use than the additive model, and the discussion here will focus almost exclusively on the multiplicative model.

The *trend* component of a time series reflects the effects of any long-term factors on the series. Analysis of trend involves searching for an equation that will suitably describe trend (assuming that trend is, in fact, present in the data). The trend component may be linear or it may not. Some commonly encountered nonlinear trend functions are illustrated in Figure 3–7. A simple plot of the data can often reveal the nature of the trend component.

A linear trend line can be obtained by using a least squares approach. The line has the equation

$$y_t = a + bt \qquad (3\text{--}7)$$

where

$t = 1,2,3, \ldots$
b = Slope of the line
a = Value of y when $t = 0$

The coefficients of the equation, a and b, can be determined using these equations:

$$b = \frac{n\,\Sigma ty - \Sigma t\,\Sigma y}{n\,\Sigma t^2 - (\Sigma t)^2} \qquad (3\text{--}8)$$

$$a = \frac{\Sigma y - b\,\Sigma t}{n} \qquad (3\text{--}9)$$

where n = Number of data points

Computations are aided by use of the values provided in Table 3–2.

FIGURE 3–7

Graphs of Some Common Nonlinear Trends

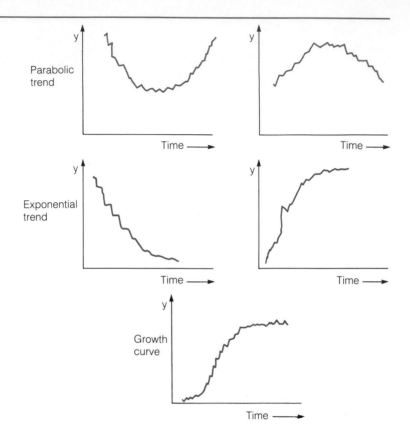

TABLE 3–2

Values of Σt and Σt^2

n	Σt	Σt^2
1	1	1
2	3	5
3	6	14
4	10	30
5	15	55
6	21	91
7	28	140
8	36	204
9	45	285
10	55	385
11	66	506
12	78	650
13	91	819
14	105	1,015
15	120	1,240
16	136	1,496
17	153	1,785
18	171	2,109
19	190	2,470
20	210	2,870

EXAMPLE 6

Annual demands for riding lawn mowers for the past 14 years are shown in the table below. Compute a least squares trend line for the data and use the trend line to predict sales for the following (15th) year.

Year	1	2	3	4	5	6	7	8	9	10	11	12	13	14
Demand (units)	32	28	30	34	30	43	36	42	42	55	47	56	54	57

Solution

The computations necessary for a least squares trend line are:

t	y	ty
1	32	32
2	28	56
3	30	90
4	34	136
5	30	150
6	43	258
7	36	252
8	42	336
9	42	378
10	55	550
11	47	517
12	56	672
13	54	702
14	57	798
	586	4,927

FIGURE 3–8

A Plot of the Data and Trend Line Supports Use of a Linear Model

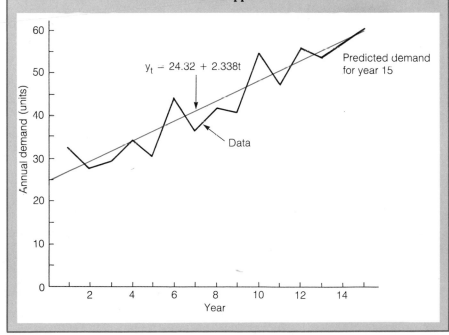

$y_t = 24.32 + 2.338t$

Predicted demand for year 15

Data

EXAMPLE 6 (concluded)
From Table 3–2, for $n = 14$, we find:

$$\Sigma t = 105 \quad \text{and} \quad \Sigma t^2 = 1{,}015$$

Then

$$b = \frac{14(4{,}927) - 105(586)}{14(1{,}015) - 105(105)} = 2.338$$

$$a = \frac{586 - 2.338(105)}{14} = 24.32.$$

Thus, the least squares equation is $y_t = 24.32 + 2.338t$.
The predicted sales for the following period are: $y_{15} = 24.32 + 2.338(15) = 59.39$, or about 59 mowers. As a check on the validity of a linear model, the data are plotted in Figure 3–8.

As an example of a nonlinear trend, suppose we consider how a *parabola* might be fitted to a series of observations. The parabola has the form $y_t = a + bt + ct^2$ with $t = 0$ at the *center* of the data.

The coefficients of the equation, *a, b,* and *c,* are found using these equations:

$$b = \frac{\Sigma ty}{\Sigma t^2}, \quad c = \frac{n\Sigma t^2\Sigma y - \Sigma t^2\Sigma y}{n\Sigma t^4 - (\Sigma t^2)^2}, \quad a = \frac{\Sigma y - c\Sigma t^2}{n} \qquad \textbf{(3–10)}$$

EXAMPLE 7
The table below illustrates computations for fitting a parabola to time series data.[2] The last column in the table shows computed values that were obtained using the least squares equation.

Period	Demand (y)	t	ty	t^2	t^2y	t^4	y_t
1	82	−6	−492	36	2,952	1,296	77.11
2	64	−5	−319	25	1,600	625	70.83
3	70	−4	−280	16	1,120	256	65.52
4	60	−3	−160	9	540	81	61.18
5	58	−2	−116	4	232	16	57.81
6	53	−1	−53	1	53	1	55.41
7	60	0	0	0	0	0	53.98
8	50	1	50	1	50	1	53.52
9	55	2	110	4	220	16	54.03
10	52	3	156	9	468	81	55.51
11	62	4	248	16	992	256	57.96
12	60	5	300	25	1,500	625	61.38
13	64	6	384	36	2,304	1,296	65.77
	790	0	−172	182	12,031	4,550	

[2] The procedure assumes an *odd* number of years. Consult a statistics textbook for the procedure for an even number of years.

EXAMPLE 7 *(concluded)*

The coefficients are:

$$b = \frac{\Sigma ty}{\Sigma t^2} = \frac{-172}{182} = -.945$$

$$c - \frac{n\Sigma t^2 y - \Sigma t^2 \Sigma y}{n\Sigma t^4 - (\Sigma t^2)^2}$$

$$= \frac{13(12,031) - 182(790)}{13(4,550) - 182(182)} = .485$$

$$a = \frac{\Sigma y - c\Sigma t^2}{n} = \frac{790 - .485(182)}{13} = 53.98$$

Predicted demand for the next period is: $y_7 = 53.98 - .945(7) + .485(7)^2 = 71.13$. A plot of the original and computed values suggests that the parabola fits the data fairly well (see Figure 3–9).

It is important to recognize that future *predicted* values will continue to increase, so that extended use of the parabola for prediction is somewhat questionable. However, the data may turn out to be cyclical (i.e., repeat a pattern similar to that observed over the 13 periods for which data exist). In that case, the parabola could be used to describe the cycles, although *it will not identify turning points.*

FIGURE 3–9

The Parabola Provides a Reasonably Good Fit to the Data Points

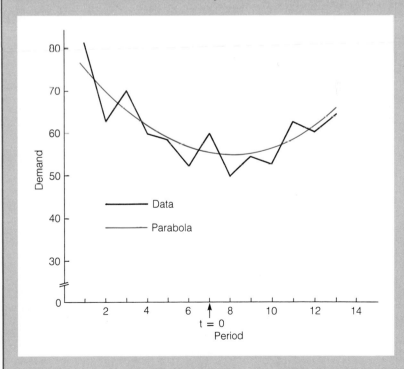

Seasonal relatives give an indication of the extent to which values of a time series will tend to deviate from a trend due to seasonal factors. Relatives are expressed as percentages of trend (or average, if there is no trend), and there will be one relative for each season. Thus, for monthly data, there will be 12 relatives, for quarterly data, there will be 4 relatives.

Obtaining estimates of seasonal relatives can be conceptually demonstrated using a linear trend line. Assume that a series consists only of a linear trend with seasonal and random elements. Using the multiplicative model, we can represent the series as $Y = T \times S \times r$. Hence, the trend component can be removed from the data by a division process. Dividing both sides of the equation by the trend component produces a series made up entirely of seasonality and random variations:

$$\frac{Y}{T} = \frac{T \times S \times r}{T} = S \times r \qquad (3\text{--}11)$$

EXAMPLE 8

Quarterly demand for word processing systems sold through a branch office are shown in the table. Based upon previous experience, the manager believes that cyclical variations are not present in demand. Determine seasonal (quarterly) relatives for demand.

Year	Quarter	t	Demand (units)
1	1	1	14
	2	2	18
	3	3	35
	4	4	46
2	1	5	28
	2	6	36
	3	7	60
	4	8	71
3	1	9	45
	2	10	54
	3	11	84
	4	12	88
4	1	13	58

Solution

A least squares trend line can be determined for the data: $y_t = 14.27 + 4.96t$. Once the equation has been determined, it can be used to compute the trend value for each period:

For $t = 1$, $y_t = 14.27 + 4.96\,(1) = 19.23$
For $t = 2$, $y_t = 14.27 + 4.96\,(2) = 24.19$
For $t = 3$, $y_t = 14.27 + 4.96\,(3) = 29.15$
etc.

EXAMPLE 8 *(concluded)*

These values are shown in column 3 of Table 3–3. The percentage of seasonal deviation for each period can be found by dividing the trend estimate into the original data. These values are shown in column 4 of Table 3–3.

TABLE 3–3

Computations for Example 8

t	Data	$(y_t = 14.27 + 4.96t)$ Trend	Data/Trend
1	14	19.23	.728
2	18	24.19	.744
3	35	29.15	1.201
4	46	34.11	1.349
5	28	39.07	.717
6	36	44.03	.818
7	60	48.99	1.225
8	71	53.95	1.316
9	45	58.91	.764
10	54	63.87	.845
11	84	68.83	1.220
12	88	73.79	1.193
13	58	78.75	.737

Some of the inherent randomness can be removed from the seasonal estimates by averaging. This requires grouping the seasonals by quarter (i.e., all first quarter values are averaged, all second quarter values are averaged, and so on):

		Quarter	
1	*2*	*3*	*4*
.728	.744	1.201	1.349
.717	.818	1.225	1.316
.764	.845	1.220	1.193
.737	2.407	3.646	3.858
2.946			
$\bar{x}$: .737	.802	1.215	1.286

These four values should sum to 4.00 (monthly seasonals should add to 12.00), but actually sum to 4.04, probably due to rounding. By multiplying each quarterly seasonal by 4.00/4.04, we can adjust the seasonals so they will add to 4.00. The adjusted values are: $S_1 = .730$, $S_2 = .794$, $S_3 = 1.203$, and $S_4 = 1.27$. These values can be interpreted in the following manner. The first quarter relative of .730 means that on the average, demand in first quarters equals

FIGURE 3–10

Quarterly Unit Sales for Word Processing Systems

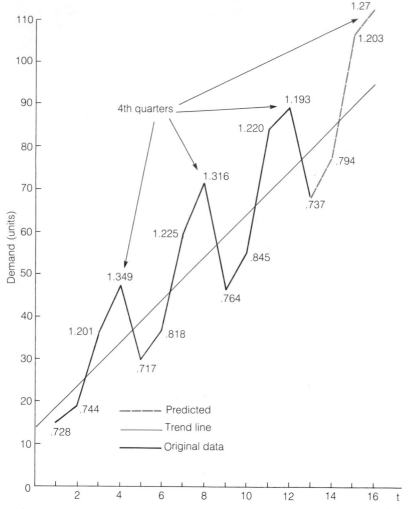

The numbers indicate the ratio of each data point to the trend line value at that time.

73 percent of the trend value. Similarly, the second quarter relative of .794 means that second quarter demand averages about 79 percent of the trend value, and so on.

Figure 3–10 presents the data and trend line for Example 8. The numbers beside the data points represent the ratio of the data to the corresponding trend value for that time period. Notice that the approximate position of the data (above or below the trend line) is the same each time a quarter repeats. For example, fourth quarters are indicated on the graph to illustrate the point. The graph also shows predicted values for the next three quarters. These were obtained by using the trend and seasonal relatives, as illustrated in the next example.

EXAMPLE 9

Using the seasonal relatives and trend line from the previous example, predict demand for word processing systems for the next three periods.

Solution

The next three periods have trend values of:

Period 14:　$14.27 + 4.96(14) = 83.71$,
Period 15:　$14.27 + 4.96(15) = 88.67$, and
Period 16:　$14.27 + 4.96(16) = 93.63$.

The forecast for each period involves adjusting the trend estimates so that the forecast includes seasonality. Period 14 is the second quarter for that year, and the forecast is: Trend estimate × Seasonal relative = $83.71(.794) = 66.47$. Similarly, period 15 is the third quarter of the year, so the forecast is: $88.67(1.203) = 106.67$, and the forecast for period 16 is: $93.63(1.270) = 118.91$. (For practical purposes forecasts are often rounded to the nearest integer.)

Note that for monthly (quarterly, etc.) data that have a parabolic trend, seasonal relatives can be obtained by substituting that trend for a linear trend and following the procedure previously described.

While the use of a linear trend line is intuitively appealing, it is more common in practice to use a *centered moving average* (i.e., positioned in the *middle* of the data used to compute the average instead of *projected* as in forecasting) to eliminate trend from a time series, for several reasons. One is that cycles may be present, which would distort the computation of seasonal relatives. Another reason is that a centered moving average can handle changes in trend, which is something the least squares approaches will not do. In order to remove trend, the length of the moving average must equal the number of periods in a season. A computational difficulty that occurs when there is an *even* number of periods in a season (e.g., 4 quarters, 12 months) is that the centered moving average will not "line up" with an original data value (e.g., a 4-period, centered moving average will fall *between* the 2d and 3d periods). In other words, there will not be any original value into which the centered average can be divided. This problem is overcome by an additional computation: a centered 2-period moving average of the initial 4- or 12-period moving average. (Note this additional moving average is not required for seasons with an odd number of periods.)

EXAMPLE 10

The table below illustrates the use of a 4-period moving average to remove trend from the sales data for the word-processing data.

Year	Quarter	Demand	MA_4	MA_2	$Demand/MA_2$
1	1	14			
	2	18			
	3	35	28.25	30.00	1.17
	4	46	31.75	34.00	1.35
2	1	28	36.25	39.38	.71
	2	36	42.50	45.63	.79
	3	60	48.75	50.88	1.18
	4	71	53.00	55.25	1.29
3	1	45	57.50	60.50	.74
	2	54	63.50	65.63	.82
	3	84	67.75	69.38	1.21
	4	88	71.00		
4	1	58			

	Quarter		
1	*2*	*3*	*4*
.71	.79	1.17	1.35
.74	.82	1.18	1.29
1.45	1.61	1.21	2.64
		3.56	
$\bar{x}$: .725	.805	1.187	1.320

The sum of these relatives is 4.037. Multiplying each by 4.00/4.037 will make the total 4.00. The resulting relatives are: quarter 1: .718; quarter 2: .798; quarter 3: 1.176; quarter 4: 1.308.

Note that these relatives are similar to, but not identical to, those produced using the trend line. The moving average is not quite as efficient in removing the trend as the least squares equation is. However, for the reasons mentioned above, the moving average approach is generally felt to be superior.

For *cyclical variations* that are fairly regular, the analysis of cycles is essentially identical to the analysis of seasonality, where the length of a "season" become the length of the cycles. Unfortunately, cycles are not usually highly regular in either length or amplitude. Sometimes leading indicators can be identified, which will provide some advance warning of cyclical turning points.[3] The

---

[3] See the section on regression analysis using indicators.

U.S. Department of Commerce publishes a list of leading cyclical indicators, which might be useful. At other times, experience and judgment may prove useful in identifying the length and turning points of cycles.

Other Techniques for Time Series

A number of other techniques that can be used to analyze time series data are beyond the scope of this text. However, one of these, the *Box-Jenkins technique,* is worthy of note because of its increasing popularity and its ability to provide accurate forecasts.

The main advantage of the Box-Jenkins method is that it is better able to handle data that include complex patterns than the techniques described previously. Also, the resulting forecasts often possess a high degree of accuracy compared to alternative methods. The main disadvantages of the technique relate to processing costs and complexity. The computations are fairly long and involved, and a computer program is essential. Furthermore, it is virtually impossible to communicate the assumptions that must be satisfied in order to obtain valid results to users who do not possess considerable mathematical sophistication.

If you are interested in learning more about this technique, consult the first reference at the end of this chapter.

ASSOCIATIVE FORECASTING TECHNIQUES

Associative techniques rely on identification of related variables that can be used to predict values of the variable of interest. For example, sales of beef may be related to the price per pound charged for beef as well as the prices of substitutes like chicken, pork, and lamb; real estate prices are usually related to property location; and crop yields are related to soil conditions, as well as amounts and timing of water and fertilizer applications.

The essence of associative techniques is the development of an equation that summarizes the effects of *predictor* variables. The primary method of analysis is known as *regression.* Although a detailed explanation of regression analysis is beyond the scope of this text, a brief overview of regression is given. This should suffice to place this approach into perspective relative to the other forecasting approaches described in the chapter.

Simple Linear Regression

The simplest and most widely used form of regression involves a linear relationship between two variables. A plot of the values might appear like that shown in Figure 3–11. The objective in linear regression is to obtain an equation of a straight line that minimizes

FIGURE 3–11

A Straight Line Is
Fitted to a Set of
Sample Points

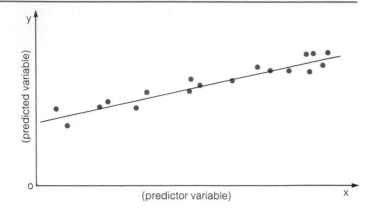

the sum of squared vertical deviations of points around the line.
This least squares line has the equation

$$y_c = a + bx \qquad (3–12)$$

where

$y_c =$ The predicted (dependent) variable
$x =$ The predictor (independent) variable
$b =$ Slope of the line
$a =$ Value of y_c when $x = 0$ (i.e., the height of the line at the y intercept)

(Note that it is conventional to represent values of the predicted variable on the y-axis and values of the predictor variable on the x-axis.) A graph of a linear regression line is illustrated in Figure 3–12.

FIGURE 3–12

Equation of a Straight
Line

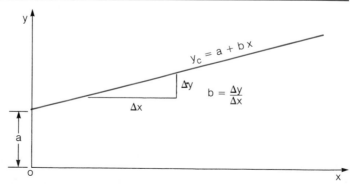

The line intersects the y axis where $y = a$. The slope of the line $= b$.

The coefficients a and b of the line are computed using these two equations:

$$b = \frac{n(\Sigma xy) - (\Sigma x)(\Sigma y)}{n(\Sigma x^2) - (\Sigma x)^2} \qquad (3\text{--}13)$$

$$a = \frac{\Sigma y - b\,\Sigma x}{n} \qquad (3\text{--}14)$$

where

$$n = \text{Number of paired observations}$$

EXAMPLE 11

Healthy Hamburgers has a chain of 12 stores in northern Illinois. Sales figures and profits for the stores are given in the table below. Obtain a regression line for the data and predict profit for a store assuming sales of $10 million.

Sales, x (millions)	Profits, y (millions)
$ 7	$.15
2	.10
6	.13
4	.15
14	.25
15	.27
16	.24
12	.20
14	.27
20	.44
15	.34
7	.17

Solution

First, plot the data and decide if a linear model is reasonable (i.e., do the points seem to scatter around a straight line? Figure 3–13 suggests they do.) Next, compute the quantities Σx, Σy, Σxy, and Σx^2. Calculations are shown for these quantities in Table 3–4. One additional calculation, Σy^2, is included for later reference. Substituting into the equations, we find:

$$b = \frac{n(\Sigma xy) - (\Sigma x)(\Sigma y)}{n(\Sigma x^2) - (\Sigma x)^2} = \frac{12((35.29) - 132(2.71)}{12(1796) - 132(132)} = .01593$$

$$a = \frac{\Sigma y - b(\Sigma x)}{n} = \frac{271 - .01593(132)}{12} = .0506$$

Thus, the regression equation is: $y_c = .0506 + .01593x$. For sales of $x = 10$ (i.e., $10 million), estimated profit is: $y_c = .0506 + .01593(10) = .2099$, or $209,900. (It may appear strange to you that substituting $x = 0$ into the equation produces a predicted profit of $50,600, because

EXAMPLE 11 *(concluded)*
FIGURE 3–13

A Linear Model Seems Reasonable

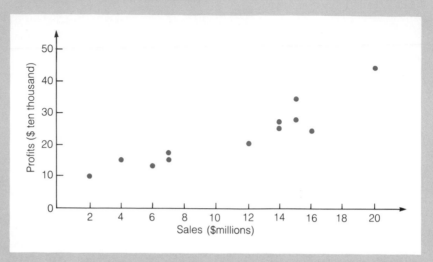

TABLE 3–4

**Calculations for Regression
Coefficients for Healthy
Hamburgers**

x	y	xy	x^2	y^2
7	.15	1.05	49	.0225
2	.10	.20	4	.0100
6	.13	.78	36	.0169
4	.15	.60	16	.0225
14	.25	3.50	196	.0625
15	.27	4.05	225	.0729
16	.24	3.84	256	.0576
12	.20	2.40	144	.0400
14	.27	3.78	196	.0729
20	.44	8.80	400	.1936
15	.84	5.10	225	.1156
7	.17	1.19	49	.0289
132	2.71	35.29	1796	.7159

it seems to suggest that amount of profit will occur with no sales.
However, the value of $x = 0$ is *outside of the range of observed values.*
The regression line should only be used for the range of values it
was developed from; the relationship may be nonlinear outside that
range. The purpose of the a value is simply to establish the height
of the line where it crosses the y-axis.)

The accuracy of regression estimates depends on the extent that sample data scatter around the line: the greater the scatter, the less accurate estimates will be. Scatter can be summarized using the standard error of estimate, s_e, where

$$s_e = \sqrt{\frac{\Sigma y^2 - a\Sigma y - b\Sigma xy}{n-2}} \qquad (3\text{--}15)$$

For the Healthy Hamburgers example, the standard error of estimate is

$$s_e = \sqrt{\frac{.7159 - .0506(2.71) - .01593(35.29)}{12-2}} = .04074 \text{ or } \$40,740.$$

A confidence interval for the predicted value of y (i.e., y_c) for a given value of x (i.e., x_g) can be obtained using the equation

$$\text{Confidence interval} = y_c \pm t s_{reg} \qquad (3\text{--}16)$$

where

$$s_{reg} = s_e \sqrt{1 + \frac{1}{n} + \frac{(x_g - \bar{x})^2}{\Sigma x^2 - [(\Sigma x)^2/n]}}$$

and

$\bar{x} = $ Mean of x's

$x_g - $ Some given value of x

$t = $ Standardized value obtained from a t-table

For convenience, some selected values of t are listed in Table 3–5.

TABLE 3–5

Selected Values of t **for 95 Percent Confidence Intervals**	*Degrees of freedom*	t
	5	2.57
	6	2.45
	7	2.37
	8	2.31
	9	2.25
	10	2.23
	11	2.20
	12	2.18

Degrees of freedom $= n - 2$.

For the Healthy Hamburgers data, s_{reg} for $x_g = 10$ is

$$s_{reg} = .04074 \sqrt{1 + 1/12 + \frac{(10-11)^2}{1796 - (132)^2/12}} = .04245$$

A 95 percent confidence interval for the predicted value of y is:

$$y_c \pm t(s_{reg}) = (.0506 + .01593(10)) \pm 2.23 \, (.04245)$$
$$= .2099 \pm .0947 \text{ or } .1152 \text{ to } .3046$$

That is, estimated profit on sales of $10 million is $209,900, and on the basis of the sample data we are 95 percent confident that actual profits will be in the range of $115,200 to $304,600.

It is interesting to note how wide the confidence interval is in this case, because after a certain point an interval can be so wide that it is meaningless. Although the interval here is somewhat wider than we would like, it does give an indication of the extent to which profits could vary on sales of $10 million.

Because the regression equation is developed from sample data that include random variability, there is always the risk that no real relationship exists between the variables. In that case, the average y would produce comparable predictions, so the added cost and effort of regression could be avoided. A simple test can be used to determine if a *significant* relationship exists (i.e., that the slope is nonzero):

$$t_{test} = b/s_b \qquad\qquad (3\text{--}17)$$

where

$$b = \text{Slope of line}$$

$$s_b = s_e \sqrt{\frac{1}{\Sigma x^2 - [(\Sigma x)^2/n]}}$$

For Healthy Hamburgers, the standard error of the slope, s_b, is:

$$s_b = .04074 \sqrt{\frac{1}{1796 - (132)(132)/12}} = .0022$$

$$t_{test} = b/s_b = .01593/.0022 = 7.24$$

This value must be compared to one found in a t-table (see Table 3–5) using the appropriate degrees of freedom. Conclude the relationship is significant if $t_{test} > t_{Table\ 3\ -5}$. (If $n > 30$, a z value obtained from the normal table can be used in place of t.) Since $t_{test} = 7.24$ and $t_{Table\ 3-5} = 2.23$, we can conclude that there *is* a relationship between the two variables.

One application of regression in forecasting relates to the use of indicators. These are uncontrollable variables that tend to lead or precede changes in a variable of interest. For example, changes in the federal reserve's discount rate may influence certain business activities. Similarly, an increase in housing starts during the spring and summer months may lead to increased demand for appliances, carpets, furniture, and similar items in the fall and winter months.

Careful identification and analysis of indicators may yield insight into possible future demand in some situations. There are numerous published indexes from which to choose.[4] Among them are the following:

Net change in inventories on hand and on order.
Interest rates for commercial loans.
Industrial output.
Consumer price index.
The wholesale price index.
Stock market prices.

Other potential indicators are population shifts, local political climates, and activities of other firms. (e.g., The opening of a shopping center may result in increased sales for nearby businesses.)

In order for an indicator to be valid, these things are required:

1. There should be a logical explanation for a relationship between movements of an indicator and movements of the variable of interest.
2. Movements of the indicator must precede movements of the dependent variable by enough time so that the forecast isn't outdated before it can be acted upon.
3. There should be a fairly high *correlation* between the two variables.

Correlation measures the strength and direction of relationship between two variables. Correlation can range from −1.00 to +1.00. A correlation of +1.00 indicates that changes in one variable are always matched by changes in the other; a correlation of −1.00 indicates increases in one variable are matched by decreases in the other; and a correlation close to zero indicates little *linear* relationship between two variables. The correlation between two variables can be computed using the equation

$$r = \frac{n(\Sigma xy) - (\Sigma x)(\Sigma y)}{\sqrt{n(\Sigma x^2) - (\Sigma x)^2} \cdot \sqrt{n(\Sigma y^2) - (\Sigma y)^2}} \qquad (3\text{--}18)$$

> **EXAMPLE 12**
>
> Sales of 19-inch color television sets and three-month lagged unemployment are shown on page 142. Determine if unemployment levels can be used to predict demand for 19-inch color TVs, and if so, derive a predictive equation

---

[4] See, for example, *The National Bureau of Economic Research, The Survey of Current Business, The Monthly Labor Review,* and *Business Conditions Digest.*

EXAMPLE 12 (continued)

Period	1	2	3	4	5	6	7	8	9	10	11
Units sold.	20	41	17	35	25	31	38	50	15	19	14
Unemployment (three-month lag). .	7.2	4.0	7.3	5.5	6.8	6.0	5.4	3.6	8.4	7.0	9.0

Solution

1. Plot the data to see if a linear model seems reasonable. In this case, a linear model seems appropriate *for the range of the data.*

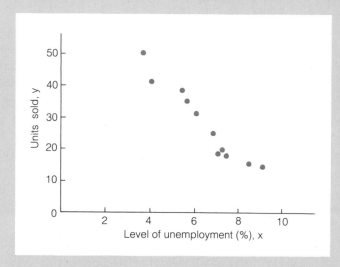

2. Compute the correlation coefficient in order to confirm that it is not close to zero.

x	y	xy	x^2	y^2
7.2	20	144.0	51.8	400
4.0	41	164.0	16.0	1,681
7.3	17	124.1	53.3	289
5.5	35	192.5	30.3	1,225
6.8	25	170.0	46.2	625
6.0	31	186.0	36.0	961
5.4	38	205.2	29.2	1,444
3.6	50	180.0	13.0	2,500
8.4	15	126.0	70.6	225
7.0	19	133.0	49.0	361
9.0	14	126.0	81.0	196
70.2	305	1,750.8	476.3	9,907

$$r = \frac{11(1,750.8) - 70.20(305)}{\sqrt{11(476.3) - (70.2)^2} \cdot \sqrt{11(9,907) - (305)^2}} = -.966$$

This is a fairly high correlation.

3. Compute the regression line:

> **EXAMPLE 12 (concluded)**
>
> $$b = \frac{11(1,750.8) - 70.2(305)}{11(476.3) - 70.2(70.2)} = -6.9145$$
>
> $$a = \frac{305 - (-6.9145)(70.2)}{11} = 71.854$$
>
> $$y = 71.85 - 6.91x$$
>
> Note that the equation pertains only to unemployment levels that are in the range 3.6 to 9.0, since sample observations covered only that range. In addition, if you suspect that r is close to zero, test the slope, b, for significance; r is significant when b is.

Comments on the Use of Linear Regression Analysis

Use of simple regression analysis implies that certain assumptions have been satisfied. Basically, these are:

1. Variations around the line are random. If they are, no patterns such as cycles should be apparent when the line and data are plotted.
2. Deviations around the line should be normally distributed. A concentration of values close to the line with a small proportion of larger deviations supports the assumption of normality.
3. Predictions are being made only within the range of observed values.

If the assumptions are satisfied, regression analysis can be a powerful tool. Particularly useful are the confidence intervals for predicted values. To obtain the best results, observe the following:

1. Always plot the data to verify that a linear relationship is appropriate.
2. Always test the relationship (slope) for significance.
3. The data may be time-dependent. Check this by plotting the dependent variable versus time; if patterns appear, use analysis of time series instead of regression.
4. A small correlation may imply that other variables are important.

In addition, note these weaknesses of regression:

1. Simple linear regression applies only to linear relationships with *one* independent variable.
2. A considerable amount of data is needed to establish the relationship; in practice, say 20 or more observations.
3. All observations are weighted equally.

4. The cost and complexity involved make this technique unattractive for situations that require forecasts for many individual items.

Curvilinear and Multiple Regression Analysis

Simple linear regression may prove inadequate to handle certain problems because a linear model is inappropriate or because more than one predictor variable is involved. When nonlinear relationships are present, curvilinear regression is called for, while models that involve more than one predictor require the use of multiple-regression analysis. Both of these techniques are beyond the scope of this text. However, you should be aware of the fact that such models are being used. For the most part the computations lend themselves more to computers than to hand computations. This usually adds to the cost of the forecast, as does the acquisition of additional data called for by the use of multiple-predictor variables. In each case, it is necessary to weigh the additional cost and effort required against potential improvements in accuracy of predictions.

ACCURACY AND CONTROL OF FORECASTS

One of the most important aspects of any forecast is the amount of error associated with it, where error is defined as the difference between a predicted value and the actual result:

$$\text{Error} = \text{Actual} - \text{Forecast}$$

There are two somewhat different ways in which forecast errors influence decisions. One is in making a choice between various forecasting alternatives, and the other is in evaluating the success or failure of a technique in use. We shall begin by examining two ways for summarizing forecast error over time and discover how that information can be applied to a choice among forecasting alternatives. Then we shall consider several methods for controlling forecasts (i.e., evaluating the performance of a given forecasting method in use).

Measuring the Accuracy of Forecasts

There are two aspects of forecast accuracy that have potential significance in deciding among forecasting alternatives. One is the historical-error performance of a forecast, and the other is the ability of a forecast to respond to changes.

Two commonly used measures for summarizing historical errors are the mean absolute deviation (MAD) and the mean squared error (MSE). MAD is the average error, and MSE is the average of squared errors. The formulas used to compute MAD[5] and MSE are:

---

[5] The absolute value, represented by the two vertical lines, ignores minus signs: all data are treated as positive values. For example, −2 becomes +2.

$$MAD = \frac{\Sigma|\text{Actual} - \text{forecast}|}{n} \qquad \text{(3–19)}$$

$$MSE = \frac{\Sigma(\text{Actual} - \text{forecast})^2}{n - 1} \qquad \text{(3–20)}$$

The sample standard deviation, *s,* equals the square root of MSE. The following example illustrates the computation of MAD and MSE.

EXAMPLE 13
Compute MAD and MSE for the data given below:

Period	Actual	Forecast	(A–F) error	|Error|	Error²
1	217	215	2	2	4
2	213	216	−3	3	9
3	216	215	1	1	1
4	210	214	−4	4	16
5	213	211	2	2	4
6	219	214	5	5	25
7	216	217	−1	1	1
8	212	216	−4	4	16
			−2	22	76

Solution
Using the figures shown in the table above,

$$MAD = \frac{\Sigma|e|}{n} = \frac{22}{8} = 2.75$$

$$MSE = \frac{\Sigma e^2}{n - 1} = \frac{76}{8 - 1} = 10.86$$

From a computational standpoint, the difference between these two measures is that one weights all errors evenly (MAD) while the other weights errors according to their *squared* values (MSE). If forecast errors are normally distributed and have a mean of zero, the values of MAD and MSE will be related:

$$1.25 \times MAD \approx \sqrt{MSE}$$

Note, for example, the numbers obtained in the preceding example:

$$1.25 \times MAD = 3.44$$

while

$$\sqrt{MSE} = 3.30$$

You might say that the values are approximately equal.

One way these measures are used is to compare alternative forecasting methods. For instance, using either MAD or MSE, a manager could compare the results of exponential smoothing with alphas of .1, .2, and .3 and select the one that yielded the *lowest* MAD or MSE for a given set of data.

In some instances, historical-error performance is secondary to the ability of a forecast to respond to changes in data patterns. Choice among alternative methods would then focus on the cost of not responding quickly to a change relative to the cost of responding to changes that are not really there (i.e., to random fluctuations).

Overall, the operations manager must settle on the relative importance of historical performance versus responsiveness as well as on whether to use MAD or MSE to measure historical performance.

Controlling the Forecast

It is necessary to monitor forecast errors to insure that the forecast is performing adequately. This can be accomplished by comparing forecast errors to predetermined values, or action limits, as illustrated in Figure 3–14. Errors that fall within the limits would be judged acceptable while errors outside of either limit would signal that corrective action is needed. Basically, errors that fall within the limits are regarded as *random deviations,* while errors outside the limits are regarded as evidence of more than just randomness.

Forecasts can be monitored using either *tracking signals* or *control charts.*

A *tracking signal* focuses on the ratio of *cumulative* forecast error to the corresponding value of MAD:

$$\text{Tracking signal} = \frac{\Sigma(\text{Actual} - \text{Forecast})}{\text{MAD}} \qquad (3\text{--}21)$$

The resulting values are compared to predetermined limits. These are based on judgment and experience, and often range from ±3 to ±8. We shall use limits of ±4 for the most part. These are roughly comparable to 3 standard deviation limits. Values *within* the limits suggest—but do not guarantee—that the forecast is performing adequately. After an initial value of MAD has been computed, MAD can be updated using exponential smoothing:

$$MAD_t = MAD_{t-1} + \alpha(|\text{Actual} - \text{Forecast}|_t - MAD_{t-1}) \qquad (3\text{--}22)$$

The *control chart* approach involves setting upper and lower limits for *individual* forecast errors (instead of cumulative errors, as is the case with a tracking signal). The limits are multiples of the square root of MSE. This method assumes the following:

1. Forecast errors are randomly distributed around a mean of zero.
2. The distribution of errors is normal.

FIGURE 3–14

Monitoring Forecast Errors

In effect, the square root of MSE is an estimate of the standard deviation of the distribution of errors. That is,

$$s = \sqrt{MSE} \qquad\qquad (3\text{–}23)$$

Recall that for a normal distribution, approximately 95 percent of the values (errors in this case) can be expected to fall within limits of $0 \pm 2s$ and that approximately 99 percent of the values can be expected to fall within $\pm 3s$ of zero. Hence, if the forecast is "in control," 99 percent or 95 percent of the errors should fall within the limits, depending on whether $3s$ or $2s$ limits are being used. Points that fall outside these limits should be regarded as evidence that corrective action is needed (i.e., that the forecast is not performing adequately). Figure 3–14 illustrates this concept.

When using a control chart, it can be very informative to plot the errors. A plot helps visualize the process and will enable you to check for possible patterns *within the limits* that would suggest an improved forecast is possible.[6]

EXAMPLE 14

Monthly sales of leather jackets at the Lucky Leather Shoppe for the past 24 months are shown below, as well as the forecasts and errors for those months. Determine if the forecast is working using these approaches:

1. A tracking signal, beginning with month 10, updating MAD with exponential smoothing. Use limits of ± 4 and alpha $= .2$.
2. A control chart with 2-sigma (i.e., $2s$) limits.

---

[6] The theory and application of control charts as well as various methods for detecting patterns in the data are covered in more detail in Chapter 15 on quality assurance.

EXAMPLE 14 (continued)

Month	A (sales)	F (forecast)	A–F (error)	$\|e\|$	Cum $\|e\|$
1	47	43	4	4	4
2	51	44	7	7	11
3	54	50	4	4	15
4	55	51	4	4	19
5	49	54	−5	5	24
6	46	48	−2	2	26
7	38	46	−8	8	34
8	32	44	−12	12	46
9	25	35	−10	10	56
10	24	26	−2	2	58
11	30	25	5	5	
12	35	32	3	3	
13	44	34	10	10	
14	57	50	7	7	
15	60	51	9	9	
16	55	54	1	1	
17	51	55	−4	4	
18	48	51	−3	3	
19	42	50	−8	8	
20	30	43	−13	13	
21	28	38	−10	10	
22	25	27	−2	2	
23	35	27	8	8	
24	38	32	6	6	
			−11		

Solution

a. The sum of absolute errors through the 10th month is 58. Hence, the initial MAD is $58/10 = 5.8$. The subsequent MADs are updated using the formula $MAD_{new} = MAD_{old} + .2(\|e\| - MAD_{old})$. The results are shown in the table below.

The tracking signal for any month is:

$$\frac{\text{Cumulative error at that month}}{\text{Updated MAD at that month}}$$

t month	$\|e\|$	$MAD_t = MAD_{t-1}$ $+.2(\|e\| - MAD_{t-1})$	Cumu- lative error	Tracking signal = Cumulative error$_t \div MAD_t$
10 . . .			−20	−20/5.800 = −3.45
11 . . .	5	5.640 = 5.8 + .2(5 − 5.8)	−15	−15/5.640 = −2.66
12 . . .	3	5.112 = 5.640 + .2(3 − 5.64)	−12	−12/5.112 = −2.35
13 . . .	10	6.090 = 5.112 + .2(10 − 5.112)	−2	−2/6.090 = −0.33
14 . . .	7	6.272 = 6.090 + .2(7 − 6.090)	5	5/6.272 = 0.79
15 . . .	9	6.818 = 6.272 + .2(9 − 6.272)	14	14/6.818 = 2.05
16 . . .	1	5.654 = 6.818 + .2(1 − 6.818)	15	15/5.654 = 2.65
17 . . .	4	5.323 = 5.654 + .2(4 − 5.654)	11	11/5.323 = 2.07
18 . . .	3	4.858 = 5.323 + .2(3 − 5.323)	8	8/4.858 = 1.65
19 . . .	8	5.486 = 4.858 + .2(8 − 4.858)	0	0/5.486 = 0.00
20 . . .	13	6.989 = 5.486 + .2(13 − 5.486)	−13	−13/6.989 = −1.86
21 . . .	10	7.591 = 6.989 + .2(10 − 6.989)	−23	−23/7.591 = −3.03

EXAMPLE 14 (concluded)

t month	$|e|$	$MAD_t = MAD_{t-1}$ $+.2|e|MAD_{t-1})$	Cumu-lative error	Tracking signal $=$ Cumulative $error_t \div MAD_t$
22 . . .	2	$6.472 = 7.591 + .2(\ 2 - 7.591)$	-25	$-25/6.472 = -3.86$
23 . . .	8	$6.778 = 6.472 + .2(\ 8 - 6\ 472)$	-17	$-17/6.778 = -2.51$
24 . . .	6	$6.622 = 6.778 + .2(\ 6 - 6.778)$	-11	$-11/6.622 = -1.66$

Since the tracking signal is within ±4 limits, there is no evidence of a problem.

b. (1) Check to make sure that the average error is approximately zero, since a large average would suggest a biased forecast.

$$\text{Average error} = \frac{\Sigma \text{ errors}}{n} = \frac{-11}{24} = -.46 \text{ [OK]}$$

(2) Compute sigma:

$$s = \sqrt{\frac{\Sigma e^2}{n-1}} = \sqrt{\frac{4^2 + 7^2 + 4^2 + 4^2 + (-5)^2 + \ldots + 8^2 + 6^2}{24 - 1}} = 7.10$$

(3) Determine $2s$ control limits:

$$0 \pm 2s = 0 \pm 2.(7.10) = -14.2 \text{ to } + 14.2$$

(4) *(a)* Check to see if all errors are within the limits. (They are.)

    (b) Plot the data (see below) and check for nonrandom patterns. Note the strings of positive and negative errors. This suggests nonrandomness (and that an improved forecast would be possible). The tracking signal did not reveal this.

In terms of comparing the two approaches, a tracking signal tends to be sensitive to trends in the data, to forecast bias (i.e., a forecast that is consistently above or below actual—see Figure 3–15), and to long cycles. Control charts are also sensitive to trends and to large forecast errors. Control charts are not particularly sensitive to bias, while a tracking signal cannot easily reveal that large positive and negative forecast errors are canceling each other out.

FIGURE 3–15

**A Forecast is Biased if
It Results in Errors
That Are Consistently
Positive or Negative**

CHOOSING A FORECASTING TECHNIQUE

There are many different kinds of forecasting techniques available, and no one technique works best in every situation. In selecting a technique for a given situation, the manager or analyst must take a number of factors into consideration.

Perhaps the two most important factors are cost and accuracy. How much money is budgeted for generating the forecast? What are the possible costs of error, and what are the possible benefits that might accrue from an accurate forecast? Generally speaking, accuracy improvements imply higher costs, so it is important to weigh cost-accuracy trade-offs carefully. The best forecast is not necessarily the most accurate, or the least costly; rather it is some combination of accuracy and cost deemed best by management.

Other factors include the availability of historical data, the availability of computers, the ability of decision makers to utilize certain techniques, the time needed to gather data, analyze it, and prepare the forecast, and any prior experience with a technique. The forecast horizon is important because some techniques are more suited to long-range forecasts while others work best for the short range. For example, moving averages and exponential smoothing are essentially short-range techniques, since they produce forecasts for the *next* period, while trend equations can be used to project over much longer time periods. Several of the qualitative techniques are well-suited to long-range forecasts because they do not require historical data. The Delphi technique and executive opinion methods are often used for long-range planning. Since new products and services lack historical data, forecasts must be made on the basis of subjective estimates. In many cases, experience with similar items can be relevant. Table 3–6 provides some additional perspectives on forecasts in terms of the forecast horizon.

In some instances, a manager may decide to use more than one forecasting technique. The purpose would be to obtain independent forecasts. If the different methods produced approximately the same predictions, that would lend additional confidence to the re-

TABLE 3–6

Forecast Factors by Range of Forecast

Factor	*Short range*	*Intermediate range*	*Long range*
1. Frequency	Often	Occasional	Infrequent
2. Level of aggregation	Item	Product family	Total output Type of product/service
3. Type of model	Smoothing Projection Regression	Projection Seasonal Regression	Managerial Judgment
4. Degree of management involvement	Low	Moderate	High
5. Cost per forecast	Low	Moderate	High

sults; if there was disagreement among the forecasts, that would indicate that perhaps additional analysis was needed.

The following section outlines some additional considerations that pertain both to choosing a forecasting methodology and to preparing a forecast.

Elements of a Good Forecast

A properly prepared forecast must fulfill certain requirements:

1. The forecast should be *timely*. Usually, a certain amount of time is needed in order to respond to the information contained in a forecast. For example, capacity cannot be expanded overnight, nor can inventory levels be changed immediately. Hence, the forecasting horizon must cover the time necessary to implement possible changes.

2. The forecast should be *accurate,* and the degree of accuracy should be stated. This will enable users to plan for possible errors and will provide a basis for comparing alternative forecasts.

3. The forecast should be *reliable;* it should work. A technique that sometimes provides a good forecast and sometimes a poor one will leave users with the uneasy feeling that they are liable to get burned every time a new forecast is issued.

4. The forecast should be in *meaningful units.* Financial planners need to know how many *dollars* will be needed, production planners need to know how many *units* will be needed, and schedulers need to know what *machines* and *skills* will be required. Hence, choice of units will depend on user needs.

5. The forecast should be *in writing.* While this will not guarantee that all concerned are using the same information, it will at least increase the likelihood of it. In addition, a written forecast

will permit an objective basis for evaluating the forecast once actual results are in.

6. The forecasting technique should be *simple to understand and use.* Users often lack confidence in forecasts based on sophisticated techniques because they do not understand the circumstances in which the techniques are appropriate and the limitations of the techniques; misuse of techniques is an obvious consequence. Not surprisingly, fairly crude forecasting techniques enjoy widespread popularity because users are more comfortable using them.

USING FORECAST INFORMATION

A manager can take a *reactive* or a *proactive* approach to a forecast. A reactive approach views forecasts as probable descriptions of future demand and reacts to meet that demand (e.g., adjust production rates, adjust inventories, adjust the work force.). Conversely, a proactive approach seeks to actively influence demand (e.g., advertising, pricing, product or service changes.).

Generally speaking, a proactive approach would require either an explanatory model (e.g., regression) or a subjective assessment of the influence on demand. It is possible, then, that a manager might use two forecasts: one to predict what will happen under the status quo and then a second one based on a "what if . . ." approach if the results of the status quo forecast are unacceptable.

SUMMARY

Forecasts are vital inputs for both the design and the operation of productive systems because they help managers to anticipate the future.

Forecasting techniques can be classified as either qualitative or quantitative. Qualitative techniques rely on judgment, experience, and expertise to formulate forecasts, while quantitative techniques rely on the use of historical data or associations among variables to develop forecasts. Some of the techniques are quite simple, and others are quite complex. Some work better than others, but no technique works all the time. Moreover, all forecasts include a certain degree of inaccuracy, and some allowance should be made for this. And all techniques assume that the same underlying causal system that existed in the past will continue to exist in the future.

The qualitative techniques described in this chapter include consumer surveys, sales force estimates, executive opinions, and manager and staff opinions. Two major quantitative approaches are described: analysis of time series data and associative techniques.

The time series techniques rely strictly on the examination of historical data; predictions are made by projecting past movements of a variable into the future without consideration of specific factors that might influence the variable. Associative techniques attempt to explicitly identify influencing factors and to incorporate that information into equations that can be used for predictive purposes.

Because all forecasts tend to be inaccurate, it is important to provide a measure of accuracy for each forecast. Several measures of forecast accuracy can be computed. These are often used to help managers evaluate the performance of a given technique as well as to choose among alternative forecasting techniques. Control of forecasts involves deciding whether or not a forecast is performing adequately, using either a control chart or a tracking signal.

Selection of a forecasting technique involves choosing a technique that will serve its intended purpose at an acceptable level of cost and accuracy.

The various forecasting techniques are summarized in Table 3–7.

TABLE 3–7

Forecasting Approaches	*Approaches*	*Brief description*
	Qualitative approach	
	Judgmental methods	
	Consumer surveys	Questioning consumers on future plans
	Sales force composites	Joint estimates obtained from salespeople
	Executive opinion	Finance, marketing, and manufacturing managers join to prepare forecast
	Delphi technique	Series of questionnaires answered anonymously by managers and staff; successive questionnaires are based on information obtained from previous surveys
	Outside opinion	Consultants or other outside experts prepare the forecast
	Quantitative approach	
	Time series	
	Naive	Next value in a series will equal the previous value
	Moving averages	Forecast is based on an average of recent values
	Exponential smoothing	Sophisticated form of averaging
	Classical decomposition	Series is separated into trend, seasonal, and cyclical components
	Associative models	
	Simple regression	Values of one variable are used to predict values of another variable
	Multiple regression	Two or more variables are used to predict values of another variable

1. *Exponential smoothing.* Using an alpha of .5, prepare a forecast for period 6 using the information given in the table below:

Period	Number of complaints
1	60
2	65
3	55
4	58
5	64

Solution

$n = 2/.5 - 1 = 3$ periods

$$\text{Initial forecast (period 4):} \frac{60 + 65 + 55}{3} = 60$$

$$F_5 = F_4 + \alpha(A_4 - F_4) = 60 + .50(58 - 60) = 59$$
$$F_6 = F_5 + \alpha(A_5 - F_5) = 59 + .50(64 - 59) = 61.5$$

2. *Time series analysis.* Apple's Citrus Fruit Farm ships boxed fruit anywhere in the continental United States. Using the information below, forecast shipments for the first four months of 1989.

Month	Seasonal relative
Jan.	1.2
Feb.	1.3
Mar.	1.3
Apr.	1.1
May	.8
Jun.	.7
Jul.	.8
Aug.	.6
Sep.	.7
Oct.	1.0
Nov.	1.1
Dec.	1.4

Monthly forecast equation:

$$y_t = 402 + 3t$$

where $t_0 =$ Jan. 1987

$y_t =$ Number of shipments

Solution

a. Determine trend amounts for the first four months of 1989. January 1989: $t = 24$, February 1989: $t = 25$, etc. Thus,

$$Y_{Jan.\ 1989} = 402 + 3(24) = 474$$
$$Y_{Feb.\ 1989} = 402 + 3(25) = 477$$
$$Y_{Mar.\ 1989} = 402 + 3(26) = 480$$
$$Y_{Apr.\ 1989} = 402 + 3(27) = 483$$

b. Multiply each monthly trend value by the corresponding seasonal relative for that month.

Month	Seasonal relative	Forecast
Jan.	1.2	474(1.2) = 568.8
Feb.	1.3	477(1.3) = 620.1
Mar.	1.3	480(1.3) = 624.0
Apr.	1.1	483(1.1) = 531.3

3. *Time series analysis.* Develop a linear trend line for the quarterly data given below and then use the trend equation to estimate seasonal relatives. Plot the trend line and the data on a single graph as a check for linearity.

Quarter	Demand	Quarter	Demand
1	63	11	66
2	64	12	68
3	58	13	80
4	60	14	81
5	75	15	74
6	70	16	75
7	64	17	87
8	67	18	84
9	80	19	76
10	74	20	74

Solution

a. Determine the trend equation:

t	y	ty
1	63	63
2	64	128
3	58	174
4	60	240
5	75	375
6	70	420
7	64	448
8	67	536
9	80	720
10	74	740
11	66	726
12	68	816
13	80	1040
14	81	1134
15	74	1110
16	75	1200
17	87	1479
18	84	1512
19	76	1444
20	74	1480
	1,440	15,785

(Note: Using Table 3–2 we obtain $\Sigma t = 210$ and $\Sigma t^2 = 2870$.)

$$b = \frac{n\,\Sigma ty - \Sigma t\,\Sigma y}{n\,\Sigma t^2 - (\Sigma t)^2} = \frac{20(15,785) - 210(1440)}{20(2870) - 210(210)} = 1.0$$

$$a = \frac{\Sigma y - b\Sigma t}{n} = \frac{1440 - 1.0(210)}{20} = 61.5$$

Thus, the trend equation is: $y_t = 61.5 + 1.0t$

b. The trend line and the original data are shown in the graph below.

c. Obtain estimates of quarterly relatives by dividing actual data for each quarter by the trend estimate for that quarter. Then average the first quarter values to obtain an overall estimate of that relative, average all the second quarter relatives to obtain the overall estimate of the second quarter relative, and so on for the third and fourth quarter relatives.

Quarter	Data	Trend value	Data/Trend
1	63	62.5	1.01
2	64	63.5	1.01
3	58	64.5	.90
4	60	65.5	.92
5	75	66.5	1.13
6	70	67.5	1.04
7	64	68.5	.93
8	67	69.5	.96
9	80	70.5	1.13
10	74	71.5	1.03
11	66	72.5	.91
12	68	73.5	.93
13	80	74.5	1.07
14	81	75.5	1.07
15	74	76.5	.97
16	75	77.5	.97
17	87	78.5	1.11
18	84	79.5	1.06
19	76	80.5	.94
20	74	81.5	.91

Grouping the estimates by quarter and averaging, we have:

I	II	III	IV
1.01	1.01	.90	.92
1.13	1.04	.93	.96
1.13	1.03	.91	.93
1.07	1.07	.97	.97
1.11	1.06	.94	.91
5.45	5.21	4.65	4.69
$\bar{x}$: 1.09	1.04	.93	.94

Thus, the quarter relative is 1.09 for the first quarter, 1.04 for the second, and so on.

4. *Regression analysis.* A large midwestern retailer has developed a linear relationship that summarizes the effect of advertising expenditures on sales volume, as shown in the graph below. Using the graph, determine an equation of the form $y = a + bx$ that describes this relationship.

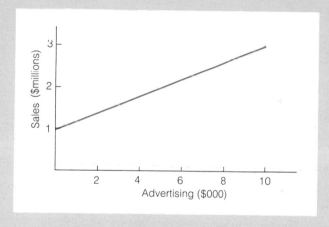

Solution

The linear equation has the form $y = a + bx$ where a is the value of y when $x = 0$ (i.e., where the line intersects the y axis) and b is the slope of the line (the amount by which y changes for a one-unit change in x).

Accordingly, $a = 1$ and $b = (3 - 1)/(10 - 0) = .2$, so $y = a + bx$ becomes $y = 1 + .2x$. Note: $(3 - 1)$ is the change in y.

5. *Regression analysis.* The owner of a small hardware store has noted a sales pattern for window locks that seems to parallel the number of break-ins reported each week in the newspaper. The data are:

Sales. . . .	46	18	20	22	27	34	14	37	30
Break-ins . . .	9	3	3	5	4	7	2	6	4

a. Plot the data to determine which type of equation, linear or nonlinear, is appropriate.

b. Obtain a regression equation for the data.

c. Test for significance.

d. Estimate sales if break-ins are 5.

e. Place a 95 percent confidence interval around the estimate of sales for five break-ins.

Solution

a.

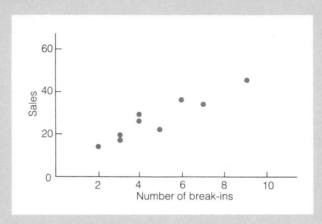

b. The computations for a straight line are:

x	y	xy	x^2	y^2
9 . . .	46	414	81	2116
3 . . .	18	54	9	324
3 . . .	20	60	9	400
5 . . .	22	110	25	484
4 . . .	27	108	16	729
7 . . .	34	238	49	1,156
2 . . .	14	28	4	196
6 . . .	37	222	36	1,369
4 . . .	30	120	16	900
43	248	1,354	245	7,674

$$b = \frac{n(\Sigma xy) - (\Sigma x)(\Sigma y)}{n(\Sigma x^2) - (\Sigma x)^2} = \frac{9(1,354) - 43(248)}{9(245) - 43(43)} = 4.275$$

$$a = \frac{\Sigma y - b(\Sigma x)}{n} = \frac{248 - 4.275(43)}{9} = 7.129$$

Hence, the equation is: $y_c = 7.129 + 4.275x$.

c. To test for significance, first compute s_e and then s_b:

$$s_e = \sqrt{\frac{\Sigma y^2 - a\Sigma y - b\Sigma xy}{n-2}} = \sqrt{\frac{7674 - 7.129(248) - 4.275(1354)}{9-2}} = 4.092$$

$$s_b = s_e \sqrt{\frac{1}{\Sigma x^2 - [(\Sigma x)^2/n]}} \qquad = 4.092\sqrt{\frac{1}{245 - [(43)^2/9]}} = .651$$

Then compute

$$t = b/s_b = 4.275/.651 = 6.57$$

Since this greatly exceeds 2.0, conclude the slope is nonzero.

d. For $x = 5$, $y_c = 7.129 + 4.275(5) = 28.50$.

e. From Table 3–5 for *d.f.* $= n - 2 = 7$, $t = 2.37$. The confidence interval for 95 percent is:

$$y_c \pm ts_{reg} = 28.50 \pm 2.73 \left[4.092 \sqrt{1 + \frac{1}{9} + \frac{(5 - {}^{43}\!/_9)^2}{245 - [(43)^2/9]}} \right]$$

$$= 28.50 \pm 10.23 \text{ or } 18.27 \text{ to } 38.73$$

6. *Accuracy and control of forecasts.* The marketing manager of a large manufacturer of industrial pumps must choose between two alternative forecasting techniques. Both techniques have been used to prepare forecasts for a six-month period. Using MAD as a criterion, which technique has the better performance record?

		Forecast	
Month	Demand	Technique 1	Technique 2
1.	492	488	495
2.	470	484	482
3.	485	480	478
4.	493	490	488
5.	498	497	492
6.	492	493	493

Solution

a. Check to see that each forecast has an average error of approximately zero. (See computations below.)

b. Select the one with the smallest mean absolute error:

Month	Demand	Technique 1	e	$|e|$	Technique 2	e	$|e|$
1 . . .	492	488	4	4	495	−3	3
2 . . .	470	484	−14	14	482	−12	12
3 . . .	485	480	5	5	478	7	7
4 . . .	493	490	3	3	488	5	5
5 . . .	498	497	1	1	492	6	6
6 . . .	492	493	−1	1	493	−1	1
			−2	28		+2	34

$$MAD_1 = \frac{\Sigma |e|}{n} = \frac{28}{6} = 4.67$$

$$MAD_2 = \frac{\Sigma |e|}{n} = \frac{34}{6} = 5.67$$

Technique 1 is superior in this comparison, although six observations would generally be too few on which to base a realistic comparison.

7. Given the sales data below, prepare a naive forecast for each of the 10 years and determine if the forecast is in control. Use 2 sigma control limits.

Year	Unit sales	Year	Unit sales
1. . . .	320	6. . . .	318
2. . . .	326	7. . . .	310
3. . . .	310	8. . . .	316
4. . . .	317	9. . . .	314
5. . . .	315	10. . . .	317

Solution

a. Prepare the naive forecast, which is actual sales of the previous year. Begin with year 2, since no information is given for sales prior to year 1. Compute and square the forecast errors:

Year	Sales	Forecast	Error	Error squared
1	320	—		
2	326	320	6	36
3	310	326	−16	256
4	317	310	7	49
5	315	317	−2	4
6	318	315	3	9
7	310	318	−8	64
8	316	310	6	36
9	314	316	−2	4
10	317	314	3	9
			−3	467

b. Compute the standard deviation of forecast errors:

$$s_f = \sqrt{\frac{\Sigma e^2}{n-1}} = \sqrt{\frac{467}{9-1}} = 7.64$$

Two-sigma limits are: $\pm 2(7.64) = -15.28$ to $+15.28$.

c. Note that the forecast error for year 3 is below the lower bound, so the forecast is not in control. Possibly using a moving average or exponential smoothing would achieve a better forecast since there does not appear to be any trend present.

DISCUSSION AND REVIEW QUESTIONS

1. Which approach to forecasting, quantitative or qualitative, is superior?
2. What are the main advantages that quantitative techniques for forecasting have over qualitative techniques? What limitations do quantitative techniques have?
3. List the specific weaknesses of each of these approaches to developing a forecast:
   a. Consumer surveys.
   b. Salesforce composite.
   c. Committee of managers or executives.
4. Briefly describe the Delphi technique. What are some of its main benefits and weaknesses?
5. What is the purpose of establishing control limits for forecasts?
6. What factors would you consider in deciding whether to use wide or narrow control limits for a forecast?
7. Contrast the use of MAD and MSE in evaluating forecasts.

8. What advantages does exponential smoothing have over moving averages as a forecasting tool?
9. How does the number of periods in a moving average affect the responsiveness of the forecast?
10. What factors enter into the choice of a value for the smoothing constant in exponential smoothing?
11. How does the decomposition approach to analysis of time series data differ from other methods that use historical data?
12. Explain how using a centered moving average with a length equal to length of a season eliminates seasonality from a time series.
13. Contrast the terms *sales* and *demand*.
14. Contrast the reactive and proactive approaches to forecasting. Give several examples of types of organizations or situations in which each type is used.

PROBLEMS

1. National Mixer, Inc., carries a line of electric blenders. Given the monthly sales data below:
   a. Compute a three-month and five-month moving average.
   b. Plot the original data and the two moving averages on the same graph.
   c. What effect does the number of periods in a moving average have on the extent of smoothing?

Month	Demand (000 units)	Month	Demand (000 units)
Jan.	20	Jul.	18
Feb.	24	Aug.	21
Mar.	18	Sept.	24
Apr.	14	Oct.	22
May	25	Nov.	28
June	20	Dec.	32

2. National Mixer, Inc., also sells can openers. Monthly sales for a six-month period were as follows:

Month	Sales (000 units)
Mar.	18
Apr.	15
May	20
Jun.	18
Jul.	22
Aug.	20

   a. Plot the monthly data on a sheet of graph paper.
   b. Forecast September sales volume using each of the following:
      (1) A linear trend equation.
      (2) A five-month moving average.
      (3) A weighted moving average with weights of .1, .1, .3, and .5 with the heaviest weight for the most recent period.
      (4) Exponential smoothing with a smoothing constant equal to .20, assuming a March forecast of 20.
      (5) The naive approach.
   c. Which method seems least appropriate? Why?
   d. What does the use of the term *sales* rather than *demand* presume?

3. Monthly sales of snowmobiles for a suburban Toronto dealer for the past year are shown below:

Month	Units sold	Month	Units sold
Jan.	92	Jul.	4
Feb.	88	Aug.	3
Mar.	80	Sept.	6
Apr.	60	Oct.	12
May	10	Nov.	25
Jun.	1	Dec.	82

   a. Smooth this data using a three-month *centered* moving average.
   b. Plot the original sales data and the centered moving average on the same graph.
   c. Would it make sense to use a three-month moving average to *predict* sales for the following January? Explain.

4. A dry cleaner uses exponential smoothing to forecast usage of equipment at its main plant. August usage was forecast to be 88 percent of capacity, while actual usage was 89.6 percent of capacity. Forecasts use a smoothing constant of .1
   a. Prepare a forecast for September.
   b. Assuming actual September usage of 92 percent, prepare a forecast for October usage.

5. The owner of Wine Sales & Service is contemplating the use of exponential smoothing to forecast wine sales. Demand for the preceding eight years is shown below.
   a. Forecast demand for next year using alpha equal to .4.
   b. What would the naive forecast for the next year be?

Year	Demand (000 cases)
1	800
2	810
3	808
4	812
5	810
6	825
7	811
8	804

6. Tread-On-Us Carpet & Tile Company sold 700,000 square feet of carpet last year, 800,000 square feet the year before, and 600,000 square feet the year before that. Using a three-year moving average, predict carpet sales for this year. Then, assuming actual sales for this year turn out to be 780,000 square feet, predict sales for next year.

7. A cosmetics manufacturer's marketing department has developed a linear trend equation that can be used to predict annual sales of its popular Hand & Foot Cream:

$$y_t = 80 + 15t$$

where

   $y_t =$ Annual sales in 1,000 bottles
   $t_o = 1977$

   a. Are annual sales increasing or decreasing? By how much?
   b. Predict annual sales for 1990 using the equation above.

8. A management consultant, using historical sales data, has developed a predictive equation for sales of white pine trees for a tree farm:

$$y_t = 480 - 50t + 10t^2$$

where

   $y_t =$ Number of trees sold in year t
   $t = 0$ at 1978

   a. Plot the equation for years 1973 to 1988.
   b. Forecast sales of white pine trees for 1990.

9. The equation below summarizes the trend portion of quarterly sales of automatic dishwashers over a long cycle. Sales also exhibit seasonal variations. Using the information given, prepare a forecast of sales for each quarter of 1989.

$$y_t = 40 - 6.5t + 2t^2$$

where

   $y_t =$ Unit sales
   $t = 0$ at 4th quarter of 1986

Quarter	Relative
1	1.1
2	1.0
3	.6
4	1.3

10. From the graph below, determine the linear equation of the trend line using 1971 as the base year for Glib Sales, Inc.

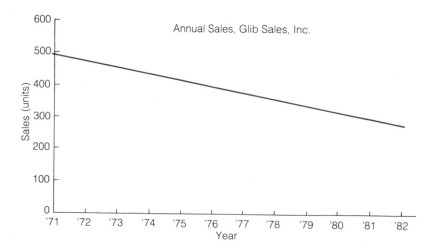

11. Freight-car loadings over a 12-year period at a busy port are given below:

Year	Number (00)	Year	Number (00)
1	220	7	350
2	245	8	360
3	280	9	400
4	275	10	380
5	300	11	420
6	310	12	450

a. Compute a linear trend line for freightcar loadings. Use year zero as the base year.
b. Plot the trend line and the original data on a single sheet of graph paper.
c. Shade in deviations around the trend line. Does it appear from this that cyclical variations were present?
d. Use the trend equation to predict loadings for year 15.

12. For each of the following sets of data, plot the data and decide which of these models would appropriately describe the data: (1) linear, (2) parabolic, (3) other.

a. t	y	b. t	y
1	61	1	90
2	65	2	70
3	70	3	60
4	80	4	50
5	87	5	49
6	94	6	47
7	96	7	44
8	93	8	40
9	90	9	36
10	83	10	33
11	80	11	30
12	75	12	28
13	70	13	26
14	63	14	25
15	58	15	25
		16	24

c. t	y	d. t	y
1	40	1	8
2	35	2	10
3	32	3	13
4	27	4	16
5	20	5	17
6	20	6	16
7	16	7	18
8	17	8	17
9	15	9	16

t	y	t	y
10	19	10	18
11	23	11	22
12	26	12	24
13	30	13	26
14	34	14	30

13. Develop a linear trend equation for the data on bread deliveries given below and use it to predict deliveries for periods 11 through 14.

Period	Dozen deliveries
1	200
2	214
3	211
4	228
5	235
6	222
7	248
8	241
9	253
10	267

14. Use trend-adjusted smoothing with $\alpha_1 = .3$ and $\alpha_2 = .2$ to smooth the bread delivery data in the preceding problem. Use an initial forecast of 200.

15. Refer to the freight-car loading data in Problem 11. Because of the apparent trend in that data, the manager has decided to use trend-adjusted exponential smoothing to predict future loading demand.
   a. Assume an initial forecast of 220 loadings. Use trend-adjusted smoothing with these constants: (1) $\alpha_1 = .2$, $\alpha_2 = .2$, (2) $\alpha_1 = .4$, $\alpha_2 = .2$, and (3) $\alpha_1 = .4$, $\alpha_2 = .35$.
   b. Which of the combinations in part *a* is the most accurate? Explain.
   c. Construct a control chart for each combination with 3-sigma limits and plot the errors on their respective control charts. What do the plots reveal?

16. Fit a least squares parabola of the form $y_t = a + bt + ct^2$ to the sales data given below and use the resulting equation to predict sales for the next two periods.

Period	Number sold
1	54
2	48
3	37
4	34
5	24
6	28
7	25
8	30
9	36

17. The data below represent annual housing starts for five New York state cities (Albany, Buffalo, Rochester, Syracuse, and Yonkers) for a 25-year period:

Year	Number of units
1	6,247
2	3,593
3	4,243
4	4,951
5	3,363
6	3,492
7	4,347
8	2,708
9	3,533
10	3,448
11	2,434
12	3,406
13	3,189
14	4,505
15	2,763
16	4,822
17	2,626
18	2,702
19	4,320
20	2,828
21	7,372
22	7,639
23	7,455
24	2,810
25	1,509

a. On a single sheet of graph paper, plot the housing starts and a three-year centered moving average.

b. Shade in the deviations around the moving average. Does it appear that cycles are present?

c. Fit a parabola of the form $y_t = a + bt + ct^2$ to the data, and shade in deviations around the line. Does it appear that cycles are present?

d. Using MAD as your criterion, which approach is better in terms of historical performance, the three-year moving average or the parabola?

e. Determine if the forecast is performing adequately at year 25 under the moving average forecast by computing the tracking signal.

18. Coal shipments from Mountain Coal Company's No. 4 Mine for the past seven years are listed below.

Year	Tons shipped (000)
1	405
2	410
3	415
4	415
5	412
6	420
7	424

a. Explain why simple exponential smoothing would not be an appropriate forecasting method.

b. Use an appropriate technique to develop a forecast for the next three years.

19. Obtain estimates of daily relatives for the number of customers at a restaurant for the evening meal, given the data below. (Hint: Use a seven-day moving average.)

Day	Number served
1	80
2	75
3	78
4	95
5	130
6	136
7	40
8	82
9	77
10	80
11	94
12	125
13	135
14	42
15	84
16	77
17	83
18	96
19	135
20	140
21	37
22	87
23	82
24	98
25	103
26	144
27	144
28	48

20. Lawn-mower sales for a dealer in Orange County, California for this past year are shown in the table below, along with monthly (seasonal) relatives, which are supplied to the dealer by the regional distributor.

Month	Units sold	Index
Jan.	640	.80
Feb.	648	.80
Mar.	600	.80
Apr.	761	.94
May	735	.89
Jun.	850	1.00
Jul.	765	.90
Aug.	1,000	1.17
Sept.	1,038	1.20
Oct.	1,026	1.14
Nov.	967	1.20
Dec.	1,107	1.23

a. Plot the data.
b. De-seasonalize lawn-mower sales.
c. Plot the de-seasonalized data on the same graph as the original data. Comment on the two graphs.

21. Long-Life Insurance has developed a linear model that it uses to determine the amount of straight life insurance a family of four should have, based on the current age of the head of the household. The equation is:

$$y = 32 - .1x$$

where

$y = $ Insurance needed ($000)
$x = $ Current age of head of household

a. Plot the relationship on a piece of graph paper.
b. Use the equation to determine the amount of straight life insurance to recommend for a family of four if the head of the household is 30 years old.

22. Timely Transport provides local delivery service for a number of downtown and suburban businesses. Delivery charges are based on distance and weight involved for each delivery: 10 cents per lb. and 15 cents per mile. In addition, there is a $10 storage and handling fee per parcel.
a. Develop an expression that summarizes delivery charges.

b. Determine the delivery charge for transporting a 40-pound parcel 26 miles.

23. The values below represent summary information produced by a regression analysis of cash flow relative to sales.

$$n = 14, \ \Sigma x = 50, \ \Sigma x^2 = 1,700, \ \Sigma xy = 1,540,$$
$$\Sigma y = 200, \ \Sigma y^2 = 4,400$$

a. Determine the least squares equation.
b. Compute the correlation coefficient.
c. Is the slope of the line significantly different from zero? Is the correlation significantly different from zero? Explain briefly.

24. The manager of a seafood restaurant was to establish a pricing policy on lobster dinners. Experimenting with prices has produced the following data:

Average number sold per day, y	Price, x
200	$6.00
190	6.50
188	6.75
180	7.00
170	7.25
162	7.50
160	8.00

a. Plot the data and a regression line on the same graph.
b. Using the regression equation, obtain a 95 percent confidence interval for estimated demand for a price of $7.00.
c. Compute the correlation coefficient and interpret it.

25. The data below were collected during a study of consumer buying patterns.

Observation	x	y
1	15	74
2	25	80
3	40	84
4	32	81
5	51	96
6	47	95
7	30	83
8	18	78
9	14	70
10	15	72
11	22	85
12	24	88
13	33	90

a. Plot the data.
b. Fit a linear regression line to the data using the least squares method.
c. Is the slope of the line significantly different from zero?
d. Use the equation determined in part b to predict the value of y for $x = 41$.
e. Determine a 95 percent confidence interval for the predicted value of y for $x = 41$.

26. Lovely Lawns, Inc., intends to use sales of lawn fertilizer to predict lawn-mower sales. The store manager feels that there is probably a six-week lag between fertilizer sales and mower sales. The pertinent data are shown below:

Period	Fertilizer sales (tons)	Number of mowers sold (six-week lag)
1	1.6	10
2	1.3	8
3	1.8	11
4	2.0	12
5	2.2	12
6	1.6	9
7	1.5	8

a. Compute the correlation between the two variables. Does it appear that there is a relationship between these variables that will yield good predictions?
b. Use the least squares method to obtain a linear regression line for the data.
c. Predict lawn-mower sales for the first week in August, given fertilizer sales six weeks earlier of two tons.

27. The owner of a specialty shop that is only open three days a week has recorded the number of sales transactions over the last five weeks for each of the two shops he owns. Those figures are reproduced here.

Shop 1

Week	Thurs.	Fri.	Sat.
1	244	275	281
2	250	277	285
3	249	280	288
4	253	285	292
5	258	287	295

Shop 2

Week	Thurs.	Fri.	Sat.
1	182	221	234
2	188	218	242
3	185	223	238
4	184	220	236
5	180	221	240

The owner wants to use seasonal (daily) relatives to help schedule employees. Develop daily relatives for each shop.

28. Forecast the number of transactions for the following week for each of the shops in the preceding problem using these techniques:
a. A naive approach.
b. A trend/seasonal approach. (Hint: see Problem 9.)

29. The manager of a travel agency has been using a seasonally adjusted forecast to predict demand for packaged tours. The actual and predicted values are shown below:

Period	Demand	Predicted
1	129	124
2	194	200
3	156	150
4	91	94
5	85	80
6	132	140
7	126	128
8	126	124
9	95	100
10	149	150
11	98	94
12	85	80
13	137	140
14	134	128

a. Compute MAD for the fifth period, then update it period-by-period using exponential smoothing with an alpha of .3.
b. Compute a tracking signal for periods 5 through 14 using the initial and updated MADs.
c. Plot the tracking signal on a graph using action limits of ±3. What can you conclude?

30. Two independent methods of forecasting based upon judgment and experience have been prepared each month for the past 10 months. The forecasts and actual sales are shown on the next page.

Month	Sales	Forecast 1	Forecast 2
1	770	771	769
2	789	785	787
3	794	790	792
4	780	784	798
5	768	770	774
6	772	768	770
7	760	761	759
8	775	771	775
9	786	784	788
10	790	788	788

a. Compute the MSE and MAD for each forecast. Does either method seem superior? Explain.

b. Compute a tracking signal for the 10th month for each forecast. What does it show? (Use action limits of ±4.)

c. Compute 2-sigma control limits for each forecast. Are they in control? Explain.

d. Prepare a naive forecast for periods 2–11 using the given sales data. Compute each of the following: (1) MSE, (2) MAD, (3) tracking signal at month 10, and (4) 2-sigma control limits. How do the naive results compare with the other two forecasts?

31. The classified department of a monthly magazine has used a combination of a quantitative and a qualitative method to forecast sales of advertising space. Results over a 20-month period are as follows:

Month	Error
1	−8
2	−2
3	4
4	7
5	9
6	5
7	0
8	−3
9	−9
10	−4
11	1
12	6
13	8
14	4
15	1
16	−2
17	−4
18	−8
19	−5
20	−1

a. Compute a tracking signal for months 11 through 20. Compute an initial value of MAD for month 11 and then update it for each month using exponential smoothing with $\alpha = .1$. What can you conclude? Assume limits of ±4.

b. Construct a control chart with 2-sigma limits. What can you conclude?

c. Plot the errors on the control chart. Are the errors random? What is the implication of this?

SELECTED BIBLIOGRAPHY

Box, G. E. P., and G. Jenkins. *Time Series Analysis: Forecasting and Control.* San Francisco: Holden-Day, 1970.

Chambers, John C.; S. K. Mullick; and Donald D. Smith. "How to Choose the Right Forecasting Technique." *Harvard Business Review,* July–August 1971, pp. 45–74.

Hanke, John E., and Arthur G. Reitsch. *Business Forecasting.* Boston: Allyn & Bacon, 1981.

Levenbach, Hans, and James P. Cleary. *The Modern Forecaster: The Forecasting Process through Data Analysis.* Belmont, Calif.: Lifetime Learning Publications, 1984.

Riggs, James L. *Production Systems: Planning, Analysis, and Control.* 3d ed. New York: John Wiley & Sons, 1981.

Stevenson, William J. *Business Statistics: Concepts and Applications.* 2d ed. New York: Harper & Row, 1985.

Sullivan, William G., and W. Wayne Claycombe. *Fundamentals of Forecasting.* Reston, Va.: Reston Publishing, 1977.

Tersine, R. J., and W. Riggs. "The Delphi Technique: A Long-Range Planning Tool." *Business Horizons* 19, no. 2, 1976.

Wheelwright, Steven C.; Spyros Madridakis; and Victor McGee. *Forecasting: Methods and Applications.* 2d ed. New York: John Wiley & Sons, 1983.

Case

Watch Our Forecasts Grow

The annual budget meeting of a large commercial bank had just ended, and from the looks on their faces, it was obvious that Bud Thompson and Brad Smith were quite disappointed with the outcome. Brad was in charge of the commercial loan department, and Bud was director of personnel for the bank. Brad remarked, somewhat dryly, "What do they think we are, miracle workers?"

"I know what you mean," Bud responded. "Even if demand turns out to be lower than my forecast, I am still going to need those funds."

When they met for coffee the next morning, Bud offered a suggestion: "You know my brother, Bob, the salesman? I mentioned our little problem to him, and he said that most of the salesmen he knows tack on an additional 10 to 20 percent to their forecasts. Maybe we should do the same. That way, even if they cut us back a bit, we would still get more than we do now. And who knows, demand might be higher than normal. And even if it isn't, I'm sure we will be able to come up with a reasonable explanation."

"I don't know if that would be wise," countered Brad. "You know how the old man pours over those figures before our meetings. I wouldn't want to have him come down on me in a meeting. But I'll tell you one thing," he continued. "If there is a substantial increase in demand, we could be in a real bind. By the time we can gear up, National will have grabbed a huge chunk of our accounts."

"It's a tricky business," Bud commented. "You're damned if you do and damned if you don't!"

Questions

1. Do you feel that inflated forecasts would be an appropriate alternative in this situation? Explain. Would inflated forecasts ever be appropriate? Why or why not?

2. What action could Bud and Brad take to try to improve the situation? Support your answer.

3. In what ways are banks similar to other organizations in terms of developing and using forecasts?

Part III

Design of Production Systems

Production system design encompasses decisions involving:

1. Capacity planning (Chapter 4).
2. Location planning (Chapter 5).
3. Product and service design (Chapter 6).
4. Facilities layout (Chapter 7).
5. Design of work systems (Chapter 8).

Design decisions are not something that occur only when an organization is initially formed. Rather, they continue to be made periodically throughout the life of the organization. The importance of these decisions is related to the cost they often entail, the long-term commitments they often require, the constraints they place on the ongoing operations of the organization, and the difficulty in reversing them once they have been executed.

These areas are not always under the direct control of the operations manager. Nonetheless, the operations manager usually has some say in these matters, especially since they play a major role in setting the stage on which the operations manager must perform.

Capacity decisions create limits on the ability of the system to provide goods and services. Capacity and location decisions both influence operating costs, and location decisions also have an effect on transportation costs, labor supply and cost, material costs, and access to markets. Product and service design often are the focal point of system design since they represent the purpose of the system. Layout decisions affect the flow of work through the system. Work design focuses on the human component of production systems and how that component interfaces with other aspects of the system. It also involves a focus on productivity improvements.

Design decisions are primarily *strategic* in nature. They have a major impact on production systems.

Chapter 4

Capacity Planning: Facilities and Equipment

After completing this chapter, you should be able to:

1. Explain the importance of capacity planning.
2. Discuss ways of measuring and defining capacity and give examples.
3. Briefly explain the differences between short-term and long-term capacity requirements.
4. Describe some of the factors that determine effective capacity.
5. Discuss the important considerations involved in developing desirable capacity alternatives.
6. Briefly describe four approaches that are useful for evaluating capacity alternatives.

INTRODUCTION, 174

PRODUCT/SERVICE CHOICES, 174

IMPORTANCE OF CAPACITY DECISIONS, 175

DEFINING AND MEASURING CAPACITY, 176

DETERMINANTS OF EFFECTIVE CAPACITY 178

DETERMINING CAPACITY REQUIREMENTS, 181
    Long-Term Considerations, 181
    Short-Term Considerations, 182

DEVELOPING CAPACITY ALTERNATIVES, 183

EVALUATING ALTERNATIVES, 186
    Cost-Volume Analysis, 187
    Financial Analysis, 190
    Decision Theory, 191
    Queuing Theory, 192

SUMMARY, 192
SOLVED PROBLEMS, 193
DISCUSSION AND REVIEW QUESTIONS, 193
PROBLEMS, 194
SELECTED BIBLIOGRAPHY, 195
SUPPLEMENT: FINANCIAL ANALYSIS, 197

Product and service choices and capacity decisions are the most basic decisions managers must make, for they determine the nature and size of a production system.

In this chapter we examine the importance of capacity decisions, the measurement of capacity, how capacity requirements are determined, and the development and evaluation of capacity alternatives.

INTRODUCTION

The term *capacity* refers to an upper limit or ceiling on the load that an operating unit can handle. The operating unit might be a plant, a department, a machine, a store, or a worker. The load can be specified either in terms of inputs or outputs. For instance, a machine may be able to process 45 pounds of raw materials per hour. Hence, its input capacity is 45 pounds per hour. Another machine might produce 18 castings per hour; its capacity in terms of the castings output is 18 pieces per hour. The choice of input or output capacity is sometimes a matter of choice, and sometimes it is dictated by the situation, as we shall see.

The capacity of an operating unit is an important piece of information for planning purposes: it enables managers to quantify production capability, either in terms of inputs or outputs, and thereby to make other decisions or plans related to those quantities.

This chapter explores the issue of capacity planning as it pertains to facilities and equipment selection. The basic questions in capacity planning of any sort are the following:

1. What kind of capacity is needed?
2. How much is needed?
3. When is it needed?

The question of what kind of capacity is needed relates to the products and services that management intends to produce or provide. Hence, in a very real sense, capacity planning is governed by those choices.

The quantity and timing of capacity are also important. These questions involve a number of considerations, but the primary factor relates to predicted quantity and timing of *demand.* A related issue is whether demand is expected to be relatively constant or whether it will increase or perhaps be cyclical in nature.

PRODUCT/SERVICE CHOICES

The most fundamental decisions in any organization relate to the products and/or services it will offer. Virtually all other decisions relative to capacity, facilities, location, and the like are governed by product and service choices. Thus, a decision to produce high-quality steel will necessitate certain types of processing equipment and certain kinds of labor skills, and will suggest certain types of arrangement of facilities. It will influence the size and type of building as well as the plant location. Notice how much different each of these factors would be in another situation in which the choice is to operate a family restaurant and how still different each of these factors would be in another situation in which the choice is to operate a hospital. As you can clearly see, the selection of products and services is fundamental to other decisions.

In some instances product or service choices are made very infrequently, while in others they are made much more regularly as part of an ongoing process. Generally speaking, the factors that influence this frequency are the stability of demand, the rate of technological change in both equipment and product design, and competitive factors. Other factors relate to the type of product or service and whether style changes are important, as they are, say, for automobiles and clothing. In any case, it is important for management to periodically review product and service choices in order to assure that changes will be made when they are needed for cost, competitive effectiveness, or other reasons.

IMPORTANCE OF CAPACITY DECISIONS

Capacity decisions are perhaps the most fundamental of all the design decisions managers are called upon to make. One reason for the importance of capacity decisions relates to their potential impact on the ability of the organization to meet future demands for products or services; capacity essentially limits the rate of output possible. A second reason for the importance of capacity stems from the relationship between capacity and operating costs. Ideally, capacity and demand requirements will be matched, which will tend to minimize operating costs. In practice, this is not always achieved, either because actual demand differs from expected demand or because demand tends to vary (e.g., cyclically). In that case, a decision might be made that would attempt to balance the costs of over- and undercapacity. Still a third reason for the importance of capacity decisions is the initial cost involved. Capacity is usually a major determinant of that cost. Typically, the greater the capacity of a productive unit, the greater its cost. This does not necessarily imply a one-for-one relationship; larger units tend to cost *proportionately* less than smaller units. A fourth reason for the importance of capacity decisions stems from the long-term commitment of resources that is often required and the fact that once implemented, it may be difficult or impossible to modify those decisions without incurring major costs.

DEFINING AND MEASURING CAPACITY

Capacity often refers to an upper limit on the *rate* of output. Even though this seems to be simple enough, there are subtle difficulties in actually measuring capacity in certain cases. These difficulties arise because of different interpretations of the term capacity and problems with identifying suitable measures for a specific situation.

When selecting a measure of capacity, it is important to choose one that does not require revision. For example, dollar amounts are often a poor measure of capacity (e.g., capacity of $30 million a year) because price changes would necessitate continual updating of that measure.

In situations where only one product or service is involved, the capacity of the productive unit may be expressed in terms of that item. However, when multiple products or services are involved—as is often the case—using a single measure of capacity based on units of output can be misleading. For example, an appliance manufacturer may produce both refrigerators and freezers. If the output rates for these two products are different, it would not make sense to simply state capacity in units without reference to either refrigerators or freezers. The problem is compounded if the firm in question has other products. One possible solution is to state capacities in terms of each product. Thus, the firm may be able to produce 100 refrigerators per day *or* 80 freezers per day. In some cases this approach is helpful, but in others it is not. For instance, in a situa-

TABLE 4–1

Examples of Commonly Used Measures of Capacity

Type of business	Measure of capacity	
	Resources available	Output
Automobile manufacturing.	Manhours, machine hours	Number of cars or trucks per shift
Steel mill.	Size of furnace	Tons of steel per week
Oil refinery	Size of refinery	Gallons of fuel oil per day
Farm	Number of acres, cows	Tons of grain per year, gallons of milk per week
Restaurant	Number of tables	Number of meals served per day
Theater	Number of seats	Number of performances per week
Retail sales	Size of display area, number of cashiers	Units sold per day

tion where an organization has many different products or services, it may not be practical to list all of the relevant capacities. This is especially true if there are frequent changes in the mix of output, because this would necessitate a continually changing composite index of capacity. The preferred alternative in such cases is to use a measure of capacity that refers to *availability of resources.* Thus, a hospital has a certain number of beds, a factory has a certain number of machine hours available, and a bus has a certain number of seats and a certain amount of standing room.

No single measure of capacity will be appropriate in every situation. Rather, the measure of capacity must be somewhat tailored for the situation at hand. Table 4–1 provides some examples of commonly used measures of capacity.

Up to this point, we have been using a working definition of capacity. While it is functional, it could stand some refinement. There are, in fact, three different definitions of capacity that are useful. They are:

1. *Design capacity.* This is the maximum output that can possibly be attained.
2. *Effective capacity.* The maximum possible output given a product mix, scheduling difficulties, machine maintenance, quality factors, and so on.
3. *Actual output.* This is the rate of output actually achieved. It cannot exceed effective capacity and is often less than effective capacity due to breakdowns, defective output, shortages of materials, and similar factors.

Design capacity is the maximum rate of output that might be achieved under ideal conditions. Effective capacity is usually less than design capacity (it cannot exceed design capacity) owing to realities of changing product mix, the need for periodic maintenance of equipment, lunch breaks, coffee breaks, problems in scheduling and balancing operations, and similar circumstances. Actual output cannot exceed effective capacity and is often less than effective capacity because of machine breakdowns, absenteeism, and other problems outside of the control of the operations manager.

These different measures of capacity are useful in defining two measures of system effectiveness: efficiency and utilization. *Efficiency* is the ratio of actual output to effective capacity while *utilization* is the ratio of actual output to design capacity. Thus:

$$\text{Efficiency} = \frac{\text{Actual output}}{\text{Effective capacity}}$$

$$\text{Utilization} = \frac{\text{Actual output}}{\text{Design capacity}}$$

It is quite common for managers to focus exclusively on efficiency, but in many instances, such emphasis can be misleading. This happens when effective capacity is low compared to design capacity. In those cases, a high efficiency would seem to indicate effective use of resources when that is not the case. The following example illustrates this point.

EXAMPLE 1

Given the information below, compute the efficiency and the utilization of the vehicle repair department:

$$\text{Design capacity} = 80 \text{ trucks per day}$$
$$\text{Effective capacity} = 40 \text{ trucks per day}$$
$$\text{Actual output} = 36 \text{ units per day}$$

Solution

$$\text{Efficiency} = \frac{\text{Actual output}}{\text{Effective capacity}} = \frac{36 \text{ units per day}}{40 \text{ units per day}} = 90\%$$

$$\text{Utilization} = \frac{\text{Actual output}}{\text{Design capacity}} = \frac{36 \text{ units per day}}{80 \text{ units per day}} = 45\%$$

Thus, compared to the effective capacity of 40 units per day, the 36 units per day looks pretty good, but compared to the design capacity of 80 units per day, the 36 units per day appears much less impressive although somewhat more meaningful.

Because effective capacity acts as a lid on actual output, the real key to improving capacity utilization is to increase effective capacity. Consider the following example. George H. wants to travel from his home in Washington, D.C., to his sister's home in Baltimore, which is 60 miles away. He could borrow his son's bike or borrow his son's car. Instead of using the bike and concerning himself with pedaling as *efficiently* as possible, he could make the trip in less time (same output in a shorter time) by using the car.

Hence, increasing utilization depends on being able to increase effective capacity, and this requires a knowledge of what is constraining effective capacity. The following section explores some of the main determinants of effective capacity.

DETERMINANTS OF EFFECTIVE CAPACITY

Many decisions made with respect to system design have an impact on capacity. The same is true for many operating decisions. Some of these factors are briefly described below and then elaborated on at other points in the book. The main factors relate to the following:

1. Facilities.
2. Products or services.
3. Processes.
4. Human considerations.
5. Operations.
6. External forces.

Facilities factors. The design of facilities, including size and provision for expansion, is very important. Locational factors, such as transportation costs, distance to market, labor supply, energy sources, and room for expansion are also important. Likewise, layout of the work area often determines how smoothly work can be performed, and environmental factors such as heating, lighting, and ventilation also play an important role in determining whether personnel can perform effectively or whether they must struggle to overcome poor design characteristics.

Product/service factors. Product or service design can have a tremendous influence on capacity. For example, when items are highly similar, the ability of the system to produce those items is generally much greater than when successive items tend to differ. For example, a restaurant that offers a limited menu can usually prepare and serve meals at a faster rate than a restaurant with a very extensive menu. Generally speaking, the more uniform the output, the more opportunities there are for standardization of methods and materials, which lead to greater capacity. The particular mix of products or services rendered must also be considered since different items will have different rates of output.

Process factors. The quantity capability of a process is perhaps an obvious determinant of capacity. A more subtle determinant is the influence of output *quality.* For instance, if quality of output does not meet quality standards, the rate of output will be slowed by the need for inspection and rework activities.

Human factors. The tasks that comprise a job, the variety of activities involved, and the training, skill, and experience required to perform a job all have an impact on the potential and actual output. In addition, employee motivation has a very basic relationship to capacity, as do absenteeism and labor turnover.

Operation factors. If there are any differences in equipment capabilities for alternative pieces of equipment and/or for differences in job requirements, there can be scheduling problems. Inventory stocking decisions, late deliveries, and acceptability of purchased materials and parts can all influence effective capacity. Quality inspection and control procedures also have an impact on effective capacity.

An example of inventory problems having a negative impact on capacity occurred when General Motors first introduced its front wheel drive cars. Unexpected high demand created by shortages and rapid price increases of gasoline exceeded the supply of cars. Company officials lamented the fact that they could not take advantage of the opportunity to increase sales because of a shortage of component parts that the company could not quickly overcome. Thus, insufficient capacity in one area affected overall capacity.

External factors.   Product standards, especially minimum quality and performance standards, can restrict management's options in increasing and using capacity. Thus, pollution standards on either products or equipment often reduce effective capacity. So, too, does paperwork required by government regulatory agencies by engaging employees in nonproductive activities. A similar effect occurs when a union contract limits the number of hours and type of work an employee may do.

A summary of these factors is presented in Table 4–2.

TABLE 4–2

Factors that Determine Effective Capacity	A. Facilities 　1. Design 　2. Location 　3. Layout 　4. Environment B. Product/service 　1. Design 　2. Product or service mix C. Process 　1. Quantity capabilities 　2. Quality capabilities D. Human factors 　1. Job content 　2. Job design 　3. Training and experience 　4. Motivation 　5. Compensation 　6. Learning rates 　7. Absenteeism and labor turnover E. Operational 　1. Scheduling 　2. Materials management 　3. Quality assurance 　4. Maintenance policies 　5. Equipment breakdowns F. External factors 　1. Product standards 　2. Safety regulations 　3. Unions 　4. Pollution control standards

DETERMINING CAPACITY REQUIREMENTS

Capacity planning decisions involve both long-term and short-term considerations. Long-term considerations relate to the overall *level* of capacity, such as facility size, while short-term considerations relate to probable *variations* in capacity requirements created by such things as seasonal, random, and irregular fluctuations in demand. Because the time intervals covered by each of these categories can vary significantly from industry to industry, it would be misleading to attempt a precise definition for these terms. Nevertheless, the distinction will serve as a framework within which to discuss capacity planning.

Long-Term Considerations

Long-term capacity needs are determined by forecasting demand over a time horizon and then converting those forecasts into capacity requirements. Some of the basic demand patterns that might be identified by a forecast are illustrated in Figure 4–1. In addition to these basic patterns are more complex patterns, such as a combination of cycles and trends.

When trends are identified, the fundamental issues are (1) how long the trend might persist, since few things last forever and (2) the slope of the trend. If cycles are identified, interest focuses on (1) the approximate length of the cycles, since cycles are rarely

FIGURE 4–1

Some Possible Demand Patterns

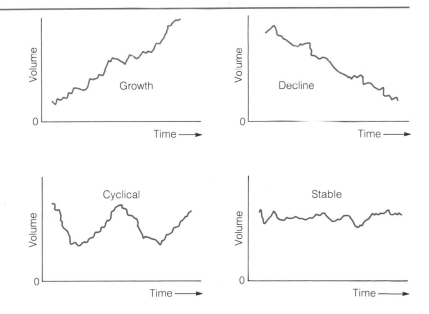

uniform in duration and (2) the amplitude of the cycles (i.e., deviation from average).

Short-Term Considerations

Short-term capacity needs are less concerned with cycles or trends than with seasonal variations and other variations from average. These deviations are particularly important because they can place a severe strain on a system's ability to satisfy demand at some times and yet result in idle capacity at other times.

Seasonal patterns can be identified using standard forecasting techniques. Although commonly thought of as annual fluctuations, seasonal variations are often reflected in monthly, weekly, and even daily capacity requirements. Table 4–3 provides some examples of items that tend to exhibit seasonal demand patterns.

When time intervals that are too short to have seasonal variations are analyzed, variations in demand may often be described by probability distributions such as the normal, uniform, or Poisson distributions. For example, the amount of coffee served during the midday meal at a luncheonette may be described by a normal distribution with a certain mean and standard deviation. The number of customers that enter a branch of a bank on Monday mornings may be described by a Poisson distribution with a certain mean. It does not follow, however, that *every* instance of random variability will lend itself to description by a standard statistical distribution. Service systems in particular tend to experience these kinds of variations in capacity requirements unless requests for service can be scheduled. Production systems, because of their typical isolation from customers and the more uniform nature of production, are less likely to experience them. Queuing models are sometimes useful in analyzing service systems.

Perhaps the most troublesome variations are the irregular ones, because they are virtually impossible to predict. They are created by such diverse forces as freak storms that disrupt normal routines, foreign political turmoil that can cause oil shortages, major equipment breakdowns, discovery of health hazards (nuclear accidents,

TABLE 4–3

Examples of Seasonal Demand Patterns	*Period*	*Items*
	Year	Beer sales, toy sales, airline traffic, clothing, vacations, tourism, power usage, gasoline consumption, sports and recreation, education
	Month	Welfare and social security checks, bank transactions
	Week	Retail sales, restaurant meals, automobile traffic, automotive rentals, hotel registrations
	Day	Telephone calls, power usage, automobile traffic, public transportation, classroom utilization, retail sales, restaurant meals

unsafe chemical dumping grounds, carcinogens in food and drink), and so on.

DEVELOPING CAPACITY ALTERNATIVES

Aside from the general considerations outlined in Chapter 1 regarding the development of alternatives (i.e., conduct a reasonable search for possible alternatives, consider doing nothing, take care not to overlook nonquantitative factors), there are some specific considerations revelant to developing capacity alternatives. Among the considerations that are discussed below are the following:

1. Design flexibility into systems.
2. Take a big-picture approach to capacity changes.
3. Prepare to deal with capacity "chunks."
4. Attempt to smooth out capacity requirements.
5. Identify the optimal operating level.

The long-term nature of many capacity decisions and the risks inherent in long-term forecasts suggest potential benefits from designing flexible systems. For example, in many instances provision for future expansion in the original design of a structure can be obtained at a small price compared to what it would cost to remodel an existing structure that did not have such a provision. Hence, if future expansion of a restaurant seems likely, water lines, power hookups, and waste disposal lines can be put in place initially so that if expansion becomes a reality, tearing up the existing structure can be minimized. Similarly, a new golf course may start as a 9-hole operation, but unless provision is made for future expansion by obtaining options on adjacent land, it may never progress to a larger (18-hole) course. Other considerations in flexible design involve layout of equipment, location, equipment selection, production planning, scheduling, and inventory policies. These are discussed in later chapters.

In developing capacity alternatives it is important to consider how parts of the system interrelate. For example, a decision to increase the number of rooms that a motel has should also take into account probable increased demands for parking, entertainment and food, and housekeeping. This is a "big-picture" approach.

Capacity increments are often acquired in fairly large chunks rather than smooth increments, making it difficult to achieve a match between desired capacity and feasible capacity. For instance, the desired capacity of a certain operation may be 55 units per hour. But suppose that machines used for this operation are able to produce 40 units per hour each. One machine by itself would cause capacity to be 15 units per hour short of what is needed, but two machines would result in an excess capacity of 25 units per hour. And the illustration becomes even more extreme if the topic shifts, say, to open-hearth furnaces or the number of airplanes needed to provide a desired level of capacity.

Unevenness in capacity requirements can create certain problems. For instance, during periods of inclement weather public transportation ridership tends to increase substantially relative to periods of pleasant weather. Consequently, the system tends to alternate between underutilization and overutilization. Increasing the number of buses or subway cars will reduce the burden during periods of heavy demand, although this will aggravate the problems of overcapacity at other times, and most certainly add to the cost of operating the system. Unfortunately, there do not seem to be any simple solutions to these kinds of problems.

The unevenness in demand for products and services can be traced to a variety of sources. The bus-ridership problem is weather-related to a certain extent, but in part demand could be considered to be random (i.e., vary because of chance factors). Still another source of varying demand is seasonality. However, seasonal variations are generally easier to cope with than random variations because they are *predictable*. Consequently, allowances can be made in planning and scheduling activities and inventories. Even so, seasonal variations can still pose problems because of their uneven demands on the system; at certain times the system will tend to be overloaded, while at certain other times it will tend to be underloaded. One possible approach to this problem is to try to identify products or services that have complementing demand patterns (i.e., patterns that tend to offset each other). For instance, demand for snow skis and demand for water skis might complement each other: demand for water skis is greater in the spring and summer months, and demand for snow skis is greater in the fall and winter months. The same might apply to heating and air conditioning equipment. The ideal case is one in which products or services with complementing demand patterns involve the use of the same resources but at different times, so that overall capacity requirements remain fairly stable. Figure 4–2 illustrates complementing demand patterns.

Other possible strategies for handling variations in a narrower time frame include subcontracting, working overtime, and using inventories to absorb demand fluctuations. These and other strategies are discussed in more detail in later chapters.

Production units typically have an ideal or optimal level of operation in terms of unit cost of output. At the ideal level, cost per unit is the lowest for that production unit; larger or smaller rates of output will result in a higher unit cost. This concept is illustrated

FIGURE 4–2

**A and B Have
Complementing
Demand Patterns**

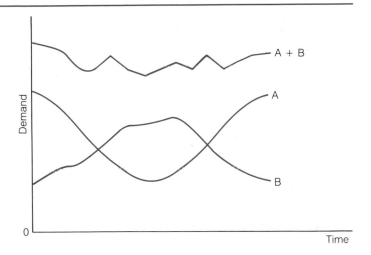

in Figure 4–3. Notice how unit costs rise as the rate of output varies from the optimum level.

The explanation for the shape of the cost curve follows: At low levels of output, the costs of facilities and equipment must be absorbed (paid for) by very few units. Hence, the cost per unit is high. As output is increased, there are more units to absorb the "fixed" cost of facilities and equipment, so unit costs decrease. However, beyond a certain point, unit costs will start to rise. To be sure, the fixed costs are being spread over even more units, so that does not account for the increase. Other factors then become important, such

FIGURE 4–3

**Production Units Have
an Optimal Rate of
Output for Minimum
Cost**

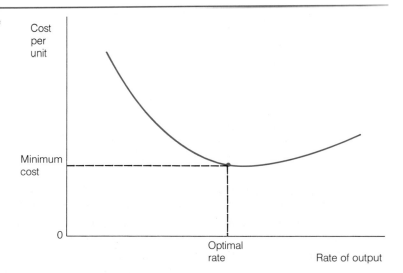

FIGURE 4–4

Minimum Cost and Optimal Operating Rate are Functions of Size of a Production Unit

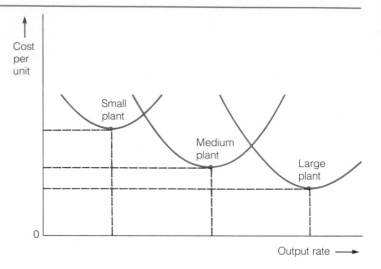

as worker fatigue, equipment breakdowns, the loss of flexibility, which leaves less of a margin for error, and generally more difficulty in coordinating operations.

The optimal operating rate and the amount of the minimum cost both tend to be a function of the general capacity of the operating unit. As the general capacity, say, of a plant, increases, the optimal output rate increases, and the minimum cost for the optimal rate decreases. Thus, larger plants tend to have higher optimal output rates and smaller minimum costs than smaller plants. These points are illustrated in Figure 4–4.

In choosing the capacity of an operating unit, management must take these relationships into account along with the availability of financial and other resources and forecasts of expected demand. In order to do this, it is necessary to determine enough points for each size facility to be able to make a comparison among different sizes. In some instances facility sizes are givens, whereas in others, facility size is a continuous variable (i.e., any size can be selected). In that case an ideal facility size can be selected. In most instances, though, a choice must be made from given sizes, and none may have a minimum at the desired rate of output.

EVALUATING ALTERNATIVES

Alternatives for future capacity need to be examined from a number of different perspectives. Most obvious, perhaps, are economic considerations: Will an alternative be economically feasible? How much will it cost? How soon can we have it? What will operating and maintenance costs be? What will the useful life be? Will it be compatible with present personnel and present operations? Less obvious, but nonetheless important, is possible negative public opinion. For instance, the decision to build a new power plant is almost sure to stir up reaction, whether it is to be coal-fired, hydroelectric, or nuclear. Any option that has the possibility of disrupting lives and property is bound to generate hostile reactions. Construction of new facilities may necessitate moving personnel to a new location. Embracing a new technology may mean retraining certain people and even terminating some people. Relocation can cause unfavorable reactions, particularly if a town is about to lose a major employer. Conversely, community pressure in a new location may arise if the presence of the company is viewed unfavorably (noise, traffic, pollution).

There are a number of techniques that are useful in evaluating capacity alternatives from an economic standpoint. Some of the more common ones are cost-volume analysis, financial analysis, decision theory, and queuing analysis. Cost-volume analysis is described in this chapter. Financial analysis is mentioned briefly and described in more detail in the chapter supplement, and decision theory and queuing theory are described in other chapters.

Cost-Volume Analysis

Cost-volume analysis, or *break-even analysis,* as it is commonly referred to, focuses on relationships between cost, revenue, and volume of output. The purpose of cost-volume analysis is to estimate the income of an organization that will occur under different operating conditions. It can be particularly useful as a tool for comparing capacity alternatives.

Use of the technique requires identification of all costs related to the production of a given product. These costs are then assigned to one of two categories: fixed costs or variable costs. *Fixed costs* are those that tend to remain constant regardless of volume of output. Examples include rental costs, property taxes, equipment costs, heating and cooling expenses, and certain administrative costs. *Variable costs* vary directly with volume of output. The major components of variable costs are generally materials and labor costs. It is assumed that variable cost per unit remains the same regardless of volume of output.

The total cost associated with a given volume of output is equal to the sum of the fixed cost and the variable cost per unit times volume.

$$\text{Total cost} = \text{Fixed cost} + \text{Variable cost per unit} \times Q \text{ units}$$

Figure 4–5A shows the relationship between volume of output and fixed costs, total variable costs, and total (fixed plus variable) costs.

FIGURE 4–5

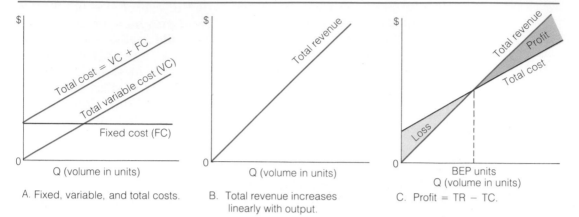

A. Fixed, variable, and total costs.

B. Total revenue increases linearly with output.

C. Profit = TR − TC.

Revenue per unit, like variable cost per unit, is assumed to be the same regardless of quantity of output. Thus, it too will have a linear relationship to output, as illustrated in Figure 4–5B. It is assumed that all of the output can be sold. The total revenue associated with a given quantity of output, Q, is:

$$\text{Total revenue} = \text{Revenue per unit} \times Q$$

Figure 4–5C describes the relationship between profit—which is the difference between total revenue and total (i.e., fixed plus variable) cost—and volume of output. The volume at which total costs and total revenue are equal is referred to as the *break-even point (BEP)*. When volume is less than the break-even point, there is a loss rather than a profit, while for volume greater than the break-even point, there is a profit. The greater the deviation from this point, the greater the profit or loss. Total profit can be computed using the formula:

$$\begin{aligned}
\text{Profit} &= \text{Total revenue} - \text{Total cost} \\
&= \text{Rev per unit} \times Q \text{ units} - (\text{Fixed cost} \\
&\quad + \text{Variable cost per unit} \times Q \text{ units})
\end{aligned}$$

The required volume needed to generate a specified profit is:

$$\text{Volume} = \frac{\text{Specified profit} + \text{Fixed cost}}{\text{Revenue per unit} - \text{Variable cost per unit}}$$

A special case of this is the volume of output needed in order for total revenue to equal total cost. This is the break-even point, and it can be computed using the formula:

$$Q_{BEP} = \frac{\text{Fixed cost}}{\text{Revenue per unit} - \text{Variable cost per unit}}$$

TABLE 4–4

Summary of Break-Even Formulas

FC = Fixed costs
VC = Variable cost per unit
TC = Total cost
Rev = Revenue per unit
Q = Quantity of output

Q_{BEP} = Break-even quantity
TR = Total revenue
P = Profit
SP = Specified profit

1. $TC = FC + VC \times Q$
2. $TR = Rev \times Q$
3. $P = TR - TC = Rev \times Q - (FC + VC \times Q) = Q(Rev - VC) - FC$

4. $Q_{BEP} = \dfrac{FC}{Rev - VC}$

5. Volume needed to generate a specified profit:

$$Q = \frac{SP + FC}{Rev - VC}$$

The break-even symbols and formulas are summarized in Table 4–4. The use of these formulas is illustrated in the following example.

EXAMPLE 2

Old-Fashioned Berry Pies, Ltd., currently operates a single bakery but is now considering a second location in a new shopping mall. The owner, S. Simon, estimates that fixed costs would be $3,000 per week and that labor and materials to produce pies at that location will be 60 cents per pie. Pies will be sold for $1.60 each.

1. What number of pies must be sold in order to break even?
2. What profit (or loss) would there be on sales of 10,000 pies in one week?
3. What volume would be required in order to realize a profit of $12,000?

Solution

1. $FC = \$3,000$, $VC = \$0.60$ per unit, $Rev = \$1.60$ per unit

$$Q_{BEP} = \frac{FC}{Rev - VC} = \frac{\$3,000}{\$1.60 - \$0.60} = 3,000 \text{ pies per week.}$$

2. Profit $= (Rev \text{ per unit}) \times Q - (FC + (VC \text{ per unit}) \times Q)$
   $= \$1.60(10,000) - (\$3,000 + \$0.60(10,000))$
   $= \$7,000.$

3. Volume $= \dfrac{SP + FC}{Rev \text{ per unit} - VC \text{ per unit}} = \dfrac{\$12,000 + \$3,000}{\$1.60 - \$0.60}$

   $= 15,000$ pies.

Before using the break-even model, it is necessary to make certain that the assumptions of the model are reasonably satisfied. The assumptions are:

1. One product is involved.
2. Everything that is produced can be sold.
3. The variable cost per unit is the same regardless of the volume.
4. Fixed costs do not change with volume changes.
5. The revenue per unit is the same regardless of volume.

Cost-volume analysis can be a valuable tool for comparing location decisions. As is the case with any quantitative tool, it is important to consider if the assumptions on which the technique is based are reasonably satisfied for a particular situation. For example, revenue per unit or variable cost per unit are not always constant. In addition, fixed costs may not be constant over the range of possible output. If demand is subject to random variations, it will be necessary to take that into account in the analysis. Cost-volume analysis requires that fixed and variable costs can be separated, and this can sometimes be exceedingly difficult to accomplish.

Cost-volume analysis works best when one or a few products that have the same cost characteristic are involved. Otherwise, the analysis can become fairly complex, although it is not impossible to deal with such cases.

In any case an important benefit of cost-volume considerations is the conceptual framework it provides for integrating cost, revenue, and profit estimates into capacity decisions.

Financial Analysis A problem that is universally encountered by managers is how to allocate scarce funds. A common approach is to use *financial analysis* to rank investment proposals. At this point, it may not be necessary to go into much detail about these methods. However, for those so inclined, the chapter supplement describes some of the techniques commonly used for financial analysis and provides examples of each.

The purpose of this section is to define some of the terms that are used elsewhere in the reading material and to provide some perspective on where financial analysis methods fit into the spectrum of evaluation techniques available to managers.

Two important terms in financial analysis are *cash flow* and *present value.*

Cash flow refers to the difference between the cash received from sales (of goods, services) and other sources (e.g., sale of old equipment) and the cash outflow for labor, materials, overhead, and taxes.

Present value expresses in current value the sum of all future cash flows of an investment proposal.

The three most commonly used methods of financial analysis are *payback, present value,* and *internal rate of return.*

Payback is a crude but widely used method that focuses on the length of time it will take for an investment to return its original cost. For example, an investment with an original cost of $6,000 and a monthly net cash flow of $1,000 has a payback period of six months. Payback ignores the *time value of money.* Its use is easier to rationalize for short-term projects than long-term ones. However, some now feel that use of this method is one of the contributing factors in the failure of U.S. firms to match productivity increases achieved by other nations.

The *present value (PV)* method summarizes the initial cost of an investment, its estimated annual cash flows, and any expected salvage value into a single value called the *equivalent current value,* taking into account the time value of money (i.e., interest rates).

The *internal rate of return (IRR)* summarizes the initial cost, expected annual cash flows, and estimated future salvage value of an investment proposal into an *equivalent interest rate.* In other words, this method identifies the rate of return that equates the estimated future returns and the initial cost.

These techniques are appropriate when there is a high degree of *certainty* associated with estimates of future cash flows. In many instances operations managers and other managers must deal with situations that can be better described by risk or uncertainty. The certainty methods are described in the chapter supplement, while methods for dealing with financial analysis under conditions of risk or uncertainty are often handled using decision theory.

Decision Theory   Decision theory is a helpful tool for financial comparison of alternatives under conditions of either risk or uncertainty. It is suited to capacity decisions as well as to a wide range of other decisions managers are called upon to make. Decision theory was described in Chapter 2, but the same approaches can be applied to capacity decisions. Some of the problems at the end of this chapter require the use of decision theory. There would be little benefit from repeating the discussion that appears in Chapter 2. Suffice it to say that decision theory is an important managerial tool for capacity decisions.

Queuing Theory   Queuing theory is often useful for designing service systems. Waiting lines have a tendency to form in a wide variety of service systems (e.g., airport ticket counters, telephone calls to a cable television company, and hospital emergency rooms). The lines are symptoms of bottleneck operations. Queuing theory is useful in helping managers choose a capacity level that will be cost effective through balancing the cost of having customers wait with the cost of providing additional capacity. Queuing theory can aid in the determination of expected costs for various levels of service capacity.

This topic is described in detail in a later chapter.

SUMMARY

Capacity refers to a system's potential for producing goods or delivering services over a specified time interval. Capacity decisions are doubly important: capacity limitations act as a ceiling on output, and capacity is a major determinant of operating costs.

As a general rule, a variety of factors interfere with capacity utilization, so that effective capacity is somewhat less than design capacity. These factors involve such things as facilities design and layout, human factors, product/service design, equipment failures, scheduling problems, and quality considerations.

Capacity planning involves long-term and short-term considerations. Long-term concern relates to the overall level of capacity, while short-term concern relates to variations in capacity requirements due to seasonal, random, and irregular fluctuations in demand. Ideally, capacity will match demand, since it is typically most efficient to operate at or close to full capacity. For this reason, there is a close link between forecasting and capacity planning, particularly in the long term. In the short term, emphasis shifts to describing and coping with variations in demand.

Development of capacity alternatives is enhanced by taking a systems approach to planning, by recognizing that capacity increments are often acquired in chunks, by designing flexible systems, and by considering product/service complements as a way of dealing with various patterns of demand.

Evaluating capacity alternatives contains both quantitative and qualitative aspects. Quantitative analysis usually reflects economic factors, while qualitative considerations include such intangibles as public opinion and personal preferences of managers. Cost-volume analysis, financial analysis, decision theory, and queuing theory are possible tools for analyzing alternatives.

SOLVED PROBLEMS

1. A small firm produces and sells novelty items in a five-state area. The firm expects to consolidate assembly of its electric turtle line at a single location, instead of the current situation, which consists of three widely scattered operations. The leading candidate location will have a monthly fixed cost of $42,000 and variable costs of $3 per turtle. Turtles sell for $7 each. Prepare a table that shows total profits, fixed costs, variable costs, and revenues for monthly volumes of 10,000, 12,000, and 15,000 units.

Solution

Given: Revenue = $7 per unit
Variable cost = $3 per unit
Fixed cost = $42,000 per month

$$\text{Profit} = \text{Revenue} \times \text{Volume} - (\text{Fixed cost} + VC \times \text{Volume})$$

$$\text{Total cost} = FC + VC$$

Volume	Total revenue	Total VC	Fixed cost	Total cost	Total profit
10,000	$ 70,000	$30,000	$42,000	$72,000	$-2,000
12,000	84,000	36,000	42,000	78,000	6,000
15,000	105,000	45,000	42,000	87,000	18,000

2. (Refer to the previous problem.) Develop an equation that can be used to compute profit for any volume using the information in the previous problem, and use that equation to determine profit for the case where volume equals 22,000 units.

Solution

$$\text{Profit} = \$7/\text{unit} \times Q - (\$42,000 + \$3/\text{unit} \times Q)$$

where Q = volume.
For Q = 22,000, profit is

$$\$7(22,000) - (\$42,000 + \$3 \times 22,000) = \$46,000.$$

DISCUSSION AND REVIEW QUESTIONS

1. Contrast *design* and *effective* capacity.
2. List and briefly explain three factors that may inhibit capacity utilization.
3. How do long-term and short-term capacity considerations differ?
4. Give two examples of items that exhibit these seasonal demand patterns: *(a)* annual, *(b)* monthly, *(c)* weekly, and *(d)* daily.
5. Give some examples of ways that flexibility can be built into system design.
6. Why is it important to adopt a *big-picture* approach to capacity planning?
7. What is meant by *capacity in chunks* and

why is that a factor in capacity planning?

8. What kinds of capacity problems are currently being experienced by many elementary and secondary schools? What are some of the alternatives being used to deal with those problems?

9. How can a systems approach to capacity planning be useful?

10. How do capacity decisions influence productivity?

PROBLEMS

1. A producer of pottery is considering the addition of a new plant to absorb the backlog of demand that now exists. The primary location being considered will have fixed costs of $9,200 per month and variable costs of 70 cents per unit produced. Each item is sold to retailers at a price that averages 90 cents.
   a. What volume per month is required in order to break even?
   b. What profit would be realized on a monthly volume of (1) 61,000 units? (2) 87,000 units?
   c. What volume would be needed to obtain a profit of $16,000 per month?
   d. What volume is required to provide a revenue of $23,000 per month?
   e. Plot the total cost and total revenue lines.

2. A small firm intends to increase the capacity of a bottleneck operation by adding a new machine. Two alternatives, A and B, have been identified, and the associated costs and revenues have been estimated: annual fixed costs would be $40,000 for A and $30,000 for B; variable costs per unit would be $10 for A and $12 for B; and revenue per unit would be $15 for A and $16 for B.
   a. Determine each alternative's break-even point in units.
   b. At what volume of output would the two alternatives yield the same profit?
   c. If expected annual demand is 12,000 units, which alternative would yield the higher profit?

3. A producer of felt-tip pens has received a forecast of a demand of 30,000 pens for the coming month from its marketing department. Fixed costs of $25,000 per month are allocated to the felt-tip operation, and variable costs are 37 cents per pen.
   a. Find the break-even quantity if pens sell for $1 each.
   b. What price must pens be sold for to obtain a monthly profit of $15,000, assuming that estimated demand materializes?

4. A real estate agent is considering installing a cellular telephone in his car. There are three billing plans to choose from, all of which involve a weekly charge of $20. Plan A has a cost of $.45 a minute for daytime calls and $.20 a minute for evening calls. Plan B has a charge of $.55 a minute for daytime calls and a charge of $.15 a minute for evening calls. Plan C has a flat rate of $80 with 200 minutes of calls allowed per week and a cost of $.40 per minute beyond that, day or evening.
   a. Determine the total charge under each plan for this case: 120 minutes of day calls, 40 minutes of evening calls in a week.
   b. Prepare a graph that shows total weekly cost for each plan versus daytime call minutes.
   c. If the agent will use the service mainly for daytime calls, over what range of call minutes will each plan be optimal?

5. (Refer to the previous question.) Suppose that the agent expects both day and eve-

ning calls. At what point (i.e., proportion of call minutes for daytime calls) would he be indifferent between plans A and B?

6. Good Labels, Inc., supplies labels for wine bottles to regional vineyards. Increased demand for wine is expected to exceed label capacity in the near future. Consequently, Good Labels is exploring several options for increasing its capacity relative to doing nothing. Net present values (in $ millions) for the various options are shown in a table below. Which option would be indicated under each of these conditions:

   a. The firm uses maximax?
   b. The firm uses maximin.
   c. The firm uses maximum expected value and probabilities of the demands listed are equally likely?
   d. The firm uses maximum expected value and $P(40) = .2$, $P(45) = .4$, $P(50) = .3$, and $P(55) = .1$?

	Demand (boxes per day)			
Options	40	45	50	55
Do nothing . .	$0	5	5	5
Expand . . .	−5	0	5	10
Additional plant . . .	−20	−5	10	25

7. A regional airline has recently added a "long-hop" commuter route and is now considering the purchase of a jet to use on that route. Information concerning the estimated payoffs under various levels of customer demand are shown for the alternatives being considered. The figures have been adjusted for purchase cost of the planes. What alternative would be appropriate if the decision criterion is:

   a. Maximax?
   b. Maximin?
   c. Minimax regret?
   d. Maximum expected value if probabilities for low, moderate, and high demand, respectively, are: (1) .1, .4, and .5? (2) .2, .3, and .5?

	Demand		
	Low	Moderate	High
Do nothing.	$ 2*	$3	$ 3
Buy 80 passenger . .	0	4	6
Buy 120 passenger . .	(5)	0	7
Buy 200 passenger . .	(10)	1	10

   * Net present value in $ millions.

8. A motel has received numerous complaints from potential guests whose reservations could not be honored due to overbooking. Discussions with the assistant manager of the motel have revealed that each overbooking results in a loss of profit and goodwill that has a value of $30. Thus, if two rooms are overbooked, the loss will be $60. On the other hand, the assistant manager estimates that "no-shows" reflect a profit loss of $12 each.

   a. Construct a payoff matrix for overbooking strategies of 0, 1, 2, 3, and 4 for 0 through 5 no shows.
   b. What decision should be made if the criterion is (1) maximax? (2) maximin?
   c. If no-show probabilities for 0, 1, 2, 3, 4, and 5 are .2, .3, .2, .1, .1, and .1 respectively, which strategy would be selected in order to minimize expected loss?

SELECTED BIBLIOGRAPHY

Abramowitz, Irving. *Production Management: Concepts and Analysis for Operation and Control.* New York: The Ronald Press, 1967.

Adam, Everette E., Jr., and Ronald J. Ebert. *Production and Operations Management: Concepts, Models and Behavior.* 2d ed. Englewood, Cliffs, N.J.: Prentice-Hall, 1982.

Buffa, Elwood, and James S. Dyer. *Essentials of Management/Operations Research.* New York: John Wiley & Sons, 1978.

Monks, Joseph G. *Operations Management: Theory and Problems.* New York: McGraw-Hill, 1982.

Moore, Franklin, and Thomas E. Hendrick. *Production/Operations Management.* 9th ed. Homewood, Ill.: Richard D. Irwin, 1985.

Financial Analysis

TERMINOLOGY, 198

    Economic Life, 198
    Net Cash Flow, 198
    Salvage Value, 198
    Depreciation, 199
    Time Value of Money, 199

TAX CONSIDERATIONS, 201

METHODS OF EVALUATION, 201

    Payback Period, 201
    Net Present Value, 202
    Internal Rate of Return, 207

SUMMARY, 209

SOLVED PROBLEMS, 210

DISCUSSION AND REVIEW QUESTIONS, 211

PROBLEMS, 211

SELECTED BIBLIOGRAPHY, 213

After completing this supplement, you should be able to:

1. Define or explain these terms:
   a. Economic life.
   b. Cash flow.
   c. Salvage value.
   d. Depreciation.
   e. Time value of money.
2. Give examples of decisions that require the operations manager to use financial analysis.
3. Describe and use each of these methods of evaluation:
   a. Payback.
   b. Net present value.
   c. Internal rate of return.

In both the public and private sectors, operations managers must continually make decisions concerning the allocation of funds among investment alternatives. In private firms the objective is to obtain a reasonable return on owners' capital, while in public organizations the objective is usually to provide a given level of service at the lowest cost or to obtain the highest possible level of service for a given cost.

Typical investment decisions usually involve the following:

1. Acquisition of facilities.
2. Acquisition of equipment.
3. Revision or expansion of existing facility layout.
4. Research and development.
5. Make or buy.
6. New products.
7. Repair and maintenance of equipment and facilities.

In comparing investment alternatives, operations managers generally take into account the economic life of an investment, its initial cost, the expected cash flows, depreciation and taxes, salvage values, and the time value of money. Before turning to the methods they might use to evaluate alternatives, it will be helpful to briefly review some of the terms commonly used in financial analysis.

TERMINOLOGY

The purpose of these brief definitions is to establish a common basis for discussion of methods of evaluation.

Economic Life

The *economic life* of an asset or other investment alternative is the period of time that it will perform a useful service to the organization. It can differ from the *accounting life* of an asset (period of time over which the asset is depreciated) as well as the *productive life* of an asset (period of time over which the asset could perform). The productive life of equipment often exceeds its useful (economic) life to the organization because technological changes make the original equipment obsolete or because the needs of the organization change. The accounting life of an asset is often a matter of tax laws and tax strategies.

Net Cash Flow

Net cash flow is the annual difference between revenues and expenses related to an investment proposal. Although cash flows might occur throughout the year, for purposes of financial analysis they are treated as occurring at the end of the year.

Salvage Value

The *salvage value* is generally the estimated income that will be received from the sale of an asset. Sometimes this will be a negative amount (e.g., the organization must incur a cost in disposing of the asset).

Depreciation

Depreciation is an accounting term that relates to an annual reduction in the value of an asset on the books of a firm. A detailed discussion of depreciation is beyond the scope of this text. However, the importance of depreciation in terms of financial analysis should be noted: Depreciation has an effect on income taxes, which in turn affect the actual cash flow, even though depreciation itself is *not* a cash flow.

Time Value of Money

The timing of cash flows from an asset has a lot to do with the desirability of the investment. Investment alternatives that produce the same total returns, but with differing times, are not usually equally attractive, due to the time value of money. The *time value of money* refers to the fact that money can be invested (e.g., in new investments, deposited in a bank account) to produce a return. The timing of cash flows of an investment proposal is important because the sooner the money becomes available, the sooner it can be used for other worthwhile purposes.

Consider this example. You are given a choice of receiving $100 now, or $100 in two years. Suppose that you will not need this money for another two years, so if you receive it now you will put it into a bank account that yields 6 percent a year. If you decide to take the money now and deposit it in the bank, the future value, *F*, after *one* year will equal the present value, *P* ($100), plus a dividend equal to the amount deposited times the interest rate, *i*. Thus:

$$F_1 = \$100 + \$100(.06) = \$106$$

Assuming the total amount remained in the account for the second year, the interest would be paid on $106 for the second year, and the account balance at the end of that year would be:

$$F_2 = \$106 + \$106(.06) = \$112.36$$

Hence, by receiving the money at the present time and investing it, you would have $12.36 *more* than if you chose to take the $100 at the end of the second year.

In general, the future value after one year can be determined using the formula:

$$F_1 = P + Pi$$
$$= P(1 + i)$$

where

F_1 = Future value at the end of period 1
P = Present value
i = Interest rate

FIGURE 4S–1

Cash Values in Given
Years Can Be Restated
Relative to the Present
Time or Some Point in
the Future

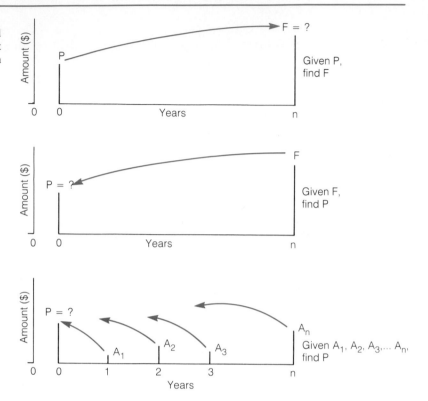

For year 2, the formula becomes:

$$F_2 = P(1+i) + P(1+i)i$$
$$= P(1+i)(1+i)$$
$$= P(1+i)^2$$

In a similar fashion, the total value after n years would be:

$$F_n = P(1+i)^n$$

An interesting question is to consider what the present value of the other alternative is (i.e., receive $100 at the end of two years). In other words, what sum of money, invested for two years at 6 percent interest, would produce $100?

A general formula for P, given F, n, and i, can be derived by solving the general formula for F in terms of P. That is: $F_n = P(1+i)^n$. Solving for P yields:

$$P = \frac{F_n}{(1+i)^n}$$

Hence, the required sum needed now to produce a future value of $100 in two years is:

$$P = \frac{\$100}{(1 + .06)^2} = \$89$$

An extension of this concept involves determining either the present or the future value of a series of annual amounts, $A_1, A_2, \ldots, A_n$, which may or may not be equal. You will see in the next section how to do this. For now, it will be instructive to compare these three concepts: given F, find P; given P, find F; and given A, find P. These are illustrated in Figure 4S–1.

TAX CONSIDERATIONS

Federal income taxes can have important implications in financial decision making. Tax rates and provisions for applying them change from time to time, so precise statements about tax laws are difficult to make. Nonetheless, certain observations concerning taxes can be made.

Taxes and depreciation on plant and equipment are closely linked. Depreciation allows companies to write off a portion of an investment against current income. This reduces the amount of taxable income and thereby frees up funds for other uses (e.g., invest in additional equipment). Generally speaking, analysis of investment alternatives on a before-tax basis leads to the same ranking as an after-tax basis, although differences may occur in cases where lease versus buy is involved. Consequently, because it is less complicated to use before-tax analysis, or to assume taxes have already been handled, we can avoid a detailed discussion of income taxes. However, a consideration of taxes is important in choosing a method of depreciation, since different methods will generally result in different tax consequences in certain years. In other words, choice of depreciation methods can result in shifting the tax burden to different years, and this can have important benefits in terms of cash flow by preserving funds that would otherwise have to be paid out in the form of income taxes.

Also, in certain years, businesses have been allowed to take an *investment tax credit,* which is a direct reduction in *taxes.* Again, the underlining philosophy is to encourage business investment.

METHODS OF EVALUATION

We shall examine three commonly used methods for evaluating alternatives: payback period, present value, and internal rate of return.

Payback Period

This is a crude, but widely used, method for evaluating the desirability of a financial investment. As its name implies, it focuses on the length of time it will take to recoup the original investment.

EXAMPLE S–1

Determine the payback period for each of the investment proposals shown below, given their estimated cash flows. Assume each requires an initial investment of $40,000.

Year	A	B	C
1	$10,000	$20,000	$ 1,000
2	10,000	20,000	5,000
3	10,000	2,000	10,000
4	10,000	1,000	20,000
5	10,000	100	40,000
6	10,000	0	80,000

Solution

Calculate the cumulative cash flows for each alternative and note when the cumulative amount equals the original investment. Hence,

Year	A	B	C
1	$10,000	$20,000	$ 1,000
2	20,000	40,000	6,000
3	30,000	42,000	16,000
4	40,000		36,000
5			76,000

Thus, A's payback period is exactly four years, B's is exactly two years, and C's is between four and five years. From a payback standpoint, the most attractive alternative is B, while C is the least attractive.

One obvious disadvantage of the payback method is that it does not consider cash flows beyond the payback period. Nor does it take salvage value into account. In the preceding example, note that B's cash flows are quite small beyond the payback period, in contrast to C's, which get larger and larger. Another disadvantage is that no allowance is made for the time value of money, at least not directly. Indirectly, the rationale of the payback approach is to recoup the initial investment as quickly as possible to have the funds available for future opportunities. In fact, this method is especially appealing to firms that have a cash shortage. Other firms like its simplicity, and many firms like to use it in situations where the payback period is fairly short (e.g., six months to a year).

Net Present Value   The present value method involves finding the present value of each of the future cash flows (including salvage value) and summing the results. The *net present value* of an alternative is equal to this sum minus the initial cost of the proposed investment:

$$\text{Net present value} = \frac{\text{Present value of}}{\text{future cash flows}} - \text{Initial cost}$$

TABLE 4S–1

Present Value of an Annuity of $1: Given equal A's, Find P

Year	5%	6%	7%	8%	9%	10%	12%	14%	16%	18%	20%	24%	28%	32%	36%
1	0.952	0.943	0.935	0.926	0.917	0.909	0.893	0.877	0.862	0.847	0.833	0.806	0.781	0.758	0.735
2	1.859	1.833	1.808	1.783	1.759	1.736	1.690	1.647	1.605	1.566	1.528	1.457	1.392	1.332	1.276
3	2.723	2.673	2.624	2.577	2.531	2.487	2.402	2.322	2.246	2.174	2.106	1.981	1.868	1.766	1.674
4	3.546	3.465	3.387	3.312	3.240	3.170	3.037	2.914	2.798	2.690	2.589	2.404	2.241	2.096	1.966
5	4.329	4.212	4.100	3.993	3.890	3.791	3.605	3.433	3.274	3.127	2.991	2.745	2.532	2.345	2.181
6	5.076	4.917	4.766	4.623	4.486	4.355	4.111	3.889	3.685	3.498	3.326	3.020	2.759	2.534	2.339
7	5.786	5.582	5.389	5.206	5.033	4.868	4.564	4.288	4.039	3.812	3.605	3.242	2.937	2.678	2.455
8	6.463	6.210	5.971	5.747	5.535	5.335	4.968	4.639	4.344	4.078	3.837	3.421	3.076	2.786	2.540
9	7.108	6.802	6.515	6.247	5.985	5.759	5.328	4.946	4.607	4.303	4.031	3.566	3.184	2.868	2.603
10	7.722	7.360	7.024	6.710	6.418	6.145	5.650	5.216	4.833	4.494	4.193	3.682	3.269	2.930	2.650
11	8.306	7.887	7.499	7.139	6.805	6.495	5.988	5.453	5.029	4.656	4.327	3.776	3.335	2.978	2.683
12	8.863	8.384	7.943	7.536	7.161	6.814	6.194	5.660	5.197	4.793	4.439	3.851	3.387	3.013	2.708
13	9.394	8.853	8.358	7.904	7.487	7.103	6.424	5.842	5.342	4.910	4.533	3.912	3.427	3.040	2.727
14	9.899	9.295	8.745	8.244	7.786	7.367	6.628	6.002	5.468	5.008	4.611	3.962	3.459	3.061	2.740
15	10.380	9.712	9.108	8.559	8.060	7.606	6.811	6.142	5.575	5.092	4.675	4.001	3.483	3.076	2.750
16	10.838	10.106	9.447	8.851	8.312	7.824	6.974	6.265	5.669	5.162	4.730	4.033	3.503	3.088	2.758
17	11.274	10.477	9.763	9.122	8.544	8.022	7.120	6.373	5.749	5.222	4.775	4.059	3.518	3.097	2.763
18	11.690	10.828	10.059	9.372	8.756	8.201	7.250	6.467	5.818	5.273	4.812	4.080	3.529	3.104	2.767
19	12.085	11.158	10.336	9.604	8.950	8.365	7.366	6.550	5.877	5.316	4.844	4.097	3.539	3.109	2.770
20	12.462	11.470	10.594	9.818	9.128	8.514	7.469	6.623	5.929	5.353	4.870	4.110	3.546	3.113	2.772
25	14.094	12.783	11.654	10.675	9.823	9.077	7.843	6.873	6.097	5.467	4.948	4.147	3.564	3.122	2.776
30	15.373	13.765	12.409	11.258	10.274	9.427	8.055	7.003	6.177	5.517	4.979	4.160	3.569	3.124	2.778

There are essentially two kinds of situations that arise in terms of annual cash flows:

1. Annual cash flows are all the same amount.
2. Annual cash flows are not all equal.

In the first situation a single computation is required; in the second a separate computation is usually required for each cash flow (i.e., the present value of each cash flow must be determined). In both cases the actual determination of the present values is greatly simplified by the use of tables. In order to use the tables, decide which of these two situations describes the problem. In the first situation, use Table 4S–1. Find the factor in the table for the number of years and the cost of capital (e.g., for $n = 2$ and $i = 5$ percent, the factor is 1.859). Multiply this factor by the annual cash flow to determine the present value.

EXAMPLE S–2

   Determine the net present value of a proposal that has an economic life of nine years, an initial cost of $30,000, and an annual cash flow of $10,000. The firm's cost of capital is 12 percent.

Solution

   $n = 9$, $A = \$10,000$, Initial cost $= \$30,000$, and $i = 12\%$.

1. Find the *annuity* factor from Table 4S–1: 5.328.
2. Find the present value of cash flows: $10,000(5.328) = \$53,280$.
3. Determine the net present value: $53,280 - \$30,000 = \$23,280$.

In the second case, a separate computation must be made for each cash flow.

EXAMPLE S–3

   A newspaper is considering two investment proposals for a new piece of equipment. Proposal A has an initial cost of $2,000, and proposal B has an initial cost of $1,000. Given the cash flow information below and the firm's cost of capital of 10 percent, determine which proposal has the higher present value.

	Cash flows	
Year	*Proposal A*	*Proposal B*
1	$1,000	$2,000
2	2,000	1,000
3	3,000	800
4		100

EXAMPLE S–3 (concluded)

Solution

Using Table 4S–2, find the *present value factor* for each in the 10 percent column. Multiply that amount by the year's cash flow and sum the results. Subtract the initial cost from the sum to obtain the net present value:

1. Find the present value of cash flows.

	Proposal A			Proposal B		
Year	Cash flow	× PVF =	PV	Cash flow	× PVF =	PV
1.	$1,000	.909	$ 909	$2,000	.909	$1,818
2.	2,000	.826	1,652	1,000	.826	826
3.	3,000	.751	2,253	800	.751	601
4.				100	.683	68
			$4,814			$3,313

2. Subtract the initial investments to find the present value of each investment:

$$\text{Proposal A:} \quad \$4,814 - \$2,000 = \$2,814$$
$$\text{Proposal B:} \quad \$3,313 - \$1,000 = \$2,313$$

Hence, proposal A has a higher present value.

If it happens that an investment is expected to have a uniform cash flow but a different salvage value, the uniform flows can be handled using Table 4S–1 and the salvage value using Table 4S–2. Then add the results

EXAMPLE S–4

$$\text{Annual cash flow} = \$5,000 \qquad i = 14\%$$
$$\text{Initial cost} = \$12,000 \qquad n = 10$$
$$\text{Salvage value} = \$2,000 \text{ in year 10}$$

Find the net present value.

Solution

1. Find the present value of the equal cash flows using Table 4S–1:

$$P = \$5,000(5.216) = \$26,080$$

2. Find the present value of the salvage using Table 4S–2:

$$P = \$2,000(0.270) = \$540$$

3. Determine the net present value:

$$\text{Net present value} = (\$26,080 + \$540) - \$12,000 = \$14,620$$

TABLE 4S–2

Present Value of $1: Given F, Find P

Year	5%	6%	7%	8%	9%	10%	12%	14%	15%	16%	18%	20%	24%	28%	32%	36%	40%
1	0.952	0.943	0.935	0.926	0.917	0.909	0.893	0.877	0.870	0.862	0.847	0.833	0.806	0.781	0.758	0.735	0.714
2	0.907	0.890	0.873	0.857	0.842	0.826	0.797	0.769	0.756	0.743	0.718	0.694	0.650	0.610	0.574	0.541	0.510
3	0.864	0.840	0.816	0.794	0.772	0.751	0.712	0.675	0.658	0.641	0.609	0.579	0.524	0.477	0.435	0.398	0.364
4	0.823	0.792	0.763	0.735	0.708	0.683	0.636	0.592	0.572	0.552	0.516	0.482	0.423	0.373	0.329	0.292	0.260
5	0.784	0.747	0.713	0.681	0.650	0.621	0.567	0.519	0.497	0.476	0.437	0.402	0.341	0.291	0.250	0.215	0.186
6	0.746	0.705	0.666	0.630	0.596	0.564	0.507	0.456	0.432	0.410	0.370	0.335	0.275	0.227	0.189	0.158	0.133
7	0.711	0.665	0.623	0.583	0.547	0.513	0.452	0.400	0.376	0.354	0.314	0.279	0.222	0.178	0.143	0.116	0.095
8	0.677	0.627	0.582	0.540	0.502	0.467	0.404	0.351	0.327	0.305	0.266	0.233	0.179	0.139	0.108	0.085	0.068
9	0.645	0.592	0.544	0.500	0.460	0.424	0.361	0.308	0.284	0.263	0.226	0.194	0.144	0.108	0.082	0.063	0.048
10	0.614	0.558	0.508	0.463	0.422	0.386	0.322	0.270	0.247	0.227	0.191	0.162	0.116	0.085	0.062	0.046	0.035
11	0.585	0.527	0.475	0.429	0.388	0.350	0.287	0.237	0.215	0.195	0.162	0.135	0.094	0.066	0.047	0.034	0.025
12	0.557	0.497	0.444	0.397	0.356	0.319	0.257	0.208	0.187	0.168	0.137	0.112	0.076	0.052	0.036	0.025	0.018
13	0.530	0.469	0.415	0.368	0.326	0.290	0.229	0.182	0.163	0.145	0.116	0.093	0.061	0.040	0.027	0.018	0.013
14	0.505	0.442	0.388	0.340	0.299	0.263	0.205	0.160	0.141	0.125	0.099	0.078	0.049	0.032	0.021	0.014	0.009
15	0.481	0.417	0.362	0.315	0.275	0.239	0.183	0.140	0.123	0.108	0.084	0.065	0.040	0.025	0.016	0.010	0.006
16	0.458	0.394	0.339	0.292	0.252	0.218	0.163	0.123	0.107	0.093	0.071	0.054	0.032	0.019	0.012	0.007	0.005
17	0.436	0.371	0.317	0.270	0.231	0.198	0.146	0.108	0.093	0.080	0.060	0.045	0.026	0.015	0.009	0.005	0.003
18	0.416	0.350	0.296	0.250	0.212	0.180	0.130	0.095	0.081	0.069	0.051	0.038	0.021	0.012	0.007	0.004	0.002
19	0.386	0.331	0.276	0.232	0.194	0.164	0.116	0.083	0.070	0.060	0.043	0.031	0.017	0.009	0.005	0.003	0.002
20	0.377	0.319	0.258	0.215	0.178	0.149	0.104	0.073	0.061	0.051	0.037	0.026	0.014	0.007	0.004	0.002	0.001
25	0.295	0.233	0.184	0.146	0.116	0.092	0.059	0.038	0.030	0.024	0.016	0.010	0.005	0.002	0.001	0.000	0.000
30	0.231	0.174	0.131	0.099	0.075	0.057	0.033	0.020	0.015	0.012	0.007	0.004	0.002	0.001	0.000	0.000	0.000

Among the disadvantages of the present value approach are the assumption that funds can be reinvested as they are received at the cost of capital and the fact that it does not consider the length of time needed to recoup the original cost. Its advantages are that it incorporates a time-value dimension, it facilitates total value comparisons among alternatives, and it can handle uneven cash flows.

Internal Rate of Return

Another popular method used to evaluate investment alternatives involves finding the interest rate that will equate the present value of future cash flows with the initial investment. The resulting interest rate is called the *internal rate of return* (IRR).

When annual expected cash flows are equal and there is no expected salvage value, computations are straightforward. Simply compute the ratio of the initial cost to the annual cash flow and then refer to Table 4S–1 to determine the approximate interest rate for the specified life of the investment. That is:

$$PVA_n = \frac{\text{Initial investment}}{\text{Annual cash flow}} = \frac{I}{A}$$

where

PVA_n = Present value factor for n years found in Table 4S–1

EXAMPLE S–5

An automatic bottlecapping machine requires an initial investment of $9,000. During its estimated useful life of 11 years, it will provide an annual cash flow of $1,800. At the end of 11 years, the machine will have no salvage value. Determine the internal rate of return.

Solution

$$I = \$9,000$$
$$A = \$1,800$$
$$n = 11 \text{ years}$$
$$\frac{I}{A} = \frac{\$9,000}{1,800} = 5.00$$

Referring to Table 4S–1 for row $n = 11$, we find $PVA = 5.029$ for $i = 16$ percent and $PVA = 4.656$ for $i = 18$ percent. Since the computed value is approximately 5.029, we conclude the IRR is approximately 16 percent.

When cash flows are nonuniform and/or when salvage value is nonzero, determination of the IRR is a good deal more complex and involves a trial and error search for the approximate interest rate. A present value computation of each cash flow must be done for a number of i's until the approximate value of i can be narrowed down, using Table 4S-2.

EXAMPLE S-6

An investment proposal will have cash flows of $2,000 in the first year, $5,000 in the second, $4,000 in the third, and a salvage value of $1,000 in fourth. Initial cost is $10,000. Determine the approximate internal rate of return.

Solution

Try several i's (perhaps 6 percent and 10 percent):

Year	Cash flow	6 percent	10 percent
1 . . .	$2,000	.943 = 1,886	.909 = 1,818
2 . . .	5,000	.890 = 4,450	.826 = 4,130
3 . . .	4,000	.840 = 3,360	.751 = 3,004
4 . . .	1,000	.792 = 792	.683 = 683
		10,488	9,635

A rate of 6 percent results in a value that is slightly greater than the initial cost, while the 10 percent rate results in a value that is slightly less than the initial cost. Thus, a rate between these two would be appropriate. A rate of 8 percent resulted in $10,048 (calculations not shown), so we can conclude the internal rate of return is approximately 8 percent.

Several points related to the IRR are worth noting:

1. The internal rate of return and present value methods often yield the same choice in an evaluation of alternatives.
2. Some organizations have a threshold for the IRR below which investments are not considered.
3. Financial calculators and computer programs greatly simplify determination of the internal rate of return.

The disadvantages of the internal rate of return method are that it does not consider the *amount* involved, nor does it indicate the payback period. Its advantages are that it permits comparisons among alternatives, it adjusts for the time value of money, and it can be compared to the firm's cost of capital (which can serve as a lower threshold for acceptable investments).

SUMMARY

Operations managers rely on financial analysis to help them in ranking investment proposals in order to allocate limited funds. The underlying theme of financial analysis is that money has a time value: a dollar today is worth more than a dollar five years from today because today's dollar can be *invested* (i.e., it has the potential to produce additional gains). Using financial techniques, managers can compare alternative investment proposals, which often differ in terms of useful life, amount of initial investment required, amounts and distributions of annual cash flows, salvage value, and interest rates. Three widely used methods of evaluation are described in this supplement: payback, present value, and internal rate of return.

Financial Analysis

1. Recreation-Can-Be-Fun, Inc., has developed a proposal to erect a temporary indoor tennis court. Profit projections are $5,000 for the first year of operation and $2,000 for years two through five. The structure will be dismantled at the end of the fifth year at a contracted cost of $3,000. Initial cost is $7,500.

   a. What is the present value of this proposal for a cost of capital of 16 percent?

   b. What rate of return would equate the cash flows to the original cost?

Solution

The cash flows are:

Year	Cash flow
1	$5,000
2	2,000
3	2,000
4	2,000
5	−1,000

For fifth year, $2,000 − $3,000 = $−1,000.
$I = $7,500$, $n = 5$.

a. $i = 16$ percent.

Year	Cash flow	PFV (Table 4S–2)	PV = Cash flow × PVF
1	$5,000	.862	$4,310
2	2,000	.743	1,486
3	2,000	.641	1,282
4	2,000	.552	1,104
5	−1,000	.476	− 476
			$7,706
			−7,500
			$ 206

b. Noting that the present value is close to zero at $i = 16$ percent and observing that increasing the interest rate causes a decrease in present value, we can try $i = 18$ percent:

Year	Cash flow	PVF (Table 4S–2)	PV
1	$5,000	.847	$4,235
2	2,000	.718	1,436
3	2,000	.609	1,218
4	2,000	.516	1,032
5	−1,000	.437	− 437
			$7,484
			−7,500
			$ −16

Hence, the IRR is approximately 18 percent.

2. Determine the present value of an investment that has an initial cost of $9,300, zero salvage value, and cash flows of $4,000 per year for the first two years of the investment, then $1,000 for the next five years, and nothing after that point, if the cost of capital is 14 percent.

Solution

The problem can be simplified by viewing the cash flows as two annuities: one of $3,000 per year and the other of $1,000 per year:

Year	Cash flow	→	Annuity 1	Annuity 2
1.	$4,000		$3,000	$1,000
2.	4,000		3,000	1,000
3.	1,000			1,000
4.	1,000			1,000
5.	1,000			1,000
6.	1,000			1,000
7.	1,000			1,000

Then:

$$PV = \$3,000 \times (PVA: n = 2, i = 14\%) + \$1,000$$
$$\times (PVA: n = 7, i = 14\%) - \$9,300$$

From Table 4S–1, for $n = 2$ and $i = 14\%$, $PVA = 1.647$.
For $n = 7$ and $i = 14\%$, $PVA = 4.288$.
Thus,

$$PV - \$3,000 \times 1.647 + \$1,000 \times 4.288 - \$9,300 = \$-71$$

DISCUSSION AND REVIEW QUESTIONS

1. Briefly define or explain each of these terms:
   a. Cash flow.
   b. Salvage value.
   c. Economic life.
   d. Depreciation.
   e. Time value of money.

2. What are the advantages and disadvantages of each of these methods of evaluation?
   a. Payback.
   b. Present value.
   c. Internal rate of return.

PROBLEMS

1. A dairy cooperative is considering construction of a processing plant, which will require an outlay of $2.1 million initially. Annual income from the plant is expected to be $300,000. Plant life will be 15 years. Determine the internal rate of return on

   this investment for each of these cases:
   a. The plant is expected to have no salvage value.
   b. A salvage value of $250,000 is anticipated.

2. In the previous problem, (a) determine the

payback period, and *(b)* determine the present value assuming a cost of capital of 10 percent for each salvage value.

3. A photo finisher must decide whether to lease or buy a delivery van that will have an expected useful life of four years. Purchased cost would be $8,000, and salvage value is estimated at $1,500. Two lease options are available: A requires a downpayment of $4,000 initially and an annual payment of $1,000; B requires an initial payment of $5,000 and an annual payment of $600. The firm's cost of capital is 14 percent. Which alternative is best?

4. City Hospital is currently involved in a campaign to update its X-ray diagnostic equipment. Two machines are being considered. Machine A would require an initial investment of $24,000 and return $5,000 yearly for 10 years. Machine B would return $6,000 per year for 12 years with an initial investment of $30,000. Assume the cost of capital is 12 percent. Determine the present value of each machine for these cases:

    a. Neither machine has any salvage value.

    b. A will have a salvage value of $4,000, and B will have a salvage value of $3,000.

5. Determine the payback periods for machines A and B in the preceding problem.

6. Determine the internal rate of return for each of the investment proposals shown below.

		Proposal	
	A	*B*	*C*
Initial amount. . .	$60,000	$60,000	$50,000
Cash flow			
(per year)			
1	20,000	20,000	20,000
2	30,000	40,000	20,000
3	30,000	30,000	20,000
4	10,000	−10,000	20,000

7. Compute the present value for each proposal in the previous problem using a cost of capital of 18 percent.

8. Commercial Utilities is considering a proposed $6.4-million coal-fired power plant, which will have an expected operating life of 30 years. Estimated annual returns after taxes and depreciation are $0.8 million for the first 10 years, $1.0 million for the next 5 years, and $0.7 million for the remaining years. A salvage value of $2.0 million is projected.

    a. Determine the present value of the proposal for interest rates of (1) 12 percent and (2) 16 percent.

    b. What is the approximate internal rate of return for the power plant?

    c. Determine the payback period for this investment.

9. A bank manager of a suburban branch of a large savings bank is currently considering two proposals for meeting increased demand for bank services. Proposal 1 would involve a remodeling of the bank; proposal 2 would involve installation of automatic equipment and different processing routines than are now being used. Substantial retraining costs would be associated with the second proposal. The manager foresees three possible future states of nature, *A, B,* and *C,* with estimated likelihoods of .20 for *A,* .30 for *B,* and .50 for *C.* Net cash flows under each state of nature for each proposal's life are shown below. If the manager's decision criterion is maximum expected present value, which proposal should be selected? Why? Assume a cost of capital of 16 percent.

Remodel: Initial cost = $80,000.

Year	*A*	*B*	*C*
1	$40*	$60	$50
2	40	60	50
3	40	40	50
4	40	30	50
5	40	20	−10

* Net cash flows in $000s.

Automate: Initial cost = $120,000.

Year	*A*	*B*	*C*
1	$50	$40	$40
2	50	45	40
3	50	50	50
4	50	55	60
5	50	60	60

SELECTED BIBLIOGRAPHY

Anthony, Robert N., and James S. Reece. *Management Accounting Principles.* 3d ed. Homewood, Ill.: Richard D. Irwin, 1975.

Bierman, H., and S. Smidt. *The Capital Budgeting Decision.* 6th ed. New York: Macmillan, 1984.

Chase, Richard B., and Nicholas J. Aquilano. *Production and Operations Management.* 4th ed. Homewood, Ill.: Richard D. Irwin, 1985.

Grant, Eugene L.; W. Grant Ireson; and Richard R. Leavenworth. *Principles of Engineering Economy.* 6th ed. New York: Ronald Press, 1976.

Horngren, Charles T. *Cost Accounting: A Managerial Emphasis.* 4th ed. Englewood Cliffs, N.J.: Prentice-Hall, 1977.

Weston, J. Fred, and Eugene F. Brigham. *Essentials of Managerial Finance.* 4th ed. Hinsdale, Ill.: Dryden Press, 1979.

Chapter 5

Location Planning

After completing this chapter, you should be able to:

1. List some of the main reasons why organizations become involved in location decisions.
2. Explain why location decisions are important.
3. Discuss the options that are generally available in location decisions.
4. Describe some of the major factors that affect location decisions.
5. Outline the decision process that is generally followed in these kinds of decisions.
6. Use the techniques presented to solve typical problems.

THE NEED FOR LOCATION DECISIONS, 216

THE NATURE OF LOCATION DECISIONS, 217

Importance of Location Decisions, 217
Objectives of Location Decisions, 217
Location Options, 217

GENERAL PROCEDURE FOR MAKING LOCATION DECISIONS, 218

FACTORS THAT AFFECT LOCATION DECISIONS, 219

Regional Factors, 219
Community Considerations, 222
Site-Related Factors, 223

EVALUATING LOCATION ALTERNATIVES, 225

Locational Break-Even Analysis, 225
The Transportation Model, 227
Factor Rating, 228

SUMMARY 229

SOLVED PROBLEMS, 231

DISCUSSION AND REVIEW QUESTIONS, 232

PROBLEMS, 232

SELECTED BIBLIOGRAPHY, 234

CASE: RADIO SHACK INTERNATIONAL, 234

SUPPLEMENT: THE TRANSPORTATION MODEL, 237

When a well-known real estate broker was asked what the three most important determinants of value of a property are, he said, "That's easy. Location, location, and location."

Evidently in the residential market, location is a rather important factor. Although factors such as the style of house, number of bedrooms and bathrooms, how well it has been maintained, and how modern the kitchen is undoubtedly enter into the picture, obviously some locations will be more desirable than others.

In many respects, the choice of location for a business organization is every bit as important as it is for a house, although for different reasons.

Location decisions represent an integral part of the strategic planning process of virtually every organization. Although it might appear that location decisions are mostly one-time problems pertaining to new organizations, the fact is that existing organizations often have a bigger stake in these kinds of decisions than new organizations have.

This chapter explores the issue of location analysis. It begins with a brief overview of the reasons firms become involved in location decisions, the nature of these decisions, and a general procedure for developing and evaluating location alternatives.

THE NEED FOR LOCATION DECISIONS

Existing organizations become involved in location decisions for a variety of reasons. Firms such as banks, fast-food chains, supermarkets, and retail stores view locations as a marketing strategy, and they look for locations that will help them to expand their markets. Basically, the location decisions in those cases reflect *addition* of new locations to an existing system.

A similar situation occurs when an organization experiences a growth in demand for its products or services that cannot be satisfied by expansion at an existing location. The addition of a new location to complement an existing system is often a realistic alternative.

Some firms become involved in location decisions through depletion of basic inputs. For example, fishing and logging operations are often forced to relocate due to the temporary exhaustion of fish or forests at a given location. Mining operations and petroleum operations face the same sort of situation, although usually over a longer horizon.

For other firms, a shift in their markets causes them to consider relocation, or the costs of doing business at a particular location reach a point where other locations begin to look more attractive.

THE NATURE OF LOCATION DECISIONS

Location decisions for many types of businesses are made rather infrequently, but they tend to have a significant impact on the organization. In this section we shall look at the importance of location decisions, the usual objectives managers have when making location choices, and some of the options that are open to them.

Importance of Location Decisions

There are two primary reasons that make location decisions a highly important part of production systems design. One is that they entail a long-term commitment, which makes mistakes difficult to overcome. The other is that location decisions often have an impact on operating costs (both fixed and variable) and revenues as well as on operations. For instance, a poor choice of location might result in excessive transportation costs, a shortage of qualified labor, loss of competitive advantage, inadequate supplies of raw materials, or some similar condition that would be detrimental to operations.

Objectives of Location Decisions

As a general rule, profit-oriented organizations base their decisions on profit potential, while nonprofit organizations strive to achieve a balance between cost and the level of customer service they provide. It would seem to follow, then, that these organizations would attempt to identify the "best" location available. However, this is not necessarily the case.

In many instances there may not be one location that is significantly better than the others. Or there may be numerous acceptable locations from which to choose, as evidenced by the fact that successful organizations can be found in a wide variety of locations. Furthermore, the number of possible locations that would have to be examined in order to find the best location would usually be too large to make an exhaustive search practical. Consequently, most organizations do not set out with the intention of identifying the *one best* location; rather, they hope to find a number of *acceptable* locations from which to choose—and to avoid choosing a location that will create future problems.

Location Options

There are essentially four options that managers can consider in location planning. One is to expand an existing facility. This option can be attractive if there is adequate room for expansion, especially if the location has desirable features that are not readily available elsewhere. Furthermore, expansion costs are often less than for other alternatives.

Another option is to add new locations while retaining existing ones, as is done in many retail operations. In such cases, it is essential to take into account what the impact will be on the *total system*.

For instance, opening a new store in a shopping mall may simply draw customers who already patronize an existing store in the same chain rather than expand the market. On the other hand, adding locations can be a defensive strategy designed to maintain a market share or to prevent competitors from entering a market.

A third option is to shut down at one location and move to another. An organization must weigh the costs of a move and the resulting benefits against the costs and benefits of remaining in an existing location. As previously mentioned, a shift in markets, exhaustion of raw materials, and the cost of operations often cause firms to seriously consider this option.

Finally, organizations have the option of doing nothing. If a detailed analysis of potential locations fails to uncover benefits that would make one of the previous three alternatives attractive, a firm may decide to maintain the status quo, at least in the short run.

GENERAL PROCEDURE FOR MAKING LOCATION DECISIONS

The way in which organizations approach location decisions often depends on the size of the organization and the nature or scope of its operations. New or small organizations tend to adopt a rather informal approach to location decisions. New firms typically locate in a certain area simply because that is where the owner lives. Similarly, managers of small firms often want to keep operations in their own backyard, so they tend to focus almost exclusively on local alternatives. Large established companies, particularly ones that already operate in more than one location, tend to take a more formal approach. Moreover, they generally consider a wider range of geographic locations. The discussion here pertains mainly to a formal approach to location decisions.

The general procedure for making location decisions usually consists of the following steps:

1. Determine the criteria that will be used to evaluate location alternatives, such as increased revenues or community service.
2. Identify factors that are important, such as location of markets or raw materials.
3. Develop location alternatives:
    a. Identify the general region for a location.
    b. Identify a small number of community-site alternatives.
4. Evaluate the alternatives and make a selection.

Step 1 is simply a matter of managerial preference. Steps 2 through 4 may need some elaboration.

FACTORS THAT AFFECT LOCATION DECISIONS

Many factors can influence location decisions. However, it often happens that one or a few factors are so important that they tend to dominate the location decision. For example, in manufacturing, the potentially dominating factors usually include availability of an abundant energy supply, abundant water supply, and nearness to raw materials. Thus, nuclear reactors require large amounts of water for cooling, heavy industries such as steel and aluminum production need large amounts of electricity, and so on. Transportation costs can also be a major factor in location decisions. In non-manufacturing organizations, possible dominating factors are market related and include such things as traffic patterns, convenience, and competitors' locations, as well as nearness to the market. For example, car rental agencies locate near airports and midcity, since that is where their business comes from.

Once the most important factors have been determined, organizations typically try to narrow the search for suitable alternatives to one geographic region. Then a small number of community-site alternatives are sought and subjected to detailed analysis. Community and site factors are often so intertwined that it makes more sense to consider them jointly than to attempt to first decide on a community and then try to find an acceptable site.

Regional Factors

The primary regional factors involve raw materials, markets, and labor considerations.

1. *Location of raw materials.* There are three primary reasons why firms locate near or at their source of raw materials: necessity, perishability, and transportation costs. In the *necessity* category are mining operations, farming, forestry, and fishing. Obviously, such operations must locate where the raw materials are. In the *perishability* category are canning or freezing of fresh fruit and vegetables, processing of dairy products, baking, and so on. *Transportation costs* are important in cases where processing eliminates much of the bulk connected with a raw material, making it much less expensive to transport the product or material after processing. Examples of this include aluminum reduction, cheese making, and paper production. In situations where inputs come from different locations, some firms choose to locate near the geographic center of the sources. For instance, steel producers use large quantities of coal and iron ore, and many are located somewhere between the Appalachian coal fields and places where the iron ore is mined. Transportation costs are often the reason that vendors locate near their major customers. Moreover, regional warehouses are used by supermarkets and other retail operations to supply multiple outlets.

Often the choice of new locations and additional warehouses reflect the locations of existing warehouses or retail outlets.

2. *Location of markets.* Profit-oriented firms often locate near the markets they intend to serve as part of their *competitive strategy,* while nonprofit organizations choose locations relative to the *needs of the users* of their services. Other factors sometimes include distribution costs or the perishability of a finished product.

Retail sales and services are usually found near the center of the markets they serve. Examples include fast-food restaurants, service stations, dry cleaners, and supermarkets. Quite often their products and those of their competitors are so similar that they rely on convenience to attract customers. Hence, these businesses seek locations with high population densities or high traffic. The competition/convenience factor is also important in locating banks, hotels and motels, auto repair shops, drugstores, newspaper boxes, and shopping centers. Similarly, doctors, dentists, and lawyers typically serve clients who reside within a limited area, as do barbers and beauticians.

Competitive pressures for retail operations can be extremely important factors. In some situations a market served by a particular location may be too small to justify two or more competitors (e.g., one hamburger stand per block), so that a search for potential locations would tend to concentrate on locations without competitors. In other cases the opposite might be true: it could be desirable to locate near competitors. Large department stores often locate near each other, and small stores like to locate in shopping centers with large "anchor" stores. The large stores are able to attract large numbers of shoppers who become potential purchasers in the smaller stores or in the other large stores.

Some firms must locate close to their markets because of the perishability of their products. Examples include bakeries, flower shops, and stores that sell fresh seafood. For other types of firms, distribution costs are the main factor in closeness to market. For example, sand and gravel dealers usually serve a limited area because of the high distribution costs associated with their products. Still other firms require close customer contact, so they too tend to locate within the area they expect to serve. Typical examples include tailor shops, home remodeling, home repair services, cabinet making, rug cleaning, and lawn and garden services.

Locations of many government services are near the markets they are designed to serve. Hence, post offices are typically scattered throughout large metropolitan areas. Police, fire, and emergency health care locations are frequently selected on the basis of client needs. For instance, fire stations would tend to locate in areas of high hazards, police patrols often concentrate on high crime areas, and emergency health care facilities are usually found in central locations because they provide ready access from all directions.

3. *Labor factors.* The primary labor considerations relate to the cost and availability of labor, wage rates in an area, labor productivity and attitudes toward work, and whether there is a serious potential for problems with unions.

Labor costs can be very important for organizations that are labor-intensive. The shift of the textile industry from the New England states to southern states was partly due to labor costs.

Skills of potential employees may be a factor, although some companies prefer to train their new employees rather than to rely on previous experience alone. Increasing specialization in many industries makes this possibility even more likely than in the past. While most companies concentrate on the supply of blue-collar workers, some firms are more interested in scientific and technical people as potential employees, and they look for areas with high concentrations of those types of workers.

Worker attitudes towards turnover, absenteeism, and similar factors may differ among potential locations. For example, workers in large urban centers may exhibit different attitudes than workers who reside in small towns or in rural areas. Furthermore, attitudes in different parts of the country, or in different countries, may be markedly different in this respect.

Some companies offer their current employees jobs when they move to a new location. However, in many instances employees are reluctant to move, especially if it means leaving families and friends. Furthermore, in families with two wage earners, relocation would require that one wage earner must give up a job and then attempt to find another job in the new location.

4. *Other factors.* Climate and taxes sometimes play a role in location decisions. For example, a string of unusually severe winters may cause some firms to seriously consider moving to a milder climate, especially if delayed deliveries and work disruptions caused by inability of employees to get to work have been frequent occurrences. Similarly, the business and personal income taxes in some northern states reduce their attractiveness as potential places for companies seeking new locations. Many companies have been attracted to the Sun Belt states by ample supplies of low-cost energy or labor, by the climate, and by tax considerations.

The growth in multinational operations over the past several decades is evidence of the importance of foreign locations. Some firms are attracted to *foreign locations* because those countries have important deposits of aluminum, copper, timber, oil, or other natural resources. Other firms view foreign locations as a way to expand their markets, while still others are attracted by ample supplies of labor. Some countries may offer financial incentives to companies in order to create jobs for their people. Developing countries may establish tariffs to protect their young industries from outside competition, which may also reduce the amount of "foreign" competition a firm must face if it located in such a country. However, the Fisher-Price Toy Company factory in Atamoros, Mexico is not allowed to sell the Muppet toys it makes in Mexico. In fact, under a trade agreement between the United States and Mexico, U.S. companies are encouraged to locate factories in Mexico and allowed to import raw materials duty-free, but they are required to export all of their output.

Many developing countries offer an abundant supply of cheap labor. For example, most of the clothes sold in the United States carry labels indicating that they were made in Korea, Hong Kong, or Taiwan. In some instances it can be less expensive to ship raw materials or semifinished goods to foreign countries for fabrication and assembly and then to ship them to their final destinations than to produce them in the United States. However, it is essential to recognize that the final cost per unit is the most important factor. In many cases the low cost of labor in a foreign country can be offset by low productivity; although labor costs in the United States are often high by foreign standards, *U.S. productivity is among the highest in the world.*

A firm contemplating a foreign location must carefully weigh the potential benefits against the potential problems it might encounter. One of the major factors is the stability of a country's government and its attitude towards American firms. Import restrictions can pose problems in terms of bringing in equipment and spare parts.

Some of the potential problems with a foreign location relate to language and cultural differences between the United States and the host country. American firms often find it necessary to use American technical personnel, but find that it is sometimes difficult to convince workers to move to a foreign country because they may have to leave their families behind or else subject them to substandard housing or educational systems. Companies usually exert additional efforts to reduce these obstacles. They are also improving their efforts to see to it that the people they send abroad are familiar with local customs and have a reasonable facility with the language of the host country.

Community Considerations

Many communities actively try to attract new businesses because they are viewed as potential sources of future taxes and as sources of new job opportunities. However, communities do not, as a rule, want firms that are going to create pollution problems or otherwise lessen the quality of life in the community. Local groups may actively seek to exclude certain companies on such grounds, and a considerable amount of effort may be required on the part of the company to convince local officials that the company will be a "responsible citizen." Furthermore, some organizations discover that even though overall community attitude is favorable, there may still be considerable opposition to specific sites from nearby residents who object to possible increases in levels of noise, traffic, or pollution. Examples of this include resistance to airport expansion, changes in zoning, construction of nuclear facilities, and highway construction.

From a company standpoint, there are a number of factors that determine the desirability of a community as a place for its workers and managers to live. They include facilities for education, shopping, recreation, transportation, religious worship, entertainment, the quality of police, fire, and medical services, local attitudes towards the company, and the size of the community. Community size can be particularly important if a firm will be a major employer in the community, because a future decision to terminate or reduce operations in that location could have a serious impact on the local economy.

Other community-related factors involve the cost and availability of utilities, environmental regulations, taxes (state and local, direct and indirect), and existence of development support (bond issues, tax abatement, low-cost loans, and grants).

Site-Related Factors

The primary considerations related to sites involve land, transportation, and zoning or other restrictions.

Evaluation of potential sites may require consulting with engineers or architects, especially in the case of heavy manufacturing, or when large buildings or facilities with special requirements are to be erected. Soil conditions, load factors, and drainage rates can be critical and often necessitate certain kinds of expertise in evaluation.

Because of the long-term commitment usually required, land costs may be secondary to other site-related factors, such as room for future expansion, current utility and sewer capacities and any limitations on these that could hinder future growth, and sufficient parking space for employees and customers. In addition many firms find access roads for trucks or rail spurs important.

Industrial parks may be worthwhile alternatives for firms involved in light manufacturing or assembly work, as well as for warehouse operations and customer service facilities. Typically the land is already developed, power, water, and sewer hookups have been attended to, and zoning restrictions do not require special attention. On the negative side, industrial parks may place restrictions on the kinds of activities that can be conducted there, and that can limit options for future development of a firm's products and services as well as the processes it can consider. In addition, in some cases there can be rather stringent regulations governing the size, shape, and architectural features of buildings, which limits managerial choice in these matters, and there may not be an adequate allowance for possible future expansion.

For firms with executives who travel frequently, the size and nearness of the airport or train station as well as travel connections can be important, although schedules and connections are subject to change.

A summary of the factors that affect location decisions is provided in Table 5–1.

TABLE 5–1

Factors that Affect Location Decisions

Level	Factors	Considerations
Region/country	Location of raw materials or supplies	Proximity, modes and costs of transportation, quantity available
	Location of markets	Proximity, distribution costs, target market, trade practices/restrictions
	Labor	Availability (general and for specific skills), age distribution of work force, attitudes toward work, union or nonunion, productivity, wage scales, unemployment compensation laws
Community	Facilities	Schools, churches, shopping, housing, transportation, entertainment, etc.
	Services	Medical, fire and police
	Attitudes	Pro/con
	Taxes	State/local, direct and indirect
	Environmental regulations	State/local
	Utilities	Cost and availability
	Development support	Bond issues, tax abatement, low-cost loans, grants
Site	Land	Cost, degree of development required, soil characteristics, room for expansion, drainage, parking
	Transportation	Type (access roads, rail spurs, air freight)
	Environmental/legal	Zoning restrictions

EVALUATING LOCATION ALTERNATIVES

This section contains descriptions of two techniques that can be used to help managers evaluate location alternatives. The first technique is an extension of cost-volume analysis and relates to evaluation on economic terms. The second approach is more general in that it offers managers a way to combine both qualitative and quantitative inputs in the decision framework.

Locational Break-Even Analysis

The economic comparison of location alternatives is facilitated by the use of cost-volume-profit analysis, which is referred to as *locational break-even analysis*. The analysis can be done numerically or graphically. The graphical approach will be demonstrated here because it enhances understanding of the concept and because it provides an indication of the ranges over which one of the alternatives is superior to the others.

The procedure for locational break-even analysis involves these steps:

1. Determine the fixed costs and the variable costs associated with each location alternative.
2. Plot the total cost lines for all location alternatives on the same graph.
3. Determine which location has the lowest total cost for the expected level of output.

This method assumes the following:

1. Fixed costs are constant for the range of probable output.
2. Variable costs are linear for the range of probable output.
3. The required level of output can be closely estimated.
4. Only one product is involved.

EXAMPLE 1

Fixed and variable costs for four potential plant locations are shown below:

Location	Fixed cost per year	Variable cost per unit
A	$250,000	$11
B	110,000	30
C	150,000	20
D	200,000	35

a. Plot the total cost curves for these locations on a single graph.
b. Identify the range of output for which each alternative is superior (i.e., has the lowest total cost).

EXAMPLE 1 (continued)

c. If expected output at the selected location is to be 8,000 units per year, which location would provide the lowest total cost?

Solution

a. To plot the total cost lines, select an output that is approximately equal to the expected output level (e.g., 10,000 units per year). Compute the total cost for each location at that level:

Fixed cost + Variable cost = Total cost

A	$250,000 +	$11(10,000) =	$360,000
B	100,000 +	30(10,000) =	400,000
C	150,000 +	20(10,000) =	350,000
D	200,000 +	35(10,000) =	550,000

Plot each location's fixed cost (at Output = 0) and the total cost at $10,000 and connect with a straight line. (See the accompanying graph.)

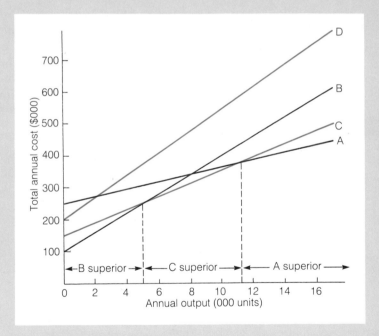

b. The *approximate* range for which the various alternatives will yield the lowest costs are shown on the graph. Note that location D is never superior. The *exact* ranges can be determined by finding the output level at which lines *B* and *C* and lines *C* and *A* cross. To do this, set their total cost equations equal and solve for *Q*, the break-even output level. Thus, for *B* and *C* we have:

EXAMPLE 1 *(concluded)*

$$
\begin{array}{cc}
(B) & (C) \\
\$100,000 + \$30Q = \$150,000 + \$20Q
\end{array}
$$

Solving for Q, we find $Q = 5,000$ units per year.
   For C and A we have:

$$
\begin{array}{cc}
(C) & (A) \\
\$150,000 + \$20Q = \$250,000 + \$11Q
\end{array}
$$

Solving for Q, we find $Q = 11,111$ units per year.
  c. From the graph we can see that for 8,000 units per year location
    C would provide the lowest total cost.

In a situation where the expected level of output is close to the middle of the range over which an alternative is superior, the choice is readily apparent. If the expected level of output is very close to the edge of a range, that simply means that the two alternatives will yield comparable annual costs, and so management would be indifferent in choosing between the two *in terms of total cost*. However, it is important to recognize that in most situations, other factors besides costs must also be considered. A general scheme for including a broad range of factors is presented later in this section. Before turning to that, let's consider another kind of cost that is often considered in location decisions, transportation costs.

The Transportation Model

Transportation costs sometimes play an important role in location decisions. These can stem from either the movement of raw materials or the movement of finished goods. If the facility will be a sole source or destination of the shipments, then the transportation costs can be included in a locational break-even analysis by incorporating the transportation cost per unit being shipped into the variable cost per unit. (If raw materials are involved, the transportation cost must be converted into *unit costs* in terms of units of *output* in order to correspond to other variable costs.)

When a problem involves shipments of goods from multiple sending points to multiple receiving points and a new location (sending or receiving point) is to be added to the system, a separate analysis of transportation should be undertaken. In such instances the *transportation model* of linear programming can be very helpful. It is a special-purpose algorithm that can be used to determine the minimum possible transportation cost that would result if a potential new location were to be added to an existing system. It can also be used if a *number* of new facilities are to be added or if an entire new system is being developed. The model is used to analyze each of the configurations being considered, and it reveals the minimum costs that each would entail. This information can then be included in the evaluation of location alternatives.

A description of the procedure for the transportation model and examples of its use in location decisions are the subject of the supplement to this chapter. A solved problem at the end of this chapter illustrates how results of a transportation analysis can be combined with the results of a locational break-even analysis.

Factor Rating   A typical location decision involves both qualitative and quantitative inputs, and these tend to vary from situation to situation depending on the needs of each particular organization. *Factor rating* is a general approach that is useful both for evaluating a given alternative and for comparing alternatives. The value of factor rating is that it provides a rational basis for evaluation and it facilitates comparison among alternatives by establishing a *composite* value for each alternative that summarizes all related factors. Factor rating enables decision makers to incorporate their personal opinions as well as quantitative information into the decision process.

The following procedure is used to develop a factor rating:

1. Determine the factors that are relevant (e.g., location of market, water supply, parking facilities, revenue potential).
2. Assign a weight to each factor that indicates its relative importance compared to all other factors. Typically, weights sum to 1.00.
3. Decide on a common scale for each factor (e.g., 0 to 100).
4. Score each location alternative.
5. Multiply the factor weight by the score for each factor, and sum the results for each location alternative.
6. Choose the alternative with the highest composite score. This procedure is illustrated in the next example.

EXAMPLE 2

A small manufacturing firm has recently decided to expand its operations to include several new lines, which it hopes to produce in a separate location because of space limitations in its existing plant. The rating sheet shown on the next page illustrates relevant factors, factor weightings, and actual ratings for two alternative locations, along with the necessary computations to obtain composite scores for each alternative.

EXAMPLE 2 *(concluded)*
Rating Analysis Worksheet

Factor	Weight	Scores (out of 100)		Weighted scores	
		Alt. 1	Alt. 2	Alternative 1	Alternative 2
Nearness to raw material	.10	100	60	.10(100) = 10.0	.10(60) = 6.0
Labor costs	.05	80	80	.05(80) = 4.0	.05(80) = 4.0
Water supply	.40	70	90	.40(70) = 28.0	.40(90) = 36.0
Transportation costs	.10	86	92	.10(86) = 8.6	.10(92) = 9.2
Climate	.20	40	70	.20(40) = 8.0	.20(70) = 14.0
Taxes	.15	80	90	.15(80) = 12.0	.15(90) = 13.5
	1.00			70.6	82.7

Thus, Alternative 2 is better because it has the higher composite score.

In some cases managers may prefer to establish minimum *thresholds* for composite scores. If an alternative fails to meet that minimum, it can be rejected without further consideration. If none of the alternatives meet the minimum, this means that either additional alternatives must be identified and evaluated, or that the minimum threshold must be reevaluated.

SUMMARY

Location decisions confront both new and existing organizations. Factors such as growth, market shifts, depletion of raw materials, and the introduction of new products and services are some of the reasons organizations become involved with location decisions. The importance of these decisions is underscored by the long-term commitment they typically involve and by their potential impact on the operating system.

The primary options available to existing organizations in terms of location are to expand an existing location, move to a new location completely, or maintain existing facilities while adding another facility in a new location.

Among the major factors that influence location decisions in practice are location of raw materials and sources of supply, labor supply, market considerations, community-related factors, site-related factors, and climate. Foreign locations may be attractive in terms of labor costs, abundance of raw materials, or as potential markets for a firm's products or services. Problems that are sometimes encountered in foreign countries involve language differences, cultural differences, anti-American sentiments, and political instability.

A common approach to narrowing the range of location alternatives is to first identify a country or region that seems to satisfy overall needs and then to identify a number of community-site alternatives for more in-depth analysis. There are a variety of methods used to evaluate location alternatives. The ones described in the chapter include locational break-even analysis and factor rating. The transportation model is briefly mentioned, and a more complete description of it is the subject of the chapter supplement.

1. A farm implements dealer is seeking a fourth warehouse location to complement three existing warehouses. There are three potential locations: Charlotte, Atlanta, and Columbia, S.C. Charlotte would involve a fixed cost of $4,000 per month and a variable cost of $4 per unit; Atlanta would involve fixed costs of $3,500 per month and a variable cost of $5 per unit; and Columbia would involve a fixed cost of $5,000 per month and a variable cost of $6 per unit. Use of the Charlotte location would increase system transportation costs by $19,000 per month, while Atlanta would add $22,000 per month and Columbia would add $18,000 per month to transportation costs. Which location would result in the lowest total cost to handle 800 units per month?

Solution

Given: Volume = 800 units per month

	FC per month	VC per unit	Transportation cost per month
Charlotte	$4,000	$4	$19,000
Atlanta	3,500	5	22,000
Columbia	5,000	6	18,000

Monthly total cost = FC + VC + Transportation cost

Charlotte:	$4,000 + $4 per unit × 800 units + $19,000 = $26,200
Atlanta:	3,500 + 5 per unit × 800 units + 22,000 = 29,500
Columbia:	5,000 + 6 per unit × 800 units + 18,000 = 27,800

Hence, Charlotte would result in the lowest total cost for this monthly volume.

2. A small printing firm is about to lose its lease, so it must move to another location. Two sites are currently under consideration. Site A would have fixed costs of $8,000 per month, while site B would have fixed costs of $9,400 per month. Variable costs are expected to be $5 per unit at site A and $4 per unit at site B. Monthly demand has been steady at 8,800 units for the last several years and is not expected to deviate from that amount in the foreseeable future. Assume units sell for $6 per unit. Determine which location would yield the higher profits under these conditions.

Solution

Profit = (Revenue per unit) × Q − [FC + (VC per unit) × Q]

Site	Revenue	FC	VC	Monthly profit
A	$52,800	$8,000	$44,000	$ 800
B	$52,800	$9,400	$35,200	$8,200

Hence, site B is expected to yield the higher monthly profit.

231

DISCUSSION AND REVIEW QUESTIONS

1. In what ways can the location decision have an impact on the productive system?
2. How would you respond to this statement? "The importance of the location decision is often vastly overrated; the fact that virtually every type of business is located in every section of the country means there should be no problem in finding a suitable location."
3. What are the community factors that influence location decisions?
4. In what ways are manufacturing and non-manufacturing location decisions similar? Different?
5. What are some of the potential benefits of locating in foreign countries? What are some of the possible drawbacks?
6. What is location rating and how does it work?
7. Outline the general approach for developing location alternatives.
8. What are the basic assumptions in locational break-even analysis?

PROBLEMS

1. A newly formed firm must decide on a plant location. There are two alternatives under consideration: locate near the major raw materials or locate near the major customers. Locating near the raw materials will result in lower fixed and variable costs than locating near the market, but the owners feel there would be a loss in sales volume because of the tendency of customers to favor local suppliers. Revenue per unit will be $185 in either case. Using the information below, determine which location would produce the greater profit.

	Omaha	Kansas City
Annual fixed costs ($ millions)	$1.2	$1.4
Variable cost per unit	$36	$47
Expected annual demand (units)	8,000	12,000

2. The owner of Genuine Subs, Inc., hopes to expand her present operation by adding one new outlet. Three locations have been studied. Each would have the same labor and material costs (food, serving containers, napkins, etc.) of $0.76 cents per sandwich. Sandwiches sell for $1.65 each in all locations. Rent and equipment costs would be $5,000 per month for location A, $5,500 per month for B, and $5,800 per month for location C.

   a. Determine the volume necessary at each location in order to realize a monthly profit of $10,000.
   b. If expected sales at A, B, and C are 21,000 per month, 22,000 per month, and 23,000 per month, respectively, which location would yield the greatest profits?

3. A small producer of machine tools wants to move to a larger building. Two alternatives have been identified. Location A would have fixed costs of $800,000 per year and variable costs of $14,000 per unit, while Location B would have annual fixed costs of $920,000 and variable costs of $13,000 per unit. The finished items sell for $17,000 each.

   a. At what volume of output would the two locations have the same total cost?
   b. For what range of output would location A be superior? For what range would B be superior?

4. A company that produces pleasure boats has recently decided to expand one of its lines. Current facilities are insufficient to handle the increased work load, so the company is considering three alternatives, A (new location), B (subcontract), and C (expand existing facilities).

Alternative A would involve substantial fixed costs but relatively low variable costs; fixed costs would be $250,000 per year, and variable costs would be $500 per boat. Subcontracting would involve a cost per boat of $2,500, while expansion would require an annual fixed cost of $50,000 and a variable cost of $1,000 per boat.

a. For what range of output would each alternative yield the lowest total cost?

b. Which alternative would yield the lowest total cost for an expected annual volume of 150 boats?

c. What other factors might be considered in choosing between expansion and subcontracting?

5. Rework part *b* of the previous problem using this additional information: Expansion would result in an increase of $70,000 per year in transportation costs, subcontracting would result in an increase of $25,000 per year, and adding a new location would result in an increase of $4,000 per year.

6. A firm that has recently experienced an enormous growth rate is seeking to lease a small plant in either Memphis, Biloxi, or Birmingham. Prepare an economic analysis of the three locations given the following information: Annual costs for building, equipment, and administration would be $40,000 for Memphis, $60,000 for Biloxi, and $100,000 for Birmingham. Labor and material are expected to be $8 per unit in Memphis, $4 per unit in Biloxi, and $5 per unit in Birmingham. The Memphis location would increase system transportation costs by $50,000 per year, the Biloxi location would increase them by $60,000 per year, and the Birmingham location would increase those costs by $25,000 per year. Expected annual volume is 10,000 units.

7. A retired auto mechanic hopes to open his own rustproofing shop. Customers would be area new car dealers. Two locations are being considered, one in the center of the city and one on the outskirts of the city. The in-city location would involve fixed monthly costs of $7,000 and labor, materi-

als, and transportation costs of $30 per car. The outside location would have fixed monthly costs of $4,700 and labor, materials, and transportation costs of $40 per car. Dealer price at either location will be $90 per car.

a. Which location will yield the greatest profit if monthly demand is (1) 200 cars? (2) 300 cars?

b. At what volume of output will the two sites yield the same monthly profit?

8. For each of the four types of organizations shown, rate the importance of each of the factors listed, using L = Low importance, M = Moderate importance, and H = High importance, in terms of making location decisions.

Factor	Local bank	Steel mill	Food warehouse	Public school
1. Convenience for customers				
2. Attractiveness of building				
3. Nearness to raw materials				
4. Large amounts of power				
5. Pollution controls				
6. Labor cost and availability				
7. Transportation costs				
8. Construction costs				

9. Using the factor ratings shown below, determine which location alternative should be chosen on the basis of maximum composite score, A, B, or C.

Factor (100 points each)	Weight	A	B	C
Convenient.	.15	80	70	60
Parking facilities	.20	72	76	92
Display area	.18	88	90	90
Shopper traffic	.27	94	86	80
Operating costs	.10	98	90	82
Neighborhood.	.10	96	85	75
	1.00			

10. A manager has received an analysis of several cities being considered for a new

office complex. The data (10 points maximum) are:

Factor	Location		
	A	B	C
Business services	9	5	5
Community services	7	6	7
Real estate cost	3	8	7
Construction costs	5	6	5
Cost of Living	4	7	8
Taxes	5	5	4
Transportation	6	7	8

a. If the manager weights the factors equally, how would the locations stack up?

b. If business services and construction costs are given weights that are double the weights of the others, how would the locations stack up?

SELECTED BIBLIOGRAPHY

Adam, Everette E., Jr., and Ronald J. Ebert. *Production and Operations Management: Concepts, Models and Behavior.* Englewood Cliffs, N.J.: Prentice-Hall, 1978.

Buffa, E. S. *Operations Management: Problems and Models.* 3d ed. New York: John Wiley & Sons, 1972.

————, and A. E. Bogardy. "When Should a Company Manufacture Abroad?" *California Management Review,* 2, 1060.

————, and J. S. Dyer. *Management Science/Operations Research: Model Formulation and Solution Methods.* Santa Barbara, Calif: Wiley/Hamilton, 1977.

Reed, R., Jr. *Plant Location, Layout, and Maintenance.* Homewood, Ill.: Richard D. Irwin, 1967.

Schmenner, R. W. "Look Beyond the Obvious in Plant Location." *Harvard Business Review,* January–February 1979, pp. 126–32.

Schollhammer, H. *Locational Strategies of Multinational Firms.* Los Angeles: Center for International Business, Los Angeles World Trade Center, 1974.

"What Management Needs to Know before Picking a Plant Site." *Dun's Review,* October 1979, p. 14 ff.

Case

Radio Shack International *

In 1973, Radio Shack opened its first European store in Belgium. In 1977, the organization had 459 overseas outlets but had not added

---

* "Radio Shack's Rough Trip," *Business Week,* May 30, 1977, p. 55. Reproduced by permission from *The Modern Manager* by Edgar F. Huse, copyright © 1979 by West Publishing Company. All rights reserved.

a new store in 18 months. In addition, it had lost $21 million from its European operations in the previous three years.

Charles D. Tandy had spent 13 years building Radio Shack into the leading merchandiser of amateur electronic gear in the United States. He bought Radio Shack Corporation in 1963 when it was in trouble. In the first nine months of fiscal 1977, the 6,000-store chain had earnings of $56.2 million on revenues of $732.6 million— respective increases of 14 percent and 32 percent. Retail stores accounted for 95 percent of the company's earnings and revenues.

Radio Shack's success in the United States appears to be a combination of well-located stores, discount prices, a wide product mix, and heavy advertising. Charles Tandy believes that this approach will work in Europe and that the four years of heavy losses are only temporary. Basically, he says, "I see nothing different about the people in Europe from the people in the United States." As a result, he plans to continue with the same strategies.

Others suggest that the problem is more fundamental—that discounting methods that work in the United States will not attract Europeans, who are highly brand and quality conscious. In a blitz operation, the European market was blanketed with hundreds of stores, many in poor locations.

In many cases, local laws and customs were overlooked or disregarded. When the first store was opened in Belgium, for example, Tandy overlooked a law that requires a government tax stamp on window signs. In Holland, the first Christmas promotion was geared to December 25. The company was not aware that the Dutch exchange holiday gifts on St. Nicholas Day, usually celebrated on December 6. In Germany, one of the biggest losses occurred when Radio Shack gave away flashlights to promote its stores—and was served with an injunction for violating German sales laws.

In the United States, citizens band radios are Radio Shack's best-selling item, accounting for 22 percent of sales. Belgium, Britain, and Holland bar citizens band radios; and various laws have curbed the sale of other items as well.

European competitors suggest that Europeans are willing to pay premium prices for top quality items and that Radio Shack's image as a discount house keeps customers away. The quality image is especially strong in France, where Radio Shack has only eight stores (none of which is in Paris).

Despite the losses, sales are slowly increasing; and Tandy is optimistic that his basic strategy will work. In fact, he predicts that the foreign operation will be profitable in two years.

Questions

1. How might planning be different in Europe than in the United States?

2. What recommendations would you have for Tandy after reading this chapter? Is he being optimistic or realistic in his planning?

3. What steps would you take to increase sales and profitability? What would you want to know about the different European countries?

4. What implications does this case have for other international operations?

The Transportation Model

INTRODUCTION 238

OBTAINING AN INITIAL SOLUTION, 240
    The Northwest-Corner Method, 240
    The Vogel Approximation Method, 242
    The Intuitive Approach, 245

TESTING FOR OPTIMALITY, 246
    Evaluating Empty Cells: The Stepping-Stone Method 247
    Evaluating Empty Cells: The MODI Method, 253

OBTAINING AN IMPROVED SOLUTION, 255

SPECIAL PROBLEMS, 259
    Unequal Supply and Demand, 259
    Degeneracy, 262

SUMMARY OF PROCEDURE, 263
LOCATION DECISIONS, 263
OTHER APPLICATIONS, 266
SOLVED PROBLEMS, 267
DISCUSSION AND REVIEW QUESTIONS, 273
PROBLEMS, 273
SELECTED BIBLIOGRAPHY, 275

INTRODUCTION

The transportation model is a technique that identifies the lowest cost plan for distributing stocks of goods or *supplies* from multiple origins to multiple destinations that *demand* the goods. For instance, a firm might have three factories that are all capable of producing *identical* units of the same product and four warehouses that stock or demand those products, as depicted in Figure 5S–1. The transportation model can be used to determine how to allocate the supplies available from the various factories to the warehouses that stock or demand those goods in such a way that total shipping cost (time, distance, etc.) is minimized. Usually analysis of the problem will produce a shipping plan that pertains to a period of time (day, week), although once the plan is established, it would generally not change unless or until one or more of the parameters of the problem (supply, demand, unit shipping cost) changed.

While the diagram in Figure 5S–1 illustrates the nature of the problem, in many real-life cases managers must sometimes deal with allocation problems that are considerably larger in scope. For instance, consider the case of a beer maker with four or five breweries and hundreds or even thousands of distributors, or the case of an automobile manufacturer with eight assembly plants scattered throughout the United States and Canada and the thousands of

FIGURE 5S–1

The Transportation Problem Involves Determining an Optimum Arrangement for Shipping from Multiple Sources to Multiple Destinations

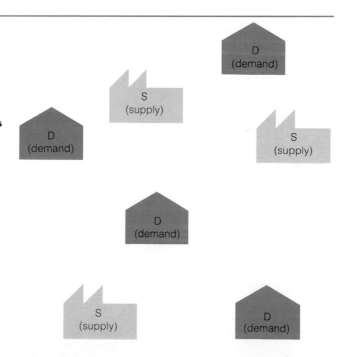

TABLE 5S–1

A Transportation Matrix

dealers that must be supplied with those cars. In such cases the ability to identify an optimal solution makes the transportation model quite important.

The shipping (supply) points can be factories, warehouses, departments, or any other place from which goods are sent. Destinations can be factories, warehouses, departments, or other points that receive goods. The information needed to use the model consists of the following:

1. A list of the origins and each one's capacity or supply quantity per period.
2. A list of the destinations and each one's demand per period.
3. The unit cost of shipping items from each origin to each destination.

This information is arranged into a *transportation matrix* such as the one shown in Table 5S–1.

The transportation model is one of a class of linear programming models, so named because of the linear relationships among problem variables. In the transportation model, transportation costs are treated as a direct linear function of the number of units shipped. For instance, if the unit cost to ship is $7 and 10 units are shipped, the cost would be 10($7) = $70. If 20 units are shipped, the cost would be 20($7) = $140. Hence, the cost per unit being shipped is the same regardless of the amount shipped.

Use of the transportation model implies that certain assumptions are satisfied. The major ones are:

1. The items to be shipped are homogeneous (i.e., are the same regardless of their source or destination).
2. Shipping cost per unit is the same regardless of the number of units shipped.
3. There is only one route or mode of transportation being used between each source and each destination.

The transportation method is an iterative process. It starts with the development of a feasible solution, which is then sequentially tested and improved until an optimum solution is obtained. The description of the technique on the following pages focuses on each of the major steps in the process in this order:

1. Obtaining an initial solution.
2. Testing the solution for optimality.
3. Improving suboptimal solutions.

OBTAINING AN INITIAL SOLUTION

In order to begin the process, it is necessary to develop a feasible distribution plan. There are a number of different methods for obtaining such a plan. The discussion here will focus on three widely used approaches: the northwest-corner method, the Vogel approximation method (VAM), and the intuitive approach. VAM is a heuristic approach that yields an initial solution which is often optimum or near-optimum. In many cases the intuitive approach also will do this. The northwest-corner method is much less efficient; it merely provides a convenient starting point. Even so, if offers an easy-to-understand approach that merits consideration. Each method will be demonstrated using the matrix illustrated in Table 5S–1.

These methods require that total supply equal total demand. If you refer to Table 5S–1, you will see that they are equal. Later you will learn what to do if they are not equal.

The Northwest-Corner Method

1. The northwest-corner method begins with the cell that is in the upper left-hand (northwest) corner of the matrix, allocating (assigning) as many units as possible to that cell. Factory 1 can supply 100 units, but warehouse A only needs 80 units. Hence, assign 80 units to cell 1–A, completely exhausting A's demand and leaving factory 1 with a supply of 20 units (see Table 5S–2).
2. Staying in row 1, moving to column B, we see that warehouse B has a demand for 90 units, 20 of which can be supplied

TABLE 5S–2

**Northwest-Corner
Solution**

by factory 1. Assigning 20 units to cell 1–B exhausts 1's supply and leaves warehouse B with a demand for 70 additional units.

3. Staying in column B and dropping down to row 2, we observe that factory 2 has a supply of 200 units. Assigning 70 units to cell 2–B satisfies B's demand and leaves factory 2 with 130 units.

4. Staying in row 2 and moving to column C, we observe that warehouse C has a demand for 120 units, which can be filled by factory 2. Assigning 120 units to cell 2–C satisfies C's demand and still leaves factory 2 with 10 units.

5. Staying in row 2 and moving to column D, we find that warehouse D has a demand of 160 units. Assigning 10 units to cell 2–D exhausts factory 2's supply and leaves D with a need for an additional 150 units.

6. The remaining demand of warehouse D for 150 units can be just satisfied by factory 3's supply. This is a consequence of starting with equal supply and demand. Hence, assign 150 units to be shipped from factory 3 to warehouse D.

Is this distribution plan optimum (i.e., does it minimize transportation costs)? In a moment we shall see how to test it to determine if further improvements are possible. In the meantime it will be instructive to compute the transportation costs associated with this initial solution. The cost for each cell is the product of units assigned to that cell and the unit transportation cost for the cell. Empty cells have no cost. Thus:

Total cost

1–A . . .	80($4)	=	$ 320
1–B . . .	20($7)	=	140
2–B . . .	70($3)	=	210
2–C . . .	120($8)	=	960
2–D . . .	10($8)	=	80
3–D . . .	150($5)	=	750
			$2,460

As previously mentioned, the northwest-corner method is merely a convenient way to obtain a feasible solution. Because it does not take costs into account, it frequently does not yield an optimum solution. Note, for example, that with the given supplies and demands, the same solution would be generated even if the costs were quite different. It will be interesting, then, to see how well the intuitive method and VAM do, since they explicitly take costs into account in obtaining an initial solution.

The Vogel Approximation Method

The *Vogel approximation method (VAM)* uses information about transportation costs in making distribution assignments. It does not consider costs directly. Instead, it focuses on the cost penalty that would be incurred if the second best cell in any row or column were used rather than the first. For example, in the problem being considered, the two lowest-cost cells in row 1 are $1 and $4. The *penalty* that would be incurred if for some reason cell 1–D were not used would be $4 − $1 = $3 per unit. In the VAM procedure the cost penalties for each row and column are determined. The largest penalty directs attention to a certain row or column in which to make the initial assignment. This process is repeated until all of the supplies have been allocated to cells.

TABLE 5S–3

Step 1 of VAM Solution: Compute Cost Penalty for Each Origin and Destination, and Identify the Largest Penalty (Circled)

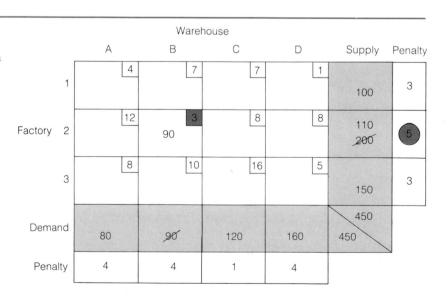

The actual procedure consists of the following steps:

1. Compute the difference between the two lowest costs in each row and column (see Table 5S–3).
2. Identify the row or column with the largest difference. In this case it is row 2 with a penalty of $5. (If a tie exists, select the row or column that has the cell with the smallest transportation cost. If a tie still exists, choose one arbitrarily.)
3. For the row or column selected, allocate as many units as possible to the cell with the lowest cost. Eliminate the row or column that is exhausted (satisfied) from further consideration. Cell 2–B has the lowest cost in row 2. Warehouse B has a demand of 90 units, and factory 2 has a supply of 200 units. Hence, the most that can be shipped is 90 units, and column B is eliminated from further consideration; see Table 5S–3.
4. Repeat steps 1–3 for the remaining rows, columns, and cells until the entire supply has been allocated (and demand has been satisifed, since it is assumed that supply and demand are equal).

The remaining allocations are made as follows. A second set of penalties is calculated for the remaining costs. There is a tie for the largest difference; both columns 1 and 4 have penalties of $4. Check each column to see which has the smallest cost. It is column

TABLE 5S–4

		Warehouse A	Warehouse B	Warehouse C	Warehouse D	Supply	Penalty 1	Penalty 2
Factory	1	4	7	7	1 / 100	~~100~~	3	3
	2	12	3 / 90	8	8	110 / ~~200~~	(5)	0
	3	8	10	16	5	150	3	3
Demand		80	~~90~~	120	60 / ~~160~~	450 / 450		
Penalty	1	4	4	1	4			
	2	4	–	1	(4)			

TABLE 5S–5

	Warehouse A	B	C	D	Supply	Penalty 1	2	3
Factory 1	4	7	7	1 100	~~100~~	3	3	—
Factory 2	12	3 90	8 110	8	~~110~~ ~~200~~	(5)	0	0
Factory 3	8 80	10	16 10	5 60	150	3	3	3
Demand	80	~~90~~	10 ~~120~~	60 ~~160~~	450 / 450			
Penalty 1	4	4	1	4				
Penalty 2	4	—	1	(4)				
Penalty 3	4	—	(8)	3				

4 with a cost in cell 1–D of $1. Allocate as many units as possible to that cell. Factory 1 has a supply of 100 while warehouse D has a demand of 160 units. Therefore, allocate 100 units. Eliminate row 1 from further consideration and adjust the demand of column D to reflect this allocation (see Table 5S–4).

Compute penalties for remaining rows and columns. The largest penalty is for column C with $8. The cell in column C with the smallest cost is cell 2–C. Allocate 110 units, which exhausts factory 2's supply and leaves warehouse C with a demand of 10 units, which still needs to be met (see Table 5S–5).

At this point only cells in the *last row* remain for consideration. Fill them as needed: 80 units in 3–A, 10 units in 3–C, and 60 units in 3–D. This completes the allocations. The VAM solution is shown in Table 5S–6.

Thus we have our initial feasible solution. Whether or not it can be improved upon must still be determined.

The total cost for this solution is computed as follows:

Cell	Quantity	Unit cost	Shipping cost
1–D	100	$ 1	$ 100
2–B	90	3	270
2–C	110	8	880
3–A	80	8	640
3–C	10	16	160
3–D	60	5	300
			$2,350

TABLE 5S–6

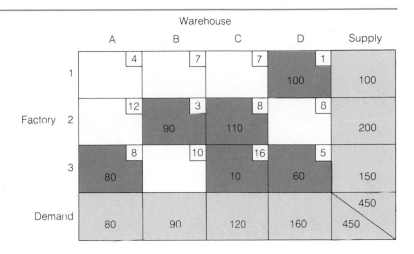

Note that this represents a saving of $110 over the northwest-corner solution, which had a total cost of $2,460.

The Intuitive Approach

This approach is somewhat similar to VAM in that it takes cell costs into consideration in making quantity assignments. The procedure involves the following:

1. Identify the cell with the lowest cost.
2. Allocate as many units as possible to that cell and cross out the row or column (or both) that is exhausted by this.
3. Find the cell with the next lowest cost from among the *feasible* cells.
4. Repeat steps 3 and 4 until all units have been allocated.

Thus, cell 1–D has the lowest cost ($1) (see Table 5S–7A), and we can allocate 100 units, which will exhaust the supply of factory 1 and rule out further consideration of any cells in that row. The next lowest cost is $3 in cell 2–B. Allocating 90 units exhausts the demand of warehouse B and leaves factory 2 with a supply of 110 units. The next lowest cost in a feasible cell is $5 in cell 3–D. Allocating 60 units exhausts the demand of D and leaves factory 3 with a supply of 90. Continuing in this manner, we end up with the shipping arrangement shown in Table 5S–7B, which is identical to that obtained using VAM. This is not always the case, but these approaches often yield the same initial solution when applied to elementary problems. Generally speaking, VAM is preferred because it is more likely to yield a better solution.

We must now determine if this initial solution obtained using VAM and the intuitive method is optimum.

TABLE 5S–7

A. Data from Table 5S–1

B. Initial Allocation Using Intuitive Approach

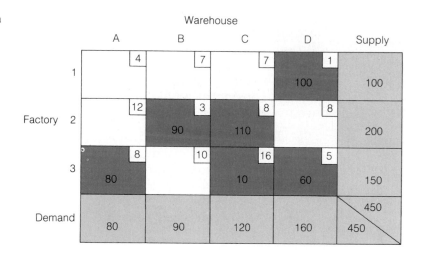

TESTING FOR OPTIMALITY

Testing for optimality and revising suboptimal solutions is the same regardless of how the initial solution was developed (e.g., northwest-corner method or VAM). The process involves analysis of each *unused* or empty cell to determine if there is a potential for reducing the total cost of the solution. This is accomplished by transferring one unit into an empty cell and noting the impact this has on costs. If costs are increased, then this implies that using the cell would increase total costs. If costs remain the same, this would imply that an alternative option with the same total cost as the current plan exists. However, if analysis reveals a cost decrease, this implies that an improved solution is possible. The test for optimality requires that *every* unused cell be evaluated for potential improvement. Either of two methods can be used: stepping-stone or MODI.

Evaluating Empty Cells: The Stepping-Stone Method

In the stepping-stone method, cell evaluation proceeds by borrowing one unit from a full cell and using it to assess the impact that shifting units into the empty cell would produce. For instance, if a shift of one unit causes an increase of $5, then it can be assumed that total costs would be increased by $5 times the number of units shifted into the cell. Obviously such a move would be unwise since the objective is to *decrease* costs.

The name *stepping-stone* derives from early descriptions of the method that likened the procedures to crossing a shallow pond by stepping from stone to stone. Here, the occupied cells are the "stones"; shifting units into empty cells requires borrowing units from occupied cells. In order to maintain the balance of supply and demand for every row and column, a shift of one unit into an empty cell requires a series of shifts from other occupied cells.

The best way to understand the evaluation process is to consider a simple example. Suppose we want to evaluate cell 1–A (see Table 5S–8). We must shift one unit into that cell, which would imply that one unit will be shipped from factory 1 to warehouse A. However, factory 1 has only 100 units it can ship, and all are allocated to warehouse D. Therefore, in order to ship one unit to A, we borrow a unit from cell 1–D. This creates two problems. One is that column A now has one extra unit and column D is short one unit (i.e., A has 1 + 80 = 81 units but needs only 80 units, and D has 99 + 60 = 159 but needs 160 units). We can remedy these problems by

TABLE 5S–8

Evaluation Path for Cell 1–A

subtracting one unit from cell 3–A and adding it to cell 3–D; this gives column A a total of $1 + 79 = 80$ and column D a total of $99 + 61 = 160$. (Note that instead of actually making each addition or subtraction of the one unit, a $+$ or $-$ sign is simply inserted in the appropriate cell to signify the operation.)

Let's see what effect such a shift would have on costs. For each cell that added a unit, the cost will increase by the transportation cost for that cell, while for cells that gave up a unit, costs will decrease by the cell's transportation cost. We can summarize this with a *T account* as follows.

Cell 1–A

	$+$		$-$
(1–A)	+4	(1–D)	−1
(3–D)	+5	(3–A)	−8
	+9		−9

0

Thus, shifting units around this path would have no impact whatsoever on transportation costs. Use of cell 1–A would be an equivalent-cost alternative. Management may prefer to use it for other reasons, or management may prefer to stay with the original solution. In any case, knowledge of such alternatives gives a certain degree of added flexibility in decision making.

So far, we have not discovered any improvement potential. But there are still five unused cells that must be analyzed. However, before evaluating the remaining empty cells, it is important to mention that constructing paths using stepping-stones requires a minimum number of stones and that unless that number exist, it will be impossible to evaluate all the empty cells in this manner. The number of occupied cells must equal the sum of the number of rows and columns minus one: $R + C - 1$ where $R = $ Number of rows and $C = $ Number of columns. Hence, in this example $R = 3$ and $C = 4$, so we must have $3 + 4 - 1 = 6$ used or completed cells (which we do have). If there are too few occupied cells, the matrix is said to be *degenerate*. A method for overcoming this problem is explained later in this supplement.

For now, let's continue evaluating the unused cells. Suppose we now consider cell 2–A. Begin by adding a unit to the empty cell. Moving to the right in row 2, we have what seems to be a choice: borrow a unit from 90 or from 110. However, borrowing from 90 will leave column B one unit short, and since adding and borrowing must involve occupied cells and there are no others in the B column, the 90 cannot be used. Instead, we must borrow from the 110 and add one unit to the 10 in cell 3–C. We can complete our path back to the original cell by subtracting a unit from the 80 units in cell 3–A. The $+/-$ path is shown in Table 5S–9. The impact on total cost for the path associated with cell 2–A would be:

TABLE 5S–9

Evaluation Path for Cell 2–A

Cell 2–A

	+		–
(2–A)	+12	(2–C)	−8
(3–C)	+16	(3–A)	−8
	+28		−16

+12

This means that for every unit shifted into cell 2–A, the total cost would *increase* by $12. Hence, we should avoid shipping units from factory 2 to warehouse A.

At this point, let's pause for a moment and consider some helpful rules for obtaining evaluation paths, since you may still be a little unsure of how to actually do it.

---

1. Start by placing a + sign in the cell you wish to evaluate.
2. Move horizontally (or vertically) to a completed cell. Choose a cell that will permit your next move to another completed cell. Assign a − sign to the cell.
3. Change direction and move to another completed cell. Again, choose one that will permit your next move. Assign a + sign to the cell.
4. Continue this process of moving to completed cells and alternating + and − signs until you can complete a closed path back to the original cell. Make only horizontal and vertical moves.
5. You may find it helpful to place a small dot or checkmark in cells that have been evaluated to help keep track of them.

Let's try another one, say, 3–B. Start by placing a + sign in cell 3–B. Move to the 90 in cell 2–B and place a − sign there. Move to

TABLE 5S–10

**Evaluation Path for
Cell 3–B**

• Previously evaluated

the 110 in cell 2–C and place a + sign there. Move to cell 3–C and give it a − sign. The path is shown in Table 5S–10. This one was fairly easy. Let's see what the impact on cost would be:

Cell 3–B

	+		−
(3–B)	+10	(2–B)	−3
(2–C)	+8	(3–C)	−16
	+18		−19

$$\boxed{-1}$$

TABLE 5S–11

**Evaluation Path for
Cell 2–D**

• Previously evaluated

TABLE 5S-12

Evaluation Path for
Cell 1-B

• Previously evaluated

The −1 indicates that for each unit we can shift into cell 3–B, our cost will decrease by $1. Hence, if we could shift 100 units, we could save $100 over the present solution. However, at this point we are not ready to make any changes since there may be some other empty cell that would yield an even greater savings, and we can only make one shift at a time.

Evaluation of cell 2–D is quite similar to the evaluation of cell 3–B. The evaluation path is shown in Table 5S–11. The cost impact would be:

Cell 2-D

+		−	
(2–D)	+8	(3–D)	−5
(3–C)	+16	(2–C)	−8
	+24		−13

+11

Thus, no improvement is possible.

There are two cells remaining to be evaluated, 1–B and 1–C. Let's consider 1–B first. It is a little more involved than the previous paths. Begin by placing a + in cell 1–B. Move to cell 1–D (100) and give it a −. Move vertically to 3–D (60 units) and give it a +. Move to the left and put a − in cell 3–C (10 units). Move up to 110 and put a + in that cell. Move to the left to 90 units (cell 2–B) and give it a − sign, completing the path. The path is shown in Table 5S–12. The cost impact of the path would be:

Cell 1–B

+		–	
(1–B)	+7	(1–D)	–1
(3–D)	+5	(3–C)	–16
(2–C)	+8	(2–B)	–3
	+20		–20

0

Again, no improvement is possible using this cell path.

The last empty cell a 1–C. Its evaluation path is shown in Table 5S–13: begin with 1–C as +, 1–D as –, 3–D as +, and 3–C as –. The cost impact would be:

Cell 1–C

+		–	
(1–C)	+7	(1–D)	–1
(3–D)	+5	(3–C)	–16
	+12		–17

(–5)

Hence, for each unit we can transfer into this empty cell, we improve the cost by $5.

At this point, each of the unused cells has been evaluated. The resulting cost are summarized below.

Cell . . .	1–A	2–A	3–B	2–D	1–B	1–C
Cost . . .	0	+12	(–1)	+11	0	(–5)

Cells with a positive total do not present opportunities for improvements. The fact that 1–A and 1–B are both zero indicates that at

TABLE 5S–13

Evaluation Path for Cell 1–C

●Previously evaluated

least one other equivalent alternative exists. The interesting fact here is that two cells have negative evaluations, indicating that the present solution is not an optimum. In the next section you will learn how to develop an improved solution.

Evaluating Empty Cells: The MODI Method

Another method for evaluating empty cells is the *modified distribution method (MODI)*. It involves computing row and column index numbers that can be used for cell evaluation. In many respects it is simpler than the stepping-stone method because it avoids having to trace cell evaluation paths. However, the cell evaluations it produces are identical to those obtained using the stepping-stone method. Note, though, that if a solution is not optimal, *one* stepping-stone path must be traced to obtain an improved solution. This is explained in detail in the next section.

The MODI procedure consists of these steps:

1. Make an initial allocation using northwest corner, VAM, or intuitive. Check for degeneracy and adjust if necessary.
2. Obtain a cost value for each row and column. Do this using only *completed* cells. Note that there will always be at least one completed cell in each row and in each column.
   a. Begin by assigning a zero to the first row. Thus, $R_1 = 0$.
   b. Determine the column cost value for any completed cells in row 1 using the relationship: column cost = cell cost − row cost. For example, if a cell cost is $8 per unit, the column cost will be $8 − 0 = 8$.
   c. Each new column value will permit the calculation of *at least* one new row value, and vice versa. Continue until all rows and columns have cost values, using only completed cells.
3. Obtain cell evaluations for *empty* cells using the relationship:

$$\text{Cell evaluation} = \frac{\text{Cell}}{\text{cost}} - \frac{\text{Row}}{\text{cost}} - \frac{\text{Column}}{\text{cost}}$$

Obtain these in any order.

Comments:

1. Row or column values may be positive, negative, or zero.
2. A reallocation requires that new row and column cost values be calculated.

Let's see how the MODI method can be used for cell evaluations. We begin by assigning a zero to row 1 (see Table 5S–14). Since we can only work with occupied cells and since cell 1–D is the only such cell in row 1, we focus on it. Since the sum of the row

TABLE 5S–14

MODI Index Numbers

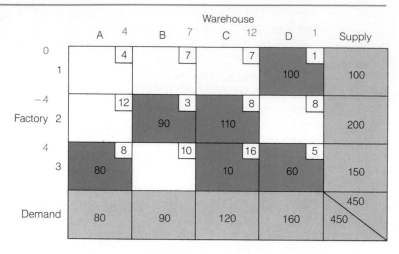

and column index numbers must add to the cell cost (which is 1), we can see that the index number for column D must be 1. There are no other occupied cells in row 1, so we shift to column D, cell 3–D. Again, the sum of the row and column index numbers must add to the cell cost (which is 5). Since the column index for D is 1, the index number for row 3 must be 4: $4 + 1 = 5$.

We can use this row 3 index number and the other two occupied cells in row 3 to obtain index numbers for columns A and C. For column A, the A index number plus 4 must equal the 1–A cell cost of 8. Hence, the index for A is 4: $4 + 4 = 8$. For C, the index plus 4 must equal 16, hence the index number is 12.

Next, for row 2, using cell 2–C and a C index of 12, the row index is -4. Then, using cell 2–B, the column index is 7: $7 + (-4) = 3$. This completes the row and column index numbers.

The cell evaluation for each empty cell is determined by subtracting from the cell cost of the empty cell the sum of the row and column index numbers:

$$\text{Cell evaluation} = \text{Cell cost} - (\text{Row index} + \text{Column index}).$$

This is shown in Table 5S–15.

TABLE 5S–15

MODI Cell Evaluation

Cell	Evaluation
1–A	$4 - [0 + 4] = 0$
1–B	$7 - [0 + 7] = 0$
1–C	$7 - [0 + 12] = -5$
2–A	$12 - [-4 + 4] = 12$
2–D	$8 - [-4 + 1] = 11$
3–B	$10 - [4 + 7] = -1$

Note that these agree with the evaluations obtained using the stepping-stone method. Again, because some evaluations are negative, the solution is not optimal.

OBTAINING AN IMPROVED SOLUTION

The presence of negative cell evaluations is evidence that an improved solution is possible. By the same token, if no negatives appear, an optimum has been achieved.

In this case there are two cells with negative evaluations, 3–B with a value of -1 and 1–C with a value of -5. Select the largest of these for improvement (i.e., 1–C) and ignore any others.

The implication of the -5 is that a savings of $5 per unit will be realized for every unit that can be shifted into cell 1–C. Recall the path used to evaluate the cell; it is reproduced below. In the course of the evaluation, a single unit was added or subtracted to certain cells, as denoted by the + and − signs. We want to repeat that procedure, but instead of shifting *one* unit, we want to shift *as many as possible*. The *quantities* in the cells that have − signs (i.e., 10 in cell 3–C and 100 in cell 1–D) are potential candidates for shifting, since the − implies units are subtracted from those cells. It is the *smaller* of these quantities that is the limiting factor. That is, we can subtract 10 from both numbers (10 and 100), but if we try to subtract 100 from both, we end up with 0 and −90. The negative would imply shipping from the warehouse back to the factory! Hence, 10 units can be shifted. In general, shift the minimum quantity that occupies a negative position in the ± path.

To accomplish the shift, add 10 units to each cell that has a + sign and subtract 10 units from each cell with a − sign. (Because

TABLE 5S—16

Evaluation Path for
Cell 1–C (See A) and
Reallocation of 10
Units around the Path
(See B)

TABLE 5S–17

Revised Solution

the signs alternate, the row and column totals will still be satisfied. This is shown in Table 5S–16.)

The improved solution is shown in Table 5S–17. The total costs are:

			Total cost
1–C.	10($7)	=	$ 70
1–D.	90($1)	=	90
2–B.	90($3)	=	270
2–C.	110($8)	=	880
3–A.	80($8)	=	640
3–D.	70($5)	=	350
			$2,300

Note that the revised solution has a total cost that is $50 less than the previous solution ($2,300 versus $2,350), which is exactly equal to the cell evaluation value times the number of units shifted: -5×10 units $= -\$50$.

Is this the optimum? Once again, we must evaluate each empty cell to determine if further improvements are possible. Recall that it is necessary to check to see that there are enough completed cells to allow all empty cells to have evaluation paths. Thus,

$$R + C - 1 = 3 + 4 - 1 = 6$$

Since there are six completed cells, the second round of cell evaluations can proceed. The cell paths and their values are shown in Tables 5S–18 to 5S–23. Since all are either zero or positive, this solution is the optimum. Note: MODI could have been used instead of stepping-stone.

Evaluation of Cell 1-A

Evaluation of Cell 1-B

Previously evaluated

Evaluation of Cell 2-A

Evaluation of Cell 2–D

TABLE 5S–22

Evaluation of Cell 3–B

TABLE 5S–23

Evaluation of Cell 3–C

SPECIAL PROBLEMS

Not all transportation problems are as straightforward to deal with as the one just presented. Various irregularities often crop up, which require certain adjustments before a solution can be obtained. Two of the most common irregularities are unequal supply and demand and *degeneracy,* a term that refers to an insufficient number of completed cells to evaluate every empty cell.

Unequal Supply and Demand

A frequently encountered situation is one in which supply and demand are not equal. Table 5S–24 illustrates such a case: total supply (capacity) of the two sources is 200 units, while total demand of the destinations is only 170. Hence, there is a deficiency in demand of 30 units. This condition can be remedied by adding a *dummy* destination with a demand equal to the difference between supply and demand. Since there is no such destination, no units will actu-

TABLE 5S–24

Supply Exceeds Demand by 30 Units

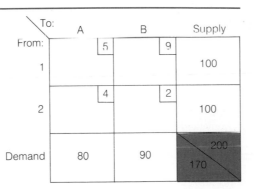

TABLE 5S–25

A Dummy Column with a Demand of 30 Units Is Added to the Matrix; Dummy Cell Costs Are Zero

TABLE 5S–26

Units in the Dummy Column Are Not Shipped; Factory 1 Will Ship Only 70 Units

From: \ To:	A	B	Dummy	Supply
1	70 [5]	[9]	30 [0]	100
2	10 [4]	90 [2]	[0]	100
Demand	80	90	30	200 / 200

TABLE 5S–27

Demand Exceeds Supply by 50 Units

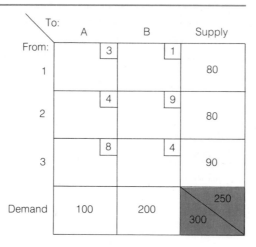

From: \ To:	A	B	Supply
1	[3]	[1]	80
2	[4]	[9]	80
3	[8]	[4]	90
Demand	100	200	250 / 300

TABLE 5S–28

A Dummy Row with a Supply of 50 Units Is Added to the Matrix so Supply Will Equal Demand

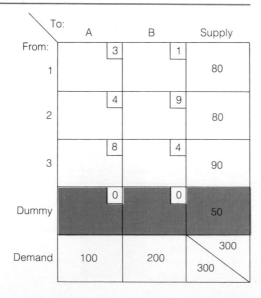

From: \ To:	A	B	Supply
1	[3]	[1]	80
2	[4]	[9]	80
3	[8]	[4]	90
Dummy	[0]	[0]	50
Demand	100	200	300 / 300

ally be shipped, and unit shipping costs for each dummy cell are $0. This is illustrated in Table 5S–25.

Once the dummy has been added, the transportation method can then be applied in the usual manner. The final solution will have a total number of units assigned to the dummy that equals the original difference between supply and demand (see Table 5S–26). These numbers indicate which source(s) (e.g., factories) will hold the extra units or will have excess capacity. In the example shown factory 1 will ship only 70 units even though it has the capacity to ship 100 units.

A similar situation exists when demand exceeds supply (see Table 5S–27). In those cases a dummy *row* (e.g., factory) with a supply equal to the difference between supply and demand must be added (see Table 5S–28). Again, units will not actually be shipped, so transportation costs are $0 for each cell in the dummy row. Units in the dummy row in the final solution indicate the destinations that will not receive all the units they desire and the amount of the shortage for each. For example, Table 5S–29 indicates that A will be 20 units short and B 30 units short.

The total transportation cost for this distribution plan is:

				Total cost
1–B.	. . .	80($1)	=	$ 80
2–A.	. . .	80($4)	=	320
3–B.	. . .	90($4)	=	360
Dummy–A.	. . .	20($0)	=	0
Dummy–B.	. . .	30($0)	=	0
				$760

TABLE 5S–29

Units in the Dummy Row Will Not Be Shipped: A Will Receive 100 − 20 = 80 Units and B Will Receive 200 − 30 = 170 Units

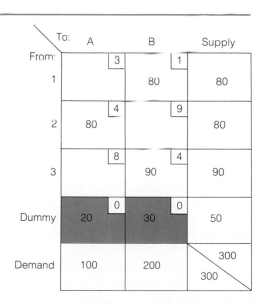

TABLE 5S–30

There Are Too Few Completed Cells; Some Empty Cells Cannot Be Evaluated

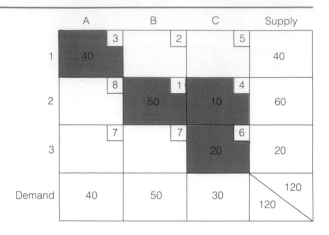

Degeneracy

We have seen that the transportation method involves evaluation of empty cells using completed cells as "stepping-stones." A degenerate situation exists if there are too few completed cells to allow all necessary paths to be constructed. The condition occurs if an allocation (other than the last one) exhausts *both* the row (supply) and the column (demand) quantities. It can occur in an initial solution or in subsequent solutions, so it is necessary to test for degeneracy after each iteration using $R + C - 1$.

An example of a matrix with too few completed cells is shown in Table 5S–30. Note that there are only four completed cells although the necessary number is five: $3 + 3 - 1 = 5$. Because of this, it is impossible to develop an evaluation path for cells 1–B, 1–C, 2–A, or 3–A. The situation can be remedied by placing a very small quantity, represented by the symbol ϵ, into one of the empty cells and then treating it as a completed cell. The quantity is so small that it is negligible; it will be ignored in the final solution.

The idea is to select a position for ϵ that will permit evaluation of all remaining empty cells. For example, putting it in cell 3–A will permit evaluation of all empty cells (see Table 5S–31). Some experimentation may be needed to find the best spot for ϵ, since not every cell will enable construction of evaluation paths for the remaining cells. Moreover, avoid placing ϵ in a minus position of a cell path that turns out to be negative because reallocation requires shifting the smallest quantity in a minus position. Since the smallest quantity is ϵ, which is essentially zero, no reallocation will be possible.

The cell evaluations (not shown) are all positive, so this solution is optimum. (Note that cell 3–A is considered to be a completed cell and is therefore *not* evaluated.)

TABLE 5S–31

Cell 3–A Becomes a Completed Cell with the Addition of a Very Small Quantity, Represented by the Symbol ε

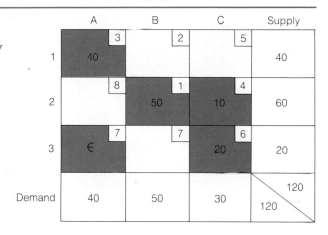

SUMMARY OF PROCEDURE

1. Make certain that supply and demand are equal. If they are not, determine the difference between the two amounts. Create a dummy source or destination with a supply (or demand) equal to the difference so that demand and supply are equal.

2. Develop an initial solution using either VAM, the northwest-corner method, or the intuitive approach.

3. Check to see that the number of completed cells is equal to $R + C - 1$. If it isn't, the solution is degenerate and will require insertion of a minute quantity, ε, in one of the empty cells.

4. Evaluate each of the empty cells. If any evaluations turn out to be negative, an improved solution is possible. Identify the cell that has the largest negative evaluation. Reallocate units around its evaluation path.

5. Repeat steps 3 and 4 until all cells have zero or positive values. When that occurs, the optimum solution has been achieved.

LOCATION DECISIONS

The transportation model can be used to compare location alternatives in terms of their impact on the total distribution costs for a system. The procedure involves working through a separate problem for each location being considered and then comparing the resulting total costs. Let's consider a simple example of this.

TABLE 5S–32

**Supply Exceeds
Demand by 30 Units**

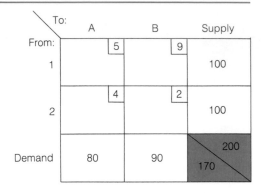

A previous example dealt with unequal supply and demand. The original matrix is reproduced below. (See Table 5S–32.) Suppose the firm has recently decided to open a third distribution center that will have an expected demand of 30 units, which will result

TABLE 5S–33

Transportation Costs for Boston and Albany	*Cost per unit to Boston*	*Cost per unit to Albany*
	From:	From:
	1 . . . $3	1 . . . $4
	2 . . . $6	2 . . . $1

TABLE 5S–34

**Optimum Plan Using
Boston Warehouse**

TC: 70 ($5) = 350
    30 ($3) = 90
    10 ($4) = 40
    90 ($2) = 180
            ‾‾‾‾‾
             $660

TABLE 5S–35

Optimum Plan Using Albany Warehouse

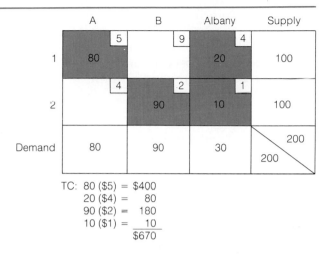

TC: 80 ($5) = $400
20 ($4) =   80
90 ($2) = 180
10 ($1) =   10
          $670

in equality of supply and demand. The question is whether to locate in a suburb of Boston or in Albany, New York. The transportation costs for each location are shown in Table 5S–33. In order to determine which will yield the lower transportation costs for the system, we must work the problem twice—once using the Boston costs and once using the Albany costs. The resulting optimum solution for each location and its total cost are shown in Tables 5S–34 and 5S–35. The total cost with the Boston location is $10 less than with the Albany location, making Boston the better location *on the basis of transportation cost.* Of course, we have already seen that there are many aspects of location decisions, and transportation cost is only one of them. There may be other, more important factors that favor one location over the other.

You may also be wondering how important a difference of $10 is. Remember that this is simply an example designed to demonstrate use of the method in location decisions. Of course, if an actual situation produced such a small difference, for practical purposes the location would undoubtedly be rated even in terms of transportation costs. However, suppose the units of supply and demand are in hundreds. Then the cost difference would be 100 ($10) = $1,000. In addition, the supply and demand quantities are generally for a short period of time (e.g., week, month, or quarter). Consequently, the difference on an annual basis would be much larger. For instance, if the amounts are in hundreds of units per week, the annual difference would be $1,000(52) = $52,000, which would undoubtedly be regarded as significant.

If there are other costs that differ among locations, such as production costs, these can easily be included in the analysis, provided they can be determined on a per unit basis. In that regard, it should be noted that merely adding or subtracting a constant to all cost values in any row or column will not affect the optimum solution, so any additional costs should only be included if they have a varying effect within a row or column.

OTHER APPLICATIONS

We have seen how the transportation model can be used to minimize the costs associated with distributing goods, and we have seen how the model can be used for comparing location alternatives. You should be aware of the fact that the model is also used in a number of other ways. For example, in a slight variation of the model, profits can be used in place of costs. In such cases the largest profit can be subtracted from each of the other cell profits, and the remaining values (opportunity costs) can be treated in the same manner that shipping costs were.

Some of the other uses of the model include production planning and scheduling (see Chapter 9), problems involving assignment of personnel or jobs to certain departments or machines (see Chapter 12), capacity planning, and transshipment problems.[1]

The use of the transportation model for capacity planning parallels its use for location decisions. Proposed capacity alternatives can be subjected to transportation analysis to determine which one would generate the lowest total shipping cost. For example, it is perhaps intuitively obvious that a factory or warehouse that is close to its market—or has low transportation costs for some other reason—should probably have a larger capacity than other locations. Of course, many problems are not so simple, and they require actual use of the model.

---

[1] Transshipment relates to problems with major distribution centers which in turn redistribute to smaller market destinations. See, for example, H. Wagner, *Principles of Management Science* (Englewood Cliffs, N.J.: Prentice-Hall, 1975).

1. Use the VAM technique to develop an initial solution to the problem shown below, and then determine if the solution is optimum. If it is not, develop the optimum solution.

To:	A	B	Supply
From: 1	6	9	75
2	5	3	75
Demand	80	90	

Solution

a. First check to see if supply and demand are equal. Total demand = 170, Total supply = 150. Therefore, it will be necessary to create a dummy destination with zero transportation costs in each of its cells (see matrix below).

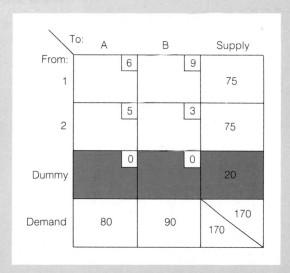

b. Develop the initial solution using VAM:
    (1) Compute the difference between the two lowest costs in each column and each row.

(2) Identify the row or column that has the largest difference (column 1 with a difference of $5).

(3) Assign as many units as possible to the cell with the lowest cost (cell Dummy–A). Assign 20 units; supply is the limiting factor.

(4) Cross out the row or column that is completely exhausted (Dummy row).

(5) Continue until all assignments have been made (i.e., all rows and columns exhausted). (See matrix below.)

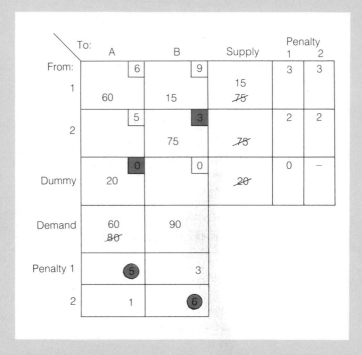

c. Check for degeneracy. It is not degenerate since the number of completed cells equals $3 + 2 - 1 = 4$.

d. Determine if the solution is optimum; evaluate each of the empty cells (see below). Since one cell has a negative value, this is not the optimum solution.

Cell 2–A		*Dummy–B*	
+	−	+	−
5	6	0	0
9	3	6	9
14	9	6	−9
+5		⊖	

e. Develop an improved solution. This requires retracing the evaluation path for the negative cells and noting the quantities in the − positions (20 and 15). Shift the smaller of these (15) around the path, subtracting from a − position and adding to each + position. The original and revised values are shown on page 269.

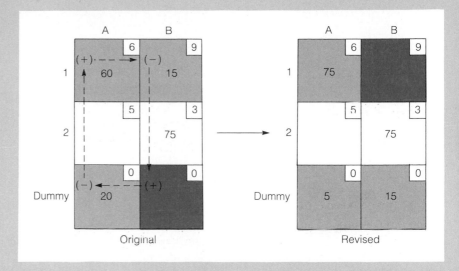

f. Check for degeneracy. ($R + C - 1 = 4$: not degenerate)

g. At this point, both empty cells have positive values. Hence, the revised solution is optimum.

Cell 2–A		*Cell 1–B*	
+	−	+	−
5	3	9	0
0	0	0	6
$\overline{5}$	$\overline{-3}$	$\overline{9}$	$\overline{-6}$
+2		+3	

h. Compute the total cost:

$$75(\$6) + 75(\$3) + 5(\$0) + 15(\$0) = \$675.$$

2. A firm that specializes in nonferrous casting must decide between locating a new foundry in either Chicago or Detroit. Transportation costs from each proposed location to existing warehouses are shown below along with transportation costs for existing locations for a certain type of casting. Use VAM to obtain the initial solution and determine which location would produce the lowest total cost. Each will be able to supply 25,000 units per month.

From Detroit to	*Cost per unit*	*From Chicago to*	*Cost per unit*
A	$10	A	$12
B	8	B	13
C	15	C	5

From: \ To:	A	B	C	Supply (hundreds of units/month)
Foundry 1	17	10	6	30
Foundry 2	7	12	14	20
Demand (hundreds of units/month)	25	10	40	

Warehouse is the heading over columns A, B, C.

Solution

This decision requires solving two transportation problems, one using Detroit costs and the other using Chicago costs.

a. Set up the two transportation matrices.

Detroit

	A	B	C	Supply
1	17	10	6	30
2	7	12	14	20
Detroit	10	8	15	25
Demand	25	10	40	

Chicago

	A	B	C	Supply
1	17	10	6	30
2	7	12	14	20
Chicago	12	13	5	25
Demand	25	10	40	

Warehouse is the heading over columns A, B, C in both matrices.

b. Solve each problem. The required steps are:
(1) Check to see that supply and demand are equal (they are).
(2) Use VAM to obtain the initial solution (see below).
(3) Check for degeneracy (both are OK; see below).
(4) Evaluate the empty cells to determine if the initial solution is optimum (Detroit is, Chicago is not).
(5) Reallocate Chicago matrix, check for degeneracy (OK) and evaluate empty cells (no negatives, so optimum).
(6) Compute the total cost for each problem (Detroit: $600; Chicago: $520). Chicago yields lower total cost (see below).

Detroit:
(a) VAM solution.

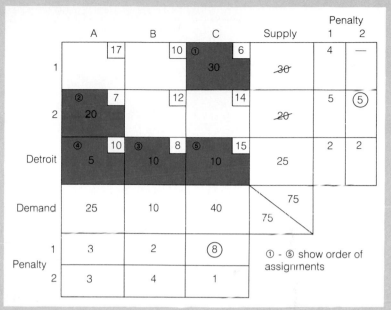

Detroit tableau (VAM solution)

	A	B	C	Supply	Penalty 1	Penalty 2
1	17	10	① 6 — 30	30̶	4	—
2	② 7 — 20	12	14	2̶0̶	5	⑤
Detroit	④ 10 — 5	③ 8 — 10	⑤ 15 — 10	25	2	2
Demand	25	10	40	75 / 75		
Penalty 1	3	2	⑧			
Penalty 2	3	4	1			

① - ⑤ show order of assignments

(b) Degenerate? $R + C - 1 = 3 + 3 - 1 = 5$ (OK).

(c) Cell evaluations

1–A		1–B		2–B		2–C	
+	−	+	−	+	−	+	−
17	6	10	6	12	8	14	15
15	10	15	8	10	7	10	7
32	16	25	14	22	15	24	22
+16		+11		+7		+2	

Since all are positive, this is the optimum distribution plan.

Chicago:
(a) VAM solution.

	A	B	C	Supply	Penalty 1	Penalty 2
1	⑤ 17 — 5	④ 10 — 10	③ 6 — 15	30	4	4
2	② 7 — 20	12	14	20	5	5
Chicago	12	13	① 5 — 25	25	⑦	—
Demand	25	10	40	75 / 75		
Penalty 1	5	2	1			
Penalty 2	⑩	2	8			

① - ⑤ show order of assignments

(b) Degenerate? $R + C - 1 = 3 + 3 - 1 = 5$ (OK).

(c) Cell evaluations

2–B		2–C		Chicago–A		Chicago–B	
+	−	+	−	+	−	+	−
12	7	14	7	12	17	13	10
17	10	17	6	6	5	6	5
29	17	31	13	18	22	19	15
+12		+18		$\overline{-4}$		+4	

The negative value for Chicago–A indicates this is not the optimum solution.

(d) Reallocate 5 units (smallest quantity in − path position) around the Chicago–A evaluation path. The revised solution is shown below.

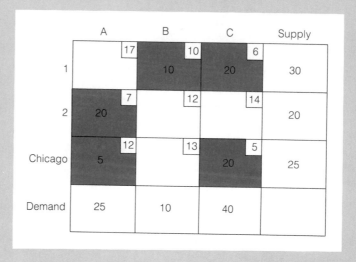

(e) Check for degeneracy: $R + C - 1 = 5$ (OK).

(f) Cell evaluations:

1–A		2–B		2–C		Chicago–B	
+	−	+	−	+	−	+	−
17	6	12	10	14	5	13	10
5	12	6	5	12	7	6	5
22	18	12	7	26	12	19	15
+4		30	22	+14		+4	
		+8					

Since all evaluations are positive, this is the optimum. Compute total costs for each plan:

Detroit	*Chicago*
30($6) = $180	10($10) = $100
20($7) = 140	20($6) = 120
5($10) = 50	20($7) = 140
10($8) = 80	5($12) = 60
10($15) = 150	20($5) = 100
$600	$520

Chicago has lower monthly costs. Note that total costs are in hundreds (i.e., Detroit cost is $60,000 per month, and Chicago cost is $52,000 per month).

DISCUSSION AND REVIEW QUESTIONS

1. What information is needed to use the transportation method?
2. What check must be made before proceeding to develop an initial solution? What corrective action might need to be taken?
3. Would it ever make sense to have a situation that required both a dummy row and a dummy column? Explain briefly.
4. What is *linear* in a transportation problem?
5. Why do the + and − signs alternate in cell evaluation paths?
6. How do you know if a solution is optimum?
7. What does a zero value for an evaluation path indicate?
8. If a solution is not optimum:
   a. How do you decide which empty cell to shift units into?
   b. How do you know which cells to include in the shifting operation?
   c. How do you decide how many units to shift?
9. What is meant by the term *degeneracy*? How is it corrected?
10. How is the transportation method useful in location decisions? How does use of the transportation method in location decisions differ from its use as a tool to develop an optimum distribution plan for a given set of sources and destinations?
11. How are total costs determined for a given distribution plan?
12. What interpretation is given to quantities allocated to dummy destinations? Dummy sources?
13. What is the MODI method? How does it differ from the stepping-stone method?

PROBLEMS

1. Obtain the optimal distribution plan for the transportation problem shown below. Develop the initial solution using:
   a. The northwest-corner method.
   b. Vogel's approximation method.
   c. The intuitive approach.
   Use the stepping-stone method for cell evaluations.
2. A given shipping combination may be undesirable for a reason other than shipping cost. Use of that combination can be avoided by replacing that cell's unit cost with a relatively larger cost. Assume cell 3–C in the previous problem is such a case. Assign a unit cost of $100 to that cell, and find the minimum cost solution using VAM for the initial allocations.
3. Given the transportation problem shown, do each of the following:
   a. Develop an initial feasible solution using each of the three methods described in this supplement.
   b. Use stepping-stone to evaluate the northwest-corner solution.
   c. Repeat part b using MODI.
   d. Find the optimal solution.

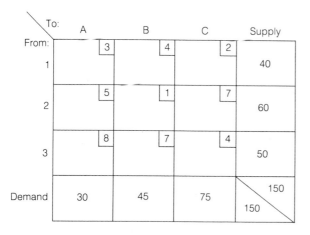

To:	A	B	C	D	Supply
1	18	12	14	16	40
2	24	24	27	33	80
3	42	34	31	26	130
Demand	90	80	30	50	

4. Refer to the previous problem. Due to a temporary condition, origin 3 has experienced a capacity reduction of 20 units per period. Using VAM to develop an initial solution, determine a temporary distribution plan that will minimize transportation costs.

5. Using VAM to generate an initial solution, determine the optimal distribution plan for the problem shown below, and compute the total cost for that plan. Use the MODI method for cell evaluation.

To: From:	A	B	C	D	Supply
1	14	24	18	28	48
2	17	18	25	16	56
3	30	16	22	30	32
Demand	41	34	35	20	

6. Refer to the previous problem. The market supplied by destination D is experiencing a period of rapid growth. Projected demand is for 60 units per period. A new factory with a capacity of 50 units is planned for one of two locations, Baltimore or Philadelphia. Transportation costs are as shown below. Which location would result in the lowest total cost? Use the MODI method for cell evaluation.

From Baltimore to	Cost per unit	From Philadelphia to	Cost per unit
A . . .	$18	A	$31
B . . .	16	B	25
C . . .	22	C	19
D . . .	27	D	20

7. Determine the optimum shipping plan for the transportation matrix below. Use VAM to develop the initial solution. What is the total cost for your plan?

To: From:	Dallas	Buffalo	Miami	Supply
Chicago	4	9	6	25
Milwaukee	12	10	7	55
Cleveland	11	5	8	40
Demand	35	40	45	

8. A toy manufacturer wants to open a third warehouse that will be used to supply three retail outlets. The new warehouse will have a capacity to supply 500 units of backyard playsets per week. Two locations are being studied, N1 and N2. Transportation costs for location N1 to stores A, B, and C would be $6, $8, and $7 respectively, while for location N2 the costs would be $10, $6, and $4 respectively. The existing system is shown below. Use VAM to develop an initial solution. Which location would result in the lowest transportation costs for the system?

		Store		Capacity
To: From:	A	B	C	(units/week)
Warehouse 1	8	3	7	500
Warehouse 2	5	10	9	400
Demand (units/week)	400	600	350	

9. A large firm is contemplating construction of a new manufacturing facility. The two leading locations are Toledo and Cincinnati. The new factory would have a supply capacity of 160 units per week. Transportation costs from each potential location are shown below along with transportation costs for existing locations. Using VAM to develop an initial solution, determine which location would provide the lowest transportation costs.

From Toledo to	Cost per unit	From Cincinnati to	Cost per unit
A . .	$18	A . . .	$ 7
B . .	8	B . . .	17
C . .	13	C . . .	13

	A	B	C	Supply (Units/week)
1	10	14	10	210
2	12	17	20	140
3	11	11	12	150
Demand (Units/week)	220	220	220	

10. A large retailer is planning to open a new store. Three locations are currently under consideration: South Coast Plaza, Fashion Island, and Laguna Hills. Transportation costs for the locations are shown below along with costs, demands, and supplies for existing locations and warehouses (origins). Each of the locations has a demand potential of 300 units per week. Use VAM to develop the initial solution. Which location would yield the lowest transportation costs for the system?

From warehouse	To SCP	FI	LH
1	$ 4	$7	$5
2	11	6	5
3	5	5	6

	A	B	Supply (Units/week)
1	15	9	660
2	10	7	340
3	14	18	200
Demand (Units/week)	400	500	

SELECTED BIBLIOGRAPHY

Bierman, Harold; Charles P. Bonini; and Warren H. Hausman. *Quantitative Analysis for Business Decisions.* 6th ed. Homewood, Illinois: Richard D. Irwin, 1981.

Eppen, G. D., and F. J. Gould. *Introductory Management Science.* Englewood Cliffs, N.J.: Prentice-Hall, 1984.

Levin, Richard I.; Charles A. Kirkpatrick; and David Rubin. *Quantitative Approaches to Management.* 5th ed. New York: McGraw-Hill, 1982.

Wagner, Harvey. *Principles of Management Science.* Englewood Cliffs, N.J.: Prentice-Hall, 1970.

Chapter 6

Product and Service Design

After completing this chapter, you should be able to:

1. Identify some of the reasons organizations become involved with product and service design.
2. Describe the contributions of R&D to product and service design.
3. Explain the concept of standardization and discuss the advantages and disadvantages of standardization.
4. Discuss the concept of modular design, including its advantages and disadvantages.
5. Define reliability, perform simple reliability computations, and suggest possible ways of improving reliability.

THE NEED FOR PRODUCT/SERVICE DESIGN, 278

    Product Life Cycles, 281

RESEARCH AND DEVELOPMENT, 282

STANDARDIZATION, 283

    Modular Design, 284
    Metric Conversion, 284

COMPUTER-AIDED DESIGN (CAD), 285

RELIABILITY, 288

    Measuring Reliability, 289
    Improving Reliability, 296

SUMMARY, 297

SOLVED PROBLEMS, 299

DISCUSSION AND REVIEW QUESTIONS, 302

PROBLEMS, 302

SELECTED BIBLIOGRAPHY, 305

READING: TOYING WITH HIGH-TECH, 305

The essence of any organization is the products or services it offers. Moreover, there is a close link between the *design* of these products or services and the realization of the goals of the organization. Because of this, organizations have a vital stake in product and service design. Two primary concerns are *function* and *cost.*

In this chapter we shall consider the need for product and service design, the function of research and development, the concept of standardization, and the concept of reliability.

THE NEED FOR PRODUCT/SERVICE DESIGN

At first glance, it might seem that the matter of product or service design is a one-time necessity for new items, and that once it is done, no further attention would be needed. Practically speaking, this is not usually the case. The business environment in which most organizations must operate is fairly dynamic, so that questions related to product and service design have a tendency to arise at any time. Pressures for design changes can come from customers, competitors, legal sources, and from within the organization.

Customers may indicate their dissatisfaction with a particular design either through direct complaints to the organization or some regulatory body, or indirectly through decreased purchases of the item. Thus, organizations often become involved in redesign to improve sales or to respond to complaints.

In competitive situations, organizations often strive to increase profits and market share by building a better mousetrap, which then forces competitors to reevaluate their own designs in a never-ending battle. Hence, as soon as one bank comes up with a promotional gimmick, such as free checking or bank-by-mail, its competitors are sure to follow. Likewise, if one supermarket offers double couponing, competitors may follow suit for fear of losing their market shares.

Organizations are faced with an increasing array of government agencies established to regulate their activities. Among the more familiar ones are the Food and Drug Administration, the Environmental Protection Agency, the National Highway Safety Commission, and the Consumer Products Safety Commission. Bans on cyclamates, red food dye, phosphates, and nitrites in recent years have sent designers scurrying back to their drawing boards to find alternative designs that will prove acceptable to both the government regulators and their customers. Similarly, pollution standards for automobiles and safety features like seat belts, safety glass, and energy absorbing bumpers and frames have had a substantial impact on automotive design. Much attention has been directed toward the design of toys with the idea of removing sharp edges, small pieces that can cause choking, and removal of toxic materials. In the construction field government regulations often require the use of lead-free paint, safety glass in entranceways, access to public buildings for handicapped persons, and standards for insulation, electrical wiring, plumbing, and so on.

In some cases the cost or shortage of raw materials can necessitate design changes. For instance, gasoline shortages and price increases spurred efforts to develop fuel-efficient cars as well as the development of alternative sources of energy.

Product liability can be a strong incentive for design improvement. Product liability means that a manufacturer is liable for any injuries or damages caused by a faulty product, either because of poor workmanship or poor design. In recent years many business firms have become involved in lawsuits related to their products, including the Firestone Tire & Rubber Co. (which underwent a major recall of its tires), the Ford Motor Co. (concerning among others, the gas tank of its Pintos), General Motors Corp. (steering problems with its Corvair), manufacturers of hairdryers (asbestos particles), toy manufacturers, and countless others. Still another consideration is the implied warranties created by state laws under the *Uniform Commercial Code,* which says, in effect, that products carry an implication of *merchantability* and *fitness* (i.e., the product must be usable for its intended purposes).

The suits and potential suits have resulted in increases in legal and insurance costs, expensive settlements with injured parties, and costly recalls. Moreover, increasing consumer awareness of product safety increases the risk of adversely affecting product image and subsequent demand for a producer's products.

Because of these factors, it is extremely important to design products that are reasonably safe and free of hazards. When hazards do exist, it is necessary to install safety guards or other devices for reducing accident potential. Adequate warning notices of risks must also be provided. Consumer groups, business firms, and various government agencies often work together to develop industry-wide standards that will help avoid some of the hazards. Major advances have been made in the area of toy manufacturing in terms of safety standards.

It is interesting to reflect on the role of operations-management people in product and service design, since operations will have the ultimate responsibility for *converting* the design into reality. During the conversion process, design errors and deficiencies are frequently detected, and ideas for improvements are generated. Many of the mistakes can be avoided by involving operations personnel in the design stages. In fact, it often happens that when operations people are not consulted during product or service design, they become involved by *initiating* redesign efforts.

FIGURE 6–1

Differing Views of Design Created through Lack of Information

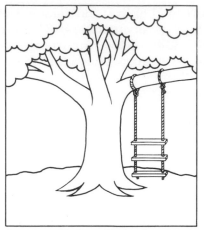

As proposed by the marketing department.

As specified in the product request.

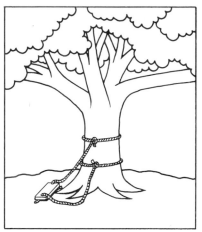

As designed by the senior designer.

As produced by manufacturing.

As used by the customer.

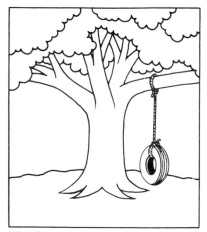

What the customer wanted.

Source: Educational Exploration Center *Newsletter,* Minneapolis, Minnesota.

Finally, a humorous look at some of the different ways that various individuals and departments in the design process can interpret the "design" is illustrated in Figure 6–1. The obvious point is that there must be sufficient information to determine what the customer wants as well as communication and agreement among those responsible for designing, producing, and marketing the product or service.

Product Life Cycles

Many new products experience a life cycle in demand. When they are first introduced, they may be treated as curiosities. Demand is generally low at this point because potential buyers have not had much time to familiarize themselves with the item. Many also realize from previous experience that all of the bugs have probably not been ironed out and that the price may drop after the introductory period. With the passage of time, production and design improvements usually create a more reliable and less costly product. Demand then grows for these reasons and because of the increasing awareness of the product or service. At the next stage in the life cycle the product reaches maturity: There are few if any design changes, and demand levels off. Eventually, the market becomes saturated, which leads to a decline in demand. These stages in the cycle are illustrated in Figure 6–2.

In the last stage of a life cycle, some firms adopt a *defensive research* posture whereby they attempt to prolong the useful life of a product or service by one or more of the following: improving the reliability of the product, reducing costs of producing the item (and hence, the price), redesigning the item, or changing the packaging.

FIGURE 6–2

Products or Services May Exhibit Life Cycles over Time

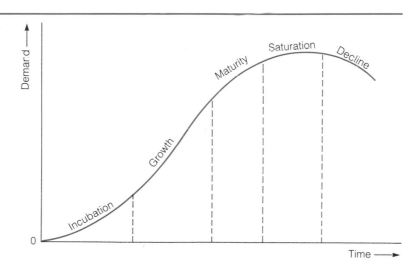

Of course, not all products go through such a life cycle. For example, wooden pencils, paper clips, nails, knives, forks and spoons, drinking glasses, and other similar items don't seem to exhibit life cycles. But most new products seem to. Some current examples of items in various stages of life cycles include slide rules, black-and-white televisions, textbook editions, computers, calculator models, kitchen-floor coverings, and TV series.

It is important to recognize that wide variations exist in the amount of time a particular product takes to pass through a given phase of its life cycle; some products pass through various stages in a relatively short period of time while others take considerably longer. Often it is a matter of the basic *need* for the item and the *rate of technological change.* For instance, some toys, novelty items, and style items have a life cycle of less than one year, while other, more crucial items such as slide rules, may last for 50 years or more before yielding to technological change.

RESEARCH AND DEVELOPMENT

Most of the recent developments in semiconductors, medical technology, communications, and space technology can be traced to research and development (R&D). The costs of much of these efforts were so great that only the largest companies and the government could afford to underwrite their expense. The research projects from which these and countless other scientific advancements have sprung are typically conducted by colleges and universities, research foundations, and large corporations. Some have come from basic research while others, perhaps the majority, have come about through applied research and development. *Basic* research is research that is intended to advance scientific knowledge (i.e., advance the state of the art), and it generally does not have any specific commercial purposes. *Applied* research is designed to produce commercial benefits. *Development* involves converting the results of applied research into useful commercial applications.

Because basic research does not yield results that might be considered immediately useful, only the largest companies, foundations, and the government can afford to underwrite such efforts. Applied research and development, because of its commercial possibilities, appeals more to smaller organizations. Even then, costs can be prohibitive, leading some to adopt a design-by-imitation approach. This is readily evident, for example, in the field of electronics.

The benefits of successful R&D can be tremendous. Some research leads to patents with the potential for licensing and royalties.

However, many discoveries are either not patentable or else companies don't wish to divulge details of their ideas and so do not follow the patent route. Even so, the first organization to bring a new product or service to the market generally stands to profit from it before the others can catch up. (Recall the earlier discussion of life cycles: early products may be priced higher because a temporary monopoly exists until competitors bring their versions out.)

There are also a number of substantial risks involved in R&D. For example, an oil company may spend $5 million to drill a well even though the probability of success might be less than 10 percent. The fact is that most projects that have high potential gains also have high potential losses. Moreover, many projects must be terminated when it appears that they are not likely to yield enough to make them attractive.

STANDARDIZATION

A major contributing factor to the high rate of productivity achieved by industrialized nations is the standardization of parts. *Standardization* means that parts are made to conform to a specified standard, and regardless of when or where such a part has been made, it can be interchanged with another part of the same type and serve just as well. Because of this, parts do not have to be custom-produced for a product, which would be a slow and expensive procedure. Instead, large volumes of standardized parts can be produced and used for subsequent assembly operations and for replacements in the field, thus permitting many economies in designing, fabricating, storing, inspecting, assembling, and repairing parts.

One of the main disadvantages of standardization is that it reduces the potential variety of products, reducing the appeal to the widest range of customers. Generally consumers must accept the standardized version or nothing at all. Another disadvantage is that a design may be frozen before it has been adequately improved. Once standardized, there are compelling arguments for avoiding design modifications. A familiar example of this is the keyboard arrangement of a typewriter. Research has demonstrated that much more efficient arrangements are possible, but the cost of replacing or changing those already in service plus the need to retrain typists would entail a tremendous burden. Similarly, U.S.-made color TVs have a standard scanning rate (lines per inch) that is lower than foreign-made televisions, resulting in poorer resolution. Again, early freezing of the design is partly to blame.

The main advantages and disadvantages of standardization are outlined in Table 6–1.

TABLE 6–1

Advantages and Disadvantages of Standardization

Advantages:
1. Fewer parts to deal with in inventory and in manufacturing.
2. Reduces training costs and time.
3. Purchasing, handling, and inspection procedures become more routine.
4. Many orders can be filled from inventory.
5. Provides opportunities for long production runs and automation.
6. Fewer parts justifies increased expenditures on perfecting designs and improving quality-control procedures.

Disadvantages:
1. Designs may be frozen with too many imperfections remaining.
2. High cost of design changes increases resistance to improvements.
3. Decreased variety results in less consumer appeal.

Modular Design

Modular design is essentially standardization in chunks. Modules represent groupings of component parts into subassemblies, usually to the point where the individual parts lose their separate identity. One familiar example of modular design is a television set with easily removed control panels. Computers, too, have modular parts that can be replaced if they become defective. By arranging modules in different configurations, different computer capabilities can be obtained. Modular design is also found in the construction industry. One firm in Rochester, New York makes prefabricated motel rooms complete with wiring, plumbing, and even room decorations in its factory and then moves the complete rooms via rail to the construction site where they are integrated into the structure.

One advantage of modular design is that failures are often easier to diagnose and remedy because there are fewer pieces to investigate compared to a nonmodular design. Similar advantages are found in ease of repair and replacement by removing the faulty module and replacing it with a good one. The manufacture and assembly of modules generally involves simplifications: Fewer parts are involved, so purchasing and inventory control become more routine, fabrication and assembly operations become more standardized, and training costs often are less.

The main disadvantages of modular design stem from the decrease in variety that results because the number of possible configurations of modules is much less than the number of configurations based on individual components. Another disadvantage that is sometimes encountered is the inability to disassemble a module in order to replace a faulty part; consequently, the entire module must be scrapped—usually a more costly procedure.

Metric Conversion

In 1975 Congress enacted legislation calling for voluntary conversion to the metric system of measurement from the present English system. At the time this was regarded as a move to achieve standardization among industrial nations; most other countries use the metric system.

Since that time there has been some change, although perhaps not as swift as most thought it would be, mainly because of the costs associated with converting tools and equipment and because of public resistance. Some of the difficulty relates to a controversy over whether to completely convert to a metric system, discarding present sizes and quantities, or whether to partially convert by relabeling current sizes and quantities. For instance, should milk and soft drinks be bottled and sold in liter-size containers, as some soft drink manufacturers are now doing, or would it be sufficient to relabel current sizes to reflect metric values (e.g., a quart would become .95 liters)? A complete conversion would be more in line with the original intention and result in fewer sizes than now exist. Relabeling would involve considerably less tooling and equipment changes, making it less costly and much easier to convert.

Other resistance to metric conversion comes from adults who will have to learn a whole new system of weights and measures and even from businesses, because of the training requirements such a move would involve.

Furthermore, during the changeover period, it is highly likely that some firms will make the conversion more rapidly than others. This may create a situation in which firms, especially suppliers, will have to provide some customers with metric sizes and others with English sizes. In addition, dual dimensioning on blueprints and machinery will be necessary during the conversion.

Thus, while it appears that metric conversion has certain advantages for American industry, the cost burden and problems in actually making the conversion create a sizable degree of inertia that must be reckoned with by both government and business.

COMPUTER-AIDED DESIGN (CAD)

Computers are being increasingly used for product design, particularly for manufacturing. *Computer-aided design (CAD)* uses computer graphics for product design. The designer can modify an existing design or create a new one on a CRT by means of a light pen, a keyboard, joysticks, or similar device. Once entered into the computer, the designer can maneuver the design on the screen: it can be rotated to provide the designer with different perspectives, it can be split apart to give the designer a view of the inside, and a portion of it can be enlarged for closer examination. When the design has been completed, the designer can obtain a printed version of the design. In addition, the design can be filed electronically, making it accessible to manufacturing personnel and others in the firm who have need for this sort of information (e.g., marketing).

An increasing number of products are being designed in this way. Some of the products include transformers, automobile parts, aircraft parts, integrated circuits, and electric motors.

A major benefit of CAD is the increased productivity of designers. No longer is it necessary to laboriously prepare mechanical drawings of products or parts and revise them repeatedly to correct errors or incorporate revisions. A rough estimate is that CAD increases the productivity of designers from 3 to 10 times. A second major benefit of CAD is the creation of a data base for manufacturing that can supply needed information on product geometry and dimensions, tolerances, material specifications, and so on. It should be noted, however, that such a data base is necessary in order for CAD to function and that this entails a considerable amount of effort.

Some CAD systems allow the designer to perform engineering and cost analyses on proposed designs. For instance, the computer can determine the weight and volume of a part and do stress analysis as well. When there are a number of alternative designs, the computer can quickly go through the possibilities and identify the best one, given the designer's criteria.

The following reprint gives some indication of the breadth of use of computer-aided design. The article refers to CAD–CAM; the CAM stands for computer-aided manufacturing.

Computers Speed the Design of More Workaday Products

The same computer technology used to design cars and missiles now is being used to design sneakers and spoons. The reason: Computer-aided design and manufacturing systems have become cheaper and easier to use, encouraging even decidedly low-tech companies to trade their drafting tables for computer terminals.

"CAD–CAM companies have been beating down our doors for years," says Alfred Zeien, vice chairman of Gillette Co., whose Braun subsidiary in West Germany uses computers to design hair dryers and electric shavers. "We were finally convinced they could deliver."

Other makers of workaday products also have been convinced. Hasbro Bradley Inc. uses computers to design parts for GI Joe aircraft carriers; Craft Patterns does the same for dog houses. ITT Corp.'s computers draw fire hydrants; Oneida Ltd.'s make spoons and forks.

Computers take the drudgery out of design. Instead of laboriously drawing and redrawing blueprints, engineers create designs electronically and alter them at the push of a few buttons. Some computer programs also analyze the designs to see how well they handle stress or changes in temperature. Manufacturers say that encourages experimentation, yields better quality goods, and helps them introduce products more quickly.

"It allows us to try blue-sky projects," says W. David Lee, who heads a product development group at the Arthur D. Little Inc. consulting firm. Using computerized design techniques, Mr. Lee's group produced a U.S. Army canteen that keeps coffee warm for eight hours in arctic temperatures and a gas stove that needs less insulation for Maytag Co.'s Hardwick Stove division.

Walter Stewart, a senior vice president at Oneida, says that adding CAD–CAM is "a matter of survival." Oneida estimates that it takes 70 weeks to design and produce a flatware set using conventional methods—nearly twice the time of Asian competitors who work longer hours and, Oneida contends, produce lower-quality goods. To compete better, Oneida began in 1983 to use computers to design flatware and to make dies that punch out stainless steel forks and knives.

As a result, Oneida says it now can match the turnaround time of its Asian competitors on some items. It also can bid on rush jobs that it might otherwise lose. Last summer, for instance, it produced spoon designs using the hot-selling Care Bear characters for General Mills Inc. in only two days. Oneida also says that more precise tooling reduces the number of imperfections in the flatware which must be laboriously ground or polished out.

Manufacturers also use CAD–CAM to customize products. The Kennedy Valve unit of ITT designs fire hydrants by piecing together computer drawings of different size nozzles and pipes. "It's like working with building blocks," says Bruce Platusich, manager of product engineering.

In a more sophisticated application, privately owned Techmedica Inc., Camarillo, Calif., produces artificial bones by computer. Techmedica uses cross-sections of a patient's bone produced by a CT scan, or computer tomography, as a basis for the bone design. The computer then directs a machine that cuts the replacement bone out of a block of titanium alloy.

Anthony Hedley, director of surgical research at the Huntington Arthritis Center in Phoenix, says Techmedica can deliver an artificial bone in two weeks—a fraction of the time of suppliers that aren't computerized. As a result of the speeded up delivery and precision design, he says, some bone cancer patients are spared amputations.

Manufacturers also say CAD–CAM fattens their profit margins. By reducing product development time with computers, Gillette says it can quickly "abort" a project that doesn't meet cost goals. Hasbro Bradley says it can gear up faster for mass production by using computers to design molds.

"With some toys you can sell all you can make by Thanksgiving," says Hugh Maxwell, Hasbro Bradley's senior vice president for operations. If the company can produce a mold just one week faster, he estimates, it can sell another $300,000 worth of some toys.

But CAD–CAM has some shortcomings. Longtime employees sometimes resist learning the technology. And because the systems are so complex, they can be out of commission as much as 30 percent of the time, says Harley Shaiken, a Massachusetts Institute of Technology researcher. Among reasons for the downtime, he says, are computer breakdowns, inexperienced workers, and management failure to devise schedules that take advantage of the technology. (Confirms Henry Eichfeld, an official at Computervision Corp., a large CAD–CAM maker: "Thirty percent downtime isn't atypical for the world of data processing.")

What's more, whatever cost savings result from the use of CAD–CAM don't necessarily translate into lower prices for consumers. Converse Inc., for instance, uses computers to design sneakers. But John O'Neil, president, says the company's large investment in CAD–CAM "means the cost of speeding up the process won't be reflected in the cost of the shoe."

Brian Smith, president of privately owned Craft Patterns, St. Charles, Illinois, has another problem with CAD–CAM. He says that he can only use his company's $165,000 design system at night because it saps too much power from the main computer. But he isn't complaining. He says the alternatives—using pen and ink to design woodworking patterns for dog houses, high chairs, and other furniture—"is a total mess."

Source: Bob Davis, "Computers Speed the Design of More Workaday Products," *The Wall Street Journal,* January 18, 1985, p. 25. Reprinted by permission of *The Wall Street Journal.* © Dow Jones & Company, Inc., 1985. All rights reserved.

RELIABILITY

Reliability is a measure of the ability of a product, part, or system to perform its intended function under a prescribed set of conditions. The importance of reliability is underscored by the fact that prospective buyers use it when comparing alternatives and sellers use it as one determinant of price. Also, it can have an impact on repeat sales, it can reflect on the producer's image, and there may be legal implications if it is too low.

There are three important dimensions of reliability:

1. Reliability as a probability.
2. Definition of failure.
3. Prescribed operating conditions.

If an item has a reliability of, say, .90, this means that the probability it will function as intended is 90 percent and that the probability it will fail is $1 - .90 = 10$ percent. Hence, it is expected that on the average 1 of every 10 such items will fail, or equivalently, that the item will fail on the average of once in every 10 trials. Similarly, a reliability of .985 would imply 15 failures per 1,000 parts or trials.

The term *failure* is used to describe a situation in which an item does not perform as intended. This includes not only those instances in which the item does not function at all, but also instances in which performance is substandard and instances in which the item functions in a way not intended. For example, a smoke alarm might fail to respond to the presence of smoke (not operate at all), or it might sound an alarm that is too faint to provide an adequate warning (substandard performance), or it might sound an alarm even though no smoke is present (an unintended response).

Reliabilities are always specified with respect to some set of conditions, called *normal operating conditions*. These can include load, temperature, and humidity ranges, as well as operating procedures and maintenance schedules. Failure of users to heed such conditions often results in premature failure of parts or complete systems. For example, using a passenger car to tow heavy loads causes excess wear and tear on the drive train; driving over potholes or curbs often results in untimely tire failure; and using a calculator to drive nails usually has a marked impact on its usefulness for performing mathematical exercises.

Measuring Reliability

Engineers and designers have a number of techniques at their disposal for assessing the reliability of parts, products, and systems. However, a discussion of those techniques is not really within the scope of this text. Instead, let us turn our attention to the issue of measuring overall product or system reliability.

Two alternative approaches to operationally defining reliability are:

1. The probability the product or system will function on any given trial.
2. The probability that the product or system will function for a given length of time.

The first approach focuses on a *point in time* and is often used when a system must operate for one or a relatively few number of times. The second approach focuses on the *length of service*. The distinction will become more evident as we examine each of these approaches in more detail.

The probability that a product or system will perform on a given trial is a function of the reliabilities of its component parts and how they are interrelated. Suppose a system is composed of two components and that *both* must operate in order for the system to function. The system reliability is then the *product* of the reliabilities of the components. Thus, if *P(A)* = .9 and *P(B)* = .8, the system has a probability of .72.

Similarly, if three components with reliabilities of .9, .8, and .9 must all work, the system reliability is .648:

It is interesting to note that even though the individual components of a system might have high reliabilities, the system as a whole may have considerably less reliability because all components that are in series (as the ones above are) must function. Furthermore, as the number of series components increases, the system reliability decreases even more. For example, a system comprised of eight components in series, each with a reliability of .99, has a reliability of only $.99^8 = .923$.

Obviously, many products and systems have a large number of component parts that must all operate, and some way to increase overall reliability is needed. One approach is to use *redundancy* in the design. This involves providing backup parts for some items. Consider the case of a component with a reliability of .9 and a backup with a reliability of .8 that automatically switches on if the original fails. The probability that the original part functions is .90. Of the 10 percent probability of failure (i.e., $1 - .9$), 80 percent of those will be "saved" by the backup. Hence, the resulting probability for this pair is $.9 + .8(.1) = .98$.

EXAMPLE 1

Determine the reliability of the system shown below.

Solution

The system can be reduced to a series of three components:

The system reliability is then the product of these:

$$.98 \times .99 \times .996 = .966$$

The second way of looking at reliability involves the incorporation of a time dimension: Probabilities are determined relative to a specified length of time. This approach is commonly used in product warranties, which pertain to a given period of time after purchase of a product.

A typical profile of product failure rate over time is illustrated in Figure 6–3. Because of its shape, it is sometimes referred to as a "bathtub curve." It often happens that a number of items fail shortly after they are put into service, not because they wear out, but simply because they are defective to begin with. The rate of such failures decreases rapidly once the truly defective items are weeded out. During the second phase there are few failures because

FIGURE 6–3

Failure Rate Is a Function of Time

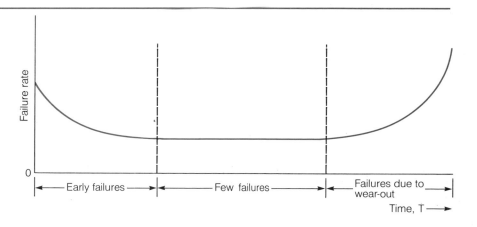

FIGURE 6–4

An Exponential
Distribution

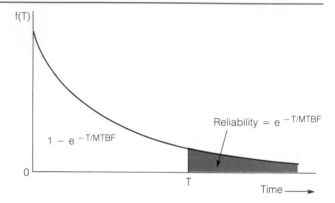

most of the defective items have been eliminated and it is too soon to encounter items that fail because they have worn out. In some cases this second phase can cover a relatively long period of time. In the third and final phase failures due to wear-out occur, and the failure rate increases.

Information on the distribution and length of each phase requires the collection of historical data and analysis of that data. It often turns out that the *mean time between failures* (MTBF) can be modeled by a negative exponential distribution, such as that depicted in Figure 6–4. Equipment failures as well as product failures may occur in this pattern. In such cases the exponential distribution can be used to determine various probabilities of interest. The probability that equipment or a product put into service at time 0 will fail *before* some specified time, *T,* is equal to the area under the curve between 0 and *T. Reliability* is concerned with the probability that a product will last *at least* until time *T;* reliability is equal to the area under the curve *beyond T.* (Note that the total area under the curve in each phase is treated as 100 percent for computational purposes.) Observe that as the specified length of service increases, the area under the curve to the right of that point (i.e., the reliability) decreases.

Determining values for the area under a curve to the right of a given point, *T,* is a relatively simple matter using a table of exponential values. An exponential distribution is completely described using a single parameter, the distribution mean, which reliability engineers often refer to as the mean time between failures. Using the symbol *T* to represent length of service, we can easily determine the probability that failure will not occur before time *T* (i.e., the area in the right tail):

$$P(\text{no failure before } T) = e^{-T/MTBF}$$

where

$$e = \text{Natural logarithm, } 2.7183 \ldots .$$
$$T = \text{Length of service before failure}$$
$$MTBF = \text{Mean time between failures}$$

The probability that failure will occur before time T is 1.00 minus that amount:

$$P(\text{failure before time } T) = 1 - e^{-T/MTBF}$$

Selected values of $e^{-T/MTBF}$ are listed in Table 6–2.

TABLE 6–2

Values of $e^{-T/MTBF}$

T/MTBF	$e^{-T/MTBF}$	T/MTBF	$e^{-T/MTBF}$
.10	.9048	3.60	.0273
.20	.8187	3.70	.0247
.30	.7408	3.80	.0224
.40	.6703	3.90	.0202
.50	.6065	4.00	.0183
.60	.5488	4.10	.0166
.70	.4966	4.20	.0150
.80	.4493	4.30	.0136
.90	.4066	4.40	.0123
1.00	.3679	4.50	.0111
1.10	.3329	4.60	.0101
1.20	.3012	4.70	.0091
1.30	.2725	4.80	.0082
1.40	.2466	4.90	.0074
1.50	.2231	5.00	.0067
1.60	.2019	5.10	.0061
1.70	.1827	5.20	.0055
1.80	.1653	5.30	.0050
1.90	.1496	5.40	.0045
2.00	.1353	5.50	.0041
2.10	.1255	5.60	.0037
2.20	.1108	5.70	.0033
2.30	.1003	5.80	.0030
2.40	.0907	5.90	.0027
2.50	.0821	6.00	.0025
2.60	.0743	6.10	.0022
2.70	.0672	6.20	.0020
2.80	.0608	6.30	.0018
2.90	.0550	6.40	.0017
3.00	.0498	6.50	.0015
3.10	.0450	6.60	.0014
3.20	.0408	6.70	.0012
3.30	.0369	6.80	.0011
3.40	.0334	6.90	.0010
3.50	.0302	7.00	.0009

EXAMPLE 2

By means of extensive testing, a manufacturer has determined that its Super Sucker Vacuum Cleaner models have an expected life that is exponential with a mean of four years. Find the probability that one of these cleaners will experience its first breakdown:

1. After the initial four years of service.
2. Before four years of service are completed.
3. Not before six years of service.

Solution

$$MTBF = 4 \text{ years}$$

a. $T = 4$ years, $T/MTBF = \dfrac{4 \text{ years}}{4 \text{ years}} = 1.0$.

From Table 6–2, $e^{-1.0} = .3679$.

b. The probability of failure before $T = 4$ years is $1 - e^{-1}$ or $1 - .3679 = .6321$.

c. $T = 6$ years, $T/MRBF = \dfrac{6 \text{ years}}{4 \text{ years}} = 1.50$.

From Table 6–2, $e^{-1.5} = .2231$.

Product life can sometimes be modeled by a normal distribution. Obtaining probabilities involves the use of a table (refer to Table B in the Appendix). The table provides areas under a normal curve from (essentially) the left end of the curve to a specified point, z, where z is a *standardized* value computed using the formula:

$$z = \frac{T - \text{Mean wear-out time}}{\text{Standard deviation of wear-out time}}$$

FIGURE 6–5

A Normal Curve

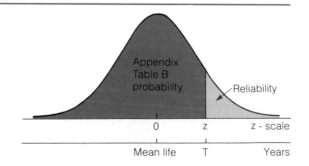

Thus, in order to work with the normal distribution, it is necessary to know the mean of the distribution and its standard deviation. A normal distribution is illustrated in Figure 6–5. Appendix Table B yields normal probabilities (i.e., the area that lies to the left of z). To obtain a probability that service life will not exceed some value, T, compute z and refer to the table. To find the reliability for time T, compute z, obtain the probability from Table B for the area to the left of z, and subtract from 100 percent. To obtain the value of T that will provide a given probability to either the right or left of that service life, locate the nearest probability under the curve *to the left* in Table B. Then use the corresponding z in the above formula and solve for T.

EXAMPLE 3

The mean life of a certain ball bearing can be modeled using a normal distribution with a mean of six years and a standard deviation of one year. Determine each of the following:

a. The probability that a ball bearing will fail *before* seven years of service.
b. The probability that a ball bearing will fail *after* seven years of service (i.e., find its *reliability*).
c. The service life that will provide a reliability of 90 percent.

Solution

Given: Wear-out mean = 6 years
            Wear-out standard deviation = 1 year
            Wear-out life is normally distributed

a. Compute z and use it to obtain the probability directly from Table B (see diagram).

$$z = \frac{7-6}{1} = +1.00$$

Thus, $P(T < 7) = .8413$.

EXAMPLE 3 *(concluded)*

b. Subtract the probability determined in part *a* from 100 percent (see diagram).

$1.00 - .8413 = .1587$

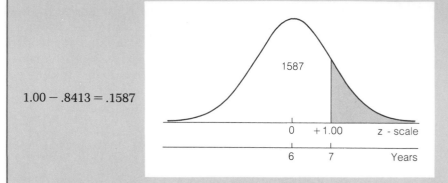

c. Turn to the normal table (Appendix Table B) and find the value of z that corresponds to an area under the curve of $100\% - 90\% = 10\%$ (see diagram).

$$z = -1.28 = \frac{T - 6}{1}$$

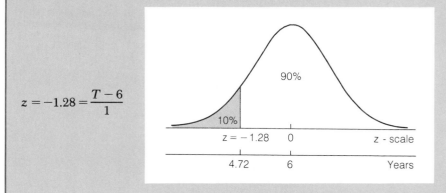

Solving for T we find $T = 4.72$ years.

Improving Reliability

Reliability can be improved in a number of ways, some of which are listed in Table 6–3.

Because overall system reliability is a function of the reliability of individual components, improvements in their reliability can increase system reliability. Unfortunately, inadequate production or assembly procedures can negate even the best of designs, and this is often a source of failures. Part of the burden of reducing product failures lies with the quality-control system, which must

TABLE 6–3

Potential Ways to Improve Reliability

1. Improve component design.
2. Improve production and/or assembly techniques.
3. Improve testing.
4. Use redundancy.
5. Improve preventive maintenance procedures.
6. Improve user education.
7. Improve system design.

inspect output and indicate if changes are needed. As we have just seen, system reliability can be increased by the use of backup components. Failures in actual use can often be reduced by upgrading user education and refining maintenance recommendations or procedures. Finally, it may be possible to increase the overall reliability of the system by simplifying the system (and thereby reducing the number of components that could cause the system to fail) or altering component relationships (e.g., increasing the reliability of interfaces).

Perhaps the fundamental issue in improving reliability is: how much reliability is needed? The answer depends on the potential benefits of improvements and on the cost of those improvements. Generally speaking, reliability improvements become increasingly costly. Thus, while initial benefits may increase at a much faster rate than costs, eventually the reverse is true. The optimum level of reliability is the point where the incremental benefit received equals the incremental cost of obtaining it.

SUMMARY

Product and service design often plays a central role in system design because the other aspects of the system must be designed with respect to the general products and services involved. Due to the ever-changing nature of the environment in which organizations must function, product and service design is subject to continual pressures for design improvements.

Research and development activities are one approach to new products. Because of the inherent costs involved, the number of firms that can afford R&D is limited. Another approach involves design by imitation. Regardless of whether firms undertake research themselves or use the services of other organizations, the value of removing uncertainty from a risk situation can be determined.

Two key aspects of product design relate to standardization and reliability. Standardization yields economies based on uniformity of output and related activities but results in a decrease in the amount of variety possible. Modular design is one form of standardization. Measuring and improving reliability are important aspects of successful systems design.

The primary concerns in product design are function and cost (manufacturability).

1. A product design engineer must decide whether a redundant component is cost-justified in a certain system. The system in question has a critical component that has a probability of .98 of operating. System failure would involve a cost of $2,000. A switch could be added to the system that would automatically transfer the system to the backup component in the event of a failure for a cost of $100. Should the backup be added if the backup probability is also .98?

   Solution:

   Since no probability is given for the switch, we must assume its probability of operating when needed is 100 percent. The expected cost of failure (i.e., without the backup) is $2,000(1 − .98) = $400.
   With the backup, the probability of *not* failing would be:

   $$.98 + .02(.98) = .9996.$$

   Hence, the probability of failure would be $1 − .9996 = .0004$. The expected cost of failure with the backup would be the added cost of the backup plus the failure cost:

   $$\$100 + \$2,000(.0004) = \$100.80.$$

   Since this is less than the cost without the backup, it appears that adding the backup is definitely cost-justifiable.

2. Due to the extreme cost of interrupting production, a firm has two standby machines available in case a particular machine suffers a breakdown. The machine in use has a reliability of .94, and the backups have reliabilities of .90 and .80. In the event of a failure, either backup can be pressed into service, and if it fails, the other backup can be used. Compute the system reliability.

   Solution

   $$R_1 = .94, \; R_2 = .90, \text{ and } R_3 = .80$$

   The system can be depicted in the manner shown:

$$R_{system} = R_1 + R_2(1 - R_1) + R_3(1 - R_2)(1 - R_1)$$
$$= .94 + .90(1 - .94) + .80(1 - .90)(1 - .94) = .9988$$

3. A hospital has three *independent* fire alarm systems, with reliabilities of .95, .97, and .99. In the event of a fire, what is the probability that a warning would be given?

Solution

A warning would *not* be given if all three alarms failed. The probability that at least one alarm would operate is $1 - P$(none operate):

$$P(\text{none operate}) = (1 - .95)(1 - .97)(1 - .99) = .000015$$
$$P(\text{warning}) = 1 - .000015 = .999985$$

4. A weather satellite has an expected life of 10 years from the time it is placed into earth orbit. Determine its reliability for the lengths of service given below:

a. 5 years　　**b.** 12 years　　**c.** 20 years　　**d.** 30 years

(Assume the exponential distribution is appropriate.)

Solution

$$MTBF = 10 \text{ years}$$

Compute the ratio $T/MTBF$ for $T = 5$, 12, 20, and 30 and obtain the values of $e^{-T/MTBF}$ from Table 6–2. The solution is summarized in the table below:

	T		$MTBF$	$T/MTBF$	$e^{-T/MTBF}$ *(from Table 6–2)*
a.	5.	. . . .	10	0.50	.6065
b.	12.	. . . .	10	1.20	.3012
c.	20.	. . . .	10	2.00	.1353
d.	30.	. . . .	10	3.00	.0498

5. What is the probability that the satellite described in the previous example will fail between 5 years and 12 years after being placed into earth orbit?

Solution

$$P(5 \text{ years} < \text{Failure} < 12 \text{ years}) = P(\text{failure after 5 years})$$
$$- P(\text{failure after 12 years})$$

Using the probabilities shown in the previous solution, we find:

$$P(\text{failure after 5 years}) = .6065$$
$$-P(\text{failure after 12 years}) = \underline{.3012}$$
$$.3053$$

The corresponding area under the curve is illustrated below:

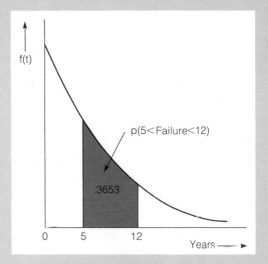

6. One line of radial tires produced by a large company has a wear-out life that can be modeled using a normal distribution that has a mean of 25,000 miles and a standard deviation of 2,000 miles. Determine each of the following:

a. The percentage of tires that can be expected to wear out within ± 2,000 miles of the average. (i.e., between 23,000 miles and 27,000 miles).

b. The percentage of tires that can be expected to fail between 26,000 miles and 29,000 miles.

Solution

Notes: (1) Miles are analogous to time and are handled in exactly the same way time is, (2) the term *percentage* refers to a *probability*.

a. The phrase "within ± 2,000 miles of the average" translates to "within one standard deviation of the mean" since a standard deviation equals 2,000 miles. Therefore, the range of z is $z = -1.00$ to $z = +1.00$, and the area under the curve *between* those points is found by finding the difference between $P(z < +1.00)$ and $P(z < -1.00)$ using values obtained from Appendix Table B:

$$P(z < +1.00) = .8413$$
$$-P(z < -1.00) = .1587$$
$$\overline{P(-1.00 < z < +1.00) = .6826}$$

b. Wear-out mean = 25,000 miles
Wear-out standard deviation = 2,000 miles

$$P(26,000 < \text{wear-out} < 29,000 = P(z < z_{29,000}) - P(z < z_{26,000})$$

$$z_{29,000} = \frac{29,000 - 25,000}{2,000} = +2.00 \to .9772 \text{ (Appendix Table B)}$$

$$z_{26,000} = \frac{26,000 - 25,000}{2,000} = +0.50 \to .6915 \text{ (Appendix Table B)}$$

The difference is .9772 − .6915 = .2857, which is the expected percentage that will wear out between 26,000 miles and 29,000 miles.

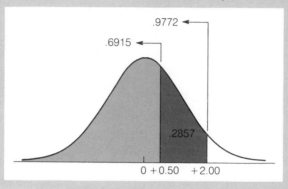

DISCUSSION AND REVIEW QUESTIONS

1. What are some of the factors that cause organizations to redesign their products and services?
2. Contrast applied research and basic research.
3. What is CAD? Describe some of the ways it can be used by a product designer.
4. What are some of the main advantages and disadvantages of standardization?
5. What is modular design and what are its main advantages and disadvantages?
6. Define the term *reliability*.
7. Explain why it is that a product or system might have an overall reliability that is low even though it is made up of components that have fairly high reliabilities.
8. What are some of the ways that reliability can be improved?
9. What is meant by the term *product life cycle*? Why would this be a consideration in product design?
10. Why is R&D a key factor in productivity improvement? What are some of the ways R&D contributes to productivity improvements?
11. What is *redundancy,* and how can it improve product design?

PROBLEMS

1. Consider the following system:

   ─────[.90]──────────[.90]─────

   Determine the probability that the system will operate under each of these conditions:
   a. The system as shown.

b. Each system component has a backup that has a probability of .90 and an 100 percent reliable switch.

c. Backups with .90 probability and a switch that is 99 percent reliable.

2. A product is comprised of four parts. In order for the product to function properly in a given situation, each of the parts must function. Two of the parts each have a probability of .96 of doing that and two have a probability of .99. What is the overall probability that the product will function properly?

3. A system consists of three identical components. In order for the system to perform as intended, all of the components must perform. Each will have the same probability of performance. If the system is to have a probability of performing of .92, what is the minimum probability of performing needed by each of the individual components?

4. A product engineer has developed the following equation for the cost of a system component: $C = (10P)^2$, where C is the cost in dollars and P is the probability that the component will operate as expected. The system is comprised of two identical components, which must both operate in order for the system to operate. The engineer can spend $173 for the two components. To the nearest two decimals, what is the largest component probability that can be achieved?

5. The guidance system of a ship is controlled by a computer that has three major modules. In order for the computer to function properly, all three modules must function. Two of the modules have reliabilities of .97, and the other has a reliability of .99.
   a. What is the reliability of the computer?
   b. A backup computer identical to the one being used will be installed to improve overall reliability. Assuming the new computer automatically functions if the main one fails, determine the resulting reliability.

c. If the backup computer must be activated by a switch in the event that the first computer fails and the switch has a reliability of .98, what is the overall reliability of the system? Note: *Both* the switch and the backup computer must function in order for the backup to take over.

6. One of the industrial robots being designed by a leading producer of servomechanisms has four major components. Component reliabilities are .98, .95, .94, and .90. All of the components must function in order for the robot to operate effectively.
   a. Compute the reliability of the robot.
   b. Designers want to improve the reliability by adding a backup component. Due to space limitations, only one backup can be added. The backup for any component will have the same reliability as the unit it is a backup for. Which component should get the backup in order to achieve the highest reliability?
   c. If one backup that has a reliability of .92 can be added to any one of the main components, which one should get it in order to obtain the highest overall reliability?

7. A production line is comprised of three machines, A, B, and C with reliabilities of .99, .96, and .93 respectively. The machines are arranged in such a way that if one breaks down, the others must also shut down. Engineers are weighing two alternative designs for increasing the line's reliability. Plan 1 involves adding an identical backup *line,* while plan 2 involves providing a backup for each *machine.* In either case, three machines, A, B, and C would be used with reliabilities equal to the original three.
   a. Which plan will provide the higher reliability?
   b. Explain why the two reliabilities are not the same.
   c. What other factors might enter into the decision of which plan to adopt?

8. A water treatment plant has five major

components that must all function in order for the plant to operate as intended. Assuming that each component of the system will have the same reliability, what is the minimum reliability each one must have in order for the overall system to have a reliability of .98?

9. Repeat the previous problem under the condition that one of the components will have a backup that has a reliability equal to that of any one of the other components.

10. Hoping to increase the chances of reaching a performance goal, the director of a research project has assigned three separate research teams the same task. The director estimates that the team reliabilities are .9, .8, and .7 for successfully completing the task in the allotted time. Assuming that the teams work independently, what is the probability that the task will not be completed in time?

11. An electronic chess game has a useful life that is exponential with a mean of 30 months. Determine each of the following:
    a. The probability that any given unit will operate for at least these times: (1) 39 months, (2) 48 months, (3) 60 months.
    b. The probability that any given unit will fail sooner than: (1) 33 months, (2) 15 months, (3) one half year.
    c. After what length of service will the percentage of units that have failed approximately equal: (1) 50 percent? (2) 85 percent? (3) 95 percent? (4) 99 percent?

12. A manufacturer of programmable calculators is attempting to determine a reasonable warranty period for a new model it will introduce shortly. The manager of product testing has indicated that the calculators have an expected life of 30 months. The manufacturer will replace calculators that fail during the warranty period at no charge. Assume product life can be described by an exponential distribution.
    a. If the warranty period is set equal to the expected life of the calculator, what percentage of those sold would

be expected to fail during the warranty period?
    b. What warranty period would result in a failure rate of approximately 10 percent?

13. Lucky Lumen lightbulbs have an expected life that is exponentially distributed with a mean of 5,000 hours. Determine the probability that one of these lightbulbs will last:
    a. At least 6,000 hours.
    b. No longer than 1,000 hours.
    c. Between 1,000 hours and 6,000 hours.

14. Planetary Communications, Inc., intends to launch a satellite that will enhance reception of television programs in Alaska. According to its designers, the satellite will have an expected life of six years. Assume the exponential distribution applies. Determine the probability that it will function for each of these time periods:
    a. More than nine years.
    b. Less than 12 years.
    c. More than 9 years but less than 12 years.
    d. At least 21 years.

15. An office manager has received a report from a consultant that includes a section on equipment replacement. The report indicates that typewriters have a service life that is normally distributed with a mean of 41 months and a standard deviation of 4 months. On the basis of this information, determine the percentage of typewriters that can be expected to fail in these time periods:
    a. Before 38 months of service.
    b. Between 40 and 45 months of service.
    c. Within ±2 months of the mean life.

16. According to a study underwritten by a major television manufacturer, its 19-inch color-TV picture tubes have a mean service life that can be modeled by a normal distribution that has a mean of six years and a standard deviation of one-half year.
    a. What reliability can you assign to these service lives: (1) Five years? (2) Six years? (3) Seven and one-half years?
    b. If the manufacturer sets a warranty

period of four years on these picture tubes, what percentage can be expected to fail from wear-out during the warranty period?

17. In the previous problem, what warranty period would achieve an expected wear-out rate of *(a)* 2 percent? *(b)* 5 percent?

SELECTED BIBLIOGRAPHY

Bierman, Harold Jr.; Charles P. Bonini; and Warren H. Hausman. *Quantitative Analysis for Business Decisions.* 6th ed. Homewood, Ill.: Richard D. Irwin, 1981.

Gerstenfeld, Arthur. *Effective Management of Research and Development.* Reading, Mass.: Addison-Wesley Publishing, 1970.

Groover, Mikell P. *Automation, Production Systems, and Computer-Aided Manufacturing.* Englewood Cliffs, N.J.: Prentice-Hall, 1980.

————, and E. W. Zimmers, Jr. *CAD/CAM: Computer-Aided Design and Manufacturing.* Englewood Cliffs, N.J.: Prentice-Hall, 1984.

Hare, Van Court, Jr. *Systems Analysis: A Di-*

agnostic Approach. New York: Harcourt Brace Jovanovich, 1967.

Hopeman, Richard J. *Production and Operations Management.* 4th ed. Columbus, Ohio: Charles E. Merrill Publishing, 1980.

Kushner, Lawrence M. "Product Safety Standards and Product Innovation, Too." *Harvard Business Review,* July–August 1980, p. 36.

Malott, Robert H. "Let's Restore Balance to Product Liability Law." *Harvard Business Review,* May–June 1983, p. 66.

Moore, Franklin G., and Thomas E. Hendrick. *Production/Operations Management.* 8th ed. Homewood, Ill.: Richard D. Irwin, 1980.

Starr, Martin K. *Operations Management.* Englewood Cliffs, N.J.: Prentice-Hall, 1978.

Reading

Toying with High-Tech

Andrew Pollack

What do you do with an exotic metal alloy that has the ability to "remember" its original shape and return to that shape when heated?

In the United States, the answer is: Use it to make pipe joints in fighter planes and think about using it for satellites that could be launched in compact form and would unfold automatically in space.

But in Japan, the answer is: Use the alloy to make eyeglass frames, air-conditioner louvers, and a toy in which a boy's head and a girl's head are separated by a wire made of the alloy. When the toy is dunked in hot water, the wire returns to a ring shape, bringing the heads together in a kiss.

The example illustrates a major difference between the two nations, which are now vying for world supremacy in high technology.

In the United States, technological emphasis is often on a big military or space project, with little regard for immediate commercial applications.

In Japan, which has no big military or space programs, the emphasis is overwhelmingly on commercial uses, particularly for consumers. Technology advances bit by bit, tested at each step in a variety of applications, some of them exceedingly trivial. Indeed, the Japanese have a penchant for finding low-tech applications for high-tech products.

"We are now in the age of popularization of advanced technology," said Masanori Moritani, senior researcher at the Nomura Research Institute, a division of the Nomura Securities Co. "Especially in Japan, companies are very eager to apply advanced technology."

James C. Abegglen, a Japan watcher associated with the Boston Consulting Group, agreed: "The Americans go for the home run. The Japanese get singles and steal bases."

Other examples of the difference in approach abound:

In the United States, one of the first feasible uses of solar electricity generation was to provide power to satellites. Japan came up with a more down-to-earth application—the solar-powered calculator. Now companies here are coming out with the solar-powered radio, the solar-powered watch, and the solar-powered rechargeable battery recharger.

In the United States more than half the market for graphite composite materials—lightweight but strong materials being used as substitutes for metal—is for aerospace and aircraft uses. In Japan, 80 percent of the market is for tennis racquets, golf clubs and other sports equipment, which account for but a small part of its American use.

In the United States, laser development has facilitated everything from surgery to fusion energy, and now lasers may be used for weapons to destroy enemy missiles. Japan produces the only existing consumer products using lasers—the laser videodisk system and the digital audiodisk system.

In new ceramics, the United States has emphasized military uses and the space shuttle heat shield. Japanese companies have come up with ceramic scissors, ballpoint pen tips, and sake warmers.

Which approach, the home run or the barrage of singles, will win the game is hotly debated, with each nation wishing it had some of the attributes of the other.

Some American electronics executives question the value of devoting so much technological research to military and space efforts with little commercial value. Many Japanese executives, however, are envious of the American system's ability to make great advances and are worried that their consumer-based technology is too limited.

Aside from Japan's lack of big military or space programs, another reason for the emphasis on consumer applications is that technology development programs run by the Ministry of International Trade and Industry do not always provide much money, despite the publicity they receive. So companies must find other ways to pay for technology development quickly.

"Whether we like it or not, our research efforts must be directed at smaller versions, to find a way to earn some profit," said Kazuo Iga, director of the corporate products development division of the Matsushita Electric Industrial Co. His company uses the shape memory alloy to make air-conditioner louvers that change direction depending on the temperature, directing hot air down to warm a room and cool air up to cool it.

Moreover, the intensely competitive nature of the Japanese consumer electronics industry leads each company to employ new technologies, no matter how frivolously, to make its product stand out. This practice is abetted by the Japanese love of novelty. One product, for example, is a voice-activated cradle, which starts rocking when the baby cries.

Such experimentation often produces benefits in allowing companies to hone their technology and reduce costs by mass production. "You can develop a high-technology base by developing low-technology products with high volume," said Bruce F. Rubinger, director of studies for the Global Competitiveness Council, a research organization in Boston.

Solar energy is an example. The Sanyo Electric Co. is producing four million solar batteries for calculators each month. Now it thinks it has forced the cost down enough to introduce a solar roof tile to provide electricity for homes.

In ceramics, as well, some experts think small consumer applications can help develop more serious ones.

The Japanese are even starting to apply their civilian technology to military systems, spurred in part by an agreement last year with the United States calling for more cooperation in defense technology.

Devices used to record images in video cameras have potential uses for missile guidance systems. Mitsubishi Heavy Industries has been approached by General Motors for help in designing tank transmissions.

Questions:

1. What is the author's main point?
2. Can you think of any other examples that support the author's contention? Can you think of any that contradict it?
3. Can you offer any other thoughts on this subject?

Chapter 7

Facilities Layout

After completing this chapter, you should be able to:

1. Briefly describe the main features of continuous, intermittent, and project processing.
2. List the primary advantages and limitations of both continuous and intermittent layouts.
3. Solve simple line balancing problems.
4. Develop simple process layouts.
5. Describe new approaches to production.

INTRODUCTION, 310

The Need for Layout Decisions, 310

TYPES OF PROCESSING, 311

Continuous Processing, 311
Intermittent Processing, 311
Projects, 312

BASIC LAYOUT TYPES, 312

Product Layouts, 312
Process Layouts, 315
Fixed-Position Layouts, 316
Combination Layouts, 317

NEW APPROACHES TO PRODUCTION, 318

Computer-Aided Manufacturing, (CAM), 318
Cellular Manufacturing, 321
Group Technology, 323
Flexible Manufacturing Systems, 325

LINE BALANCING, 325

Other Factors, 334

DESIGNING PROCESS LAYOUTS, 335

Measures of Effectiveness, 336
Information Requirements, 337
Minimizing Transportation Costs or Distances, 338
Closeness Ratings, 340
Computer Analysis, 343

SUMMARY, 344

SOLVED PROBLEMS, 346

DISCUSSION AND REVIEW QUESTIONS, 348

PROBLEMS, 349

SELECTED BIBLIOGRAPHY, 352

READING: THE TECHNOCRATIC HAMBURGER, 353

This chapter is the fourth one of a series of chapters on design of operating systems. The previous chapters dealt with location, products, and capacity planning; this chapter examines layout design. Layout concerns the configuration of departments, work centers, and equipment, with particular emphasis on movement of work (customers or materials) through the system. Decisions in any one of these four design areas usually have impacts on the others. Thus, both layout and location decisions affect capacity. Conversely, efforts to increase capacity may involve modifications in layout and changes in location. Moreover, any time a new location is established or products or services are introduced or changed, there are layout implications.

This chapter describes the main types of layout designs along with models used to evaluate design alternatives. The chapter begins with a discussion of the basic types of processing that can be done by operating systems since type of processing is usually the main determinant of layout design.

INTRODUCTION

As in other areas of system design, layout decisions are important for three basic reasons: (1) they require substantial investments of both money and effort, (2) they involve long-term commitments, which make mistakes difficult to overcome, and (3) they have a significant impact on the cost and efficiency of short-term operations. In addition, personnel may resist changes to an existing layout because such changes often require them to alter daily routines or to undergo retraining.

The Need for Layout Decisions

The need for layout planning can arise as part of the design of new facilities as well as the redesign of existing facilities. In the latter instance, the most common reasons for redesign of layouts include the following:

1. Inefficient operations (e.g., high cost, bottlenecks).
2. Accidents or safety hazards.
3. Changes in the design of products or services.
4. The introduction of new products or services.
5. Changes in the volume of output or mix of outputs.
6. Changes in methods or equipment.
7. Changes in environmental or other legal requirements.
8. Morale problems (e.g., lack of face-to-face contact).

Naturally, the reasons for layout redesign influence the objectives being sought. For instance, if morale or safety problems exist, the objectives of a new layout plan would include remedying those problems. Even so, the main objectives in the majority of layout analyses relate to minimizing either the cost of materials handling or the movement of customers within a system, along with concerns for productivity and other operating characteristics of the system.

TYPES OF PROCESSING

There are basically three types of processing systems: continuous, intermittent, and project. Continuous systems are highly specialized systems designed to provide high volumes of output for one or a few standardized items. Intermittent systems are more generalized, making them more suited to handle lower volumes of items that present a variety of processing requirements. Project systems have limited life spans and are best suited for complex, special-purpose jobs. Each of these systems is briefly described below.

Continuous Processing

Continuous processing systems are sometimes referred to as *flow* systems because of the rapid rate items move through the system. This form of processing is used when highly standardized products or services are involved. The highly repetitive nature of operations lends itself to specialization of both labor and equipment. Because of the division of labor, there are usually low-skill labor requirements. Specialized equipment, on the other hand, although expensive, can usually be justified by the high volumes often characteristic of such systems because the overall cost per unit is relatively low. Typewriters, radios and TVs, telephone equipment, and calculators are examples of products that are often mass produced using a continuous processing system. As a general rule, such products are made for inventory rather than for customer order. Examples in the service area are less plentiful. They include programs for mass inoculations, automatic car washes, mechanical harvesters, mail service, and fast-food operations.

Intermittent Processing

Intermittent processing gets its name from the short runs associated with low-volume jobs. In addition to relatively low volumes of output, these systems are characterized by general-purpose equipment that can satisfy a variety of processing requirements, semiskilled or skilled workers who operate the equipment, and a narrower span of supervision than most continuous systems. Differences in job-processing requirements present routing and scheduling challenges, as well as a frequent need to adjust equipment settings or make other alterations for successive jobs. In manufacturing systems items are often processed in batches or lots, although in non-manufacturing applications processing occurs both by lots and on an individual basis. Processing cost per unit is generally higher than it would be under continuous processing. Typical examples of intermittent processing include textbook production, bakeries, health-care systems, and educational systems. In some cases the outputs are made for inventory (clothing, automobile tires) while in others they are designed to meet customer needs (health care) or specifications (special tools, parts, or equipment). Marketing efforts in such systems are often directed towards promoting system capabilities or customized services.

Projects

Project systems are set up to handle complex jobs that involve unique sets of activities. Examples include large or unusual construction projects, new product development or promotion, planning and coordinating space missions, and organizing and handling the logistics of disaster relief efforts. Because of their limited life span and the nonrepetitive nature of activities, these systems differ considerably from continuous and intermittent processing systems. Projects are discussed at length in Chapter 13.

BASIC LAYOUT TYPES

There are three basic types of layouts, and these correspond roughly to the three types of processing systems. *Product layouts,* for example, are most conducive to continuous processing, *process layouts* are used for intermittent processing, and *fixed-position layouts* are used when projects require layouts, although not all projects do. In addition, fixed-position layouts find applications in other situations, as you will soon discover. The characteristics of each layout type will be described below, along with the advantages and disadvantages associated with each of these layouts. Hybrid layouts, which are combinations of these pure types, are also briefly described.

Product Layouts

Product layouts are used to achieve a smooth and rapid flow of large volumes of products or customers through a system. This is made possible by highly standardized products or services that require highly standardized (repetitive) processing operations. A job is divided into a series of standardized tasks, permitting specialization of both labor and equipment. The large volumes handled by these systems usually make it economical to invest substantial sums of money in equipment and in job design. Because only one or a few very similar items are involved, it is feasible to arrange an entire layout to correspond to the technological processing requirements of the product or service involved. For instance, if a portion of a manufacturing operation required the sequence mill-drill-deburr, the appropriate pieces of equipment would be arranged in

FIGURE 7–1

A Flow Line for Production or Service

that same sequence. Moreover, because each item follows the same sequence of operations, it is often possible to utilize fixed-path material-handling equipment such as conveyors to transport items between operations. The resulting arrangement forms a line like the one depicted in Figure 7–1. In manufacturing environments the lines are referred to as *production lines* or *assembly lines,* depending on the type of activity involved. In nonmanufacturing the term *line* may or may not be used. For instance, it is common to refer to a cafeteria line as such, but not usually to refer to a car wash in this way, although from a conceptual standpoint, the two are nearly identical. Figure 7–2 illustrates a typical cafeteria serving line layout. Examples of this type of layout tend to be less plentiful in nonmanufacturing because processing requirements usually exhibit too much variability to make standardization feasible. Without high standardization, many of the benefits of continuous processing are lost. When lines are used, certain compromises may be made. For instance, an automatic car wash provides equal treatment to all cars—the same amount of soap and water and scrubbing—even though cars may differ considerably in cleaning needs. As a result, some very dirty cars do not come out completely clean, while relatively clean cars that go through the system mean some waste of soap, water, and energy.

Product layouts achieve a high degree of both labor and equipment utilization, and that tends to offset the high equipment costs usually associated with this type of layout. Because items move quickly from operation to operation, investment in work-in-process is often minimal. However, operations are so closely tied to each

FIGURE 7–2

Cafeteria Line

other that there is a high vulnerability to shut down the entire system due to either mechanical failure or high absenteeism. Maintenance procedures are geared to this. Preventive maintenance—periodic inspection and replacement of worn parts or those with high failure rates—is used to reduce the probability of breakdowns during operations. Of course, no amount of preventive activity can completely eliminate failures, so measures designed to provide quick repair must also be taken, which include maintaining an inventory of spare parts and having repair personnel available to quickly restore equipment to normal operation. These procedures are fairly expensive: Because of the specialized nature of equipment, problems become more difficult to diagnose and resolve, and spare parts inventories can be extensive.

The main advantages of product layouts can be summarized as:

1. A high rate of output.
2. Low unit costs due to high volume.
3. Labor specialization reduces training costs and time and results in a wide span of supervision.
4. Material-handling costs are low per unit, and material handling is simplified because units follow the same sequence of operations.
5. There is a high utilization of labor and equipment.
6. Routing and scheduling are encompassed in the initial design of the system and do not require much attention once the system is in operation.
7. Accounting, purchasing, and inventory control are fairly routine.

The primary disadvantages of product layouts include:

1. The intensive division of labor usually creates dull, repetitive jobs, which do not provide much opportunity for advancement and may lead to morale problems.
2. Low-skilled workers may exhibit little interest in maintaining equipment or in quality of output.
3. The system is fairly inflexible to either changes in the volume of output or changes in product or process design.
4. The system is highly susceptible to shutdowns caused by equipment breakdowns or excessive absenteeism.
5. Preventive maintenance, the capacity for quick repairs, and spare parts inventories are necessary expenses.
6. Incentive plans tied to individual output are impractical since they would tend to cause variations among outputs of individual workers that would adversely affect high utilization of labor and equipment.

Process Layouts   Process layouts are designed to facilitate processing items or providing services that present variations in their processing requirements. The layouts feature departments or other functional groupings in which similar kinds of activities are performed. For example, machine shops usually have separate departments for milling, grinding, drilling, and so on. Items that require those operations are frequently moved in batches to the departments in a sequence dictated by technical considerations. Different products may present quite different processing requirements and sequences of operations. Consequently, variable-path material-handling equipment (forklift trucks, jeeps, tote boxes) is needed to handle the variety of routes and items. The use of general-purpose machines provides the flexibility necessary to handle a wide range of processing requirements. Workers who operate the equipment are usually skilled or semiskilled. Figure 7–3 illustrates the departmental arrangement typical of process layouts.

Process layouts are also common in nonmanufacturing environments. Examples include hospitals, colleges and universities, banks, auto repair shops, airlines, and public libraries. For instance, hospitals have departments or other units that specifically handle surgery, maternity, pediatrics, psychiatric, emergency, and geriatric care. Similarly, universities have separate schools or departments that concentrate on such areas of study as business, engineering, science, and math. Most business organizations have administrative departments like accounting and payroll.

Because process layouts arrange equipment by type rather than according to processing sequence, the system is much less vulnerable to shutdown caused by either mechanical failure or absentee-

FIGURE 7–3

A Process Layout Is Typified by Departmental Work Centers

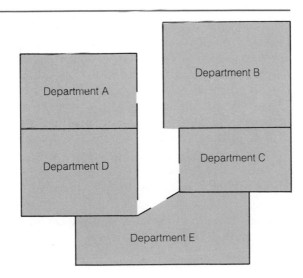

ism. In manufacturing systems, especially, idle equipment is usually available to replace machines that are temporarily out of service. Moreover, since items are often processed in lots, there is considerably less interdependence between successive operations than with a product layout. Maintenance costs tend to be lower because the equipment is less specialized than with product layouts, and grouping of machinery permits repair personnel to become somewhat specialized in handling repairs. And machine similarity reduces the necessary investment in spare parts. On the negative side, routing and scheduling must be done on a continual basis in order to accommodate the variety of processing demands typically imposed on these systems. Material handling is inefficient, and unit handling costs are generally much higher than in product layouts. In-process inventories can be substantial due to lot processing. Furthermore, it is not uncommon for such systems to have equipment utilization rates under 50 percent because of routing and scheduling complexities related to the variety of processing demands being handled.

In sum, the advantages of process layouts include:

1. Systems can handle a variety of processing requirements.
2. The system is not particularly vulnerable to equipment failures.
3. General-purpose equipment is often less costly than the specialized equipment used in product layouts and is easier and less costly to maintain.
4. It is possible to use individual incentive systems.

Disadvantages of process layouts include:

1. In-process inventory costs can be high if batch processing is used in manufacturing systems.
2. Routing and scheduling pose continual challenges.
3. Equipment utilization rates are low.
4. Material handling is slow and inefficient and more costly per unit than under product layouts.
5. Job complexities often reduce the span of supervision and result in higher supervisory costs than product layouts do.
6. Special attention for each product or customer (routing, scheduling, machine setups, and so on) and low volumes result in higher unit costs than with product layouts.
7. Accounting, inventory control, and purchasing are much more involved than under product layouts.

Fixed-Position Layouts

In fixed-position layouts the product or other item being worked on remains stationary, and workers, materials, and equipment are moved about as needed. This is in marked contrast to both product and process layouts. Almost always, the nature of the product dictates this kind of arrangement; weight, size, bulk, or some other factor makes it undesirable or extremely difficult to attempt to move the product. Fixed-position layouts are used in large construction projects (buildings, power plants, dams), shipbuilding, and production of large aircraft and the rockets used to launch space missions. In those instances, attention is focused on timing of material and equipment deliveries so as not to clog up the work site and to avoid having to relocate materials and equipment around the work site. Lack of storage space can present significant problems, for example, at construction sites in crowded urban locations. Because of the many diverse activities being carried out on large projects and because of the wide range of skills required, special efforts are needed to coordinate the activities, and the span of control can be quite narrow. For these reasons, the administrative burden is often much higher than it would be under either of the other layout types. Material handling may or may not be a factor: In many cases there is no tangible product involved (e.g., designing a computerized inventory system). When goods and materials are involved, material handling often resembles process-type variable-path, general-purpose equipment, even though the actual equipment used might differ somewhat, depending on the nature of the work. Projects might require use of earth-moving equipment and trucks to haul materials to, from, and around the work site, for example.

Fixed-position layouts are widely used for farming, firefighting, road building, home building, remodeling and repair, and drilling for oil. In each case there are compelling reasons for bringing workers, materials, and equipment to the "product's" location instead of the other way around.

Combination Layouts

The three basic layout types are ideal models that may be altered to satisfy the needs of a particular situation. In fact, it is not unusual to discover layouts that represent some combination of the pure types described above. For instance, supermarket layouts are essentially of a process nature, and yet we find most use fixed-path material-handling devices such as roller-type conveyors both in the stockroom and at checkouts and belt-type conveyors at the cash registers. Hospitals also use the basic process arrangement, although frequently patient care involves more of a fixed-position approach, which has nurses, doctors, medicines, and special equipment brought to the patient. By the same token, faulty parts made by a continuous system may require off-line reworking, which involves customized processing. And one frequently observes use of conveyors in both farming and construction activities.

NEW APPROACHES TO PRODUCTION

This section describes some of the latest production technology, including computer-aided manufacturing (CAM), robotics, cellular manufacturing, group technology, and flexible manufacturing systems.

Computer-Aided Manufacturing (CAM)

The term *computer-aided manufacturing (CAM)* refers to the use of computers in process control, ranging from numerically controlled (N/C) machines to robots to automated assembly systems. These systems replace human functions with machine functions. They have the advantage of reducing labor, handling dangerous, dirty, or boring tasks, and yielding high, consistent quality. As you might suppose, such equipment can be very expensive.

Numerically controlled machines are programmed to follow a set of processing instructions that are based on mathematical relationships that tell the machine the details of operations that are to be performed. The instructions are stored on a device such as a floppy disk, magnetic tape, or microprocessor. Although N/C machines have been used for many years; they are an important part of new approaches to manufacturing. Individual machines may have their own computer, which is referred to as *computerized numerical control (CNC)*. Or one computer may control a number of N/C machines, which is referred to as *direct numerical control (DNC)*.

The use of *industrial robots* in manufacturing is increasing. A robot consists of three parts: A mechanical arm, a power supply, and a controller. Unlike film versions of robots, which vaguely resemble human beings, industrial robots are much less glamorous in appearance and much less mobile: most robots are stationary except for their movable "arms."

Robots are used to handle a wide variety of tasks, including welding, assembly, loading and unloading machines, painting, and testing. They relieve humans from heavy or dirty work; robots are typically used to eliminate drudgery tasks.

Some uses of robots are fairly simple, whereas others are much more complex. At the lowest level are robots that follow a fixed set of instructions. Next are programmable robots, which can repeat a set of movements after being led through the sequence. In effect, these robots "play back" a mechanical sequence much as a video recorder plays back a visual sequence. At the next higher level are robots that follow instructions from a computer. At the top end are robots that can recognize objects and make certain decisions.

Robots move in one of two ways. Point-to-point robots move to predetermined points, perform a specified operation, and then move

FIGURE 7–4

**Examples of Robot
"Hands"**

Special hand with one
movable jaw
> A hand with single-acting
> jaw should be considered
> when there is any access
> underneath a part, as
> when it is on a rack.
> Where this hand can be
> applied, it will scoop up a
> part quite quickly. Sim-
> plicity of the design makes
> this one of the most
> economical hands.

Special hand for cartons
> The dual-jaw hand will
> open wide to grasp
> inexactly located objects
> of light weight. Lifting and
> placement of cardboard
> cartons is an application.
> Actuators and jaws can
> be remounted in any of
> several positions on the
> fixed back plate, making it
> practical for the same
> dual-jaw hand to move
> large cartons on one
> day and smaller cartons
> the next.

Special hand with modular
gripper
> This special hand, with pair
> of pneumatic actuators, is
> one of the many special
> hand designs for industrial
> robots. It would be suitable
> for parts of light weight.
> Lifting capacity is depen-
> dent upon friction devel-
> oped by the fingers, but
> heavier parts could be
> handled if the fingers
> could secure a more posi-
> tive purchase—as under a
> flange or lip.

FIGURE 7–5

Work Comes to Robot

on to the next point and perform another operation, and so on. Continuous-path robots follow a continuous (moving) path while performing an operation.

Robots can be powered in one of three ways: pneumatically (air-driven), hydraulically (fluids under pressure), or electronically.

Figures 7–4 through 7–7 illustrate robots. Table 7–1 describes in more detail some of the various kinds of robots currently being used.

FIGURE 7–6

Robots on an Assembly Line

FIGURE 7-7

Typical Articulations of a Playback Robot with Point-to-Point Control

a) EXTEND AND RETRACT ARM
(Out - in = 0)

b) ELEVATE AND DEPRESS ARM
(Down - up = D)

c) ROTATE LEFT OR RIGHT
(Rotate = R)

d) TURN ON HAND ASSEMBLY AXIS
(Swivel = S)

e) PIVOT HAND ASSEMBLY
(Bend = B)

Source: Reprinted by permission of the publisher, from *Robotics In Practice*, by Joseph F. Engelberger, p. 26 © 1980 Joseph F. Engelberger. Published by AMACOM, a division of American Management Associations, New York. All rights reserved.

Cellular Manufacturing

Process layouts and product layouts represent two ends of a continuum from small batches to continuous production. Process layouts are conducive to the production of a wider range of products or services than product layouts, which is desirable from a consumer standpoint where customized products are often in demand. However, process layouts tend to be less efficient than product layouts, and they involve higher unit production costs than product layouts and sometimes lower quality. Some manufacturers are attempting to move away from process layouts in an effort to capture some of the benefits of product layouts. Ideally, a system would be flexible and yet be efficient with low unit production costs. Cellular manufacturing, group technology, and flexible manufacturing systems represent efforts to move toward this ideal.

TABLE 7-1

Industrial Robots	*Industrial robots* all have armlike projections and grippers that perform factory work customarily done by humans. The term is usually reserved for machines with some form of built-in control system and capable of stand-alone operation. But in Japan, it also includes manipulators operated by humans, either directly or remotely.

A pick-and-place robot is the simplest version, accounting for about one third of all U.S. installations. The name comes from its usual application in materials handling: picking something from one spot and placing it at another. Freedom of movement is usually limited to two or three directions—in and out, left and right, and up and down. The control system is electromechanical. Prices range from $5,000 to $30,000.

A servo robot is the most common industrial robot because it can include all robots described below. The name stems from one or more servomechanisms that enable the arm and gripper to alter direction in midair, without having to trip a mechanical switch. Five to seven directional movements are common, depending on the number of "joints," or articulations, in the robot's arm.

A programmable robot is a servo robot directed by a programmable controller that memorizes a sequence of arm-and-gripper movements; this routine can then be repeated perpetually. The robot is reprogrammed by leading its gripper through the new task. The price range is $25,000 to $90,000.

A computerized robot is a servo model run by a computer. The computer controller does not have to be taught by leading the armgripper through a routine; new instructions can be transmitted electronically. The programming for such "smart" robots may include the ability to optimize, or improve, its work-routine instructions. Prices start at about $35,000.

A sensory robot is a computerized robot with one or more artificial senses, usually sight or touch. Prices for early models start at about $75,000.

An assembly robot is a computerized robot, probably a sensory model, designed specifically for assembly-line jobs. For light, batch-manufacturing applications, the arm's design may be fairly anthropomorphic.

Cellular manufacturing is a type of layout in which one or a variety of machines are grouped together into what is referred to as a *cell.* Groupings are determined by the operations needed to perform work for a set of similar items, or *part families,* that require similar processing. In effect, the cells become miniature versions of product layouts. The cells can consist of one machine, a group of machines with no conveyorized movement of parts between machines (automatic transfer), or a flow line connected by a conveyor line. A comparison of a typical functional (process) layout and a cellular manufacturing layout is given in Figure 7–8. Observe that in the cellular layout, machines are arranged to handle all of the operations necessary for a group (family) of similar parts. Thus, all of the parts follow the same route, although minor variations (e.g., skip an operation) are possible. In contrast, the functional layout involves multiple paths for parts. Moreover, there is little effort or need to identify part families; the distinction in the figure is merely for purposes of comparison.

There are numerous benefits of cellular manufacturing. These

FIGURE 7–8

**Comparison
of Functional
and Cellular
Manufacturing
Layouts**

Functional layout

Cellular manufacturing layout

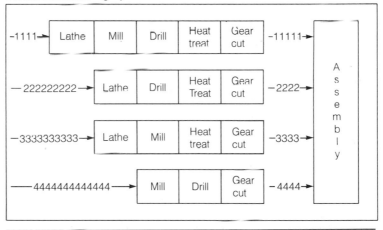

Source: Adapted from D. Fogarty, and T. Hoffman, *Production and Inventory Management* (Cincinnati: South-Western Publishing, 1983), p. 472.

relate to the grouping of equipment. They include faster throughput time, less material handling, less work in process inventory, and reduced setup time.

**Group
Technology**

In order to use cellular manufacturing, there must be groups of items that have similar processing characteristics. Moreover, these items must be identified. The grouping process is known as *group technology,* which involves indentifying items that have similarities in either *design characteristics* or in *manufacturing character-*

FIGURE 7–9

A Group of Parts with Similar Manufacturing Process Requirements but Different Design Attributes

Source: Mikell P. Groover, *Automation, Production Systems, and Computer-Aided Manufacturing* © 1980, p. 540. Reprinted by permission of Prentice-Hall, Inc., Englewood Cliffs, New Jersey.

istics and grouping them into part families. Design characteristics would include size, shape, and function; manufacturing or processing characteristics would involve the type and sequence of operations required. In many cases design and processing characteristics are correlated, although this is not always the case. Thus, design families may be different than processing families. Figure 7–9 illustrates a group of parts that have similar processing characteristics but different design characteristics.

Once similar items have been identified, items can be classed according to their families, and a coding system can be developed. The coding system facilitates retrieval from a data base for purposes of design and manufacturing. For instance, a designer can readily determine if there is an existing part that is similar or identical to one that had to be designed. It may happen that an existing part, with some modification, would be satisfactory. This greatly enhances the productivity of design. Similarly, planning manufacturing for a new part would involve matching it with one of the part families in existence, thereby alleviating much of the burden of specifying processing details.

The conversion to group technology and cellular manufacturing involves a systematic analysis of parts in order to identify the part families. This often represents a major undertaking; it is a time-consuming job that involves the analysis of a considerable amount of data. Three primary methods for accomplishing this are visual inspection, examination of design and production data, and production flow analysis.

Visual inspection is the least accurate of the three but also the least costly and simplest to perform. Examining design and production data is more accurate but much more time-consuming. It is perhaps the most commonly used method of analysis. Production flow analysis involves examination of operation sequences and machine routings to uncover similarities. Hence, the analysis has a manufacuring perspective and not a design perspective. Moreover, the operation sequences and routings are taken as givens; in reality the existing procedures may be far from optimal.

Conversion to cellular manufacturing can involve costly realignment of equipment. Consequently, a manager must weigh the benefits of a switch from a process layout to a cellular one against the costs of moving equipment as well as the cost and time needed for grouping parts.

Flexible Manufacturing Systems

Flexible manufacturing systems (FMS) are more fully automated versions of cellular manufacturing: A computer controls the transfer of parts from machine to machine as well as the start of work at each machine. These systems are also referred to as *computer-integrated manufacturing* (CID). As you might suspect, these systems are quite expensive. However, they enable manufacturers to achieve some of the benefits of product layouts with small batch sizes and much greater flexibility with a system that is capable of operating with little or no human intervention.

LINE BALANCING

Many of the benefits of a product layout relate to the ability to divide required work up into a series of elemental tasks that can be performed quickly and routinely by low-skilled workers or by specialized equipment. The durations of these elemental tasks typically range from as little as a few seconds to as much as 15 minutes or more. Most of the times are so brief that it would be impractical to assign only one task to each worker. For one thing, most workers would quickly become bored by the limited job requirements. For another, the number of workers required to complete even a simple product or service would be enormous. Instead, tasks are usually grouped into manageable bundles that are assigned to work stations manned by one or two operators.

The process of deciding how to assign tasks to work stations is referred to as *line balancing*.

The goal of line balancing is to obtain task groupings that represent approximately equal time requirements. This minimizes the idle time along the line and results in a high utilization of labor and equipment. Idle time occurs if task times are not equal among work stations because some stations will have the capability to produce at higher rates than others. These "fast" stations will experience periodic waits for the output from slower stations, or else be forced into idleness to avoid buildups of work between stations. Unbalanced lines are undesirable both from the point of inefficient utilization of labor and equipment and because they may create morale problems for workers at the slower stations who must work continuously.

Lines that are perfectly balanced will have a smooth flow of work because activities along the line can be synchronized to achieve a maximum utilization of labor and equipment. The major obstacle in attaining a perfectly balanced line is the inability to obtain task bundles that have the same durations. One reason for this is the fact that it may not be feasible to combine certain activities into the same bundle either because of differences in equipment requirements or because the activities are not compatible (e.g., risk of contamination of painting from sanding). Another reason is that differences among elemental task lengths can not always be overcome by grouping tasks. Still a third reason for the inability to perfectly balance a line is that a required technological sequence may prohibit otherwise desirable task combinations. For instance, consider a series of three operations that have durations of two minutes, four minutes, and two minutes, as shown below. Ideally, the first and third operations could be combined at one work station and have a total time equal to that of the second operation. However, it may not be possible to combine the first and third operations. For instance, in the case of an automatic car wash, scrubbing and drying operations could not be realistically combined at the same work station due to the need to rinse cars between these two operations.

We can gain some insight into task grouping by considering a simple example.

Suppose that the work required to fabricate a certain product can be divided up into five elemental tasks, with the task times and precedence relationships as shown below.

Two important pieces of information in any listing of elemental task times are the sum of the task times and the length of the longest elemental task. The longest task (one minute in this case) indicates the *minimum* possible *cycle time* (the time interval between units coming off the line), while the sum of the times indicates the *maximum* cycle time that would make sense. For example, combining the tasks at a single work station would require a cycle time of two and a half minutes, since that is how long it would take to produce one unit. At the other extreme, even by assigning each task to a different work station, the cycle time could not be less than one minute, since the third task requires that length of time. The maximum and minimum cycle times are important because they can be used to determine upper and lower bounds on a line's output potential. Daily capacity, for example, can be found by dividing operating time per day by a line's cycle time:

$$\text{Output} = \frac{OT}{CT} \tag{7-1}$$

where

OT = Operating time per day
CT = Cycle time

For instance, assume that the line will operate for eight hours per day (480 minutes). With a cycle time of 1.0 minute, output would be:

$$\frac{480 \text{ minutes per day}}{1.0 \text{ minute per unit}} = 480 \text{ units per day}$$

With a cycle time of 2.5 minutes, the output would be:

$$\frac{480 \text{ minutes per day}}{2.5 \text{ minutes per unit}} = 192 \text{ units per day}$$

Assuming that no parallel activities are to be employed (e.g., two lines), the output selected for the line must fall in the range of 192 units per day to 480 units per day.

As a general rule, the cycle time is determined by the desired output. That is, a desired output level is selected, and the cycle time is computed. If the cycle time does not fall within the maximum and minimum bounds, the desired output rate must be revised. The cycle time can be computed using this formula:

$$CT = \frac{OT}{D} \qquad (7\text{–}2)$$

where D = Desired output rate

For example, suppose that the desired output rate is 480 units. Using the formula above, we can compute the necessary cycle time:

$$\frac{480 \text{ minutes per day}}{480 \text{ units per day}} = 1.0 \text{ minutes per unit.}$$

The number of work stations that will be needed is a function of both the desired output rate and our ability to combine elemental tasks into work stations. The *minimum* number of stations necessary to provide a specified rate of output can be determined as follows:

$$N = \frac{D \times \Sigma t}{OT} \qquad (7\text{–}3)$$

where

N = Minimum number of stations
D = Desired output rate
Σt = Sum of task times
OT = Operating time

Suppose the desired rate of output is the maximum of 480 units per day.[1] (This will require a cycle time of 1.0 minute.) The minimum number of stations required to achieve this goal is:

$$N = \frac{480 \text{ units per day} \times 2.5 \text{ minutes per unit}}{480 \text{ minutes per day per station}} = 2.5 \text{ stations}$$

Because 2.5 stations is not feasible, it is necessary to *round up* to three stations. The *actual* number of stations used will equal or exceed three, depending on how successful we are in grouping the tasks into work bundles.

---

[1] At first glance, it might seem that the desired output would logically be the maximum possible output. However, you will soon learn why that is not always the best arrangement.

EXAMPLE 1

Combine the five elemental tasks described in the preceding illustration into three work stations. Assign tasks to work stations according to precedence, beginning with the first task. Use a cycle time of 1.0 minute.

Solution

The cycle time of 1.0 minute represents an upper constraint on the sum of task times assigned to any work station. With this in mind, we assign the first two tasks to the first work station since their times sum to 0.8 minute. Obviously, the next task must be assigned to a separate work station because its length equals the cycle time. The remaining two tasks can be assigned to the third work station for a station time of 0.7 minute. The resulting assignments are illustrated below.

Since the goal of line balancing is to minimize idle time, the percentage of idle time associated with a given assignment of tasks to work stations is of particular interest. The idle time per cycle for each station is:

$$\text{Idle time per station} = \text{Cycle time} - \text{Station time}$$

The idle times for the above assignments are shown in the table below:

Station	Station time	Station idle time
1	0.8	0.2
2	1.0	0.0
3	0.7	0.3
		0.5

The percentage of idle time is the ratio of idle time per cycle to total time available per cycle:

$$\text{Percentage of idle time} = \frac{\text{Idle time per cycle}}{N \times CT} = \frac{0.5}{3(1.0)} = 16.7 \text{ percent}$$

Note that an idle percentage of zero means the line is perfectly balanced.

The extent to which work stations can be *packed* influences both the number of stations needed and the percentage of idle time.

EXAMPLE 2

Assign the given tasks to work stations in a way that minimizes idle time and compute the resulting percentage of idle time. (Note that the total task times and the longest task time are the same as in the preceding example.) Assume $D = 480$ units per day.

Solution

An output of 480 units per day will require a cycle time of 1.0 minute:

$$CT = \frac{\text{Operating time per day}}{\text{Desired output rate}} = \frac{480 \text{ minutes per day}}{480 \text{ units per day}} = 1.0$$

Assign tasks, beginning with the first task. The first station will consist solely of the first task because the second task's time equals the cycle time. The second station will consist of the second task; the third station will consist of the third and fourth tasks; and a fourth station will be required to handle the last task. These assignments are shown below:

The resulting idle times for this assignment are:

Station	Station time	Station idle time
1	0.3	0.7
2	1.0	—
3	0.7	0.3
4	0.5	0.5
		1.5

The percentage of idle time is:

$$\text{Percentage of idle time} = \frac{\text{Idle time per cycle}}{N \times CT} = \frac{1.5}{4(1.0)} = 37.5 \text{ percent}$$

Note that the overall efficiency is lower in Example 2 than it was in Example 1 (the percentage of idle time is greater), even though the sum of the task times and the cycle time are identical. The reason for the decrease in efficiency can be attributed to the use of a fourth work station for the second example. Of course, that station was unavoidable because of the inability to obtain as high a degree of packing of the first three stations as was possible in Example 1.

This brings us back to the question of whether the selected level of output should equal the maximum output possible. The minimum number of work stations needed is a function of the desired output rate:

$$N = \frac{D \times \Sigma t}{OT}$$

Therefore, a lower rate of output may produce a need for fewer stations. Hence, the manager must consider whether the potential savings that could be realized by having fewer work stations would be greater than the decrease in contribution resulting from producing fewer units.

The preceding examples serve to illustrate some of the fundamental concepts of line balancing. Nonetheless, as compared to most real-life situations, they are rather simple; the number of branches and tasks involved are often much greater than in these examples. Consequently, the job of line balancing can be a good deal more complex than you might suspect. In fact, in many instances the number of alternatives for grouping tasks is so great that it would be virtually impossible to conduct an exhaustive review of all possibilities. For this reason, many real-life problems of any magnitude are solved using *heuristic* approaches. The purpose of the heuristic approaches is to reduce the number of alternatives that must be considered, but they do not guarantee an optimum solution.

Some of the heuristic rules used in practice are:

1. Assign tasks to work stations, longest tasks first, and continue until all tasks have been assigned.
2. Assign tasks in order of most number of following tasks.
3. Assign tasks in order of most number of preceding tasks.
4. Assign tasks according to *positional weight*, which is the sum of a task's time and the times of all following tasks.

Unfortunately none of these rules works all the time, so it is usually necessary to try several rules in the hopes of discovering a good solution to a problem. Although heuristic rules do not guarantee an optimal solution to line-balancing problems, they often provide reasonably good solutions with a limited amount of effort. Moreover, they are intuitively appealing: The rules offer rational, step-by-step handling of fairly complex problems.

Computerized approaches to the line-balancing problem may incorporate heuristic rules such as those listed above, or they may use dynamic programming.[2]

It can be helpful in line balancing to work with a *precedence diagram,* which shows the sequence of operations. This diagram can easily be constructed from a list of sequential activities. The following example illustrates the use of such a diagram and the use of one of the heuristic rules for task assignments. (See also Solved Problem 1.)

EXAMPLE 3

Using the information contained in the table shown, do each of the following:

1. Draw a precedence diagram.
2. Assuming an eight-hour workday, compute the cycle time needed to obtain an output of 400 units per day.
3. Determine the minimum number of work stations required.
4. Assign tasks to work stations using this rule: Assign tasks according to greatest number of following tasks.

Task	Immediate predecessor	Task time
a	—	0.2
b	a	0.2
c	—	0.8
d	c	0.6
e	b	0.3
f	d,e	1.0
g	f	0.4
h	g	0.3
		$\Sigma t = \overline{3.8}$

Solution

1. Drawing a precedence diagram is a relatively straight-forward task. Begin with activities with no predecessors. We see from the list that *a* and *c* have no immediate predecessors. Now we build from here.

---

[2] See, for example, M. Held, R. M. Karp, and R. Sharesian, "Assembly-Line Balancing: Dynamic Programming with Precedence Constraints," *Operations Research* 11, no. 3 (May–June 1963).

EXAMPLE 3 *(continued)*

b follows *a* and
d follows *c*

e follows *b*

f follows *e* and *d*

g follows *f* and *h*
follows *g*

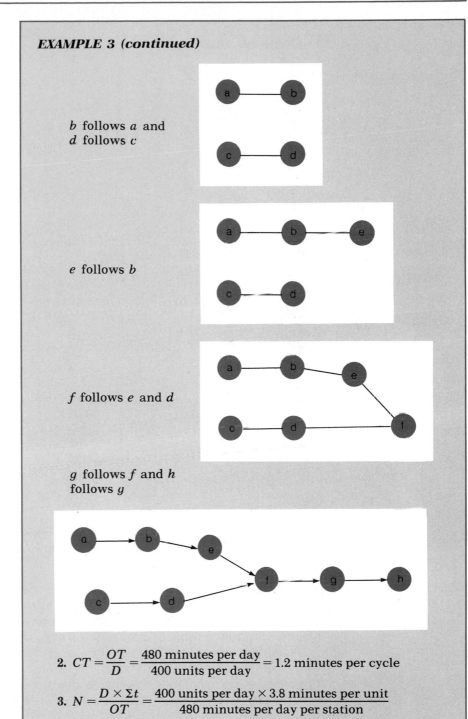

2. $CT = \dfrac{OT}{D} = \dfrac{480 \text{ minutes per day}}{400 \text{ units per day}} = 1.2 \text{ minutes per cycle}$

3. $N = \dfrac{D \times \Sigma t}{OT} = \dfrac{400 \text{ units per day} \times 3.8 \text{ minutes per unit}}{480 \text{ minutes per day per station}}$

$= 3.17 \text{ stations (round to 4).}$

EXAMPLE 3 (concluded)

4.

Station	Task	Time (minutes)	Remaining time	Remaining feasible tasks	Task with most followers
1	a	0.2	1.0	b,c	(tie)*
	c	0.8	0.2	b,d	b
	b	0.2	0.0	None	
2	d	0.6	0.6	e	e
	e	0.3	0.3	None	
3	f	1.0	0.2	None	
4	g	0.4	0.8	h	h
	h	0.3	0.5	None	

* Tiebreaker: Assign task with longest processing time first.

These assignments are shown in the diagram below. If you look carefully at this solution, you may discover that it can be improved upon. Thus, this solution is not necessarily an optimal solution. The point is that one should not expect that heuristic solutions will produce optimum solutions, they merely provide a practical way to deal with what can be a highly complex problem that does not lend itself to optimizing techniques.

Other Factors

The preceding discussion on line balancing presents a relatively straightforward approach to approximating a balanced line. In practice, the ability to do this usually involves additional considerations, some of which are technical, and some of which are not.

Technical considerations include such factors as skill requirements of different tasks. If skill requirements of tasks are quite different, it may not be feasible to place them in the same work station. Similarly, if the tasks themselves are in conflict, such as sanding and painting or use of fire and use of volatile liquids, it may not be feasible to place them in the same work station, or even in nearby stations.

Although it can be convenient to treat assembly operations as if they occur at the same rate time after time, it is more realistic to admit that whenever humans are involved, variability in task completion times will occur. The reasons for the variations are numerous, including such factors as fatigue, boredom, and non-work-related thoughts. Hence, even in a "perfectly balanced line" the actual performance may not reflect perfect balance. Likewise, absenteeism can affect line balance.

Thus, developing a workable plan for balancing a line requires consideration of other factors besides precedence relationships such as human factors, equipment and space limitations, and incompatible operations.

DESIGNING PROCESS LAYOUTS

The main issue in design of process layouts concerns the relative positioning of the departments involved. As illustrated in Figure 7–10, a list of departments must be assigned to a list of locations. The problem is to develop a reasonably good layout; some combinations will be more desirable than others. For example, some departments may benefit from adjacent locations while others should be separated. Painting and sanding departments that are too close to each other could cause painting to be contaminated by particles from the sanding operations. Conversely, two departments may share some of the same equipment, and so would benefit from being placed close together.

Layouts can also be influenced by such external factors as the locations of entrances, loading docks, elevators, windows, and areas of reinforced flooring.

In a few instances, such as laying out supermarkets, gas stations, and fast-food chains, there are sufficient numbers of installations with similar characteristics to justify development of standardized layouts. A good example of standardized layouts is provided by

FIGURE 7–10

Work Centers Must Be Assigned to Locations

Locations			Work centers to be assigned
A	B	C	1
			2
			3
D	E	F	4
			5
			6

McDonald's hamburger outlets. The use of the same basic pattern in all outlets facilitates construction of new structures and employee training. Food preparation, taking orders, and serving customers follows the same pattern throughout the chain. Moreover, installation and service of equipment are also standardized. Supermarkets also benefit from standardized layouts, although in a different respect. Customers acquainted with the layout of any store in the chain can readily locate desired items in other stores in the chain. In addition, most supermarkets locate departments such as meat, produce, and bakery around the perimeter of the store with wide aisles to permit customers to ponder choices and to achieve customer circulation throughout the store. Bread and milk are often placed away from the entrance in order to expose customers who stop in just to pick up those items to additional merchandise.

The majority of layout problems involve single locations rather than multiple locations, and they present unique combinations of factors that do not lend themselves to a standardized approach. Consequently, these layouts require customized designs.

The major obstacle in finding the most efficient layout of departments is the large number of assignments that are possible. For example, there are over 50,000 different ways that nine departments can be assigned to nine locations if the locations form a single line. Different location configurations (e.g., nine departments in a 3×3 grid) often reduce the number of possibilities, as do any special requirements (e.g., the stamping department may have to be assigned to a location with reinforced flooring). Still, the remaining number of layout possibilities usually is too large to allow each one to be examined, even with computer assistance. Unfortunately, no algorithms exist that can identify the best layout arrangement under all circumstances. Often planners must rely on heuristic rules to guide trial-and-error efforts to obtain a satisfactory solution to each problem.

Measures of Effectiveness

One advantage of process layouts is their ability to satisfy a variety of processing requirements. Customers or materials in these systems require different operations and different sequences of operations, which causes them to follow different paths through the system. Materials-oriented systems necessitate the use of variable-path material-handling equipment to move materials from work center to work center, while in customer-oriented systems, people must travel or be transported from work center to work center. In both cases, transportation costs or time can be significant. Because of this factor, one of the major objectives in process layout is to minimize either transportation cost, distance, or time. This is usually accomplished by locating departments with relatively high interdepartmental work flows as close together as possible.

Other measures that may be used to choose among alternative layouts include initial costs in setting up the layout, expected operating costs, the amount of effective capacity created, and the ease with which the system could be modified if the need arose.

In situations that involve efforts to improve an existing layout, costs of relocating any work center must be weighed against the potential benefits of such a move.

Information Requirements

The design of a process layout requires the following information:

1. A list of departments or work centers to be arranged, their approximate dimensions, and the dimensions of the building or buildings that will house the departments.
2. A projection of future work flows between the various work centers.
3. The distance between locations and the cost per unit of distance to move loads between various locations.
4. The amount of money to be invested in the layout.
5. A list of any special considerations (e.g., heavy equipment will require reinforced flooring and separate sanding and painting operations to avoid contamination).

An ideal situation would be to first develop a layout and then design the physical structure around that layout, because this would permit maximum flexibility in design. In fact, this procedure is often followed when new facilities are being constructed. Nonetheless, many layouts must be developed in situations where there is an existing structure. In those instances, floor space, the dimensions of the building, locations of entrances and elevators, and other similar factors must often be carefully weighed in designing the layout.

FIGURE 7-11

Buildings Can Have a Variety of Shapes

Some of the building shapes encountered during layout development are illustrated in Figure 7–11. Multiple-level structures pose special problems for layout planners.

Minimizing Transportation Costs or Distances

The most common goals in designing process layouts relate to minimization of transportation costs or distances traveled. In such cases it can be very helpful to summarize the necessary data in *from-to* charts like those illustrated in Tables 7–2 and 7–3. Table 7–2 indicates the distance between each of the locations, and Table 7–3 indicates actual or projected work flows between each pair. For instance, the distance chart reveals that a trip from location A to location B will involve a distance of 20 meters. (Distances are often measured between department centers.) Oddly enough, the length of a trip between location A and B may differ depending on the *direction* of the trip due to one-way routes, escalators, or other factors. To simplify the discussion, we shall assume equality of distances between any two locations. However, it would not be realistic to assume that interdepartmental work flows are equal; there is no reason to suspect that department 1 will send as much work to department 2 as that department sends to 1. For example, several departments may send goods to packaging, but packaging may send only to the shipping department.

Transportation costs can also be summarized in from-to charts, but to avoid the added complexity that would entail, we shall assume that costs are a direct, linear function of distance.

TABLE 7–2

Distance between Locations (Meters)

		Location		
From	To	A	B	C
A		—	20	40
B		20	—	30
C		40	30	—

TABLE 7–3

Interdepartmental Work Flow (Loads per Day)

		Department		
From	To	1	2	3
1		—	10	80
2		20	—	30
3		90	70	—

EXAMPLE 4

Assign the three departments shown in Table 7–3 to locations A, B, and C, which are separated by the distances shown in Table 7–2, in such a way that transportation cost is minimized. Use this heuristic: Assign departments with the greatest interdepartmental work flows first.

Solution

Ranking departments according to highest work flows and locations according to highest interlocation distances helps in making assignments. If interlocation distances are independent of direction of flow, work flows between departments can be summed to achieve a clearer picture of the need for closeness. Thus:

Trip	Distance (meters)	Department pair	Work Flow	
A–B	20	3–1	90	} 170
B–A	20	1–3	80	
B–C	30	3–2	70	} 100
C–B	30	2–3	30	
A–C	40	2–1	20	} 30
C–A	40	1–2	10	

From these listings we can see that departments 1 and 3 have the highest interdepartmental work flows and that locations A and B are the closest. Thus, it would seem reasonable to consider assigning 1 and 3 to locations A and B, although it is not yet obvious which department should be assigned to which location. Further inspection of the work-flow list reveals that 2 and 3 have higher work flows than 1 and 2, and so 2 and 3 should probably be located more closely than 1 and 2. Hence, it would seem reasonable to place 3 between 1 and 2, or at least *centralize* that department with respect to the other two. The resulting assignments might appear as illustrated in Figure 7–12.

Note that work flows between departments in the diagram are the sum of the flow each way (e.g., the 170 between 1 and 3 is the combined flow of 90 loads from 3 to 1 and 80 loads from 1 to 3).

FIGURE 7–12

Interdepartmental Work Flows for Assigned Departments

EXAMPLE 4 *(concluded)*

If we assume that the cost per meter to move any load is $1, we can compute the total daily transportation cost for this assignment by multiplying each department's number of loads by the trip distance and summing those quantities:

Depart- ment	Number of loads to:	Location	Distance to:	Loads × Distance
1	2: 10	A	C: 40	10 × 40 = 400
	3: 80		B: 20	80 × 20 = 1,600
2	1: 20	C	A: 40	20 × 40 = 800
	3: 30		B: 30	30 × 30 = 900
3	1: 90	B	A: 20	90 × 20 = 1,800
	2: 70		C: 30	70 × 30 = 2,100
				7,600

At $1 per load-meter, the cost for this plan would be $7,600 per day, and even though it might appear that this arrangement yields the lowest transportation cost, we cannot be absolutely positive of that without actually computing the total cost for every alternative and comparing it to this one. While we could do so in this case where the number of alternatives is quite small (i.e., there are 3! = 6 possible arrangements), the point is that in problems with more departments, the number rapidly becomes too large to even consider examining every alternative. Instead, we must rely on the choice of reasonable heuristic rules such as those demonstrated above to guide us to a solution that will be satisfactory, if not optimal.

Closeness Ratings

Even though the preceding approach is widely used, it suffers from the limitation of being able to focus on only one objective, whereas many situations actually involve multiple criteria. Richard Muther developed a more general approach to the problem, which allows for subjective input from analysts or managers that indicates the relative importance of each combination of department pairs.[3] That information is then summarized in a grid like the one shown in Figure 7–13. The grid is read in the same way that the mileage chart on a road map is, except that letters appear at the intersections rather than distances. The letters represent the importance of closeness for each department pair, with A being the most important and X being an undesirable pairing. Thus, in the grid we can see that it is "absolutely necessary" to locate 1 and 2 close to each other because there is an A at the intersection of those departments on the grid. On the other hand, we also can see that 1 and 4 should not be close together because their intersection has an X. In practice,

[3] R. Muther, *Systematic Layout Planning* (Boston: Industrial Education Institute, 1961).

FIGURE 7–13

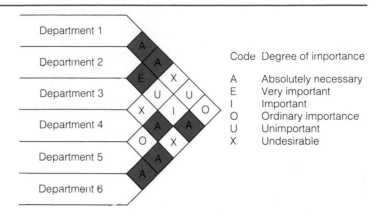

Code	Degree of importance
A	Absolutely necessary
E	Very important
I	Important
O	Ordinary importance
U	Unimportant
X	Undesirable

the letters on the grid are often accompanied by numbers that indicate the reason for each assignment, although they are omitted here to simplify the illustration. Muther suggests the following list:

1. Use same equipment or facilities.
2. Share the same personnel or records.
3. Sequence of work flow.
4. Ease of communication.
5. Unsafe or unpleasant conditions.
6. Similar work performed.

As with the previous examples, no optimizing algorithm exists, so trial-and-error alternatives must be developed and compared using heuristic rules.

EXAMPLE 5

Assign the six departments in the preceding grid to a 2 × 3 set of locations using the heuristic rule: Assign critical departments first.

Solution

Critical pairs of departments are those with A or X ratings. We can prepare a list of those by referring to the grid:

A's	X's
1–2	1–4
1–3	3–6
2–6	3–4
3–5	
4–6	
5–6	

Next, form cluster of A links, beginning with the department that appears most frequently in the A list (in this case, 6). For instance:

EXAMPLE 5 (concluded)

Take the remaining A's in order and add on to this main cluster where possible, rearranging the cluster where necessary to achieve this. Form separate clusters for departments that do not link with the main cluster. In this case, they all link with the main cluster:

Next, graphically portray the X's:

Observe that as it stands, the cluster of A's also satisfies the X separations, and it is a fairly simple exercise to fit the cluster into a 2×3 arrangement:

1	2	6
3	5	4

It is interesting to note that the lower-level ratings have also been satisfied with this arrangement, even though no attempt was made to explicitly consider these E and I ratings. Naturally not every problem will yield the same results, so it may be necessary to do some additional juggling to see if improvements can be made, keeping in mind that the A and X assignments deserve the greatest consideration.

Note that departments are considered close not only when they touch side to side, but also if they touch corner to corner.

The value of this rating approach lies in the fact that it permits the use of multiple objectives and subjective inputs. Its limitations relate to the use of subjective inputs in general: they are imprecise and unreliable.

Computer Analysis

The size and complexity of process layout problems led to the development of a number of computerized packages during the late 1960s. Three of the most well-known packages are ALDEP, CORELAP, and CRAFT.

ALDEP (automated layout design program) and CORELAP (computerized relationship layout planning) both use preferences ratings (A-E-I-O-U-X format) and either building or space requirements. ALDEP processing involves an initial random selection of a department and location and then a search of remaining departments' closeness ratings with the chosen department to assign nearby locations. That procedure is continued until all departments have been assigned. The completed layout is evaluated and scored according to how well the preferences have been satisfied. The program is rerun a number of times, and the best layout is identified. CORELAP processes location assignments using the preference ratings to order choice of departments. Hence, the program begins with a department pair that has an A rating, then another A pair, and so on, until all A relationships have been assigned. Next, the E-relationship pairs are assigned, and so on down the line until all departments have been assigned to locations.

CRAFT (computerized relative allocation of facilities technique) seeks to minimize material flow cost. The program requires information on material flow rates between departments, unit-distance transportation costs, and an initial layout. The program exchanges department pairs until no further improvement can be achieved. The output is a printout of a rectangular layout that may or may not be optimal.

The obvious advantage of computerized analyses of layout problems is the ability to handle large problems and to consider many different layout alternatives. Even so, in most instances the results of computer analysis require additional manual adjustments before they can be used. In some cases this is due to irregularly shaped layouts produced by the program, while in others there is the need to check the logic of certain assignments. In the case of the CRAFT program, where the analyst must submit an initial feasible layout, different layouts will sometimes lead to different final solutions, so the experience and judgment of the analyst in preparing the initial layout can be an important factor. Moreover, manual adjustment of computer output also can benefit from an experienced analyst.

Other computer programs also exist to handle layout assignments, and it is highly likely that additional packages will be developed in the future. While current programs can not guarantee optimum solutions to problems, it is impossible to predict what course new program developments will take. For the present it appears that knowledge and experience are valuable resources for dealing with process layout problems.

SUMMARY

Layout decisions are an important aspect of the design of productive systems, affecting operating costs and efficiency. Layout decisions are interrelated with decisions involving location, products or services, and capacity.

A major determinant of layout design is the type of processing required of a system. The three basic types are continuous, intermittent, and project. Continuous processing is characterized by a high volume of one or a few similar products or services. Intermittent processing provides the processing capability needed to deal with a broader range of products or services than continuous processing allows. Projects are used to plan and coordinate complex jobs with relatively brief life spans. Product layouts are typically used for continuous processing, process layouts for intermittent, and fixed-position layouts for projects, although some projects do not require layouts. Product layouts are geared to high-volume output of standardized items. Workers and equipment are arranged according to the technological sequence required by the product or service involved. Emphasis in design is on work flow through the system. Very often specialized processing and handling equipment is used. Although costly, such equipment contributes to rapid processing, and the resulting high volume of output means cost per unit is relatively low. Product layouts are highly vulnerable to breakdowns, and preventive maintenance is often used to reduce the occurrence of breakdowns.

Process layouts involve grouping of like activities into departments or other work centers. Such systems can handle a wide range of processing requirements and are less susceptible to breakdowns. However, the variety of processing requirements necessitates continual routing and scheduling and the use of variable-path material-handling equipment. Also, the rate of output of such systems is generally much lower than that of product layouts. Fixed-position layouts are used when size, fragility, cost, or other factors makes it undesirable or impractical to move a product through a system. Instead, workers, equipment, and materials are brought to the product.

The main design efforts in product layout development focus on dividing up the work required to produce a product or service into a series of tasks that are as nearly equal as possible in an effort to achieve a high degree of utilization of labor and equipment. In process layout, design efforts often focus on the relative positioning of departments to minimize transportation costs or to meet other requirements concerning nearness of certain department pairs.

Many layout problems possess such a large number of possible alternatives that it is virtually impossible to examine each one. Instead, heuristic rules are used to guide discovery of alternatives, which are usually satisfactory, although not necessarily optimal. Computer packages are available to reduce the effort required to obtain solutions to layout problems. For the most part, these, too, rely on heuristic methods.

1. The tasks shown in the precedence diagram below are to be assigned to work stations with the intent of minimizing idle time. Management has designated an output rate of 275 units per day. Assume 440 minutes available per day.
   a. Determine the appropriate cycle time.
   b. What is the minimum number of stations possible?
   c. Assign tasks using the "positional weight" rule: Assign tasks with highest following times (including its own time) first. Break ties using greatest number of following tasks.

Solution

a. $CT = \dfrac{\text{Operating time}}{\text{Desired output}} = \dfrac{440 \text{ minutes per day}}{275 \text{ units/per day}} = 1.6 \text{ minutes}$

b. $N = \dfrac{\text{Desired output} \times \Sigma t}{\text{Operating time}} = \dfrac{275 \text{ per day} \times 4.2}{440 \text{ minute/per day}} = 2.6 \text{ (round to 3)}$

c.

Station	Task	Time remaining	Feasible next task
1	b	3.2	a
	a	1.8	c
	c	1.5	None
2	d	2.6	e
	e	1.1	g
	g	0.9	None
3	f	1.4	h
	h	0.8	i
	i	0.3	None

The resulting assignments are shown below.

(Note that the time needed to produce 275 units will be 275×1.5 minutes = 412.5 minutes. With 440 minutes per day available, this leaves 27.5 minutes of "slack." This time could be used for work breaks, for equipment maintenance, or to produce additional units.

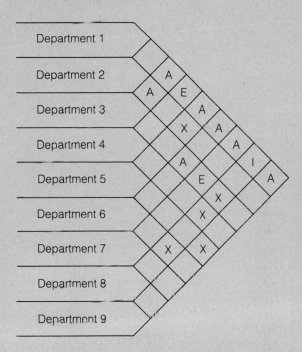

2. Assign nine departments to locations in a 3×3 grid so that the closeness ratings in the matrix below are satisfied. (The unimportant and ordinary-importance pair ratings have been omitted to simplify the example.) The location of department 4 must be in the upper right-hand corner of the grid to satisfy a town ordinance.

Solution

Note that department 1 has many A ratings, making it a strong candidate for the center position in the grid. We can form a cluster of departments that should be close together.

Next, we can identify departmental pairings that should be avoided:

These departments should be spaced around the perimeter of the grid. After a bit of juggling, the final grid shown below emerged. Check it against the rating matrix to see if it satisfies the ratings.

2	3	4
9	1	6
8	7	5

DISCUSSION AND REVIEW QUESTIONS

1. Briefly describe each of the three basic types of processing systems.
2. Briefly describe each of the three basic layout types.
3. What are the main advantages of a product layout? The main disadvantages?
4. What are the main advantages of a process layout? The main disadvantages?
5. What is the goal of line balancing? What happens if a line is unbalanced?
6. Why are routing and scheduling continual problems under a process layout?
7. Compare equipment maintenance strategies in product and process layouts.
8. Briefly outline the impact that job sequence has on each of the layout types.
9. City Transportation Planning Committee must make a decision on whether to begin a long-term project to build a subway system or to upgrade bus service. Since you are an expert in fixed-path and variable-path material-handling equipment, your counsel has been sought on this matter. How would you compare the advantages and limitations of subway versus bus?
10. Identify the fixed-path and variable-path material-handling equipment commonly found in supermarkets.
11. What are *heuristic approaches* and why are they used in designing layouts?
12. Why are product layouts rarely used in nonmanufacturing environments?
13. According to a recent study by the Alliance of American Insurers, it would cost approximately $26,000 in parts and labor to replace a totally wrecked Chevrolet Citation that sold new for about $7,000. Explain some of the reasons for this large discrepancy in terms of the processes used to assemble the original car versus those required to reconstruct the wrecked car.
14. What are some of the ways that layout can help or hinder productivity?

PROBLEMS

1. An assembly line with 17 tasks is to be balanced. The longest task is 2.4 minutes, and the sum of task times is 18 minutes. The line will operate for 450 minutes per day.
   a. Determine the minimum and maximum cycle times.
   b. What range of output is theoretically possible for the line?
   c. What is the minimum number of stations needed if the maximum output rate is to be sought?
   d. What cycle time will provide an output rate of 125 units per day?
   e. What output potential will result if the cycle time is (1) 9 minutes? (2) 15 minutes?

2. A large manufacturer of plastic saddles is planning to add a new line of multicolored saddles, and you have been asked to balance the process, given the task times and precedence relationships shown below. Assume that cycle time is to be the minimum length possible.

Task	Length (minutes)	Immediate predecessor
a	0.2	
b	0.4	a
c	0.3	—
d	1.3	b,c
e	0.1	--
f	0.8	e
g	0.3	d,f
h	1.2	g

   Do each of the following:
   a. Draw the precedence diagram.
   b. Assign tasks to stations, longest times first.
   c. Determine the percentage of idle time.
   d. Compute the rate of output that could be expected for this line assuming a 420-minute working day.

3. In the previous problem.
   a. What is the shortest cycle time that will permit use of only two work stations? Is this cycle time feasible? Identify the tasks you would assign to each station.
   b. Determine the percentage of idle time that would result if two stations were to be used.
   c. What would the daily output be under this arrangement?
   d. Determine the output rate that would be associated with the maximum cycle time.

4. As part of a major plant renovation project, the industrial engineering department has been asked to balance a revised assembly operation to achieve an output of 480 units per eight hour day. Task times and precedence relationships are shown in the table below.

Task	Duration (minutes)	Follows Task
a	0.1	—
b	0.2	a
c	0.1	b
d	0.2	—
e	0.6	d
f	0.6	c
g	0.5	e,f

   Do each of the following:
   a. Draw the precedence diagram.
   b. Determine the maximum cycle time.
   c. Determine the minimum number of stations needed.
   d. Assign tasks to stations on the basis of greatest number of following tasks; use longest processing time as a tiebreaker. If ties still exist, assume indifference in choice.
   e. Compute the percentage of idle time for the assignment in part d,
   f. Assign tasks to work stations using the rule: Assign tasks in order of greatest number of preceding tasks, using the same tiebreaker as in d.
   g. Compute the percentage of idle time for the assignment in part f.

5. The 12 tasks with times and precedence requirements as shown in the table below are to be assigned to work stations using a cycle time of 1.5 minutes. Three heuristic rules will be tried: (1) greatest posi-

tional weight, (2) greatest number of following tasks, and (3) longest task first.

In each case the tiebreaker will be shortest task time.

Task	Length (minutes)	Follows
a	0.1	—
b	0.2	a
c	0.9	b
d	0.6	c
e	0.1	—
f	0.2	d,e
g	0.4	f
h	0.1	g
i	0.2	h
j	0.7	i
k	0.3	j
l	0.2	k

a. Draw the precedence diagram for this line.

b. Assign tasks to stations under each of the three rules.

c. Compute the percentage of idle time for each rule.

6. Arrange six departments into a 2×3 grid so that these conditions are satisfied: 1 close to 2, 5 close to 6, 2 close to 5, and 3 not close to 1.

7. Using the information given in the preceding problem, develop a Muther-type grid using the letters A, O, and X. Assume any pair combinations not mentioned have an O rating.

8. Using the information in the grid below, determine if the department locations shown are appropriate. If they are not, modify the assignments so that the conditions are satisfied.

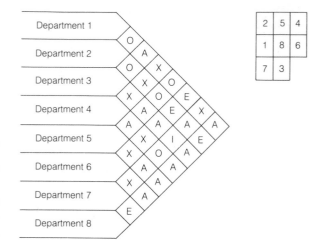

9. Arrange the eight departments shown in the accompanying Muther grid into a 2×4 format. Note: Department 1 must be in the location shown.

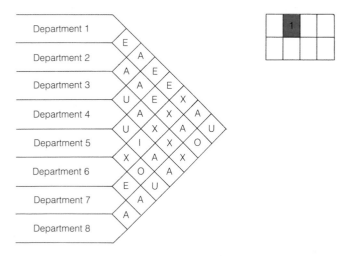

10. Arrange the departments so they satisfy the conditions shown in the rating grid

into a 3 × 3 format. Place department 5 in the lower left corner of the 3 × 3 grid.

A	B	C
D	E	F

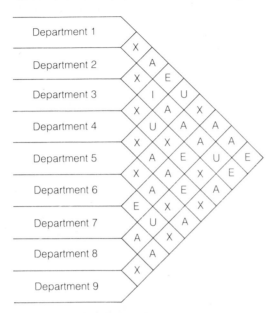

11. Assign six work centers to locations A–F given the information below so that the total distance traveled is minimized. Assume work center 6 must be in location A. Compute the total cost of your plan if the transportation cost is $2 per load per foot. Assume the reverse distances are equal (e.g., *B* to *A* = 50 feet = *A* to *B*)

		Distances between locations (feet)				
From	To	A	B	C	D	E	F
A		—	50	100	50	80	130
B			—	50	90	40	70
C				—	140	60	50
D					—	50	120
E						—	50
F							—

		Number of trips per day between centers				
From	To	1	2	3	4	5	6
1		—	90	25	23	11	18
2		35	—	8	5	10	16
3		37	2	—	1	0	7
4		41	12	1	—	4	0
5		14	16	0	9	—	3
6		32	38	13	2	2	—

12. Eight work centers must be arranged in an L-shaped building. The locations of centers 1 and 3 are designated as shown in the accompanying diagram. Assuming transportation costs are $1 per load per meter, develop a suitable layout that minimizes transportation costs using the given information below. Compute the total cost.

		Distances (meters)							
From	To	A	B	C	D	E	F	G	H
A		—	40	40	60	120	80	100	110
B			—	60	40	60	140	120	130
C				—	45	85	40	70	90
D					—	40	50	40	45
E						—	90	50	40
F							—	40	60
G								—	40
H									—

Assume the reverse distances are the same.

		Loads per day							
From	To	1	2	3	4	5	6	7	8
1		—	10	5	90	365	135	125	0
2		0	—	140	10	0	35	0	120
3		0	220	—	110	10	0	0	200
4		0	110	240	—	10	0	0	170
5		5	40	100	180	—	10	40	10
6		0	80	40	70	0	—	10	20
7		0	45	20	50	0	40	—	20
8		0	0	0	20	0	0	0	—

13. Develop a process layout that will minimize the total distance traveled by patients at a medical clinic using the information below on projected departmental visits by patients and distance between locations. Assume a distance of 35 feet be-

tween the reception area and each potential location. Use the format shown below.

Distance between locations (feet)

From \ To	A	B	C	D	E	F
A	—	40	80	100	120	160
B		—	40	60	80	120
C			—	20	40	80
D				—	20	40
E					—	40
F						—

Trips between departments (per day)

From \ To	1	2	3	4	5	6	Reception
Reception	10	10	200	20	0	100	—
1	—	0	0	80	20	40	10
2	0	—	0	0	0	20	40
3	40	0	—	10	190	10	10
4	30	50	0	—	10	70	0
5	60	40	60	30	—	20	10
6	10	100	0	20	0	—	30

layout's congestion in the halls, the new lab manager has requested an assignment that will minimize traffic between offices. In addition, movement in the halls is restricted to a counterclockwise route. Develop a suitable layout using the information below.

Number of trips per day between departments

From \ To	1	2	3	4	5	6	7	8	9	10
1	—	40	1	20	20	4	0	2	6	5
2	0	—	2	15	25	10	2	12	13	6
3	50	35	—	10	13	4	0	4	7	1
4	6	1	8	—	0	14	10	20	22	11
5	3	2	7	35	—	22	5	9	19	10
6	5	5	10	0	2	—	15	0	1	20
7	20	16	50	4	9	2	—	1	3	0
8	10	6	14	2	4	44	13	—	1	25
9	5	5	18	1	2	40	30	42	—	32
10	30	30	35	20	15	5	40	10	15	—

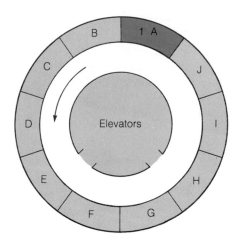

14. Ten labs will be assigned to the circular layout shown below. Recalling a similar

SELECTED BIBLIOGRAPHY

Fogarty, Donald W., and Thomas R. Hoffman. *Production and Inventory Management.* Cincinnati: South-Western Publishing, 1983.

Foulkes, Fred K., and J. L. Hirsch. "People Make Robots Work." *Harvard Business Review,* January–February 1984, p. 94.

Francis, R. L., and J. A. White. *Facility Layout and Location: An Analytical Approach.* Englewood Cliffs, N.J.: Prentice-Hall, 1974.

Freeman, D. R., and J. V. Jucker. "The Line Balancing Problem." *Journal of Industrial Engineering* 18 (1967), p. 361.

Gerwin, D. "Do's and Don'ts of Computerized

Manufacturing." *Harvard Business Review,* March–April 1982, pp. 107–16.

Gold, B. "CAM Sets New Rules for Production." *Harvard Business Review,* November–December 1982, pp. 88–94.

Groover, Mikell P. *Automation, Production Systems, and Computer-Aided Manufacturing.* Englewood Cliffs, N.J.: Prentice-Hall, 1980.

Helgeson, W. B., and D. P. Bernie. "Assembly Line Balancing Using the Ranked Positional Weight Technique." *Journal of Industrial Engineering* 12, no. 6 (November–December 1961).

Hendrick, T.E., and F.G. Moore. *Production/Operations Management.* 9th ed. Homewood, Ill.: Richard D. Irwin, 1985.

Hicks, P. E., and T. E. Cowan. "CRAFT-M for Layout Rearrangement." *Industrial Engineering* 8 May 1976, pp. 30–35.

Hyer, Nancy L., and Urban Wemmerlöv. *Harvard Business Review,* July–August 1984, p. 140.

Ignall, E. J. "A Review of Assembly Line Balancing." *Journal of Industrial Engineering* 16 (1965).

Kilbridge, M. D., and L. Wester. "A Heuristic Method of Assembly Line Balancing." *Journal of Industrial Engineering* 12 (July–August 1961).

Lee, R. C., and J. M. Moore. "CORELAP-Computerized Relationship Layout Planning." *Journal of Industrial Engineering* 18 (March 1967), pp. 195–200.

Mastor, A. A. "An Experimental Investigation and Comparative Evaluation of Production Line Balancing Techniques." *Management Science* 16, no. 11 (July 1970), 728–46.

Moore, J. M. *Plant Layout and Design.* New York: Macmillan, 1962.

Muther, R., and K. McPherson. "Four Approaches to Computerized Layout Planning." *Industrial Engineering* 2 (1970), p. 39–42.

Reed, R. *Plant Location, Layout and Maintenance.* Homewood, Ill.: Richard D. Irwin, 1967.

Scriabin, M., and R. C. Vergin. "Comparisons of Computer Algorithms and Visual Based Methods for Plant Layout." *Management Science* 22 (October 1975), pp. 172–81.

Vollman, Thomas E.; William L. Berry; and D. Clay Whybark. *Manufacturing and Control Systems.* Homewood, Ill.: Richard D. Irwin.

Reading

The Technocratic Hamburger

Nowhere in the entire service sector are the possibilities of the manufacturing mode of thinking better illustrated than in fast-food franchising. Nowhere have manufacturing

methods been employed more effectively to control the operation of distant and independent agents. Nowhere is "service" better.

Few of today's successful new commercial ventures have antecedents that are more humble and less glamorous than the hamburger. Yet the thriving nationwide chain of hamburger stands called "McDonald's" is a supreme example of the application of manufacturing and technological brilliance to problems that must ultimately be viewed as marketing problems. From 1961 to 1970 McDonald's sales rose from approximately $54 million to $587 million. During this remarkable ascent, the White Tower chain, whose name had theretofore been practically synonymous throughout the land with low-priced, quick-service hamburgers, practically vanished.

The explanation of McDonald's thundering success is not a purely fiscal one—i.e., the argument that it is financed by independent local entrepreneurs who bring to their operations a quality of commitment and energy not commonly found among hired workers. Nor is it a purely geographical one—i.e., the argument that each outlet draws its patronage from a relatively small geographic ring of customers, thus enabling the number of outlets easily and quickly to multiply. The relevant explanation must deal with the central question of why each separate McDonald's outlet is so predictably successful, why each is so certain to attract many repeat customers.

Entrepreneurial financing and careful site selection do help. But most important is the carefully controlled execution of each outlet's central function—the rapid delivery of a uniform, high-quality mix of prepared foods in an environment of obvious cleanliness, order, and cheerful courtesy. The systematic substitution of equipment for people, combined with the carefully planned use and positioning of technology, enables McDonald's to attract and hold patronage in proportions no predecessor or imitator has managed to duplicate. Consider the remarkable ingenuity of the system, which is worth examining in some detail:

To start with the obvious, raw hamburger patties are carefully prepacked and premeasured, which leaves neither the franchisee nor his employees any discretion as to size, quality, or raw-material consistency. This kind of attention is given to all McDonald's products. Storage and preparation space and related facilities are expressly designed for,

and limited to, the predetermined mix of products. There is no space for any foods, beverages, or services that were not designed into the system at the outset. There is not even a sandwich knife or in fact, a decent place to keep one. Thus the owner has no discretion regarding what he can sell—not because of any contractual limitations, but because of facilities limitations. And the employees have virtually no discretion regarding how to prepare and serve things. Discretion is the enemy of order, standardization, and quality. On an automobile assembly line, for example, a worker who has discretion and latitude might possibly produce a more personalized car, but one that is highly unpredictable. The elaborate care with which an automobile is designed and an assembly line is structured and controlled is what produced quality cars at low prices, and with surprising reliability considering the sheer volume of the output. The same is true at McDonald's, which produces food under highly automated and controlled conditions.

French-fried automation

While in Detroit the significance of the technological process lies in production, at McDonald's it lies in marketing. A carefully planned design is built into the elaborate technology of the food-service system in such a fashion as to make it a significant marketing device. This fact is impressively illustrated by McDonald's handling of that uniquely plebeian American delicacy, french-fried potatoes.

French fries become quickly soggy and unappetizing; to be good, they must be freshly made just before serving. Like other fast-food establishments, McDonald's provides its outlets with precut, partially cooked, frozen potatoes that can be quickly finished in an on-premises, deep-fry facility. The McDonald's fryer is neither so large that it produces too many fresh fries at one time (thus allowing them to become soggy) nor so small that it requires frequent and costly frying.

The fryer is emptied onto a wide, flat tray adjacent to the service counter. This location is crucial. Since the McDonald's practice is to create an impression of abundance and generosity by slightly overfilling each bag of french fries, the tray's location next to the service counter prevents the spillage from an overfilled bag from reaching the floor. Spillage creates not only danger underfoot but also an unattractive appearance that causes the employees to become accustomed to an unclean environment. Once a store is unclean in one particular, standards fall very rapidly and the store becomes unclean and the food unappetizing in general.

While McDonald's aims for an impression of abundance, excessive overfilling can be very costly for a company that annually buys potatoes almost by the trainload. A systematic bias that puts into each bag of french fries a half ounce more than is intended can have visible effects on the company's annual earnings. Further, excessive time spent at the tray by each employee can create a cumulative service bottleneck at the counter.

McDonald's has therefore developed a special wide-mouthed scoop with a narrow funnel in its handle. The counter employee picks up the scoop and inserts the handle end into a wall clip containing the bags. One bag adheres to the handle. In a continuous movement the scoop descends into the potatoes, fills the bag to the exact proportions its designers intended, and is lifted, scoop facing the ceiling, so that the potatoes funnel through the handle into the attached bag, which is automatically disengaged from the handle by the weight of the contents. The bag comes to a steady, nonwobbling rest on its flat bottom.

Nothing can go wrong—the employee never soils his hands, the floor remains clean, dry, and safe, and the quantity is controlled. Best of all, the customer gets a visibly generous portion with great speed, the employee

remains efficient and cheerful, and the general impression is one of extravangantly good service.

Mechanized marketing

Consider the other aspects of McDonald's technological approach to marketing. The tissue paper used to wrap each hamburger is color-coded to denote the mix of condiments. Heated reservoirs hold pre-prepared hamburgers for rush demand. Frying surfaces have spatter guards to prevent soiling of the cook's uniforms. Nothing is left to chance or the employees' discretion.

The entire system is engineered and executed according to a tight technological discipline that ensures fast, clean, reliable service in an atmosphere that gives the modestly paid employees a sense of pride and dignity. In spite of the crunch of eager customers, no employee looks or acts harassed, and therefore no harassment is communicated to the customers.

But McDonald's goes even further. Customers may be discouraged from entering if the building looks unappealing from the outside; hence considerable care goes into the design and appearance of the structure itself.

Some things, however, the architect cannot control, especially at an establishment where people generally eat in their parked cars and are likely to drop hamburger wrappings and empty beverage cartons on the ground. McDonald's has anticipated the requirement: its blacktop parking facilities are dotted like a checkerboard with numerous large, highly visible trash cans. It is impossible to ignore their purpose. Even the most indifferent customer would be struck with guilt if he simply dropped his refuse on the ground. But, just in case he drops it anyway, the larger McDonald's outlets have motorized sweepers for quick and easy cleanup.

What is important to understand about this remarkably successful organization is not only that it has created a highly sophisticated piece of technology, but also that it has done this by applying a manufacturing style of thinking to a people-intensive service situation. If machinery is to be viewed as a piece of equipment with the capability of producing a predictably standardized, customer-satisfying output while minimizing the operating discretion of its attendant, that is what a McDonald's retail outlet is. It is a machine that produces, with the help of totally unskilled machine tenders, a highly polished product. Through painstaking attention to total design and facilities planning, everything is built integrally into the machine itself, into the technology of the system. The only choice available to the attendant is to operate it exactly as the designers intended.

Questions

1. Describe McDonald's production-line approach to fast-food service.

2. What are the advantages of that approach?

3. Which operation—a takeout shop specializing in pizza, or a famous expensive restaurant with a large menu—would be most amenable to the production-line approach? Why?

4. Can you think of any other nonmanufacturing examples that parallel the MacDonald's approach?

Chapter 8

Design of Work Systems

After completing this chapter, you should be able to:

1. Briefly describe the two basic approaches to job design.
2. Discuss the advantages and disadvantages of specialization and automation.
3. Explain the term *sociotechnical system.*
4. Explain the purpose of methods analysis and describe how methods studies are done.
5. Describe four commonly used techniques for motion study.
6. Discuss the impact of working conditions on job design.
7. Define a standard time.
8. Discuss and compare time-study methods.
9. Describe work sampling and perform calculations.
10. Compare stopwatch time study and work sampling.
11. Contrast time and output pay systems.

JOB DESIGN, 360

    Specialization, 361
    Behavioral Approaches to Job Design, 363
    Automation, 364
    Sociotechnical Systems, 365
    Methods Analysis, 366
    Motion Study, 371
    Working Conditions, 374

WORK MEASUREMENT, 382

    Stopwatch Time Study, 383
    Standard Elemental Times, 390
    Predetermined Time Standards, 390
    Work Sampling, 391

COMPENSATION, 399

    Individual Incentive Plans, 401
    Group Incentive Plans, 402

SUMMARY, 402

SOLVED PROBLEMS, 404

DISCUSSION AND REVIEW QUESTIONS, 406

PROBLEMS, 407

SELECTED BIBLIOGRAPHY, 409

CASE: MAKING HOTPLATES, 410

CASE: ALLSTATE AUTOMOTIVE ANALYZERS, INC., 411

SUPPLEMENT: LEARNING CURVES, 415

This chapter concludes our discussion of the design of operations systems. Previous chapters in this part have dealt with capacity planning, location, product/service design, and layout. In this chapter we turn our attention to the design of the work system. Work design involves job design, establishment of time standards, and worker compensation.

As you read this chapter, notice how decisions in the other design areas have an impact on work systems, and how decisions on work design have an impact on the other areas. For example, product or service design decisions (e.g., operate a coal mine, offer computer dating service, sell sports equipment) in large measure determine the kinds of activities workers will be involved with. Similarly, layout decisions often influence work design. Process layouts tend to necessitate broader job content than product layouts. The implication of these interrelationships is that it is essential to adopt a systems approach to design; decisions in one area must be related to the overall system.

The importance of work system design is underscored by the fact that the organization depends on human efforts (i.e., work) to accomplish its goals. Work design is one of the oldest areas of operations management. In the past it has often been de-emphasized in operations management courses in favor of other topics. In recent years, however, there has been renewed interest in this area, which has come from somewhat different directions. Some of the interest has come about from studies that suggest a general dissatisfaction on the part of many workers with their jobs. Interest has also been sparked by increasing concerns over productivity. Paradoxically, the very jobs that yield the highest productivity levels are also the ones that appear to generate the greatest amount of worker dissatisfaction, posing somewhat of a dilemma for job designers.

JOB DESIGN

Job design is concerned with specifying the contents and methods of jobs. In general, the goal of job design is to create a work system that is productive and efficient, taking into consideration costs and benefits of various alternatives. Practically speaking, job designers are concerned with *who* will do a job, *how* the job will be done, and *where* the job will be done.

In order for job design to be successful, it must be:

1. Carried out by experienced personnel who have the necessary training and background.
2. Consistent with the goals of the organization.

3. In written form.
4. Understood and agreed to by both management and employees.

The factors that affect job design and the implications of various alternatives are often so complex that a person without a good background in job design is likely to overlook important aspects of it. Workers and managers alike should be consulted in order to take advantage of their knowledge as well as to keep them informed. Because they are intimately involved with the work, employees are frequent sources of valuable suggestions relative to job improvements. Managerial support depends on the commitment and involvement of managers in job design. It is usually easier to sell a design to these two groups if they have been included in the process. Finally, establishing a written record of the job design can serve as a basis for referral if questions arise about it.

Current practice in job design contains elements of two basic schools of thought. One might be called the *efficiency* school because it emphasizes a systematic, logical approach to job design; the other is called the *behavioral school* because it emphasizes satisfaction of wants and needs.

The efficiency approach is a refinement of Frederick Winslow Taylor's scientific management concepts and has received considerable emphasis in the past. The behavioral approach emerged during the 1950s and has continued to make inroads into many aspects of job design. One of the main contributions of the behavioral approach is that is has awakened managers to the fact that humans are complex beings and the efficiency approach may not necessarily be appropriate in every instance.

The behavioral view received a shot in the arm in 1973 when the report *Work in America* was released detailing some of the problems that currently exist in our work systems.[1] The report revealed an apparently widespread dissatisfaction on the part of workers across the spectrum of jobs. Two points were of special interest to job designers. One was that many workers felt that their jobs were not interesting; the other was that workers wanted more control over their jobs. The central issue seemed to be the degree of specialization associated with their jobs; high specialization appeared to generate the most dissatisfaction. It is noteworthy that specialization is a primary source of disagreement between the efficiency and behavioral approaches.

Specialization

Specialization is a term used to describe jobs that have a very narrow scope. Examples range from assembly lines to medical special-

---

[1] Upjohn Institute for Employment Research, *Work in America* (Cambridge, Mass.: MIT Press, 1973).

ties. College professors often specialize in teaching certain courses, some auto mechanics specialize in transmission repair, and some bakeries specialize in wedding cakes. The main rationale for specialization is the ability to concentrate one's efforts and thereby become proficient in some aspect of a product or service. Sometimes the amount of knowledge or training required of a specialist and the complexity of the work suggest that individuals who choose such work are not unhappy with their jobs. This seems to be especially true in the professions (doctors, lawyers, professors, etc.). However, at the other end of the scale are assembly-line workers, who are also specialists, although with a lot less glamor. The rationale for these highly specialized jobs is that they yield high productivity and low unit costs. In fact, such specialization is largely responsible for the high standard of living that exists today in industrial nations.

Unfortunately, many of these jobs can be described as dull, monotonous, and downright boring and are apparently the source of much of the dissatisfaction that exists in industry today. Even so, it would be wrong to conclude that all workers oppose this type of work. Some workers undoubtedly prefer a job with limited requirements and responsibility for making decisions. Others are not capable of handling jobs with larger scopes. Nonetheless, many workers are frustrated in such jobs, and this often manifests itself in a number of ways. Turnover and absenteeism are often high in these jobs. For example, in the automotive industry, absenteeism often runs as high as 20 percent or more, although not every absentee is a frustrated worker on an assembly line. Workers may also take out their frustrations by disruptive tactics, deliberate slowdowns, or poor attention to product quality.

The seriousness of some of these problems has caused job designers and others to seek ways of alleviating them. Some of those approaches are discussed below. Before turning to them, it will be

---

TABLE 8–1

Major Advantages and Disadvantages of Specialization in Business

A. Advantages:

For management	For labor
1. Simplifies training	1. Low education and skill requirements
2. High productivity	2. Minimum responsibilities
3. Low wage costs	3. Little mental effort needed

B. Disadvantages:

For management	For labor
1. Difficult to motivate quality	1. Monotonous, boring work
2. Work dissatisfaction possibly resulting in absenteeism, turnover, etc.	2. Limited opportunities for advancement
	3. Little control over work
	4. Little opportunity for self-fulfillment

Chapter 13

Project
Management

After completing this chapter, you should be able to:

1. Give a general description of PERT/CPM techniques.
2. Construct simple network diagrams.
3. List the kinds of information that a PERT or CPM analysis can provide the manager.
4. Analyze networks with deterministic times.
5. Analyze networks with probabilistic times.
6. Describe activity "crashing" and solve simple problems.
7. Discuss the behavioral aspects of projects in terms of project personnel and the project manager.

BEHAVIORAL ASPECTS OF PROJECT MANAGEMENT, 626

The Nature of Projects, 627
The Project Manager, 627
The Pros and Cons of Working on Projects, 628

PLANNING AND SCHEDULING WITH GANTT CHARTS, 628

PERT AND CPM, 630

The Network Diagram, 631
Network Conventions, 632

DETERMINISTIC TIME ESTIMATES, 634

A COMPUTING ALGORITHM, 636

Computing ES and EF Times, 636
Computing LS and LF Times, 638
Computing Activity Slack Times, 639

PROBABILISTIC TIME ESTIMATES, 640

ACTIVITIES ON NODES DIAGRAMS, 647

SIMULATION, 648

TIME-COST TRADE-OFFS—CRASHING, 649

ADVANTAGES AND LIMITATIONS OF PERT, 653

SUMMARY, 653
SOLVED PROBLEMS, 655
DISCUSSION AND REVIEW QUESTIONS, 662
PROBLEMS, 663
SELECTED BIBLIOGRAPHY, 667
CASE: THE CASE OF THE MEXICAN CRAZY QUILT, 668

Managers typically oversee a variety of operations. Some of these involve routine, repetitive activities while others tend to vary with the task. *Projects* fall under the latter heading; they are unique, one-time operations designed to accomplish a specific set of objectives in a limited time frame. Examples of projects include constructing a shopping complex, installing a new computer system, moving a firm to a new location, launching a space shuttle, and introducing a new product or service to the marketplace.

Most projects have certain elements in common. Often they involve considerable cost. They usually have a long time horizon, and they involve a large number of activities that must be carefully planned and coordinated in order for the project to be completed within time, cost, and performance guidelines. Goals must be established, and priorities must be set. Tasks must be identified, and time estimates must be made. Resource requirements must also be projected, and budgets must be prepared. Once underway, progress must be monitored to assure that project goals and objectives will be achieved.

The project approach enables an organization to focus attention and concentrate efforts on accomplishing a narrow set of objectives within a limited time and budget framework. This can produce significant benefits relative to other approaches that might be considered. Even so, projects present a manager with a host of problems that differ in many respects from those encountered with more routine types of activities. The problems of planning and coordinating project activities can be quite formidable for large projects, which typically have hundreds or even thousands of activities that must be carefully planned and monitored if a project is to proceed according to schedule and at a reasonable cost.

The chapter introduces the basic concepts of project management. It begins with a brief discussion of some of the behavioral aspects of project management, along with some of the difficulties project managers are apt to encounter. The main portion of the chapter is devoted to a description of graphical and computational methods that are used for planning and scheduling projects.

BEHAVIORAL ASPECTS OF PROJECT MANAGEMENT

Project management differs from management of more traditional activities, mainly because of its limited time framework, which gives rise to a host of rather unique problems. This section considers more fully the nature of projects and their behavioral implications. Special attention is given to the role of the project manager.

The Nature of Projects

Projects go through a series of stages (i.e., a life cycle), which include project planning, execution of major activities, and project phaseout. During this life cycle, a variety of skill requirements are involved. An analogous set of circumstances exists in constructing a house. Initially a site must be found and plans drawn up and approved by the owner and possibly a town building commission or other regulatory agency. Then a succession of personnel become involved, starting with those doing the site preparation, laying the foundation, erecting the frame, roofing, constructing exterior walls, wiring and plumbing, installing kitchen and bathroom fixtures and appliances, interior finishing work, and painting and carpeting work. Similar sequences are found on large construction projects, in R&D work, in the aerospace industry, and in virtually every other instance where projects are being used.

In effect, projects bring together personnel with diverse knowledge and skills, most of whom remain associated with the project for less than its full life. Some personnel go from project to project as their contributions become needed while others are "on loan," either on a full-time or part-time basis, from their regular jobs. The latter is usually the case when a special project exists within the framework of a more traditional organization. Certain kinds of organizations tend to be involved with projects on a regular basis. Examples include consulting firms, architects, writers and publishers, and construction firms. In fact, it is not uncommon to have organizations or departments spending virtually all of their time involved with projects, with little or no "continuous" work.

Some organizations use a *matrix organization* that allows them to integrate the activities of a variety of specialists within a functional framework. For instance, they have certain people who prepare proposals, other who concentrate exclusively on engineering, others who devote their efforts to marketing, and so on.

The Project Manager

The central figure in the project is the project manager. He or she bears the ultimate responsibility for the success or failure of the project. The role of the project manager is one of an organizer—a person who is capable of working through others to accomplish the objectives of the project.

The job of project manager can be both difficult and rewarding. The manager must coordinate and motivate people who sometimes owe their allegiance to other managers in their functional areas. In addition, the people who work on a project frequently possess specialized knowledge and skills that the project manager does not have. Nevertheless, the manager is expected to guide and evaluate their efforts. Project managers must often function in an environment that is beset with uncertainties. Even so, budgets and time constraints are usually imposed, which can create additional pressures on project personnel. Finally, the project manager may not have the authority he or she needs to accomplish all of the objectives of the project. Instead, the manager must sometimes rely on persuasion and the cooperation of others to realize project goals.

The rewards of the job of project manager come from the benefits of being associated with a successful project as well as the personal satisfaction of seeing it through to its conclusion, the challenge of the job, and working with other people.

The Pros and Cons of Working on Projects

People are selected to work on special projects because the knowledge or abilities they possess are needed on them. In some instances, however, their supervisors may be reluctant to allow them to interrupt their regular jobs, even on a part-time basis, because it may require training a new person to do a job that will be temporary. Moreover, managers don't want to lose the output of good workers. The workers, themselves, are not always eager to participate on projects, because it may mean working for two bosses, disruption of friendships and daily routines, and risking the possibility of being replaced on the current job. Furthermore, there may be fear of being associated with an unsuccessful project because of the potential adverse effect it might have on career advancement. In too many instances, when a project is phased out and the project team disbanded, team members tend to drift away from the organization for lack of a new project and the difficulty of returning to former jobs. This tendency is more pronounced after involvement with lengthy projects and is less likely to occur when a team member works on a part-time basis, although that approach has its own drawbacks in terms of divided loyalty and dual bosses.

In spite of the potential risks of being involved in a project, there are certain potential rewards that attract people to them. One is the dynamic environment that surrounds a project, often a marked contrast to the more staid environment in which some may feel trapped. Some individuals seem to thrive in more dynamic environments; they welcome the challenge of working under pressure and solving new problems. Then, too, projects may present opportunities to meet new people and to increase future job opportunities, especially if the project is at all successful. And being associated with a project can be a source of status among fellow workers. Finally, working on projects frequently inspires a team spirit, increasing morale and motivation to achieve successful completion of project goals.

PLANNING AND SCHEDULING WITH GANTT CHARTS

The Gantt chart is a popular tool for planning and scheduling *simple* projects. It enables a manager to initially schedule project activities and then to monitor progress over time by comparing planned

FIGURE 13–1

Gantt Chart for Bank Example

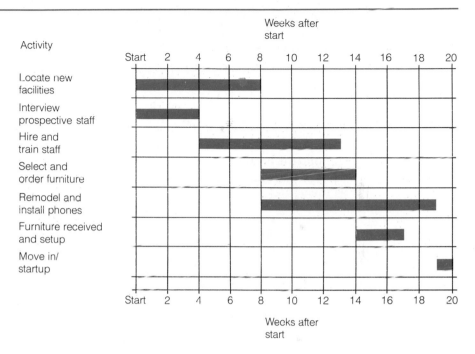

progress to actual progress. A Gantt chart for a bank's plan to establish a new direct marketing department is illustrated in Figure 13–1. In order to prepare the chart, the vice president who was in charge of the project had to first identify the major activities that would be required. Next, time estimates for each activity were made, and the sequence of activities was determined. Once completed, the chart indicated which activities were to occur, their planned duration, and when they were to occur. Then, as the project progressed, the manager was able to see which activities were ahead of schedule and which activities were delaying the project. This enabled the manager to direct attention where it was needed most to speed up the project in order to finish on schedule.

The obvious advantage of a Gantt chart is its simplicity, and this accounts for its popularity. However, Gantt charts fail to reveal certain relationships among activities that can be crucial to effective project management. For instance, if one of the early activities in a project suffers a delay, it would be important for the manager to be able to easily determine which later activities would have to be delayed *because they could not start until that activity was completed.* Conversely, some activities may safely be delayed without affecting the overall project schedule. Again, a Gantt chart does not directly reveal this. Consequently, Gantt charts are most useful for simple projects, say where activities are simultaneous or where a string of sequential activities is involved. On more complex projects, Gantt charts can be useful for initial project planning, which then gives way to the use of *networks,* the subject of the following sections.

PERT AND CPM

PERT (program evaluation and review technique) and CPM (critical path method) are two of the most widely used techniques for planning and coordinating large-scale projects. By using PERT or CPM, managers are able to obtain:

1. A graphical display of project activities.
2. An estimate of how long the project will take.
3. An indication of which activities are the most critical to timely project completion.
4. An indication of how long any activity can be delayed without lengthening the project.

PERT and CPM were developed independently during the late 1950s. PERT evolved through the joint efforts of Lockheed Aircraft, the U.S. Navy Special Projects Office, and the consulting firm of Booz, Allen & Hamilton in an effort to speed up the Polaris missile project. At the time, there was considerable concern on the part of the U.S. government that the Soviet Union might be gaining nuclear superiority over the United States, and early completion of the project was given top priority by the Department of Defense. The project was a huge one, with over 3,000 contractors involved, and many thousands of activities. The use of PERT was quite successful: PERT is generally credited for shaving two years off the length of the project. Partly for that reason, PERT or some similar technique is now required on all large government projects.

CPM was developed by J. E. Kelly of the Remington Rand Corporation and M. R. Walker of Du Pont to plan and coordinate maintenance projects in chemical plants.

Although these two techniques were developed independently, they have a great deal in common. Moreover, many of the initial differences between the two techniques have disappeared as users borrowed certain features from one technique for use with the other. For example, PERT originally stressed probabilistic activity time estimates, because the environment in which it was developed was typified by high uncertainty. In contrast, the tasks for which CPM was developed were much less uncertain, so CPM originally made no provision for variable time estimates. At present, either technique can be used with deterministic or probabilistic times. Other initial differences concerned the mechanical aspects of developing project networks. However, from a conceptual standpoint, most of these differences were relatively minor. In order to avoid confusion, we shall not delve into the differences here. For purposes of illustration, the discussion will proceed along the lines of PERT, particularly with respect to construction of precedence networks. Nonetheless, as a general rule, the comments and procedures described will apply to CPM analysis as well as to PERT analysis of projects.

The Network Diagram

One of the main features of PERT and related techniques is their use of a *network* or *precedence diagram* to depict major project activities and their sequential relationships. Recall the bank example that used a Gantt chart (see Figure 13–1). A network diagram for that same problem is shown in Figure 13–2. The diagram is composed of a number of arrows and nodes. The arrows represent the project activities. Notice how much clearer the sequential relationship of activities is with a network instead of a Gantt chart. For instance, it is apparent that ordering the furniture and remodeling both require that a location for the office has been identified. Likewise, interviewing must precede training. However, interviewing and training can take place independently of activities associated with locating a facility, remodeling, and so on. Hence, a network diagram is generally the preferred approach for visual portrayal of project activities.

You should know that there are two slightly different conventions for constructing these network diagrams. Under one convention, the *arrows* are used to designate activities, while under the other convention, the *nodes* are used to designate activities. These conventions are referred to as *activity-on-arrow (A–O–A)* and *activity-on-node* (A–O–N). In order to avoid confusion, the discussion here will focus primarily on the activity-on-arrow convention. Then, later in the chapter, a comparison of the two conventions will be

FIGURE 13–2

A Simple Project Network Diagram

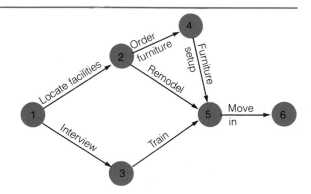

given. For now, we shall use the arrows for activities. The nodes in the A–O–A approach represent either the starting and finishing of activities, which are called *events.* The activities have associated time estimates, while the events do not.

The chart describes sequential relationships among major activities on a project. For instance, activity 2–4 cannot be started, according to the chart, until activity 1–2 has been completed. A *path* is a sequence of activities that leads from the starting node to the finishing node. Thus, the sequence 1–2–4–5–6 is a path. There are two other paths in this network: 1–2–5–6 and 1–3–5–6. The length (of time) of any path can be determined by summing the expected times of the activities on that path. The path with the longest time is of particular interest because it governs project completion time. In other words, expected project duration equals the expected time of the longest path. Moreover, if there are any delays along the longest path, there will be corresponding delays in project completion time. Conversely, attempts to shorten project completion must focus on the longest sequence of activities. Because of its influence on project completion time, the longest path is the *critical path,* and its activities are referred to as *critical activities.*

Paths that are shorter than the critical path can experience some delays and still not affect the overall project completion time as long as the ultimate path time does not exceed the length of the critical path. The allowable slippage for any path is called the path *slack;* and it reflects the difference between the length of a given path and the length of the critical path. The critical path, then, has zero slack time.

Network Conventions

Developing and interpreting network diagrams requires some familiarity with networking conventions. While there are many things that could be mentioned, the discussion here will concentrate on some of the most basic, and most common, features of network diagrams. This will provide sufficient background for understanding the basic concepts associated with precedence diagrams and allow you to solve typical problems.

One of the main features of a precedence diagram is that it reveals which activities must be performed in *sequence* (i.e., there is a precedence relationship) and which can be performed independently of each other. For example, in this diagram, activity *a* must

be completed before activity *b* can begin, and activity *b* must be completed before activity *c* can begin. If the diagram had looked like this, both activity *a* and activity *b* would have to be completed

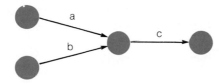

before activity *c* could begin, but *a* and *b* could be performed at the same time; performance of *a* is independent of performance of *b*.

If activity *a* must precede *b* and *c*, the appropriate network would look like this:

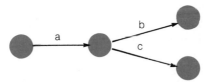

When multiple activities enter a node, this implies that all those activities must be completed before any activities that are to begin at that node can start. Hence, in this diagram, activities *a* and *b* must both be finished before either activity *c* or activity *d* can start.

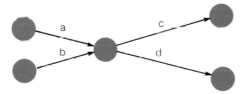

When two activities both have the same beginning and ending nodes, a *dummy* node and activity is used in order to preserve the separate identity of each activity. In the diagram below, activi-

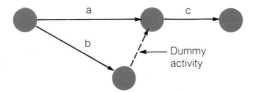

ties *a* and *b* must be completed before activity *c* can be started. Separate identities are particularly important for computer analysis, because most computer programs identify activities by their endpoints; activities with the same endpoints could not be distinguished from each other, although they might have quite different expected times.

There are actually a number of different uses of dummy activities. Another common use is depicted below:

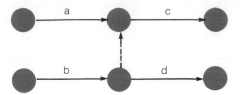

In this situation, activities *a* and *b* must both precede activity *c.* However, *d*'s start is dependent only on completion of activity *b,* and *not* on activity *a*'s completion.

The primary function of dummy activities is to clarify relationships. As far as time is concerned, a dummy activity has an activity time equal to zero.

For reference purposes, nodes are numbered, typically from left to right:

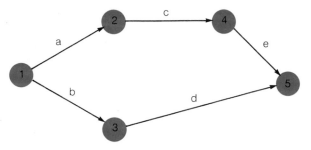

Starting and ending arrows are sometimes used during development of a network for increased clarity.

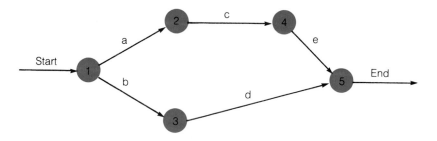

DETERMINISTIC TIME ESTIMATES

The main determinant of the way PERT and CPM networks are analyzed and interpreted is whether activity time estimates are *probabilistic* or *deterministic.* If time estimates can be made with a high degree of confidence that actual times will not differ significantly, we say the estimates are *deterministic.* On the other hand, if estimated times are subject to variation, we say the estimates are *probabilistic.* Probabilistic time estimates must include an indication of the extent of probable variation.

This section describes analysis of networks with deterministic time estimates. A later section deals with probabilistic times.

One of the best ways to gain an understanding of the nature of network analysis is to consider a simple example.

EXAMPLE 1

Given the information provided in the accompanying network diagram, determine each of the following:

a. The length of each path.
b. The critical path.
c. The expected length of the project.
d. Amount of slack time for each path.

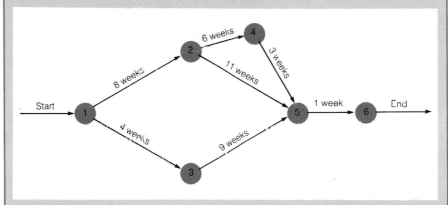

Solution

(The start and end "activities" have no times—they merely serve as reference points.)

a. As shown in the table below, the path lengths are 18 weeks, 20 weeks, and 14 weeks.
b. The longest path (20 weeks) is 1–2–5–6, so it is the critical path.
c. The expected length of the project is equal to the length of the critical path (i.e., 20 weeks).
d. The slack for each path is found by subtracting its length from the length of the critical path, as shown in the last column of the table. Note: it is sometimes desirable to know the slack time associated with individual activities. The next section describes a method for obtaining those slack times.

Path	Length (weeks)	Slack
1–2–4–5–6	$8 + 6 + 3 + 1 = 18$	$20 - 18 = 2$
1–2–5–6	$8 + 11 + 1 = 20*$	$20 - 20 = 0$
1–3–5–6	$4 + 9 + 1 = 14$	$20 - 14 = 6$

* Critical path length.

A COMPUTING ALGORITHM

Many real-life project networks are much larger than the simple network illustrated in the preceding example; they often contain hundreds or even thousands of activities. Because the necessary computations can become exceedingly complex and time-consuming, large networks are generally analyzed by computer programs rather than manually. The intuitive approach just demonstrated does not lend itself to computerization because in many instances path-sequences are not readily apparent. Instead, an algorithm is used to develop four pieces of information about the network activities:

> ES, the earliest time the activity can start, assuming all preceding activities start as early as possible.
> EF, the earliest time the activity can finish.
> LS, the latest time the activity can start and not delay the project.
> LF, the latest time the activity can finish and not delay the project.

Once these values have been determined, they can be used to find:

1. Expected project duration.
2. Activity slack time.
3. Which activities are on the critical path.

The three examples that follow illustrate how these values are computed using the precedence diagram of Example 1, which is repeated here for convenient reference.

Computing ES and EF Times

Computation of earliest starting and finishing times is aided by two simple rules:

1. The earliest finish time for any activity is equal to its earliest start time plus its expected duration, *t*:

$$EF = ES + t \qquad\qquad (13\text{--}1)$$

2. For nodes with one entering arrow: ES for activities at such nodes is equal to EF of entering arrow. For nodes with multiple entering arrows: ES for activities leaving such nodes equals the largest EF of entering arrows.

EXAMPLE 2

Compute the earliest starting time and earliest finishing time for each activity in the diagram shown in Figure 13–3.

EXAMPLE 2 (concluded)
FIGURE 13–3

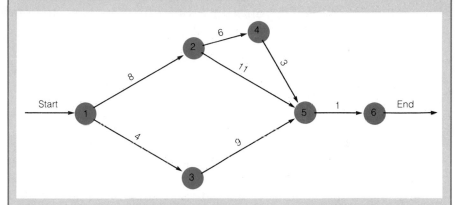

Solution

Assume an ES of 0 for activities without predecessors. Thus, activities 1–2 and 1–3, as initial activities, are assigned early starting times equal to zero. The earliest finishing times for these activities are:

$$EF_{1-2} = 0 + 8 = 8 \quad \text{and} \quad EF_{1-3} = 0 + 4 = 4$$

The EF of activity 1–2 becomes the ES for the two activities that follow it: 2–4 and 2–5. Likewise, the EF of activity 1–3 becomes the ES for activity 3–5. Thus:

$$ES_{2-4} = 8, ES_{2-5} = 8 \quad \text{and} \quad ES_{3-5} = 4$$

The corresponding EF times for these activities are:

$$EF_{2-4} = 8 + 6 = 14$$
$$EF_{2-5} = 8 + 11 = 19$$
$$EF_{3-5} = 4 + 9 = 13$$

Activity 4–5 has an early starting time equal to EF_{2-4}, or 14, and an early finish time of $14 + 3 = 17$. Finally, activity 5–6, with three predecessors, has an early starting time equal to the *largest* EF of the three activities that precede it. Hence, it has an ES of 19. Its EF time is $19 + 1 = 20$.

These results are summarized in the table below.

Activity	Duration	ES	EF
1–2	8	0	8
1–3	4	0	4
2–4	6	8	14
2–5	11	8	19
3–5	9	4	13
4–5	3	14	17
5–6	1	19	20

Note that the latest EF is the project duration. Thus, the expected length of the project is 20 weeks.

Computing LS and LF Times

Computation of the latest starting and finishing times is aided by the use of two rules:

1. The latest starting time for each activity is equal to its latest finishing time minus its expected duration:

$$LS = LF - t \qquad\qquad\qquad \textbf{(13–2)}$$

2. For nodes with one leaving arrow: LF for arrows entering that node equals the LS of the leaving arrow. For nodes with multiple leaving arrows: LF for arrows entering that node equals the smallest LS of leaving arrows.

Finding ES and EF times involves a "forward pass" through the network; finding LS and LF times involves a "backward pass" through the network. Hence, we must begin with the EF of the last activity and use that time as the LF for the last activity. Then we obtain the LS for the last activity by subtracting its expected duration from its LF.

EXAMPLE 3

Compute the latest finishing and starting times for each activity shown in Figure 13–3.

Solution

Set LF of the last activity equal to the EF of that activity. Thus,

$$LF_{5\text{-}6} = EF_{5\text{-}6} = 20 \text{ weeks}$$

Next, compute the latest starting time:

$$LS_{5\text{-}6} = LF_{5\text{-}6} - t$$
$$= 20 - 1 = 19$$

In order for activity 5–6 to be able to start no later than week 19, all immediate predecessors must finish no later than that time. Thus,

$$LF_{4\text{-}5} = LF_{2\text{-}5} = LF_{3\text{-}5} = 19$$

The respective LS times for each activity are:

$$LS_{4\text{-}5} = 19 - 3 = 16$$
$$LS_{2\text{-}5} = 19 - 11 = 8$$
$$LS_{3\text{-}5} = 19 - 9 = 10$$

Similarly, $LF_{2\text{-}4} = LS_{4\text{-}5} = 16$, and $LS_{2\text{-}4} = 16 - 6 = 10$. Hence, there are two arrows leaving node 2: 2–4 with $LS = 10$ and 2–5 with $LS =$

EXAMPLE 3 (concluded)

8. The latest finish for activity 1–2 thus becomes 8, which is the smallest LS for a leaving arrow. The LF for 1–3 is equal to the LS for 3–5:

$$LF_{1-3} = LS_{3-5} = 10$$

The LS for activity 1–3 is:

$$LS_{1-3} = 10 - 4 = 6$$

The LS for activity 1–2 is:

$$LS_{1-2} = LF_{1-2} - t$$
$$= 8 - 8 = 0$$

The LS, LF computations are summarized in the table below.

Activity	Duration	LF	LS
5–6	1	20	19
4–5	3	19	16
2–5	11	19	8
3–5	9	19	10
2–4	6	16	10
1–2	8	8	0
1–3	4	10	6

Computing Activity Slack Times

The slack time for any activity can be computed in either of two ways:

$$\text{Activity slack} = LS - ES \quad \text{or} \quad LF - EF \qquad (13\text{–}3)$$

EXAMPLE 4

Compute activity slack times for the precedence diagram of Figure 13–3.

Solution

We have the option of using either the starting times or the finishing times. Suppose we choose the starting times. Using ES times computed in Example 2 and LS times computed in Example 3, slack times are:

Activity	LS	ES	(LS − ES) Slack
1–2	0	0	0
1–3	6	0	6
2–4	10	8	2
2–5	8	8	0
3–5	10	4	6
4–5	16	14	2
5–6	19	19	0

TABLE 13–1

Computer Printout		STARTING SCHEDULE					
		EARLY		LATE			
ACTIVITY	*TIME*	*ES*	*EF*	*LS*	*LF*	*SLACK*	
1–2 . . .	8.00	0.00	8.00	0.00	8.00	0.00	
1–3 . . .	4.00	0.00	4.00	6.00	10.00	6.00	
2–4 . . .	6.00	8.00	14.00	10.00	16.00	2.00	
2–5 . . .	11.00	8.00	19.00	8.00	19.00	0.00	
3–5 . . .	9.00	4.00	13.00	10.00	19.00	6.00	
4–5 . . .	3.00	14.00	17.00	16.00	19.00	2.00	
5–6 . . .	1.00	19.00	20.00	19.00	20.00	0.00	

THE CRITICAL PATH SEQUENCE IS:

SNODE	*FNODE*	*TIME*
1	2	8.00
2	5	11.00
5	6	1.00
		20.00

The critical path using this computing algorithm is denoted by activities with zero slack time. Thus, the table in the preceding example indicates that activities 1–2, 2–5, and 5–6 are all critical activities, which agrees with the results of the intuitive approach demonstrated in Example 1.

Knowledge of individual slack times provides managers with greater detail for planning allocation of scarce resources and for directing control efforts toward those activities that might be most susceptible to delaying the project than the more simplistic intuitive approach does. In this regard, it is important to recognize that the activity slack times are based on the assumption that all other activities on the same path will be started as early as possible and not exceed their expected times. In other words, if two activities are both on the same path (e.g., activities 2–4 and 4–5 in the preceding example) and have the same slack (e.g., two weeks), this will be the total slack *available to both.* Hence, if the first activity uses all this slack, there will be zero slack for the other activity, and that much less slack for all following activities on that same path.

As noted above, this algorithm lends itself to computerization. A computer printout for this problem would appear something like the one shown in Table 13–1.

PROBABILISTIC TIME ESTIMATES

The preceding discussion assumed that activity times were known and not subject to variation. While that assumption is appropriate

FIGURE 13–4

A Beta Distribution Is Used to Describe Probabilistic Time Estimates

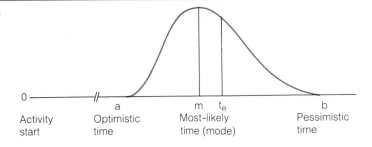

0	a	m t_e	b
Activity start	Optimistic time	Most-likely time (mode)	Pessimistic time

in some situations, there are many others where it is not. Consequently, those situations require a probabilistic approach.

The probabilistic approach involves *three* time estimates for each activity instead of one:

1. *Optimistic time:* The length of time required under optimum conditions. Represented by the letter *a*.
2. *Pessimistic time:* The amount of time that will be required under the worst conditions. Represented by the letter *b*.
3. *Most-likely time:* The most probable amount of time that will be required. Represented by the letter *m*.

These time estimates should be made by managers or others with knowledge about the project.

The *beta* distribution is commonly used to describe the inherent variability in time estimates (see Figure 13–4). Although there is no real theoretical justification for using the beta distribution, it has certain features that make it attractive in practice: The distribution can be symmetrical or skewed to either the right or left according to the nature of a particular activity, the mean and variance of the distribution can be readily obtained from the three time estimates listed above, and the distribution is unimodal with a high concentration of probability surrounding the most-likely time estimate.

Of special interest in network analysis are the average or expected time for each activity, t_e, and the variance of each activity time, σ_i^2. The expected time is computed as a weighted average of the three time estimates:

$$t_e = \frac{a + 4m + b}{6} \qquad (13\text{–}4)$$

The standard deviation of each activity's time is estimated as one sixth of the difference between the pessimistic and optimistic time estimates. (Analogously, essentially all of the area under a normal distribution lies within ± 3 standard deviations of the mean, which is a range of *six* standard deviations.) The variance is found by squaring the standard deviation. Thus:

$$\sigma^2 = \left[\frac{(b-a)}{6}\right]^2 \quad \text{or} \quad \frac{(b-a)^2}{36} \tag{13–5}$$

The size of the variance reflects the degree of uncertainty associated with an activity's time: The larger the variance the greater the uncertainty. Hence, an activity with a variance of 16 would have more uncertainty as to its eventual duration than one with a variance of, say, 6.

It is also desirable to compute the standard deviation of the expected time for *each path*. This can be accomplished by summing the variances of the activities on a path and then taking the square root of that number. That is,

$$\sigma_{\text{path}} = \sqrt{\Sigma(\text{variances of activities on path})} \tag{13–6}$$

EXAMPLE 5

The network diagram for a project is shown in the accompanying figure, with three time estimates for each activity. Activity times are in months. Do the following:

a. Compute the expected time for each activity and the expected duration for each path.
b. Identify the critical path.
c. Compute the variance for each activity and the variance for each path.

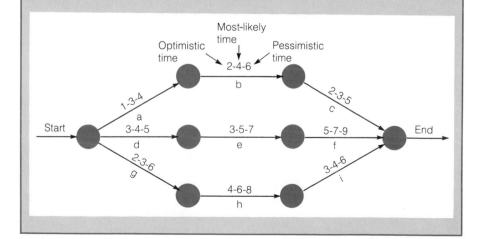

EXAMPLE 5 *(concluded)*

Solution

a.

Path	Activity	Times a m b	$t_e = \dfrac{a + 4m + b}{6}$	Path total
a–b–c	a	1 3 4	2.83 ⎫	
	b	2 4 6	4.00 ⎬	10.00
	c	2 3 5	3.17 ⎭	
d–e–f	d	3 4 5	4.00 ⎫	
	e	3 5 7	5.00 ⎬	16.00
	f	5 7 9	7.00 ⎭	
g–h–i	g	2 3 6	3.33 ⎫	
	h	4 6 8	6.00 ⎬	13.50
	i	3 4 6	4.17 ⎭	

b. The path that has the longest expected duration is the critical path. Since path d–e–f has the largest path total, it is the critical path.

c.

Path	Activity	Times a m b	$\sigma^2_{act.} = \dfrac{(b-a)^2}{36}$	σ^2_{path}	σ_{path}
a–b–c	a	1 3 4	$(4-1)^2/36 = 9/36$ ⎫		
	b	2 4 6	$(6-2)^2/36 = 16/36$ ⎬	$34/36 = .944$	.97
	c	2 3 5	$(5-2)^2/36 = 9/36$ ⎭		
d–e–f	d	3 4 5	$(5-3)^2/36 = 4/36$ ⎫		
	e	3 5 7	$(7-3)^2/30 = 16/36$ ⎬	$36/36 = 1.00$	1.00
	f	5 7 9	$(9-5)^2/36 = 16/36$ ⎭		
g -h–i	g	2 3 6	$(6-2)^2/36 = 16/36$		
	h	4 6 8	$(8-4)^2/36 = 16/36$	$41/36 = 1.139$	1.07
	i	3 4 6	$(6-3)^2/36 = 9/36$		

Knowledge of the expected path times and their standard deviations enables a manager to make probabilistic estimates of the project completion time, such as:

The probability that the project will be completed within 17 months of its start is about 84 percent.

The probability that the project will take longer than 18 months is approximately 2 percent.

Statements of this sort are based on the assumption that the duration time of a path is a random variable that is normally distributed around the expected path time. The rationale for a normal distribution is that we are summing activity times (random variables), and sums of random variables tend to be normally distributed when the number of items being summed is large. However, even when the number of items is relatively small, the normal distribution provides a reasonable approximation to the actual distribution.

The next example illustrates the use of a normal distribution to determine the probabilities for various completion times. Before we look at that example, it is important to make note of two points. One relates to *independence*. It is assumed that path duration times are independent of each other. In essence, this requires two things: Activity times are independent of each other, and each activity is only on one path. For activity times to be independent, the time for one must not be a function of another's time; if two activities were always early or late together, they would not be considered independent. The assumption of independent *paths* is usually considered to be met if only a *few* activities in a large project are on multiple paths. Even then, common sense should govern the decision of whether the independence assumption is justified.

A second important point is that a project is not completed until all of its activities have been completed, not just those on the critical path. It sometimes happens that another path requires more time than the critical path, in which case the project runs longer than expected. Hence, it can be risky to focus exclusively on the critical path. Instead, one must consider the possibility that at least one other path will delay timely project completion. This requires determining the probability that *all* paths will finish by a specified time. To do that, find the probability that each path will finish by the specified time and multiply the resulting probabilities. Note that only paths with expected times that are relatively close to that of the critical path need to be considered since it would be highly unlikely that a path with a much shorter expected time would exceed the critical path's time. A simple rule of thumb is to ignore any path if its expected time plus two of *its* standard deviations is less than the specified time. These concepts are illustrated in the following example.

EXAMPLE 6

Using the information from the preceding example, answer the following questions:

a. Can the paths be considered independent? Why?
b. Determine the probability that the project can be completed within 17 months of its start.
c. Determine the probability that the project will be completed within 15 months of its start.
d. What is the probability that the project will not be completed within 15 months of its start?

Solution

a. Yes, the paths can be considered independent since no activity is on more than one path and we have no information that would suggest that any activity times are interrelated.

EXAMPLE 6 *(continued)*

b. In order to answer questions of this nature, we must take into account the degree to which the path distributions "overlap" the specified completion time. This concept is illustrated in the accompanying figure, which shows the three path distributions, each centered on that path's expected duration, and the specified completion time of 17 months.

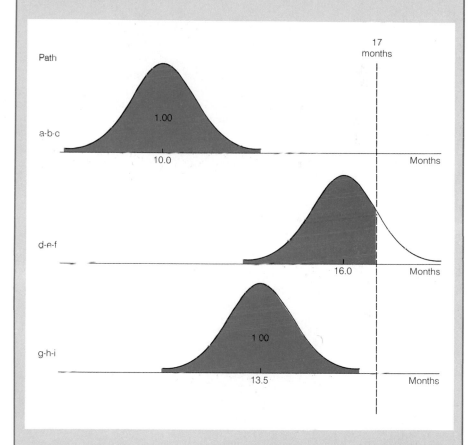

The shaded portion of each distribution corresponds to the probability that the part will be completed within the specified time. Observe that paths a–b–c and g–h–i are well enough to the left of the specified time that it is highly likely that both will be finished by month 17 but that the critical path overlaps the specified completion time. Hence, we need only consider only the distribution of path d–e–f in assessing the probability of completion by month 17. To do so, we must first compute the value of z using the relationship

EXAMPLE 6 (continued)

$$z = \frac{\text{Specified time} - \text{Expected time}}{\text{Path standard deviation}} \qquad (13\text{–}7)$$

In this instance, we find

$$z = \frac{17 - 16}{1.00} = +1.00.$$

Turning to Appendix Table B with $z = +1.00$, we see that the area under the curve to the left of z is .8413. Hence, the probability of the project finishing within 17 months of its start is 84.13 percent.

c. This question illustrates how to handle a problem in which more than one of the distributions overlaps the specified time. Note in the accompanying figure that paths d–e–f and g–h–i overlap month

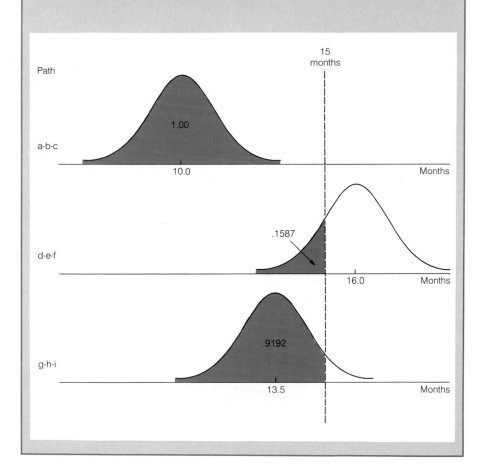

> **EXAMPLE 6 (concluded)**
>
> 15. This means that both paths have the potential for delaying the project beyond the 15 months.
>
> While the figure is useful in expressing the concept of overlapping paths, we need a more rigorous approach to determine which paths to consider and what each path's probability of completion is. This requires computing a value of z using the formula on page 646 for each path. Then, any path with a z of more than $+2.00$ is ignored; the others will be used to determine the *joint* probability of finishing by the specified time. For this problem with a specified time of 15 months, the z-values are:
>
> $$z = \frac{15 - Expected\ path\ duration}{Path\ standard\ deviation}$$
>
> | Path | |
> |------|--|
> | a–b–c | $\dfrac{15 - 10.00}{.97} = +5.15$ (ignore) |
> | d–e–f | $\dfrac{15 - 16.00}{1.00} = -1.00$ |
> | g–h–i | $\dfrac{15 - 13.50}{1.07} = +1.40$ |
>
> From Appendix Table B, the area to the *left* of $z = -1.00$ is .1587, and the area to the *left* of $z = +1.40$ is .9192. The joint probability of both finishing before month 15 is the product of these probabilities: .1587(.9192) = .1459.

ACTIVITIES ON NODES DIAGRAMS

Earlier in the chapter it was mentioned that network diagrams can be drawn with the activities on nodes (A–O–N) rather than on arrows. The result is a slightly different diagram. We can begin to get an appreciation for the differences by comparing the two approaches to a given problem. Consider this set of project activities:

Activity	Precedes
start	a,b
a	c
b	d,e
c	f
d	g
e	g
f	end
g	end

Figure 13–5 illustrates both types of networks.

FIGURE 13–5

A Comparison of the A–O–A and A–O–N Methods of Network Representation

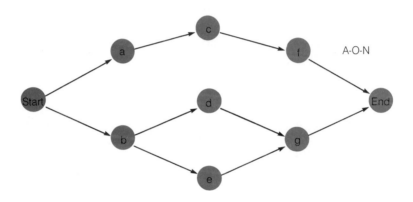

One obvious difference in the two approaches is that there are more nodes in the A–O–N approach. Generally speaking, this will be the rule. A second difference is that the A–O–A network has a dummy arrow that is necessary in order to correctly show the precedence relationship that exists. The dummy is not necessary in the A–O–N network; A–O–N networks eliminate the need for dummy activities, which is an advantage of having activities on nodes.

In practice, both approaches are used. Usually PERT/CPM computer programs can handle either convention, but some require one or the other. Often the choice of method depends more on personal preference or established procedures.

SIMULATION

The preceding section illustrated a method for computing the probability that a project would be completed in a specified length of time. That discussion assumed that the paths of the project were *independent;* that is, that the same activities were not on more than one path. If an activity were on more than one path and it happened that the completion time for that activity far exceeded its expected time, all paths that included that activity would be affected, and hence, their times would not be independent. In situations where activities are on multiple paths, one must consider if the preceding approach can be used. For instance, if only a few activities are on multiple paths, and particularly if the paths are *much* shorter than the critical path, that approach may still be reasonable. Moreover, for purposes of illustration, as in the text problems and examples, we treat the paths as being independent when, in fact, they may not be.

In practice, when *dependent* cases occur, an approach that is often used is *simulation.* It amounts to a form of repeated sampling wherein many passes are made through the PERT network. In each pass a randomly selected value for each activity time is made based on the characteristics of the activity's probability distribution (e.g., its mean, standard deviation, and distribution type). After each pass, the expected project duration is determined by adding the times along each path and designating the time of the longest path as the project duration. After a large number of such passes (say, several hundred), there is enough information to prepare a frequency distribution of the project duration times. This distribution can be used to make a probabilistic assessment of the actual project duration, allowing for the fact that some activities are on more than one path. The last problem in the Simulation Supplement in Chapter 14 illustrates this.

TIME-COST TRADE-OFFS—CRASHING

Estimates of activity times for projects usually are made for some given level of resources. In many situations it is possible to reduce the length of a project by injecting additional resources. The impetus to shorten projects may reflect efforts to avoid late penalties or to take advantage of monetary incentives for timely completion of a project, or to free resources for use on other projects. In many cases, however, the desire to shorten the length of a project merely reflects an attempt to reduce the indirect costs associated with running the project, such as facilities and equipment costs, supervision, and labor and personnel costs. Managers often have certain options at their disposal that will allow them to shorten, or *crash,* certain activities. Among the most obvious options are the use of additional funds to support additional personnel or more efficient equipment and the relaxing of some work specifications. Hence, a project manager may be able to shorten a project, thereby realizing a saving on indirect project costs, by increasing *direct* expenses to speed up the project. The goal in evaluating time-cost trade-offs is to identify a plan that will minimize the sum of the indirect and direct project costs.

In order to make a rational decision on which activities (if any) to crash, and on the extent of crashing desirable, a manager needs certain information:

1. Regular time and crash time estimates for each activity.
2. Regular cost and crash cost estimates for each activity.
3. A list of activities that are on the critical path.

Activities on the critical path are potential candidates for crashing, since shortening noncritical activities would not have an impact on total project duration. From an economic standpoint, activities should be crashed according to crashing costs: Crash those with the lowest costs first. Moreover, crashing should continue as long as the cost to crash is less than the benefits received from crashing. These benefits might take the form of incentive payments for early project completion as part of a government contract, or they might

FIGURE 13–6

Crashing Activities*

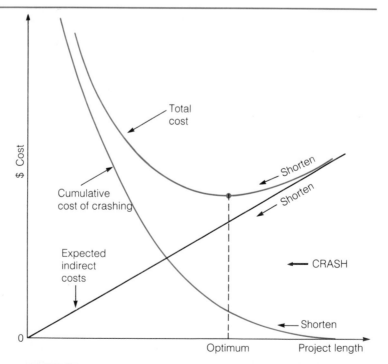

*Crashing activities reduces indirect project costs while increasing direct costs: The optimum amount of crashing results in minimizing the sum of these two types of costs.

reflect savings in the indirect project costs, or both. Figure 13–6 illustrates the basic relationships between indirect, direct, and total project costs due to crashing.

The general procedure for crashing is:

1. Obtain estimates of regular and crash times and costs for each activity.
2. Determine the lengths of all paths and path slack times.
3. Determine which activities are on the critical path.
4. Crash critical activities, in order of increasing costs, as long as crashing costs do not exceed benefits. (Note that two or more paths may become critical as the original critical path becomes shorter, so that subsequent improvements will require simultaneous shortening of two or more paths. In some cases it will be most economical to shorten an activity that is on two (or more) of the critical paths. This is true whenever the crashing cost for a joint activity is less than the sum of crashing one activity on each separate path.

EXAMPLE 7

Using the information below, develop an optimum time-cost solution. Assume that indirect project costs are $1,000 per day.

Activity	Normal time	Crash time	Cost per day to crash
a	6	6	—
b	10	8	$500
c	5	4	300
d	4	1	700
e	9	7	600
f	2	1	800

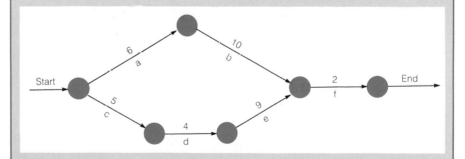

Solution

a. Determine which activities are on the critical path, its length, and the length of the other path:

EXAMPLE 7 (continued)

Path	Length
a–b–f	18
c–d–e–f . . .	20—critical path

b. Rank the critical path activities in order of lowest crashing cost and determine the number of days each can be crashed.

Activity	Cost per day to crash	Available days
c	$300	1
e	600	2
d	700	3
f	800	1

c. Begin shortening the project, one day at a time, and check after each reduction to see which path is critical. (After a certain point, another path may equal the length of the shortened critical path.) Thus:

d. (1) Shorten activity c one day at a cost of $300. The length of the critical path now becomes 19 days.

    (2) Activity c cannot be shortened any more. Shorten activity e one day at a cost of $600. The length of path c–d–e–f now becomes 18 days, which is the same as the length of path a–b–f.

    (3) Since the paths are now both critical, further improvements will necessitate shortening one activity on each.

        The remaining points for crashing and their costs are:

Path	Activity	Crash cost (per day)
a–b–f	a	No reduction possible
	b	$500
	f	800
c–d–e–f	c	No further reduction possible
	d	$700
	e	600
	f	800

    At first glance, it would seem that crashing f would not be advantageous, since it has the highest crashing cost. However, f is on both paths, so shortening f by one day would shorten *both* paths (and hence, the project) by one day for a cost of $800. The option of shortening the least expensive activity on each path would cost $500 for b and $600 for e, or $1,100. Thus, shorten f by one day. The project duration is now 17 days.

    (4) At this point, no additional improvement is feasible. The cost to crash b is $500 and the cost to crash e is $600 for a total of $1,100, and that would exceed the project costs of $1,000 per day.

    (5) The crashing sequence is summarized below:

EXAMPLE 7 *(concluded)*

		Length after crashing n *days:*		
Path	*n = 0*	*1*	*2*	*3*
a–b–f.	18	18	18	17
c–d–e–f	20	19	18	17
Activity crashed . . .		*c*	*e*	*f*
Cost		$300	$600	$800

ADVANTAGES AND LIMITATIONS OF PERT

PERT and similar project-scheduling techniques can provide important services for the project manager. Among the most useful features are:

1. Use of these techniques forces the manager to organize and quantify available information and to recognize where additional information is needed.
2. The techniques provide a graphical display of the project and its major activities.
3. They identify *(a)* activities that should be closely watched because of the potential for delaying the project and *(b)* other activities that have slack time and so can be delayed without affecting project completion time. This raises the possibility of reallocating resources in order to shorten the project.

No analytical technique is without limitations. Among the more important limitations of PERT are the following:

1. In developing the project network, one or more important activities may be omitted.
2. Precedence relationships may not all be correct as shown.
3. Time estimates usually include a fudge factor: Managers feel uncomfortable about making time estimates because they appear to commit themselves to completion within a certain time period.
4. The use of a computer is essential for large projects.

SUMMARY

Projects are comprised of a unique set of activities established to realize a given set of objectives in a limited life span. The nonroutine nature of project activities places a set of demands on the project manager, which are different in many respects than those required for the manager of more traditional operations activities, both in planning and coordinating the work and in the human problems encountered.

PERT and CPM are two commonly used techniques for developing and monitoring projects. Although each technique was developed independently and for expressly different purposes, time and practice have erased most of the original differences so that now little distinction can be made between the two. Either one provides the manager with a rational approach to project planning along with a graphical display of project activities. Both depict the sequential relationships that exist among activities and reveal to managers which activities must be completed on time in order to achieve timely project completion. Managers can use that information to direct their attention toward the most critical activities.

Two slightly different conventions can be used when constructing a network diagram. One designates the arrows as activities, the other designates the nodes as activities. To avoid confusion, this chapter emphasized only one approach, activities-on-arrows.

The task of developing and updating project networks quickly becomes complex for projects of even moderate size, so that the task is often handled through the use of computer programs, which involves the use of some computing algorithm.

A deterministic approach is used for determining project duration estimates when activity times can be fairly well established. However, when activity times are subject to some uncertainty, a probabilistic approach is more realistic, and estimates of the length of such projects should be couched in probabilistic terms.

In some instances it may be possible to shorten the length of a project by shortening one or more of the project activities. Typically, such gains are achieved by the use of additional resources, although in some cases it may be possible to transfer resources among project activities. Generally, projects are shortened to the point where the cost of additional reduction would exceed the benefit of additional reduction, or to the point where further improvements, although desirable, would be physically impossible.

1. The table below contains information related to the major activities of a research project. Use the information to do the following:
   a. Draw a precedence diagram.
   b. Find the critical path.
   c. Determine the expected length of the project.

Activity	Precedes	Expected time (days)
Start . . .	a,e,g	—
a	c,b	5
c	d	8
d	i	2
b	i	7
e	f	3
f	j	6
i	j	10
j	End	8
g	h	1
h	k	2
k	End	17

Solution

a. In constructing networks, these observations can be useful:
   (1) Activities with no predecessors are at the beginning (left side) of the network.
   (2) Activities with multiple predecessors are located at path intersections.

   Start the network diagram by identifying and charting all activities with no predecessors:

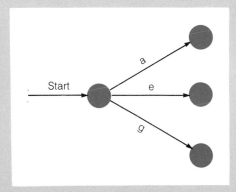

   Next, complete the diagram in sections. Go down the activity list in order when possible to avoid overlooking any activities. The process is illustrated in the following diagram.

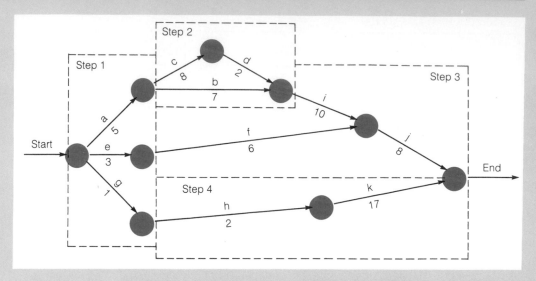

Here are some additional hints for constructing a precedence diagram:

(1) Use pencil.
(2) Start with a single node and end with a single node.
(3) Try to avoid having paths cross each other.
(4) Number nodes from left to right.
(5) Have activities going from left to right.
(6) Use only one arrow between any pair of nodes.

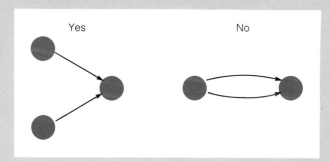

b and c.

Path	Length (days)
a–c–d–i–j*. . . .	5 + 8 + 2 + 10 + 8 = 33†
a–b–i–j.	5 + 7 + 10 + 8 = 30
e–f–j.	3 + 6 + 8 = 17
g–h–k	1 + 2 + 17 = 20

    * Critical path.
    † Expected project duration.

2. Using the computing algorithm, determine the slack for each activity for the following diagram. Identify the activities that are on the critical path.

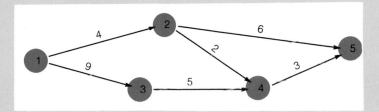

Solution

The task of determining ES, EF, LS, and LF times can be greatly simplified by setting up two brackets for each activity, as illustrated below:

The bracket at the left end of each activity will eventually be filled in with the earliest and latest *starting* times, and the bracket at the right end of each activity will be filled in with the earliest and latest *finishing* times, as symbolized below:

This is accomplished in a two-step process. First, the earliest starting times and earliest finishing times are determined, working from left to right, as shown in the diagram below.

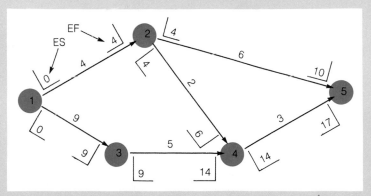

Thus, activity 1–2 can start at 0. With a time of 4, it can finish at $0 + 4 = 4$. This established the earliest start for all activities that begin at node 2. Hence, 2–5 and 2–4 can start no earlier than 4. Activity 2–5 has an early finish of $4 + 6 = 10$, and activity 2–4 has an early finish of $4 + 2 = 6$. At this point, it is impossible to say what the earliest start is for 4–5: that will depend on which activity, 3–4 or 2–4, has the latest EF. Consequently, it is necessary to compute ES and EF along the lower path. Assuming an ES of 0 for 1–3, its EF will be 9, so 3–4 will have an ES of 9 and an EF of $9 + 5 = 14$.

Considering that the two activities entering node 4 have EF times of 6 and 14, the earliest that activity 4–5 can start is the *largest* of these, which is 14. Hence, activity 4–5 has an ES of 14 and an EF of $14 + 3 = 17$.

Now compare the EFs of the activities entering the final node. The largest of these, 17, is the expected project duration.

The LF and LS times for each activity can now be determined by working backward through the network (i.e., from right to left). The LF for the two activities entering node 5 is 17—the project duration. In other words, in order for the project to finish in 17 weeks, these last two activities must both finish by that time.

In the case of activity 4–5, the LS necessary for an LF of 17 is $17 - 3 = 14$. This means that both 2–4 and 3–4 must finish no later than 14. Hence, their LF times are 14. Activity 3 has an LS time of $14 - 5 = 9$, making the LF of activity 1–3 equal to 9, and its LS equal to $9 - 9 = 0$.

Activity 2–4, with an LF time of 14, has an LS time of $14 - 2 = 12$. Activity 2–5 has an LF of 17 and therefore an LS of $17 - 6 = 11$. Thus, the latest 2–5 can start is 11, and the latest 2–4 can start is 12 in order to finish by week 17. Since activity 1–2 precedes *both* of these activities, it can finish no later than the *smaller* of these, which is 11. Hence, 1–2 has an LF of 11 and an LS of $11 - 4 = 7$.

The ES, EF, LF, and LS times are shown on the network below.

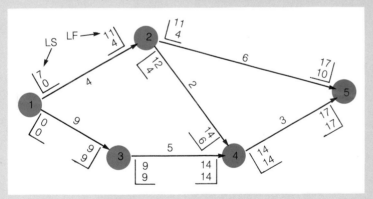

The slack time for any activity is the difference between *either* LF and EF *or* LS and ES. Thus,

Activity	LS	ES	Slack	or	LF	EF	Slack
1–2 . . .	7	0	7		11	4	7
2–5 . . .	11	4	7		17	10	7
2–4 . . .	12	4	8		14	6	8
1–3 . . .	0	0	0		9	9	0
3–4 . . .	9	9	0		14	14	0
4–5 . . .	14	14	0		17	17	0

The activities with zero slack times indicate the critical path. Thus, the critical path is 1–3–4–5.

When working problems of this nature, keep in mind the following:

a. For nodes with multiple entering activities, the ES time for leaving activities of that node is the *largest* EF of the entering activities.

b. For nodes with multiple leaving activities, the LF for an entering activity for that node is the *smallest* LS of the leaving activities.

3. Expected times and variances for the major activities of an R&D project are depicted in the PERT chart below. Determine the probability that project completion time will be:
   a. less than 50 weeks.
   b. more than 50 weeks

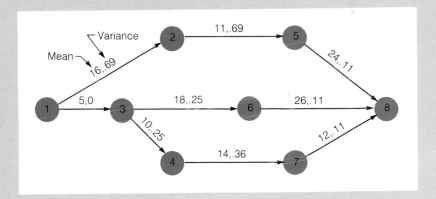

Solution

a. Compute the mean and standard deviation for each path:

Path	Expected time (weeks)	Standard deviation (weeks)
1–2–5–8	$16 + 11 + 24 = 51$	$\sqrt{.69 + .69 + .11} = 1.22$
1–3–6–8	$5 + 18 + 26 = 49$	$\sqrt{.00 + .25 + .11} = .60$
1–3–4–7–8	$5 + 10 + 14 + 12 = 41$	$\sqrt{.00 + .25 + .36 + .11} = .85$

b. Compute the z-score for each path for the length specified. Ignore the influence of any path that has a score of more than $z = +2.00$. Use

$$z = \frac{50 - t_{path}}{\sigma_{path}}$$

The probability that each path will be completed in 50 weeks or less is shown in the corresponding diagram. (Probabilities are from Appendix Table B.)

The probability that the project will be completed in 50 weeks or less depends on all three paths being completed in that time. Because the z for path 1–3–4–7–8 is greater than +2.00, it can be ignored; the probability of completion of that path in 50 weeks is close to 100 percent. It is less certain that the other two paths will be completed in that time. The probability that *both* will

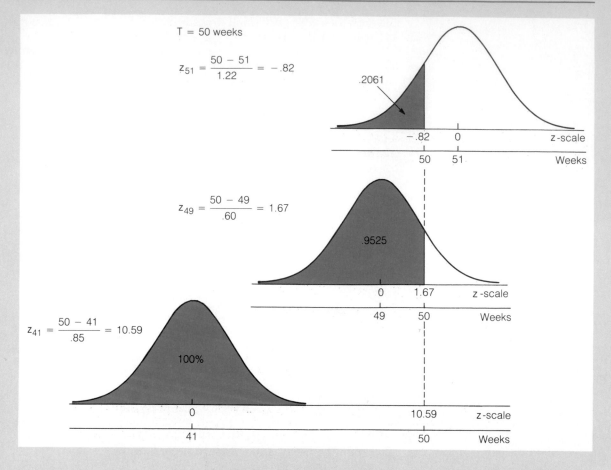

T = 50 weeks

$$z_{51} = \frac{50 - 51}{1.22} = -.82$$

.2061

$$z_{49} = \frac{50 - 49}{.60} = 1.67$$

.9525

$$z_{41} = \frac{50 - 41}{.85} = 10.59$$

100%

not exceed 50 is the *product* of their individual probabilities *of* completion. Thus, .2061(.9525) = .1963.

The probability that the project will *exceed* 50 weeks is the complement of this number, which is 1.000 − .1963 = .8037. (Note that it is *not* the product of the complements of the path probabilities.)

4. Indirect costs for a project are $12,000 per week for as long as the project lasts. The project manager has supplied the cost and time information shown below. Use the information to:

   a. Determine an optimum crashing plan.

   b. Graph the total costs for the plan.

Activity	Crashing potential (weeks)	Cost per week to crash
a	3	$11,000
b	3	3,000 first week, $4,000 others
c	2	6,000
d	1	1,000
e	3	6,000
f	1	2,000

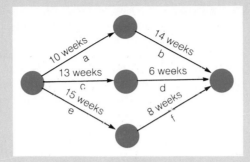

Solution

a. (1) Compute path lengths and identify the critical path:

Path	Duration (weeks)
a–b	24 (critical path)
c–d	19
e–f	23

(2) Rank critical activities according to crashing costs:

Activity	Cost per week to crash
b	$ 3,000
a	11,000

Activity b should be shortened one week since it has the lowest crashing cost. This would reduce indirect costs by $12,000 at a cost of $3,000, for a net savings of $9,000. At this point, paths a–b and e–f would both have a length of 23 weeks, so both would be critical.

(3) Rank activities by crashing costs on the two critical paths:

Path	Activity	Cost per week to crash
a–b. . . .	b	$ 4,000
	a	11,000
e–f	e	6,000
	f	2,000

Choose one activity on each path to crash: b on a–b and f on e–f for a total cost of $4,000 + $2,000 = $6,000 and a net savings of $12,000 − $6,000 = $6,000.

(4) Check to see which path(s) might be critical: a–b and e–f would be 22 weeks in length, and c–d would still be 19 weeks.

(5) Rank activities on the critical paths:

Path	Activity	Cost per week to crash
a–b. . . .	b	$ 4,000
	a	11,000
e–f	e	6,000
	f	(no further crashing possible)

Crash b on path a–b and e on e–f for a cost of $4,000 + $6,000 = $10,000, for a net savings of $12,000 − $10,000 = $2,000.

(6) At this point, no further improvement would be possible: paths a–b and e–f would be 21 weeks in length, and one activity from each path would have to be shortened. This would mean *a* at $11,000 and *e* at $6,000 for a total of $17,000, which would exceed the $12,000 potential savings in indirect costs.

b. A summary of the crashing sequence is shown below:
Length of project after crashing n weeks:

Path	$n=0$	1	2	3
a–b	24	23	22	21
c–d	19	19	19	19
e–f	23	23	22	21
Activity crashed		b	b,f	b,e
Crashing costs ($000)		3	6	10

A summary of costs for the preceding schedule would look like this:

Project length	Cumulative weeks shortened	Cumulative crashing costs ($000)	Indirect costs ($000)	Total costs ($000)
24	0	0	$24(12) = 288$	288
23	1	3	$23(12) = 276$	279
22	2	$3 + 6 = 9$	$22(12) = 264$	273
21	3	$9 + 10 = 19$	$21(12) = 252$	271
20	4	$19 + 17 = 36$	$20(12) = 240$	276

The graph of total costs is shown below.

DISCUSSION AND REVIEW QUESTIONS

1. What are some of the basic differences between project planning and scheduling and production planning and scheduling?

2. "A probabilistic approach to estimating project duration is generally preferred." Comment.

3. Identify the term being described for each of the following:

a. A sequence of activities in a project.
b. The longest time sequence of activities in a project.
c. Used when two activities have the same starting and finishing points.
d. The difference in time length of any path and the critical path.
e. Used to denote the beginning or end of an activity.
f. The statistical distribution used to describe variability of an activity time.
g. The statistical distribution used to describe project variability.
h. Shortening an activity by allocating additional resources.

4. If a path has a slack of four days, does this necessarily imply that any activity on that path can be delayed by as much as four days without delaying the project? Explain.

5. Can you envision a situation in which resources might be *subtracted* from a project in a kind of reverse time-cost trade-off? Explain briefly.

6. List the main advantages of PERT. List the main limitations.

7. What are dummy activities and why are they used?

8. Why might a probabilistic estimate of a project's completion time based solely on the variance of the critical path be misleading? Under what circumstances would it be acceptable?

9. Define each of these terms and indicate how each is determined.
a. Optimistic time estimate.
b. Most-likely time estimate.
c. Pessimistic time estimate.
d. Expected activity time.
e. Variance of an activity time.
f. Standard deviation of a path's time.

10. Could PERT or CPM be used to schedule nonproject activities? Explain your reasoning briefly.

11. Why might a person wish to be associated with a critical path activity? What are some of the reasons one might have for not wanting such an association?

12. What are some of the potential benefits of working on a special project in one's firm? What are some of the risks?

13. What are some of the aspects of the project manager's job that make it more demanding than that of a manager working in a more traditional organizational framework?

14. What is the main benefit of a project organization over more traditional forms of operations management for project work?

PROBLEMS

1. For each of the network diagrams below, determine both the critical path and the expected project duration. The quantities on the arrows represent expected activity times.

a.

b.

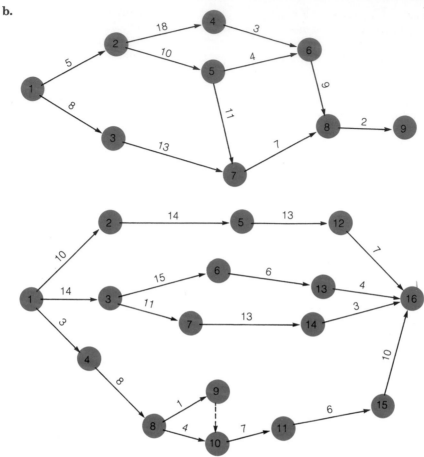

2. Using the information provided in the table below, do the following:
   a. Construct a network diagram.
   b. Determine which activities are on the critical path.
   c. Compute the length of the critical path.

Activity	Estimated time (days)
1–2	5
2–3	6
2–4	4
3–6	9
6–7	2
4–5	4
4–7	18
5–7	10

3. The information shown pertains to a project that is about to commence. As the project manager, which activities would you be concerned with in terms of timely project completion? Explain.

Activity	Precedes	Estimated time (days)
Start	a,f	—
a	b	15
b	c,d	12
c	e	6
d	End	5
e	End	3
f	g,h	8
g	i,j	8
h	j	9
i	End	7
j	k	14
k	End	6

4. Use the computational algorithm to determine the slack time for each activity in the problems listed below:
   a. Problem 1.a.
   b. Problem 1.b.

5. For each of the problems listed below, determine the following quantities for each activity: earliest start time, latest start

time, earliest finish time, latest finish time, and slack. List the activities that are on the critical path and determine the expected duration of the project.

a. Problem 2.

b. Problem 3.

6. Reconsider the network diagram of Problem 1a. Suppose that after 12 weeks activities 1–2 and 2–4 have been finished, 2–5 is 75 percent finished, and 3–6 is half finished. How many weeks after the original start time should the project be finished?

7. Three recent college graduates have formed a partnership and have opened an advertising firm. Their first project consists of the activities listed below.

   a. Draw the precedence diagram.

   b. What is the probability that the project can be completed in 24 days or less? In 21 days or less?

   c. Suppose it is now the eighth day and that activities *a* and *b* have been completed while *d* is 50 percent completed. Time estimates for the completion of *d* are 5, 6, and 7. Determine the probability of finishing the project by the 24th day and the probability of finishing by the 21st day.

		Time in days		
Activity	Pre-cedes	Opti-mistic	Most likely	Pessi-mistic
Start . .	a,b,d	—	—	—
a	c	5	6	7
b	h	8	8	11
c . . .	e	6	8	11
d . . .	f	9	12	15
e . . .	End	5	6	9
f . . .	g	5	6	7
g . . .	End	2	3	7
h . . .	i	4	4	5
i . . .	End	5	7	8

8. The new director of special events at a large university has decided to completely revamp graduation ceremonies. Toward that end, a PERT chart of the major activities has been developed. The chart has five paths with expected completion times and variances as shown in the table below. Graduation day is 17 weeks from now. Assuming the project begins now, what is the probability that the project will be completed before:

   a. Graduation time?

   b. Week 16?

   c. Week 13?

Path	Expected duration (weeks)	Variance
A . . .	10	1.21
B . . .	8	2.00
C . . .	12	1.00
D . . .	15	2.89
E . . .	14	1.44

9. The precedence diagram shown below reflects three time estimates for each activity. Determine:

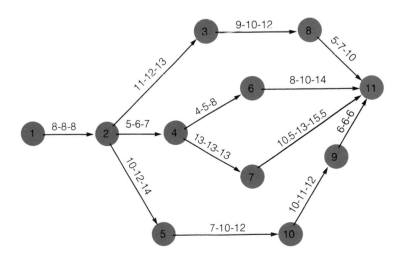

a. The expected completion time for each path and its variance.

b. The probability that the project will require more than 49 weeks.

c. The probability that the project can be completed in 46 weeks or less.

10. A project manager has compiled a list of major activities that will be required to install a computer information system in her firm. The list includes estimated completion times for activities and precedence relationships:

Activity	Precedes	Estimated times (weeks)
Start . . .	a,b,c	—
a	d,f	2–4–6
d	e	6–8–10
e	h	7–9–12
h	End	2–3–5
f	g	3–4–8
g	End	5–7–9
b	i	2–2–3
i	j	2–3–6
j	k	3–4–5
k	End	4–5–8
c	m	5–8–12
m	n	1–1–1
n . . .	o	6–7–11
o	End	8–9–13

If the project is finished within 27 weeks of its start, the project manager will receive a bonus of $1,000; and if the project is finished within 28 weeks of its start, the bonus will be $500. Find the probability of each bonus.

11. Construct an activity-on-node diagram for the set of activities listed in Problem 3.

12. Construct an activity-on-node diagram for the set of activities listed in Problem 2. In order to facilitate this, replace the activity designations (1–2, 2–3, etc.) with letters (a, b, c, etc.)

13. The project manager of a task force planning the construction of a domed stadium had hoped to be able to complete construction prior to the start of the next college-football season. After reviewing construction time estimates, it now appears that a certain amount of crashing will be needed to insure that the project is completed before the season opener. Given the time and cost estimates below, determine a minimum-cost crashing schedule that will shave five weeks off the project length.

Activity	Pre-cedes	Normal time (weeks)	Crashing costs First week	Crashing costs Second week
Start . .	a,c	—		
a . . .	b	12	$15,000	$20,000
b . . .	k	14	10,000	10,000
c . . .	d,e,f	10	5,000	5,000
d . . .	g	17	20,000	21,000
e . . .	h	18	16,000	18,000
f . . .	i	12	12,000	15,000
g . . .	m	15	24,000	24,000
h . . .	n,p	8	—	—
i . . .	j	7	30,000	—
j . . .	p	12	25,000	25,000
k . . .	End	9	10,000	10,000
m . . .	End	3	—	—
n . . .	End	11	40,000	—
p . . .	End	8	20,000	20,000

14. A construction project has indirect costs totaling $40,000 per week. Major activities in the project and their expected times are shown in the precedence diagram below.

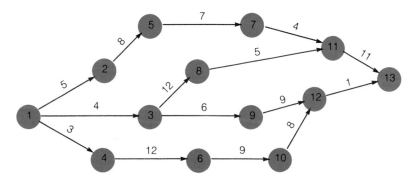

Crashing costs for each activity are listed in the table below.

Crashing costs (000)

Activity	First week	Second week	Third week
1–2 . .	$18	$22	$—
2–5 . .	24	25	25
5–7 . .	30	30	35
7–11 . .	15	20	—
11–13 . .	30	33	36
1–3 . .	12	24	26
3–8 . .	—	—	—
8–11 . .	40	40	40
3–9 . .	3	10	12
9–12 . .	2	7	10
12–13 . .	26	—	—
1–4 . .	10	15	25
4–6 . .	8	13	—
6–10 . .	5	12	—
10–12 . .	14	15	—

a. Determine the optimum time-cost crashing plan.

b. Plot the total-cost curve that describes the least expensive crashing schedule that will reduce the project length by six weeks.

SELECTED BIBLIOGRAPHY

Bierman, Harold, Jr.; Charles P. Bonini; and Warren H. Hausman. *Quantitative Analysis for Business Decisions.* 6th ed. Homewood, Ill.: Richard D. Irwin, 1981.

Burman, P. J. *Precedence Networks for Project Planning and Control.* New York: McGraw-Hill, 1972.

Buffa, Elwood, and James S. Dyer. *Essentials of Management Science/Operations Research.* New York: John Wiley & Sons, 1978.

Hoare, H. R. *Project Management Using Networks.* New York: McGraw-Hill, 1973.

Kerzner, Harold. *Project Management for Executives.* New York: Van Nostrand Reinhold, 1984.

Levin, Richard I.; Charles A. Kirkpatrick; and David S. Rubin. *Quantitative Approaches to Management.* 5th ed. New York: McGraw-Hill, 1982.

Moder, J.; E. W. Davis, and C. Phillips. *Project Management with CPM and PERT.* New York: Van Nostrand Reinhold, 1983.

Reeser, Clayton. *Management: Functions and Modern Concepts.* Glenview, Ill.: Scott, Foresman, 1973.

Wiest, J. D., and F. K. Levy. *A Management Guide to PERT/CPM.* 2d ed. Englewood Cliffs, N.J.: Prentice-Hall, 1977.

Case

The Case of the Mexican Crazy Quilt *

"The mission of the project which you will head is to get our new Mexican subsidiary company ready for take-over by Mexican managers. My hope is that you will be able to do this in about two years," explained Robert Linderman, president of Linderman Industries, Inc., to Carl Conway, newly appointed project manager for "Operation Mexicano." Conway had been hired specifically for this assignment because of his experience in managing large defense projects in the aerospace industry.

"The first thing that I will have to do is put a project team together," said Conway. "I imagine that you have in mind my drawing people from the functional divisions."

"Yes, and I have already sent memoranda to the division managers informing them that you will be asking for some of their key people to work under you for about two years," said Linderman. "In addition, I have advised them to be prepared to process work orders from Operation Mexicano with the personnel and equipment of their organizations. Later on in the project's life, you will begin to get Mexican personnel, both managers and technicians, into your organization. These people will have Mexican supervisors, but until the mission is accomplished they also will report to you. I will have to admit that you are going to have some complex authority relationships, especially as you personally will be responsible to the president of the subsidiary, Felix Delgado, as well as to me."

Conway began to make his plans for the project team. The plant building was available and empty in Mexico City, and it was important to get equipment purchased and installed as soon as possible. A plant layout would have to be prepared, but before that could be done there would have to be a manufacturing plan. Therefore, he needed to recruit an industrial engineer, a production planner, and an equipment buyer. They, in turn, would have to build their own staffs.

He made an appointment with Sam Sargis, corporate manager of industrial engineering. "I have had a preliminary talk with Bob Cates about his joining Operation Mexicano, and he is quite interested," Carl said. "Will you release him to me?"

"Why, I'm grooming Cates to take over my job when I retire," replied Sargis. "He is my best man. Let me pick someone else for you, or better still, you just tell me what industrial engineering work you want done, and I will have it done for you."

"Sorry, I want Cates," said Carl firmly. "And besides, you are not due to retire for five years. This will be good experience for him."

For production planning, Carl had in mind Bert Mill, an older man with extensive experience in managing production operations, but Mill rejected his offer. "I talked it over with my wife," he said, "and we feel that at my age I shouldn't take a chance on not having a job to come back to when Operation Mexicano is finished."

Carl next talked to Emil Banowetz, who was assistant to Jim Burke, the vice president for manufacturing, and Banowetz decided that he would like to join the project team. However, Burke told Conway that if Banowetz were forcibly taken away from him, he would give Mr. Linderman his resignation, so Carl decided to back down. He finally accepted a man that Burke recommended.

Filling the equipment buyer's slot was easy. The director of procurement phoned Carl and said that a senior buyer, Humberto Guzman, had requested permission to ask for the assignment, and that he strongly recommended him. Guzman had been purchasing agent for a large mining company in Mexico for about ten years.

Carl had about the same experiences in getting the people he wanted for the functions of engineering, quality control, cost, marketing, and advertising as he did for the first three positions; in other words, he won some confrontations with the division managers, and lost some. For personnel, he got Dr. Juan Perez, who was slated to be personnel director of the subsidiary company, to affiliate temporarily with the project team.

The first brush that Project Mexicano had in getting a functional division to do work for it came when Carl's engineering man, Frank Fong, reported to him that the engineering vice president, who was formally Fong's boss, refused to authorize top priority to the changing of dimensions in the production drawings to the metric system. Carl had to take this issue to Linderman, who ruled in his favor. The defeated vice president, of course, did not take kindly to the decision.

The next incident revolved about Carl's desire to have a pilot run of products made with metric measurements for shipment to Mexico. The purpose was to test the market acceptance of the Linderman articles. Jim Burke stated flatly that there was no way that his production workers could be trained to work with metric drawings. Carl quickly saw that this was an issue that he was not going to win, so he had his buyer, Guzman, work with the newly appointed manufacturing manager for the subsidiary in getting a run of the products subcontracted in Mexico City.

Bob Cates made a special trip from Mexico City to present Carl with an interesting problem. The Mexican industrial engineer, whom Bob was supposed to be training, had his own ideas about plant layout. When they differed from Bob's, as they usually did, he would take his complaint directly to Felix Delgado, the president of the Mexican subsidiary. Because Delgado's competence was primarily in finance, he would not know how to decide the argument and would simply table it. Carl took examples of some of the disagreements to Bob's formal boss, Sam Sargis, who quite unexpectedly ruled against Bob's proposed methods. Carl saw that there was bad feeling by Sargis against Bob for leaving his department, which boded ill for Bob's return. To solve the immediate problem, however, Carl asked Dr. Perez to try to reconcile the situation in Mexico City.

Despite these problems, and many more of a similar nature, Project Mexicano was successful, and the transition to Mexican management was made in just a little over two years. By a curious twist, through Dr. Perez' intercession Felix Delgado became very impressed by Bob Cates and convinced him to accept the job of director of industrial engineering for the Mexican company. Humberto Guzman also stayed on to head the procurement operation.

Other members of the project team were not so fortunate. Linderman Industries was laying off personnel when the project ended in 1970, and only the project production man was able to get a job in the company at as high a level as the one he had when he joined the team. The cost expert elected to leave Linderman because he said the glamor of Project Mexicano had spoiled him for any routine job.

Carl Conway had a difficult decision of his own to make. Robert Linderman said that he was extremely pleased with his performance and that something good would open up in the company for him soon. In the meantime, there was a staff assignment available for him. Carl had seen enough project managers in the aerospace industry who had figuratively rotted on staff assignments when their projects were completed to be somewhat wary.

Questions

1. Was Linderman Industries' adoption of project organization an appropriate one for getting the Mexican subsidiary started?

2. In consideration of Robert Linderman's letting the division managers know that the project manager would be asking for some of their key people, why would Conway have any difficulty in getting the ones he wanted?

3. Would you expect that many people would turn down a chance to join a project organization, as Bert Mill did?

4. Why would Conway take his problem with the engineering vice president to Linderman and have it resolved in his favor, yet back down in two disputes with the manufacturing vice president?

5. What could Linderman Industries have done to assure good jobs for the people coming off Project Mexicano, including Carl Conway, the project manager?

Chapter 14

Queuing

After completing this chapter, you should be able to:

1. Explain why waiting lines form in underloaded systems.
2. Identify the goal of queuing analysis.
3. List the measures of system performance that are used in queuing.
4. Discuss the assumptions of the basic queuing models presented.
5. Solve typical problems.

WHY IS THERE WAITING?, 675

GOAL OF QUEUING ANALYSIS, 676

SYSTEM CHARACTERISTICS, 677
 Population Source, 677
 Number of Servers (Channels), 678
 Arrival and Service Patterns, 679
 Queue Discipline, 681

MEASURES OF SYSTEM PERFORMANCE, 681

QUEUING MODELS: INFINITE–SOURCE, 682
 Basic Relationships, 683
 Model 1: Single Channel, Exponential Service Time, 685
 Model 2: Single Channel, Constant Service Time, 686
 Model 3: Multiple Channel, 687

QUEUING MODEL: FINITE SOURCE, 693

OTHER APPROACHES, 699

SUMMARY, 699
SOLVED PROBLEMS, 701
DISCUSSION AND REVIEW QUESTIONS, 703
PROBLEMS, 703
SELECTED BIBLIOGRAPHY, 705
SUPPLEMENT: SIMULATION, 707

Waiting—A New Popular Pastime Miss Manners

by Judith Martin

Many things in life are worth waiting for, but not all that long. Miss Manners would put a time limit on how long one should wait for salespeople to finish their conversations with each other before writing up one's order, or for a spouse who has departed with someone else to realize what a terrible mistake that was.

Nevertheless, waiting is now in a class with working as a popular pastime. A *waitologist* has estimated that the average adult spends one tenth of his or her waking moments waiting, at a minimum. There are waits for buses, banks, stores, theaters, gas stations, court cases, elevators, driver's licenses, and dentist appointments.

One could easily pass one's life enduring just such basic waits. But there are also intermediary waits, such as waiting for the rain to stop, and advanced waits, such as waiting for your ship to come in. Some of these go in fashions. There was a time when all of America was waiting to be discovered by a movie talent scout in a drug store, and now everyone is waiting for a television camera to come along and ask it to tell the world what it thinks.

It is the elementary, and comparatively

short-term wait with which Miss Manners is concerned. If you want to hear about the others, you will just have to wait.

It is perfectly correct, although not many people realize it, to refuse to wait on the telephone. When Miss Manners is asked "Can you hold on for a minute?" she often replies, "No," and it is too bad that the person on the other end ties up his own line by putting her on hold anyway, because that person has not waited for Miss Manners' reply.

One should also refuse to wait for inefficient or indefinite service. A restaurant should be able to tell you how long the wait will be, and a service person should not keep you waiting except to attend a previous customer.

It is rude to refuse to wait by announcing that one's needs take precedence over those of other waiting people. Miss Manners can think of no circumstances in which a person transacting the ordinary business of life can plead with legitimacy that it is more outrageous to expect him to wait than to expect it of others. "Let me go through, please—I'm in labor," perhaps, but then what are you doing at the stockings sale, anyway?

The only polite way to wait, if one must do so, is to bring one's own portable work or amusement. An unoccupied person waiting in line is by definition a potential raving maniac. A nice Jane Austen novel ready-to-go has preserved even the naturally tranquil spirits of Miss Manners. Even using conversation as a means to pass the time is dangerous, in Miss Manners' opinion. Two people quietly discussing what a shame it is to have to wait are, by that same definition, a potential mob.

The above article pokes fun at one of life's realities: having to wait in line. No doubt those waiting in line would all agree that the solution to the problem is obvious: simply add more servers or else do something to speed up service. While both ideas may be potential solutions, there are certain subtleties that must be dealt with. For one thing, most service systems have the capacity to process more customers over the long run than they are called upon to process. Hence, the problem of waiting is a short-term phenomenon. The other side of the coin is that at certain times the system is empty, and *servers* are idle waiting for customers. Thus, by increasing the service capacity, the server idle time would increase. Consequently, in designing service systems, the designer must weigh the cost of providing a given level of service capacity against the potential (implicit) cost of having customers wait for service.

The planning and analysis of service capacity frequently lends itself to queuing theory, which is a mathematical approach to the analysis of waiting lines. These waiting lines are commonly found wherever customers arrive randomly for services. Some examples of waiting lines we encounter in our daily lives include the lines at supermarket checkouts, fast-food restaurants, airport ticket counters, theaters, post offices, toll booths, and so on. In many business situations, the "customers" are not people, but orders waiting to be filled, trucks waiting to be unloaded, jobs waiting to be processed, or equipment awaiting repairs. Still other examples include ships waiting to dock, planes waiting to land, hospital patients waiting for a nurse, and cars waiting at a stop sign.

The foundation of modern theory is based on studies made in the early part of this century by Danish telephone engineer A. K. Erlang involving automatic dialing equipment. Prior to World War II, there were very few attempts to apply queuing theory to business problems. However, since that time, queuing theory has been applied to a wide range of problems.

The mathematics of queuing can be quite complex, and for that reason, the emphasis here will not be on the mathematics, but on the concepts that underlie the use of queuing in analyzing waiting-line problems. We shall rely on the use of formulas and tables for analysis.

We shall begin our discussion of queuing with an examination of what is perhaps the most fundamental issue in waiting-line theory: Why are there waiting lines?

WHY IS THERE WAITING?

Many people are surprised when they learn that waiting lines tend to form *even though a system is basically underloaded.* For example, a fast-food restaurant may have the capacity to handle an average of 200 orders per hour and yet experience waiting lines even though the average number of orders is only 150 per hour. The key word here is *average.* In reality, customers arrive at random intervals rather than at evenly spaced intervals, and some orders take longer to fill than others. In other words, both arrivals and service times exhibit a high degree of *variability*. As a result of this variability, there are times when the system becomes *temporarily overloaded,* and that gives rise to waiting lines. By the same token, there are other times when the system is idle because there are no customers. Thus, although a system may be underloaded from a *macro* standpoint, because of variabilities in arrivals and service there will be times when the system is overloaded from a *micro* standpoint. It follows, then, that in systems where variability is minimal or nonexistent (say, because arrivals can be scheduled and service time is constant), waiting lines do not ordinarily form.

GOAL OF QUEUING ANALYSIS

The goal of queuing is essentially to minimize total costs. There are two basic categories of cost in a queuing situation: those associated with customers waiting for service and those associated with capacity. Capacity costs relate to maintaining the ability to provide service. Examples include the number of bays in a car wash, the number of checkouts in a supermarket, the number of repairmen to handle equipment breakdowns, the number of lanes on a highway, and so on. Note that when a service facility is idle, there is a loss of capacity since it cannot be stored. Waiting costs include the salaries paid to employees while they wait for service (mechanics waiting for tools, the drivers of trucks waiting to unload), the cost of the space for waiting (size of doctor's waiting room, length of driveway at a car wash, fuel consumed by planes waiting to land), and any loss of business due to customers refusing to wait and possibly going elsewhere *in the future.*

A practical difficulty that is frequently encountered is pinning down the cost of customer waiting time, especially since major portions of that cost are not a part of accounting data. One approach that is sometimes used is to treat waiting times or line lengths as a policy variable: a manager simply specifies an acceptable level of waiting and directs that capacity be established to achieve that level.

The goal of queuing analysis is to balance the cost of providing a level of service capacity and the cost of customers waiting for service. This concept is illustrated in Figure 14–1. Note that as capacity increases, its cost increases. For simplicity, the increase is shown as a linear relationship, although a step function is often more appropriate. However, use of a straight line does not significantly distort the picture. As capacity increases, the number of customer waiting, and the time they wait, tends to decrease, thereby decreasing waiting costs. As is the case with trade-off cost relationships, total cost can be represented as a U-shaped curve. The goal

FIGURE 14–1

The Goal of Queuing Analysis Is to Minimize the Sum of Two Costs: Customer Waiting Costs and Service Capacity

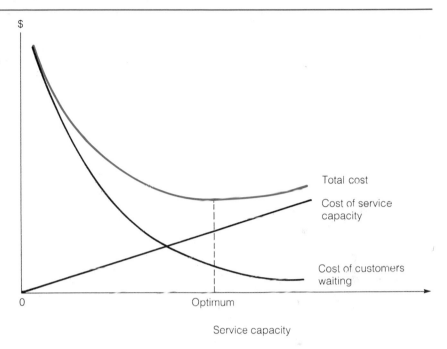

of analysis is to identify a level of service capacity that will minimize total cost. (Unlike the situation in the inventory EOQ model, the minimum point on the total cost curve is *not* usually where the two cost lines intersect.)

SYSTEM CHARACTERISTICS

There are numerous queuing models from which an analyst can choose. Naturally, much of the success of the analyst will depend on choosing an appropriate model. Model choice is dependent on the characteristics of the system under investigation. The main characteristics are:

1. The population source.
2. The number of servers (channels).
3. Arrival and service patterns.
4. The queue discipline (order of service).

Population Source

The approach used to analyze a queuing problem depends on whether or not there is a limit to the potential number of customers. There are two possibilities: *infinite source* and *finite source* populations. In an *infinite source* situation, the potential number of customers greatly exceeds system capacity. Infinite source situations exist whenever service is *unrestricted.* Typical examples include supermarkets, drugstores, banks, restaurants, theaters, amusement centers, and toll bridges. Theoretically, large numbers of customers from the "calling population" can request service at any time. When the potential number of customers is limited, a *finite source* situation exists. Examples include a repairer responsible for a certain number of machines (the potential number of machines that might need repairs at any one time cannot exceed the number of machines assigned to the repairer). Similarly, an operator may be responsible for loading and unloading a bank of four machines, a nurse may be responsible for answering patient calls for a 10-bed ward, a secretary may be responsible for taking dictation from three executives, and a company shop may perform repairs as needed on the firm's 20 trucks.

Number of Servers (Channels)

The capacity of a queuing system is a function of the capacity of each server and the number of servers being used. The terms *server* and *channel* are synonomous, and it is generally assumed that each channel can handle one customer at a time. Systems can be either *single* or *multiple* channel. (If a group of servers works together as a team, such as a surgical team, this is treated as a single-channel system.) Examples of single-channel systems are small grocery stores with one checkout counter, most theaters, single-bay car washes, and drive-in banks that have one teller. Figure 14–2 illustrates a single-channel queuing system. Examples of multiple-channel systems (those with more than one server) are commonly found in banks, at airline ticket counters, at auto service centers, and at gas stations.

A related distinction is the number of steps or *phases* in a queuing system. For example, at registration it is customary for students to go from desk to desk to have courses assigned, and to then move to final checkers and the bursar's table. Each location constitutes a separate phase where queues can (and usually do) form.

Figure 14–3 illustrates some of the most common queuing systems found in practice. Because it would not be possible to cover all of

FIGURE 14–2

A Single-Channel Queuing System

FIGURE 14–3

**Four Common
Variations of Queuing
Systems**

Single channel,
single phase

Single channel,
multiple phase

Multiple channel,
single phase

Multiple channel,
multiple phase

these cases in sufficient detail in the limited amount of space available here, our discussion will focus on *single-phase* systems.

**Arrival and
Service Patterns**

Queues are a direct result of arrival and service variability. Waiting lines are created because random, highly variable arrival and service patterns produce systems that are temporarily overloaded. In many instances the variabilities can be described by theoretical distributions. In fact, the most commonly used models assume that the customer arrival *rate* can be described by a Poisson distribution and that the service *time* can be described by a negative exponential distribution. These distributions are illustrated in Figure 14–4.

It is interesting to note that the Poisson and negative exponential distributions are alternate but equivalent ways of presenting the same basic information. If service time is exponential, then the service rate is Poisson. Similarly, if the customer arrival rate is Poisson, then the arrival time (i.e., the time between arrivals) is exponential. For instance, if a service facility can process 12 cus-

FIGURE 14–4

Poisson and Negative Exponential Distributions

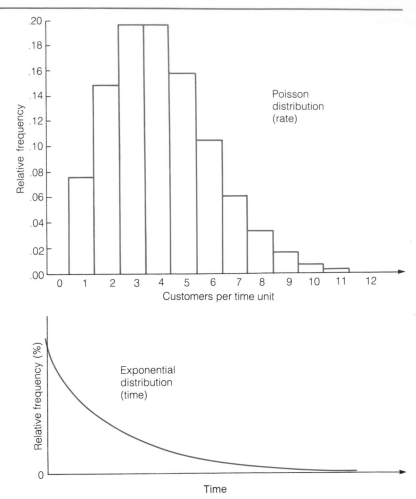

tomers per hour (rate), average service *time* is five minutes. Similarly, if the arrival rate is 10 per hour, then the average *time* between arrivals is six minutes. Hence, the models described here generally require that arrival and service *rates* lend themselves to description using a Poisson distribution, or equivalently, that interarrival and service *times* lend themselves to description using a negative exponential distribution. In practice, it is necessary to verify that these assumptions are met. Sometimes this is done by collecting data and plotting them, although the preferred approach is to use a chi-square goodness-of-fit test for that purpose. A discussion of the chi-square test is beyond the scope of this text. However, most basic statistics textbooks cover the topic.

Research has shown that these assumptions are often appropriate for customer arrivals, but are less likely to be appropriate for service. In situations where the assumptions are not reasonably satisfied, the alternative would be (1) attempt to develop a more suitable model, (2) search for a better (and usually more complex) existing model, or (3) resort to computer simulation. Each of these alternatives requires more effort or cost than the ones presented here.

Queue Discipline   All of the models described here assume that service is provided on a *first-come, first-served* basis. This is perhaps the most commonly encountered rule. We find first-come service at banks, stores, theaters, restaurants, four-way stop signs, registration lines, and so on. Examples of systems that do not serve on a first-come basis include hospital emergency rooms, rush orders in a factory, and computer processing of programs. In these and similar situations, customers do not all represent the same waiting costs; those with the highest costs (e.g., most seriously ill) are processed first, even though other customers arrived earlier.

MEASURES OF SYSTEM PERFORMANCE

The operations manager typically looks at four measures when evaluating existing or proposed service systems. Those measures are:

1. The average number of customers waiting, either in the line or in the system.
2. The average time customers wait, either in line or in the system.
3. System utilization, which refers to the percentage of capacity utilized.
4. The implied cost of a given level of capacity and its related waiting line.
5. The probability that on arrival will have to wait for service.

Of these measures, system utilization bears some elaboration. It reflects the extent to which the servers are busy rather than idle. On the surface, it might seem that the operations manager would want to seek 100 percent utilization. However, as illustrated in Figure 14–5, increases in system utilization are achieved at the expense of increases in both the length of the waiting line and the average waiting time. In fact, these values become exceedingly large as utilization approaches 100 percent. The implication is that under normal circumstances, 100 percent utilization is not a realistic goal.

FIGURE 14–5

The Average Number Waiting in Line, and the Average Time Customers Wait in Line, Increase Exponentially as the System Utilization Increases

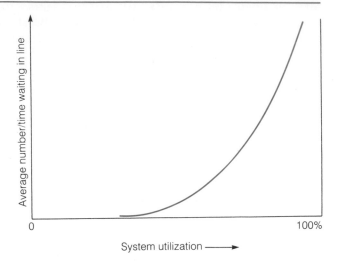

Instead, the operations manager should try to design a system that minimizes the sum of waiting costs and facility costs.

QUEUING MODELS: INFINITE-SOURCE

There are many queuing models available for a manager or analyst to choose from. The discussion here will include three of the most basic and most widely used models. The purpose is to give you an exposure to a range of models rather than to provide an extensive coverage of the field. The three models described here are listed

TABLE 14–1

Infinite-Source Symbols

Symbol	Represents
λ	Customer arrival rate
μ	Service rate
L_q	The average number of customers waiting for service
L_s	The average number of customers in the system (waiting or being served)
ρ	The system utilization
W_q	The average time customers wait in line
W_s	The average time customers spend in the system (waiting in line and service time)
$1/\mu$	Service time
P_o	The probability of zero units in the system
P_n	The probability of n units in the system
M	The number of servers/channels
L_{max}	The maximum expected number waiting in line

below. All assume a Poisson arrival rate. Moreover, the models pertain to a system operating under *steady state* conditions. That is, they assume the average arrival and service rates are stable. The models are:

1. Single channel, exponential service time.
2. Single channel, constant service time.
3. Multiple channel, exponential service time.

In order to facilitate your use of queuing models, Table 14–1 provides a list of the symbols used for the infinite-source models.

Basic Relationships

There are certain basic relationships that hold for all infinite-source models. Knowledge of these basic relationships can be very helpful in deriving desired performance measures, given a few key values. These basic relationships are:

1. The average number being served:

$$r = \frac{\lambda}{\mu} \tag{14–1}$$

Note: λ and μ must be in the same units (e.g., rate per hour, rate per minute).

2. The average number in the system:

$$L_s = L_q + r \tag{14–2}$$

3. The average time in line:

$$W_q = \frac{L_q}{\lambda} \tag{14–3}$$

4. The average time in the system, including service time:

$$W_s = W_q + \frac{1}{\mu} \tag{14–4}$$

5. System utilization:

$$\rho = \frac{\lambda}{M\mu} \tag{14–5}$$

All infinite-source models require that system utilization be less than 1.0; the models only apply to underloaded systems.

The average number waiting in line, L_q, is a key value because it is a determinant of some of the other measures of system performance, such as the average number in the system, the average time in line, and the average time in the system. Hence, L_q will usually be one of the first values to determine in problem solving.

EXAMPLE 1

Customers arrive at a bakery at an average of 18 per hour on weekday mornings. The arrival distribution can be described by a Poisson distribution with a mean of 18. Each clerk can serve a customer in an average of four minutes, and this time can be described by an exponential distribution with a mean of 4.0 minutes.

a. What are the arrival and service *rates*?
b. Compute the average number of customers being served at any time.
c. Suppose it has been determined that the average number of customers waiting in line is 3.6. Compute the average number of customers in the system (i.e., waiting in line or being served), the average time customers wait in line, and the average time in the system.
d. Determine the system utilization for M = 2, 3, and 4 servers.

Solution

a. The arrival rate is given in the problem: $\lambda = 18$ customers per hour. The service time can be changed to a comparable hourly *rate* by first restating the time in hours and then taking its reciprocal. Thus, $\dfrac{4 \text{ minutes per customer}}{60 \text{ minutes per hour}} = \dfrac{1}{15} = \dfrac{1}{\mu}$. Its reciprocal is $\mu = 15$ customers per hour.

b. $r = \dfrac{\lambda}{\mu} = \dfrac{18}{15} = 1.2$ customers.

c. Given: $L_q = 3.6$ customers.

$L_s = L_q + r = 3.6 + 1.2 = 4.8$ customers.

$W_q = \dfrac{L_q}{\lambda} = \dfrac{3.6}{18} = .20$ hours per customer, or .20 hours
$\times 60 \text{ minutes/hour} = 12 \text{ minutes}$

$W_s =$ Waiting in line plus service

$= W_q + \dfrac{1}{\mu} = .20 + \dfrac{1}{15} = .267$ hours or approximately 16 minutes.

d. System utilization is $\rho = \dfrac{\lambda}{M\mu}$

For $M = 2$, $\rho = \dfrac{18}{2(15)} = .60$

For $M = 3$, $\rho = \dfrac{18}{3(15)} = .40$

For $M = 4$, $\rho = \dfrac{18}{4(15)} = .30$

Hence, as the system capacity as measured by $M\mu$ increases, the system utilization for a given arrival rate decreases.

TABLE 14–2

Formulas for Basic Single-Server Model

Performance measure	Equation	
Average number in line	$L_q = \dfrac{\lambda^2}{\mu(\mu - \lambda)}$	(14–6)
Probability of zero units in the *system*	$P_o = 1 - \left(\dfrac{\lambda}{\mu}\right)$	(14–7)
Probability of *n* units in the *system*	$P_n = P_o \left(\dfrac{\lambda}{\mu}\right)^n$	(14–8)

Model 1: Single Channel, Exponential Service Time

The simplest model involves a system that has one server (or a single crew). The queue discipline is first-come, first-served, and it is assumed that customer arrival rate can be approximated by a Poisson distribution and service time by a negative exponential distribution. There is no limit on length of queue.

Table 14–2 lists the formulas for the single-channel model, which should be used in conjunction with formulas 14–1 through 14–5.

EXAMPLE 2

An airline is planning to open a satellite ticket desk in a new shopping plaza, staffed by one ticket agent. It is estimated that requests for tickets and information will average 15 per hour, and requests will have a Poisson distribution. Service time is assumed to be exponentially distributed. Previous experience with similar satellite operations suggests that mean service time should average about three minutes per request. Determine each of the following:

a. System utilization.
b. Percent of time the server (agent) will be idle.
c. The expected number of customers waiting to be served.
d. The average time customers will spend in the system.
e. The probability of zero customers in the system and the probability of four customers in the system.

Solution

$$\lambda = 15 \text{ per hour}$$

$$\mu = \frac{1}{\text{Service time}} = \frac{1 \text{ customer}}{3 \text{ minutes}} \times 60 \text{ minutes per hour}$$
$$= 20 \text{ customers per hour}$$

a. $\rho = \dfrac{\lambda}{M_\mu} = \dfrac{15}{1(20)} = .75$

b. Idle time $= 1 - \rho = 1 - 0.75 = 0.25$ or 25%

EXAMPLE 2 *(concluded)*

c. $L_q = \dfrac{\lambda^2}{\mu(\mu - \lambda)} = \dfrac{15^2}{20(20 - 15)} = 2.25$ customers

d. $W_s = \dfrac{L_q}{\lambda} + \dfrac{1}{\mu} = \dfrac{2.25}{15} + \dfrac{1}{20} = 0.20$ hours, or 12 minutes

e. $P_o = 1 - \dfrac{\lambda}{\mu} = 1 - \dfrac{15}{20} = .25$; $P_4 = P_o \left(\dfrac{\lambda}{\mu}\right)^4 = .25 \left(\dfrac{15}{20}\right)^4 = .079$

Model 2: Single Channel, Constant Service Time

As noted previously, waiting lines are a consequence of random, highly variable arrival and service rates. If the variability of either or both can be reduced or eliminated, waiting lines can be shortened noticeably. A case in point is a system with constant service time. The effect of a constant service time is to cut in half both the average number of customers waiting *in line* and the average time customers spend waiting *in line*. Similar improvements can be realized by smoothing arrival times (e.g., by use of appointments). In effect, the formulas 14–1 through 14–6 can be used for problems with constant service time as long as the computed value of L_q is divided by 2.

EXAMPLE 3

Wanda's Car Wash & Dry is an automatic, five-minute operation with a single bay. On a typical Saturday morning, cars arrive at a mean rate of eight per hour, with arrivals tending to follow a Poisson distribution. Find:

1. The average number of cars in line.
2. The average time cars spend in line and service.

Solution

$$\lambda = 8 \text{ cars per hour}$$
$$\mu = 1 \text{ per 5 minutes or 12 per hour}$$

a. $L_q = \dfrac{\lambda^2}{2\mu(\mu - \lambda)} = \dfrac{8^2}{2(12)(12 - 8)} = .667$ cars

b. $W_s = \dfrac{L_q}{\lambda} + \dfrac{1}{\mu} = \dfrac{.667}{8} + \dfrac{1}{12} = 0.167$ hours or 10 minutes

Model 3: Multiple Channel

A multiple-channel system exists whenever there are two or more servers working *independently* to provide service to customer arrivals. Use of the model involves the following assumptions:

1. A Poisson arrival rate and exponential service time.
2. Servers all work at the same average rate.
3. Customers form a single waiting line (in order to maintain first-come, first-served processing).

Formulas for the multiple-channel model are listed in Table 14–3.

Obviously, the multiple-channel formulas are more complex than the single-channel formulas, especially the formulas for L_q and P_o. However, these formulas are shown primarily for completeness; actual determination of their values can be made using Table 14–4, which gives values of L_q and P_o for selected values of λ/μ and M.

To use Table 14–4, compute the value of λ/μ and round according to the number of decimal places given for that ratio in the table. Then simply read the value of L_q and P_o for the appropriate number of channels, M. For instance, if $\lambda/\mu = .50$ and $M = 2$, the table provides a value of .033 for L_q and a value of .600 for P_o. These values can then be used to compute other measures of system performance. Note that the formulas in Table 14–3 and the values in Table 14–4 yield *average* amounts (i.e., expected values).

Note that Table 14–4 can also be used for single-channel problems (i.e., $M = 1$).

TABLE 14–3

Multiple-Channel Queuing Formulas

Performance measure	Equation	
Average number in line	$L_q = \dfrac{\lambda\mu\left(\dfrac{\lambda}{\mu}\right)^M}{(M-1)!(M\mu-\lambda)^2}P_o$	(14–9)
Probability of zero units in the system	$P_o = \left[\displaystyle\sum_{n=0}^{M-1}\dfrac{\left(\dfrac{\lambda}{\mu}\right)^n}{n!} + \dfrac{\left(\dfrac{\lambda^M}{\mu}\right)}{M!\left(1-\dfrac{\lambda}{M\mu}\right)}\right]^{-1}$	(14–10)
Average waiting time for an arrival not immediately served	$W_a = \dfrac{1}{M\mu-\lambda}$	(14–11)
Probability that an arrival will have to wait for service	$P_w = \left(\dfrac{\lambda}{\mu}\right)^M \dfrac{P_o}{M!\left(1-\dfrac{\lambda}{M\mu}\right)}$	(14–12)

TABLE 14–4

Infinite-Source Values for L_q and P_o given λ/μ and M

λ/μ	M	L_q	P_o	λ/μ	M	L_q	P_o	λ/μ	M	L_q	P_o
.15	1	.026	.850		3	.094	.294		5	.130	.080
	2	.001	.860		4	.016	.300		6	.034	.082
.20	1	.050	.800		5	.003	.301		7	.009	.082
	2	.002	.818	1.3	2	.951	.212	2.6	3	4.933	.035
.25	1	.083	.750		3	.130	.264		4	.658	.065
	2	.004	.778		4	.023	.271		5	.161	.072
.30	1	.129	.700		5	.004	.272		6	.043	.074
	2	.007	.739	1.4	2	1.345	.176		7	.011	.074
.35	1	.188	.650		3	.177	.236	2.7	3	7.354	.025
	2	.011	.702		4	.032	.245		4	.811	.057
.40	1	.267	.600		5	.006	.246		5	.198	.065
	2	.017	.667	1.5	2	1.929	.143		6	.053	.067
.45	1	.368	.550		3	.237	.211		7	.014	.067
	2	.024	.633		4	.045	.221	2.8	3	12.273	.016
	3	.002	.637		5	.009	.223		4	1.000	.050
.50	1	.500	.500	1.6	2	2.844	.111		5	.241	.058
	2	.033	.600		3	.313	.187		6	.066	.060
	3	.003	.606		4	.060	.199		7	.018	.061
.55	1	.672	.450		5	.012	.201	2.9	3	27.193	.008
	2	.045	.569	1.7	2	4.426	.081		4	1.234	.044
	3	.004	.576		3	.409	.166		5	.293	.052
.60	1	.900	.400		4	.080	.180		6	.081	.054
	2	.059	.538		5	.017	.182		7	.023	.055
	3	.006	.548	1.8	2	7.674	.053	3.0	4	1.528	.038
.65	1	1.207	.350		3	.532	.146		5	.354	.047
	2	.077	.509		4	.105	.162		6	.099	.049
	3	.008	.521		5	.023	.165		7	.028	.050
.70	1	1.633	.300	1.9	2	17.587	.026		8	.008	.050
	2	.098	.481		3	.688	.128	3.1	4	1.902	.032
	3	.011	.495		4	.136	.145		5	.427	.042
.75	1	2.250	.250		5	.030	.149		6	.120	.044
	2	.123	.455		6	.007	.149		7	.035	.045
	3	.015	.471	2.0	3	.889	.111		8	.010	.045
.80	1	3.200	.200		4	.174	.130	3.2	4	2.386	.027
	2	.152	.429		5	.040	.134		5	.513	.037
	3	.019	.447		6	.009	.135		6	.145	.040
.85	1	4.817	.150	2.1	3	1.149	.096		7	.043	.040
	2	.187	.404		4	.220	.117		8	.012	.041
	3	.024	.425		5	.052	.121	3.3	4	3.027	.023
	4	.003	.427		6	.012	.122		5	.615	.033
.90	1	8.100	.100	2.2	3	1.491	.081		6	.174	.036
	2	.229	.379		4	.277	.105		7	.052	.037
	3	.030	.403		5	.066	.109		8	.015	.037
	4	.004	.406		6	.016	.111	3.4	4	3.906	.019
.95	1	18.050	.050	2.3	3	1.951	.068		5	.737	.029
	2	.277	.356		4	.346	.093		6	.209	.032
	3	.037	.383		5	.084	.099		7	.063	.033
	4	.005	.386		6	.021	.100		8	.019	.033
1.0	2	.333	.333	2.4	3	2.589	.056	3.5	4	5.165	.015
	3	.045	.364		4	.431	.083		5	.882	.026
	4	.007	.367		5	.105	.089		6	.248	.029
1.1	2	.477	.290		6	.027	.090		7	.076	.030
	3	.066	.327		7	.007	.091		8	.023	.030
	4	.011	.367	2.5	3	3.511	.045		9	.007	.030
1.2	2	.675	.250		4	.533	.074	3.6	4	7.090	.011

TABLE 14–4 (*continued*)

λ/μ	M	L_q	P_o	λ/μ	M	L_q	P_o	λ/μ	M	L_q	P_o
	5	1.055	.023	4.6	5	9.289	.004	5.5	6	8.590	.002
	6	.295	.026		6	1.487	.008		7	1.674	.003
	7	.091	.027		7	.453	.009		8	.553	.004
	8	.028	.027		8	.156	.010		9	.204	.004
	9	.008	.027		9	.054	.010		10	.077	.004
3.7	4	10.347	.008		10	.018	.010		11	.028	.004
	5	1.265	.020	4.7	5	13.382	.003		12	.010	.004
	6	.349	.023		6	1.752	.007	5.6	6	11.519	.001
	7	.109	.024		7	.525	.008		7	1.944	.003
	8	.034	.025		8	.181	.008		8	.631	.003
	9	.010	.025		9	.064	.009		9	.233	.004
3.8	4	16.937	.005		10	.022	.009		10	.088	.004
	5	1.519	.017	4.8	5	21.641	.002		11	.033	.004
	6	.412	.021		6	2.071	.006		12	.012	.004
	7	.129	.022		7	.607	.008	5.7	6	16.446	.001
	8	.041	.022		8	.209	.008		7	2.264	.002
	9	.013	.022		9	.074	.008		8	.721	.003
3.9	4	36.859	.002		10	.026	.008		9	.266	.003
	5	1.830	.015	4.9	5	46.566	.001		10	.102	.003
	6	.485	.019		6	2.459	.005		11	.038	.003
	7	.153	.020		7	.702	.007		12	.014	.003
	8	.050	.020		8	.242	.007	5.8	6	26.373	.001
	9	.016	.020		9	.087	.007		7	2.648	.002
4.0	5	2.216	.013		10	.031	.007		8	.823	.003
	6	.570	.017		11	.011	.077		9	.303	.003
	7	.180	.018	5.0	6	2.938	.005		10	.116	.003
	8	.059	.018		7	.810	.006		11	.044	.003
	9	.019	.018		8	.279	.006		12	.017	.003
4.1	5	2.703	.011		9	.101	.007	5.9	6	56.300	.000
	6	.668	.015		10	.036	.007		7	3.113	.002
	7	.212	.016		11	.013	.007		8	.939	.002
	8	.070	.016	5.1	6	3.536	.004		9	.345	.003
	9	.023	.017		7	.936	.005		10	.133	.003
4.2	5	3.327	.009		8	.321	.006		11	.051	.003
	6	.784	.013		9	.117	.006		12	.019	.003
	7	.248	.014		10	.042	.006	6.0	7	3.683	.001
	8	.083	.015		11	.015	.006		8	1.071	.002
	9	.027	.015	5.2	6	4.301	.003		9	.392	.002
	10	.009	.015		7	1.081	.005		10	.152	.002
4.3	5	4.149	.008		8	.368	.005		11	.059	.002
	6	.919	.012		9	.135	.005		12	.022	.002
	7	.289	.130		10	.049	.005	6.1	7	4.394	.001
	8	.097	.013		11	.017	.006		8	1.222	.002
	9	.033	.014	5.3	6	5.303	.003		9	.445	.002
	10	.011	.014		7	1.249	.004		10	.173	.002
4.4	5	5.268	.006		8	.422	.005		11	.068	.002
	6	1.078	.010		9	.155	.005		12	.026	.002
	7	.337	.012		10	.057	.005	6.2	7	5.298	.001
	8	.114	.012		11	.021	.005		8	1.397	.002
	9	.039	.012		12	.007	.005		9	.504	.002
	10	.013	.012	5.4	6	6.661	.002		10	.197	.002
4.5	5	6.862	.005		7	1.444	.004		11	.078	.002
	6	1.265	.009		8	.483	.004		12	.030	.002
	7	.391	.010		9	.178	.004	6.3	7	6.480	.001
	8	.133	.011		10	.066	.004		8	1.598	.001
	9	.046	.011		11	.024	.005		9	.571	.002
	10	.015	.011		12	.009	.005		10	.223	.002

TABLE 14–4 *(concluded)*

λ/μ	M	L_q	P_o	λ/μ	M	L_q	P_o	λ/μ	M	L_q	P_o
	11	.089	.002		12	.077	.001		10	1.157	.0004
	12	.035	.002	7.0	8	4.447	.001		11	.471	.0004
6.4	7	8.077	.001		9	1.347	.001		12	.201	.0004
	8	1.831	.001		10	.517	.001	7.8	8	35.898	.0001
	9	.645	.002		11	.212	.001		9	3.856	.0002
	10	.253	.002		12	.088	.001		10	1.298	.0004
	11	.101	.002	7.1	8	5.270	.000		11	.525	.0004
	12	.040	.002		9	1.525	.001		12	.224	.0004
6.5	7	10.341	.001		10	.581	.001	7.9	8	75.827	.00003
	8	2.102	.001		11	.238	.001		9	4.474	.00023
	9	.730	.001		12	.099	.001		10	1.457	.00031
	10	.285	.001	7.2	8	6.314	.000		11	.586	.00035
	11	.115	.001		9	1.729	.001		12	.251	.00036
	12	.046	.001		10	.652	.001	8.0	9	5.227	.00020
6.6	7	13.770	.000		11	.268	.001		10	1.637	.00028
	8	2.420	.001		12	.112	.001		11	.653	.00031
	9	.825	.001	7.3	8	7.675	.0003		12	.280	.00033
	10	.285	.001		9	1.963	.0005	8.1	9	6.161	.00017
	11	.130	.001		10	.732	.0006		10	1.841	.00025
	12	.052	.001		11	.300	.0007		11	.728	.00028
6.7	7	19.532	.000		12	.126	.0007		12	.312	.00029
	8	2.796	.001	7.4	8	9.511	.0003	8.2	9	7.344	.00014
	9	.932	.001		9	2.233	.0005		10	2.074	.00022
	10	.363	.001		10	.820	.0006		11	.811	.00025
	11	.147	.001		11	.337	.0006		12	.347	.00026
	12	.060	.001		12	.142	.0006	8.3	9	8.884	.00011
6.8	7	31.127	.000	7.5	8	12.109	.0002		10	2.341	.00019
	8	3.245	.001		9	2.546	.0004		11	.903	.00022
	9	1.054	.001		10	.920	.0005		12	.386	.00024
	10	.409	.001		11	.377	.0005	8.4	9	10.960	.00009
	11	.167	.001		12	.160	.0005		10	2.647	.00017
	12	.068	.001	7.6	8	16.039	.0002		11	1.006	.00020
					9	2.912	.0004		12	.429	.00021
6.9	7	66.055	.000		10	1.031	.0004	8.5	9	13.891	.00007
	8	3.786	.001		11	.421	.0005		10	3.003	.00015
	9	1.191	.001		12	.179	.0005		11	1.121	.00018
	10	.460	.001	7.7	8	22.636	.0001		12	.476	.00019
	11	.188	.001		9	3.343	.0003				

EXAMPLE 4

Alpha Taxi and Hauling Company has 10 cabs stationed at the airport. It has been determined that during the late-evening hours on week nights, customers request cabs at a rate that follows the Poisson distribution with a mean of 9.6 per hour. Service time is exponential with a mean of 50 minutes per customer. Assume that there is one customer per cab. Find each of the performance measures listed in Table 14–3 and the system utilization.

EXAMPLE 4 (concluded)

Solution

$$\lambda = 9.6 \text{ per hour} \qquad M = 10 \text{ cabs (servers)}$$

$$\mu = \frac{1 \text{ customer per trip}}{50 \text{ minutes per trip} \div 60 \text{ minutes per hour}}$$
$$= 1.2 \text{ customers per hour per cab}$$

$\lambda/\mu = 8.0$. From Table 14–4, with $M = 10$: $L_q = 1.637$ and $P_o = .00028$.

a. $L_q = 1.637$ customers

b. $L_s = L_q + \dfrac{\lambda}{\mu} = 1.637 + 8.0 = 9.637$ customers

c. $W_q = L_q / \lambda = 1.637/9.6 = .17$ hours

d. $W_s = W_q + \dfrac{1}{\mu} = .17 + .833 = 1.0033$ hours

e. $P_o = .00028$ (from Table 14–4)

f. $W_a = \dfrac{1}{M\mu - \lambda} = \dfrac{1}{10(1.2) - 9.6} = .4167$ hours

g. $P_w = \left(\dfrac{\lambda}{\mu}\right)^M \dfrac{P_o}{M!\left(1 - \dfrac{\lambda}{M\mu}\right)} = (8)^{10} \dfrac{.00028}{10!\left(1 - \dfrac{9.6}{10(1.2)}\right)} = .414$

The process can also be worked in reverse. That is, an analyst can determine the capacity needed to achieve specified levels of various performance measures. This approach is illustrated in the following example.

EXAMPLE 5

Alpha Taxi and Hauling also plans to have cabs at a new rail station. The expected arrival rate is 4.8 customers per hour, and the service rate (including return time to the rail station) is expected to be 1.5 per hour. How many cabs will be needed to achieve an average time in the system of less than one hour?

Solution

$$\lambda = 4.8 \text{ customers per hour}$$
$$\mu = 1.5 \text{ customers per hour}$$
$$M = ?$$

$$r = \frac{\lambda}{\mu} = \frac{4.8}{1.5} = 3.2$$

EXAMPLE 5 *(concluded)*

Notice that unless M is at least 4, the system will be overloaded (i.e., system utilization λ/Mu will exceed 1.00. This is why the table does not have a value for M less than 4 at $r = 3.2$.

Using trial and error, beginning with $M = 4$, we find:

M	L_q	$\dfrac{L_q}{\lambda} + \dfrac{1}{\mu} = w_s$
4	2.386	$2.386/4.8 + 1/1.5 = 1.16$ hour
5	0.513	$0.513/4.8 + 1/1.5 = 0.77$ hour

Hence, five cabs will provide the desired result.

Another question that often comes up in capacity planning is the amount of space to allocate for waiting lines. Theoretically, with an infinite population source, the waiting line can become infinitely long. This implies that no matter how much space is allocated for a waiting line, one can never be completely sure that the space requirements won't exceed that amount. Nonetheless, as a practical matter, one can determine a line that will not be exceeded a specified proportion of the time. For instance, an analyst may wish to know the length of line that will probably not be exceeded 98 percent of the time, or perhaps 99 percent of the time, and use that number as a planning value.

The approximate line length that will satisfy a specified percentage can be determined by solving the following equation for n:

$$n = \frac{\log K}{\log \rho} \quad \text{or} \quad \frac{1n\ K}{1n\ \rho} \quad \text{where } K = \frac{1 - \dfrac{\text{specified}}{\text{percentage}}}{L_q(1 - \rho)} \quad (14\text{--}13)$$

The resulting value of n will usually not be integer. Generally, round *up* to the next higher integer and treat that value as n. However, as a practical matter, if the computed value of n is less than .10 above the next lower integer, round down. Thus, 15.2 would be rounded to 16, but 15.06 would be rounded to 15.

EXAMPLE 6

Determine the maximum length of a waiting line for specified probabilities of 95 percent and 98 percent for a system in which $M = 2$, $\lambda = 8$ per hour, and $\mu = 5$ per hour.

Solution

$r = \dfrac{8}{5} = 1.6 \quad$ and $\quad \rho = \dfrac{8}{2(5)} = .80$

> ### EXAMPLE 6 (concluded)
>
> From Table 14–4, $L_q = 2.844$ customers.
>
> For 95%, using Formula 14–13, $K = \dfrac{1 - .95}{2.844(1 - .80)} = .088$.
>
> Then $n = \dfrac{1n\ .088}{1n\ .80} = \dfrac{-2.4304}{-\ .2231} = 10.89$, which rounds to 11.
>
> For 98%, $K = \dfrac{1 - .98}{2.844(1 - .80)} = .035$.
>
> Then $n = \dfrac{1n\ .035}{1n\ .80} = \dfrac{-3.352}{-\ .2231} = 15.03$, which rounds to 15.

QUEUING MODEL: FINITE SOURCE

The finite-source model is appropriate for cases in which the calling population is limited to a relatively small number of potential calls. For instance, one person may be responsible for handling breakdowns on 15 machines. Hence, the size of the calling population is 15. There may be more than one server or channel, though. For instance, due to a backlog of machines awaiting repairs, the manager might authorize an additional person to work on repairs.

A major difference between the finite- and infinite-source models is that the arrival rate of customers in a finite situation is *dependent* on the length of the waiting line: the arrival rate decreases as the length of the line increases simply because there is a decreasing proportion of the population left to generate calls for service. The limit occurs when *all* of the limited population are waiting in line: at that point the arrival rate is zero since no additional units can arrive.

Because the mathematics of the finite-source model can be quite complex, finite-queuing tables are often used in conjunction with simple formulas to analyze these systems. Table 14–5 contains a list of the key formulas and definitions. You will find it helpful to study the diagram of a cycle that is presented in the table.

Table 14–6 is an abbreviated finite queuing table that is used to obtain values of D and F. (Most of the formulas require a value of F.) In order to use the finite queuing table, follow this procedure:

1. List the values for:

    N, population size.
    M, number of servers/channels.

T, service time.

U, time between calls for service, per customer.

2. Compute the service factor, $X = \dfrac{T}{T + U}$.

3. Locate the section of the finite queuing tables for N.

4. Using the value of X as the point of entry, find the values of D and F that correspond to M.

5. Use the values of N, M, X, D, and F as needed to compute the desired measures of system performance.

TABLE 14–5

Finite-Source Queuing Formulas and Notation

Formulas			*Notation†*
Service factor	$X = \dfrac{T}{T + U}$	(14–14)	D = Probability that a customer will have to wait in line
Average number waiting	$L = N(1 - F)$	(14–15)	F = Efficiency factor: 1—percentage waiting in line
Average waiting time	$W = \dfrac{L(T + U)}{N - L} = \dfrac{T(1 - F)}{XF}$	(14–16)	H = Average number of customers being served
Average number running	$J = NF(1 - X)$	(14–17)	J = Average number of customers not in line or in service
Average number being serviced	$H = FNX$	(14–18)	L = Average number of customers waiting for service
Number in population	$N = J + L + H$	(14–19)	M = Number of service channels

N = Number of potential customers
T = Average service time
U = Average time between customer service requirements per customer
W = Average time customers wait in line
X = Service factor

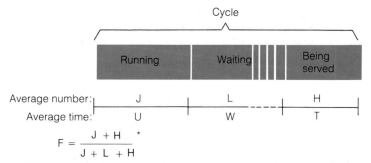

$$F = \dfrac{J + H}{J + L + H} \quad ^*$$

* The purpose of this formula is to provide an understanding of F. Because the value of F is needed to compute J, L, and H, the formula cannot be used to actually compute F. The finite queuing tables must be used for that purpose.

---

† Adapted from L. G. Peck and R. N. Hazelwood, *Finite Queuing Tables* (New York: John Wiley & Sons, 1958).

TABLE 14–6

Finite Queuing Tables

POPULATION 5

X	M	D	F
.012	1	.048	.999
.019	1	.076	.998
.025	1	.100	.997
.030	1	.120	.996
.034	1	.135	.995
.036	1	.143	.994
.040	1	.159	.993
.042	1	.167	.992
.044	1	.175	.991
.046	1	.183	.990
.050	1	.198	.989
.052	1	.206	.988
.054	1	.214	.987
.056	2	.018	.999
.056	1	.222	.985
.058	2	.019	.999
.058	1	.229	.984
.060	2	.020	.999
.060	1	.237	.983
.062	2	.022	.999
.062	1	.245	.982
.064	2	.023	.999
.064	1	.253	.981
.066	2	.024	.999
.066	1	.260	.979
.068	2	.026	.999
.068	1	.268	.978
.070	2	.027	.999
.070	1	.275	.977
.075	2	.031	.999
.075	1	.294	.973
.080	2	.035	.998
.080	1	.313	.969
.085	2	.040	.998
.085	1	.332	.965
.090	2	.044	.998
.090	1	.350	.960
.095	2	.049	.997
.095	1	.368	.955
.100	2	.054	.997

X	M	D	F
.100	1	.386	.950
.105	2	.059	.997
.105	1	.404	.945
.110	2	.065	.996
.110	1	.421	.939
.115	2	.071	.995
.115	1	.439	.933
.120	2	.076	.995
.120	1	.456	.927
.125	2	.082	.994
.125	1	.473	.920
.130	2	.089	.993
.130	1	.489	.914
.135	2	.095	.993
.135	1	.505	.907
.140	2	.102	.992
.140	1	.521	.900
.145	3	.011	.999
.145	2	.109	.991
.145	1	.537	.892
.150	3	.012	.999
.150	2	.115	.990
.150	1	.553	.885
.155	3	.013	.999
.155	2	.123	.989
.155	1	.568	.877
.160	3	.015	.999
.160	2	.130	.988
.160	1	.582	.869
.165	3	.016	.999
.165	2	.137	.987
.165	1	.597	.861
.170	3	.017	.998
.170	2	.145	.985
.170	1	.611	.853
.180	3	.021	.999
.180	2	.161	.983
.180	1	.638	.836
.190	3	.024	.998
.190	2	.177	.980
.190	1	.665	.819
.200	3	.028	.998

X	M	D	F
.200	2	.194	.976
.200	1	.689	.801
.210	3	.032	.998
.210	2	.211	.973
.210	1	.713	.783
.220	3	.036	.997
.220	2	.229	.969
.220	1	.735	.765
.230	3	.041	.997
.230	2	.247	.965
.230	1	.756	.747
.240	3	.046	.996
.240	2	.265	.960
.240	1	.775	.730
.250	3	.052	.995
.250	2	.284	.955
.250	1	.794	.712
.260	3	.058	.994
.260	2	.303	.950
.260	1	.811	.695
.270	3	.064	.994
.270	2	.323	.944
.270	1	.827	.677
.280	3	.071	.993
.280	2	.342	.938
.280	1	.842	.661
.290	3	.079	.992
.290	2	.362	.932
.290	1	.856	.644
.300	4	.010	.999
.300	3	.086	.990
.300	2	.382	.926
.300	1	.869	.628
.310	4	.011	.999
.310	3	.094	.988
.310	2	.402	.919
.310	1	.881	.613
.320	4	.012	.999
.320	3	.103	.987
.320	2	.422	.912
.320	1	.892	.597

X	M	D	F
.330	4	.012	.999
.330	3	.112	.986
.330	2	.442	.904
.330	1	.902	.583
.340	4	.013	.999
.340	3	.121	.985
.340	2	.462	.896
.340	1	.911	.569
.360	4	.017	.998
.360	3	.141	.981
.360	2	.501	.880
.360	1	.927	.542
.380	4	.021	.998
.380	3	.163	.976
.380	2	.540	.863
.380	1	.941	.516
.400	4	.026	.997
.400	3	.186	.972
.400	2	.579	.845
.400	1	.952	.493
.420	4	.031	.997
.420	3	.211	.966
.420	2	.616	.826
.420	1	.961	.471
.440	4	.037	.996
.440	3	.238	.960
.440	2	.652	.807
.440	1	.969	.451
.460	4	.045	.995
.460	3	.266	.953
.460	2	.686	.787
.460	1	.975	.432
.480	4	.053	.994
.480	3	.296	.945
.480	2	.719	.767
.480	1	.980	.415
.500	4	.063	.992
.500	3	.327	.936
.500	2	.750	.748
.500	1	.985	.399
.520	4	.073	.991
.520	3	.359	.927

X	M	D	F
.520	2	.779	.728
.520	1	.988	.384
.540	4	.085	.989
.540	3	.392	.917
.540	2	.806	.708
.540	1	.991	.370
.560	4	.098	.986
.560	3	.426	.906
.560	2	.831	.689
.560	1	.993	.357
.580	4	.113	.984
.580	3	.461	.895
.580	2	.854	.670
.580	1	.994	.345
.600	4	.130	.981
.600	3	.497	.883
.600	2	.875	.652
.600	1	.996	.333
.650	4	.179	.972
.650	3	.588	.850
.650	2	.918	.608
.650	1	.998	.308
.700	4	.240	.960
.700	3	.678	.815
.700	2	.950	.568
.700	1	.999	.286
.750	4	.316	.944
.750	3	.763	.777
.750	2	.972	.532
.800	4	.410	.924
.800	3	.841	.739
.800	2	.987	.500
.850	4	.522	.900
.850	3	.907	.702
.850	2	.995	.470
.900	4	.656	.871
.900	3	.957	.666
.900	2	.998	.444
.950	4	.815	.838
.950	3	.989	.631

TABLE 14–6 (*continued*)

X	M	D	F	X	M	D	F	X	M	D	F	X	M	D	F
POPULATION 10				.064	2	.119	.995	.125	3	.100	.994	.180	2	.614	.890
					1	.547	.940		2	.369	.962		1	.975	.549
.016	1	.144	.997	.066	2	.126	.995		1	.878	.737	.190	5	.016	.999
.019	1	.170	.996		1	.562	.936	.130	4	.022	.999		4	.078	.995
.021	1	.188	.995	.068	3	.020	.999		3	.110	.994		3	.269	.973
.023	1	.206	.994		2	.133	.994		2	.392	.958		2	.654	.873
.025	1	.224	.993		1	.577	.931		1	.893	.718		1	.982	.522
.026	1	.232	.992	.070	3	.022	.999	.135	4	.025	.999	.200	5	.020	.999
.028	1	.250	.991		2	.140	.994		3	.121	.993		4	.092	.994
.030	1	.268	.990		1	.591	.926		2	.415	.952		3	.300	.968
.032	2	.033	.999	.075	3	.026	.999		1	.907	.699		2	.692	.854
	1	.285	.988		2	.158	.992	.140	4	.028	.999		1	.987	.497
.034	2	.037	.999		1	.627	.913		3	.132	.991	.210	5	.025	.999
	1	.302	.986	.080	3	.031	.999		2	.437	.947		4	.108	.992
.036	2	.041	.999		2	.177	.990		1	.919	.680		3	.333	.961
	1	.320	.984		1	.660	.899	.145	4	.032	.999		2	.728	.835
.038	2	.046	.999	.085	3	.037	.999		3	.144	.990		1	.990	.474
	1	.337	.982		2	.196	.988		2	.460	.941	.220	5	.030	.998
.040	2	.050	.999		1	.692	.883		1	.929	.662		4	.124	.990
	1	.354	.980	.090	3	.043	.998	.150	4	.036	.998		3	.366	.954
.042	2	.055	.999		2	.216	.986		3	.156	.989		2	.761	.815
	1	.371	.978	.090	1	.722	.867		2	.483	.935		1	.993	.453
.044	2	.060	.998	.095	3	.049	.998		1	.939	.644	.230	5	.037	.998
	1	.388	.975		2	.237	.984	.155	4	.040	.998		4	.142	.988
.046	2	.065	.998		1	.750	.850		3	.169	.987		3	.400	.947
	1	.404	.973	.100	3	.056	.998		2	.505	.928		2	.791	.794
.048	2	.071	.998		2	.258	.981		1	.947	.627		1	.995	.434
	1	.421	.970		1	.776	.832	.160	4	.044	.998	.240	5	.044	.997
.050	2	.076	.998	.105	3	.064	.997		3	.182	.986		4	.162	.986
	1	.437	.967		2	.279	.978		2	.528	.921		3	.434	.938
.052	2	.082	.997		1	.800	.814		1	.954	.610		2	.819	.774
	1	.454	.963	.110	3	.072	.997	.165	4	.049	.997		1	.996	.416
.054	2	.088	.997		2	.301	.974		3	.195	.984	.250	6	.010	.999
	1	.470	.960		1	.822	.795		2	.550	.914		5	.052	.997
.056	2	.094	.997	.115	3	.081	.996		1	.961	.594		4	.183	.983
	1	.486	.956		2	.324	.971	.170	4	.054	.997		3	.469	.929
.058	2	.100	.996		1	.843	.776		3	.209	.982		2	.844	.753
	1	.501	.953	.120	4	.016	.999		2	.571	.906		1	.997	.400
.060	2	.106	.996		3	.090	.995		1	.966	.579	.260	6	.013	.999
	1	.517	.949		2	.346	.967	.180	5	.013	.999		5	.060	.996
.062	2	.113	.996		1	.861	.756		4	.066	.996		4	.205	.980
	1	.532	.945	.125	4	.019	.999		3	.238	.978		3	.503	.919

TABLE 14–6 (concluded)

X	M	D	F	X	M	D	F	X	M	D	F	X	M	D	F
.260	2	.866	.732	.340	6	.049	.997	.480	8	.015	.999	.600	6	.518	.915
	1	.998	.384		5	.168	.983		7	.074	.994		5	.795	.809
.270	6	.015	.999		4	.416	.938		6	.230	.973		4	.953	.663
	5	.070	.995		3	.750	.816		5	.499	.916		3	.996	.500
	4	.228	.976		2	.968	.584		4	.791	.799	.650	9	.021	.999
	3	.537	.908	.360	7	.014	.999		3	.961	.621		8	.123	.988
	2	.886	.712		6	.064	.995		2	.998	.417		7	.353	.954
	1	.999	.370		5	.205	.978	.500	8	.020	.999		6	.651	.878
.280	6	.018	.999		4	.474	.923		7	.093	.992		5	.882	.759
	5	.081	.994		3	.798	.787		6	.271	.966		4	.980	.614
	4	.252	.972		2	.978	.553		5	.553	.901		3	.999	.461
	3	.571	.896	.380	7	.019	.999		4	.830	.775	.700	9	.040	.997
	2	.903	.692		6	.083	.993		3	.972	.598		8	.200	.979
	1	.999	.357		5	.247	.971		2	.999	.400		7	.484	.929
.290	6	.022	.999		4	.533	.906	.520	8	.026	.998		6	.772	.836
	5	.093	.993		3	.840	.758		7	.115	.989		5	.940	.711
	4	.278	.968		2	.986	.525		6	.316	.958		4	.992	.571
	3	.603	.884	.400	7	.026	.998		5	.606	.884	.750	9	.075	.994
	2	.918	.672		6	.105	.991		4	.864	.752		8	.307	.965
	1	.999	.345		5	.292	.963		3	.980	.575		7	.626	.897
.300	6	.026	.998		4	.591	.887		2	.999	.385		6	.870	.792
.300	5	.106	.991		3	.875	.728	.540	8	.034	.997	.750	5	.975	.666
	4	.304	.963		2	.991	.499		7	.141	.986		4	.998	.533
	3	.635	.872	.420	7	.034	.993		6	.363	.949	.800	9	.134	.988
	2	.932	.653		6	.130	.987		5	.658	.867		8	.446	.944
	1	.999	.333		5	.341	.954		4	.893	.729		7	.763	.859
.310	6	.031	.998		4	.646	.866		3	.986	.555		6	.939	.747
	5	.120	.990		3	.905	.700	.560	8	.044	.996		5	.991	.625
	4	.331	.957		2	.994	.476		7	.171	.982		4	.999	.500
	3	.666	.858	.440	7	.045	.997		6	.413	.939	.850	9	.232	.979
	2	.943	.635		6	.160	.984		5	.707	.848		8	.611	.916
.320	6	.036	.998		5	.392	.943		4	.917	.706		7	.879	.818
	5	.135	.988		4	.698	.845		3	.991	.535		6	.978	.705
	4	.359	.952		3	.928	.672	.580	8	.057	.995		5	.998	.588
	3	.695	.845		2	.996	.454		7	.204	.977	.900	9	.387	.963
	2	.952	.617	.460	8	.011	.999		6	.465	.927		8	.785	.881
.330	6	.042	.997		7	.058	.995		5	.753	.829		7	.957	.777
	5	.151	.986		6	.193	.979		4	.937	.684		6	.995	.667
	4	.387	.945		5	.445	.930		3	.994	.517	.950	9	.630	.938
	3	.723	.831		4	.747	.822	.600	9	.010	.999		8	.934	.841
	2	.961	.600		3	.947	.646		8	.072	.994		7	.994	.737
.340	7	.010	.999		2	.998	.435		7	.242	.972				

Source: From L. G. Peck and R. N. Hazelwood, *Finite Queuing Tables* (New York: John Wiley & Sons, 1958).

EXAMPLE 7

One operator loads and unloads a bank of five machines. Service time is exponentially distributed with a mean of 10 minutes per cycle. Machines run for an average of 70 minutes between loading and unloading, and this time is also exponential.

Find:

1. The average number of machines waiting for the operator.
2. The expected number of machines running.
3. Average downtime.
4. The probability that a machine will not have to wait for service.

Solution

$N = 5$ $\quad\quad\quad\quad M = 1$

$T = 10$ minutes

$U = 70$ minutes

$$X = \frac{T}{T + U} = \frac{10}{10 + 70} = .125$$

From Table 14–6, with $N = 5$, $M = 1$, and $X = .125$

$$D = .473 \text{ and } F = .920$$

a. Average number waiting, $L = N(1 - F) = 5(1 - .92) = 0.40$ machines.

b. Expected number running, $J = NF(1 - X) = 5(.92)(1 - .125) = 4.025$ machines.

c. Downtime = Waiting time + Service time

Waiting time, $W = \dfrac{L(T + U)}{N - L} = \dfrac{.40(10 + 70)}{5 - .40} = 6.957$ minutes

Downtime = 6.957 minutes + 10 minutes = 16.957 minutes

d. Probability of not waiting = 1 − Probability of waiting

$$= 1 - D$$
$$= 1 - .473 = .527$$

EXAMPLE 8

Suppose that in the previous example, operators are paid $10 per hour, and machine downtime costs $16 per hour. Should the department add another operator if the goal is cost minimization?

Solution

Compare the total cost of the present system with the expected total cost of the proposed system:

	M	Average number down $N - J$	Average down cost (per hour) $(N - J)\$16$	Operator cost (per hour)	Total cost (per hour)
(opt)	1	.975	$15.60	$10	$25.60
	2	.651	10.42	20	30.42

Hence, the present system is superior because its total cost is less than the expected total cost using two operators.

OTHER APPROACHES

The discussion in this chapter has focused on designing service systems that achieve a balance between service capacity and customer waiting time. The implication is that an appropriate level of service capacity can be determined. In certain instances such an approach may not be practical, for a variety of reasons. One is that the system may be currently in operation and indicated design changes may be too costly or there may be space restrictions such that changes cannot reasonably be made. One alternative that is particularly suited for queuing systems in which the customers are actually people rather than inanimate objects is to provide some form of diversion so that the waiting time becomes more tolerable. For example, magazines and newspapers can be placed in waiting rooms, as is usually the case in doctors' and dentists' offices. Auto repair shops sometimes use radio or television, and airlines may provide in-flight movies to help occupy the time. Airlines also serve meals and snacks, which also helps to make the time spent waiting more pleasant. Some less-obvious measures include placing mirrors where people wait for elevators and asking people to fill out forms, which makes waiting somewhat constructive.

Carrying this concept one step further, it is sometimes possible to derive some benefit from customer waiting. For instance, supermarkets position impulse items near checkout counters and gain additional sales, banks advertise current rates and place brochures describing bank services within easy reach of waiting customers, and restaurants have bars where customers can relax and spend money while waiting for their tables.

The implication in these approaches is that imagination and creativity can often play an important role in system design and that purely mathematical approaches are not the only tools worth considering.

SUMMARY

Analysis of waiting lines can be an important aspect of the design of service systems. Waiting lines have a tendency to form in such systems even though in a macro sense the system is underloaded. The arrival of customers at random times and variability of service times combine to create temporary overloads. When this happens, waiting lines appear. By the same token, at various times, the servers will be idle.

A major consideration in the analysis of queuing systems relates to whether the number of potential customers is limited (finite-source) or whether entry to the system is unrestricted (infinite-source). Four basic queuing models are described in the chapter: three dealing with infinite source populations and one dealing with finite source populations. In general, the models assume that customer arrival rates can be described by a Poisson distribution and that service time can be described by a negative exponential distribution.

1. *Infinite-source.* One of the features of a new machine shop will be a well-stocked tool crib. The manager of the shop must decide on the number of attendants needed to staff the crib. Attendants will receive $9 per hour in salary and fringe benefits. Mechanics' time will be worth $30 per hour, which includes salary and fringe benefits plus lost work time caused by waiting for parts. Based on previous experience, the manager estimates requests for parts will average 18 per hour with a service capacity of 20 requests per hour per attendant. How many attendants should be on duty if the manager is willing to assume that arrival and service rates will be Poisson distributed? (Assume the number of mechanics is very large—so an infinite source model is appropriate.)

Solution

$$\lambda = 18 \text{ per hour}$$
$$\mu = 20 \text{ per hour}$$

The solution requires a trial-and-error approach that reveals the total cost of feasible alternatives (i.e., a utilization less than 100 percent), and selection of the lowest cost alternative. Note that the total-cost curve will always be U-shaped; increase the number of servers until the total cost shows an increase over the previous value. The optimum will be the number of servers that produced the previous total cost value. Thus,

Number of servers, M	$L_q{}^*$	$L_q + \dfrac{\lambda}{\mu} = L_s$	[$M(\$9)$] Server cost (per hour)	[$L_s\,(\$30)$] Mechanic cost (per hour)	Total cost (per hour)
1	8.1	$8.1 + .9 = 9.0$	$ 9	$270	$279
2	.229	$.229 + .9 = 1.129$	$18	$ 33.87	$ 52†
3	.03	$.03 + .9 = .93$	$27	$ 27.9	$ 55†

* L_q: From Table 14–4 with $r = \dfrac{\lambda}{\mu} = \dfrac{18}{20} = .9$

† Rounded.

Hence, two servers will produce the lowest total cost.

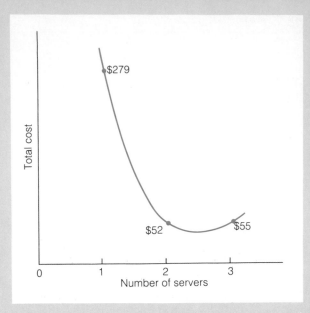

2. *Infinite-source.* The following is a list of service *times* for three different operations:

Operation	Service time
A	8 minutes
B	1.2 hours
C	2 days

    a. Determine the service *rate* for each operation.
    b. Would the calculated rates be different if these were *interarrival times* rather than service times?

    Solution
    a. The service rate is the reciprocal of service time. Thus, the rates are:
        A: 1/8 per minute = .125 per minute, or .125/min. × 60 min./hr. = 7.5 per hour
        B: 1/1.2 per hour = .833 per hour
        C: 1/2 per day = .50 per day
    b. No, in either case the rate is simply the reciprocal of the time.

3. *Finite-source.* A group of 10 machines is loaded and unloaded by one of three servers. The machines run for an average of six minutes per cycle, and average time to unload and reload is nine minutes. Both times can be described by an exponential distribution. While running, the machines produce at a rate that would yield 16 units per hour if they did not have to pause to wait for a server and be loaded and unloaded. What is the average hourly output of each machine when waiting and serving are taken into account?

Solution

$$T = 9 \text{ minutes}$$

$$U = 6 \text{ minutes.} \quad X = \frac{T}{T+U} = \frac{9}{9+6} = .60$$

$$M = 3 \text{ servers. From Table 14–6, } F = .500$$

$$N = 10 \text{ machines}$$

a. Compute the average number of machines running:

$$J = NF(1-X) = 10(.500)(.40) = 2$$

b. Determine the percentage of machines running and multiply by output while running:

$$\frac{J}{N} \times (16 \text{ per hour}) = \frac{2}{10} \times (16 \text{ per hour}) = 3.2 \text{ per hour}$$

DISCUSSION AND REVIEW QUESTIONS

1. In what kinds of situations is queuing analysis most appropriate?
2. Why do waiting lines form even though a service system is underloaded?
3. What are the most common measures of system performance in a queuing analysis?
4. What effect would decreasing arrival and service variability have on the effective capacity of a system?
5. What approaches do supermarkets use to try to offset variations in customer traffic intensity?
6. Contrast *finite* and *infinite* population sources.

7. Will doubling the service rate of a single-channel system reduce the average waiting time in line by a factor of one half? Explain briefly.
8. In a multiple-channel system, what is the rationale for having customers wait in a single line as is now being done in many banks and post offices, rather than multiple lines? (Hint: the *average* waiting time is unaffected.)
9. What happens to the length of a waiting line in a highly variable (queuing) setting if a manager attempts to achieve a high percentage of capacity utilization?

PROBLEMS

1. Repair calls are handled by one repairman at a photocopy shop. Repair time, including travel time, is exponentially distributed with a mean of two hours per call. Requests for copier repairs come in at a mean rate of three per eight-hour day (assume Poisson). Determine the following:
   a. The average number of customers awaiting repairs.
   b. System utilization.
   c. The amount of time during an eight-hour day that the repairman is not out on a call.
   d. The probability of two or more customers in the system.

2. A vending machine dispenses hot chocolate or coffee. Service time is 30 seconds per cup and is constant. Customers arrive at a mean rate of 80 per hour, and this rate is Poisson distributed. Determine:
   a. The average number of customers waiting in line.

  b. The average time customers spend in the system.
  c. The average number in the system.
3. A small town with one hospital is supplied ambulance service via the hospital's two ambulances. Requests for ambulances during nonholiday weekends average 0.8 per hour and tend to be Poisson distributed. Travel and assistance time averages one hour per call and follows an exponential distribution. Find:
  a. System utilization.
  b. The average number of customers waiting.
  c. Average customer waiting time.
  d. The probability that *both* ambulances will be busy when a call comes in.
4. The information below pertains to telephone calls to a motel switchboard on a typical Tuesday. Determine the average time callers wait to have their calls completed for each period and the probability that a caller will have to wait for each period.

Period	Incoming rate (calls per minute)	Service rate (calls per minute per operator)	Number of operators
Morning . . .	1.8	1.5	2
Afternoon . . .	2.2	1.0	3
Evening . . .	1.4	0.7	3

5. For each case in the previous problem, determine the maximum line length for a probability of 96 percent.
6. Trucks arrive at the loading dock of a wholesale grocer at the rate of 1.2 per hour. A single crew consisting of two men can load trucks at the rate of 2 per hour. Crew members receive $10 per hour in wages and fringe benefits, and trucks and drivers reflect an hourly cost of $60. The manager is thinking of adding another member to the crew. The service rate would then be 2.4 trucks per hour. Treat this as a single-channel system, and assume rates are Poisson. Would the third crew member be economical? Would a fourth member be justifiable if the resulting service capacity was 2.6 trucks per hour?

7. A branch location of a large savings bank is open on Saturdays from 10 A.M. until 2 P.M. During that time, four tellers are on duty. Tellers can handle customer deposits and withdrawals at the rate of 28 customers per hour each. Customers arrive to do their banking at the rate of 84 per hour during this period. Determine each of the following, assuming arrival and service rates are Poisson:
  a. The average number of customers waiting in line for a teller.
  b. The expected length of time customers wait in the system.
  c. The average waiting time for customers who are not served immediately.
  d. The maximum number waiting for a confidence (probability) of 97 percent.
8. During slow hours, a certain post office branch uses three clerks, each of whom can process customers at a rate of 1.26 per minute (Poisson). The average time between customer arrivals is 25 seconds (exponential). Determine each of the following:
  a. System utilization.
  b. The percentage of time clerks are idle.
  c. The average number of customers in line and the average time they will wait.
  d. The maximum number waiting for a probability of 98 percent.
  e. The manager is contemplating using only two clerks. How much impact would this have on the average number waiting in line, the average waiting time, and the maximum number waiting (98 percent probability)?
9. One field representative services five customers for a computer manufacturer. Customers request assistance at an average (Poisson distributed) rate of once every four working days. The field representative can handle an average (Poisson distributed) of one call per day. Determine:
  a. The expected number of customers waiting.
  b. How long customers must wait, on the average, from the time a request for

service is made until the service has been completed.

   c. The percentage of time the service rep will be idle.

   d. By how much would your answer to part **a** be reduced assuming a second field rep was added?

10. Two operators handle adjustments for a group of 10 machines. Adjustment time is exponentially distributed and has a mean of 14 minutes per machine. The machines operate for an average of 86 minutes between adjustments. While running, each machine can turn out 50 pieces per hour. Find:

   a. The probability that a machine will have to wait for an adjustment.

   b. The average number of machines waiting for adjustment.

   c. The average number of machines being serviced.

   d. The expected hourly output of each machine, taking adjustments into account.

   e. Machine downtime represents a cost of $70 per hour, while operator cost (including salary and fringe benefits) is $15 per hour. What is the optimum number of operators?

11. One operator services a bank of five machines. Machine running time and service time are both exponential. Machines run for an average of 90 minutes between service requirements, and service time averages 35 minutes. The operator receives $10 per hour in salary and fringe benefits, while machine downtime costs $35 per hour per machine.

   a. If each machine produces 60 pieces per hour while running, find the average hourly output of each machine when waiting and service times are taken into account.

   b. Determine the optimum number of operators.

12. The manager of a regional warehouse must decide on the number of loading docks to request for a new facility in order to minimize the sum of dock costs and driver/truck costs. The manager has learned that each driver/truck combination represents a cost of $300 per day and that each dock plus loading crew represents a cost of $1,100 per day. How many docks should be requested if trucks arrive at the rate of four per day, each dock can handle five trucks per day, and both rates are Poisson?

13. For the preceding problem, if the cost for waiting space is $100 per day, how many docks would be optimum if a probability of .95 is used for the maximum line length?

SELECTED BIBLIOGRAPHY

Buffa, Elwood. *Operations Management.* 3d ed. New York: John Wiley & Sons, 1972.

Chase, Richard, and Nicholas Aquilano. *Production and Operations Management.* 3d ed. Homewood, Ill.: Richard D. Irwin, 1981.

Griffin, W. *Queuing: Basic Theory and Applications.* Columbus, Ohio: Grid Publishing, 1978.

Hillier, Frederick S., and Gerald J. Lieberman. *Introduction to Operations Research,* 3d ed. San Francisco: Holden-Day, 1980.

Peck, L. G., and R. N. Hazelwood. *Finite Queuing Tables.* New York: John Wiley & Sons, 1958.

Simulation

STEPS IN THE SIMULATION PROCESS, 708

MONTE CARLO SIMULATION, 710
   Simulating Theoretical Distributions, 716

SIMULATION APPLICATIONS, 721

COMPUTER SIMULATION, 721

ADVANTAGES AND LIMITATIONS OF USING SIMULATION, 722

SOLVED PROBLEMS, 725

DISCUSSION AND REVIEW QUESTIONS, 727

PROBLEMS, 728

SELECTED BIBLIOGRAPHY, 731

After completing this section, you should be able to:

1. Explain what is meant by the term *simulation.*
2. List some of the reasons for simulation's popularity.
3. Explain how and why random numbers are used in simulations.
4. Outline the advantages and limitations of simulation as a tool for decision making.
5. Describe the alternatives that a manager would reject *before* choosing simulation as a decision-making tool.
6. Solve typical problems that require the use of simulation.

Simulation is a descriptive technique that involves developing a model of a process and then conducting experiments on the model in order to evaluate its behavior under certain conditions. Unlike many of the other models that have been described in this text, simulation is not an optimizing technique. In fact, simulation does not produce a solution, per se. Instead, it enables decision makers to test *their* solutions on a model that reasonably duplicates a real process; simulation models enable decision makers to experiment with decision alternatives using a "what-if" approach.

The use of simulation as a decision-making tool is fairly widespread. As a matter of fact, you are undoubtedly familiar with some of the ways it is used. For instance, space engineers simulate space flight in laboratories to permit future astronauts to become accustomed to working in a weightless environment. Similarly, airline pilots often undergo extensive training with simulated landings and takeoffs before being allowed to try the real thing. Many universities use *management games* as a means of simulating business environments. Tire designers evaluate alternative tread designs using machines that simulate conditions that produce tire wear and handling problems. Of course, there are many other examples of applications of simulation techniques. These few are mentioned to illustrate the nature and diversity of their use.

There are a number of reasons for the popularity of simulation. Among the most important ones are:

1. Many situations are too complex to permit development of a mathematical solution. The degree of simplification needed would seriously affect the results in most cases. However, simulation models are often able to capture the richness of a situation without sacrificing simplicity, thereby enhancing the decision process.

2. Simulation models are fairly simple to use and to understand.

3. Simulation enables the decision maker to conduct experiments that will help in understanding the model's behavior while avoiding the risks that would be inherent in conducting tests on the model's real-life counterpart.

4. Extensive computer software packages are available, making it easy to use fairly sophisticated models.

5. Simulation can be used for a wide range of situations.

6. There have been numerous successful applications of these techniques.

STEPS IN THE SIMULATION PROCESS

Regardless of the type of simulation involved, there are certain basic steps that all simulation models go through:

1. Identify the problem and set objectives.
2. Develop the simulation model.
3. Test the model to be sure that it reflects the system being studied.
4. Develop one or more experiments (conditions under which the model's behavior will be examined).
5. Run the simulation and evaluate the results.
6. Repeat steps 4 and 5 until satisfied with the results.

The first step in problem solving of any sort is to clearly *define the problem and set objectives* that the solution is intended to achieve, and simulation is no exception to this. A clear statement of the objectives can provide not only guidance of model development but also the basis for evaluation of the success or failure of a simulation. In general the goal of a simulation study is to determine how a system will behave under certain conditions. The more specific a manager is about what he or she is looking for, the better the chances that the simulation model will be designed to accomplish that. Toward that end, the *scope* and *level of detail* of the simulation must be decided on. This will provide an indication of the degree of complexity the model will need as well as the information requirements of the study.

The next step in simulation is *model development.* Typically this involves making decisions on the structure of the model and then writing a computer program to carry out the simulations. (Note that for instructional purposes, the examples and problems in this chapter are primarily *manual,* but in most real-life applications, computers are used to conduct the simulations. This stems from the need for large numbers of runs, the complexity of simulations, and the need for record keeping of results.) Data gathering is an important aspect of model development. The amount and type of data needed are a direct function of the scope and level of detail of the simulation. The data are needed both for model development and evaluation. Naturally, the model must be designed so that it will enable evaluation of key decision alternatives.

The *validation* phase is closely related to model development. Its main purpose is to help determine if the model adequately depicts real system performance. This is usually accomplished by comparing the results of simulation runs with known performance of the system under the same circumstances. If such a comparison cannot be made, say because real-life data are difficult or impossible to obtain, an alternative is to employ a test of reasonableness. This means that the judgment and opinion of individuals familiar with the system or similar systems are relied upon for confirmation that the results are plausible and acceptable. Still another aspect of validation is careful consideration of the assumptions of the model and the values of parameters used in testing the model. Again, the judgment and opinion of those who are familiar with the real-life system, and those who must use the results, is essential. Finally, note that model development and model validation go hand in hand: model deficiencies uncovered during validation prompt model revisions, which lead to the need for further validation efforts and perhaps further revisions.

The fourth step in simulation is *designing experiments*. Experiments are the essence of a simulation. They help answer the "what if . . . ?" questions posed in simulation studies. By going through the process, the manager or analyst is able to learn about system behavior.

The fifth step in simulation is to *run the simulation* model. If a simulation model is deterministic and all parameters are known and constant, only a single run will be needed for each "what if . . . ?" question. If the simulation is probabilistic, with parameters subject to random variability, multiple runs will be needed to obtain a clear picture of the results. In this text probabilistic simulations are the focal point of the discussion, and we shall limit comments to that sort of simulation. Probabilistic simulation is essentially a form of random sampling, with each run representing one observation. Consequently, statistical theory can be used to determine appropriate sample sizes. In effect, the larger the degree of variability inherent in simulation results, the greater the number of simulation runs needed in order to achieve a reasonable level of confidence that the results are truly indicative of model behavior.

The last step in the simulation process is to analyze and interpret the results. Interpretation of the results depends to a large extent on the degree to which the simulation model approximates reality; the closer the approximation, the less will be the need for "adjusting" the results. Moreover, the closer the approximation of the model to reality, the less the risk inherent in applying the results.

MONTE CARLO SIMULATION

There are many different kinds of simulation techniques. Our discussion will focus on probabilistic simulation using the *Monte Carlo* method. The technique gets its name from the famous Mediterranean resort often associated with games of chance. In fact, the chance element is an important aspect of Monte Carlo simulation; this approach can only be used when a process has a *random,* or chance component.

In the Monte Carlo method, a probability distribution is developed that reflects the random component of the system under study. Random samples taken from this probability distribution are analogous to observations made on the system itself. As the number of observations increases, the results of the simulation will tend to more closely approximate the random behavior of the real system, provided an appropriate model has been developed. Sampling is accomplished by the use of random numbers.

The basic steps in the process are as follows:

1. Identify a probability distribution for each random component of the system.
2. Work out an assignment so that intervals of random numbers will correspond to the probability distribution.
3. Obtain the random numbers needed for the study.
4. Interpret the results.

The random numbers used in Monte Carlo simulation can come from any source that will exhibit the necessary randomness. Typically, they come from one of two sources: large studies depend on computer-generated random numbers, while small studies may make use of numbers from a table of random digits like the one shown in Table 14S–1. The digits are listed in pairs for convenience, but can be used singly, in pairs, or in whatever grouping might be called for in a given problem.

There are two important features of sets of random numbers that are essential to simulation. One is that the numbers are uniformly distributed. This means that for any size grouping of digits (e.g., two-digit numbers), every possible outcome (e.g., 34, 89, 00) has the same probability of appearing. The second feature of these sets is that there are no discernable patterns in sequences of numbers that would enable one to predict future numbers in the sequence (hence the name *random* digits). This feature holds for any sequence of numbers; the numbers can be read across rows as well as up or down columns.

TABLE 14S–1

Random Digits

	1	2	3	4	5	6	7	8	9	10	11	12
1	18	20	84	29	91	73	64	33	15	67	54	07
2	25	19	05	64	26	41	20	09	88	40	73	34
3	73	57	80	35	04	52	81	48	57	61	29	35
4	12	48	37	09	17	63	94	08	28	78	51	23
5	54	92	27	61	58	39	25	16	10	46	87	17
6	96	40	65	75	16	49	03	82	38	33	51	20
7	23	55	93	83	02	19	67	89	80	44	99	72
8	31	96	81	65	60	93	75	64	26	90	18	59
9	45	49	70	10	13	79	32	17	98	63	30	05
10	01	78	32	17	24	54	52	44	28	50	27	68
11	41	62	57	31	90	18	24	15	43	85	31	97
12	22	07	38	72	69	66	14	85	36	71	41	58

An important point in using the table is to avoid always starting in the same spot, because that would result in the same sequence of numbers each time. Various methods exist for choosing a random starting point. One involves using the serial number of a dollar bill to select the row, column, and direction of number selection. Another approach is to use rolls of a die to choose the starting point. The importance of this not withstanding, for our purposes the starting point will be specified in each example or problem so that we may all obtain the same results.

The process of simulation will become clearer as we work through some simple problems.

EXAMPLE S–1

The manager of a machine shop is concerned about machine breakdowns. A decision has been made to simulate breakdowns for a 10-day period. Historical data on breakdowns over the last 100 days is given in the table below:

Number of breakdowns	Frequency
0	10
1	30
2	25
3	20
4	10
5	5
	100

Simulate breakdowns for a 10-day period. Read two-digit random numbers from Table 14S–1, starting at the top of column 1 and reading down.

Solution

a. Develop a cumulative probability distribution for breakdowns:
  (1) Convert frequencies into probabilities by dividing each frequency by the sum of the frequencies. Thus, 10 becomes 10/100 = .10, 30 becomes 30/100 = .30, and so on.
  (2) Develop cumulative probabilities by successive summing. The results are shown in the following table:

Number of breakdowns	Frequency	Probability	Cumulative probability
0	10	.10	.10
1	30	.30	.40
2	25	.25	.65
3	20	.20	.85
4	10	.10	.95
5	5	.05	1.00
	100	1.00	

EXAMPLE S–1 (continued)

b. Assign random number intervals so that they correspond to the cumulative probabilities for breakdowns. (Note: two-digit numbers are used because the probabilities are given to two decimal places.) We want there to be a 10 percent probability of obtaining the event "0 breakdowns" in our simulation. Therefore, we must designate 10 percent of the possible random numbers as corresponding to that event. Since the numbers are evenly distributed between 00 and 99 (i.e., there are 100 two-digit numbers), we assign the 10 numbers 00 to 09 to that event.

Similarly, we assign the numbers 10 to 39 to "one breakdown," the numbers 40 to 64 to "two breakdowns," the numbers 65 to 84 to "three breakdowns," the numbers 85 to 94 to "4 breakdowns" and 95 to 99 to "five breakdowns." (Notice that the ending number of each random number interval is one less than the cumulative probability and that each interval begins at the cumulative probability for the last event, except the first one, which begins at 00.) The results are shown below.

Number of breakdowns	Frequency	Probability	Cumulative probability	Corresponding random numbers
0	10	.10	.10	00 to 09
1	30	.30	.40	10 to 39
2	25	.25	.65	40 to 64
3	20	.20	.85	65 to 84
4	10	.10	.95	85 to 94
5	5	.05	1.00	95 to 99
	100	1.00		

c. Obtain the random numbers from Table 14S–1, column 1, as specified in the problem:

18   25   73   12   54   96   23   31   45   01

d. Convert the random numbers into numbers of breakdowns:

18 falls in the interval 10 to 39 and corresponds, therefore, to one breakdown in day 1.

25 falls in the interval 10 to 39, which corresponds to one breakdown on day 2.

73 corresponds to three breakdowns on day 3.

12 corresponds to one breakdown on day 4.

54 corresponds to two breakdowns on day 5.

96 corresponds to five breakdowns on day 6.

23 corresponds to one breakdown on day 7.

31 corresponds to one breakdown on day 8.

45 corresponds to two breakdowns on day 9.

01 corresponds to no breakdowns on day 10.

EXAMPLE S–1 (concluded)
These results are summarized in the table below.

Day	Random number	Simulated number of breakdowns
1	18	1
2	25	1
3	73	3
4	12	1
5	54	2
6	96	5
7	23	1
8	31	1
9	45	2
10	01	0
		$\overline{17}$

The mean number of breakdowns for this 10-period simulation is $17/10 = 1.7$ breakdowns per day. Compare this to the *expected* number of breakdowns based on the historical data:

$$0(.10) + 1(.30) + 2(.25) + 3(.20) + 4(.10) + 5(.05) = 2.05 \text{ per day}$$

Several comments come to mind at this point:

1. This simple example is intended to illustrate the basic concepts of Monte Carlo simulation. If our only goal was to estimate the average number of breakdowns, we would not have to simulate; we could base the estimate on the historical data alone.
2. The simulation should be viewed as a *sample;* it is quite likely that additional runs of 10 numbers would produce different means.
3. Because of the variability inherent in the results of small samples, it would be unwise to attempt to draw any firm conclusions from them; in an actual study, much larger sample sizes would be used.

In some cases it can be helpful to construct a flowchart that describes a simulation. This is especially true if the simulation will involve periodic updating of system values (e.g., amount of inventory on hand), as illustrated in the following example.

EXAMPLE S–2
The manager of a small truck-dealership wants to acquire some insight into how a proposed policy for reordering trucks might affect order frequency. Under the new policy, two trucks are to be ordered

EXAMPLE S–2 (continued)

whenever the number of trucks on hand is five or less. Due to the nearness of the dealer to the home office, orders can be filled overnight. According to the dealer's records, the probability distribution for daily demand is as shown below:

x demand	$P(x)$
0	.50
1	.40
2	.10

1. Construct a flowchart that describes a 10-day simulation.
2. Use two-digit random numbers from Table 14S–1, column 11, reading down. Assume a beginning inventory of 7 trucks.

Solution

a.

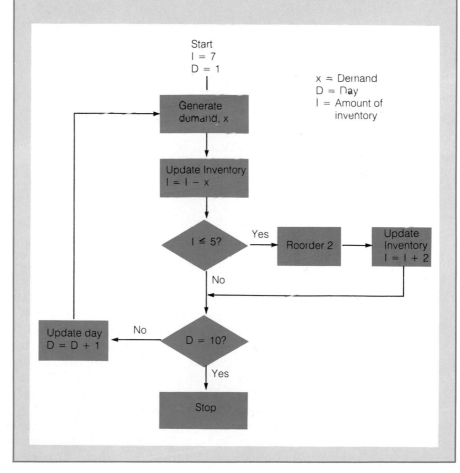

EXAMPLE S–2 (concluded)

b. (1) Assign digits to probabilities:

x	P(x)	Cumulative P(x)	Digits
0 . .	.50	.50	00–49
1 . .	.40	.90	50–89
2 . .	.10	1.00	90–99

(2) Obtain random numbers, convert to demand, update inventory accordingly, and reorder when necessary:

Day	Random number	x demand	Beginning inventory	Ending inventory
1	54	1	7	6
2	73	1	6	5 (reorder 2; new beginning inventory = 5 + 2)
3	29	0	7	7
4	51	1	7	6
5	87	1	6	5 (reorder 2; new beginning inventory = 5 + 2)
6	51	1	7	6
7	99	2	6	4 (reorder 2; new beginning inventory = 4 + 2)
8	18	0	6	6
9	30	0	6	6
10	27	0	6	6

Simulating Theoretical Distributions

In many instances a simulation will involve the use of theoretical distributions. Among the most frequently encountered theoretical distributions are the Poisson, normal, and exponential distributions. Consequently, an ability to simulate these distributions will greatly enhance knowledge and appreciation of simulation.

In order to simulate a Poisson distribution, the mean of the distribution is required. Knowledge of the mean enables one to obtain cumulative probabilities for the distribution from Appendix Table C, which provide the basis for random number assignments. Table 14S–1 can be used to obtain random numbers. Since the probabilities in Appendix Table C are three-digit numbers, three-digit random numbers must be read from Table 14S–1 in order to achieve correspondence. The following example illustrates these concepts.

EXAMPLE S–3

The number of lost-time accidents at a large plant has been determined from historical records to be two per day. Moreover, it has been determined that this accident rate can be well-approximated by a Poisson distribution that has a mean of 2.0. Simulate five days of accident experience for the plant. Read random numbers from columns 1–2.

Solution

First, obtain the cumulative distribution from Appendix Table C for a mean of 2.0 and make the range assignments:

x	Cumulative probability	Random number ranges
0	.135	000 to 134
1	.406	135 to 405
2	.677	406 to 676
3	.857	677 to 856
4	.947	857 to 946
5	.983	947 to 982
6	.995	983 to 994
7	.999	995 to 998
8	1.000	999

Next, obtain three-digit numbers from Table 14S–1. Reading from columns 1–2 as instructed, we find 182, 251, 735, 124, and 549.

Finally, convert the random numbers into number of lost-time accidents using the established set of ranges. Hence, since 182 falls in the second range, it corresponds to one accident on day 1. Likewise, the second random number, 251, falls in the same range, indicating one accident on day 2. The 735 falls between 677 and 856, which corresponds to three accidents on day 3; the 124 corresponds to 0 accidents on day 4; and 549 corresponds to two accidents on day 5.

The normal distribution can be important in many problems. There are a number of ways to simulate a normal distribution, but perhaps the simplest is to use a table of normally distributed random numbers, such as Table 14S–2. The basis of the table is a normal distribution with a mean of 0 and a standard deviation of 1.00. Like all such tables, the numbers are arranged randomly, so that when read in any sequence they duplicate "randomness." In order to use the table we must have the parameters of a normal distribution (i.e., its mean and standard deviation) in mind. Numbers obtained from the random number table can then be converted into "actual" values by multiplying the standard deviation by the random number and adding this amount to the mean. That is:

$$\text{Simulated value} = \text{Mean} + \text{Random number} \times \text{Standard deviation} \quad \text{(14S–1)}$$

TABLE 14S–2

Normally Distributed Random Numbers

	1	2	3	4	5	6	7	8	9	10
1	1.46	0.09	−0.59	0.19	−0.52	−1.82	0.53	−1.12	1.36	−0.44
2	−1.05	0.56	−0.67	−0.16	1.39	−1.21	0.45	−0.62	−0.95	0.27
3	0.15	−0.02	0.41	−0.09	−0.61	−0.18	−0.63	−1.20	0.27	−0.50
4	0.81	1.87	0.51	0.33	−0.32	1.19	2.18	−2.17	1.10	0.70
5	0.74	−0.44	1.53	−1.76	0.01	0.47	0.07	0.22	−0.59	−1.03
6	−0.39	0.35	−0.37	−0.52	−1.14	0.27	−1.78	0.43	1.15	−0.31
7	0.45	0.23	0.26	−0.31	−0.19	−0.03	−0.92	0.38	−0.04	0.16
8	2.40	0.38	−0.15	−1.04	−0.76	1.12	−0.37	−0.71	−1.11	0.25
9	0.59	−0.70	−0.04	0.12	1.60	0.34	−0.05	−0.26	0.41	0.80
10	−0.06	0.83	−1.60	−0.28	0.28	−0.15	0.73	−0.13	−0.75	−1.49

In effect, the random number equates to a normal z value, which indicates how far a particular value is above or below the distribution mean.

EXAMPLE S–4

It has been determined that the time required to perform a certain task can be described by a normal distribution that has a mean of 30 minutes and a standard deviation of four minutes. Simulate times for three jobs using the first three values in column 1 of Table 14S–2.

Solution

The first three values are: 1.46, −1.05, and 0.15. The simulated values are:

$$\text{For } \;\;1.46, 30 + 1.46(4) = 35.84 \text{ minutes}$$
$$\text{For } -1.05, 30 - 1.05(4) = 25.80 \text{ minutes}$$
$$\text{For } \;\;0.15, 30 + 0.15(4) = 30.60 \text{ minutes}$$

It is important to recognize that the last example involves a continuous variable, whereas the previous examples have involved discrete variables. (Remember that discrete variables typically take on only integer values while continuous variables can take on integer and noninteger values.) Whenever possible, a model of a continuous variable should be able to simulate noninteger values as well as integer values.

Another continuous type of distribution we can consider is the uniform distribution, in which values may occur anywhere over a continuous range between two extremes, a and b, as illustrated in Figure 14S–1.

FIGURE 14S–1

A Uniform
Distribution

Simulated values for a uniform distribution are determined in this way:

(14S–2)

Simulated value $= a + (b - a)$ (random number as a percentage)

Converting the random number to a percentage simply involves placing a decimal point at the left of the number. For example, 77 becomes .77.

EXAMPLE S–5

Job times vary uniformly between 10 and 15 minutes. Use Table 14S–1 to simulate job times for four jobs. Read numbers from column 9 going down.

Solution

$$a = 10 \text{ minutes}, b = 15 \text{ minutes, so } a - b = 5 \text{ minutes.}$$

a. Obtain the random numbers: 15, 88, 57, and 28.
b. Convert to simulated values:

Random number	Computation	Simulated value (minutes)
15	$10 + 5(.15)$ =	10.75
88	$10 + 5(.88)$ =	14.40
57	$10 + 5(.57)$ =	12.85
28	$10 + 5(.28)$ =	11.40

A third continuous distribution is the exponential distribution. We shall concern ourselves with simulating values of *negative* exponential distributions, as portrayed in Figure 14S–2.

With a negative exponential distribution, the probability is fairly high that the random variable will assume a value close to zero. Moreover, the probability decreases as the specified value of the random variable increases. The probability that a random variable will take on a value greater than some specified value t, given

FIGURE 14S–2

A Negative
Exponential
Distribution

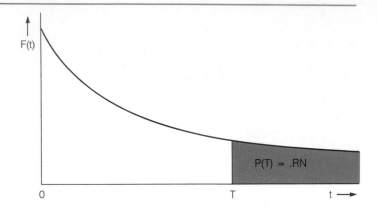

that the variable can be described by an exponential distribution with a mean equal to $\frac{1}{\lambda}$, is given by the equation

$$P(T) = e^{-\lambda t} \qquad \text{(14S–3)}$$

To simulate exponential values, we select a random number, place a decimal point at the left of it, set this equal to the probability P(T), and solve the above equation for t. The result is a simulated value from an exponential distribution with a mean of λ.

We can obtain an expression for t by taking the natural logarithm of both sides of the equation. Thus, with P(T) = .RN, we have

$$1n(.RN) = 1n(e^{-\lambda t})$$

The natural logarithm of a power of e is equal to the power itself, so

$$1n(.RN) = 1n(e^{-\lambda t}) = -\lambda t.$$

$$\text{Then } t = -\frac{1}{\lambda} 1n(.RN). \qquad \text{(14S–4)}$$

This concept is illustrated in Figure 14S–2.

Values of random numbers can be obtained using Table 14S–1, as demonstrated in the following example.

EXAMPLE S–6

Times between breakdowns of a certain type of equipment can be described by an exponential distribution with a mean of five hours. Simulate the time between two breakdowns. Read two-digit random numbers from column 3 of Table 14S–1.

> **EXAMPLE S–6 (concluded)**
> **Solution**
>
> $\frac{1}{\lambda} = 5$ hours. The random numbers are 84 and 05. Using equation (14S–4), the simulated times are:
>
> For 84, $t = -5[1n(.84)] = -5[-.1744] = .872$ hours.
> For 05, $t = -5[1n(.05)] = -5[-2.9957] = 14.979$ hours.
>
> Note that the smaller the value of the random number, the larger the simulated value of t.

SIMULATION APPLICATIONS

Simulation has applications across a broad spectrum of operations management problems. In some instances the simulations are quite modest, while in others they are rather involved. Their usefulness, however, depends on the degree to which decision makers are able to answer their "what if . . ." questions.

Generally speaking, the simulation approach is used either because optimization techniques are unavailable or because the assumptions required by an optimizing technique are not reasonably satisfied in a given situation. Queuing problems are a good example of the latter reason. Although waiting-line problems are pervasive, the rather restrictive assumptions of arrival and service distributions in many cases are simply not met. Very often, analysts will then turn to simulation as a reasonable alternative for obtaining descriptive information about the system in question.

If you were to go down the list of operations management topics, you would find that most have simulation applications. For instance, simulation is often helpful in product design and testing, layout of facilities, line balancing, job design, aggregate planning, testing alternative inventory policies, scheduling, and project management. Actually, the list is quite long. The books and articles noted in the bibliography of this chapter give an indication of the richness and breadth of those applications and offer the interested reader an opportunity to explore this fascinating and useful subject in more detail.

COMPUTER SIMULATION

Although the emphasis in this supplement has been on manual simulation in order to convey its main concepts, most real-life simulations involve the use of a computer. Computers offer relatively quick and easy means of obtaining results. Many real-life applications involve fairly complex simulation models that have substantial record-keeping requirements, and computers offer a practical way to do this.

Over the years a number of simulation languages have been developed that make the task of writing simulation programs much simpler than the use of such standard programming languages as FORTRAN and BASIC. Some of the more widely used specialty languages include SIMSCRIPT, GPSS, GASP, and DYNAMO. In addition, there are a number of other simulation packages, some of which have very narrow focuses that relate to queuing or network problems. Most of the simulation packages have certain features in common. For example, they generally provide for random number generation from a variety of statistical distributions as well as collection and tabulation of simulation results and time keeping.

It should be noted that some managers prefer to write their own simulations, or have a member of their staff do so, using a standard programming language rather than a simulation language. In cases where simulation is used infrequently, it can be more practical to use that approach rather than to go through the time and effort to use a specialty language. Similarly, for simple problems, the slight inefficiency related to the use of a standard language is not usually an important consideration.

ADVANTAGES AND LIMITATIONS OF USING SIMULATION

Among the main advantages of simulation are the following:

1. It lends itself to problems that are difficult or impossible to solve mathematically.
2. It permits an analyst to experiment with system behavior while avoiding the risks that would be inherent in experimenting with the actual system.
3. It compresses time so that managers can quickly discern long-term effects.
4. It can serve as a valuable tool for training decision makers by building up their experience and understanding of system behavior under a wide range of conditions.

There are also certain limitations associated with simulation. Some of the chief limitations are:

1. Simulation does not produce an optimum solution; it merely indicates an *approximate* behavior for a given set of inputs.
2. A large-scale simulation can require considerable effort to

develop a suitable model as well as considerable computer time to obtain simulations.

3. Monte Carlo simulation is applicable only in situations that have elements that can be described by random variables.

Because simulation produces an *approximate* answer rather than an exact solution and because of the cost of running a simulation study, simulation is not generally the first choice of a decision maker. Instead, depending on the complexity of the situation, intuitive or analytical methods should first be investigated. Very often in simple cases, an intuitive solution will be acceptable. In more complex cases, an analytical solution would be preferable, assum-

FIGURE 14S–3

Choosing a Solution Technique

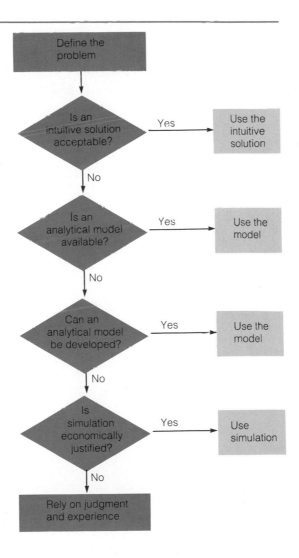

ing an appropriate technique is available. If not, it may be feasible to attempt to develop an analytical model that could be used to generate a solution. If these measures are rejected, simulation becomes the next logical possibility. However, its use may not be economically justifiable, in which case the decision maker will have to resort to the use of judgment and experience. In effect, after reevaluating all the alternatives, the decision maker must revert to an intuitive solution, even though initially that approach did not appear acceptable. This process is outlined in Figure 14S–3.

1. The number of customers who arrive at a transmission repair shop can be described by a Poisson distribution that has a mean of three per hour. Assuming the distribution holds for an entire eight-hour day, simulate customer arrivals for the first four hours of a day. Read random numbers from Table 14S–1, columns 4 and 5, going down.

Solution

a. Obtain cumulative probabilities of the Poisson distribution from Appendix Table C for the mean specified. (Those values are given below for convenience.)

x	Cumulative probability
0	.050
1	.199
2	.423
3	.647
4	.815
5	.916
6	.966
7	.988
8	.996
9	.999
10	1.000

b. Obtain the random numbers: 299, 642, 350, and 091. (Note: three-digit numbers are needed because the probabilities are given to three decimal places.)

c. Convert the random numbers into number of arrivals: First, place a decimal point in front of each random number. Then note where each number falls in the cumulative probability list. For instance, .299 falls between .199 and .423, or between $x = 1$ and $x = 2$. Assign the larger x value to that random number (i.e., interpret this to mean two customers arrive in the first hour). Similarly, .642 is interpreted to mean three customers arrive in the second hour; .350 implies two customers in the third hour, and .091 implies one customer in the fourth hour. (Note: If a random number turns out to be exactly equal to one of the cumulative probabilities, round up to the next largest x value. For example, the random number .199 would be interpreted as *two* customers per hour.)

In sum, the number of customers per hour for the four-hour simulation is:

Hour	Number of arrivals
1	2
2	3
3	2
4	1

2. Jobs arrive at a work station at fixed intervals of one hour. Processing time is approximately normal and has a mean of 56 minutes per job and a standard deviation of four minutes per job. Using the fifth row of the table of normally distributed random numbers (14S–2), simulate the processing times for four jobs and determine the amount of operator idle time and job waiting time. Assume the first job arrives at time $= 0$.

Solution

a. Obtain the random numbers from the table: 0.74, −0.44, 1.53, and −1.76.

b. Convert the random numbers into simulated processing times:

Random number	Compu-tation	Simulated time
0.74	$56 + 4(\ 0.74) =$	58.96
−0.44	$56 + 4(-0.44) =$	54.24
1.53	$56 + 4(\ 1.53) =$	62.12
−1.76	$56 + 4(-1.76) =$	48.96

Note that three of the times are less than the interarrival times for the jobs, meaning the operator may be idle after those three jobs. One time exceeds the one-hour interval, so the next job must wait, and possibly the job following it if the waiting plus processing time exceeds 60 minutes.

c. Compute waiting/idle times:

Job number	Arrives at	Processing time, t (minutes)	$60-t$ Operator idle (minutes)	$t-60$ Next job waits (minutes)
1	0	58.96	1.04	—
2	60	54.24	5.76	—
3	120	62.12	—	2.12
4	180	48.96	8.92	—
			15.72	2.12

3. The time between mechanics' requests for tools in a large plant is normally distributed with a mean of 10 minutes and a standard deviation of 1 minute. The time to fill requests is also normal with a mean of nine minutes per request and a standard deviation of one minute. Mechanics' waiting time represents a cost of $2 per minute, and servers represent a cost of $1 per minute. Simulate arrivals for the first nine mechanic requests and their service times, and determine the mechanics' waiting time assuming one server. Would it be economical to add another server? Explain. Use Table 14S–2, column 8 for requests and column 9 for service.

Solution

a. Obtain random numbers and convert to times [see columns *(a)* and *(b)* in the following table for requests and columns *(f)* and *(g)* for service].

	Customer arrivals				Service		
(a)	*(b)*	*(c)*	*(d)*	*(e)*	*(f)*	*(g)*	*(h)*
		(cumulative time)	*(e − c) Customer*				*(e + g)*
Random →	*Time between*	*Arrival*	*waiting*	*Service*	*Random →*	*Service*	*Service*
number	*arrivals*	*time*	*time*	*begins*	*number*	*time*	*ends*
−1.12	8.88	8.88	0.00	8.88	1.36	10.36	19.24
−0.62	9.38	18.26	0.98	19.24	−0.95	9.05	28.29
−1.20	8.80	27.06	1.23	28.29	0.27	9.27	37.56
−2.17	7.83	34.89	2.67	37.56	1.10	10.10	47.66
0.22	10.22	45.11	2.55	47.66	−0.59	8.41	56.07
0.43	10.43	55.54	0.53	56.07	1.15	10.15	66.22
0.38	10.38	65.92	0.30	66.22	−0.04	8.96	75.18
−0.71	9.39	75.31	0.00	75.31	−1.11	7.89	83.20
−0.26	9.74	85.05	0.00	85.05	0.41	8.59	93.64
			8.26				

b. Determine arrival times [column *(c)*] by successive adding of times between arrivals in column *(b)*.

c. Use arrival times for service start *unless service is still in progress on a previous request.* In that case, determine how long the arrival must wait [column *(e − c)*]. Column *(e)* values are the sum of starting time and service time [column *(g)*], which is the time service ends [column *(h)*]. Thus, service on each new request begins [column *(e)*] at the same time that service on the previous request [column *(h)*] ends.

d. The simulation and resulting waiting times for the first nine arrivals are shown in the table. Total waiting time is 8.26 minutes.

e. The total cost for the 93.64 minutes (end of service on the ninth request) of the simulation is:

Waiting cost. . .   8.26 minutes at $2 per minute = $ 16.52
Server cost . . .   93.64 minutes at $1 per minute =   93.64
                                                        $110.16

f. Usually, a second simulation with two servers would be needed (but with the same arrival times so that the results would be comparable). However, in this case it is apparent that a second server would increase server cost by about $93, but could not eliminate more than $16.52 of waiting cost. Hence, the second server would not be justified.

DISCUSSION AND REVIEW QUESTIONS

1. What is a *simulation?*
2. What are some of the primary reasons for the widespread use of simulation techniques in practice?
3. What are some of the ways simulation can be used?
4. What role do random numbers play in Monte Carlo simulations?
5. How would you respond to this comment?

"I ran the simulation several times, and each run gave me a different result. Therefore, the technique does not seem to be useful. I need answers!"

6. Briefly discuss the main advantage of simulation.

7. What are some of the limitations of simulation as a tool for decision making?

PROBLEMS

1. The number of jobs received by a small shop is to be simulated for an eight-day period. The shop manager has collected the following data:

Number of jobs	Frequency
2 or less	0
3	10
4	50
5	80
6	40
7	16
8	4
9 or more	0
	200

Use the third column of Table 14S–1 and read two-digit numbers, going down. Determine the average number of jobs per day for the eight-day simulation period.

2. Jack M. sells insurance on a part-time basis. His records on the number of policies sold per week over a 50-week period are given in the table below:

Number sold	Frequency
0	8
1	15
2	17
3	7
4	3
	50

Simulate three five-day periods: use Table 14S–1, column 6 for the first simulation, column 7 for the second, and column 8 for the third. In each case, read two-digit numbers, beginning at the *bottom* of the column and going *up*. For each simulation, determine the percentage of days that two or more policies are sold.

3. After a careful study of requests for a special tool at a large tool crib, an analyst has concluded that demand for the tool can be adequately described by a Poisson distribution with a mean of two requests per day. Simulate demand for a twelve working day period for this tool using Table 14S–1. Read three-digit numbers from columns 5 and 6 combined, starting at the *top* and reading *down* (e.g., 917, 264, 045).

4. The number of lost-time accidents at a logging firm can be described using a Poisson distribution that has a mean of four accidents per month. Using the last two columns of Table 14S–1 (e.g., 540, 733, 293), simulate accidents for a 12-month period.

5. The time a physician spends with patients can be modeled using a normal distribution that has a mean of 20 minutes and a standard deviation of 2 minutes. Using the table of normally distributed random numbers (14S–2), simulate the times the doctor might spend with the next seven patients. Use column 4 of the table, start at the bottom of the column and read up.

6. Jobs are delivered to a work station at random intervals. The time between job arrivals tends to be normally distributed with a mean of 15 minutes and a standard deviation of 1 minute. Job processing time is also normally distributed with a mean of 14 minutes per job and a standard deviation of 2 minutes.

   a. Using Table 14S–2, simulate the arrival and processing of five jobs. Use column 4 of the table for job arrival times and column 3 for processing times. *Start each column at row 4.* Find the total times jobs wait for processing.

   b. The company is considering the use of new equipment that would result in processing time that is normal with a mean of 13 minutes and a standard deviation of 1 minute. Job waiting represents a cost of $3 per minute, and the new equipment would represent an additional cost of $.50 per minute. Would the equipment be cost justified? (Note: use the same arrival *times* and the same *random numbers* for processing times.)

7. Daily usage of sugar in a small bakery can be described by a uniform distribution

with end points of 30 pounds and 50 pounds. Assuming usage is independent of the day of the week, simulate daily usage for a 10-day period. Read four-digit numbers from Table 14S–1, columns 5 and 6, going up, starting at the bottom.

8. Weekly usage of spare parts for a specialized machine can be described by a Poisson distribution with a mean of 2.8 parts per week. Lead time to replenish the supply of spare parts is two weeks (constant). Simulate the total usage of parts during lead time 10 times and then determine the frequency of lead-time demands (i.e., what percentage of times was the demand equal to 2, 3, 4, etc.?) Read four-digit numbers from Table 14S–1, columns 8 and 9, going down.

9. (Computer exercise.) Repeat the previous problem for 100 lead-time periods.

10. A repair shop breaks an average of 0.6 tools per day. The average number of days required to obtain replacements is six. (Parts are delivered by mail once each day.) Both breakages and delivery times can be described by Poisson distributions. Tools are reordered whenever three or more must be replaced. Simulate.
   a. Draw a flowchart to describe this process.
   b. Simulate breakage, ordering, and receipt for a 12-day period. Read three-digit numbers from Table 14S–1, columns 5 and 6 going down (e.g., 917, 264), for tool breakage, and columns 7 and 8 going down (e.g., 643, 200) for delivery time. Assume zero tools in inventory to start.

11. (Computer exercise.) Repeat the previous problem for 150 days.

12. Customers arrival randomly at a catalog department of a large store. The time between arrivals varies uniformly between 10 and 20 minutes. Service time is normal with a mean of 15 minutes and a standard deviation of 2 minutes.
   a. Simulate processing and waiting times for nine customers. Read three-digit numbers going down columns 9 and 10, Table 14S–1, for arrivals (e.g.,

156, 884, 576). Use column 8, Table 14S–2, for processing time.
   b. If management can reduce the range of arrival times to between 13 and 17 minutes, what would the impact be on customer waiting times? [Use the same service times and the same random numbers for arrival times from part (a).] Round arrival times to two decimal places.

13. Probabilities have been determined for the movements of the ball in a pinball game, as shown below, along with the points awarded if the ball strikes a given position. Simulate the paths of three balls and compute the number of points awarded for each ball. Use column 1 of Table 14S–1 for the first ball, column 2 for the second ball, and column 3 for the third ball, reading down the columns.

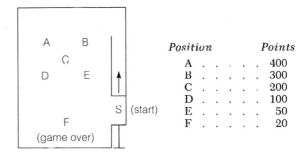

Position					Points
A	.	.	.	.	400
B	.	.	.	.	300
C	.	.	.	.	200
D	.	.	.	.	100
E	.	.	.	.	50
F	.	.	.	.	20

Path	Probability	Path	Probability
S to A	.30	C to A	.10
B	.30	B	.15
C	.25	C	.20
D	.10	D	.15
E	.04	E	.25
F	.01	F	.15
A to A	.25	D to A	.10
B	.25	B	.05
C	.25	C	.25
D	.10	D	.20
E	.10	E	.25
F	.05	F	.15
B to A	.30	E to A	.05
B	.20	B	.10
C	.20	C	.15
D	.15	D	.15
E	.10	E	.20
F	.05	F	.35

(Hint: Construct a cumulative probability distribution for each of the six cases. Each new random number indicates the next position to move to. Each ball must start at S.)

14. Repeat the previous problem using columns 1, 2, and 3 for the next three balls, reading *up* from the bottom.

15. An analyst found that the length of telephone conversations in an office could be described by an exponential distribution with a mean of 4 minutes. Reading two-digit random numbers from Table 14S–1, column 6, simulate the length of 5 calls and compute the simulated average time. Why is the simulated average different than the mean of 4 minutes?

16. The length of time between calls for service of a certain piece of equipment can be described by an exponential distribution with a mean of 40 minutes. Service time can be described by a normal distribution with a mean of 8 minutes and a standard deviation of 2 minutes. Simulate the time until the first breakdown and the times between four breakdowns as well as the four service times. For breakdowns, read two-digit numbers from Table 14S–1, row 7, and for service times, read numbers from Table 14S–2, row 8.

17. The number of jobs per day that a repair shop gets can be described by a Poisson distribution with a mean of 3.0. Repair time per job can be described by an exponential distribution with a mean of 6 hours. Simulate the number of jobs received for a four-day period and the repair time for each job. What is the simulated total repair time per day? For number of jobs received, read two-digit numbers from Table 14S–1, row 1, and for repair times, read two-digit numbers from row 2 of the same table.

18. A service operation consists of three steps. The first step can be described by a uniform distribution that ranges between 5 and 9 minutes. The second step can be described by a normal distribution with a mean of 7 minutes and a standard deviation of 1 minute, and the third step can

be described by an exponential distribution with a mean of 5 minutes. Simulate three cycles reading two-digit numbers from Table 14S–1, row 4 for step 1, Table 14S–2, row 6 for step 2, and two-digit numbers from column 4 of Table 14S–1 for step 3. Determine the simulated time for each of the three cycles.

19. A project consists of eight major activities, as illustrated in the accompanying diagram. Activity times are normally distributed with means and standard deviations as shown in the following table. Note that there are two paths *through* the project: 1–2–3–5 and 1–2–4–5. Project duration is defined as the largest sum of times along a path. Simulate 12 times for each activity. Use columns 1 and 2 of Table 14S–2 for activity 1–2, columns 3 and 4 for activity 2–3, columns 5 and 6 for activity 2–4, columns 7 and 8 for activity 3–5, and columns 9 and 10 for activity 4–5. Determine the project duration for each of the 12 sets and then prepare a frequency distribution of project duration. Use categories of 25 to less than 30, 30 to less than 35, 35 to less than 40, 40 to less than 45, and 45 or more. Determine the proportion of time that a simulated duration of less than 40 days occurred. How might this information be used?

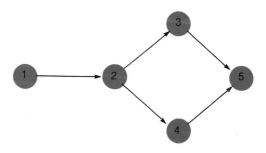

Activity	Mean	Standard deviation
1–2	10 days	2 days
2–3	12	2
2–4	15	3
3–5	14	2
4–5	8	1

SELECTED BIBLIOGRAPHY

Barton, R. *A Primer on Simulation and Gaming.* Englewood Cliffs, N.J.: Prentice-Hall, 1970.

Buffa, Elwood. *Operations Management.* 3d ed. New York: John Wiley & Sons, 1972.

Chase, Richard, and Nicholas Aquilano. *Production and Operations Management.* 3d ed. Homewood, Ill.: Richard D. Irwin, 1981.

Graybeal, W., and U. Pooch. *Simulation: Principles and Methods.* Cambridge: Winthrop Publishers, 1980.

Hillier, Fredericks S., and Gerald J. Lieberman. *Introduction to Operations Research.* 2d ed. San Francisco: Holden-Day, 1974.

Law, A. M., and W. D. Kelton. *Simulation Modeling and Analysis.* New York: McGraw-Hill, 1982.

Meier, R. C.; W. T. Newell; and H. L. Pazer. *Simulation in Business and Economics.* Englewood Cliffs, N.J.: Prentice-Hall, 1969.

Schmidt, J. W., and R. E. Taylor. *Simulation and Analysis of Industrial Systems.* Homewood, Ill. Richard D. Irwin, 1970.

Shannon, Robert E. *Systems Simulation: The Art and Science.* Englewood Cliffs, N.J.: Prentice-Hall, 1975.

Smith, David E. *Quantitative Business Analysis.* New York: John Wiley & Sons, 1977.

Watson, Hugh J. *Computer Simulation in Business.* New York: John Wiley & Sons, 1981.

Chapter 15

Quality Assurance

After completing this chapter, you should be able to:

1. Define the term quality and tell why quality is important for the organization.
2. Discuss the determinants of quality and some of the avenues available for improving quality.
3. Describe quality circles and their potential benefits.
4. Discuss the major inspection decisions managers must make.
5. Contrast variables and attributes inspection.
6. Describe the major features of acceptance sampling.
7. Differentiate between acceptance sampling and process control.
8. List and briefly explain the elements of the control process.
9. Explain how control charts are used to monitor a process and the concepts that underlie the use of control charts.
10. Use and interpret control charts.
11. Use run tests to check for nonrandomness in process output.

INTRODUCTION, 734

Defining Quality, 734

THE IMPORTANCE OF QUALITY, 737

DETERMINANTS OF QUALITY, 739

THE EVOLUTION OF QUALITY CONTROL, 741

IMPROVING QUALITY, 742

QUALITY OF CONFORMANCE, 749

INSPECTION, 750

How Much to Inspect and How Often, 750
Where in the Process to Inspect, 752
Centralized versus On-Site Inspection, 753
Attributes versus Variables Inspection, 753

ACCEPTANCE SAMPLING, 753

Sampling Plans, 754
Operating Characteristic Curve, 755
Average Quality of Inspected Lots, 761

PROCESS CONTROL, 763

The Control Process, 763
Variations and Control, 764
Control Charts, 765
Control Charts for Variables, 766
Control Charts for Attributes, 772
Tolerances, Control Limits, and Process Variability, 775
Run Tests, 777

SUMMARY, 780

SOLVED PROBLEMS, 783

DISCUSSION AND REVIEW QUESTIONS, 788

PROBLEMS, 788

SELECTED BIBLIOGRAPHY, 792

CASE: MARION CAMP MEMORIAL HOSPITAL, 793

CASE: ANYONE FOR SUSHI? 794

Establishing quality levels for goods or services and assuring that those levels are achieved are vital tasks for virtually every type of business organization and government agency. Quality—or lack of quality—can have far-reaching consequences. In profit-oriented firms, quality can have a strong impact on differentiation among competitors and, ultimately, on the profits and losses firms experience. This is true whether the firm is engaged in manufacturing, banking, transportation, tourism, health care, or repair work. By the same token, quality is important in nonprofit organizations such as schools, state and local governments, federal agencies, and the like, where political, economic, and social pressures have an impact. Moreover, social services, including public safety, postal services, waste removal and disposal, highway planning and construction, and fire protection are coming under increasing scrutiny, both in terms of cost and quality. In addition, legal and professional standards may fix minimum acceptable quality levels.

Quality assurance is concerned with the entire range of production, beginning with product or service design, continuing through the transformation process, and extending to service after delivery. The current view of quality assurance is that in order for it to be successful, it must be all-inclusive.

The chapter begins with a definition of quality, a list of reasons for the importance of quality, a discussion of the major determinants of quality, and an outline of some ways of improving quality. Since measurement is a key factor in control, the subject of inspection is discussed, with emphasis on the major managerial decisions that must be made. The remainder of the chapter is divided into two parts. The first of these is acceptance sampling, which relates to inspection of lots or batches of previously produced goods or services. The second part concerns process control, which involves monitoring an ongoing process for the purpose of deciding when corrective action is necessary so that *future* output will be acceptable.

INTRODUCTION

Decisions on quality are among the most important ones that managers are called upon to make. In this section we examine how quality is defined and why decisions on quality are so important.

Defining Quality   The term *quality* is used in a variety of ways. Sometimes it refers to *grade* of a product, as in USDA PRIME and grade A eggs. At other times it refers to materials, workmanship, or special features, such as "fine leather," "expertly handcrafted," or "waterproof." As a practical matter, we can think of two major categories of quality: quality of *design* and quality of *conformance.*

Quality of design refers to the intention of the designer to include or exclude certain features in a good or service. For instance, the general purpose of an automobile is to provide transportation. However, models and manufacturers differ in terms of size, comfort, fuel economy, appearance, roominess, road handling ability, and performance. These are the result of deliberate choices made by designers that affect the quality of design.

Quality of conformance refers to the degree to which goods and services conform to (i.e., achieve) the intent of design. This is affected by such factors as the capability of equipment used to produce the good or service, the training and skills of workers, the extent to which design lends itself to production, the degree of monitoring of output to assess conformance, and motivation of workers.

Both aspects of quality are important; the best design in the world cannot overcome poor workmanship, nor can workmanship, however good, overcome a poor design. Since the remainder of the chapter concentrates on achieving quality of conformance, it will be helpful to at least mention some of the salient aspects of quality of design.

Design choices are usually the result of marketing input (what can we sell?) and manufacturing (what can we produce?). Naturally, a firm has to consider if it can produce at a cost that will enable it to make a reasonable profit. Maximizing profit generally does not mean achieving the highest design quality that is technically feasible. Consumers would not generally appreciate that level of quality, nor would they be willing to pay the price. Thus, it may be technically feasible to produce a stick of bubblegum that would retain its flavor forever, but at $300 a piece, not many people would stand in line to buy it. Hence, the goal of selecting the design quality is to maximize the difference between the cost to provide quality and the value (price) to the consumer. This is illustrated in Figure 15–1.

From the consumers' perspective, what is desired is a reasonable quality level and a reasonable price. Generally speaking, consumers are interested in one or more of the following, depending on the item in question: how it looks, how well it works, and how long it will last. In other words, the quality of a good or service is often perceived by the consumer in terms of:

1. Appearance.
2. Operation.
3. Reliability.

These are viewed by consumers as determinants of "fitness for use."

FIGURE 15–1

The Optimum Design Quality

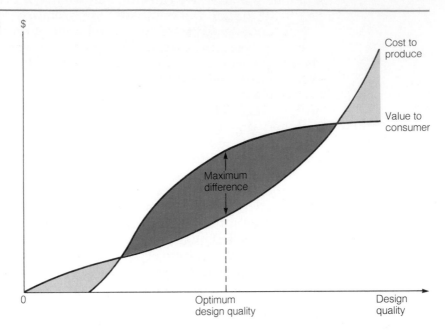

Table 15–1 illustrates how these three dimensions of quality might apply to a color TV, clothing, and a restaurant meal.

In some cases, one or two of these dimensions might be considerably more important than the other one or two. For example, a painting would be judged primarily on appearance, attic insulation on how well it insulates (operation), and a truck tire on how long it lasts; the other dimensions tend to be secondary in such cases. On the other hand, there are many examples of products or services

TABLE 15–1

Examples of Dimensions of Quality

Product/service	Appearance	Operation	Reliability
Color TV	Cabinetry, position of controls, exterior workmanship	Clarity, sound, ease of adjustment, reception, realistic colors	Frequency of repair
Clothing	Seams matched, no loose threads or missing buttons, pattern matched, fit, style	Warm/cool, resistance to wrinkles, color-fastness	Durability
Restaurant meal . .	Color, arrangement, atmosphere, cleanliness, friendliness of servers	Taste and consistency of food	Indigestion?

in which all three dimensions are important, including automobiles, kitchen appliances, housepaint, and dental care.

In essence, quality can be defined in terms of how well a product or service serves its intended function.

THE IMPORTANCE OF QUALITY

As a rule, consumers are influenced by three major factors when making buying decisions: price, availability, and quality. Hence, to compete effectively in the marketplace, businesses must pay careful attention to these factors; the decisions and tradeoffs managers make will be a major determinant of demand for a firms' goods and services.

It is important for management to recognize the different ways in which the quality of a firm's products or services can affect the organization and to take this into account in developing and maintaining a quality assurance program. Some of the major ways that quality affects an organization are:

1. Reputation and image.
2. Liability.
3. Productivity.
4. Costs.

An organization's *reputation and image* are generally associated with the cost and quality of the goods or services it provides. Failure to devote adequate attention to quality can damage the organization's image and perhaps lead to a decreased share of the market in the case of a profit-oriented firm or increased criticism and/or controls in the case of a government agency or other nonprofit organization. In many instances consumers are unable to assess product quality directly. Instead, they tend to rely on price, brand name, and a company's reputation when making choices.

Organizations must pay special attention to their potential *liability* due to damages or injuries resulting from either faulty design or poor workmanship. This applies to both products and services. Thus, a poorly designed steering arm on a car might cause the driver to lose control of the car, but so could improper assembly of the steering arm. However, the net result is the same. Similarly, a tree surgeon may be called to cable a tree limb. If the limb later falls and causes damage to a neighbor's car, the accident might be traced to a poorly designed procedure for cabling or to improper workmanship. Liability for poor quality has been well-established in the courts. The organization's liability costs can often be substantial, especially if large numbers of items are involved, as is the case in the automobile industry, or if potentially widespread injury or damage (e.g., an accident at a nuclear power plant) is involved. Negligence is often a key issue, although "foreseeable" use or misuse can also be an important issue. Express written warranties as well as implied warranties generally warrant the product as safe when used as intended. The courts have tended to extend this to uses that are *foreseeable,* even if the product has been used incorrectly or misused. In the health care field, medical malpractice claims and insurance costs are having an impact on skyrocketing costs and have drawn the attention of both doctors and legislators.

Productivity and quality are often closely related. Poor quality can adversely affect productivity during the manufacturing process if parts are defective and have to be reworked, or if an assembler has to try a number of parts before finding one that fits properly. Similarly, poor quality in tools and equipment can lead to injuries and defective output, which must be reworked or scrapped, thereby reducing the amount of usable output for a given amount of input. Conversely, improving and maintaining good quality can have a positive effect on productivity.

Poor quality increases certain *costs* incurred by the organization. These include scrap and rework costs, warranty costs, replacement and repair costs after purchase, and any other costs expended in transportation, inspection in the field, and payments to customers or discounts used to offset the inferior quality. In some instances the costs can be substantial. Liability claims and legal expenses are perhaps obvious. However, other costs can also be substantial, even if those two items are not factors. For instance, rework costs involve the salaries of workers and the additional resources needed to perform the rework (e.g., equipment, energy, raw materials). Beyond those costs are such items as inspection of reworked parts, disruption of schedules, the added cost of parts and materials in inventory waiting for reworked parts, and the paperwork needed to keep track of the items until they can be integrated back into the process. Aside from these out-of-pocket costs are *opportunity costs* related to lost sales due to dissatisfied customers who switch their business to competitors.

Quality also has *international* implications. If a company is to compete effectively in the world marketplace, its products must compare favorably with its competitors' products in terms of price, quality, and availability. If the products of a country's major industries are consistently inferior to those of other industrial nations, that country can lose out at home and abroad. The result will be a drain of capital needed for construction of facilities and to provide employment opportunities for its people. This points up the need for government and industries to recognize the importance of the quality issue and to work together to improve the quality of products and services. Favorable tax status and support of research are two possible avenues. Another is encouragement and support of exchange programs that enable manufacturers to acquire firsthand information on techniques used in other countries.

DETERMINANTS OF QUALITY

A few pages back it was noted that the ultimate definition of quality is consumer perception of how well a product or service does—or will—perform its intended function, and that performance often manifests itself in terms of such dimensions as appearance, operation, and reliability.

Any realistic effort to achieve specific quality goals, or to improve quality, must be predicated on the factors that determine quality. The degree to which a product or service successfully satisfies its intended purpose has four primary determinants. They are:

1. Design.
2. Conformance to design.
3. Consumer education.
4. Service after delivery.

These four determinants essentially define the scope of quality assurance.

The design phase is the starting point for the level of quality that is eventually achieved. Design involves decisions regarding specific characteristics of a product or service (size, shape, location, and so on), as well as methods, materials, processes, and equipment that will be employed. Design decisions must take into account the wants and needs of the consumer (perhaps determined by market research), production and service capabilities, safety and liability both during production and after delivery, and projected costs, profits, or other relevant considerations.

Poor design can result in difficulties in production or service. For example, materials might be difficult to obtain, specifications might be difficult to meet, or procedures difficult to follow. Moreover, if a design is inadequate or inappropriate for the circumstances, the best workmanship in the world may not be enough to achieve the desired quality. Thus, we cannot expect a surgeon to achieve good results if the given tools or procedures are inadequate. Likewise, it is wrong to criticize a social service agency for failure to achieve specified results if funding is inadequate. This can occur if local funding does not enable the agency to meet state mandated guidelines.

Once the desired quality level has been specified, the responsibility for quality becomes one of conformance, which involves assuring that operations follow through as intended. This involves workmanship, inspection, and corrective action when necessary.

As noted, the importance of workmanship is equivalent to the importance of design—the best design in the world can be easily negated by inferior workmanship. Furthermore, it matters not to the consumer whether poor quality is due to design or workmanship, the end result is the same. Good workmanship is the product of selection and training of employees, supervision of work, and development and maintenance of favorable attitudes toward quality standards.

Inspection and control are vital links in quality assurance. The objective of inspection is to provide an indication to management when output does not conform to expectation. Even with good design and workmanship, problems can still occur that will lead to poor quality. For example, equipment can malfunction, materials received from suppliers can be inferior or incorrect, materials can deteriorate after being received, tools can wear out more quickly than expected, and human beings can make mistakes. Consequently, it is necessary to inspect at least a portion of the output at various stages of completion, partly to correct defects that have already occurred, but primarily to know when corrective action is needed to avoid future deficiencies. Whenever problems are discovered, it becomes necessary to undertake appropriate corrective action. This typically involves an investigation into the causes, a selection of an action that can be expected to rectify the situation, implementation of the corrective action, and following up to insure that the desired changes have been realized.

The determination of quality does not stop once the product or service has been sold or delivered. Customer education is necessary to increase (but not guarantee) the chances that a product will be used for its intended purposes and used in such a way that it will continue to function properly and safely. (Companies involved in liability litigation often argue that injuries and damages occurred because the user misused the product.) Much the same reasoning can be applied to services. If customers, patients, clients, etc., are not clearly informed on what they should or should not do, there is the danger that they will take some action that will adversely affect quality. Typical examples include the doctor who fails to specify that a medication should be taken *before* meals and *not* with orange juice, the TV installer who doesn't take enough time to show the owner how to properly adjust the color, the attorney who neglects to inform a client of a deadline for filing a claim, and so on.

Much consumer education takes the form of printed instructions and labeling. Thus, it is important for manufacturers to assure that directions for unpacking, assembling, using, maintaining, and adjusting the product—and what to do if something goes wrong (e.g., flush eyes with water, call a physician, induce vomiting, do not induce vomiting, nontoxic, disconnect set immediately, no consumer-serviceable parts) are *clearly visible* and *easily understood*.

Products do not always perform as expected, and services do not always yield the desired results, for a variety of reasons. Whatever the reason, it is important from a quality standpoint to remedy the situation, either through recall and repair of the product, adjustment, replacement or buyback, or reevaluation of a service and then doing whatever is necessary to bring the product or service up to standard.

While each of the above factors is an important determinant of quality, it is important to recognize that *management* has the ultimate responsibility for quality; it is management that initially establishes the desired level of quality being sought, and management that provides the necessary funding for selection and training of workers, for inspection and control, and for follow-up after delivery to correct problems. Furthermore, management is responsible for creating a supportive environment and for conveying to employees the importance of quality and seeing that employees reflect this in their work.

THE EVOLUTION OF QUALITY CONTROL

Prior to the Industrial Revolution, production was carried out by skilled craftsmen. Pride of workmanship and reputation often provided the necessary motivation to see that a job was done right. Lengthy apprenticeships required by guilds caused this attitude to carry over to new workers. Moreover, one person or a small group of people were responsible for an entire product.

The Industrial Revolution was accompanied by a division of labor, and each worker was responsible for only a small portion of each product. Pride of workmanship became less meaningful since workers could not readily identify with the final product. The responsibility for quality control shifted to the foremen. Inspection was either nonexistent or haphazard, although in some instances 100 percent inspection was used.

In 1924 W. Shewhart of Bell Telephone Laboratories introduced statistical control charts that could be used to monitor production. Then around 1930 H. F. Dodge and H. G. Romig, also of Bell Labs, introduced tables for acceptance sampling. However, statistical quality control procedures were not widely used until World War II, when the U.S. government began to require vendors to use them.

Just after the war the American Society for Quality Control was founded. Throughout the years, the society has promoted quality control with its publications, conferences, and training programs.

During the 1950s and 60s, W. Edwards Deming is credited with introducing statistical quality control methods to Japanese manufacturers. Prior to that time, much of the output by the Japanese was of inferior quality. However, by the late 1970s, the Japanese began to acquire a reputation for high quality in automobiles, appliances, steel, and electronics, some of which can be attributed to quality control efforts. Now, Japanese manufacturers are formidable competitors in the world marketplace. One consequence is that manufacturers in other industrialized countries have intensified their efforts to improve the quality of their products.

The current thinking on achieving consistently high levels of quality in both goods and services requires more of a *total* approach to quality, from the design, procurement, production, and delivery stages to service after the sale as well as consumer education. More and more, firms that overlooked the importance of quality are recognizing its importance and attempting to achieve higher quality levels.

IMPROVING QUALITY

For many reasons, most organizations are constantly striving to improve the quality of their products or services. Competitive pressures, complaints from clients or customers, professionalism, and the desire to increase sales and/or market share all have a potential for instigating quality improvements. Some of the major sources of improvements are research and development, competitors, customers, and employees.

Research and development involves exploring new or different designs for products or services or new and different equipment, materials, processes, methods, or packaging that have the potential for yielding quality improvements. Organizations are sometimes reluctant to commit large sums of money to these efforts because of the high risks of failure (i.e., not obtaining the desired results), because the funds are needed elsewhere, or because stockholders often prefer the more tangible returns afforded by higher dividends. During the 70s, the amount of funding large corporations allocated to R&D decreased steadily. However, more and more companies are beginning to recognize the merits of research and development and are committing the necessary funds.

Competitors are often sources for quality improvements, although at first glance, it may seem unethical to adopt another firm's ideas. To be sure, patent and copyright laws are designed to provide protection from the wholesale absorption of another's technology or techniques. However, there is nothing inherently wrong with noting how a competitor is able to achieve higher reliability, or that the competitor uses special packaging to reduce damage during shipment, or that the competitor uses newer and more efficient methods, or offers free in-home repair service. In other words, it is often possible to accomplish the same results without violating another's rights. Other examples of this include observing that a competitor offers more convenient sizes, expends more effort to educate customers in the use of the product, or uses better materials or ingredients.

Customers or consumers can often be a valuable source of ideas for quality improvement, either via suggestions they offer or via complaints received. Through careful analysis, perhaps using follow-up surveys, much can be learned about how users perceive quality and what changes they would be receptive to. Professional societies use customer or patient complaints to identify potential sources of poor quality and usually attempt to institute corrective measures.

Employees can often provide suggestions for improvements both in the design of a product or service and in the way the product or service is processed. One obvious advantage that workers possess is that they are intimately familiar with the process and the product or service, which can give them valuable insight that other sources may lack. Some organizations have made use of employee suggestions right along, while many others have more or less tended to ignore this input. Fortunately, more and more organizations are beginning to recognize the potential of employee suggestions. One of the ways companies are tapping this potential is with the use of *quality circles,* which are voluntary groups of employees who get together periodically to discuss ways of improving both the quality of the product they produce and ways of improving working conditions. This can also yield indirect benefits by improving worker attitudes about quality. Japan is noted for its use of quality circles, and some American firms are patterning their quality circles along the same lines as the Japanese. One possible benefit of management's support and encouragement of these groups is that it communicates to employees the importance of quality in the eyes of management, and this can motivate them in their own work as well as motivate them to search for ways of improving output. Another possible benefit often noted is the potential for making the worker feel like an important part of the system, one whose opinion and counsel are sought on something that is important to the organization. However, quality circles are neither a panacea nor a "quick fix," as the following reprint explains.

Quality Control Circles: They Work and Don't Work

Kenichi Ohmae

Quality control circles, so spectacularly successful in Japan in recent years, hold little promise of short-term gains. They take generations to bear fruit, and cannot be expected to succeed if they are ordered by edict. Moreover, the scope of their achievement, though impressive over time, is limited.

A QC circle is a group of about 10 relatively autonomous workers from the same division of a company who volunteer to meet for an hour or so once or twice a month. After work (usually they are paid overtime), they discuss ways to improve the quality of their products, the production process in their part of the plant, and the working environment. Their long-term objective is to build a sense of responsibility for improving quality, but the immediate goal is to exchange ideas in a place uninhibited by barriers of age, sex, or company rank.

Japan's experience has revealed several preconditions for the success of QC circles. Some may be indigenous.

First, the work force must be intelligent and reasonably well-educated. Members of the circles must be able to use statistical and industrial engineering analysis. They must know what it takes to make things work on a nuts and bolts level, and they must be able to brainstorm together. It is no coincidence that the Japanese companies that have been most successful with these circles and other participatory methods for improving productivity (Hitachi, Teijin, Asahi Glass, and Nippon Kokan) are also well-known for their fine recruiting and internal training programs.

Second, management must be willing to trust workers with cost data and important information, and to give them the authority to implement their ideas. At Japanese companies with successful QC programs, managers have tended to work their way up through the ranks: They really believe in their work force. It is no surprise to them that groups of workers, if given information and authority to experiment by trial and error, will be able to reduce downtime, waste, or reworking—the sorts of questions that the circles are most effective in addressing.

Third, workers must be willing and eager to cooperate with each other. Unlike the suggestion box and other worker incentive programs that reward individuals, QC programs reward groups. A genuine "team spirit" is therefore necessary: Workers must be willing to express themselves and find fulfillment by reaching agreement.

Moreover, if authority in production decisions is to be decentralized down to the level of these circles, then the circles have to be able to cooperate with each other lest they work at cross-purposes. Unless there is a spirit of cooperation within the work force, an attitude that talking a problem through with peers is more rewarding than taking it up to management, a company is better off using individual carrots instead of the circles. Otherwise, it may find night shifts undoing the improvements of day shifts.

One of the most important features of QC circles in Japan is that they did not originate with senior management. They spring rather from a voluntary, grass-roots movement of workers and middle managers from across the nation.

The spearhead has been the Union of Japanese Scientists and Engineers, or Nikka-

Giren. In 1962 it began publishing a magazine, later named FQC, which called for quality control circles among factory workers and foremen and helped precipitate a change from the Western concept of quality control as the prerogative of technical experts. The magazine circulated widely among industrial workers, who bought it themselves (it cost them about the same as a pack of cigarettes) rather than receiving it through their employers, and read it together—in a circle. The magazine, together with a generation of supervisors familiar with QC concepts from the 50s, helped initiate massive training of non-supervisors.

The Nikka-Giren Union continues to have great influence. It publishes case histories of successful QC circles and sponsors regional and national conferences, where circle participants from different companies share their experiences.

Since most Japanese companies are very secretive with each other, this openness seems a paradox. But the movement was initially popular in the steel and ship-building industries, where there was a tradition of letting other companies freely inspect production methods and facilities. Had the movement started in the Japanese camera or auto industry, it is doubtful whether the current openness and cross-fertilization would have developed. Today, cross-fertilization is one of the keys to the success of the circles in Japan—the exchanges not only encourage but also keep workers interested in the process.

Quality control circles don't run themselves. They must be revitalized. Most important is the specific set of goals they are given and a strong manager who coordinates QCC changes with corporate objectives. In companies that use both the suggestion box and quality control circle, management can gather directly from workers ideas that may require significant capital expenditures and at the same time use suggestion box successes to encourage QCC efforts.

Management spends more time today on sustaining existing circles than starting new ones, understanding that their effects are incremental and cumulative. In 1951 Toyota received 700 proposals from its new worker participation program. Today it gets 500,000 per year, which saves a reported $230 million.

But there are limits to what the circles can do. The abrupt quantum leaps in cost reduction that the Japanese have achieved in industries as diverse as steel and consumer electronics do not result from QC circles. Instead they come from major strategic decisions about new technologies and plants and entirely new ways of producing and delivering a product.

At Ricoh, for example, it wasn't a circle that figured out how to redesign the business system by changing the technology manufacturing, and marketing to completely change the game in plain paper copiers. Nor was it the circles that led to the elimination of inventory ("Kanban" system) at Toyota. QC circles, composed of workers from a single division, can't come up with these bold strokes.

A single-minded focus

Nor can they replace strategy. Indeed in many industries a single-minded focus on productivity improvements and concomitant quality control activities may be less important for success than focused R & D and targeted marketing.

Quality control circles work best when they are part of what the Japanese call total quality control, which embraces concerns about the entire spectrum of a business. And they are one of a number of productivity improvement techniques that work best when put together. As the Japanese would say, it's like collecting dust to make a mountain. But somebody has to envision the mountain, and know which way the wind is blowing.

Management is the key factor in quality improvements. It is management that decides if quality improvements are needed, which sources will be used, and how much emphasis will be placed on achieving them. Hence, if quality circles are formed but management pays only lip service to them while ignoring their advice, that approach is doomed to failure. Although it might seem irrational for management to ignore employee input, you have to realize that some managers are fearful of permitting employees to have a say in how things are done because they feel they will lose control of the situation or be criticized for not recognizing the potential improvements themselves. Also, some managers prefer to retain all initiative for changes and improvements rather than share it with others.

Similarly, a doctor may receive complaints from patients or staff, but choose to ignore them or attempt to rationalize his or her behavior instead of making an effort to improve the situation. The same can be said for teachers, lawyers, dentists, and other professionals.

When consumers encounter substandard quality in either goods or services, there is a tendency to blame workers' attitudes. However, workers generally reflect the attitudes of their managers and/or lack training, which is also the responsibility of management. Hence, management is the key factor in improving and maintaining quality output.

Dr. W. Edwards Deming suggests a number of actions that management can take to improve quality.[1] Among them are:

1. Adopt a long-term perspective.
2. Don't go along with the philosophy of an "irreducible percentage of defectives."
3. Demand quality from vendors.
4. Use statistical methods to identify sources of poor quality and then take corrective action. Train employees to use statistical techniques.
5. Improve supervision.
6. Don't emphasize output at the expense of good quality.
7. Make sure that employees have the proper training to do their jobs.

Other points can be added to the list. An important one is for top management to visibly support quality efforts. Philip Crosby offers some additional suggestions.[2] Among them are:

---

[1] W. Edwards Deming, "Dr. Deming's Cure for U.S. Management," *WARD'S Auto World,* November 1981, p. 16.

[2] Philip Crosby, *Quality without Tears:* The Art of Hassle-Free Management McGraw-Hill, 1984.

1. Top management must demonstrate its commitment to quality and its willingness to give support to achieve good quality.
2. Management must be persistent in efforts to achieve good quality.
3. Management must spell out very clearly what it wants in the way of quality and what workers must do to achieve that.
4. Make it right the first time.

Reading ——————————————————————

Cause of Quality-Control Problems Might Be Managers—Not Workers

Ed Bean

A company's widgets continue to roll off the assembly line with loose screws and flaky paint. Who is at fault?

The stubborn union? The slipshod school system? Careless suppliers?

Blame the chairman and the chief executive officer, suggest quality experts.

Too many companies, consultants say, still equate quality control with having more inspectors at the end of the assembly line. Or with plastering factory walls with posters that exhorted employees to take pride in their work.

Those old notions of quality control came under scrutiny as the Japanese carved out even bigger niches in the U.S. markets. Following the doctrines of such consultants as W. Edwards Deming, the 84-year-old crusader for quality and productivity and the man who often gets credit for much of Japan's success with quality control, more U.S. companies are now controlling quality through prevention.

That means better training for workers. It may mean re-engineering the product and re-designing the workplace. Above all, it means reshaping attitudes, from board room to loading dock, so that quality becomes more important than getting the product out the door. On all these fronts, consultants say, management has to take the initiative.

Outside help

Tennant Co., a Minneapolis manufacturer of maintenance equipment for industrial floors, was one of the earliest U.S. companies to adopt such tactics. Too many of its machines were rolling off the assembly line with defects, says John Davis, Tennant manager for quality. In 1979 the company sought outside help.

Tennant became the first client of Philip Crosby, a management consultant in Winter Park, Florida. Since 1979, Mr. Crosby has advised more than 350 companies on quality control. His theory: A company gets what it asks for. If management decides it can live with a 10 percent defect rate, management will get a 10 percent defect rate.

Mr. Crosby advised Tennant to start its quality program by assigning a dollar value to the additional production time and service visits caused by defects. Study groups by workers and managers then identified specific problems.

Leaking joints in hydraulic lines were a consistent headache. A study group found that management hadn't adequately trained assembly workers how to install the joints. Further study showed that Tennant engineers hadn't kept up with the latest technology in hydraulics circuits. Relations with suppliers of the joints were simplified when the number of suppliers was reduced to 2 from 16. The company also reduced the variety of joints it used.

Mr. Davis warns that self-examination can be painful. Suppliers were often blamed for the poor quality of some parts. But when Tennant discussed its problems with suppliers, the company found that it often hadn't given accurate specifications. In some cases, Tennant was using parts that unnecessarily exceeded specifications.

By the end of 1984, manufacturing defects had decreased 52 percent. The cost of correcting errors (the company calls it the "cost of quality") was cut to 8.9 percent of sales at the end of 1984, down from 17 percent in 1980. The company's goal: reduce that to 2.5 percent by 1988. But such progress hasn't come easily. "We grossly underestimated the time required to implement this," Mr. Davis says.

All of the company's 1,200 employees received at least 40 hours of classroom training in the first year, and much more time was devoted to studying business and production processes. The big change, though, was reshaping attitudes so that employees realized management was giving quality more than lip service. "People had a lot of questions," says Mr. Davis. "Are you going to provide us with the tools we need? How will it impact my performance review? Is this a one-shot deal?"

Carolina Freight Corp., a Cherryville, N.C., trucking company, also had problems convincing employees that its new push for quality wasn't just a fad. Middle and lower-level managers, like dock supervisors, were the most skeptical, says Doug Wiles, Carolina's director of quality. To prove its committment, the company spent about $250,000 on its program in the first year.

The company, which started thinking about quality in late 1983, sought help from Leadership Education & Development Services Inc., management consultants in Orlando, Fla.

The biggest concern at Carolina and most other trucking companies was claims for damages and shortages. Although a forklift driver or dock worker often seemed to be the culprit, the company eventually recognized that the workers had received little training in the art of loading a trailer.

Many problems were embarrassingly simple: Someone didn't pay attention. The company found that late deliveries usually were caused by someone failing to read the paperwork that listed when a shipment was promised. Drivers ran out of fuel because broken fuel gauges were never repaired. The latter was a $25,000-a-year inconvenience that disappeared.

Other problems required more sophisticated approaches. Haphazard routing that often left trucks half empty was corrected with computer scheduling.

Like Tennant, Carolina is finding that quality programs only work if everyone from the chief executive to the hourly employee is involved. "We used to think mistakes were just a part of doing business," Mr. Wiles says.

The chief executive's response to such a challenge may determine how a company regards quality, says David Garvin, a Harvard University associate professor who has studied quality in the U.S. and Japan. "He may make speeches about quality and say he's interested but I look at how he spends his time. If he meets with the quality people once every six months, he's not serious. If he sits down with them once a week for three hours, that's a good indicator."

Traditional views

Even with a strong commitment, a company shouldn't expect to see big improvements for several years, Mr. Garvin says. U.S. managers have traditionally viewed quality control as a defensive strategy to control costs, he says. Now, he says, management must learn that quality is becoming a competitive strategy that will separate the winners from the losers.

Tennant Co. had so many outside executives ask about its quality program that it organized a conference several years ago where companies could share information. Last year the two-day meeting attracted 170 executives. This fall Tennant is expecting 600.

Mr. Garvin thinks U.S. industry is making great strides, particularly auto and electronics companies. But he cautions that they're shooting at a moving target. The Japanese are also getting better.

Mr. Crosby, the consultant, estimates that the U.S. auto industry is about 60 percent of the way in its bid to catch the Japanese. But too much of the improvement has come with better inspection, rather than prevention, he laments. "It's been plain old hard work, like dragging a sled behind you with no wheels."

When Detroit does achieve parity with its foreign competition, consumers will forgive and forget, Mr. Crosby says. "It's like Scrooge," he says. "As soon as he changed, everyone accepted him and forgot he had been rotten for 20 years."

QUALITY OF CONFORMANCE

The remainder of the chapter deals with quality of conformance, which refers to making sure that goods and services have "fitness for use" (i.e., that they conform to the intent of design).

There are three points in the production process where monitoring takes place: before production, during production, and after production. The logic of checking conformance before production is to make sure that inputs are acceptable. The logic of checking conformance during production is to make sure that the conversion of inputs into outputs is proceeding in an acceptable manner. The logic of checking conformance of output is to make a final check on conformance before passing goods on to customers.

Monitoring both before and after production involves *acceptance sampling* procedures, while monitoring during the production process is referred to as *process control*. These procedures are explained in detail in the following pages. Figure 15–2 gives an overview of where these two procedures are applied in the production process.

FIGURE 15–2

Acceptance Sampling and Process Control

For both acceptance sampling and process control, inspection provides key data for decision making.

INSPECTION

In order to determine if a process is functioning as intended, or that a shipment of raw materials or final products does not contain more than a specified percentage of defectives, it is necessary to physically examine at least some of the items in question. The purpose of inspection is to provide information concerning the degree to which items conform to a standard. The basic issues in inspection are:

1. How much to inspect and how often.
2. At what points in the process inspection should occur.
3. Whether to inspect in a centralized location or on-site.
4. Whether to inspect attributes or variables.

Consider, for example, inspection at an intermediate step in the manufacture of electric typewriters. Because inspection costs are often significant, the question naturally arises as to whether it is necessary to inspect every typewriter, or whether a small sample of typewriters will suffice. Moreover, while there are numerous points in the production process where inspections could be made, it is not generally cost-effective to inspect at every point. Hence, the question of which points to inspect at. Once these have been identified, a decision must be made on whether to remove the typewriters from the line and take them to a lab where specialized equipment might be available to run certain tests, or whether to test them where they are being made. These points are expanded upon below.

How Much to Inspect and How Often

The amount of inspection can range from no inspection whatsoever to inspecting each item numerous times. Low cost, high-volume items such as paper clips, roofing nails, and wooden pencils often require little inspection because (1) the cost associated with passing defectives is quite low and (2) the processes that produce these items are usually highly reliable, so that defectives are rare anyway. Conversely, high cost, low-volume items that have large costs associated with passing defectives often require more intensive inspections. Thus, critical components of a manned-flight space vehicle are closely scrutinized because of the risk to human safety and the high cost of mission failure.

The majority of quality control applications lies somewhere between these two extremes. Most require some inspection, but it is

FIGURE 15–3

The Amount of Inspection Is Optimul when the Sum of the Cost of Inspection and of Passing Defectives Is Minimized

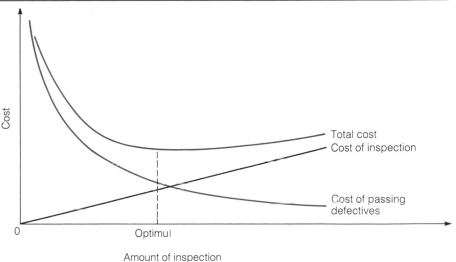

neither possible nor economically feasible to critically examine each and every part or activity for control purposes. The cost of inspection, resulting interruptions of a process or delays caused by inspection, and the manner of testing typically outweigh the benefits of 100 percent inspection. However, the cost of letting undetected defectives slip through is high enough so that inspection cannot be completely ignored. The amount of inspection needed is governed by the costs of inspection and the expected costs of passing defective items. As illustrated in Figure 15–3, if inspection activities increase, inspection costs increase but the costs of unde tected defectives decrease. The goal, of course, is to minimize the *sum* of these two costs. In other words, it may not pay to attempt to catch *every* defective, particularly if the cost of inspection exceeds the penalties associated with letting some defectives get through.

As a rule, operations that have a high proportion of human involvement necessitate more inspection effort than mechanical operations because mechanical operations tend to be more reliable than human ones.

The frequency of inspection depends largely on the rate at which a process may go out of control, or the number of lots being inspected. A stable process will necessitate only infrequent checks, while an unstable one, or one that has recently given trouble, will require more frequent checks. Likewise, many small lots will require more samples than a few large lots because it is important to obtain sample data from each lot.

**Where in the
Process to Inspect**

In many operations there are a large number of possible inspection points. Because each inspection adds to the cost of the product or service, it is important to restrict inspection efforts to the points where they can do the most good. In manufacturing, some of the typical inspection points are:

1. *Raw materials and purchased parts.* There is little sense in paying for goods that do not meet quality standards and little sense in expending time and effort on material that is bad to begin with.

2. *Finished products.* Customer satisfaction and the firm's image are at stake here, and repairing or replacing products in the field is usually a good deal more costly than at the factory. Likewise, the seller is usually responsible for shipping costs on returns, and payments may be held up pending delivery of satisfactory goods.

3. *Before a costly operation.* The point is not to waste costly labor or machine time on items that are already defective.

4. *Before an irreversible process.* In many cases items can be reworked up to a certain point, but beyond that point, they cannot. For example, pottery can be reworked prior to firing. After that,

TABLE 15–2

**Examples of
Inspection Points in
Service Organizations**

Type of business	Inspection points	Characteristics
Fast-food	Cashier	Accuracy
	Counter area	Appearance, productivity
	Eating area	Cleanliness, no loitering
	Building and grounds	Appearance, safety hazards
	Kitchen	Cleanliness, purity of food, food storage, health regulations
	Parking lot	Safe, well-lighted
Hotel/motel	Accounting/billing	Accuracy, timeliness
	Building and grounds	Appearance and safety
	Main desk	Appearance, waiting times, accuracy of bills
	Maid service	Completeness, productivity
	Personnel	Appearance, manners, productivity
	Reservations/occupancy	Over/underbooking, percent occupancy
	Restaurants	Kitchen, menus, meals, bills
	Room service	Waiting time, quality of food
	Supplies	Ordering, receiving, inventories
Supermarket	Cashiers	Accuracy, courteous, productivity
	Deliveries	Quality, quantity
	Produce	Freshness, well-stocked
	Aisles and stockrooms	Uncluttered
	Inventory control	Stock-outs
	Shelf stock	Ample supply, rotation of perishables
	Shelf displays	Appearance
	Checkouts	Waiting time
	Shopping carts	Good working condition, ample supply, theft/vandalism
	Parking lot	Safe, well-lighted
	Personnel	Appearance

defectives must be discarded or sold as seconds at a lower price.

5. *Before a covering process.* Painting, plating, and assemblies often hide defects.

In the service area, inspection points are incoming purchased materials and supplies, personnel, service interfaces (e.g., service counter), and outgoing completed work (e.g., repaired appliances, automobiles). Table 15–2 illustrates a number of examples.

Each situation is different. The operations manager must weigh the costs and benefits of inspections at each potential point in a process in deciding where to assign inspections.

Centralized versus On-Site Inspection

Some situations require that inspections be done *on site.* For example, inspecting the hull of a ship for cracks requires inspectors to visit the ship. At other times, specialized tests can best be performed in a lab. This is the case, for example, with many medical tests, and it also applies to various tests in business and industry (analyzing food samples, testing metals for hardness, running viscosity tests on lubricants, and so on).

The central issue in the decision of whether to inspect on site is whether the advantages of specialized lab tests are worth the time and interruption needed to obtain the results. Arguments favoring on-site inspection are quicker decisions and avoidance of introduction of extraneous factors (e.g., damage or other alteration of samples during transportation to the lab). On the other hand, specialized equipment and a more favorable testing environment (less noise and confusion, vibrations, dust, and workers "helping" with inspections) offer strong arguments for using a lab.

Attributes versus Variables Inspection

Quality characteristics are the focal point of inspection. They can be classified as either *attributes* or *variables.* Attributes yield pass-fail data, such as defective-nondefective, acceptable-not acceptable. Thus, attribute data are *count* data. For attribute data, a *discrete* distribution such as the binomial or Poisson serves as the basis for statistical inference. Variables can be present in varying degrees (e.g., length, height, thickness, tensile strength). As such, they must be *measured* rather than counted. Often, a normal distribution serves as the basis for statistical inference.

Inspection and control procedures differ somewhat, depending on whether the quality characteristic of interest is an attribute or a variable.

ACCEPTANCE SAMPLING

Acceptance sampling is a form of inspection applied to lots or batches of products that have been previously produced, rather than to items that are part of an ongoing process. In the majority of cases, the lots represent incoming purchased items or final products awaiting shipment to warehouses or customers. The purpose of acceptance sampling is to decide if a lot satisfies predetermined standards. Lots that are judged to satisfy standards are passed or *accepted,* while those that do not are *rejected.* Rejected lots may be subjected to 100 percent inspection, or they may be returned to the supplier for credit or replacement (especially if destructive testing is involved).

Acceptance-sampling procedures are most useful when one or more of the following conditions exist:

1. A large number of items must be processed in a short period.
2. The cost consequences of passing defectives is low.
3. Destructive testing is required.
4. Fatigue or boredom caused by inspecting large numbers of items lead to inspection errors.

Acceptance-sampling procedures can be applied to both attribute and variable inspection. However, inspection of attributes is perhaps more widely used in practice, and for purposes of illustration, the discussion here will focus exclusively on attribute-sampling plans.

Sampling Plans

Sampling plans specify the lot size, N, the sample size, n, the number of samples to be taken, and the acceptance/rejection criterion. There are a variety of sampling plans in use. Some plans call for selection of a single sample while others call for two or more samples, depending on the nature of the plan. Some of these different kinds of plans are briefly described in the following paragraphs.

Single-sampling plans. In a single-sampling plan, one random sample is drawn from each lot, and every item in the sample is examined and classified as either "good" or "defective." If any sample contains *more* than a specified number of defectives, c, that lot is rejected.

Double-sampling plans. In a double-sampling plan, there is the opportunity to take a second sample if the results of an initial sample are inconclusive. For example, if the quality of the initial sample is high, the lot can be accepted without need for a second sample. Likewise, if the quality in the initial sample is poor, sampling can also be terminated and the lot rejected. For results between those two cases, a second sample must be taken and the items inspected, after which the lot is either accepted or rejected on the basis of the evidence obtained from both samples. A double-sampling plan specifies the lot size, the size of the initial sample and accept/reject criteria for the initial sample (e.g., $c_1 = 2$, $c_2 = 5$: if two or less defectives are found, accept the lot; if more than five defectives are found, reject the lot; and if three, four, or five defectives are found, take a second sample), and the size of the second sample and a single acceptance number (e.g., $c_3 = 6$: accept the lot if the total number of defectives found in both samples is six or less, otherwise, reject the lot).

Multiple-sampling plans. Multiple sampling plans are very similar to double-sampling plans, except that more than two samples may be required. A sampling plan will specify each sample size and two limits for each sample. The values increase with the number of samples. If, for any sample, the cumulative number of defectives found (i.e., in the present sample plus those found in all previous samples) exceeds the upper limit specified for that sample, sampling is terminated, and the lot is rejected. If the cumulative number of defectives is less than or equal to the lower limit, sampling is terminated, and the lot is passed. Otherwise, another sample is taken. The process continues until the lot is either accepted or rejected.

Choosing a plan. The cost and time required for inspection often dictate the kind of sampling plan used. The two primary considerations are the number of samples needed and the total number of observations required. Single-sampling plans involve only a single sample, but the sample size is large relative to the total number of observations taken under double- or multiple-sampling plans. In a situation where the cost to obtain a sample is relatively high compared to the cost of analyzing the observations, a single-sampling plan would be more desirable. For instance, if a sample of moon soil is needed, clearly the cost of returning for a second or third sample would far outweigh the cost of analyzing a single large sample. Conversely, in situations where item inspection costs are relatively high, such as destructive testing, it may be better to use double or multiple sampling, because the average number of items inspected per lot will be lower. This stems from the fact that if the lot quality is either very good or very poor, this will often show up initially, and sampling can be terminated.

Operating Characteristic Curve

An important feature of a sampling plan is how well it discriminates between lots of high quality and lots of low quality. The ability of a sampling plan to discriminate is described by its *operating characteristic (OC) curve.* A typical curve for a single-sampling plan is shown in Figure 15–4. The curve shows the probability that use of the sampling plan will result in lots with various *fraction defective* being accepted. For example, we can see from the graph that a lot with 3 percent defectives (i.e., a fraction defective of .03) would have a probability of about .90 of being accepted (and hence, a probability of $1.00 - .90 = .10$) of being rejected. Note that there is a downward relationship; as lot quality decreases, the probability of acceptance decreases, although the relationship is not linear.

FIGURE 15–4

A Typical OC Curve for Proportions

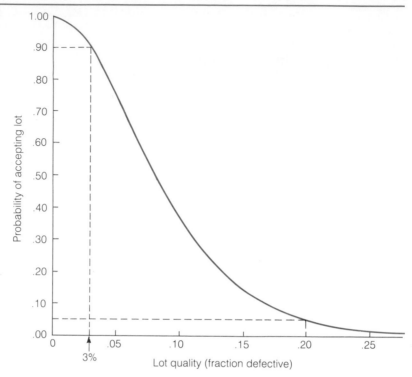

For instance, if a lot contains 20 percent defectives, the probability of acceptance drops to about .04.

It is interesting to note that even lots that contain more than 20 percent defectives still have some probability of being accepted, while lots with as few as 3 percent defectives stand some chance of being rejected. In other words, a sampling plan does not provide perfect discrimination between good and bad lots; some low-quality lots will invariably be accepted while some lots with very good quality will invariably be rejected.

The degree to which a sampling plan discriminates between good and bad lots is a function of the steepness of the graph's OC curve: The steeper the curve, the more discriminating the sampling plan. This is illustrated in Figure 15–5. Note the curve for an ideal plan (i.e., one that can discriminate perfectly between good and bad lots). In order to achieve that, it would be necessary to inspect 100 percent of each lot. Obviously, if you are going to do that, theoretically *all* of the defectives can be eliminated (errors and boredom might result in a few defectives remaining). However, the point is that 100 percent inspection provides a perspective from which to view the OC curves of other sampling plans.

FIGURE 15–5

**The Steeper the OC
Curve, the More
Discriminating the
Sampling Plan**

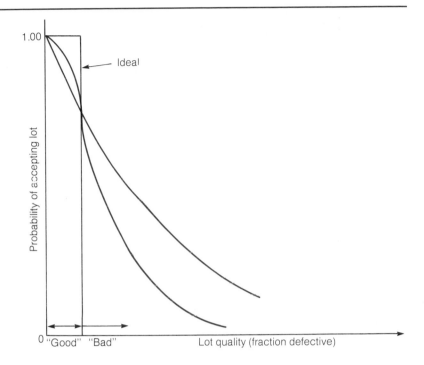

It should be noted that the cost and the time that would be needed to conduct 100 percent inspection often rule out 100 percent inspection, as does destructive testing, leaving acceptance sampling as the only viable alternative.

For these reasons, consumers are generally willing to accept lots that contain small percentages of defective items as "good," especially if the cost related to a few defectives is low. Often this percentage is in the neighborhood of 2 percent to 4 percent defective. This figure is known as the *acceptable quality level* (AQL). Because of the inability of random sampling to clearly identify lots that contain more than this specified percentage of defectives, consumers recognize that some lots that actually contain more will be accepted. However, there is usually an upper limit on the percentage of defectives that a consumer is willing to tolerate in accepted lots. This is known as the *lot tolerance percent defective* (LTPD). Thus, the consumer would like quality equal or better than the AQL, and is willing to live with some lots with quality as poor as the LTPD, but would prefer not to accept any lots that have a defective percentage that exceeds the LTPD. The probability that a lot that contains the lot tolerance percent defective will be accepted is known as the *consumer's risk,* or beta (β), or a *Type II error,* and the probabil-

FIGURE 15–6

The AQL Indicates "Good" Lots, and LTPD Indicates "Bad" Lots

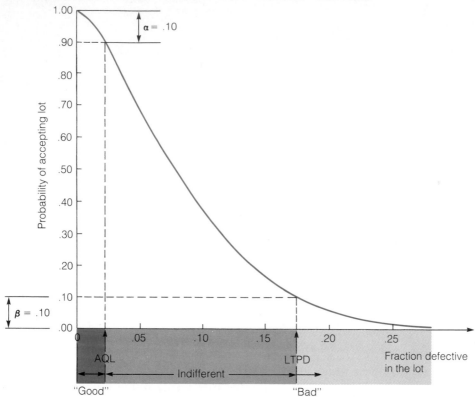

ity that a lot that contains the acceptable quality level will be rejected is known as the *producer's risk,* or alpha (α), or a *Type I error.* Sampling plans are frequently designed so that they have a producer's risk of 5 percent and a consumer's risk of 10 percent, although many other combinations are also used. It is possible to use trial and error to design a plan that will provide selected values for alpha and beta given the AQL and the LTPD. However, standard references such as the government MIL-STD Tables are widely used to obtain sample sizes and acceptance criteria for sampling plans. Figure 15–6 illustrates an OC curve with the AQL, LTPD, producer's risk, and consumer's risk.

A certain amount of insight can be gained by actually constructing an OC curve. Suppose we want the curve for a situation in which a sample of $n = 10$ items is drawn from lots containing $N = 2,000$ items, and lots are accepted if no more than $c = 1$ defective is found. Because the sample size is small relative to the lot size, it is reasonable to use the binomial distribution to obtain the probabilities that a lot will be accepted for various lot qualities.[3] A portion of the cumulative binomial table found in Appendix Table D is reproduced below to facilitate the discussion.

Portion of a Cumulative Binomial Table (from Appendix Table D)

	n	x	.05	.10	.15	.20	.25	.30	.35	.40	.45	.50	.55	.60
	10 . . .	0	.5987	.3487	.1969	.1074	.0563	.0282	.0135	.0060	.0025	.0010	.0003	.0001
$c = 1$	$\rightarrow$	1	.9139	.7361	.5443	.3758	.2440	.1493	.0860	.0464	.0233	.0107	.0045	.0017
		2	.9885	.9298	.8202	.6778	.5256	.3828	.2616	.1673	.0996	.0547	.0274	.0123
		3	.9990	.9872	.9500	.8791	.7759	.6496	.5138	.3823	.2660	.1719	.1020	.0548

In order to use the table, we select various lot qualities (value of p listed across the top of the table), beginning with .05, and find the probability that a lot with that percentage of defectives

FIGURE 15–7

OC Curve for $n = 10$, $c = 1$

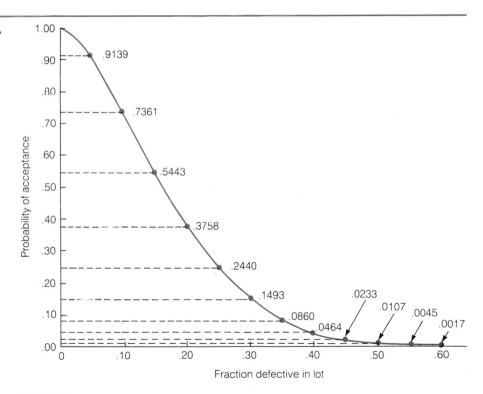

would be accepted (i.e., the probability of finding 0 or 1 defective in this case). Hence, for $p = .05$, the probability of one or less defectives is .9139. For a lot with 10 percent defectives (i.e., a fraction defective of .10), the probability of 1 or less defectives drops to .7361, while for 15 percent defectives, the probability of acceptance is .5443. In effect, we simply read the probabilities across the row for $c = 1$. By plotting these points (e.g., .05 and .9139, .10 and .7361) on a graph and connecting them, we can obtain the OC curve illustrated in Figure 15–7.

When $n > 20$ and $p < .05$, the Poisson distribution is useful in constructing operating characteristic curves for proportions. In effect, the Poisson distribution is being used to approximate the binomial distribution. The Poisson approximation involves treating the mean of the binomial distribution (i.e., np) as the mean of the Poisson (i.e., μ):

$$\mu = np \qquad (15\text{--}1)$$

As with the binomial distribution, various values of lot quality, p, will be selected, and the probability of accepting a lot (i.e., finding two or less defectives) will be determined by referring to the cumulative Poisson table. Values of p in increments of .01 are often used in this regard. The following example illustrates this use of the Poisson table.

EXAMPLE 1

Use the cumulative Poisson table to construct an OC curve for this sampling plan:

$N = 5,000$
$n = 80$
$c = 2$

Solution

Selected values of p	$\mu = np$	P_{ac} [$P(x \leq 2)$ from Appendix Table C]
.01	$80(.01) = 0.8$	.953
.02	$80(.02) = 1.6$	.783
.03	$80(.03) = 2.4$	.570
.04	$80(.04) = 3.2$	.380
.05	$80(.05) = 4.0$	.238
.06	$80(.06) = 4.8$	.143
.07	$80(.07) = 5.6$	.082
.08	$80(.08) = 6.4$	.046

EXAMPLE 1 (concluded)

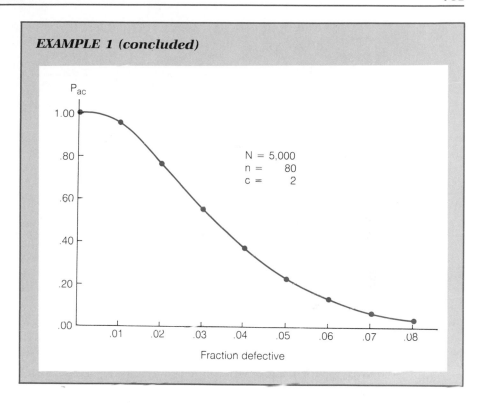

Operating characteristic curves can be constructed for variables-sampling plans as well as for attributes-sampling plans. It is beyond the scope of this presentation to go into detail on this. The purpose here is merely to illustrate the concept of an OC curve and to show how its construction is based on an underlying *sampling distribution.*

Average Quality of Inspected Lots

An interesting feature of acceptance sampling is that the level of inspection automatically adjusts to the quality of lots being inspected, assuming rejected lots are subjected to 100 percent inspection. The OC curve reveals that the greater the percentage of defectives in a lot, the less likely the lot is to be accepted. Generally speaking, good lots have a high probability of being accepted, and bad lots have a low probability of being accepted. If the lots being inspected are mostly good, few will end up going through 100 percent inspection. But the poorer the quality of the lots, the greater the number of lots that will come under closer scrutiny. This tends to improve overall quality of lots by weeding out defectives. In this way, the level of inspection is affected by lot quality.

If all lots have some given percentage of defectives, $p,$ the average outgoing quality (AOQ) of the lots can be computed using the formula below, assuming defectives are replaced with good items.

$$AOQ = P_{ac} \times p \left(\frac{N - n}{N} \right) \qquad (15\text{--}2)$$

where

P_{ac} = Probability of accepting the lot
  p = Fraction defective
  N = Lot size
  n = Sample size

In practice, the last term is often omitted since it is usually close to 1.0, and therefore has little effect on the resulting values. The formula becomes:

$$AOQ = P_{ac} \times p \qquad (15\text{--}3)$$

Use this formula for computing AOQ values instead of the preceding one.

By allowing the percentage, p, to vary, a curve such as the one in the following example can be constructed in the same way that an OC curve is constructed. The curve illustrates the point that if lots are very good or very bad, the average outgoing quality will be high. The maximum point on the curve becomes apparent in the process of calculating values for the curve.

EXAMPLE 2

Construct the AOQ curve for this situation:

$$N = 500, \; n = 10, \; c = 1$$

Solution

Let values of p vary from .05 to $\underset{\text{.40}}{\cancel{.50}}$ in steps of .05. The probabilities of acceptance, P_{ac}, can be read from Appendix Table D.

$$AOQ = P_{ac} \times p$$

p	P_{ac}	AOQ
.05	.9139	.046
.10	.7361	.074
.15	.5443	.082
.20	.3758	.075
.25	.2440	.061
.30	.1493	.045
.35	.0860	.030
.40	.0464	.019

EXAMPLE 2 (concluded)

The average outgoing quality limit (AOQL) appears to be just above 8 percent.

PROCESS CONTROL

Process control is concerned with assuring that *future* output is acceptable. Toward that end, periodic samples of process output are taken and evaluated. If the output is acceptable, the process is allowed to continue; if the output is not acceptable, the process is stopped, and corrective action is instituted. The primary tool of evaluation is the control chart.

The Control Process

The basic elements of control are the same, whether the intent is to control quality, costs, manpower, accidents, or anything else. In each case, effective control requires these steps:

1. Define.
2. Measure.
3. Compare to a standard.
4. Evaluate.
5. Take corrective action if necessary.
6. Evaluate corrective action.

Define in as much detail as possible what it is that is to be controlled. It is not sufficient, for example, to simply refer to a painted surface. The paint can have a number of characteristics that might be of interest, such as its thickness, resistance to fading or chipping, and hardness. Different characteristics may require different approaches for control purposes.

Only those characteristics that can be counted or measured are candidates for control. Thus, it will be important to consider how measurement will be accomplished.

There must be a standard of comparison that can be used to evaluate the measurements. This will relate to the level of quality being sought.

A definition of *out-of-control* must be established. Even a process that is functioning as it should will not yield output that conforms exactly to a standard, simply because of the natural (i.e., random) variations that are inherent in all processes, whether they are manual or mechanical. In other words, a certain amount of variation is inevitable. The main task of quality assurance is to distinguish between random variability and nonrandom variability, because nonrandom variability means that a process is out of control.

In the event that a process is judged to be out-of-control, corrective action must be taken. This involves uncovering the cause of nonrandom variability (worn equipment, incorrect methods being used, failure to follow specified procedures, and so on).

In order to assure that corrective action is effective, it is necessary to closely monitor the output of a process for a sufficient period of time to verify that the problem has been eliminated.

In a nutshell, then, control is achieved by inspecting a portion of the goods or services, comparing the results to a predetermined standard, evaluating departures from the standard, taking corrective action when necessary, and following up to assure that problems have been corrected.

Variations and Control

All processes that provide a product or service exhibit a certain amount of variation that is inherent or "natural" in their output. The variations are created by the combined influences of countless minor factors, each one so unimportant that even if it could be identified and eliminated, the decrease in process variability would be negligible. In effect, this natural or *inherent* variability cannot be reduced—the operations manager must learn to live with it. It is often referred to as *random* or *chance* variability. The amount of inherent variability differs from process to process; some have more and some have less. For instance, older machines often exhibit a higher degree of natural variability than newer machines, partly because of worn parts and partly because newer machines may incorporate design improvements, which lessen variability.

A second kind of variability is called *assignable variation.* Unlike natural variation, the main sources of assignable variation can usually be identified (assigned to a specific cause) and eliminated. Such factors as tool wear, equipment that needs adjustment, defective materials, and human factors (carelessness, fatigue, failure to follow correct procedures, and so on) are commonly encountered sources of assignable variations.

In terms of quality control, a process that exhibits only random variability is said to be statistically *in control,* while one that exhibits nonrandom (i.e., assignable) variations is said to be *out of control.* The objective of quality control is to distinguish between the two kinds of variations so that appropriate corrective action can be taken when necessary to insure desirable future output.

Control Charts

Control charts are graphical tools that are used to differentiate between random and nonrandom process output. There are different kinds of control charts (e.g., mean charts, range charts) for different kinds of situations. Each of these charts is constructed in a slightly different way. However, on the surface they are quite similar. Each chart has a center line, which represents the process average, and an upper and lower line *(control limits),* which define the range of random output. Use of the charts involves taking periodic samples, computing the appropriate sample statistic (e.g., sample mean for a mean chart, sample range for a range chart), and plotting that value on the chart. Values that fall within the control limits suggest (but do not prove) that the process is in control (i.e., process variations are random), while one or more values on or outside of the control limits suggests the process is out of control (i.e., process variations are nonrandom). For example, consider the control chart for means illustrated in Figure 15–8. Because all of the sample means fall within the control limits, it appears the process is statistically stable, or "in control." A second means chart is illustrated in Figure 15–9. Unlike the previous one, this chart has a sample mean that is beyond the upper control limit, which suggests that the process not "in control."

Underlying every control chart is a related sampling distribution

FIGURE 15–8

Since All of the Sample Means Are within the Control Limits, It Appears That the Process Is Performing Properly

FIGURE 15–9

The Process Is Out of Control

(based on sample size and type of data—e.g., means) that indicates the extent to which sample statistics like the mean or range will tend to vary from the process average solely as a result of chance. In effect, the sampling distribution provides a *standard of comparison* against which sample statistics can be judged: Those which fall within the bounds (control limits) of the sampling distribution suggest randomness, while those beyond the bounds suggest non-random output.

We shall consider four commonly used control charts: mean, range, percent defective, and number of defects. The first two pertain to variables, and the last two pertain to attribute or count data. Recall that variables generate continuous data (e.g., thickness, length, weight), and that attribute data involves counting the number of occurrences in a sample (e.g., five defectives in a sample of 200).

Control Charts for Variables

Mean and range charts are used to monitor variables. Control charts for means reflect the *central tendency* of a process, while control charts for the range reflect process dispersion. These two charts are described below.

Mean charts. Mean control charts, or $\bar{x}$ *(x-bar)* charts, are based on a normal distribution. The theoretical foundation for this is the *central limit theorem,* which says roughly that the distribution of sample means taken from a process will be normal if the process distribution is normal, and approximately normal even if the process is nonnormal, if the sample size is large enough. In most cases, a sample size of 30 is large enough, and often sample sizes in the range of 10 to 20 observations will suffice. Not only is the sampling distribution normal, its variability is also less than the variability of the process being sampled. These concepts are illustrated in Figure 15–10.

FIGURE 15-10

The Sampling Distribution of Means Is Normal, and It Has Less Variability than the Process

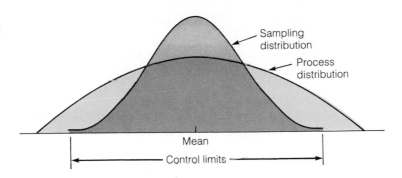

Control limits are based on the sampling distribution, and in effect, each sample mean plotted on a control chart represents a test of whether the process mean has shifted (see Figure 15–11).

In selecting control limits, it is important to recognize that just because all observations are within the limits, this does not guarantee that assignable variations are not present, and that just because an observation appears outside one of the control limits, this does not guarantee that assignable variations are present. For example, if 2-sigma limits are used, 95.5 percent of the sample means should be within the limits, and 4.5 percent should be outside of the limits, when *only* random variations are present. Using wider limits (e.g., 3 sigma limits) will reduce the risk of concluding that the process is out of control when in fact only random variations account for points outside the control limits. However, wider limits make it more difficult to detect nonrandom variations when they occur. Thus, the process average might shift (assignable cause of variation) enough to be readily apparent at the 2-sigma level, but not at the 3-sigma level. Hence, the risk with wide limits is that assigna-

FIGURE 15-11

Each Observation on a Control Chart *Tests* Whether the Process Average Has Changed

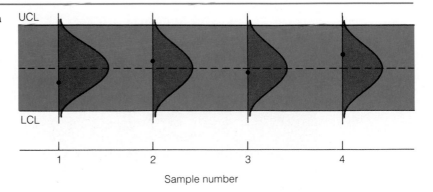

ble variations may go unnoticed. Concluding a process is out of control when it really isn't is called a *Type I error,* and concluding it is in control when it isn't is called a *Type II error.* In theory, the costs of these two kinds of error should be balanced when selecting control limits. However, in practice either 2- or 3-sigma limits are commonly used, partly because of the difficulties associated with determining what probability of a Type II error is appropriate.

If the process standard deviation is known (there may be considerable historical data on which to base this value), control limits can be computed using these formulas:

$$\text{Upper control limit: } \bar{\bar{x}} + z\sigma_{\bar{x}}$$

$$\text{Lower control limit: } \bar{\bar{x}} - z\sigma_{\bar{x}}$$

(15–4)

where $\sigma_{\bar{x}} = \sigma/\sqrt{n}$

and

$\sigma_{\bar{x}} =$ Standard deviation of
       distribution of sample means
$\sigma =$ Process standard deviation
$n =$ Sample size
$z =$ Standard normal deviate
$\bar{\bar{x}} =$ Mean of sample means

The following example illustrates the use of these formulas.

EXAMPLE 3

A process for making aluminum rods has a mean of 2 centimeters. The process variability is approximately normal and has a standard deviation of 0.1 centimeters. Determine control limits that will include 99.74 percent of sample means if the process is generating random output for:

1. $n = 16$.
2. $n = 25$.

Solution

$$\bar{\bar{x}} = 2 \text{ cm}, \sigma = 0.1 \text{ cm}, z = 3 \text{ (From Appendix Table A)}$$
$$UCL = \bar{\bar{x}} + z\,(\sigma/\sqrt{n}\,)$$
$$LCL = \bar{\bar{x}} - z\,(\sigma/\sqrt{n}\,)$$

1. $n = 16$, $UCL = 2 + 3(0.1/\sqrt{16}) = 2 + 0.075 = 2.075$
       $LCL = 2 - 3(0.1/\sqrt{16}) = 2 - 0.075 = 1.925$

2. $n = 25$, $UCL = 2 + 3(0.1/\sqrt{25}) = 2 + 0.06 = 2.06$
       $LCL = 2 - 3(0.1/\sqrt{25}) = 2 - 0.06 = 1.94$

Note that increasing the sample size results in control limits that are closer to the process mean.

TABLE 15–3

Factors for 3-Sigma Control Limits for $\bar{x}$- and R-Charts

Number of observations in subgroup n	Factor for $\bar{x}$-chart A_2	Factors for R chart	
		Lower control limit D_3	Upper control limit D_4
2	1.88	0	3.27
3	1.02	0	2.57
4	0.73	0	2.28
5	0.58	0	2.11
6	0.48	0	2.00
7	0.42	0.08	1.92
8	0.37	0.14	1.86
9	0.34	0.18	1.82
10	0.31	0.22	1.78
11	0.29	0.26	1.74
12	0.27	0.28	1.72
13	0.25	0.31	1.69
14	0.24	0.33	1.67
15	0.22	0.35	1.65
16	0.21	0.36	1.64
17	0.20	0.38	1.62
18	0.19	0.39	1.61
19	0.19	0.40	1.60
20	0.18	0.41	1.59

Source: Adapted from Eugene Grant and Richard Leavenworth, *Statistical Quality Control*, 5th ed. (New York: McGraw-Hill, 1980).

In the event that the process standard deviation is unknown, the sample *range* can be used as a measure of process variability. The appropriate formulas for the control limits are:

$$UCL = \bar{\bar{x}} + A_2\bar{R}$$
$$LCL = \bar{\bar{x}} - A_2\bar{R}$$

(15–5)

Values of A_2 can be obtained from Table 15–3.

EXAMPLE 4

Twenty samples of $n = 8$ have been taken from a milling process. The average sample range for the 20 samples was 0.016 centimeters, and the average mean was 3 centimeters. Determine 3-sigma control limits for this process.

Solution

$\bar{\bar{x}} = 3$ cm., $\bar{R} = .016$, from Table 15–3, $A_2 = 0.37$ for $n = 8$

$$UCL = \bar{\bar{x}} + A_2\bar{R} = 3 + 0.37(.016) = 3.006 \text{ cm.}$$
$$LCL = \bar{\bar{x}} - A_2\bar{R} = 3 - 0.37(.016) = 2.994 \text{ cm.}$$

Range charts.   Control charts for the range are used to monitor
process variability; they are sensitive to changes in process dispersion. Although the underlying sampling distribution is not normal,
the concepts for use of range charts are much the same as those
for use of means charts. Control limits for range charts are found
using the average sample range in conjunction with the formulas:

$$UCL_R = D_4\overline{R}$$
$$LCL_R = D_3\overline{R}$$

(15–6)

where values of D_3 and D_4 are obtained from Table 15–3.

EXAMPLE 5

Twenty-five samples of $n = 10$ observations have been taken from
a milling process. The average sample range was 0.01 centimeter.
Determine upper and lower control limits for sample ranges.

Solution
$\overline{R} = .01$ cm., $n = 10$

From Table 15–3, for $n = 10$, $D_4 = 1.78$, and $D_3 = 0.22$

$$UCL_R = 1.78(.01) = .0178 \text{ or } .018$$
$$LCL_R = 0.22(.01) = .0022 \text{ or } .002$$

In the preceding example, a sample range of 0.018 centimeters
or more would suggest that the process variability had increased.
A sample range of 0.002 or less would imply that the process variability had decreased. In the former case, this would mean that the
process was producing too much variation and we would want to
investigate this in order to remove the cause of variation. In the
latter instance, even though decreased variability is desirable, we
would want to determine what was causing it. Perhaps an improved
method has been used, in which case we would want to identify
it. Possibly the improved quality has come at the expense of productivity, which would not generally be desirable. Or this may only
be a random occurrence. We would expect these about 1 percent
of the time. Hence, it can be instructive to investigate points beyond
the lower limit as well as the upper limit in a range chart.

Using mean and range charts.   Mean control charts and range control charts provide different perspectives on a process. Mean charts
are sensitive to shifts in the process mean while range charts are
sensitive to changes in process dispersion. Because of the difference
in perspective, both types of charts might be used to monitor the
same process. The logic of using both is readily apparent in Figure
15–12. In 15–12A, the mean chart picks up the shift in the process

FIGURE 15–12

Mean and Range Charts Used Together Complement Each Other

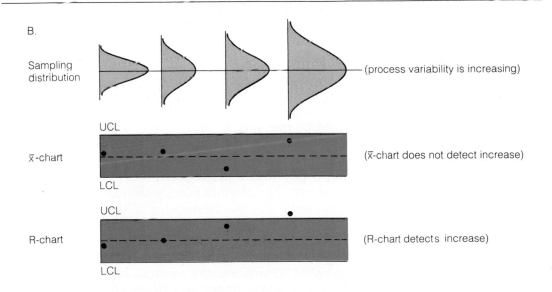

mean, but because the dispersion is not changing, the range chart fails to indicate a problem. Conversely, in 15–12B, a change in process dispersion is less apt to be detected by the mean chart than by the range chart. Hence, use of both charts provides more complete information than either chart alone. Even so, in some cases a single chart may suffice. For example, a process may be more susceptible to changes in the process mean than it is to changes in dispersion, so it might not be necessary to monitor dispersion. Because of the time and cost involved in constructing control charts, gathering the necessary data, and evaluating the results, only those aspects of a process that have a tendency to cause problems should be monitored.

Once control charts have been set up, they can serve as a basis for deciding when to interrupt a process and search for assignable causes of variation. In order to initially determine control limits, the following procedure can be used:

1. Obtain 20 to 25 samples. Compute the mean and range of each sample and the average mean and range for all samples.
2. Establish preliminary control limits for the mean and range using the above formulas and graph them.
3. Plot the sample means on the mean chart and the sample ranges on the range chart and note if any points fall outside of the control limits.
4. If all points are within limits, assume that the process is in control. If not, investigate and correct assignable causes of variation. Then discard those points for which assignable causes have been found and recompute the control limits, or resume the process and collect another set of observations upon which control limits can be based.

Control Charts for Attributes

Control charts for attributes are used when the process characteristic is *counted* rather than measured. For example, the number of defective items in a sample would be counted, whereas the length of each item would be measured. There are two types of attribute control charts, one for the percentage of defective items in a sample (a p-chart) and one for the number of defects (called a c-chart). A p-chart is appropriate when both the defectives and nondefectives can be counted. For instance, if glass bottles are inspected for chipping and cracking, *both* the good bottles and the defective ones can be counted. However, one can count the number of accidents that occur during a given period of time, but *not* the number of accidents that did not occur. Similarly, one can count the number of scratches on a polished surface, the number of bacteria present in a water sample, and the number of crimes committed during the month of August, but not be able to count the number of nonoccurences. In such cases, a *c-chart* is appropriate.

p-chart. A p-chart is used to monitor the proportion of defectives generated by a process. The theoretical basis for a p-chart is the binomial distribution, although for large sample sizes, the normal distribution provides a good approximation to it. Conceptually, a p-chart is constructed and used in much the same way that a mean chart is.

The center line on a p-chart is the average fraction defective in the sample, $\bar{p}$. The standard deviation of the sampling distribution can be estimated using the formula:

$$\hat{\sigma}_p = \sqrt{\frac{\bar{p}(1-\bar{p})}{n}}$$

Control limits are computed using the formulas:

$$UCL_p = \bar{p} + z\,\hat{\sigma}_p$$

$$LCL_p = \bar{p} - z\,\hat{\sigma}_p$$

(15–7)

EXAMPLE 6

Using the information below, construct a control chart that will describe 95.5 percent of the chance variation in the process when the process is in control. Each sample contains 100 items.

Sample	Number of defectives	Sample	Number of defectives
1	14	11	8
2	10	12	12
3	12	13	9
4	13	14	10
5	9	15	11
6	11	16	10
7	10	17	8
8	12	18	12
9	13	19	10
10	10	20	16
			$\overline{220}$

Solution

z for 95.5% is 2.00 (from Appendix Table A)

$$\bar{p} = \frac{\text{Total number of defectives}}{\text{Total number of observations}} = \frac{220}{20(100)} = 0.11$$

$$\hat{\sigma}_p = \sqrt{\frac{\bar{p}(1-\bar{p})}{n}} = \sqrt{\frac{.11(1-.11)}{100}} = .03$$

Control limits are:

$$UCL_p = \bar{p} + z\,(\hat{\sigma}_p) = .11 + 2.00(.03) = .17$$

$$LCL_p = \bar{p} - z\,(\hat{\sigma}_p) = .11 - 2.00(.03) = .05$$

Plotting the control limits and the sample percentages, we can see that the process is initially in control, although the last point is close to the upper limit.

EXAMPLE 6 (concluded)

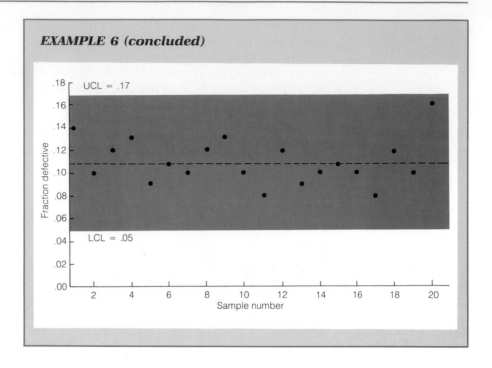

---

c-chart.　　When the goal is to control the number of defects per unit, a c-chart is used. Units might be automobiles, hotel rooms, typed pages, or rolls of carpet. The underlying sampling distribution is the Poisson distribution. Use of the Poisson distribution assumes that defects occur over some *continuous* region and that the probability of more than one defect at any particular spot is negligible. The mean number of defects per unit is $\bar{c}$, *and the standard deviation is* $\sqrt{\bar{c}}$. For practical reasons, the normal approximation to the Poisson is used. The control limits are:

$$UCL_c = \bar{c} + 3\sqrt{\bar{c}}$$
$$LCL_c = \bar{c} - 3\sqrt{\bar{c}}$$

（15–8）

This will include about 99 percent of the output for a stable process.

EXAMPLE 7

Rolls of coiled wire are monitored using a c-chart. Eighteen rolls have been examined, and the number of defects per roll have been recorded, as shown below. Is the process in control? Plot the values on a control chart.

EXAMPLE 7 (concluded)

Sample	Number of defects	Sample	Number of defects
1	3	10	1
2	2	11	3
3	4	12	4
4	5	13	2
5	1	14	4
6	2	15	2
7	4	16	1
8	1	17	3
9	2	18	$\underline{1}$
			45

Solution

$$\bar{c} = 45/18 = 2.5$$

$$UCL_c = \bar{c} + 3\sqrt{\bar{c}} = 2.5 + 3\sqrt{2.5} = 7.24$$

$$LCL_c = \bar{c} - 3\sqrt{\bar{c}} = 2.5 - 3\sqrt{2.5} = -2.24 \rightarrow 0$$

When the computed lower control limit is negative, the effective lower limit is zero, since negative observations cannot occur. (The reason the calculation sometimes produces a negative lower limit is due to the use of the normal distribution to approximate the Poisson distribution: The normal is symmetrical while the Poisson is not symmetrical when $\bar{c}$ is close to zero.)

Tolerances, Control Limits, and Process Variability

There are three commonly used terms that refer to the variability of process output. Each term relates to a slightly different aspect of that variability, so it is important to differentiate between these terms.

Tolerances are specifications established by engineering design or customer requirements. They indicate a range of values in which individual units of output must fall in order to be acceptable.

Control limits are statistical limits that reflect the extent to which *sample statistics* such as means and ranges can vary due to randomness alone.

Process variability refers to the natural or inherent variability in a process.

Control limits and process variability are directly related: control limits are based on sampling variability, and sampling variability is a function of process variability. This relationship can be seen in the way control limits are calculated. For example, control limits for an $\bar{x}$-chart are computed using the formula:

$$\text{Control limits} = \frac{\text{Process}}{\text{mean}} \pm z \frac{\text{Process variability}}{\sqrt{n}}.$$

On the other hand, there is no direct link between tolerances and either control limits or process variability. Tolerances are specified in terms of a product or service, and not in terms of the *process* by which the product of service is generated. Hence, in a given instance, the output of a process may or may not conform to specifications, *even though the process may be statistically "in control."* For example, consider the three cases illustrated in Figure 15–13. In the first case, process capability and output specifications are well matched, so that nearly all of the process output can be expected to meet the specifications. In the second case, the process variability is much less than what is called for, so that virtually 100 percent of the output should be within tolerance. However, in the third case, the specifications are tighter than what the process is capable of, so that even when the process is functioning as it should, a sizable percentage of the output will fail to meet the speci-

FIGURE 15–13

Process Capability and Specifications May or May Not Match

A. Process variability
   matches specifications

B. Process variability
   well within specifications

C. Process variability
   exceeds specifications

fications. In other words, in the third case, the process could be "in control" and still be generating unacceptable output. Thus, we cannot automatically assume that a stable process will provide desired output. Instead, we must specifically check to see if a process is capable of meeting specifications, and not simply set up a control chart to monitor it.

Run Tests

When a process is stable, or in statistical control, the output it generates will exhibit natural variability over a period of time. The presence of patterns, such as trends, cycles, or bias in the output, indicates that assignable, or nonrandom, causes of variation exist. Hence, a process that produces output with such patterns is not in a state of statistical control. This is true even though all of the points on a control chart are within the control limits. For this reason, it is usually prudent to subject control chart data to run tests to determine if patterns can be detected.

A *run* is defined as a sequence of observations with a certain characteristic followed by one or more observations with a different characteristic. The characteristic can be anything that is observable. For example, in the series A A A B there are two runs; the first is a run of three As followed by a run of one B. Underlining each run often helps in counting them. In the series <u>A A</u> <u>B B</u> <u>A</u> there are three runs, as indicated by the underlining.

Two useful run tests involve examination of the number of runs *up and down* and the number of runs with respect to the *median*.[4] In order to count these runs, it becomes necessary to first transform the data into a series of U's and D's (for Up and Down) and into a series of A's and B's (for Above and Below the median). Consider the sequence below, which has a median of 36.5. With respect to the median, the first two values are below it, the second two are above it, the second to last is below, and the last is above. There are four runs:

$$25 \quad 29 \quad 42 \quad 40 \quad 35 \quad 38$$
$$\underline{B \quad B} \quad \underline{A \quad A} \quad \underline{B} \quad \underline{A}$$

In terms of up and down, there are three runs in the same data:

$$25 \quad 29 \quad 42 \quad 40 \quad 35 \quad 38$$
$$- \quad \underline{U \quad U} \quad \underline{D \quad D} \quad \underline{U}$$

(The first value does not receive either a U or a D, since nothing precedes it.)

To determine if any patterns are present in control chart data, one must transform the data into both A's and B's and U's and

---

[4] The median and mean are approximately equal for control charts. The use of the median depends on its ease of determination; use the mean instead of the median *if it is given.*

D's and then count the number of runs in each case. These numbers must then be compared to the number of runs that would be expected in a completely random series. For both the median and the up/down run tests, the expected number of runs is a function of the number of observations in the series. The formulas are:

$$E(r)_{med} = \frac{N}{2} + 1 \tag{15-9a}$$

$$E(r)_{u/d} = (2N - 1)/3 \tag{15-10a}$$

where N is the number of observations.

The actual number of runs in any given set of observations will tend to vary from the expected number, due to chance and to any patterns that might be present. Chance variability is measured by the standard deviation of runs. The formulas are:

$$\sigma_{med} = \sqrt{\frac{N-1}{4}} \tag{15-9b}$$

$$\sigma_{u/d} = \sqrt{\frac{16N - 29}{90}} \tag{15-10b}$$

Distinguishing between chance variability and patterns requires use of the sampling distributions for median runs and for up/down runs. Both distributions are approximately normal. Consequently, we know, for instance, that 95.5 percent of the time a process that is random will produce an observed number of runs that is within two standard deviations of the expected number. If the observed number of runs falls in that range, we can conclude that there are probably no nonrandom patterns; for observed numbers of runs beyond such limits, we begin to suspect that patterns are present. Hence, either too few or too many runs can be an indication of nonrandomness.

In practice, it is often easiest to compute the number of standard deviations, z, that an observed number of runs differs from the

FIGURE 15-14

A Sampling Distribution for Runs Is Used to Distinguish between Chance Variation and Patterns

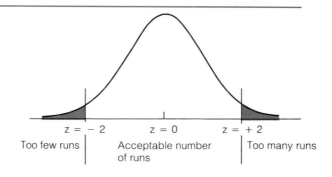

$z = -2$ $z = 0$ $z = +2$

Too few runs   Acceptable number of runs   Too many runs expected. This z would then be compared to the value ±2(z for 95.5%) or some other desired value (e.g., ±1.96 for 95%, ±2.33 for 98%). A test z that exceeds these limits indicates patterns are present. (See Figure 15–14.) The computation of z takes the form:

$$z_{test} = \frac{\text{Observed number of runs} - \text{Expected number of runs}}{\text{Standard deviation of number of runs}}$$

For the median and up/down tests, z is found using the formulas:

$$\text{Median} \qquad z = \frac{r - [(N/2) + 1]}{\sqrt{(N - 1)/4}} \qquad \qquad (15\text{–}11)$$

$$\text{Up and down} \qquad z = \frac{r - [(2N - 1)/3]}{\sqrt{(16N - 29)/90}} \qquad \qquad (15\text{–}12)$$

where

$N = $ Total number of observations
$r = $ Observed number of runs of either A's and B's or U's and D's, depending on which test is involved.

It is desirable to apply both run tests to any given set of observations because each test is different in terms of the types of patterns it can detect. Sometimes both will pick up a certain pattern, but sometimes only one will detect nonrandomness. If either does, the implication is that some sort of nonrandomness is present in the data.

EXAMPLE 8

Twenty sample means have been taken from a process. The means are shown below. Use a median and up/down runs test with $z = 2$ to determine if assignable causes of variation are present. Assume the median is 11.0.

Solution

The means are marked according to above/below median and up/down. The solid lines represent the runs.

Sample	A/B	Mean	U/D	Sample	A/B	Mean	U/D
1	B	10.0	—	11	B	10.7	D
2	B	10.4	U	12	A	11.3	U
3	B	10.2	D	13	B	10.8	D
4	A	11.5	U	14	A	11.8	U
5	B	10.8	D	15	A	11.2	D
6	A	11.6	U	16	A	11.6	U
7	A	11.1	D	17	A	11.2	D
8	A	11.2	U	18	B	10.6	D
9	B	10.6	D	19	B	10.7	U
10	B	10.9	U	20	A	11.9	U

A/B: 10 runs   U/D: 17 runs

EXAMPLE 8 *(concluded)*

The expected number of runs for each test is:

$$E(r)_{med} = \frac{N}{2} + 1 = \frac{20}{2} + 1 = 11$$

$$E(r)_{u/d} = \frac{2N - 1}{3} = \frac{2(20) - 1}{3} = 13$$

The standard deviations are:

$$\sigma_{med} = \sqrt{\frac{N - 1}{4}} = \sqrt{\frac{20 - 1}{4}} = 2.18$$

$$\sigma_{u/d} = \sqrt{\frac{16N - 29}{90}} = \sqrt{\frac{16(20) - 29}{90}} = 1.80$$

The z_{test} values are:

$$z_{med} = \frac{10 - 11}{2.18} = -.46$$

$$z_{u/d} = \frac{17 - 13}{1.80} = +2.22$$

Although the median test does not reveal any pattern, since its z_{test} value is less than ± 2, the up/down test does. Its value exceeds $+2$. Consequently, we conclude that nonrandom variations are present in the data, and hence, that the process is not in control.

If ties occur in either test (e.g., a value equals the median, or two values in a row are the same), assign A/B or U/D in such a manner that z_{test} is as large as possible. If z_{test} still does not exceed ± 2 (± 1.96, etc.) then you can be reasonably confident that a conclusion of nonrandomness is justified.

SUMMARY

Quality assurance is a comprehensive approach to quality that begins with product or service design, continues through the transformation process, and extends to service after delivery.

Among other things, successful quality assurance depends on clear definition of what constitutes desired quality. The chapter discusses quality definition as well as the determinants of quality and potential sources of ideas for improving quality. The remainder of the chapter is devoted to quality of conformance.

The primary concern of quality control is the assurance that goods and services conform to standards. Quality control efforts are directed toward detecting departures from standards and instituting corrective or remedial action whenever it becomes necessary. Since it is not usually feasible to examine every single item, the task of identifying departures from standards relies on inspection of sampled items.

Quality control is largely based on statistical procedures. There are two main areas of quality control: acceptance sampling and process control. Acceptance sampling involves sampling previously produced output with the goal of deciding whether to pass or reject an entire lot. Operating characteristic curves can be used to describe the ability of a given sampling plan to discriminate between good and bad lots. Sampling plans exist for both variables and attributes. This chapter focused on single-sampling plans for percent defectives since they are widely used and easily understood.

Process control involves the monitoring of an ongoing process, partly to check on current quality, but primarily to determine if future output is likely to be acceptable. The main tool is the control

TABLE 15–4

Summary of Quality Assurance Formulas

Acceptance sampling	$AOQ = P_{ac} \times p$

Control charts

Chart	Symbol	Control limits
Mean	$\overline{x}$	$\overline{\overline{x}} \pm z \dfrac{\sigma}{\sqrt{n}}$ or $\overline{\overline{x}} \pm A_2 \overline{R}$
Range	R	$UCL = D_4 \overline{R},\ LCL = D_3 \overline{R}$
Percent defective	p	$\overline{p} \pm z \sqrt{\dfrac{\overline{p}(1-\overline{p})}{n}}$
Number of defects	c	$\overline{c} \pm z \sqrt{\overline{c}}$

Run tests

Name	Number of runs		Standard deviation	z
	Observed	*Expected**		
Median	r	$\dfrac{N}{2} + 1$	$\sqrt{\dfrac{N-1}{4}}$	$\dfrac{r - [(N/2) + 1]}{\sqrt{(N-1)/4}}$
Up/down	r	$\dfrac{(2N-1)}{3}$	$\sqrt{\dfrac{16N - 29}{90}}$	$\dfrac{r - [(2N-1)/3]}{\sqrt{(16N-29)/90}}$

chart, which is a graphical aid for distinguishing between random variations in output and those which can be traced to specific causes and eliminated. Four different control charts were described: means, ranges, fraction defectives, and number of defects. Control charts are based on sampling distributions that indicate the extent of chance or random variation. Run tests are sometimes used in conjunction with control charts to check for patterns in sample data that would suggest nonrandomness.

The formulas used in this chapter are summarized in Table 15–4.

1. *Inspection.* A process for manufacturing shock absorbers for light trucks produces 5 percent defectives. Inspection cost per shock is $0.40, and 100 percent inspection generally catches all defectives, due to the nature of the inspection and the small volume produced. Any defectives installed on trucks must eventually be replaced at a cost of $12 per shock. Is 100 percent inspection justified?

   Solution

   Five percent of the output is defective. The expected cost per shock for replacement is thus 0.05($12) = 60 cents. Since this is greater than the inspection cost per shock of 40 cents, 100 percent inspection is justified.

2. *Acceptance sampling.* Shipments of 300 boxes of glassware are received at a warehouse of a large department store. Random samples of five boxes are checked and the lot rejected if more than one box reveals breakage. Construct the OC curve for this plan.

   Solution

   When the sample size is less than five percent of the lot size, the binomial distribution can be used to obtain P_{ac} for various lot percentage defectives. Here, $n/N = 5/300 = .017$, so the binomial can be used. A portion of the cumulative binomial table is shown on pages 784 and 785. Note that $c = 1$.

   The table indicates that $P_{ac} = .9974$ when lot quality is 5 percent defective, .9185 for 10 percent defective, .8352 for 15 percent, and so on. The resulting curve is:

Lot fraction defective

N = 300
n = 5
c = 1

Cumulative Binomial Probabilities

n	x	.05	.10	.15	.20	.25	.30	.35
					$p =$ *Fraction defective*			
5 . . .	0	.7738	.5905	.4437	.3277	.2373	.1681	.1160
$c = 1$ →	1	.9974	.9185	.8352	.7373	.6328	.5282	.4284
	2	.9988	.9914	.9734	.9421	.8965	.8369	.7648
	3	1.0000	.9995	.9978	.9933	.9844	.9692	.9460
	4	1.0000	1.0000	.9999	.9997	.9990	.9976	.9947
	5	1.0000	1.0000	1.0000	1.0000	1.0000	1.0000	1.0000

3. Develop the AOQ curve for the previous problem.

   Solution

   $$AOQ = P_{ac} \times p$$

   (*Values of lot quality, p,* are taken from the portion of the binomial table shown above.)

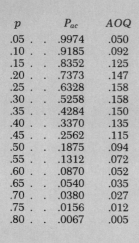

p	P_{ac}	AOQ
.05 . .	.9974	.050
.10 . .	.9185	.092
.15 . .	.8352	.125
.20 . .	.7373	.147
.25 . .	.6328	.158
.30 . .	.5258	.158
.35 . .	.4284	.150
.40 . .	.3370	.135
.45 . .	.2562	.115
.50 . .	.1875	.094
.55 . .	.1312	.072
.60 . .	.0870	.052
.65 . .	.0540	.035
.70 . .	.0380	.027
.75 . .	.0156	.012
.80 . .	.0067	.005

4. *Control charts.* An industrial process that makes 3-foot sections of plastic pipe produces pipe with an average inside diameter of 1 inch and a standard deviation of 0.05 inches.
   a. If one piece of pipe is randomly selected, what is the probability that its inside diameter will exceed 1.02 inches (assuming the population is normal)?
   b. If a random sample of 25 pieces of pipe is selected, what is the probability that the sample *mean* will exceed 1.02 inches?

   Solution

   $$\mu = 1.00", \sigma = .05"$$

   a. $z = \dfrac{x - \mu}{\sigma} = \dfrac{1.02 - 1.00}{.05} = .4$

.40	.45	.50	.55	.60	.65	.70	.75	.80
.0778	.0503	.0313	.0185	.0102	.0053	.0024	.0010	.0003
.3370	.2562	.1875	.1312	.0870	.0540	.0308	.0156	.0067
.6826	.5931	.5000	.4069	.3174	.2352	.1631	.1035	.0579
.9130	.8688	.8125	.7438	.6630	.5716	.4718	.3672	.2627
.9898	.9815	.9688	.9497	.9222	.8840	.8319	.7627	.6723
1.0000	1.0000	1.0000	1.0000	1.0000	1.0000	1.0000	1.0000	1.0000

Using Appendix Table B, $P(x > z) = 1.0000 - .6554 = .3446$

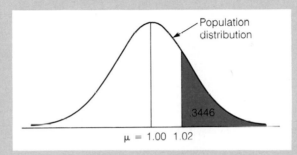

b. $z = \dfrac{\bar{x} - \mu}{\sigma/\sqrt{n}} = \dfrac{1.02 - 1.00}{.05/\sqrt{25}} = 2.00$

Using Appendix Table B,

$$P(\bar{x} > z) = 1.0000 - .9772 = .0228$$

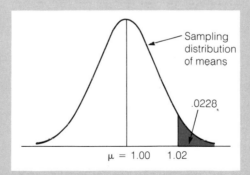

5. Drop-forged steel handles have a designed weight of 10 ounces. Five samples of four observations each have been taken. Use the sample data in conjunction with Table 15–3 to construct upper and lower control limits for both a mean and a range chart. Is the process in control?

	Sample 1	Sample 2	Sample 3	Sample 4	Sample 5
	10.2	10.3	9.7	9.9	9.8
	9.9	9.8	9.9	10.3	10.2
	9.8	9.9	9.9	10.1	10.3
	10.1	10.4	10.1	10.5	9.7
Totals	40.0	40.4	39.6	40.8	40.0

Solution

a.   Determine the mean and range of each sample.

$$\bar{x} = \frac{\Sigma x}{n}, \quad \text{Range} = \text{Largest} - \text{Smallest}$$

Sample	Mean	Range
1	40.0/4 = 10.0	10.2 − 9.8 = .4
2	40.4/4 = 10.1	10.4 − 9.8 = .6
3	39.6/4 = 9.9	10.1 − 9.7 = .4
4	40.8/4 = 10.2	10.5 − 9.9 = .6
5	40.0/4 = 10.0	10.3 − 9.7 = .6

b.   Compute the average mean and average range:

$$\bar{\bar{x}} = \frac{10.0 + 10.1 + 9.9 = 10.2 + 10.0}{5} = 50.2/5 = 10.04$$

$$\bar{R} = \frac{.4 + .6 + .4 + .6 + .6}{5} = 2.6/5 = .52$$

c.   Obtain factors A_2, D_4, and D_3 from Table 15–3 for $n = 4$:

$$A = .73, D_4 = 2.28, D_3 = 0$$

d.   Compute upper and lower limits:

$$UCL_{\bar{x}} = \bar{\bar{x}} + A_2\bar{R} = 10.04 + .73(.52) = 10.42$$
$$LCL_{\bar{x}} = \bar{\bar{x}} - A_2\bar{R} = 10.04 - .73(.52) = 9.66$$
$$UCL_R = D_4\bar{R} = 2.28(.52) = 1.19$$
$$LCL_R = D_3\bar{R} = 0(.52) = 0.$$

e.   Plot sample means and ranges on their respective control charts or otherwise verify that points are within limits.

The smallest sample mean is 9.9, and the largest is 10.2. Both are well within the control limits. Similarly, the largest sample range is 0.6, which is also within the control limits. Hence, we conclude the process is in control. Note, however, that for illustrative purposes, the number of samples was deliberately small; 20 or more samples would give a clearer indication of control limits and whether the process was in control.

6.   *Run tests.* The number of defectives per sample for 11 samples is shown below. Determine if nonrandom patterns are present in the sequence.

			Sample								
	1	2	3	4	5	6	7	8	9	10	11
Number of defectives. . .	22	17	19	25	18	20	21	17	23	23	24

Solution

Since the median isn't given, it must be estimated from the sample data. To do this, array the data from low to high; the median is the middle value. (In this case, there are an odd number of values. For an even number of values, average the middle two to obtain the median.)

Arrayed values: 17 17 18 19 20 21 22 23 23 24 25
                          (5 below)   ↑   (5 above)
                                      median

Hence, the median is 21.

Next, code the observations using *A/B* and *U/D:*

Sample	A/B	Number of defectives	U/D
1	| A	22	—
2	B	17	| D
3	B	19	| U
4	| A	25	| U
5	B	18	| D
6	B	20	| U
7	—	21	| U
8	| B	17	| D
9	A	23	| U
10	A	23	—
11	A	24	| U

Note that with each test there are tied values. How these are resolved can affect the number of observed runs. Suppose we adhere to this rule: Assign a letter (A or B, U or D) in such a way that the resulting difference between the observed and expected number of runs is as large as possible. To accomplish this, it will be necessary to initially ignore ties and count the runs to see whether there are too many or too few. Then return to the ties and make the assignments. The rationale for this rule is that it is a conservative method for retaining data; if we can conclude the data are random using this approach, we can be reasonably confident that the data are random, and not that our method "created" randomness. With this in mind, assign a B to sample 7 since the expected number of runs is:

$$E(r)_{med} = N/2 + 1 = 11/2 + 1 = 6.5$$

and the difference between the resulting 5 runs and 6.5 is greater than 6.5 and 7 (which occurs if A is used instead of B). Similarly, in the up/down test, a U for sample 10 produces 6 runs, while a D produces 8 runs. Since the expected number of runs is:

$$E(r)_{u/d} = (2N - 1)/3 = (22 - 1)/3 = 7$$

It makes no difference which one we use: They both yield a difference of one. For the sake of illustration, suppose we assign a D.

The computations for the two tests are summarized below. Since neither test reveals nonrandomness, we conclude the data are random.

	Runs observed	E(r)	σ_r	z	Conclude
Median	5	6.5	1.58	−.95	Random
Up/down	8	7.0	1.28	.78	Random

DISCUSSION AND REVIEW QUESTIONS

1. Define the term *quality*, and explain why quality is important to most organizations.
2. What are the primary determinants of quality?
3. What are some sources of ideas for improving quality?
4. Explain the term *quality circle* and list some of the potential benefits of quality circles.
5. For each item listed below, indicate how you would define quality.
   a. Family car.
   b. Lawn care.
   c. Tree.
   d. Answering service.
6. Inspection is an integral part of quality control.
   a. What level of inspection is optimal?
   b. What factors often guide the decision of how much to inspect?
   c. What are the main considerations in choosing between centralized and on-site inspection?
   d. What points are potential candidates for inspection?
7. What is meant by the term *fitness for use*?
8. How are quality and productivity related?
9. Compare and contrast *design quality* and *quality of conformance*.
10. What is the objective of acceptance sampling?
11. What is an *operating characteristic curve*?
12. What general factors govern the choice of single- versus multiple-sampling plans?
13. Briefly explain each of these terms:
   a. AOQ.
   b. AOQL.
   c. LTPD.
   d. α risk.
   e. β risk.
14. How does process control differ from lot control?
15. List the elements in the control process.
16. Quality control is an example of management by exception. Explain.
17. What are the concepts that underlie the construction and use of control charts?
18. What is the purpose of control charts?
19. Why is order of observation important in process control?
20. What is a run? How are run tests useful in process control?
21. Why is it usually desirable to use both an up/down and a median run test on the same data?
22. If neither the up/down nor the median test indicates nonrandomness, does that guarantee that the process is random? If one or both tests indicate nonrandom variations in the data, does that prove that the process is not in control? Explain.
23. Contrast *tolerances, control limits,* and *process variability.*
24. Explain this statement: "A process may be out of control even though all observations are well within the control limits."
25. A customer has recently modified specifications on a part your company supplies. The specs are now much narrower than the machine generally used for the job is capable of. Briefly discuss the alternatives the operations manager might consider to resolve this problem. (See Figure 15–13C)
26. A new order has just come into the department. The capability of the machine used for this type of work is such that virtually all of the output can be expected to be well inside of the specs. (See Figure 15–13B.)
   a. What benefits might be derived by analyzing this situation?
   b. What alternatives should be considered in this sort of situation.

PROBLEMS

1. An assembly operation for trigger mechanisms of a semiautomatic spray gun produces a small percentage of defective mechanisms. Management must decide whether to continue the current practice of 100 percent inspection or whether to

replace defective mechanisms after final assembly, when all guns are inspected. Replacement at final assembly costs $30 each; inspection during trigger assembly costs $12 per hour for labor and overhead. The inspection rate is one trigger per minute.

   a. Would 100 percent inspection during trigger assembly be justified if there are (1) 4 percent defective? (2) 1 percent defective?

   b. At what point would management be indifferent between 100 percent inspection of triggers and only final inspection?

2. Random samples of $n = 20$ circuit breakers are tested for damage caused by shipment in each lot of 4,000 received, and lots with more than one defective are pulled and subjected to 100 percent inspection.

   a. Construct the OC curve for this sampling plan.

   b. Construct the AOQ curve for this plan assuming defectives found during 100 percent inspection are replaced with good parts. What is the approximate AOQL?

3. Auditors use a technique called *discovery sampling* in which a random sample of items is inspected, and if *any* defectives are found, the entire lot of items being sampled is subjected to 100 percent inspection.

   a. Draw an OC curve for the case where a sample of 15 credit accounts will be inspected out of a total of 8,000 accounts.

   b. Draw an OC curve for the case where 150 accounts out of 8,000 accounts will be examined. (Hint: Use $p = .001, .002, .003, . . .$).

   c. Draw the AOQ curve for the preceding case and estimate the AOQL.

4. Random samples of lots of textbooks are inspected for defectives just prior to shipment to the warehouse. Each lot contains 3,000 books.

   a. On a single sheet of graph paper, construct OC curves for $n = 100$ and (1) $c = 0$, (2) $c = 1$, and (3) $c = 2$. (Hint: Use $p = .001, .002, .003, . . .$).

   b. On a single sheet of graph paper, construct OC curves for $c = 2$ and (1) $n = 5$, (2) $n = 20$, and (3) $n = 120$.

   c. Construct AOQ curves for the first two cases in part *b*.

5. Manufacturing specifications call for motor housings that weigh between 24 and 25 pounds. The housings are cast using a process that produces castings that have a mean of 24.5 pounds and a standard deviation of 0.2 pounds. The distribution of output is normal.

   a. What percentage of housings will not meet the weight specs?

   b. Determine 3 sigma control limits for this process if $n = 16$.

6. An automatic filling machine is used to fill one-liter bottles of cola. The machine's output is approximately normal with a mean of 1.0 liters and a standard deviation of 0.01 liters. Output is monitored using means of samples of 25 observations.

   a. Determine upper and lower control limits that will include roughly 95.5 percent of the sample means when the process is in control.

   b. Graph the control chart and plot these sample means: 1.005, 1.001, .998, 1.002, .995, and .999. Is the process in control?

7. A grinding and deburring operation is monitored using a mean and a range chart. Six samples of $n = 20$ observations have been obtained and the sample means and ranges computed:

Sample	Mean	Range
1	3.06	.42
2	3.15	.50
3	3.11	.41
4	3.13	.46
5	3.06	.46
6	3.09	.45

   a. Using the factors in Table 15–3, determine upper and lower limits for mean and range charts.

   b. Is the process in control?

8. Under stable conditions, 8 percent of the aluminum bowls formed on a certain piece of equipment require reworking. The process will be checked using samples of 80 bowls. Determine upper and

lower 3-sigma control limits for the proportion of output needing rework.

9. A continuous process cuts plastic tubing into nominal lengths of 80 centimeters. Samples of five observations each have been taken, and the results are listed below. Using factors from Table 15–3, determine upper and lower control limits for mean and range charts and decide if the process is in control.

Sample

1	2	3	4	5	6
79.2	80.5	79.6	78.9	80.5	79.7
78.8	78.7	79.6	79.4	79.6	80.6
80.0	81.0	80.4	79.7	80.4	80.5
78.4	80.4	80.3	79.4	80.8	80.0
81.0	80.1	80.8	80.6	78.8	81.1

10. An automatic screw machine produces 2 inch hex-nuts. Using the sample data below and $n = 200$, construct a control chart for the fraction defective using 2-sigma limits. Is the process in control? If not, eliminate any values that are outside of the limits and compute revised limits.

Sample

	1	2	3	4	5	6	7	8	9	10	11	12	13
Number of defectives	1	2	2	0	2	1	2	0	2	7	3	2	1

11. The postmaster of a small western city receives a certain number of complaints about mail delivery each day. Assume that the distribution of daily complaints is Poisson. Construct a control chart with 3-sigma limits using the data below. Is the process in control?

Day

	1	2	3	4	5	6	7	8	9	10	11	12	13	14
Number of complaints . . .	4	10	14	8	9	6	5	12	13	7	6	4	2	10

12. Construct a control chart with 3-sigma limits for the number of defects per spool of cable given the data below. Is the process in control?

Observation	Number of defects
1	2
2	3
3	1
4	0
5	1
6	3
7	2
8	0
9	2
10	1
11	3
12	1
13	2
14	0

13. During long runs of canned vegetables through a labeling machine, a few labels invariably fail to adhere properly and eventually fall off. Using the sample data below, which is based on samples of 100 observations each, construct a control chart for the fraction defective using 95 percent control limits and determine if the process is in control.

Sample	Number of defectives
1	5
2	3
3	6
4	7
5	4
6	6
7	8
8	4
9	5
10	8
11	3
12	4
13	5
14	6
15	6
16	7

14. Tolerances for a metal shaft are much wider than the process used to machine the shafts is capable of. Consequently, the decision has been made to allow the cut-

ting tool to wear a certain amount before replacement. The tool wears at the rate of 0.004 centimeters per piece. The process has a natural variation, σ, of 0.01 centimeters and is normally distributed. Tolerances are 15 to 17 centimeters and $n = 1$. For 2-sigma limits, how many can the process turn out before tool replacement becomes necessary? (See diagram.)

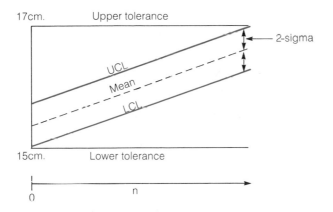

15. Tolerances for the plastic tubing mentioned in Problem 9 are 78 centimeters and 81 centimeters. Based on the data given in the problem, are the tolerances being met? Estimate the percentage of the process output that can be expected to fall within the tolerances.

16. A process that produces bars of soap is to be investigated. Historically, the process has had a standard deviation equal to .146. The means of 39 samples of $n = 14$ are shown below:

Sample	Mean		Sample	Mean
1.	3.86		21.	3.84
2.	3.90		22.	3.82
3.	3.83		23.	3.89
4.	3.81		24.	3.86
5.	3.84		25.	3.88
6.	3.83		26.	3.90
7.	3.87		27.	3.81
8.	3.88		28.	3.86
9.	3.84		29.	3.98
10.	3.80		30.	3.96
11.	3.88		31.	3.88
12.	3.86		32.	3.76
13.	3.88		33.	3.83
14.	3.81		34.	3.77
15.	3.83		35.	3.86
16.	3.86		36.	3.80
17.	3.82		37.	3.84
18.	3.86		38.	3.79
19.	3.84		39.	3.85
20.	3.87			

a. Construct an x-bar chart for this process with 3-sigma limits. Is the process in control?

b. Analyze the data using a median run test and an up/down run test. What can you conclude?

17. For each of the control charts below, analyze the data using both median and up/down run tests with $z = \pm 1.96$ limits. Are nonrandom variations present? Assume the center line is the long-term median.

18. Analyze the data in the problems listed below using median and up/down run tests with $z = \pm 2$.
    a. Problem 13.
    b. Problem 11.

19. Use both types of run tests to analyze the daily expense vouchers listed below. Assume a median of $31.

Day	Amount	Day	Amount
1 . . .	$27.69	31 . . .	40.54
2 . . .	28.13	32 . . .	36.31
3 . . .	33.02	33 . . .	27.14
4 . . .	30.31	34 . . .	30.38
5 . . .	31.59	35 . . .	31.96
6 . . .	33.64	36 . . .	32.03
7 . . .	34.73	37 . . .	34.40
8 . . .	35.09	38 . . .	25.67
9 . . .	33.39	39 . . .	35.80
10 . . .	32.51	40 . . .	32.23
11 . . .	27.98	41 . . .	26.76
12 . . .	31.25	42 . . .	30.51
13 . . .	33.98	43 . . .	29.35
14 . . .	25.56	44 . . .	24.09
15 . . .	24.46	45 . . .	22.45
16 . . .	29.65	46 . . .	25.16
17 . . .	31.08	47 . . .	26.11
18 . . .	33.03	48 . . .	29.84
19 . . .	29.10	49 . . .	31.75
20 . . .	25.19	50 . . .	29.14
21 . . .	28.60	51 . . .	37.78
22 . . .	20.02	52 . . .	34.16
23 . . .	26.67	53 . . .	38.28
24 . . .	36.40	54 . . .	29.49
25 . . .	32.07	55 . . .	30.81
26 . . .	44.10	56 . . .	30.60
27 . . .	41.44	57 . . .	34.46
28 . . .	29.62	58 . . .	35.10
29 . . .	30.12	59 . . .	31.76
30 . . .	26.39	60 . . .	34.90

20. A company has just negotiated a contract to produce a part for another firm. In the process of manufacturing the part, as the cutting tool wears, the inside diameter of successive parts becomes smaller and smaller. However, the specs are so wide relative to what the machine is capable of that it is possible to initially set the diameter at a large value and let the process run for a while before replacing the cutting tool. (This situation is somewhat similar to the one described in Problem 14.)

The inside diameter decreases at an average rate of 0.001 cm. per part, and the process has a standard deviation of 0.01 cm. The variability is approximately normal. Assuming 3-sigma control limits, how frequently must the tool be replaced if the process specs are 3 cm. and 3.5 cm., and the initial setting is the upper spec?

21. (Refer to Solved Problem 5.) Suppose the process specs are 9.65 and 10.35. Based on the data given, does it appear that the specs are being met? If not, what should one look for?

22. A production process consists of a three-step operation. The scrap rate of the first step is 10 percent, and 6 percent on the other two steps.
    a. If the desired daily output is 450 units, how many units must be started to allow for loss due to scrap?
    b. If the scrap rate on each step could be cut in half, how many units would this save in terms of the scrap allowance?
    c. If the scrap represents a cost of $10 per unit, how much is it costing the company per day for the original scrap rate?

23. (Refer to the data in Example 7.) Two additional observations have been taken. The first resulted in 3 defects and the second had 4 defects. Using the set of 20 observations, perform run tests on the data. What can you conclude about the data?

SELECTED BIBLIOGRAPHY

Duncan, A. J. *Quality Control and Industrial Statistics.* 4th ed. Homewood, Ill.: Richard D. Irwin, 1974.

Garvin, David A. "Quality on the Line." *Harvard Business Review,* September–October 1983, p. 64.

Gitlow, Howard S., and Paul T. Hertz. "Product Defects and Productivity." *Harvard Business Review,* September–October 1983, p. 131.

Grant, Eugene L., and Richard S. Leavenworth. *Statistical Quality Control.* 5th ed. New York: McGraw-Hill, 1980.

Juran, J. M. "Japanese and Western Quality—A Contrast." *Quality Progress,* December 1978, pp. 10–18.

Juran, J. M., and F. M. Gryma, Jr. *Quality Planning and Analysis.* 2d ed. New York: McGraw-Hill, 1980.

Leonard, Frank S., and W. Earl Sasser. "The Incline of Quality." *Harvard Business Review,* September–October 1982, p. 163.

Nelson, Paul C. "Current Impact of Product Liability." *Quality Progress,* August 1976, pp. 22–27.

Reddy, Jack, and Abe Berger. "Three Essentials of Product Quality." *Harvard Business Review,* July–August 1983, p. 153.

Takeuchi, Hirotaka, and John A. Quelch. "Quality Is More than Making a Good Product." *Harvard Business Review,* July–August 1983, p. 139.

Van Girch, John P. "Quality—Producer and Consumer Views." *Quality Progress,* April 1977, pp. 30–33.

Vinson, William D., and Donald F. Heany. "Is Quality Out of Control?" *Harvard Business Review,* November–December 1977, p. 114.

Case

Marion Camp Memorial Hospital

The Marion Camp Memorial Hospital provides convalescent care for patients with long-term illnesses as well as for patients who require extended periods of physical therapy. The average length of stay at the hospital is four months. The hospital is supported through a combination of state and federal funding, medicare payments, and private donations. Less than 10 percent of the hospital's revenue is derived from patients.

The hospital director, H. John ("Big Jack") Pace has become increasingly concerned with the number of complaints the hospital is receiving on various aspects of its health care, and he recently made this the main topic at the monthly staff meeting. In attendance at that meeting were Alan Carter, chief physician, Nancy Ames, supervisor of nursing, Phil Rogers, manager of support services, and Charlotte James, assistant director.

Mr. Pace began the meeting with a brief statement outlining some of the many complaints he'd received, which ranged from cold meals to beds not being changed often enough. Some of the complaints were from hospital employees themselves. Mr. Pace indicated that he hoped that this wasn't the start of a decline in the quality of health care. However, his main concern was an upcoming inspection for reaccreditation by the state. In his words, "You know how they can pick up on something like this and blow it all out of proportion."

Charlotte James, who has been investigating the problem, reported that she was having difficulties because "doctors, nurses, dieticians, and support people all have different definitions of quality." She also noted that most of the complaints seemed to relate to support services rather than medical care, and Phil Rogers tended to agree with her, but he indicated that he had not been able to "turn things around." He pointed out that support people (nurses' aids, kitchen workers, janitors, painters, etc.) were unskilled or semiskilled personnel who generally received the minimum wage. He noted that turnover was high, morale low, there were no professional standards, and few workers viewed themselves as a part of the "health-care team." According to Phil, "Most of my people are bored with their jobs, and they lack any positive attitude towards quality. In fact, I'm not even sure they know what quality means!"

At this point, Nancy Ames mentioned that her husband was involved in quality control for a local candy manufacturer, and she wondered if perhaps some of those techniques might be useful. Although she was not completely familiar with those techniques, she promised to ask her husband to drop by to discuss the problems.

Mr. Pace closed the meeting, tabling the discussion until they could meet with Mr. Ames.

The meeting with Mr. Ames took place late the following week. At the meeting, Mr. Ames stressed the importance of defining quality, illustrated the use of control charts, and wondered if some of the increase in complaints could be attributed to seasonal factors. He also suggested that the hospital develop a short questionnaire for patients and staff, which might enable them to, in his words, "get a better handle on the problems before wasting any time trying to solve them."

Question

Assume that you have been called in as a consultant on this case. Your job is to identify the main problem and to make recommendations for solving it.

Case

Anyone for Sushi?

The operations manager of a firm that produces frozen dinners had received numerous complaints about the firm's Chick-n-Gravy dinners from supermarkets that sell this item. The manager then asked Ann to investigate the matter and to report her recommendations.

Ann's first task was to sift through the list of complaints to determine what problems were generating the complaints. The majority of complaints centered on five defects: underfilled packages, a missing item, spills/mixed items, unacceptable taste, and packages improperly sealed.

Next, she took samples of dinners from the production line and examined each sample, making note of any defects that she found. A summary of those results is shown in the accompanying table:

Date	Time	Line	*Defect Observed*				
			Underfilled	Missing item	Spill/ mixed	Unacceptable taste	Improperly sealed
5/12	0900	1		√	√	√√√	
5/12	1330	2			√√		√√
5/13	1000	2				√	√√√
5/13	1345	1	√√		√√		
5/13	1530	2			√√√		√
5/14	0830	1		√√√		√√	
5/14	1100	2	√		√	√√	
5/14	1400	1			√		√
5/15	1030	1		√√		√√	
5/15	1145	2			√		
5/15	1500	1	√		√		
5/16	0845	2				√√	√√
5/16	1030	1		√√	√	√	
5/16	1400	1					
5/16	1545	2	√	√√√√√	√	√	√√

The data resulted from inspecting approximately 800 frozen dinners. What should Ann recommend to the manager?

Answers to Selected Problems

Chapter 2: Decision Making

1. **a.** Expand (80).
   b. Do nothing (50).
   c. Indifferent between Do nothing and Subcontract (55).
   d. Subcontract (10).

2. **a.** Expand (62).
   b. $9.

3. Do nothing: P (High) less than .50.
   Subcontract: .50 < P(High) < .67.
   Expand: P(High) greater than .67.

4. **a.**

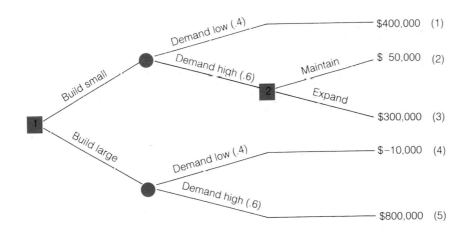

   b. $164,000

5. Large for P(low) less than .55.
   Small for P(low) greater than .55.

6. **a.** Relocate.
   b. Renew.
   c. Relocate.

7. **a.** Renew.
   c. $1,575,000.

8. Indifferent at P(approved) = .464.

9. **a.** Build large.
   b. Build small.
   c. $12.4.
   d. Build small for P(High) less than .721. Build large for P(High) greater than .721.

10. Buy 2 ($113.5).

11. Expand ($1.57).

12. $4.

Chapter 2 Supplement: Linear Programming

1. **a.** $x = 0$, $y = 12$, Profit = \$240.
    b. $A = 25.45$, $B = 18.18$, $Z = \$207.25$.

2. **a.** $T = 20$, $S = 8$, $Z = \$58.40$.
    b. $C = 4.6$, $D = 14.4$, $Z = \$24.18$.

3. $H = 132$ units, $W = 36$ units, Profit = \$6,360.

4. Deluxe = 90 lb., Standard = 60 lb., Profit = \$243.

5. $x = 327.27$, $y = 163.64$, $Z = \$1,636.36$.

6. 500 apple, 200 grape, Revenue = \$990. Fifty cups of sugar will be unused.

7. Final tableau:

C		$10	$20	$0	$0	
	Variables in solution	x	y	s_1	s_2	Solution quantity
$0	s_1	3.0	0.0	1.0	−0.5	16.0
$20	y	1.0	1.0	0.0	0.3	12.0
	Z	20.0	20.0	0.0	5.0	240.0
	$C - Z$	−10.0	0.0	0.0	−5.0	

8. **a.** (1) 485.72 to 800.
              (2) 750 to 1080.
              (3) 145.45 to infinity.
    b. (optimality).
              C_A: \$3.75 to \$12.
              C_B: \$1.50 to \$4.80.

9. Final tableau:

C		$40	$30	$0	$0	
	Variables in solution	H	W	s_1	s_2	Solution quantity
$40	H	1.0	0.0	0.3	−0.1	132
$30	W	0.0	1.0	−0.1	0.2	36
	Z	40.0	30.0	9.0	2.0	6,360
	$C - Z$	0.0	0.0	−9.0	−2.0	

a. Fabrication: 160 to 960.
        Assembly: 300 to 1800.
b. (optimality) H: \$10 to \$60.
                        W: \$20 to \$120.

10. Final tableau:

C		$4	$2	$0	$0	$0	
	Variables in solution	x	y	s_1	s_2	s_3	Solution quantity
$2	y	0.0	1.0	0.0	0.0	−0.4	163.64
$0	s_2	0.0	0.0	−0.1	1.0	1.0	695.46
$4	x	1.0	0.0	−0.0	0.0	0.3	327.27
	Z	4.0	2.0	0.0	0.0	0.4	1,636.36
	C − Z	0.0	0.0	−0.0	0.0	−0.4	

a. Casting: 32,000 to 41,016.
   Grinding: 1,555 to infinity.
   Drilling: 2,871 to 4,050.
b. (optimality).
   C_x: $2.67 to $4.50.
   C_y: $1.78 to $3.00.

11. a. Sugar: 1,150 to infinity.
    Flour: 2,070 to 2,160.
    Time: 3,300 to 4,200.
    b. C_A: $1.20 to $2.40.
    C_G: $.75 to $1.50.

12. a. Final tableau:

C		$10.5	$11.75	$10.8	$0	$0	$0	
	Variables in solution	x	y	z	s_1	s_2	s_3	Solution quantity
$0.00	s_1	0.0	5.6	1.6	1.0	−0.7	0.0	507.14
$10.50	x	1.0	1.3	1.3	0.0	0.1	0.0	178.57
$0.00	s_3	0.0	−2.1	0.9	0.0	−0.6	1.0	5.71
	Z	10.5	13.5	13.5	0.0	1.5	0.0	1875.00
	C − Z	0.0	−1.8	−2.7	0.0	−1.5	0.0	

b. Stapling, since the optimum solution
   exhausts that resource.

13. Final tableau:

C		$2.40	$2.50	$3.00	$0	$0	$0	
	Variables in solution	a	b	c	s_1	s_2	s_3	Solution quantity
$2.50	b	1.2	1.0	0.0	0.2	0.0	−0.1	80
$0.00	s_2	0.2	0.0	0.0	−0.3	1.0	−0.1	380
$3.00	c	0.0	0.0	1.0	−0.1	0.0	0.1	50
	Z	3.0	2.5	3.0	0.2	0.0	0.1	350
	C − Z	−0.6	0.0	0.0	−0.2	0.0	−0.1	

C_a (insignificance): $0 to $3.00.
C_b (optimality): $2.00 to $3.50.
C_c (optimality): $2.00 to $5.00.

14. **a.** Final tableau:

C		21	18	999	0.0	999	0.0	
	Variables in solution	x	y	a_1	s_1	a_2	s_2	Solution quantity
18	y	0.0	1.0	0.1	−0.1	−0.3	0.3	6.7
21	x	1.0	0.0	−0.1	0.1	0.7	−0.7	6.7
	Z	21.0	18.0	1.0	−1.0	8.0	−8.0	260.0
	$C - Z$	0.0	0.0	998.0	1.0	991.0	8.0	

b. Final tableau:

C		$5	$2	$3	$999	$0	$999	$0	$999	$0	
	Variables in solution	x	y	z	a_1	s_1	a_2	s_2	a_3	s_3	Solution quantity
$3	z	1.0	0.0	1.0	0.1	−0.1	−0.1	0.1	0.0	0.0	12.56
$0	s_3	2.1	0.0	0.0	−0.2	0.2	0.7	−0.7	−1.0	1.0	11.16
$2	x	−0.1	1.0	0.0	−0.2	0.2	0.2	−0.2	0.0	0.0	11.40
	Z	2.6	2.0	3.0	0.1	−0.1	0.1	−0.1	0.0	0.0	60.47
	$C - Z$	2.4	0.0	0.0	999	0.1	999	0.1	999	0.0	

Chapter 3: Forecasting

2. **b.** (1) 21.74, (2) 19, (3) 20.4, (4) 19.52, (5) 20.
   c. Demand did not exceed supply.

4. **a.** 88.16%. **b.** 88.54%.

5. **a.** Starting forecast is $(800 + 810 + 808 + 812)/4 = 807.5$; $F_9 = 809.68$ cases.
   b. 804 cases.

6. **a.** 700,000 sq. ft. **b.** 760,000 sq. ft.

7. **a.** Increasing by 15,000 bottles per year.
   b. 275 (i.e., 275,000 bottles).

8. **b.** 1,320 trees.

9. Q_1: 158; Q_2: 175; Q_3: 126; Q_4: 325.

10. $500 - 18.18t$.

11. **a.** $Y_t = 204.09 + 19.76t$. **c.** No. **d.** 500.49.

13. Y_{11}: 267.63; Y_{12}: 274.13; Y_{13}: 280.63; Y_{14}: 287.13.

14.

Period	Forecast
1	—
2	200.00
3	208.40
4	211.64
5	223.62
6	234.79
7	233.25
8	247.32
9	251.04
10	259.72
11	272.58

16. $Y_t = 27.64 - 2.60t + 1.121t^2$.

17. $Y_t = 3,518.5 - 15.64t + 9.49t^2$.

19.

Day	Relative
1	.902
2	.836
3	.919
4	1.034
5	1.416
6	1.487
7	.427

20.

Jan	800
Feb	810
Mar	750
Apr	810
May	826
Jun	850
Jul	850
Aug	855
Sep	865
Oct	900
Nov	875
Dec	900

21. **a.** $29,000.

22. **b.** $17.90.

23. **a.** $Y = 12.35 + .543x$. **b.** $r = .539$.
    c. Yes.

24. **a.** $Y = 334.57 - 22.286x$. **c.** $r = -.974$.

25. **b.** $Y = 66.33 + .584x$. **c.** Yes.
    d. 90.27 **e.** 90.27 ± 10.04.

26. **a.** $r = +.94$ **b.** $Y = .955 + 5.276x$.
   c. 11.51 mowers.

27.

	Shop 1	*Shop 2*
Thurs . . .	.92	.86
Fri.	1.03	1.03
Sat	1.05	1.11

28.

	Shop 1	*Shop 2*
Thurs . . .	258	180
Fri	287	221
Sat	295	240

29. **a.**

$MAD_5 = 5$	$T.S._5 = 1.40$
$MAD_6 = 5.9$	$T.S._6 = -.17$
$MAD_7 = 4.73$	$T.S._7 = -.63$
$MAD_8 = 3.911$	$T.S._8 = -.26$
$MAD_9 = 4.238$	$T.S._9 = -1.42$

                            etc.

30. **a.**

	MSE	*MAD*
Forecast 1	10.44	2.8
Forecast 2	42.44	3.6
Naive	156	10.7

  b.

	Shop 1	*Shop 2*
Thurs . .	265.1	191.4
Fri . . .	296.8	229.7
Sat . . .	304.4	247.7

31. **a.** Initial $MAD = 4.727$. The tracking signal for month 15 is 4.087, so at that point, the forecast would be suspect.
   b. Σ errors $= -1$, Σ errors$^2 = 573$. Control limits: 0 ± 10.98 (in control). Plot reveals cycles in errors.

Chapter 4: Capacity Planning

1. **a.** 46,000 units. **b.** (1) $3,000, (2) $8,200.
   c. 126,000 units. **d.** 25,556 units.
2. **a.** *A:* 8,000 units. **b.** 10,000 units.
       B: 7,500 units
   c. *A:* $20,000.
       B: $18,000.
3. **a.** 39,683 units. **b.** $1.71 (rounded up).
4. **a.** A: $82.
      B: $92.
      C: $100.

   c. A: 0 to less than 178.
      B: Never.
      C: 178+.
5. $\frac{1}{3}$ day, $\frac{2}{3}$ evening.
6. **a.** Additional plant. **b.** Do nothing.
   c. Do nothing.
   d. Do nothing.
7. **a.** Buy 200. **b.** Do nothing.
   c. Buy 80.
   d. (1) Buy 80.
      (2) Buy 80.
8. **b.** Overbook 1 for maximin; indifferent for maximax.
   c. Overbook 1 ($19.2).

Chapter 4 Supplement: Financial analysis

1. **a.** 11%. **b.** 12%.
2. **a.** Seven years.
   b. $PV_u = \$181,800$, $PV_b = \$241,550$
3. PV_{buy}: $7,112; PV_A: $6,914; PV_B: $6,748.40
4. **a.** PV_A: $4,250, PV_B: $7,164
   b. PV_A: $5,538, PV_B: $7,935
5. *A:* 4.8 years. *B:* 5 years.
6. *A:* 20%; *B:* 18%; *C:* 22%.
7. PV_A: $1,910; PV_B: $-13,300$; PV_C: $-3,800$
8. **a.** (1) $217,800.
      (2) $-1,346,400$.
   b. Approximately 12%.
   c. Eight years.
9. Remodel ($58,168).

Chapter 5: Location Planning

1. Kansas City: $256,000.
2. **a.** *A:* 16,854; *B:* 17,416; *C:* 17,753.
   b. *C:* $14,670.
3. **a.** 120 units. **b.** *A:* 0 to 119
                         B: 121+.
4. **a.** *B:* 0 to 33; *C:* 34 to 400;
      A: 400+.
5. *C* ($270,000).
6. Biloxi ($160,000).
7. **a.** (1) outside, (2) city. **b.** 230 cars.
9. A.
10. **a.** B = C > A.
   b. B > C > A.

Chapter 5 Supplement: The Transportation Model

1.

	A	B	C
1	15		25
2	15	45	
3			50

2.

	A	B	C
1			40
2		25	35
3	30	20	

3.

	A	B	C	D
1	10	30		
2	80			
3		50	30	50

4.

	A	B	C	D
1		40		
2	70	10		
3		30	30	50
Dummy	20			

5.

	A	B	C	D	Dummy
1	13		35		
2	28	2		20	6
3		32			

6.

	A	B	C	D	Dummy
1	41		7		
2				56	
3		32			
Balt.		2	28	4	16

7.

	A	B	C	D	Dummy
1	41		7		
2		2		54	
3		32			
Ph.			28	6	16

8.

	A	B	C	Dummy
1		500		
2	400			
New$_1$		100	350	50

	A	B	C	Dummy
1		500		
2	400			
New$_2$		100	350	50

9.

	A	B	C
1			210
2	140		
3	80	60	10
Tol.		160	

	A	B	C
1			210
2	60	80	
3		140	10
Cin.	160		

Chapter 6: Product and Service Design

1. **a.** .81   **b.** .9801   **c.** .9783
2. .9033
3. .9726
4. .93
5. **a.** .9315   **b.** .9953   **c.** .994
6. **a.** .7876
7. **a.** Plan 2 (.9934).

8. .996

9. .995

10. .006

11. **a.** (1) .2725 **b.** (1) .6671
    (2) .2019   (2) .3935
    (3) .1353   (3) .1813

   c. (1) 21 months. (3) 90 months.
     (2) 57 months. (4) 138 months.

12. **a.** .6321 **b.** 3 months or 90 days.

13. **a.** .3012 **b.** .1813 **c.** .5175

14. **a.** .2231 **b.** .8647
   c. .0878 **d.** .0302

15. **a.** .2266 **b.** .4400 **c.** .3830

16. **a** (1) .9772 **b.** Approximately zero.
    (2) .5000
    (3) .0013

Chapter 7: Facilities Layout

1. **a.** Minimum is 2.4 min., maximum is 18 min.
   b. 25 units to 187.5 units. **c.** 8.
   d. 3.6 min. **e.** (1) 50 units.
                 (2) 30 units.

2. **c.** 11.54%. **d.** 323 units per day.

3. **a.** 2.3 min. **c.** 182.6 units per day.
   d. 91.3 units per day.

4. **b.** 1 min. **c.** 3 stations

5. **c.** (1) 11.1%. (2) 11.1%. (3) 33.33%.

7.

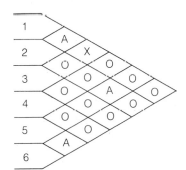

8.

3	5	4
1	8	7
6	2	

10.

3	1	8
9	7	4
5	2	6

11.

6	2	5
3	1	4

TC = $52,080.

13. A: 3; B: 5; C: 1; D: 4; E: 6; F: 2.

14. A: 1; B: 2; C: 5; D: 4; E: 9; F: 8; G: 6; H: 10; I: 7; J: 3.

Chapter 8: Design of Work Systems

1. 15.08 minutes.

2. **a.** 1.2 minutes.
   b. 1.14 minutes.
   c. 1.27 minutes.

3.

Element	OT	NT	ST
1	0.46	0.414	0.476
2	1.505	1.280	1.472
3	0.83	0.913	1.050
4	1.16	1.160	1.334

4. 5.85 minutes.

5. 7.125 minutes.

7. 57 observations.

8. 14 cycles.

9. **a.** 12%. **b.** 163 observations.

10. 377 observations.

11.

Hour	Minute
1	0
1	47
1	56
3	38
4	24
4	27
6	26
7	15

Chapter 8 Supplement: Learning Curves

1. **a.** 178.8 hours.
   b. 1,121.4 hours.
   c. 2,914.8 hours.

2. **a.** 41.47 hours.
   b. 60.55 hours.
   c. 72.20 hours.

3. **a.** 56.928 days.
   b. 42.288 days.
   c. 37.512 days.

4. **a.** $P = 85\%$.
   b. 23.5 minutes.

5. 87.9 minutes.

6. 201.26 hours.

7. **a.** 10.57 hours.
   b. 13.05 hours.
   c. 12.29 hours.

8. **a.** $128.50.
   b. 26 units.

9. 31.63 days.

10. B and C.

Chapter 9: Aggregate Planning

3. B: $18,870.
   C: $18,860.

4. $18,525.

5. $18,417.50.

6. $18,190.

7. **b.** $11,600.

8. **a.** $12,270.
   b. $12,670.

9. $12,250.

10. $12,920.

12. $124,960.

13. $123,830.

14. $124,060.

Chapter 10: Inventory Management

1. **a.** 24 bags.
   b. 12 bags.
   c. 56.
   d. $336.

2. **a.** 379.47 liters.
   b. Increase by $179.

3. **a.** 374 pots.
   b. $16.83 each.

4. $176.

5. **a.** 516.40 tons.
   b. 309.84 tons.
   c. 5.164 days.
   d. 12.91 days.

7. **a.** 4,812.
   b. 15.6.
   c. .96 days.

8. **a.** 9.
   b. 11.

9. **a.** 693 stones.
   b. 600 stones.

10. 10,000 boxes, 1.8 orders.

11. 20,000 units.

12. 1,000 seats.

13. 6,600 feet.

14. **a.** 8.39 gallons.
    b. 40 gallons.

15. **a.** 72 boxes.
    b. .0023.
    c. .0228.

16. 14 riders.

18. 749 lb.; 4.078 lb.

19. **a.** 134 rolls.
    b. 36 rolls.
    c. .055 per cycle $[\sigma_{dLT} = \sqrt{LT}\ \sigma_d]$.
    d. .9996.

20. **a.** 80 ft. per day.
    b. 301 ft.
    c. .999.

21. **a.** ROP = 77 cases.

22. K033: 581.
    K144: 458.
    L700: 0.

23. 25 dozen.

24. 9 spares.

25. 78.9 lb.

26. $4.89 per quart.

27. 5 cakes.

28. 421.5 lb.

29. **a.** $0.53 to $1.76.
    c. $56.67 to $190.00.

30. $0 to $78.03.

Chapter 11: Material Requirements Planning

1.

Level	Item	Quantity
0	P	60
1	A	120
	B	180
	H	240
2	K	120
	D	180
	E	180
	I	480

Index

A

A-B-C inventory classification, 474–75
Acceptable quality level (AQL), 757–58
Acceptance sampling, 753–63
operating characteristic curves, 755–61
sampling plans, 754–55
Accidents, 379–82
Accounting interface
with operations management, 11
with purchasing, 532
Accuracy
in forecasting, 144–46, 150–51
in time study, 383–85
in work sampling, 394–95
Activity-on-arrow (AOA), 631–62
Activity-on-node (AON), 631–32, 647–48
Additive model in forecasting, 124–25
Aggregate planning, 432–59
defined, 434–37
disaggregation, 457–59
graphical and charting techniques, 445–51
mathematical techniques, 451–57
purpose, 437–43
strategies for, 443–45
ALDAP, 343
Allowance factor in time study, 386–88
table of, 388
Allstate Automotive Analyzers, Inc., 411–14
Alpha (α)
acceptance sampling, 757–58
exponential smoothing, 118
Anyone for Sushi? 794–95

Artificial variable, 83–84
Assembly line, 313
Assembly line balancing; *see* Line balancing
Assembly-time chart, 550–51
American Production and Inventory Control Society (APICS), 544
AOQ curve, 761–63
Assignable variation, 764–65
Assignment method of linear programming, 599–603
Associative forecasts, 109, 135–44
Attributes
control charts for, 772–75
inspection of, 753–63
Automation, 318–25, 364–65
Average outgoing quality (AOQ) curve, 761–63
Average outgoing quality limit (AQL), 762–63

B

Beta distribution in PERT, 641–43
Beta (β) error, 757–58, 768
Bill of materials (BOM), 547–50
Binomial distribution, table of values, 815
Bounded rationality, 36
Bowman, E. H., 452, 456
Box-Jenkins technique, 135
Break-even analysis
in capacity planning, 187–90
in location planning, 225–27

C

CAD, 285–88
CAM, 286–88, 318–21
Capacity, 173–92; *see also* Capacity planning

Capacity—*Cont.*
decisions, importance of, 175
defining and measuring, 176–78
determinants of effective, 178–180
Capacity planning, 134–56; *see also* Capacity
developing alternatives, 183–86
evaluating alternatives, 183–92
cost-volume analysis, 187–90
decision theory, 191
financial analysis, 190, 197–209
rough-cut, 437
Capacity requirements planning, 565–67
Carrying costs, 473, 478–79
Case of the Mexican Crazy Quilt, The, 668–70
Cash flow, 190–91, 198
c-chart, 774–75
Cellular manufacturing, 321–25
Centered moving average, 133–34
Centralized inspection versus onsite inspection, 753
Centralized purchasing versus decentralized purchasing, 537–38
Central limit theorem, 766
Certainty, defined, 44
Chance variation, 764
Closeness ratings, 340–42
Compensation, 399–402
group incentive plans, 402
individual incentive plans, 401–2
Component parts, 547–49
Constraints in linear programming, 65, 67–69
Computer-aided design (CAD), 285–88

Computer-aided manufacturing (CAM), 286–88, 318–21
Computers, use of
  in MRP, 544, 567
  in operations, 25–26
Consumer education, 740–41
Consumer's risk, 631, 757–58
Continuous processing, 311
Control charts, in forecasting quality, 765–80
Control charts, in quality control, 765–80
  attribute, 772–775
  variables, 766–72
Control limits, 765–66, 776
CORELAP, 343
Corrective action, in quality control, 763–64
Correlation, 141–43
Costs
  fixed, 186–87
  variable, 186–87
Cost-volume analysis, 187–90
  assumptions of, 190
CPM; *see* PERT
CRAFT, 343
Critical activities, in PERT, 632
Critical path, 632, 635, 640
Crosby, P., 746–47
Cumulative lead time, 546
Cycles, in time series data, 713–14
Cycle time, in line balancing, 327–28
Cyclical component of time series, 86–88, 113–14, 124–25, 134–35

D

DD, due date rule for sequencing, 603–6
Decision making, 33–56
  bounded rationality, 36
  quantitative approaches, 39–40
  reasons for poor decisions, 36–37
  sensitivity analysis, 41–42
  steps in, 34–35
  suboptimization, 36–37
  systems approach, 42–43
  trade-offs, 40–41
  use of models, 37–39
Decision theory, 44–56
  decision environments, 44
  decision matrix, 45
  decision tree, 50–5
  expected monetary value (EMV), 49–52
  expected value of perfect information (EVPI), 52–53
  Laplace, 46–48
  maximax, 46–48
  maximin, 46–48

Decision theory—*Cont.*
  minimax regret, 46–48
  steps in, 45
Decomposition of a time series, 124–35
Defensive research, 281
Degeneracy, in the transportation method, 248, 262–63
Delay, unavoidable, 392
Delphi method, in forecasting, 111–13
Demand
  dependent, 467–68, 542–43
  derived, 542
  independent versus dependent, 467–68, 542–43
  lumpy, 543
Deming, W. Edwards, 742, 746
Dependent variable, 135–36
Depreciation, 199
Design versus operation of production systems, 13–15
Dewey Stapler Company, The, 527–30
Disaggregation, 457–59
Discovery sampling, problem 3, 789
Distributions; *see specific distribution name, e.g.,* Binomial distribution, 754–55
Double sampling plan, 754–55
Dummy, in linear programming; *see specific linear programming model*
Dummy activity, in PERT, 633–34

E

Early start, early finish, in PERT, 636–37
Economic life of an asset, 198
Economic order quantity (EOQ) model, 475–91
  assumptions, 476
Economic part-period, 563
Economic run size, 482–84
EEO, 25
Efficiency, 177–78
End item, 545
EOQ model, 475–91
Errors
  in forecasting, 144–50
  Type I, II, 757–58, 768
Event, in PERT, 632
Expected time, in PERT, 634–35, 641
Expected value
  Expected monetary value (EMV), 49–52
  Expected value of perfect information (EVPI), 52–53

Exponential distribution, 292–94, 679–80
  table of values, 293
Exponential smoothing, 118–24
  adjusted for trend, 122–24
  alpha (α), 118
  double, 122–24
  simple, 118–21
  smoothing constant, 118

F

Facility layout, 309–45
  basic types, 312–17
  line balancing, 325–35
  need for layout decisions, 310–11
  process layouts, 315, 335–44
  product layouts, 312–14, 325–35
  types of processing, 311–12
Factor rating, in location analysis, 328–29
FCFS rule
  in queuing, 681
  in scheduling, 603–6
Feedback, 79
Financial analysis, 190–91, 197–211
  depreciation, 199
  internal rate of return method (IRR), 191, 207–8
  net present value method, 191, 202–7
  payback period, 201–2
  tables, 203, 206
  tax considerations, 201
  terminology, 198–201
Finite source queuing model, 693–98
First come, first served rule
  in queuing, 681
  in scheduling, 603–6
Fixed order interval model, 505–7
Fixed order size model, 475–91
Fixed cost, 186–87
Flexibility, in capacity planning, 183
Flexible manufacturing systems, 325
Flow chart
  for aggregate planning, 437
  for capacity requirements planning, 566
  for MRPII, 569
Flow process chart, 367–69
Flow system, in scheduling, 593–94
Forecast horizon, 108
Forecasting; *see also* Forecasts
  approaches to, 108–9
  associative techniques, 109, 135–44
  choosing a technique, 150–53

Forecasting—*Cont.*
  controlling, 146–50
  Delphi method, 111–13
  exponential smoothing, 118–24
  forecasting process, steps in, 108
  judgmental, 109–13
  linear regression, 109, 135–44
  moving averages, 115–18
  tracking signal, 146–50
Forecasts; *see also* Forecasting
  accuracy, 107–8, 144–46
  associative, 109, 135–44
  based on historical data, 109,
    113–35
  based on judgment and opinions,
    109–113
  causal, 109, 135–44
  common features, 107–8
  consensus; *see* Delphi method
  consumer surveys, 110–11
  controlling, 146–50
  decomposition of time series,
    124–35
    additive model, 124–25
    cyclical component, 113–14,
      134–35
    multiplicative model, 125, 130–
      32
    seasonal relatives, 130–34
    trend component, 124–29
  Delphi method, 111–13
  elements of good, 151–52
  evaluation of, 144–50
  executive opinions, 111–13
  exponential smoothing, 118–24
    adjusted for trend, 122–24
    simple, 118–21
    smoothing constant, alpha, 118
  judgmental, 109–13
  meaningful units, 151
  moving average,
    centered, 133–35
    characteristics, 117–18
    simple, 116
    weighted, 116–17
  naive approach, 115
  noise in, 115–16
  panels of experts, 111–13
  parabolic, 128–29
  regression, 109, 135–44
    linear, 135–44
      assumptions, 143
      least squares equations, 125–
        28
      weaknesses of, 143–44
    multiple, 144
  reliable, 151
  salesforce composite, 110
  time series, analysis of, 113–35
    cycles, 113, 134–35
    seasonality, 113, 130–34

Forecasts—*Cont.*
  time series—*Cont.*
    trend, 113, 124–29
      linear, 125–28
      parabolic, 128–29
  tracking signal, 146–50
  trend; *see* regression *and* time
    series
  use of
    in aggregate planning, 436–37
    in capacity planning, 181–85
    in inventory management,
      472–73
Foreign locations, 221–22
Fraction defective, defined, 755;
  see also Quality control

G

Gang-process chart, 371–72
Gantt, Henry, 596
Gantt chart
  in PERT, 628–30
  in scheduling, 596–99
General purpose equipment, 311,
  315–16
Gilbreth, Frank and Lillian, 372,
  375
Graphical and charting ap-
  proaches to aggregate plan-
  ning, 445–51
Graphical linear programming,
  66–75
Group incentive plans, 402
Group technology, 323–25

H

Hackman, Richard, 364
Herzberg, Frederick, 363
Heuristic approaches
  in aggregate planning, 445–51
  in layout, 331–34, 343
  in sequencing, 603–7
Holding costs, 473, 478–79
Holt, Charles, 455
Huse, Edgar, 410

I

Incentive plans, 399–402
Independent demand, 467–68, 542–
  43
Independent variable, 135–36
Infinite source queuing models,
  682–93
Inputs in the production process,
  9–10
Inspection; *see* Quality assurance
Interarrival time, 679–80

Intermediate planning, 435–36; *see
  also* Aggregate planning
Intermittent processing, 311–12
Internal rate of return (IRR), 191,
  207–8
Inventory
  A-B-C approach, 474–75
  costs, 473
    carrying, 473, 478–79
    excess, 508
    holding, 473, 478–79
    ordering, 473, 479–80
    shortage, 473, 508
  economic order quantity models,
    475–91
  EOQ assumptions, 476
  economic run size model, 482–84
  expected number of units short,
    501–4
  fixed order interval model, 505–
    7
  formulas, table of, 514
  independent versus dependent
    demand, 467–68, 542–43
  objectives, 469–70
  priority system for, 474–75
  quantity discounts, 485–92
  reasons for holding, 468–69
  reorder point models (ROP),
    492–504
  requirements for effective man-
    agement, 470–75
  safety stock, 493–95
  service level, 495–96, 509
  total cost formula, 479–80, 485
  two-bin system, 471
  types of, 468
Inventory records file, 450
Investment proposals, methods for
  ranking
  internal rate of return, 207–8
  payback, 201
  present value, 202–7
Irregular component of a time series, 124
Isocost line, 73
Isoprofit line, 69–70

J–K

Japanese
  Just-in-time (JIT), 571–81
  kanban system, 571–81
  The Nuts and Bolts of Japan's
    Factories, 571–73
  productivity, 18–19
  quality circles, 743–46
  Quality Control Circles: They
    Work and Don't Work, 744–
    45
  Toying with High-Tech, 305–7

Job design, 360–82
  automation, 364–65
  behavioral approaches, 363–64
  methods analysis, 366–72
  motion study, 371–75
  safety, 379–82
  sociotechnical systems, 365–66
  specialization, 361–63
  working conditions, 374–82
Job enlargement, 363
Job enrichment, 363–64
Job rotation, 363
Job shop scheduling, 596–610
Jones, C. H., 456
Johnson, S. M., 608
Johnson's rule, 608–10
Just-in-time (JIT), 571–81
Kaiser plan, 402
Kanban system, 571–81
Kodak plan, 402

L

Labor specialization, 361–62
Laplace, 46–48
Late start, late finish, in PERT, 636–40
Layout of facilities, 309–45
  combination, 317
  computer analysis, 343
  fixed-position, 316–17
  process, 315, 335–44
    closeness ratings, 340–42
    measures of effectiveness, 336–37
  product, 312–14, 325–35
Leading indicators, 134–35
Lead time
  cumulative, 546
  defined, 472, 476
  variable, 493–501
Learning curves, 415–25
  table of values, 420–21
Least squares equation, 125–28
Levitt, Theodore, 353
Liability, product, 279, 737–38
Life cycle, product, 281–82
Lincoln plan, 402
Line balancing, 325–35
  cycle time, 327–28
  heuristic rules, 331–34
  minimum number of work stations, 331
Linear decision rule, 455–56
Linear programming
  in aggregate planning, 451–55
  assignment method, 599–603
  graphical method, 66–75
  simplex method, 75–92
  transportation model, 237–73

Linear regression, 135–44; *see also* Forecasts *and* Forecasting
  assumptions, 143
  test for significance, 140
  weaknesses, 143–44
Loading, 596–603
Load report, 565–67
Location planning
  break-even analysis, 225–27
  community factors, 222–23
  evaluating alternatives, 225–29
  factor rating, 228–29
  factors which affect, 219–24
  foreign locations, 221–22
  general procedure for, 218
  industrial parks, 223–24
  need for, 216
  objectives in, 217
  options, 217–18
  regional factors, 219–22
  site factors, 223–24
Lot-for-lot ordering, 553–55, 562
Lot inspection; *see* Acceptance sampling
Lot sizing
  EOQ, 475–92
  MRP, 561–65
Lot tolerance percent defective (LTPD), 757–58
Love, Stephen, 566
Low-level coding, 548–49
LTPD, 757–58
Lumpy demand, 543

M

McDonald's restaurants, 353–56
MAD, 144–49
Maintenance, preventive, 314
Make or buy, 442–43
Making Hotplates, 410
Man-machine chart, 370
Manners, Miss, 674
Manufacturing resource planning, 568–70, 579–81
Manufacturing versus service, 21–23
Marion Camp Memorial Hospital, 793–94
Marketing/operations interface, 10–11
Martin, Judith, 674
Master schedule, 458–59, 545
Material requirements planning (MRP), 540–68
  assembly-time chart, 550–51
  APICS, 544
  benefits and limitations, 567–68
  bill of materials, 547–50
  BOM; *see* Bill of materials

Material requirements planning (MRP)—*Cont.*
  capacity requirements planning, 565–67
  cumulative lead time, 546
  defined, 543–44
  gross requirements, defined, 553
  inputs, 545–50
  inventory records file, 550
  lot-sizing, 561–65
  low-level coding, 548–49
  master schedule, 458–59, 545
  net change system, 559
  net requirements, defined, 551–52
  Nuts and Bolts of Japan's Factories, The, 571–73
  Orlicky, Joseph, 544
  outputs, 545, 560
  overview of, 543–45
  parent, 548, 558
  part-period model, 563
  pegging, 558–59
  planned order receipt, 551–52
  planned order release, 551–52
  processing, 550–59
  product-structure tree, 547–48
  regenerative system, 559
  safety stock, 560–61
  safety time, 561
  scheduled receipts, 552
  time-phased requirements, 550–52
  updating the system, 559
Matrix organization, 627
Maximax decision criterion, 46–48
Maximin, 46–48
Mean absolute deviation, 144–49
Meaningful units, in forecasting, 151
Mean squared error, 144–46
Median run test, 777–80
Methods-time measurement (MTM), 390–93
Metric conversion, 284–85
Micromotion analysis, 375
MIL Standard Tables, 758
Minimax regret, 46–48
Miss Monners, 674
Models, use of in decision making, 37–39
MODI, 235–55
Modigliani, Franco, 455
Modular design, 284
Money, time value of, 199–201
Monte Carlo simulation; *see* Simulation
Most likely time, in PERT, 641
Motion economy, principles of, 372–73
Motion study, 371–75

Moving averages, 115–18, 133–35
  centered, 133–35
  simple, 116
  weighted, 116–17
MRP; *see* Material requirements
  planning
MRP II; *see* Manufacturing re-
  source planning
MSE, 144–46
MTM; *see* Methods-time measure
  ment
Multiple sampling plans, 755
Multiplicative model, in forecast-
  ing, 125, 130–32
Muth, John, 455
Muther, Richard, 340
Muther grid, 340–42

N

Naive forecast, 115
Negative exponential distribution
  in product design, 292–94
  in queuing, 679–81
  table of values, 293
Negotiated purchasing, 537
Net cash flow, 198
Net-change system, in MRP, 559
Net present value, 191, 202–207
Network; *see* PERT *and* Project
  management
Noise, in forecasting, 115–16
Normal distribution, tables, 810–
  12
Normal time, in work measure-
  ment, 385–86
Northwest corner method, trans-
  portation model, 240–42
Nuts and Bolts of Japan's Facto-
  ries, The, 571–73

O

Objective function, 64–66, 69–72
Occupational Safety and Health
  Act (OSHA), 381–82
OC curve, 755–61
Oldham, G. R., 364
Operating characteristic (OC)
  curve, 755–61
Operations management
  contemporary issues in, 24–26
  described, 6–7, 8–10, 13–24
Optimistic time, in PERT, 641
Optimized Production Technology
  (OPT), 610–11
Orlicky, Joseph, 544
OSHA (Occupational Safety and
  Health Act), 381–82
Outputs of MRP, 545, 560

P

p-chart, 772–74
Parametric production planning,
  456
Parent item, 548, 558
Part-period model, 563
Payback method, 201–2
Pegging, in MRP, 558–59
Percent defective; *see* p-chart
Performance rating, 385–86, 389
PERT; *see* Project management,
  634–54
  activity-on-arrow (AOA), 631–32
  activity-on-node (AON), 631–32,
    647–48
  advantages and limitations, 653
  beta distribution, use of, 641–43
  computing algorithm, 636–40
  crashing, 649–53
  critical path, 632, 635, 640
  deterministic time estimates,
    634–35
  dummy activity, 633–34
  most likely time, 641
  network conventions, 632–34
  optimistic time, 641
  pessimistic time, 641
  probabilistic time estimates,
    640–47
  slack, 635, 639–40
  time-cost trade-offs (crashing),
    649–53
Pessimistic time; *see* PERT
Planned order receipt, 551, 552
Planned order release, 551, 552
Plant layout; *see* Facility layout
Plossl, George, 544
Poisson table, 613
Precedence diagram
  in line balancing, 332–34
  in PERT, 631–34
Predetermined time standards,
  390–93
Predictor variable, 135–36
Present value
  defined, 191, 202–7
  table of values, 203, 206
Principles of motion economy,
  372–73
Preventive maintenance, 314
Pricebreak, 485–90
Priority
  classifications, in inventory, 474–
    75
  discipline, in queuing, 681
  rules, in sequencing, 603–10
Probabilistic time estimates, in
  PERT, 640–47
Probability distribution; *see* spe-
  cific name, e.g., Poisson

Process batch, 611
Process control, 763–80
Process layout
  described, 315
  design of, 335–44
Process variability, 764–65, 776
Producer's risk, 757–58
Productivity
  defined, 16–17
  and quality, 738
  U.S. versus Japanese, 18–19
Product layout, 312–14, 325–35
Product liability, 279, 737–38
Product life cycle, 281–82
Product and service design, 278–98
Product-structure tree, 547–48
Program evaluation and review
  technique; *see* PERT
Progress function; *see* Learning
  curves
Project management, 625–62; *see
  also* PERT
  behavioral aspects, 626–28
  Case of the Mexican Crazy Quilt,
    The, 668–70
  computing algorithm, 636–40
  nature of projects, 627
  PERT/CPM, 625–62
  project manager, 627–28
  pro's and con's of working on
    projects, 628
  time-cost trade-offs, 649–53
Purchasing, 531–39
  centralized versus decentral-
    ized, 537–38
  competitive bidding, 537
  negotiated purchasing, 537
  objectives of, 533–34
  purchasing cycle, 534–35
  value analysis, 535
  vendor analysis, 535–36

Q

Quality; *see also* Quality assurance
  and Quality control
  circles, 743–46
  control charts; *see* Quality con-
    trol
  defined, 734–37
  determinants of, 739–41
  and productivity, 738
  sources of improvements, 742–49
Quality assurance, 733–82; *see also*
  Quality *and* Quality control
  acceptance sampling, 753–63
  AOQ curve, 761–63
  AOQL, 762–63
  consumer's risk, 757–58
  LTPD, 757–58
  MIL Standard Tables, 758

Quality assurance—*Cont.*
  acceptance sampling—*Cont.*
    operating characteristic (OC)
        curve, 755–61
    producer's risk, 757–58
    sampling plans, 754–55
    when to use, 754
  Anyone for Sushi? 794–95
  conformance, quality of, 735, 749
  control charts; *see* Quality control
  Crosby, P., 746–47
  defined, 734
  Deming, W. Edwards, 742, 746
  design, quality of, 735, 739
  inspection, 750–53
    attribute versus variable, 753
    centralized versus on-site, 753
    how much and how often, 750–51
    where in the process to inspect, 752–53
  international implications, 738–39
  and liability, 737–38
  process control, 763–80; *see also* Quality control
  quality circles, 743–46
  run tests, 777–80
  sampling plans, 754–55
Quality circles, 743–46
Quality control; *see also* Quality *and* Quality assurance
  control charts, 765–80
    attribute, 772–75
    c-chart, 774–75
    control limits, 765–66, 776
    fraction defective, 755
    mean, 766–72
    out of control criteria, 764–66, 777
    p-chart, 772–74
    percent defective; *see* p-chart
    range charts, 770–72
    run tests, 777–80
    table of factors, 769
    using mean and range charts together, 771–72
    variables, 766–72
  control limits, 765–66, 776
  evolution of quality control, 741–42
  formulas, table of, 781
  inspection, 750–53; *see also* Quality assurance
  process control, 763–80
  process variability, defined, 776
  run tests, 777–80
  tolerances, defined, 776
  variations and control, 764–65
Quality of work life, 364

Quantity discounts, 485–90
Queue discipline, 681
Queuing analysis, 673–700
  arrival and service patterns, 679–81
  channel, 678
  finite source formulas, 694
  finite source model, 693–98
  finite source population, defined, 677
  finite source table, 695–97
  goal of, 676–77
  infinite source models, 682–93
    multiple channel, 687–93
    single channel, 685–86
    table of formulas, 687
    table of values, 688–90
  Manners, Miss, 674
  maximum line length, 692–93
  measures of system performance, 681–82
  models
    finite source, 693–98
    infinite source, 682–93
  multiple channel, defined, 678–79
  population source, defined, 677
  single channel model, 685–87
  system characteristics, 677–81
  system utilization, 681–82
  Waiting—A New Popular Pastime, 674

R

R & D; *see* Research and development
Radio Shack International, 234–35
Randomness, tests for
  in forecasting, 146–50
  in quality control
    control charts, 765–80
    run tests, 777–80
Random numbers
  in simulation, 710–21
  tables of
    normal, 718
    uniform, 396, 711
  in work sampling, 396–99
Random variation
  in forecasting, 146–50
  in quality control, 764–65
Range charts, 770–72
Ranging, 88–92
Rating
  closeness, in layout, 340–42
  factor, in location analysis, 228–29
  performance, 385–86, 389
Ratio-delay, 392

Redundancy
  in graphical linear programming, 93
  in product design, 290–91
Regenerative system, in MRP, 559
Regression analysis, 109, 135–44
Relative, seasonal, 130–34
Reliability, 288–97
  improving, 296–97
  measuring, 289–96
  in quality, 735–37
Reorder point (ROP) models, 492–502; *see also* Inventory
Report from the Assembly Line, 28–30
Research, defensive, 281
Research and development, 282–83
Risk, in decision making, defined, 44
Robots, 19, 25, 318–22
  list of, 322
ROP; *see* Reorder point models
Rough-cut capacity planning, 437
Run, defined, 777
Runout time, 595–96
Run size, economic, 482–84
Run tests, 777–80

S

Safety, in job design, 379–82
Safety stock, 493–95
Safety time, 561
Salvage value, 198
Sampling distribution, 761, 765–66
Sampling plans, 754–55
Scanlon plan, 402
Scheduled receipts, 552
Scheduling, 591–619
  appointment systems, 612–13
  assignment method, 599–603
  Gantt charts in, 596–99
  in high-volume systems, 593–94
  in intermediate-volume systems, 595–96
  in job shops, 596–610
  Johnson's rule, 608–10
  loading, 596–603
  multiple resources, 613–14
  priority rules, 603–10
  reservation systems, 613
  sequencing rules, 603–10
  service systems, 611–14
Seasonality, 113
Seasonal relatives, 130–34
Sensitivity analysis, 41–42
  in linear programming, 88–92
Sequencing rules, 603–10
Service
  after sale, 536, 740–41
  design, 278–82

Service—*Cont.*
  versus manufacturing, 21–23
  system scheduling, 611–14
Service level, 495–96, 509
Shadow prices, 91
Shortest processing time (SPT)
  rule, 603–7
Slack
  in linear programming, 77
  in PERT, 635, 639–40
Slack variables, 77
Simon, Herbert, 455
Simplex, 75–92
  summary of procedure, 84–85
Simulation, 707–31
  advantages and limitations, 722–
    24
  applications, 721
  computer simulation, 721–22
  defined, 708–27
  Monte Carlo, 710–21
  steps in, 708–10
Simultaneous motion (Simo)
  chart, 375
Site-related factors in location
  analysis, 223–24
Sociotechnical systems, 365–66
Specialization, 361–63
SPT rule, 603–7
Standard of comparison, in quality
  control, 763, 766
Standard elemental time, 390
Standardization, 283–84
Standard time, 382, 386–89
Statistical quality control; *see*
  Quality control
Stepping-stone method, 347–53
Stopwatch time study, 383–89
Straight piecework, 401–2
Strategic decisions, 14–15
Subcontracting, 442–43
Suboptimization, 36–37
Systems approach, 42–43

T

Tables
  annuity, 203
  learning curve coefficients, 420–
    21
  present value, 203, 206

Tables—*Cont.*
  probability, *see specific name,*
    e.g., Poisson
  queuing
    finite, 695–97
    infinite, 688–90
  Random numbers
    normally distributed, 718
    uniformly distributed, 396, 711
Tactical decisions, 15
Tax considerations, 201
Technocratic Hamburger, The,
  353–56
Therbligs, 373–75
Time and motion study; *see* Motion
  study *and* Work measurement
Time buckets, 546
Time-phased requirements, 550–
  52
Time series, defined, 113
Time series analysis, 113–35
Time study; *see* Work measure-
  ment
Time value of money, 199–201
Tippet, L. H. C., 391
Tolerances, 776
Toying with High-Tech, 305–7
Tracking signal, 146–50
Trade-offs in decision making, 40–
  41
Transfer batch, 611
Transformation process, 9–10
Transportation method of linear
  programming, 237–73
  degeneracy, 248, 262–63
  dummy, use of, 259–61
  evaluation of empty cells, 246–55
  intuitive approach, 245–46
  in location decisions, 263–66
  MODI method, 235–55
  northwest corner method, 240–
    42
  stepping-stone method, 247–53
  summary of procedure, 263
  unequal supply and demand,
    259–61
  Vogel's approximation method
    (VAM), 242–45
Trend component of time series,
  124–29
  linear, 125–28
  parabolic, 128–29

Trend line, 125–28
Two-bin system, 471
Type I error, 757–58, 768
Type II error, 757–58, 768

U

Unavoidable delay, 392
Uncertainty, in decision making,
  defined, 44
Uniform Commercial Code, 279
UPC (universal product code), 471–
  72
Utilization
  capacity, 177–78
  queuing, 681–82

V

Value analysis, 535
VAM, 242–45
Variable cost, 145–46
Variables, decision, 64–65
Variables control charts, 766–72
Variance, in PERT, 642–43
Variation
  assignable, 764–65
  random, 764
Vendor analysis, 535–36
Vogel's approximation method
  (VAM), 242–45

W–X

Wage incentive plans; *see* Incen-
  tive plans
Waiting line analysis; *see* Queuing
  analysis
Watch Our Forecasts Grow, 168
Weighted moving average, 116–17
Wight, Oliver, 544
Work in America, 361
Worker-machine chart, 370
Work measurement, 382–99
  predetermined time standards,
    390–93
  standard elemental times, 390
  stopwatch time study, 383–89
  work sampling, 391–99
    compared to time study, 399
Work sampling, 391–99
$\bar{x}$-bar chart, 766–72

*This book has been set VideoComp, in 10 and
9 point Primer, leaded 2 points. Part and chapter numbers are 20 point Zapf Demibold, and
part and chapter titles are 36 point Zapf Demibold. The size of the type page is 37 by 48 picas.*

helpful to reflect on the advantages and disadvantages of specialization, which are summarized in Table 8–1.

Behavioral Approaches to Job Design

In an effort to make jobs more interesting and meaningful, job designers frequently consider job enlargement, job rotation, job enrichment, and increased use of mechanization.

Job enlargement involves giving a worker a larger portion of the total task. This constitutes horizontal loading in the sense that the additional work is on the same skill and responsibility level as before. Schematically, this can be depicted as:

$$\longleftarrow \text{Present job} \longrightarrow$$

The goal is to make the job more interesting by increasing the variety of skills required and by providing the worker with a more recognizable contribution to the overall output. For example, in a supermarket setting instead of having employees who work exclusively in the produce or the meat department, they might have assignments that involve work in two or more of these departments. Similarly, a production worker's job might be expanded so that he or she is responsible for a *sequence* of activities instead on only one activity.

Job rotation involves having workers take turns at various jobs by periodically having them exchange jobs. This approach can be used as a way to avoid having one or a few employees stuck in boring or monotonous jobs. It works best when workers can be transferred to more interesting jobs; there is little advantage in merely having workers exchange one boring job for another. Job rotation allows workers to broaden their learning experience and enables workers to fill in for others in the event of sickness or absenteeism.

Job enrichment involves an increase in the level of responsibility for planning and coordinating tasks. In effect, it represents a vertical loading:

$$\uparrow$$

Present job

An example of this would be to permit stock clerks in supermarkets to handle reordering of goods, thus increasing their responsibilities. Job enrichment approaches focus on the motivating potential of jobs via worker satisfaction. Among the proponents of this approach is Frederick Herzberg, who published a study that indicated that factors such as achievement, recognition, and responsibility have the potential for generating satisfaction, but not dissatisfaction, while factors such as supervision, pay, and working conditions had the opposite potential: they can lead to dissatisfaction, but not

satisfaction.[2] According to this view, job enrichment could be a source of satisfaction by adding more of the factors that have satisfying potential.

In a later study, Richard Hackman and G. R. Oldham proposed that job enrichment can lead to improved worker performance if the worker perceives that the work is meaningful, perceives responsibility for the outcome, and receives knowledge of the results.[3] However, they point out that job enrichment should not be used without a careful investigation of the need for changes and of what changes are most apt to succeed. In effect, they warn that not all jobs or workers are amenable to job enrichment, nor would they necessarily benefit from enrichment. Toward that end, they have developed a questionnaire that can be used to diagnose the motivating potential of job enrichment.[4] The diagnosis focuses on four dimensions:

1. Is there a problem with motivation and job satisfaction?
2. What is the motivating potential of the job?
3. What aspects of the job are causing difficulty?
4. Will employees accept the necessary changes?

Increased use of mechanization often enables designers to free workers from repetitive work, which tends to be monotonous and boring. Increased mechanization often takes the form of automation, which is discussed more fully in the following section.

The essence of these approaches to job design is that they attempt to increase the motivational aspect of jobs by increasing worker satisfaction through the improvement in the *quality of work life.* Many firms are currently involved in or seriously considering programs related to quality of work life. In addition to the above approaches, organizations are also experimenting with choice of locations (e.g., medium-sized cities, campus-like settings when feasible), flexible work hours, and quality circles, which are described in the chapter on quality assurance.

Automation

The use of mechanical and/or electronic devices in place of human effort is referred to as *automation.* Under this heading come automatic processing equipment, computers, industrial robots, and similar devices. A key feature of these devices is their ability to exert control over a process without human intervention. There are nu-

---

[2] F. Herzberg, B. Mausner, and B. Snyderman, *The Motivation to Work* (New York: John Wiley & Sons, 1959).

[3] J. Richard Hackman, G. R. Oldham, Jane L. Pearce, and Jane Caminis, "A New Strategy for Job Enrichment," *California Management Review,* Summer 1975, pp. 57–71.

[4] J. Richard Hackman and G. R. Oldham, "Development of the Job Diagnostic Survey," *Journal of Applied Psychology* 60 (1975), pp. 159–70.

merous benefits, as well as potential drawbacks, associated with automation.

Among the benefits of automation are the following:

1. The jobs that are most susceptible to automation are those that are repetitive, boring, and monotonous. Hence, the jobs that are least desirable from a human standpoint often lend themselves to automation.
2. Automation yields a highly uniform output and generally results in higher quality compared to human-generated output.
3. The rate of output generally exceeds human capabilities.
4. Human conflicts are avoided.

Among the potential drawbacks of automation are the following:

1. The traditional argument against automation is that it displaces humans. While it has been shown that automation results in more jobs rather than less, and the jobs created are more interesting than those lost, the fact remains that workers must be retrained, which adds to the cost. Moreover, workers often tend to resist any sort of change.
2. Automated systems often involve substantial costs, and this usually means that a fairly high volume of output is needed to make the system economical.
3. Automated systems can be inflexible because they are often restricted by design to a narrow range of tasks.

Compared to American firms, the Japanese are much greater users of automated processing in the automotive and steel industries, but considerably less-automated in agriculture. The successes that the Japanese have had in the areas of quality and productivity in industrial applications of automation, and the U.S. successes in agriculture, have caused managers in many U.S. firms to give more attention to the possible benefits of automation. There has not, as yet, been a wholesale rush toward it. One possible reason is the resistance of labor unions. Another is the enormous cost involved coupled with a long period of time before payoffs can be realized. Still a third possible reason is the costs and difficulties of retraining employees and the problems associated with integrating automated systems into current operations.

Sociotechnical Systems

The *sociotechnical systems* approach is concerned with the human-technology interface. Specifically, it recognizes that choice of technology can and often does have an impact on the social structure within an organization, and that technological changes (redesign of layout, automation, introduction of new techniques) can and often do have detrimental effects on worker performance. Further-

more, proponents of this approach argue that there are often technological alternatives that would produce desired results and still be consistent with sociological considerations. Hence, the focus is on finding a design that is consistent with both technological efficiency and the existing sociological system. In many respects, this approach is very similar to job enrichment in that it seeks task variety, skill variety, task autonomy, and feedback. It goes beyond that approach in terms of giving the workers more say in how the work is actually done and in allowing workers to self-organize. Because of this, there is a certain amount of controversy surrounding the sociotechnical approach, and there has not been widespread acceptance of this approach, although some foreign firms are using it. It may be that such an approach would be more suited to Japan's work environment, where staff personnel like industrial engineers and quality-control experts are viewed as consultants, available to assist workers but not to specify work procedures. One of the major obstacles to greater use of the sociotechnical approach appears to be the reluctance of managers to entrust more of their authority to their workers. While in some cases such fears are somewhat unfounded, in other cases they are not. Consequently, much additional work remains to be done before it will be possible to say how, and to what extent, the sociotechnical system can be used in job design.

Methods Analysis

Job design often begins with a methods analysis of an overall operation. You might call it a macro view of the job. It then moves from the general to specific details of the job, concentrating on arrangement of the workplace and movements of the worker.

The need for methods analysis can come from a number of different sources, such as:

1. Changes in tools and equipment.
2. Changes in product design.
3. New products.
4. Changes in materials or procedures.
5. Government regulations or contractual agreements.

Methods analysis is done both for existing jobs and for new jobs that have not yet been performed. At first glance, it might seem strange to analyze methods of a nonexistent job. However, someone has to establish a method for a new job, and it is usually wise to have a person who is trained to handle this do it at the start rather than to allow the job to begin and then try to improve on it later.

When an existing job is involved, the procedure generally begins with the analyst observing the job as it is currently being done and then devising ways to improve the job. For a brand new job, the analyst must rely on a description of the job and an ability to

visualize the operation in advance. Methods analysis can be a good source of productivity improvements.

The basic procedure in methods analysis is to:

1. Identify the operation to be studied and gather all pertinent facts regarding tools, equipment, materials, and so on.
2. If the job is currently being done, discuss the job with the operator and supervisor to get their inputs.
3. Study and document the present method of an existing job using process charts. For new jobs, develop charts based on information about the activities involved.
4. Analyze the job.
5. Propose new methods.
6. Install the new methods.
7. Follow up installation to assure that improvements have been achieved.

Selecting the operation to study.   Sometimes a foreman or supervisor will request that a certain operation be studied. At other times, methods analysis will be part of an overall program to increase productivity and to reduce costs. Some general guidelines for selecting a job to study are to seek jobs that:

1. Have a high labor content.
2. Are done frequently.
3. Are unsafe, tiring, unpleasant, noisy.
4. Are designated as problems (e.g., quality problems, scheduling bottlenecks).

Documenting the present method.   Use charts, graphs, and verbal descriptions of the way the job is now being done. This will provide a better understanding of the job and serve as a basis of comparison against which revisions can be judged.

Analyzing the job and proposing new methods.   Analyzing the job requires that the analyst carefully consider the what, why, when, where, and who of the job. Often simply going through these questions will clarify the review process by encouraging the analyst to take a devil's-advocate attitude toward both the present and the proposed methods.

Analyzing and improving methods is facilitated by the use of various charts such as *flow process charts* and *worker-machine* charts. Another chart that is sometimes useful is a *gang process chart.*

Flow process charts are used to review and critically examine the overall sequence of an operation by focusing on either the movements of the operator or the flow of materials. These charts can be very helpful in identifying nonproductive parts of the process (e.g., delays, temporary storages, distances traveled).

FIGURE 8–1

Process Chart Symbols

Operation A large circle indicates an operation, such as	Drive nail	Mix	Type letter
Transportation An arrow indicates a transportation, such as	Move material by truck	Move material by conveyor	Move material by carrying (messenger)
Storage A triangle indicates a storage, such as	Raw material in bulk storage	Finished stock stacked on pallets	Protective filing of documents
Delay A large capital D indicates a delay, such as	Wait for elevator	Material in truck or on floor at bench waiting to be processed	Papers waiting to be filed
Inspection A square indicates an inspection, such as	Examine material for quality or quantity	Read steam gage on boiler	Examine printed form for information

FIGURE 8–2

Format of a Flow Process Chart

FLOW PROCESS CHART Job requisition of petty cash	ANALYST D. Kolb	PAGE 1 of 2	Operation	Movement	Inspection	Delay	Storage
Details of method							
Requisition made out by department head			●	⇨	□	D	▽
Put in "pick-up" basket			○	⇨	□	●	▽
To accounting department			○	⬛⇨	□	D	▽
Account and signature verified			○	⇨	■	D	▽
Amount approved by Treasurer			●	⇨	□	D	▽
Amount counted by Cashier			●	⇨	□	D	▽
Amount recorded by Bookkeeper			●	⇨	□	D	▽
Petty cash sealed in envelope			●	⇨	□	D	▽
Petty cash carried to department			○	⬛⇨	□	D	▽
Petty cash checked against requisition			○	⇨	■	D	▽
Receipt signed			●	⇨	□	D	▽
Petty cash stored in safety box			○	⇨	□	D	▼
			○	⇨	□	D	▽
			○	⇨	□	D	▽
			○	⇨	□	D	▽
			○	⇨	□	D	▽

Source: Elias M. Awad, *Systems Analysis and Design* (Homewood, Ill.: Richard D. Irwin, 1979), p. 113. © by Richard D. Irwin, Inc. Reprinted by permission.

Figure 8–1 describes the symbols used in constructing a flow process chart, and Figure 8–2 illustrates a flow process chart.

Some of the uses of flow process charts involve studying the flow of materials through a department, studying the sequence that documents or forms take, analyzing movement and care of surgical patients, layout of department and grocery stores, and mail handling.

Experienced analysts have usually developed a checklist of questions they ask themselves in order to generate ideas for improvements. Some representative questions are:

1. Why is there a delay or storage at this point?
2. How can travel distances be shortened or avoided?
3. Can materials handling be reduced?
4. Would a rearrangement of the workplace result in greater efficiency?
5. Can similar activities be grouped?
6. Would the use of additional or improved equipment be helpful?
7. Does the worker have any ideas for improvements?

A *worker-machine chart* is helpful for visualizing the portions of a work cycle during which an operator and equipment are busy or idle. The analyst can easily see when the operator and machine are working independently as well as when their work overlaps or is interdependent. One use of this type of chart is to determine how many machines or how much equipment the operator can manage.

An example of a worker-machine chart is presented in Figure 8–3. Among other things, the chart highlights worker and machine utilization.

FIGURE 8–3

Worker-Machine Chart

Product: Produce			Operator: L.W.
Process:			Charted by: R.G.

Step	Employee	Time (seconds)	Machine
1	Accepts produce from customer and places on scale	0	
		1	
2	Punches in price/lb	2	
3		3	Calculates and displays total price
4	Removes produce	4	
5	Notes price and marks on produce	5	
		6	
6	Hands produce to customer	7	
		8	

Summary

	Employee		Machine	
	Time (seconds)	%	Time (seconds)	%
Work	7	87.5	1	12.5
Idle	1	12.5	7	87.5

Another multiactivity chart is the *gang process chart.* It is useful in coordinating and analyzing a *team* of workers because it provides a cross-sectional view of the work at any point. The chart also reveals individual utilizations. An example of this kind of chart is shown in Figure 8–4.

Installing the improved method. Successful implementation of the proposed methods changes requires convincing management of the desirability of the new method and obtaining the cooperation of the worker. If the worker has been consulted throughout the process and has made suggestions that are incorporated in the proposed changes, this part of the task will be considerably easier than if the analyst has assumed sole responsibility for the development of the proposal.

If the proposed method constitutes a major change from the way the job has been performed in the past, workers may have to undergo a certain amount of training, and full implementation may take some time to achieve.

The follow-up. In order to insure that changes have been made and that the proposed method is functioning as expected, the analyst should review the operation after a reasonable period and consult again with the operator.

Motion Study

Motion study is the systematic study of the human motions used to perform an operation. The purpose is to eliminate unnecessary motions and to identify the best sequence of motions for maximum efficiency. Hence, motion study can be an important avenue for productivity improvements. Present practice evolved from the work of Frank Gilbreth, who originated the concepts in the bricklaying trade in the early part of this century. Through the use of motion-study techniques, Gilbreth is generally credited with increasing the average number of bricks laid per hour by a factor of three, even though he was not a bricklayer by trade. When you stop to realize that bricklaying had been carried on for centuries, Gilbreth's accomplishment is even more remarkable.

There are a number of different techniques that motion-study analysts can use to develop efficient procedures. The most used techniques are:

1. Motion-study principles.
2. Analysis of therbligs.
3. Micromotion study.
4. Charts.

The work of Gilbreth laid the foundation for development of *motion-study principles,* which are guidelines for designing motion-efficient work procedures. The guidelines are divided into three categories: principles for use of the body, principles for arrange-

FIGURE 8–4

Multiactivity Chart (Gang Process): Hydraulic Extrusion Process, Proposed Method

Machine operation	Time	Press operator operation	Time	Assistant press operator operation	Time	Dummy knocker operation	Time	Pull-out man operation	Time
Elevate billet	.07	Elevate billet	.07	Grease die and position back in die head	.12	Position shell on small press	.10	Pull rod toward cooling rack	.20
Position billet	.08	Position billet	.08	Walk to furnace	.05	Press dummy out of shell	.12		
Position dummy	.04	Position dummy	.04						
Build pressure	.05	Build pressure	.05	Rearrange billets in furnace	.20	Dispose of shell	.18	Walk back toward press	.15
				Return to press	.05				
Extrude	.45	Extrude	.45	Idle time	.09	Dispose of dummy and lay aside tongs	.12	Grab rod with tongs and pull out	.45
					.19	Idle time	.23		
Unlock die	.06	Unlock die	.06		.10	Grab tongs and move to position	.05		
Loosen and push out shell	.10	Loosen and push out shell	.10	Run head and shell out	.11	Guide shell from sheat to small press	.20		.11
Withdraw ram and lock die in head	.15	Withdraw ram and lock die in head	.15	Shear rod from shell	.04				.09
				Pull die off end of rod	.05				
Working time	1.00 minute		1.00 minute		.91 minute		.77 minute		1.00 minute
Idle time	0		0		.09 minute		.23 minute		0 minute

Source: Benjamin W. Niebel, *Motion and Time Study*, 6th ed. (Homewood, Ill.: Richard D. Irwin, 1976), p. 132. © 1976 by Richard D. Irwin, Inc. Reprinted by permission.

TABLE 8–2

Motion-Study Principles	Human body

Human body
1. Begin and end motions of both hands at the same time.
2. Do not allow both hands to be idle at the same time except during rest periods.
3. Make sure that motions of arms are in opposite and symmetrical directions and at the same time.
4. Confine hand and body motions to the simplest movements that will do the work.
5. Use momentum to assist where helpful but reduce it if it must be overcome by muscular effort.
6. Use smooth, continuous curved motions in preference to straight-line motions that involve sudden changes in direction.
7. Remember that ballistic motions are faster, easier, and more accurate than controlled movements.
8. Arrange work to permit use of natural rhythm wherever possible.
9. Keep eye fixations as few and as close together as possible.

Workplace
10. Keep all tools and materials in a definite and fixed place.
11. Keep tools, materials, and controls close to the point of use.
12. Use gravity feed bins and containers to deliver material close to the point of use.
13. Use drop deliveries wherever possible.
14. Locate materials and tools to permit the best sequence of motions.
15. Provide proper illumination, heating, and ventilation.
16. Arrange the height of the workplace and the chair so that alternate sitting and standing is easily possible.
17. Provide a chair that permits good posture for every worker.

Tools and equipment
18. Relieve the hands of all work that can be done by jigs, fixtures, and foot-operated devices.
19. Combine two or more tools wherever possible.
20. Pre-position tools and materials to reduce motions of searching, finding, and selecting as much as possible.
21. Distribute the load on each finger in accordance with the inherent capabilities of the fingers.
22. Locate levers, crossbars, and handwheels so that the operator can manipulate them with the least change in body position and with the greatest mechanical advantage.

Source: Ralph M. Barnes, *Motion and Time Study: Design and Measurement of Work,* 6th ed. (New York: John Wiley & Sons, 1968), p. 220. Reprinted by permission of the publisher.

ment of the workplace, and principles for the design of tools and equipment. The principles are listed in Table 8–2.

In developing work methods that are motion efficient, some of the things the analyst tries to do are:

1. Eliminate unnecessary motions.
2. Combine activities.
3. Reduce fatigue.
4. Improve the arrangement of the workplace.
5. Improve the design of tools and equipment.

Therbligs are basic elemental motions. The name *therblig* is Gilbreth, spelled backwards (except for the *th*). The idea behind the

development of therbligs was to break jobs down into minute elements and base improvements on analysis of these basic elements be eliminating, combining, or rearranging them.

Although a complete description of therbligs would be outside of the scope of this text, a representative sample of some common ones will give you some idea of the nature of these basic elemental motions.

Search implies hunting for an item with hands and/or the eyes.
Select means to choose from a group of objects.
Grasp means to take hold of an object.
Hold refers to retention of an object after it has been grasped.
Transport loaded means movement of an object after hold.
Release load means to deposit the object.

Some other therbligs are *inspect, position, plan, rest,* and *delay.*

Description of a job using therbligs often involves a substantial amount of work. However, for short, repetitive jobs, therbligs analysis may be justified.

Frank Gilbreth and his scientist wife, Lillian, were also responsible for introducing motion pictures for studying motions, called *micromotion study.* This approach is used not only in industry but in many other areas of human endeavor such as sports and health care. Use of the camera and slowmotion replays enable analysts to study motions that would otherwise be too rapid to see. In addition, the resulting films provide a permanent record that can be referred to for training workers and analysts as well as for settling job disputes involving work methods.

The cost of micromotion study limits its use to repetitive activities, where even minor improvements can yield substantial savings owing to the number of times an operation is repeated, or where other considerations justify its use (e.g., surgical procedures).

Motion-study analysts often use charts as a tool for analyzing and recording motion studies. Activity charts and process charts such as those described a few pages back can be quite helpful. In addition, a *simo chart,* like the one shown in Figure 8–5 can be used to study simultaneous motions of the hands. These charts are invaluable in studying operations like typing, sewing, surgical and dental procedures, and certain assembly operations.

Working Conditions

Working conditions are an important aspect of job design. Physical factors such as temperature, humidity, ventilation, illumination, color, and noise can have a significant impact on worker performance in terms of productivity, quality of output, and accidents.

1. *Temperature and humidity.* Although human beings can function under a fairly wide range of temperatures, work performance tends to be adversely affected unless temperatures are kept

FIGURE 8–5

A Simultaneous-Motion Chart

SIMO CHART

OPERATOR: Ken Reisch
DATE: May 21,
OPERATION: Assembly
PART: Lace Finger
METHOD: Proposed
CHART BY: Joseph Riley

TIME SCALE (winks)	ELEMENT TIME	LEFT-HAND DESCRIPTION	SYMBOL	MOTION CLASS	SYMBOL	RIGHT-HAND DESCRIPTION	ELEMENT TIME	TIME SCALE (winks)
4548	12	Reach for finger	RE		RE	Reach for finger	12	4548
4560	19	Grasp finger	G		G	Grasp finger	19	4560
4579	31	Move finger	M		M	Move finger	31	4579
4610	75	Position and release finger	P RL		P RL	Position and release finger	75	4610
4685	15	Reach for clamp	RE		RE	Reach for clamp	15	4685
4700	15	Grasp clamp	G		G	Grasp clamp	15	4700
4715								4715
7541	12	Grasp assembly	G		G	Grasp assembly	12	7541
	18	Move and release assembly	M RL		M RL	Move and release assembly	18	
7559								7559

SUMMARY

%	TIME	LEFT HAND SUMMARY	SYM.	RIGHT HAND SUMMARY	TIME	%
8.56	249	Reach	RE	Reach	245	8.4
7.49	218	Grasp	G	Grasp	221	7.5
12.16	354	Move	M	Move	413	14.2
30.45	887	Position	P	Position	1124	38.7
39.3	1145	Use	U	Use	876	30.1
1.03	30	Idle	I	Idle	0	0.0
.96	28	Release	RL	Release	32	1.1
100.0	3011		TOTALS		3011	100.0

Source: B. W. Niebel, *Motion and Time Study,* 6th ed. (Homewood, Ill.: Richard D. Irwin, 1976, p. 204) © 1976 by Richard D. Irwin, Inc. Reprinted by permission.

within a very narrow *comfort band.* While individuals tend to differ in terms of what they consider comfortable ranges, it is generally agreed that office workers and others who exert little physical effort on the job function best when temperatures are between 65° F. and 72° F. For moderately strenuous activities, temperatures in the range of 60° F. to 70° F. are preferable, while for very strenuous activities, temperatures in the range of 55° F. to 65° F. are best.

Heating and cooling are less of a problem in offices than they are in factories and other work environments where high ceilings allow heat to rise and where there is often a constant flow of trucks and other moving and handling equipment through large doors. This makes it difficult to maintain a constant temperature. Solutions range from selection of suitable clothing to space heaters and other localized heating or cooling devices.

Humidity is generally an important variable in maintaining a comfortable working environment. Humidities in the range of 30 percent to 50 percent are most conducive to comfort, although as a general rule, choice of temperature levels depends on humidity levels because humans tend to be more sensitive to variations in temperature at high humidities than at lower humidities. Therefore, high humidity will require more cooling on a warm day, and more heating on a cold day, than low humidity.

2. *Ventilation.* Unpleasant and noxious odors can be distracting as well as dangerous to workers. Moreover, unless smoke and dust are periodically removed, the air can quickly become stale and unpleasant. Large fans and air conditioning equipment are often used to exchange and recondition the air.

3. *Illumination.* The amount of illumination required depends largely on the type of work being performed. The more detailed the work, the higher the level of illumination needed for adequate performance. Other important considerations are the amount of glare and contrast. From a safety standpoint, good lighting in halls and stairways and other dangerous points is important. However, because illumination is expensive, high illumination in all areas is not generally desirable.

Sometimes natural daylight can be used as a source of illumination. Not only is it free, but it also provides some psychological benefits. Workers in windowless rooms may feel "cut off" from the outside world and experience various psychological problems. However, the inability to control natural light (e.g., cloudy days) can result in dramatic changes in light intensity.

4. *Color.* There are two features of color that are important in job design. One is the ability of colors to affect moods and feelings, and the other is the visual discriminations it permits.

Color produces emotional and psychological effects in many situations. Some of the effects of the various colors are:

Red conveys warmth, action, and stimulation. It is a high-visibility color.

Yellow is also a high-visibility color. It can give the impression of cheerfulness and freshness.

Blue is a low-visibility color. It may convey coolness and may promote thoughtfulness or depression.

Green is another low-visibility color. It is often associated with calm and restfulness.

Brown is a natural color. Earth tones impart a natural, peaceful feeling. It is a low-visibility color.

Orange is a high-visibility color that attracts attention more than any other color. It imparts feelings of warmth and stimulation.

The implications for job designers relate to the type of atmosphere and emotions that are best suited for the job. Red is generally taboo in hospitals, while green is widely used. Bright colors lend themselves to coloring the surroundings where jobs involve a high degree of creativity, while browns are used to convey peaceful surroundings, and blues are more appropriate where quiet deliberations are involved. Of course, these are only broad generalizations, but the point is that colors should be a part of job design.

Colors are also used to designate safe and hazardous areas or conditions. Some of the common uses are:

Red is frequently used for fire protection equipment, gasoline storage containers, danger signs, emergency warning lights, and hot pipes.

Yellow indicates caution. It is frequently used to designate walkways, edges of stairs, corners and ends of loading docks. Heavy equipment, school buses, and forklifts are usually yellow because of its high visibility.

Blue is sometimes used to mark control devices, water pipes, and valves.

Green is used to designate safety areas or equipment.

Purple is used for radiation hazards.

Orange is frequently used to indicate dangerous parts of equipment and safety starting buttons and switches.

Color coding is also used as a means of identifying electrical wiring, especially where a number of different wires might need to be traced through partitions or equipment.

5. *Noise and vibration.* Noise is unwanted sound. It is caused by vibrations of machines or equipment as well as by humans. Noise can be annoying or distracting, leading to errors and accidents. It can also damage or impair hearing if it is loud enough. Figure 8–6 illustrates loudnesses of some typical sounds.

FIGURE 8–6

Decibel Values of Typical Sounds (dbA)

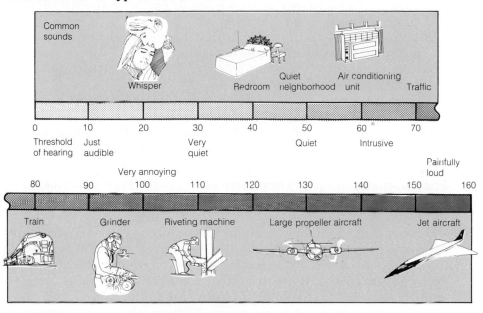

Source: B. W. Niebel, *Motion and Time Study,* 6th ed. (Homewood, Ill.: Richard D. Irwin, 1976), p. 221. © 1976 by Richard D. Irwin, Inc. Reprinted by permission.

Successful sound control begins with measurement of the offending sounds. In a new operation, selection and placement of equipment can eliminate or reduce many potential problems. In the case of existing equipment, it may be possible to redesign the equipment or substitute other equipment. In some instances the source of noise can be isolated from other work areas. If that isn't feasible, acoustical walls and ceilings or baffles that deflect sound waves may prove useful. Sometimes the only alternative is to provide protective devices for those in the immediate vicinity (e.g., personnel who guide jet aircraft into landing gates wear protective devices over their ears).

Vibrations can be a factor in job design even without a noise component, so merely eliminating sound may not be sufficient in every case. Vibrations can come from tools, machines, vehicles, human activity, air conditioning systems, pumps, and other sources. Corrective measures include padding, stabilizers, shock absorbers, cushioning, and rubber mountings.

6. *Workbreaks.* The frequency, length, and timing of workbreaks can have a significant impact on both productivity and quality of output. One indication of the relationship between worker efficiency and workbreaks is illustrated in Figure 8–7. It reveals

FIGURE 8–7

A Typical Relationship between Worker Efficiency and the Time of Day

Source: B. W. Niebel, *Motion and Time Study,* 6th ed. (Homewood, Ill.: Richard D. Irwin, 1976), p. 243. © 1976 by Richard D. Irwin, Inc. Reprinted by permission.

that efficiency generally declines as the day wears on, but it also shows how breaks for lunch and rest can cause an upward shift in efficiency.

An important variable in the rate of decline and potential effects of workbreaks is the amount of physical and/or mental requirements of the job. Steelworkers, for instance, may need rest breaks of 15 minutes per hour due to the heavy nature of their jobs. Physical effort is not the only condition that indicates workbreaks. People working at CRTs also need periodic breaks. Moreover, you have undoubtedly experienced the benefits of study breaks.

7. *Safety.* Worker safety is perhaps one of the most basic issues in job design. This is an area that needs constant attention from management, employees, and designers. Workers can not be effectively motivated if they feel they are in physical danger.

From an employer standpoint, accidents are undesirable because they are expensive (insurance and compensation), they usually involve damage to equipment and/or products, they require hiring, training, and makeup work, and generally interrupt work. From a worker standpoint, accidents mean physical suffering, mental anguish, potential loss of earnings, and disruption of the work routine.

It is generally agreed that the two basic causes of accidents are worker *carelessness* and accident *hazards.* Under the heading of carelessness come unsafe acts. Examples include driving at high speeds, drinking and driving, failure to use protective equipment,

overriding safety controls (e.g., taping control buttons down), disregarding safety procedures (e.g., running, throwing objects, cutting through, failing to observe one-way signs), improper use of tools and equipment, and failure to use reasonable caution in danger zones. Unsafe conditions include unprotected pulleys, chains, material-handling equipment, machinery, and so on. Also, poorly lighted walkways, stairs, and loading docks constitute hazards. Toxic wastes, gases and vapors, and radiation hazards must be contained. In many instances, these cannot be detected without special equipment, so they would not be obvious to workers or emergency personnel. Protection against hazards involves use of proper lighting, clearly marking danger zones, use of protective equipment (e.g., hardhats, goggles, ear muffs, gloves, heavy shoes and clothing), safety devices (e.g., machine guards, dual control switches that require an operator to use both hands), emergency equipment (e.g., emergency showers, fire extinguishers, fire escapes) and thorough instruction in safety procedures and use of regular and emergency equipment. Housekeeping (clean floors, open aisles, waste removal, etc.) is another important safety factor.

An effective program of safety and accident control requires the cooperation of both workers and management. Workers must be trained in proper procedures and attitudes, and they can contribute to a reduction in hazards by pointing out hazards to management. Management must enforce safety procedures and use of safety equipment. If supervisors allow workers to ignore safety procedures or look the other way when they see violations, workers will be less likely to take proper precautions. Some firms use contests that compare departmental safety records. However, accidents cannot be completely eliminated, and a freak accident may seriously affect worker morale and might even contribute to additional accidents. Posters can be very effective, particularly if they communicate in specific terms *how to avoid accidents.* For example, the admonition to "be careful" is not nearly as effective as "wear hardhats," "walk, don't run," "hold on to rail," and so on.

Effective accident control begins with measurement of accident experience. Commonly used measures include frequency of accidents, severity, and average seriousness. Accidents that cause serious injury and loss of work time beyond the day of the injury are called *lost-time accidents,* and these cases are the ones generally used to quantify experience, although minor accidents can serve as a warning of impending major accidents. Frequency, severity, and seriousness are defined as follows:

$$Frequency = \text{Number of lost-time accidents per million labor-hours worked}$$

$$Severity = \text{Number of days lost per million labor-hours worked}$$
$$Average\ seriousness = \text{Severity} \div \text{Frequency}$$

Use of hours worked is standard practice because it allows for meaningful comparisons based on *exposure*. However, the last measure, average seriousness, avoids the need to determine the number of hours worked. The frequency of accidents is useful as a measure of how often accidents are occurring; severity can be high because of numerous accidents with little time lost per accident or because of one or two very serious accidents. The lost-time figure is based on the number of days a worker is actually absent from his regular job plus possible standard charges based on the nature of the injury. For instance, loss of a portion of a finger or toe results in a specified charge of lost-time in addition to time actually lost.

Accident measures are necessary to assess a department's or company's experience over time, as well as to judge the experience of a company against that of the industry as a whole. In other words, frequency and severity of accidents vary by type of work; the nature and seriousness of accident hazards in electrical work, office work, logging, steel work, and so on are quite different. In order to get a clear picture of any firm's accident experience, it is necessary to compare its record with other firms engaged in the same type of business, since jobs in these firms will have the same hazards. In addition, accident records can be used to help management pinpoint areas where corrective action is needed, although it is infinitely better to *prevent* accidents rather than emphasize corrective action. Still, hazards are not always obvious, and corrective action can prevent *future* accidents.

The importance of safety considerations in systems design was heightened by the enactment of the Occupational Safety and Health Act (OSHA) in 1970. The law was intended to ensure that workers in all organizations have healthy and safe working conditions. It provides specific safety regulations as well as inspectors to see that they are adhered to. Inspections are carried out randomly and to investigate complaints of unsafe conditions. OSHA officials are empowered to issue warnings, impose fines, and even to invoke court-ordered shutdowns for unsafe conditions.

Early experience with OSHA was mixed. Although OSHA caused a general improvement in working conditions and safety records, sometimes overzealous inspectors demanded strict compliance with regulations. Moreover, many employers felt that certain regulations were too detailed and unrealistic in terms of costs and benefits. Congress subsequently ordered OSHA to eliminate nuisance regulations and to try to be more realistic in administering federal regulations.

OSHA must be regarded as a major factor in terms of its influence on operations-management decisions in all areas relating to worker safety. OSHA has promoted the welfare and safety of workers in its role as a catalyst, often spurring companies to make changes that they knew were needed but "hadn't gotten around to making yet."

WORK MEASUREMENT

Job design and methods analysis concentrate on *how* a job is done. Work measurement is concerned with determining the *length of time* it should take to complete the job. Job times are vital inputs for manpower planning, estimating labor costs, scheduling, budgeting, and designing incentive systems. Moreover, from the workers' standpoint, time standards provide an indication of expected output. Time standards reflect the amount of time it should take an average worker to do a given job working under typical conditions. The standards include expected activity time plus allowances for probable delays.

More formally, a *standard time* is the amount of time it should take a qualified worker to complete a specified task, working at a sustainable rate, using given methods, tools and equipment, raw material inputs, and workplace arrangement. Whenever a time standard is developed for a job, it is essential to provide a complete description of the parameters of the job because the actual time to do the job is sensitive to all of these factors; changes in any one of the factors can materially affect time requirements. For instance, changes in product design or changes in the way a job is performed brought about by a methods study should trigger a new time study to update the standard time. As a practical matter, though, minor changes are occasionally made that do not justify the expense of restudying a job. Consequently, the standards for many jobs may be slightly inaccurate. Periodic time studies may be used to update the standards.

There are a number of different ways organizations develop time standards. While some small manufacturers and service organizations rely on subjective estimates of job times, the most commonly used methods of work measurement are:

1. Stopwatch time study.
2. Historical times.
3. Predetermined data.
4. Work sampling.

Each of these techniques is described in some detail on the following pages, beginning with time study.

Stopwatch Time Study

Stopwatch time study was formally introduced by Frederick Winslow Taylor late in the last century. Today it is the most widely used method of work measurement. It is especially appropriate for short, repetitive tasks.

Stopwatch time study involves developing a time standard based on observations of one worker taken over a number of cycles. Once established, it is then applied to the work of all others in the organization who perform the same task. The basic steps in a time study are:

1. Define the task to be studied and inform the worker who will be studied.
2. Determine the number of cycles to observe.
3. Time the job and rate the worker's performance.
4. Compute the standard time.

The analyst who will study the job should be thoroughly familiar with it since it is not unknown for workers to attempt to include extra motions during the study in the hope of gaining a standard that allows more time per piece (i.e., the worker will be able to work at a slower pace and still meet the standard). Furthermore, the analyst will want to check to see if the job is being performed efficiently before setting the time standard.

In most instances an analyst will want to break all but very short jobs down into basic elemental motions (e.g., reach, grasp) and obtain times for each element. There are several reasons for this. One is that some elements are not done in every cycle, and the breakdown enables the analyst to get a better perspective on them. Another is that the worker's proficiency may not be the same for all elements of the job, so an elemental breakdown becomes necessary. Still a third reason for an elemental breakdown is to build a file of elemental times that can be used to set times for other jobs. This use will be described a bit later.

It is important to inform the worker who will be observed about the study in order to avoid suspicion or misunderstandings. Workers sometimes feel uneasy about being studied, and they may fear changes that might result. The analyst should make an attempt to discuss these things with the worker prior to studying the operations to allay such fears and to enlist the cooperation of the worker.

The *number of cycles* that must be timed is a function of three things: (1) the variability of observed times, (2) the desired accuracy, and (3) the desired level of confidence for the estimated job time. Very often the desired accuracy is expressed as a percentage of the mean of the observed times. For example, the goal of a time study may be to achieve an estimate that is within ±10 percent of the actual mean. The sample size that will be needed to achieve that goal can be determined using this formula:

Sample size
$$n = \left(\frac{zs}{a\overline{x}}\right)^2 \qquad \text{(8–1)}$$

where

$z =$ Number of normal standard deviations needed for desired confidence

$s =$ Sample standard deviation

$a =$ Desired accuracy percentage

$\overline{x} =$ Sample mean

Typical values of z used in this computation are:[5]

Desired confidence percent	z-value
90	1.65
95	1.96
95.5	2.00
98	2.33
99	2.58

Of course, the value of z for any desired confidence can be obtained from the normal table in the Appendix, Table A or Table B.

An alternate formula that is used when the desired accuracy is stated as an *amount* (e.g., within one minute of the true mean) instead of a percentage is:

$$n = \left(\frac{z\,s}{e}\right)^2 \qquad \text{(8–2)}$$

where

$e =$ Accuracy or maximum error desired

In order to make a preliminary estimate of sample size it is typical to take a small number of observations (say 10 to 20) and then compute values of $\overline{x}$ and s to use in the formula for n. Toward the end of the study, the analyst may want to recompute n using revised estimates of $\overline{x}$ and s based on the increased data available.

EXAMPLE 1

A time study analyst wants to estimate the time required to perform a certain job. A preliminary study yielded a mean of 6.4 minutes and a standard deviation of 2.1 minutes. The desired confidence is 95 percent. How many observations will be needed (including those already taken) if the desired maximum error is *(a)* ±10 percent of the sample mean? *(b)* one half minute?

---

[5] Theoretically, a t-value rather than a z should be used because the population standard deviation in unknown. However, the use of z is simpler and provides reasonable results when the number of observations is 30 or more. In practice, z is used almost exclusively.

EXAMPLE 1 (concluded)

a. $s = 2.1$ minutes $z = 1.96$
   $\bar{x} = 6.4$ minutes $a = 10\%$

$$n = \left(\frac{z\,s}{a\,\bar{x}}\right)^2 = \left(\frac{1.96(2.1)}{.10(6.4)}\right)^2 = 41.36 \text{ (round to 42)}$$

b. $e = 0.5$ $n = \left(\frac{z\,s}{e}\right)^2 = \left(\frac{1.96(2.1)}{0.5}\right)^2 = 67.77 \text{ (round to 68)}$

In an actual situation, the analyst would not be "given" the value of s but would be expected to compute it from sample data. This can be done using either of two formulas:

$$s = \sqrt{\frac{\Sigma(x_i - \bar{x})^2}{n-1}} \quad \text{or} \quad s = \sqrt{\frac{\Sigma x_i^2 - (\Sigma x_i)^2/n}{n-1}}. \tag{8-3}$$

An example of this computation is provided in the Solved Problems section at the end of this chapter.

Development of a time standard involves computation of three times: the *observed time* (OT), the *normal time* (NT) and then the *standard time* (ST).

Observed time.   The observed time is simply the average of the observed times. Thus,

$$OT = \frac{\Sigma x_i}{n} \tag{8-4}$$

where

   OT = Observed time
   Σx_i = Sum of observed times
   n = Number of observations

Normal time.   The normal time is the observed time adjusted for worker performance. It is computed by multiplying the observed time by a *performance rating*. That is,

$$NT = OT \times PR \tag{8-5}$$

where

   NT = Normal time
   PR = Performance rating

This assumes that a single performance rating has been made for the entire job. If ratings are made on an element by element basis, the normal time is obtained by multiplying each element's average time by its performance rating and summing those values:

$$NT = \Sigma(\bar{x}_j \cdot PR_j) \tag{8-6}$$

where

$\overline{x}_j$ = Average time for element j
PR_j = Performance rating for element j

The reason for including this adjustment factor is that the worker being observed may be working at a rate that is different from a "normal" rate, either because of an attempt to deliberately slow the pace or because the worker's natural abilities differ from the "norm." For this reason, an efficiency factor, or *performance rating,* is made by the observer to adjust the observed times to an "average" pace. For instance, a performance rating of 0.9 indicates a pace that is 90 percent of normal, while a rating of, say, 1.05 indicates a pace that is slightly faster than normal. For long jobs, each element may be rated, while for short jobs, a single rating may be made for an entire cycle.

In assessing performance, the analyst must compare the observed performance to his or her concept of normal. Obviously, there is room for debate about what constitutes normal performance, and performance ratings are sometimes the source of considerable conflict between labor and management. While no one has been able to suggest a way around these subjective evaluations, sufficient training and periodic *recalibration* of analysts using training films can provide a high degree of consistency in the ratings of different analysts.

Standard time. Normal time is the length of time a worker should take to perform a job if there are no delays or interruptions. It does not take into account such factors as personal delays (getting a drink of water or going to the restroom), unavoidable delays (machine adjustments and repairs, talking to a supervisor, waiting for materials), or rest breaks. The standard time for a job is the normal time adjusted for these delays using an allowance factor:

$$ST = NT \times AF \qquad\qquad (8\text{--}7)$$

where

ST = Standard time
AF = Allowance factor

The allowance factor can be computed in one of two ways, depending on how allowances are specified. If allowances are based on the *job time,* the allowance factor must be computed using the formula:

$$AF_{Job} = 1 + A \qquad\qquad (8\text{--}8)$$

where

AF = Allowance factor
A = Allowance percentage based on job time

If allowances are based on a percentage of the time worked (i.e., the *workday*), the appropriate formula is:

$$AF_{Day} = \frac{1}{1 - A} \tag{8-9}$$

where

A = Allowance percentage based on workday.

Some typical allowance percentages (A) are listed in Table 8–3.

EXAMPLE 2

Compute the allowance factor for these two cases:

a. The allowance is 20 percent of *job* time.
b. The allowance is 20 percent of *work* time.

Solution

$$A = 0.20$$

a. $AF = 1 + A = 1.20$, or 120%.

b. $AF = \dfrac{1}{1 - A} = \dfrac{1}{1 - 0.20} = 1.25$, or 125%.

EXAMPLE 3

A time study of an assembly operation yielded the observed times shown below, for which the analyst gave a performance rating of 1.10. Using an allowance of 15 percent of *job* time, determine the appropriate standard time for this operation.

Observation	Time (minutes)	Observation	Time (minutes)
1	4.20	6	4.18
2	4.15	7	4.14
3	4.08	8	4.14
4	4.12	9	4.19
5	4.15		37.35

Solution

$$n = 9, \; PR = 1.10, \text{ and } A = 0.15$$

a. $OT = \dfrac{\Sigma \text{ times}}{n} = \dfrac{37.35}{9} = 4.15$ minutes

b. $NT = OT \times PR = 4.15(1.10) = 4.565$ minutes
c. $ST = NT \times (1 + A) = 4.565(1.15) = 5.25$ minutes.

TABLE 8–3

Typical Allowance Percentages for Working Conditions

			Percent
A.	Constant allowances:		
	1.	Personal allowance	5
	2.	Basic fatigue allowance	4
B.	Variable allowances:		
	1.	Standing allowance	2
	2.	Abnormal position allowance:	
		a. Slightly awkward	0
		b. Awkward (bending)	2
		c. Very awkward (lying, stretching)	7
	3.	Use of force or muscular energy (lifting, pulling, or pushing):	
		Weight lifted, pounds:	
		5	0
		10	1
		15	2
		20	3
		25	4
		30	5
		35	7
		40	9
		45	11
		50	13
		60	17
		70	22
	4.	Bad light:	
		a. Slightly below recommended	0
		b. Well below	2
		c. Quite inadequate	5
	5.	Atmospheric conditions (heat and humidity)—variable	0–10
	6.	Close attention:	
		a. Fairly fine work	0
		b. Fine or exacting	2
		c. Very fine or very exacting	5
	7.	Noise level:	
		a. Continuous	0
		b. Intermittent—loud	2
		c. Intermittent—very loud	5
		d. High-pitched—loud	5
	8.	Mental strain:	
		a. Fairly complex process	1
		b. Complex or wide span of attention	4
		c. Very complex	8
	9.	Monotony:	
		a. Low	0
		b. Medium	1
		c. High	4
	10.	Tediousness:	
		a. Rather tedious	0
		b. Tedious	2
		c. Very tedious	5

Source: B. W. Niebel, *Motion and Time Study,* 6th ed. (Homewood, Ill.: Richard D. Irwin, 1976), p. 380. © 1976 by Richard D. Irwin, Inc. Reprinted by permission.

TABLE 8–4

Summary of Time Study Computations

A. Sample size

$$n = \left(\frac{z \cdot s}{a \cdot \bar{x}} \right)^2 \qquad (8\text{–}1)$$

$$n = \left(\frac{z \cdot s}{e} \right)^2 \qquad (8\text{–}2)$$

B. Observed time

$$OT = \frac{\Sigma x_i}{n} \qquad (8\text{–}4)$$

C. Normal time

$$NT = OT \cdot PR \qquad (8\text{–}5)$$

D. Standard time

$$ST = NT \cdot AF \qquad (8\text{–}7)$$

where

$$AF_{Job} = (1 + A) \qquad (8\text{–}8)$$

$$AF_{Day} = \frac{1}{(1 - A)} \qquad (8\text{–}9)$$

Symbols

$a =$ Allowable error as a percentage of average time
$A =$ Allowance percentage
$AF =$ Allowance factor
$AF_{Job} =$ Allowance expressed as a percentage of job time
$AF_{Day} =$ Allowance expressed as a percentage of working day
$n =$ Number of observations needed
$NT =$ Normal time
$OT =$ Observed, or average, time
$s =$ Standard deviation of observed times
$x_i =$ Time for ith observation $(i = 1,2,3, \ldots , n)$
$ST =$ Standard time

The formulas and symbols used for time study computations are summarized in Table 8–4.

In spite of the obvious benefits that can be derived from work measurement using time study, there are also some limitations that must be mentioned. One limitation relates to the subjective nature of performance rating. This has created innumerable conflicts between labor and management and in some companies is a continual sore spot. Another limitation is the fact that only those jobs that can be observed can be studied. This eliminates most managerial and creative jobs that involve mental as well as physical aspects. In addition, the cost of making the study rules out its use for irregular operations and infrequently occurring jobs. Finally, it disrupts the normal work routine, and workers resent it in many cases.

Standard Elemental Times

Standard elemental times are derived from a firm's own historical time-study data. Over the years a time-study department can accumulate a file of elemental times that are common to many jobs. After a certain point, many such times can be taken from the file instead of having to go through a complete time study to get them, although others may require actual timing.

The procedure for using standard elemental times consists of the following steps:

1. Analyze the job to identify the standard elements.
2. Check the file to see which elements have historical times and record them. Use time study to obtain others, if necessary.
3. Modify the file times if necessary (explained below).
4. Sum the elemental times to obtain the normal time and factor in allowances to obtain the standard time.

In some cases the file times may not pertain exactly to a specific task. For instance, standard elemental times might be on file for "move the tool three centimeters" and "move the tool nine centimeters," while the task in question involves a move of six centimeters. However, it is often possible to interpolate between values on file to obtain the desired time estimate.

One obvious advantage of this approach is the potential savings in cost and effort created by not having to conduct a complete time study for each job. A second advantage is that there is less disruption of work, again because the analyst does not have to time the worker. A third advantage is that performance ratings do not have to be done, they are generally *averaged* in the file times. The main disadvantages of this approach are that times may not exist for enough standard elements to make it worthwhile and the file times may be biased or inaccurate.

The method described in the following section is a variation of this that helps avoid some of these problems.

Predetermined Time Standards

Predetermined time standards involve the use of published data on standard elemental times. A commonly used system is *MTM* (methods-time measurement), which was developed in the late 1940s by the Methods Engineering Council. The MTM tables are based on extensive research on basic elemental motions and times. In order to use this approach, the analyst is required to divide the job into its basic elements (reach, move, turn, disengage), measure the distances involved (if applicable), rate the difficulty of the element, and then refer to the appropriate table of data to obtain the time for that element. The standard time for the job is obtained by adding the times for all of the basic elements. Times of the

basic elements are measured in time-measurement units (TMUs), and one TMU equals 0.0006 minutes. One minute of work may involve 100 or more basic elements, and a typical job may involve several hundred or more of these basic elements. This requires a considerable amount of skill on the part of the analyst to adequately describe the operation and develop realistic time estimates.

A few of the MTM tables are presented in Table 8–5 to give you an idea of the kind of information they provide.

A great deal of skill is required to generate a predetermined time standard. Analysts generally take training or certification courses to develop the necessary skills to do this kind of work.

Among the advantages of predetermined time standards are the following:

1. They are based upon large numbers of workers under controlled conditions.
2. The analyst is not required to rate performance in developing the standard.
3. There is no disruption of the operation.
4. Standards can be established even before a job is done.

Although proponents of predetermined standards claim that the approach provides much better accuracy than stopwatch studies, not everyone agrees with that claim. Some argue that many activity times are too specific to a given operation to be able to generalize them from published data. Others argue that different analysts perceive elemental activity breakdowns in different ways and that this adversely effects the development of times and produces varying time estimates among analysts. Still a third argument is that analysts can differ on the degree of difficulty that they assign to a given task, and thereby obtain different time standards.

Work Sampling

Work sampling is a technique for estimating the proportion of time that a worker or machine spends on various activities. Introduced by L. H. C. Tippett in 1934 in the textile industry, it is now widely used to study work activities.

Unlike time study, work sampling does not require timing an activity. In fact, it does not even involve continuous observation of the activity. Instead, an observer is required to make brief observations of a worker or machine at random intervals over a period of time and simply note the nature of the activity. For example, a machine may be "busy" or "idle"; a secretary may be typing, filing, talking on the telephone, and so on; and a carpenter may be carrying supplies, taking measurements, cutting wood, and so on. The resulting data are *counts* of the number of times each category of activity or nonactivity was observed.

Although work sampling is occasionally used to set time stan-

dards, its two primary uses are (1) ratio-delay studies, which concern the percentage of a worker's time that involves unavoidable delays or the proportion of time a machine is idle, and (2) *analysis of nonrepetitive jobs.* In a ratio-delay study, a hospital administrator, for example, might want to estimate the percentage of time that a certain piece of X-ray equipment is not in use. In a nonrepeti-

TABLE 8–5

A Portion of the MTM Tables

Table II—Move—M

Distance moved (inches)	Time TMU				Weight Allowance			Case and description
	A	B	C	Hand in motion B	Weight (pound) up to	Dy- namic factor	Static con- stant TMU	
¾ or less	2.0	2.0	2.0	1.7				
1	2.5	2.9	3.4	2.3	2.5	1.00	0	
2	3.6	4.6	5.2	2.9				A. Move object to other hand or against stop.
3	4.9	5.7	6.7	3.6	7.5	1.06	2.2	
4	6.1	6.9	8.0	4.3				
5	7.3	8.0	9.2	5.0	12.5	1.11	3.9	
6	8.1	8.9	10.3	5.7				
7	8.9	9.7	11.1	6.5	17.5	1.17	5.6	
8	9.7	10.6	11.8	7.2				B. Move object to approxi- mate or in- definite location.
9	10.5	11.5	12.7	7.9	22.5	1.22	7.4	
10	11.3	12.2	13.5	8.6				
12	12.9	13.4	15.2	10.0	27.5	1.28	9.1	
14	14.4	14.6	16.9	11.4				
16	16.0	15.8	18.7	12.8	32.5	1.33	10.8	
18	17.6	17.0	20.4	14.2				
20	19.2	18.2	22.1	15.6	37.5	1.39	12.5	
22	20.8	19.4	23.8	17.0				C. Move object to exact location.
24	22.4	20.6	25.5	18.4	42.5	1.44	14.3	
26	24.0	21.8	27.3	19.8				
28	25.5	23.1	29.0	21.2	47.5	1.50	16.0	
30	27.1	24.3	30.7	22.7				
Addi- tional	0.8	0.6	0.85		TMU per inch over 30 inches			

TABLE 8–5 *(concluded)*

Table III A—Turn—T

Weight	Time TMU for degrees turned										
	30°	45°	60°	75°	90°	105°	120°	135°	150°	165°	180°
Small—0 to 2 pounds	2.8	3.5	4.1	4.8	5.4	6.1	6.8	7.4	8.1	8.7	9.4
Medium—2.1 to 10 pounds	4.4	5.5	6.5	7.5	8.5	9.6	10.6	11.6	12.7	13.7	14.8
Large—10.1 to 35 pounds	8.4	10.5	12.3	14.4	16.2	18.3	20.4	22.2	24.3	26.1	28.2

Source: MTM Association for Standards and Research. Copyrighted by the MTM Association for Standards and Research. No reprint permission without written consent from MTM Association, 16–01 Broadway, Fair Lawn, New Jersey 07410.

tive job such as secretarial work, maintenance, and others, it can be important to establish the percentage of time an employee spends doing various tasks.

Nonrepetitive jobs typically involve a broader range of skills than repetitive jobs, and workers in these jobs are often paid on the basis of the highest skill involved. Therefore, it is important to determine the proportion of time spent on the high-skill level. For example, a secretary may take dictation, type, file, answer the telephone, schedule appointments, and do other routine office work. If the secretary spends a high percentage of time filing instead of typing or taking shorthand, the compensation should be lower than for a secretary who spends a high percentage of time typing and taking shorthand. Work sampling can be used to verify those percentages and can therefore be an important tool in developing the job description. In addition, work sampling can be part of a program for validation of job content that is needed for "bona fide occupational qualifications" (i.e., advertised jobs must require the skills that are specified).

Work sampling estimates include some degree of error; the same number of observations taken at different times during the week will probably produce slightly different estimates, and all estimates will usually differ from the actual (but unknown) values. Hence, it is important to treat work sampling estimates as *approximations* of the actual proportion of time devoted to any given activity. The goal of work sampling is to obtain an estimate that provides a specified confidence of not differing from the true value by more than a specified error. For example, a hospital administrator might request an estimate of X-ray idle time that will provide a 95 percent confidence of being within 4 percent of the actual percentage. Hence, work sampling is designed to produce a value, $\hat{p}$, which estimates the true proportion, p, within some allowable error, e: $\hat{p} \pm e$. The variability associated with sample estimates of p tends

FIGURE 8–8

A Confidence Interval
for the Estimate of the
True Proportion Is
Based on a Normal
Distribution

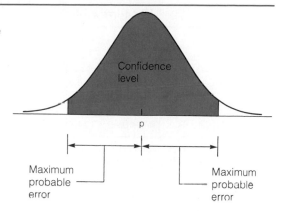

to be approximately normal for large sample sizes. Consequently, the normal distribution can be used to construct a confidence interval and to determine required sample sizes. One (nonclassical) way to view the sampling distribution is to imagine all of the *possible* true proportions that could produce a given sample value of $\hat{p}$. The result is a distribution of possible true proportions that is (1) normal and (2) centered around the sample proportion. The most likely values of the actual proportion are quite close to the sample proportion; a true value close to the center of the distribution is much more likely than a value in one of the tails. This concept is illustrated in Figure 8–8. The degree to which this distribution is narrow or spread out is a function of the sample size and p. The amount of maximum probable error is a function of both the sample size and the desired level of confidence.

For large samples the maximum error, e, can be computed using the formula:

$$e = z \sqrt{\frac{\hat{p}(1-\hat{p})}{n}}$$

(8–10)

where

   $z =$ Number of standard deviations needed to achieve desired
        confidence
   $\hat{p} =$ Sample proportion
   $n =$ Sample size

In most instances management will be required to specify the desired confidence level and the amount of allowable error, and the analyst will be required to determine a sample size that will be

sufficient to obtain those results. The appropriate value for n can be determined by solving the previous equation for n, which yields:

$$n = \left(\frac{z}{e}\right)^2 \hat{p}(1 - \hat{p}) \tag{8-11}$$

EXAMPLE 4

The manager of a small supermarket chain wants to estimate the proportion of time stock clerks spend making price changes to previously marked merchandise. The manager wants a 98 percent confidence that the resulting estimate will be within ±5 percent of the true value. What sample size should be used?

Solution

$e = 0.05$, $z = 2.33$ (see p. 384)
$\hat{p} = $ Unknown

(see p. 384)

When no sample estimate of p is available, a preliminary estimate of sample size can be obtained using $\hat{p} = 0.50$. Then, after 20 or so observations, a new estimate of $\hat{p}$ can be obtained from those observations and a revised value of n computed using the new $\hat{p}$. In fact, it would be prudent to recompute the value of n at two or three points during the study to obtain a better indication of the necessary sample size. Thus, the initial estimate of n is:

$$n = \left(\frac{2.33}{0.05}\right)^2 0.5(1 - 0.5) = 542.89, \text{ or } 543 \text{ observations}$$

Suppose that in the first 20 observations stock clerks were found to be changing prices twice, making $p = 2/20 = 0.10$. The revised estimate of n at that point would be:

$$n = \left(\frac{2.33}{0.05}\right)^2 0.1(1 - .1) = 195.44 \text{ or } 196$$

Suppose a second check is made after a total of 100 observations, and assume $\hat{p} = 0.11$ at this point (including the initial 20 observations). Recomputing n yields:

$$n = \left(\frac{2.33}{0.05}\right)^2 0.11(0.89) = 212.60 \text{ or } 213$$

Perhaps one more check might be made to settle on a final value for n. If the computed value of n is less than the number of observations already taken, sampling would be terminated at that point.

Determining the sample size is only one part of work sampling. The overall procedure consists of the following steps:

1. Clearly identify the worker(s) or machine(s) to be studied.
2. Notify the workers and supervisors of the purpose of the study to avoid arousing suspicions.
3. Compute an initial estimate of sample size, using a preliminary estimate of p if available (say, from analyst experience or past data). Otherwise, use $\hat{p} = 0.50$.
4. Develop a random observation schedule.
5. Begin taking observations. Recompute the required sample size several times during the study.
6. Determine the estimated proportion of time spent on the specified activity.

As always, careful problem definition can prevent mistakes such as studying the wrong worker or wrong activity. Similarly, it is important to inform related parties of the purpose and scope of the study in order to reduce unnecessary fears that might be generated by unannounced data collection. It is also important to obtain random observations in order to achieve valid results.

Observations must be spread out over a period of time so that a true indication of variability is obtained. If observations are bunched too closely in time there is some risk that the behaviors observed during that time will not genuinely reflect typical performance. The degree to which observations should be spread out will depend in part on the nature of the activity being studied, and a decision on this is usually best left to the analyst. Determination of a random observation schedule involves the use of a *random number table*. A random number table (see Table 8–6) consists of *unordered sequences* of numbers (i.e., *random*). Use of such tables enables the analyst to incorporate randomness into the observation schedule. Numbers obtained from the table can be used to identify observation times for a study. Any size number (i.e., any number

TABLE 8–6

Portion of a Random Number Table

	1	2	3	4	5	6
1	6912	7264	2801	8901	4627	8387
2	3491	1192	0575	7547	2093	4617
3	4715	2486	2776	2664	3856	0064
4	1632	1546	1950	1844	1123	1908
5	8510	7209	0938	2376	0120	4237
6	3950	1328	7343	6083	2108	2044
7	7871	7752	0521	8511	3956	3957
8	2716	1396	7354	0249	7728	8818
9	2935	8259	9912	3761	4028	9207
10	8533	9957	9585	1039	2159	2438
11	0508	1640	2768	4666	9530	3352
12	2951	0131	4359	3095	4421	3018

of digits read as one number) can be obtained from the table. The digits are in groups of four for convenience only. The basic idea is to obtain numbers from the table and to convert each one so that it corresponds to an observation time. There are a number of different ways to accomplish this. The approach we will use is as follows. We will obtain three sets of numbers from the table for each observation: the first set will correspond to the *day,* the second to the *hour,* and the third to the *minute* when the observation is to be made. The number of digits necessary for any set will equal the number of days in the study, the number of hours per day, and minutes per hour. For instance, if the study will cover 47 days, a two-digit number will be needed, and if the activity is performed for eight hours per day, a one-digit number will be needed for hours. Of course, since each hour has 60 minutes, a two-digit number will be needed for minutes. Thus, we would need a two-digit number for day, a one-digit number for hour, and a two-digit number for minutes. For a study that requires observations over a seven-day period in an office that works nine hours per day, one-digit numbers would be needed for days, one-digit numbers for hours, and two-digit numbers for minutes.

Suppose we want three observations in this last case (i.e., 7 days, 9 hours, 60 minutes). We might begin by first determining the days on which observations will be made, then the hours, and finally the minutes. Let's begin at the upper left-hand corner of Table 8–6 and read across: The first number is 6, which indicates day 6. The second number is 9. Since it exceeds the number of days in the study, it is simply ignored. The third number is 1, indicating day 1, and the next is 2, indicating day 2. Hence, observations will be made on days 6, 1, and 2. Next we can determine the hours. Suppose we read the second row of column 1, again obtaining one-digit numbers. We find:

$$3 \ (= \text{3d hour}), \ 4 \ (= \text{4th hour}), \ 9 \ (= \text{9th hour})$$

Moving to the next row and reading two-digit numbers, we find:

$$47 \ (= \text{47th minute}), \ 15 \ (= \text{15th minute}), \text{ and } 24 \ (= \text{24th minute})$$

Combining these results yields:

Day	Hour	Minute
6 3		47
1 4		15
2 9		24

This means that on day 6 of the study, an observation is to be made during the 47th minute of the 3d hour, on day 1 during the 15th minute of the 4th hour, and on day 2 during the 24th minute of the 9th hour. For simplicity, these times can be put in chronological order by day. Thus,

Day		Hour	Minute
1	. . . . .	4	15
2	. . . . .	9	24
6	. . . . .	3	47

A complete schedule of observations might appear like the one below after all numbers have been arranged in chronological order.

Day 1

Observa-tion	Time	Busy (√)	Idle (√)
1	8:15		
2	8:42		
3	9:02		
4	9:31		
5	9:48		
6	9:57		
7	10:20		
8	11:02		
9	11:13		
10	11:55		
11	1:29		
12	1:41		
13	2:00		
14	2:33		

Day 2

Observa-tion	Time	Busy (√)	Idle (√)
24	8:04		
25	9:15		
26	9:19		
27	9:35		
28	10:12		
29	10:27		
30	10:38		
31	10:58		
32	11:50		
33	1:14		
34	1:43		
35	1:57		
36	3:10		

The general procedure for using a random number table is to read the numbers in some sequence (across rows, down or up columns), discarding any that lack correspondence. It is important to vary the starting point from one study to the next in order to avoid taking observations at the same times, since the times would quickly become known to workers and the random element would be lost. There are various ways to choose a starting point. One is to use the serial number on a dollar bill to select a starting point. However, so that everyone ends up with the same results, you will be instructed in each problem as to the starting point and as to the direction to read in.

In sum, the procedure for identifying random times at which to make work-sampling observations involves the following steps:

1. Determine the number of days in the study and the number of hours per day. This will indicate the required number of digits for days and hours.

TABLE 8–7

Advantages and Disadvantages of Work Sampling Compared to Stopwatch Time Study

Advantages:
1. Observations are spread out over a period of time, making results less susceptible to short-term fluctuations.
2. There is little or no disruption of work.
3. Workers are less resentful.
4. Studies are less costly and less time-consuming, and the skill requirements of the analyst are much less.
5. The study can be interrupted without affecting the results.
6. Many different studies can be conducted simultaneously.
7. No timing device is required.
8. Lends itself to nonrepetitive tasks.

Disadvantages:
1. There is much less detail on the elements of a job.
2. Workers may alter their work patterns when they spot the observer, thereby invalidating the results.
3. In many cases there is no record of the method used by the worker.
4. Observers may fail to adhere to a *random* schedule of observations.
5. It is not well-suited for short, repetitive tasks.
6. Much time may be required to move from one work place to another and back to satisfy the randomness requirement.

2. Obtain the necessary number of sets for *days,* ignoring any sets which exceed the number of days.
3. Repeat the previous step for *hours.*
4. Repeat step 2 for *minutes.*
5. Link the days, hours, and minutes in the order that they were obtained.
6. Place the observation times in chronological order.

A comparison of work sampling and time study is presented in Table 8–7. It suggests that work sampling is a less-formal, less-detail approach to determining job times and that work sampling is best-suited to nonrepetitive jobs.

COMPENSATION

A significant issue that relates to the design of work systems is worker compensation. It is important for organizations to develop suitable compensation plans for their employees, especially since the success or failure of a firm will depend in large measure on the efforts of its employees. If wages are set too low, organizations may find it difficult to attract and hold competent workers and managers. Conversely, if wages are set too high, the increased costs may result in lower profits or force the organization to increase its prices, which might adversely affect demand for the organization's products or services.

Organizations use two basic systems for compensating employ-

ees: *time-based systems* and *output-based systems*. Time-based systems, also known as *hourly* and *measured daywork* systems, compensate employees for the *time* the employee has worked during a pay period. Salaried workers also represent a form of time-based compensation. Output-based, or *incentive*, systems compensate employees according to the amount of output they produce during a pay period, thereby tying pay directly to performance.

Time-based systems are more widely used than incentive systems, particularly for office, administrative, and managerial employees, but also for blue-collar workers. One of the reasons for this is that computation of wages is straightforward and managers can readily estimate labor costs for a given manpower level. Employees often prefer time-based systems because the pay is steady and they know how much they will receive for each pay period. In addition, employees may resent the pressures associated with an output-based system.

Another reason for using time-based systems is that many jobs do not lend themselves to the use of incentives. In some cases it may be difficult or impossible to measure output. For example, jobs that require creative or mental work cannot be easily measured on an output basis. Other jobs may include irregular activities or have so many different forms of output that measuring output and determining pay is fairly complex. Also, in the case of assembly lines, the use of *individual* incentives would disrupt the even flow of work. However, *group* incentives are sometimes used successfully in such cases. Finally, *quality* considerations may be more important than *quantity*. For example, in health care, greater emphasis is generally placed on the quality of patient care than on the number of patients processed.

On the other hand, there are situations in which the use of incentives is desirable. Incentives reward workers for their output, which presumably causes some workers to produce more than they might under a time-based system. The advantage is that certain (fixed) costs do not vary with increases in output, so the overall cost per unit decreases if output increases. Workers may prefer incentive systems because they see a relationship between their efforts and their pay and because it presents the opportunity for them to earn more than they might under a time-based system.

On the negative side, incentive systems involve a considerable amount of paperwork, computation of wages is more difficult than under time-based systems, output has to be measured and standards have to be set, cost-of-living increases are difficult to integrate into incentive plans, and contingency arrangements for unavoidable delays have to be developed.

The main advantages and disadvantages of time-based and output-based plans are outlined in Table 8–8.

TABLE 8–8

Comparison of Time-Based and Output-Based Pay Systems

		Management	*Worker*
A.	Time-based Advantages:	1. Stable labor costs 2. Easy to administer 3. Simple to compute pay 4. Stable output	1. Stable pay 2. Less pressure to produce than under output system
	Disadvantages:	1. No incentive for workers to increase output	1. Extra efforts not rewarded
B.	Output-based Advantages:	1. Lower cost per unit 2. Greater output	1. Pay related to efforts 2. Opportunity to earn more
	Disadvantages:	1. Wage computation is more difficult 2. Need to measure output 3. Quality may suffer 4. Difficult to incorporate wage increases 5. Increased problems with scheduling	1. Pay fluctuates 2. Workers may be penalized because of factors beyond their control (e.g., machine breakdowns)

In order to obtain the maximum benefit from an incentive plan, the plan should be:

1. Accurate.
2. Easy to apply.
3. Consistent.
4. Easy to understand.
5. Fair.

In addition, there should be an obvious relationship between effort and reward, and there should not be a limit on earnings.

Incentive systems may focus on the output of each individual or on the output of a group. Each of these approaches is briefly described below.

Individual Incentive Plans

Individual incentive plans take a variety of forms. The simplest plan is *straight piecework*. Under this plan a worker's pay is a direct linear function of his output. In the past, piecework plans were fairly popular. Now, minimum wage legislation makes them somewhat impractical. Even so, many of the plans currently in use represent variations of the straight piecework plan. They typically incorporate a base rate that serves as a floor; workers are guaranteed that amount as a minimum, regardless of output. The base rate is tied to an output standard. If the worker produces less than standard that worker will be paid at the base rate. This protects workers from pay loss due to delays, breakdowns, and similar prob-

lems. In most cases incentives are paid for output above standard, and the pay is referred to as a *bonus*.

Group Incentive Plans

Group incentive plans stress sharing of productivity gains with employees. There are a variety of plans in use. Some focus exclusively on output while others reward employees for output and for reductions in material and other costs. The four well-known plans described below reflect the main features of most of the plans currently in operation.

The *Scanlon plan* was developed by the late Joseph Scanlon during the 1930s in cooperation with the management of a machine-tool company that was on the brink of bankruptcy. The main feature of the plan was to encourage reductions in labor costs by allowing workers to share in any reductions achieved. The plan involved formation of worker committees to actively seek out areas for improvement.

The *Kaiser plan* was introduced during the 1960s. Like the Scanlon plan, it involved the use of committees to suggest ways of reducing costs with savings shared by employees. However, in addition to reductions in labor costs, it also provided for workers to share in reductions in material and supply costs.

The *Lincoln plan* was developed over a period of about 20 years (1914 to 1934) at the Lincoln Electric Company in Cleveland, Ohio. It includes profit sharing, job enlargement, and participative management. Like the other plans, it involves the use of evaluation committees to generate suggestions. The three main components of the plan are a piecework system, an annual bonus, and a stock purchase provision. Lincoln officials credit the plan with enabling the company to increase its market share and profitability and with reducing the unit cost of its basic product while competitors have experienced substantial increases in their costs.

The *Kodak plan* uses a combination of premium wage levels and an annual bonus related to company profits instead of more traditional incentives. Workers are encouraged to help set goals and to decide on what reasonable performance levels are with the idea that because of their involvement they will be more apt to produce at a premium rate.

SUMMARY

The design of work systems involves job design, work measurement, and compensation.

Job design is concerned with the content of jobs and work methods. In the past, job design has often tended to focus on efficiency. However, there now seems to be an increasing awareness of, and

an attempt to consider, the behavioral aspects of work and worker satisfaction. Current concern about productivity has thrust job design into the limelight. However, the jobs usually associated with high productivity are often the same jobs that appear to be the greatest source of worker dissatisfaction, creating somewhat of a paradox for job designers.

Methods-analysis and motion-study techniques are often used to develop the "efficiency" aspects of jobs but do not directly consider their behavioral aspects. Nonetheless, they are an important part of job design. Working conditions are also an important aspect of job design, not only because of behavioral and efficiency factors, but also because of concern for the health and safety of workers.

Work measurement is concerned with specifying the length of time needed to complete a job. Such information is vital for manpower planning, cost estimating, budgeting, scheduling, and worker compensation. Commonly used approaches include stopwatch time study and predetermined times. A related technique is work sampling, which can also be used to obtain data on activity times. More commonly, work sampling is used to estimate the proportion of time a worker spends on a certain aspect of the job.

Organizations can choose from a variety of compensation plans. It is important to do so carefully, for compensation is important to both the worker and the organization, and once adopted, it is usually difficult to substantially change a compensation plan.

1. Compute the mean and standard deviation of these observed times:

Observation	Time (minutes)
1	3.6
2	4.1
3	4.4
4	3.7
5	4.2

Solution

$$\bar{x} = \text{Average time} = \frac{3.6 + 4.1 + 4.4 + 3.7 + 4.2}{5} = \frac{20.0}{5} = 4.0$$

Using $s = \sqrt{\dfrac{\Sigma(x_i - \bar{x})^2}{n - 1}}$:

x_i	$\bar{x}$	$(x_i - \bar{x})$	$(x_i - \bar{x})^2$
3.6	4.0	−0.4	0.16
4.1	4.0	0.1	0.01
4.4	4.0	0.4	0.16
3.7	4.0	−0.3	0.09
4.2	4.0	0.2	0.04
		0.0	0.46

$$s = \sqrt{\frac{0.46}{5 - 1}} = 0.34 \text{ minutes.}$$

Using $s = \sqrt{\dfrac{\Sigma x_i^2 - (\Sigma x_i)^2/n}{n - 1}}$:

x_i	x_i^2
3.6	12.96
4.1	16.81
4.4	19.36
3.7	13.69
4.2	17.64
20.0	80.46

$$s = \sqrt{\frac{80.46 - 20^2/5}{5 - 1}}$$

$$= 0.34$$

2. An analyst has been asked to prepare an estimate of the proportion of time that a turret lathe operator spends adjusting his machine, with a 90 percent confidence level. Based upon previous experience, the analyst believes the proportion will be approximately 30 percent.

   a. If the analyst uses a sample size of 400 observations, what is the maximum probable error that will be associated with the estimate?

b. What sample size would the analyst need in order to have the maximum error be no more than ±5 percent?

Solution

$$\hat{p} = .30, \ z = 1.65 \text{ for } 90 \text{ percent confidence}$$

a. $e = z \sqrt{\dfrac{\hat{p}(1-\hat{p})}{n}} = 1.65 \sqrt{\dfrac{.3(.7)}{400}} = .038$

b. $n = \left(\dfrac{z}{e}\right)^2 \hat{p}(1-\hat{p}) = \left(\dfrac{1.65}{.05}\right)^2 (.3)(.7) = 228.69 \text{ or } 229.$

3. The owner of a large gift shop wants to estimate the proportion of time that shoppers spend in a certain part of the store. The shop is open nine hours a day, six days a week. Twelve observations will be taken over a 30-day period. Determine the random observation times using Table 8–6 and these instructions:
   a. For days, read the first two digits of column 2 going down, and then the first two digits of column 3, going down.
   b. For hours, read one-digit numbers in row 4 from left to right.
   c. For minutes, read two-digit numbers using the first two digits in column 1, going down and then the second two digits in column 1, going down.

Solution

a. Days:	**b.** Hours:	**c.** Minutes:
Random Number	*Random Number*	*Random Number*
72*	1	69†
11	6	34
24	3	47
15	2	16
72*	1	85†
13	5	39
77*	4	78†
13	6	27
82*	1	29
99*	9	85†
16	5	05
01	0‡	29
28	1	12
05		91†
27		15
19		32
09		10

* Since there will be 30 days in the study, random numbers larger than 30 are not relevant.

† There are 60 minutes per hour. Larger numbers do not correspond.

‡ The store is open nine hours per day. The numbers 1–9 correspond to the hours 1–9; zero is not applicable.

Combining these results, in the order they appeared, produces the following results:

Day	Hour	Minute
11	1	34
24	6	47
15	3	16
13	2	39
13	1	27
16	5	29
01	4	05
28	6	29
05	1	12
27	9	15
19	5	32
09	1	10

Arranging the results chronologically by day, hour, and minute (but maintaining the same *combinations*) produces this list of observation times:

Observation	Day	Hour	Minute
1	01	4	05
2	05	1	12
3	09	1	10
4	11	1	34
5	13	1	27
6	13	2	39
7	15	3	16
8	16	5	29
9	19	5	32
10	24	6	47
11	27	9	15
12	28	6	29

DISCUSSION AND REVIEW QUESTIONS

1. What is job design and why is it important?

2. What are some of the main advantages and disadvantages of specialization from a management perspective? From a worker's perspective?

3. Contrast the meanings of the terms *job enlargement* and *job enrichment*.

4. What is the purpose of job enlargement and job enrichment?

5. Explain what is meant by the term *sociotechnical approach*.

6. What are some of the ways in which automation can improve production operations? What are some of the potential problems that a manager should be aware of when considering automation?

7. Some Japanese firms have a policy of rotating their managers among the different managerial jobs. In contrast, American managers are more likely to specialize in a certain area (e.g., finance or operations). Discuss the advantages and disadvantages of each of these approaches.

8. What are motion-study principles? How are they classified?

9. What are some of the reasons that methods analyses are needed? How is methods analysis linked to productivity improvements?

10. How are devices such as flow process charts and worker-machine charts useful?

11. What is a time standard? What factors must be taken into account when developing standards?

12. What are some of the main uses of time-study information?

13. Could performance rating be avoided by studying a group of workers and averaging their times? Explain briefly.

14. If an average worker could be identified, what advantage would there be in using that person for a time study? What are some of the reasons that an average worker might not be studied?

15. What are some of the main limitations of time study?

16. Comment on the following: "At any given instant, the standard times for many jobs will not be strictly correct."
    a. Why is this so?
    b. Does this mean that those standards are worthless? Explain.

17. Why do workers sometimes resent time studies?

18. What are the advantages and disadvantages of (a) time-based pay plans and (b) incentive plans?

PROBLEMS

1. An analyst has timed a metal-cutting operation for 50 cycles. The average time per cycle was 10.40 minutes, and the standard deviation was 1.20 minutes for a worker with a performance rating of 125 percent. Assume an allowance of 16 percent of job time. Find the standard time for this operation.

2. A job was timed for 60 cycles and had an average of 1.2 minutes per piece. The performance rating was 95 percent and allowances are 10 percent, based on an eight-hour day. Determine each of the following:

    a. Observed time.
    b. Normal time.
    c. Standard time.

3. A time study was conducted on a job that contains four elements. The observed times and performance ratings for six cycles are shown below.

    a. Determine the average cycle time for each element.

    b. Find the normal time for each element.

    c. Assuming an allowance factor of 15 percent of job time, compute the standard time for this job.

4. A worker-machine operation was found to involve 3.3 minutes of machine time per cycle in the course of 40 cycles of stopwatch study. The worker's time averaged 1.9 minutes per cycle, and she was given a rating of 120 percent (machine rating is 100 percent). Assuming an allowance factor of 12 percent of labor time, determine the standard time for this job.

5. A recently negotiated union contract allows workers in a grinding department 48 minutes for rest, 20 minutes for personal time, and 28 minutes for delays for an eight-hour shift. A time-study analyst observed a job that is performed continuously and found an average time of 6.0 minutes per cycle for a worker he rated at 95 percent. What standard time is applicable for that operation?

Element	Performance rating	Observations (minutes per cycle)					
		1	2	3	4	5	6
1	90%	0.44	0.50	0.43	0.45	0.48	0.46
2	85	1.50	1.54	1.47	1.51	1.49	1.52
3	110	0.84	0.89	0.77	0.83	0.85	0.80
4	100	1.10	1.14	1.08	1.20	1.16	1.26

6. The data below represent time-study observations for a woodworking operation. Based on the observations, determine the standard time for the operation assuming an allowance of 15 percent based on job time.

Using Table 8–6, read the *last digit* going down column 4 for hour (e.g., 1 7 4 4 6 . . .), and then read across row 3 from left to right in sets of two for minutes (e.g., 47 15 24 86 . . .). Arrange the time chronologically.

Element	Performance rating	Observation (minutes per cycle)					
		1	2	3	4	5	6
1.	110%	1.20	1.17	1.16	1.22	1.24	1.15
2.	115	0.83	0.87	0.78	0.82	0.85	1.32*
3.	105	0.58	0.53	0.52	0.59	0.60	0.54

* Unusual delay; disregard time.

7. How many observations should a time-study analyst plan for in the case of an operation that has a standard deviation of 1.5 minutes per piece if the goal is to estimate the mean time per piece to within 0.4 minutes and obtain a confidence of 95.5 percent?

8. About how many work cycles should be timed in order to estimate the average cycle time to within 2 percent of the sample mean with a confidence of 99 percent if a pilot study yielded these times (minutes): 5.2, 5.5, 5.6, 5.3, 5.5, and 5.3?

9. In an initial survey designed to estimate the percentage of time air-express cargo loaders are idle, an analyst found that loaders were idle in 6 of the 50 observations.
   a. Estimate the percentage of idle time.
   b. Based on the initial results, approximately how many observations would you require in order to estimate the actual percentage of idle time to within ±5 percent with a confidence of 95 percent?

10. A certain job in an insurance office involves telephone conversations with policy holders. The office manager estimates that about half of this person's time is spent on the telephone. How many observations would be needed in a work-sampling study to estimate that time percentage to within ±6 percent and have a confidence of 98 percent?

11. Design a schedule of work-sampling observations in which there are eight observations made during one eight-hour day.

12. The manager of a large office intends to conduct a work sampling of the time the staff spends on the telephone. The observations will be taken over a period of 50 workdays. The office is open five days a week for eight hours a day. Although the study will consist of 200 random observations, in this problem you will be asked to determine times for 11 observations. Use random numbers from Table 8–6.
   a. Determine times for 11 observations. For days, read sets of two-digit numbers going across row 4 from left to right (e.g., 16 32 15 46 . . .) and do the same in row 5.
   b. For hours, read one-digit numbers going *down*, using the first digit of column 1 (e.g., 6 3 4 1 . . .).
   c. For minutes, read two-digit numbers going *up* column 4 using the first two digits (e.g., 30 46 10 . . .) and then repeat for the second two digits going *up* column 4 (e.g., 95 66 39 . . .).
   d. Arrange the combinations chronologically by day, hour, and minute.
   e. Assume March 1 is a Monday and that there are no holidays in March, April, or May. Convert your observation *days* to dates in March, April, and May.

13. A work-sampling study is to be conducted on rush-hour traffic (4 to 7 P.M.) five days per week. The study will encompass 40 days. Determine the day, hour, and minute for 10 observations using the following procedure:
   a. Read two-digit numbers going *down* the first two digits of column 5 (e.g.,

46 20 38 . . .) and then down the second two digits of that column (e.g., 27 93 56 . . .) for days.

b. For hours, read one-digit numbers going from left to right across row 1 and then across row 2. (Read only 4s, 5s, and 6s.)

c. For minutes, read two-digit numbers

going *down* column 6, first using the *last* two digits (e.g., 87 17 64 . . .) and then after exhausting those numbers, repeat using the first two digits of that column (e.g., 83 46 00 19 . . .).

Arrange your times chronologically by day, then hour, and then minute.

SELECTED BIBLIOGRAPHY

Barnes, Ralph M. *Motion and Time Study: Design and Measurement of Work.* 8th ed. New York: John Wiley & Sons, 1980.

Buffa, Elwood Spencer. *Operations Management: The Management of Productive Systems.* 2d ed. New York: John Wiley & Sons, 1980.

Chase, Richard B., and Nicholas J. Aquilano. *Production and Operations Management.* 4th ed. Homewood, Ill.: Richard D. Irwin, 1985.

Davis, L. E. "Job Satisfaction Research: The Post-Industrial View." *Industrial Relations* 10 (1971), pp. 176–93.

————, and A. B. Cherns, eds. *Quality of Working Life; Cases.* Vol. 2. New York: Free Press, 1975.

————, and J. C. Taylor, eds. *Design of Jobs.* Middlesex, Eng.: Penguin Books, 1972.

Dickson, Paul. *The Future of the Workplace.* New York: Weybright and Talley, 1975.

Foy, N., and H. Gordon. "Worker Participation: Contrasts in Three Countries." *Harvard Business Review* 54, no. 3 (May–June 1976), pp. 71–83.

Herbst, P. G. *Socio-technical Design: Strategies in Multidisciplinary Research.* London: Tavistock, 1974.

Herzberg, Frederick. "One More Time: How Do You Motivate Employees?" *Harvard Business Review,* January–February 1968.

Hopeman, Richard J. *Production and Operations Management.* 4th ed. (Columbus, Ohio: Charles E. Merrill Publishing, 1980).

Huchinson, R. D. *New Horizons for Human Factors in Job Design.* New York: McGraw-Hill, 1981.

Konz, S. *Work Design: Industrial Ergonomics.* 2d ed. New York: John Wiley & Sons, 1981.

Monks, Joseph G. *Operations Management: Theory and Problems.* New York: McGraw-Hill, 1977.

Moore, Franklin, and Thomas Hendrick. *Production/Operations Management.* 8th ed. Homewood, Ill.: Richard D. Irwin, 1980.

Mundel, Marvin E. *Motion and Time Study.* 5th ed. Englewood Cliffs, N.J.: Prentice-Hall, 1978.

Nadler, G. *Work Design.* Rev. ed. Homewood, Ill.: Richard D. Irwin, 1970.

Niebel, Benjamin W. *Motion and Time Study.* 6th ed. Homewood, Ill.: Richard D. Irwin, 1976.

Smith, George L., Jr. *Work Measurement: A Systems Approach.* Columbus, Ohio: Grid Publishing, 1978.

Van Der Zwaan, A. H. "The Sociotechnical Systems Approach: A Critical Evaluation." *International Journal of Production Research* 13, no. 2 (1975), pp. 149–63.

Vroom, V. H. *Work and Motivation.* New York: John Wiley & Sons, 1964.

Case

*Making Hotplates**

A group of 10 workers were responsible for assembling hotplates (instruments for heating solutions to a given temperature) for hospital and medical laboratory use. A number of different models of hotplates were being manufactured. Some had a vibrating device so that the solution could be mixed while being heated. Others heated only test tubes. Still others could heat solutions in a variety of different containers.

With the appropriate small tools, each worker assembled part of a hotplate. The partially completed hotplate was placed on a moving belt to be carried from one assembly stage to the next. When the hotplate was completed, an inspector would check it over to ensure that it was working properly. Then, the last worker would place it in a specially prepared cardboard box for shipping.

The assembly line had been carefully "balanced" by industrial engineers, who had used a time and motion study to break the job down into subassembly tasks, each requiring about three minutes to accomplish. The amount of time calculated for each subassembly had also been "balanced" so that the task performed by each worker was supposed to take almost exactly the same amount of time. The workers were paid a straight hourly rate.

However, there were some problems. Morale seemed to be low, and the inspector was finding a relatively high percentage of badly assembled hotplates. Controllable rejects—those "caused" by the operator rather than by faulty materials—were running about 23 percent.

After discussing the situation, management decided to try something new. The workers were called together and asked if they would like to build the hotplates individually. The workers decided they would like to try this approach, provided they could go back to the old program if the new one did not work well. After several days of training, each worker began to assemble the entire hotplate.

---

* Source: Reproduced by permission from *The Modern Manager* by Edgar F. Huse, copyright © 1979 by West Publishing Company. All rights reserved.

Based on the following articles: E. Huse and M. Beer, "An Eclectic Approach to Organizational Development," *Harvard Business Review* 49 (September–October 1971), pp. 103–12; M. Beer and E. Huse, "A Systems Approach to Organization Development," *Journal of Applied Behavioral Science* 8 (January–February 1972), pp. 79–101; and "The Drive to Make Dull Jobs Interesting," *U.S. News & World Report,* July 17, 1972, p. 50.

The change was made at about the middle of the year. Productivity climbed quickly. By the end of the year, it had leveled off at about 84 percent higher than during the first half of the year, although no other changes had been made in the department or its personnel. Controllable rejects had dropped from 23 percent to 1 percent during the same period. Absenteeism had dropped from 8 percent to less than 1 percent. The workers had responded positively to the change, and their morale was higher. As one person put it, "Now, it is *my* hotplate." Eventually, the reject rate dropped so low that all routine final inspection was done by the assembly workers themselves. The full-time inspector was transferred to another job in the organization.

Questions

1. What changes in the work situation might account for the increase in productivity and the decrease in controllable rejects?

2. What might account for the drop in absenteeism and the increase in morale?

3. What were the major changes in the situation? Which changes were under the control of the manager? Which were controlled by the workers?

4. What might happen if the workers were to go back to the old assembly line method?

Case

Allstate Automotive Analyzers, Inc. *

Allstate Automotive Analyzers manufactures a complete line of automobile testing equipment, ranging from basic timing lights and tachometers for the do-it-yourself owner-mechanic to superior quality console testers for the professional. Basic DC-powered timing lights are used to check timing, distributor action, centrifugal and vacuum advance; tachometers measure RPM, point resistance, and dwell angle. Allstate's professional quality analyzer checks the electrical output of alternators, generators, and voltage regulators and measures RPM, air-fuel ratios, and carbon monoxide levels of auto-

---

* Reproduced by permission from *Cases in Production and Operations Management,* by Joe C. Iverstine and Jerry Kinard (Columbus, Ohio: Charles E. Merrill Publishing, 1977).

mobiles. When coupled with an oscilloscope, the tune-up analyzer diagnoses coil output, spark plug voltage, polarity, point bounce, and other aspects of a secondary ignition circuit.

Allstate's products are advertised and sold nationally. Prior to the surge in prices of new cars in the early 1970s, the company was only moderately successful; following several years of significant price increases, Allstate has enjoyed strong demand for its equipment and resultant high profits. (The demand for the firm's analyzers is attributed to car-owners keeping their automobiles longer and a tendency for the owner to save on expensive tune-ups.) Unit price on the firm's testers varies from $25 for the most basic timing lights to nearly $1,000 for the firm's most sophisticated console analyzer.

For several years, management of Allstate has had a number of its manufacturing operations on individual incentives. Before an operation is placed on an incentive wage plan, however, the firm's Industrial Engineering Department thoroughly analyzes the job, establishes standardized methods of performance, and sets production standards based on accepted work measurement techniques. The firm uses motion and time study as a basis for setting productivity expectations, and it has adopted the standard hour wage incentive plan for all operations that lend themselves to incentive pay.[1]

Eligible employees of Allstate are represented by a large national labor union which has gained a reputation for hard-nosed bargaining with employers on wages, hours, and conditions of employment. As a result of the union's effective bargaining, the base rates of pay for employees of Allstate are above average for the geographic region and type of work performed. One of the key factors which the union uses in negotiating for higher base rates of pay is the "tight" production standards set by management. Such tight standards, according to the union, restrict employees from earning "bonus" pay.

Basically, the wage incentive program has been a success for the company. With the exception of one department, very few grievances are filed with the union stewards. Whenever a grievance charging unfair standards is voiced, the steward (who has been

---

[1] The standard hour plan expresses the work standard in terms of time. It incorporates a base rate of pay which workers earn if they fail to meet standards. For all productivity over standards, earnings are directly proportional to the output. For example, assume the base rate of pay for a job is $5 per hour and the time standard is one half hour per unit. If a worker produces 20 units in one day, he or she earns 10 standard hours of pay, or $50. Productivity is 125 percent of standards; hence, earnings are 125 percent of base wages.

trained in basic motion and time study) has the right to time the operation himself. Based on his analysis, the steward either processes the grievance or screens it out as being without merit or justification. A majority of the formal grievances and informal complaints over standards originate in the assembly department, where one of the union stewards works. (All stewards are regular employees of the company; each is given six hours each week for the purpose of handling union business. While conducting union business, stewards earn the base rate of pay established for their particular jobs.) This steward recently transferred to the assembly department from another operation which is not on incentive pay because it is machine controlled.

Management of Allstate contends that the existing production standards in all departments, as set by the Industrial Engineering Department, are fair. Moreover, they feel that the steward is bitter because of his inability to earn higher wages than he earned in his former job. (He cannot bump back into his old job because all other workers in that department have more seniority.) As a result of his situation, management argues, the steward continually stirs up trouble and acts as an agitator. To support its contention, management points out that most of the grievances over unjust standards never get to the second stage of the grievance procedure and, hence, are not put in writing as dictated by the union contract. Even so, the steward remains quite popular with many of his coworkers, who feel that he gives them better representation than the other stewards who "bend over backward to get along with management."

Generally, the grievances filed by employees of the assembly department are based on standards which they consider "too tight," excessive down-time resulting from mechanical failures, and the introduction of new electric power drills and other assembly tools with which they must become familiar. In addition, they complain that the motion-and-time-study engineers use their positions to intimidate and harass by continually conducting time studies (with the implied threat of reducing time and increasing productivity requirements).

On two occasions (once in the assembly department and once in a punch press operation), formal grievances led to retiming of operations and a reduction in standards. Following the change in standards, productivity increased by an average of 20 percent, thereby making the operations more costly for the company. Restriction of output, on the other hand, which results from standards that are too tight, makes it difficult for the firm to meet its production schedules. Consequently, management is baffled by the seemingly paradoxical situation.

Questions

1. Evaluate the strengths and weaknesses of the standard hour plan used by Allstate Automotive Analyzers, Inc.

2. On what basis should production standards be set? Changed?

3. Discuss the handling of grievances which arise because of "tight" standards, new assembly tools, downtime, etc.

Learning Curves

THE CONCEPT OF LEARNING CURVES, 416

APPLICATIONS OF LEARNING CURVES, 422

CAUTIONS AND CRITICISMS, 424

SOLVED PROBLEMS, 426
DISCUSSION AND REVIEW QUESTIONS, 427
PROBLEMS, 427
SELECTED BIBLIOGRAPHY, 428
CASE: PRODUCT RECALL, 429

After completing this supplement you should be able to:

1. Explain the concept of a learning curve.
2. Use the learning curve table to make activity-time projections.
3. List and briefly describe some of the main applications of learning curves.
4. Outline some of the cautions and criticisms of learning curves.

A basic consideration in the design of work systems relates to the fact that learning is usually present when humans are involved. Consequently, it can be highly desirable to be able to predict how learning will affect task times and costs. This section addresses those issues.

THE CONCEPT OF LEARNING CURVES

Human activities typically reflect an improvement when they are done on a repetitive basis: The time required to perform a task decreases with increasing repetitions. The degree of improvement and the number of tasks needed to realize the major portion of the improvement is a function of the task being done. If the task is short and somewhat routine, only a modest amount of improvement is apt to occur, and it generally occurs during the first few repetitions. On the other hand, if the task is fairly complex and has a longer duration, improvements will occur over a longer interval (i.e., a larger number of repetitions). Because of this, learning factors have little relevance for planning or scheduling routine activities, but they do have relevance for complex, repetitive activities.

Figure 8S–1 illustrates the basic relationship between the increasing repetitions and a decreasing time per repetition. It should be noted that the curve will never touch the x-axis; the time per unit will never be zero.

T. P. Wright drew attention to learning curves in a 1936 article in which he described how the direct labor cost of producing a certain airframe decreased with experience.[1] Since that time, a number of other studies have confirmed the general relationship that Wright described. Alternately referred to as a progress or improvement function, it is now widely agreed that the learning effect is the result of factors in addition to actual worker learning. Some of the improvements can be traced to preproduction factors such as selection of tooling and equipment, product design, methods analysis, and in general, the amount of effort expended prior to the start of the work. Other contributing factors may involve changes once production has begun, such as changes in methods, tooling, and design. In addition, management can be an important factor through improvements in planning, scheduling, motivation, and control.

It is interesting to note that changes made once production is underway can cause a temporary *decrease* in output rate until work-

---

[1] T. P. Wright, "Factors Affecting the Cost of Airplanes," *Journal of the Aeronautical Sciences* 3 (February 1936).

FIGURE 8S–1

The Learning Effect:
Time per Repetition
Decreases as the
Number of Repetitions
Increases

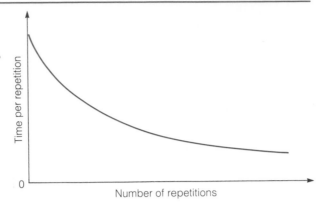

ers adjust to the change, even though they eventually lead to an increased output rate. If a number of changes are made during production, the learning curve would be more realistically described by a series of scallops instead of a smooth curve, as illustrated in Figure 8S–2. Nonetheless, it is convenient to work with a smooth curve, which can, in fact, be interpreted as the *average* effect.

From an organizational standpoint, the thing that makes the learning effect more than an interesting curiosity is its *predictability,* which becomes readily apparent if the relationship is plotted on a log-log scale (see Figure 8S–3). The straight line that results

FIGURE 8S–2

Improvements May
Create a "Scallop"
Effect in the Curve

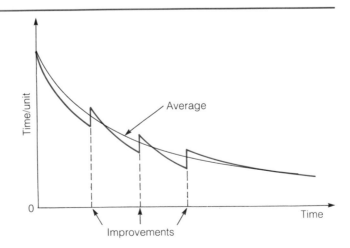

FIGURE 8S–3

On a Log-Log Graph, Learning Curves Are Straight Lines

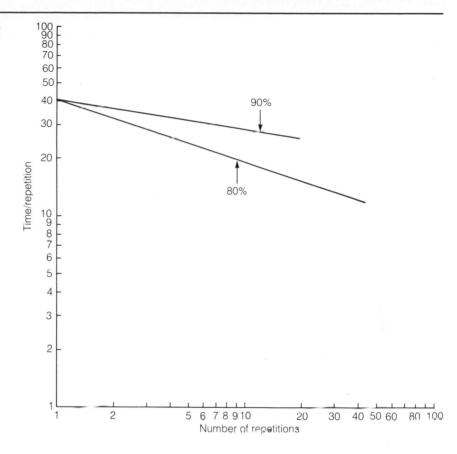

FIGURE 8S–4

After the First Unit, the Unit and Average Curves Are Parallel

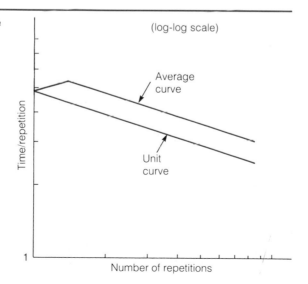

reflects a constant learning percentage, which is the basis of learning curve estimates: A *doubling* of the total number of repetitions results in a *constant* decrease in the time per repetition. This applies to *both* the *average* time and to the *unit* time, as shown in Figure 8S–4. Typical decreases range from 10 percent to 20 percent. By convention, learning curves are referred to in terms of the *complements* of their improvement rates. For example, an 80 percent learning curve denotes a 20 percent decrease in unit (or average) time with each doubling of repetitions, and a 90 percent curve denotes a 10 percent improvement rate. Thus, a 100 percent curve would imply no improvement at all.

EXAMPLE S–1

An activity is known to have an 80 percent learning curve. It has just taken a worker 10 hours to produce the first unit. Determine expected completion times for these units: the 2d, 4th, 8th, and 16th (note successive doubling of units).

Solution

Each time the cumulative output doubles, the time per unit for that amount should be approximately equal to the previous time multiplied by the learning percentage (80 percent in this case). Thus:

Unit	Unit time (hours)
1	10
2	0.8(10) = 8
4	0.8(8) = 6.4
8	0.8(6.4) = 5.12
16	0.8(5.12) = 4.096

This example illustrates an important point, and it also raises an interesting question. The point it makes is that the time reduction *per unit* becomes less and less as the number of repetitions increase. For example, the second unit required two hours less time than the first, while the improvement from the 8th to 16th unit was only a bit more than one hour. The question the example raises is: How are times for values like three, five, six, seven, and other units that don't fall into this pattern computed?

The unit time (i.e., the number of direct labor hours required) for the nth unit can be computed using the relationship:

$$T_n = T_1 \times n^b \qquad\qquad \text{(8S–1)}$$

where

T_n = Time for nth unit
T_1 = Time for first unit
b = Ln learning percent/ln 2

For example, for an 80 percent curve with $T_1 = 10$ hours, the time for the third unit would be computed as:

$$T_3 = 10(3^{\ln.8/\ln2}) = 7.02$$

In many instances it is not necessary to use the formula; values can be determined using Table 8S–1.

The table shows two things for some selected learning percentages. One is a unit value for each of the outputs listed. It enables us to easily determine how long any unit will take to produce. The second is a cumulative value, which enables us to compute the total number of hours that will be needed to complete any given number of repetitions. The computation is a relatively simple operation: Multiply the table value by the time required for the first unit.

EXAMPLE S–2

Production Airlines is negotiating a contract involving production of 20 small jets. The initial jet required 400 labor-days of direct labor. Estimate the expected number of labor-days of direct labor for (a) the 20th jet, (b) all 20 jets. Assume an 80 percent learning curve is appropriate.

Solution

Using Table 8S–1 with $n = 20$ and an 80 percent learning percentage, we find these factors: Unit = .381, Cumulative = 10.485.

a. Expected time for 20th jet: 400(.381) = 152.4 labor-days.
b. Expected total time for all 20: 400(10.485) = 4,194 labor-days.

TABLE 8S–1

Learning Curve Coefficients

Unit number	70% Unit time	70% Total time	75% Unit time	75% Total time	80% Unit time	80% Total time	85% Unit time	85% Total time	90% Unit time	90% Total time
1	1.000	1.000	1.000	1.000	1.000	1.000	1.000	1.000	1.000	1.000
2	.700	1.700	.750	1.750	.800	1.800	.850	1.850	.900	1.900
3	.568	2.268	.634	2.384	.702	2.502	.773	2.623	.846	2.746
4	.490	2.758	.562	2.946	.640	3.142	.723	3.345	.810	3.556
5	.437	3.195	.513	3.459	.596	3.738	.686	4.031	.783	4.339
6	.398	3.593	.475	3.934	.562	4.299	.657	4.688	.762	5.101
7	.367	3.960	.446	4.380	.534	4.834	.634	5.322	.744	5.845
8	.343	4.303	.422	4.802	.512	5.346	.614	5.936	.729	6.574
9	.323	4.626	.402	5.204	.493	5.839	.597	6.533	.716	7.290
10	.306	4.932	.385	5.589	.477	6.315	.583	7.116	.705	7.994

TABLE 8S–1 *(concluded)*

Unit number	70% Unit time	70% Total time	75% Unit time	75% Total time	80% Unit time	80% Total time	85% Unit time	85% Total time	90% Unit time	90% Total time
11	.291	5.223	.370	5.958	.462	6.777	.570	7.686	.695	8.689
12	.278	5.501	.357	6.315	.449	7.227	.558	8.244	.685	9.374
13	.267	5.769	.345	6.660	.438	7.665	.548	8.792	.677	10.052
14	.257	6.026	.334	6.994	.428	8.092	.539	9.331	.670	10.721
15	.248	6.274	.325	7.319	.418	8.511	.530	9.861	.663	11.384
16	.240	6.514	.316	7.635	.410	8.920	.522	10.383	.656	12.040
17	.233	6.747	.309	7.944	.402	9.322	.515	10.898	.650	12.690
18	.226	6.973	.301	8.245	.394	9.716	.508	11.405	.644	13.334
19	.220	7.192	.295	8.540	.388	10.104	.501	11.907	.639	13.974
20	.214	7.407	.288	8.828	.381	10.485	.495	12.402	.634	14.608
21	.209	7.615	.283	9.111	.375	10.860	.490	12.892	.630	15.237
22	.204	7.819	.277	9.388	.370	11.230	.484	13.376	.625	15.862
23	.199	8.018	.272	9.660	.364	11.594	.479	13.856	.621	16.483
24	.195	8.213	.267	9.928	.359	11.954	.475	14.331	.617	17.100
25	.191	8.404	.263	10.191	.355	12.309	.470	14.801	.613	17.713
26	.187	8.591	.259	10.449	.350	12.659	.466	15.267	.609	18.323
27	.183	8.774	.255	10.704	.346	13.005	.462	15.728	.606	18.929
28	.180	8.954	.251	10.955	.342	13.347	.458	16.186	.603	19.531
29	.177	9.131	.247	11.202	.338	13.685	.454	16.640	.599	20.131
30	.174	9.305	.244	11.446	.335	14.020	.450	17.091	.596	20.727
31	.171	9.476	.240	11.686	.331	14.351	.447	17.538	.593	21.320
32	.168	9.644	.237	11.924	.328	14.679	.444	17.981	.590	21.911
33	.165	9.809	.234	12.158	.324	15.003	.441	18.422	.588	22.498
34	.163	9.972	.231	12.389	.321	15.324	.437	18.859	.585	23.084
35	.160	10.133	.229	12.618	.318	15.643	.434	19.294	.583	23.666
36	.158	10.291	.226	12.844	.315	15.958	.432	19.725	.580	24.246
37	.156	10.447	.223	13.067	.313	16.271	.429	20.154	.578	24.824
38	.154	10.601	.221	13.288	.310	16.581	.426	20.580	.575	25.399
39	.152	10.753	.219	13.507	.307	16.888	.424	21.004	.573	25.972
40	.150	10.902	.216	13.723	.305	17.193	.421	21.425	.571	26.543
41	.148	11.050	.214	13.937	.303	17.496	.419	21.844	.569	27.111
42	.146	11.196	.212	14.149	.300	17.796	.416	22.260	.567	27.678
43	.144	11.341	.210	14.359	.298	18.094	.414	22.674	.565	28.243
44	.143	11.484	.208	14.567	.296	18.390	.412	23.086	.563	28.805
45	.141	11.625	.206	14.773	.294	18.684	.410	23.496	.561	29.366
46	.139	11.764	.204	14.977	.292	18.975	.408	23.903	.559	29.925
47	.138	11.902	.202	15.180	.290	19.265	.405	24.309	.557	30.482
48	.136	12.038	.201	15.380	.288	19.552	.403	24.712	.555	31.037
49	.135	12.173	.199	15.579	.286	19.838	.402	25.113	.553	31.590
50	.134	12.307	.197	15.776	.284	20.122	.400	25.513	.552	32.142
51	.132	12.439	.196	15.972	.282	20.404	.398	25.911	.550	32.692
52	.131	12.570	.194	16.166	.280	20.684	.396	26.307	.548	33.241
53	.130	12.700	.192	16.358	.279	20.963	.394	26.701	.547	33.787
54	.128	12.828	.191	16.549	.277	21.239	.392	27.094	.545	34.333
55	.127	12.955	.190	16.739	.275	21.515	.391	27.484	.544	34.877
56	.126	13.081	.188	16.927	.274	21.788	.389	27.873	.542	35.419
57	.125	13.206	.187	17.144	.272	22.060	.388	28.261	.541	35.960
58	.124	13.330	.185	17.299	.271	22.331	.386	28.647	.539	36.499
59	.123	13.453	.184	17.483	.269	22.600	.384	29.031	.538	37.037
60	.122	13.574	.183	17.666	.268	22.868	.383	29.414	.537	37.574

Use of the table requires a time for the first unit. If it happens that for some reason the completion time of the first unit is not available or if the manager believes the completion time for some later unit is more reliable, it can be used to obtain a revised estimate of the initial time, and that value can be used in conjunction with the table.

EXAMPLE S–3

The manager in the previous problem feels there were some unusual problems encountered in producing the first jet and would like to revise that estimate based on a completion time of 276 labor-days for the third jet.

Solution

The unit value for $n = 3$ and an 80 percent curve is .702 (Table 8S–1).

Divide the actual time for unit 3 by the table value to obtain the revised estimate for unit 1's time: 276 labor-days $\div$ .702 = 393.2 labor-days.

APPLICATIONS OF LEARNING CURVES

Learning curve theory has found useful applications in a number of areas, including:

1. Manpower planning and scheduling.
2. Negotiated purchasing.
3. Pricing new products.
4. Budgeting, purchasing, and inventory planning.

Knowledge of output projections in learning situations can help managers to make better decisions on how many workers they will need than basing decisions on initial output rates. Of course, managers obviously recognize that improvement will occur; what the learning curve contributes is a method for quantifying expected future improvements.

Negotiated purchasing often involves contracting to supply specialized items that may have a high degree of complexity. Examples include aircraft, computers, special-purpose equipment, and the like. The direct labor cost per unit of such items can be expected to decrease as the size of the order increases. Hence, negotiators first settle on the number of units and then negotiate price on that basis. The government requires learning-curve data on contracts that involve large, complex items. In the event of contracts that

are terminated before delivery of all units, suppliers can use learning-curve data to argue for an increase in the unit price for the smaller number of units. Conversely, the government can use that information to negotiate a lower price per unit on follow-on orders on the basis of projected additional learning gains.

Organizations must establish prices for their products and services, often well in advance of producing a new product on a large enough scale to make a firm determination of costs. Simply projecting the cost of the first few units will result in a much higher price than can be expected after a number of units have been produced. However, the manager needs to use the learning curve to avoid underpricing as well as overpricing. The manager may project initial costs, using the learning progression known to represent an organization's past experience, or else do a regression analysis of the initial results.

The learning curve projections help managers to plan costs and labor, purchasing, and inventory needs. For example, initial cost per unit will be high, and output will be fairly low, so purchasing and inventory decisions can reflect this. As productivity increases, purchasing and/or inventory actions must allow for increased usage of raw materials and purchased parts to keep pace with output. Because of learning effects the usage rate will increase over time. Hence, failure to refer to a learning curve would lead to substantial *overestimates* of labor needs and *underestimates* of the rate of material usage.

These learning principles can sometimes be useful in evaluating new workers during training periods. This can be done by measuring each worker's performance, graphing the results, and then com-

FIGURE 8S–5

Worker Learning Curves Can Help Guide Personnel Job Placement

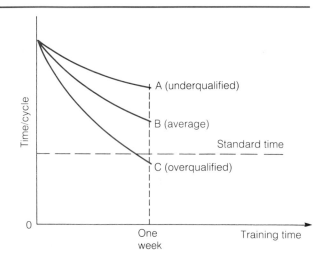

paring them to an expected rate of learning. This can reveal which workers are underqualified, average, and overqualified for a given type of work (see Figure 8S–5). Moreover, measuring a worker's progress can help predict whether the worker will make a quota within a required period of time.

CAUTIONS AND CRITICISMS

Managers who use the learning curve should be aware of its limitations and pitfalls. This section briefly outlines some of the major cautions and criticisms of learning curves.

1. Learning rates may differ from organization to organization and by type of work. Therefore, it is best to base learning rates on empirical studies rather than on assumed rates.

2. Projections based on learning curves should be regarded as *approximations* of actual times, and treated accordingly.

3. Because time estimates are based on the time for the first unit, considerable care should be taken to insure that the time is valid. It may be desirable to revise the base time as later times become available. Since it is often necessary to estimate the time for the first unit prior to production, this caution is doubly important.

4. It is entirely possible that at some point the curve might level off or even tip upward, especially near the end of a job. The potential for savings at that point is so slight that most jobs do not command the attention or interest to sustain improvements. Then too, some of the better workers may be shifted into new jobs that are starting up.

FIGURE 8S–6

Learning Curves Are Useful for Production Start-Up, But Not Usually for Mass Production

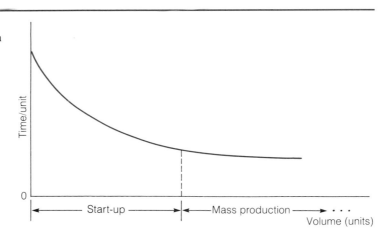

5. Some of the improvements may be more apparent than real: Improvements in times may be caused in part by *increases* in *indirect* labor costs.

6. In situations that involve mass production, learning curves may be of use in predicting how long it will take before the process stabilizes. However, for the most part, the concept does not apply to mass production because the decrease in time per unit is imperceptible for all practical purposes (see Figure 8S–6).

7. Users of learning curves sometimes fail to include carryover effects; previous experience with similar activities can reduce initial activity times, although it should be noted that the *learning rate* remains the same.

1. An assembly operation has a 90 percent learning curve. The line has just begun work on a new item, and the initial unit required 28 hours. Estimate the time that will be needed to complete:
   a. The first five units.
   b. Units 20 through 25.

   Solution

   (Use the cumulative (total) portion of the 90 percent column of Table 8S–1.)
   a. Table value: 4.339.
      Estimated time for five units: 28(4.339) = 121.49 hours.
   b. The total time for units 20 through 25 can be determined by subtraction:

		Hours
Total time for 25 units:	28(17.713) =	495.96
−Total time for 19 units:	28(13.974) =	391.27
Total time for 20 through 25:		104.69

2. A manager wants to determine an appropriate learning rate for a new type of work his firm will undertake. He has obtained completion times for the initial six repetitions of a job of this type. What learning rate is appropriate?

Unit	Completion time (hr.)
1	15.9
2	12.0
3	10.1
4	9.1
5	8.4
6	7.5

   Solution

   According to theory, the time per unit decreases at a constant rate each time the output *doubles* (e.g., unit 1 to 2, 2 to 4, and 3 to 6). The ratios of these observed times will give us an approximate rate. Thus

   $$\frac{\text{Unit } 2}{\text{Unit } 1} = \frac{12.0}{15.9} = .755; \quad \frac{\text{Unit } 4}{\text{Unit } 2} = \frac{9.1}{12.0} = .758; \quad \frac{\text{Unit } 6}{\text{Unit } 3} = \frac{7.5}{10.1} = .743.$$

   Not surprisingly, there is some variability; the rate is usually a smoothed approximation. Even so, the ratios are fairly close; a rate of 75 percent seems reasonable in this case.

DISCUSSION AND REVIEW QUESTIONS

1. If the learning phenomenon applies to all human activity, why isn't the effect noticeable in mass production or high-volume assembly work?
2. Under what circumstances might a manager prefer a learning rate of approximately 100 percent?
3. What would a learning percentage of 120 percent imply?
4. Explain how an increase in indirect labor cost can contribute to a decrease in direct labor cost per unit.
5. List the kinds of factors that create the *learning effect*.
6. Explain how changes in a process once it is underway can cause scallops in a learning curve.
7. What are some of the areas in which learning curves are useful?
8. What factors might cause a learning curve to "tip up" toward the end of a job?

PROBLEMS

1. An aircraft company has an order to refurbish the interiors of 18 jet aircrafts. The work has a learning percentage of 80. On the basis of previous experience with similar jobs, the industrial engineering department estimates that the first plane will require 300 hours to refurbish. Estimate the amount of time that will be needed to complete:
   a. The fifth plane.
   b. The first five planes.
   c. All 18 planes.
2. Estimate the time it will take to complete the 4th unit of a 12-unit job involving a large assembly if the initial unit required approximately 80 hours for each of these learning percentages:
   a. 72 percent. b. 87 percent. c. 95 percent.
3. A small contractor intends to bid on a job that will involve installation of 30 in-ground swimming pools. Because this will be a new line of work for the contractor, he believes there will be a learning effect for the job. After reviewing time records from a similar type of activity with his daughter who is majoring in operations management at a nearby university, the contractor is convinced that an 85 percent curve is appropriate. He estimates that the first pool will take his crew eight days to install. How many days should the contractor budget for:
   a. The first 10 pools?
   b. The second 10 pools?
   c. The final 10 pools?
4. A manager wants to determine an appropriate learning percentage for a certain activity. Toward that end, times have been recorded for completion of each of the first six repetitions. They are:

Repetition	Time (minutes)
1	46
2	39
3	35
4	33
5	32
6	30

   a. Determine an approximate learning percentage.
   b. Using your answer from part a, estimate the average completion time per repetition assuming a total of 50 repetitions are planned.
5. Students in an operations management class have been assigned four transportation problems by their instructor. One student noted that it took her 50 minutes to complete the first problem. Assume that the four problems are quite similar and

that a 70 percent learning curve is appropriate. How long can this student plan to spend in solving the remaining problems?

6. A subcontractor is responsible for outfitting six satellites that will be used for solar research. Four of the six have been completed in a total of 600 hours. If the crew has a 75 percent learning curve, how long should it take them to finish the last two units?

7. The fifth unit of a 40-unit job took 14.5 hours to complete. Answer the following questions assuming a 90 percent learning curve is appropriate:
   a. About how long should the last unit take to complete?
   b. How much time should it take to complete the 10th unit?
   c. Estimate the average time per unit for the 40 units.

8. The labor cost to product a certain item is $8.50 per *hour*. Job setup costs $50 and material costs are $20 per unit. Overhead is charged at a rate of 140 percent of labor, materials, and setup costs.

   The job has a 90 percent learning rate, and the foreman estimates that the initial unit will require five hours. The item can be purchased for $125 per unit.
   a. Determine the unit cost for 20 units.
   b. What is the minimum production quantity that would make production cost less than purchase cost?

9. The government agency for which a contractor has been working has notified the contractor of a desire to extend the original contract to include three additional units. The initial contract called for four units to be built and delivered. The contractor must now estimate the total time required to complete the next three units.

   Upon reviewing records for the original contract, it was discovered that data for the second unit are inaccurate and cannot be used. It is known that the first unit required 16 days, the third 12.5 days, and the fourth 11.5 days.

   Determine an estimated time for the next three units.

10. A firm has a training program for a certain operation. The progress of trainees is carefully monitored. A standard has been established that requires a trainee to be able to complete the sixth repetition of the operation in six hours or less. Those who are unable to do this are assigned to other jobs.

    Currently, three trainees have each completed two repetitions. Trainee A had times of 9 hours for the first and 8 hours for the second repetition; trainee B had times of 10 hours and 8 hours for the first and second repetition; and trainee C had times of 12 and 9 hours.

    Which trainees do you think will make standard? Explain your reasoning.

SELECTED BIBLIOGRAPHY

Abernathy, W. J. "The Limits of the Learning Curve." *Harvard Business Review,* September–October 1974, pp. 109–19.

Andress, Frank J. "The Learning Curve as a Production Tool." *Harvard Business Review,* January–February 1954, pp. 87–95.

Fabrycky, W. J., P. M. Ghare, and P. E. Torgersen. *Industrial Operations Research.* Englewood Cliffs, N.J.: Prentice-Hall, 1972.

Holdham, J. H. "Learning Curves—Their Applications in Industry." *Production and Inventory Management* (fourth quarter 1970), pp. 40–55.

Yelle, Y. E. "The Learning Curve: Historical Review and Comprehensive Survey." *Decision Sciences,* 1979, 10, pp. 302–28.

Case

Product Recall

An automobile manufacturer is conducting a product recall after it was discovered that a possible defect in the steering mechanism could cause loss of control in certain cars. The recall covers a span of three model years. The company has sent out letters to car owners promising to repair the defect at no cost at any dealership.

The company's policy is to pay the dealer a fixed amount for each repair. The repair is somewhat complicated, and the company expected learning to be a factor. In order to set a reasonable rate for repairs, company engineers conducted a number of repairs themselves. It was then decided that a rate of $88 per repair would be appropriate based on a flat hourly rate of $22 per hour and a 90 percent learning rate.

Shortly after dealers began making repairs, the company received word that several dealers were encountering resistance from workers who felt the flat rate was much too low and who were threatening to refuse to work on those jobs. One of the dealers has collected data on job times and has sent that information to the company: three mechanics each completed two repairs. Average time for the first unit was 9.6 hours, and the average time for the second unit was 7.2 hours. The dealer has suggested a rate of $110 per repair.

You have been asked to investigate the situation and to prepare a report.

Questions

1. Prepare a list of questions that you will need answers for in order to analyze this situation.

2. Prepare a list of observations regarding the information provided in the case.

3. What preliminary thoughts on solutions/partial solutions to points you have raised do you have?

Part IV

Operating and Controlling the System

The topics in this part relate to operating and controlling the production of goods and services.

The chapters in this section cover the following general topics:

1. Aggregate planning (Chapter 9).
2. Inventory management (Chapter 10).
3. Material requirements planning (Chapter 11).
4. Scheduling (Chapter 12).
5. Project management Chapter 13).
6. Queuing (Chapter 14).
7. Quality assurance (Chapter 15).

Chapter 9 serves as a link between the design decisions discussed in the previous part and the operating decisions described in the remaining chapters. It deals with intermediate-range decisions.

Chapters 10 and 11 deal with various aspects of inventories. The first of these two chapters deals with general inventory management decisions, particularly as they relate to finished goods inventories, while Chapter 11 deals with inventories in a manufacturing/assembly mode.

Chapter 12 deals with scheduling decisions involving fairly routine types of activities. Chapter 13 deals with planning and scheduling projects, which generally include many nonroutine activities.

Chapter 14 is concerned with the analysis of waiting lines, which are commonly found in service systems.

Chapter 15 discusses quality assurance, an increasingly important topic for many organizations.

Chapter 9

Aggregate Planning

After completing this chapter, you should be able to:

1. Explain what aggregate planning is and how it can be useful.
2. Identify the variables that decision makers have to work with in aggregate planning and some of the possible strategies they can use.
3. Describe some of the graphical and quantitative techniques planners use.
4. Prepare aggregate plans and compute their costs.

INTRODUCTION 434
   The Concept of Aggregation, 434

AGGREGATE PLANNING IN PERSPECTIVE, 435

AN OVERVIEW OF AGGREGATE PLANNING, 436

THE PURPOSE AND SCOPE OF AGGREGATE PLANNING, 437
   Demand and Capacity, 438
   The Purpose of Aggregate Planning, 438
   Inputs to Aggregate Planning, 438
   Decision Variables and Costs, 439

BASIC STRATEGIES FOR MEETING UNEVEN DEMAND, 443
   Choosing a Strategy, 444

TECHNIQUES FOR AGGREGATE PLANNING, 445
   Informal Techniques, 445
   Mathematical Techniques, 451

DISAGGREGATING THE AGGREGATE PLAN, 457

SUMMARY, 459
SOLVED PROBLEM, 460
DISCUSSION AND REVIEW QUESTIONS, 461
PROBLEMS, 461
SELECTED BIBLIOGRAPHY, 463

INTRODUCTION

Aggregate planning is medium-range capacity planning that typically covers a time horizon of anywhere from 3 to 18 months. The goal of aggregate planning is to achieve a production plan that will effectively utilize the organization's resources to satisfy expected demand. Planners must make decisions on output rates, employment levels and changes, inventory levels and changes, back orders, and subcontracting.

The purpose of this chapter is to introduce the concept of aggregate planning, discuss the pertinent costs and possible strategies, and illustrate some of the different approaches used in aggregate planning.

The Concept of Aggregation

Aggregate planning is essentially a big-picture approach to planning. Planners generally try to avoid focusing on individual products or services unless, of course, the organization has only one major product or service. Instead, they focus on overall, or aggregate, capacity.

Most organizations, though, offer a variety of products and/or services. For purposes of aggregate planning, it is often convenient to think of capacity in terms of labor-hours or machine hours per month, or output rates (barrels per month, units per month), without worrying about how much of this item or how much of that item will actually be involved. The reason for this approach is that it frees planners to make decisions about the use of resources in a general way without having to get into the complexities of individual product or service requirements. Often aggregation is done by product groupings, where products (or services) with similar requirements are lumped together for planning purposes. This makes the problem of obtaining an acceptable unit of aggregation easier since different product groupings may lend themselves to different aggregate measures.

It can be convenient to think of aggregate planning as a *macro approach* to developing a production plan. For instance, consider the task of planning a vegetable garden. Aggregate planning would consist of deciding on the overall size (capacity) of the garden, taking into account how much time and effort the gardener is willing to commit to the garden for preparing the soil, planting, weeding, watering, and fertilizing, as well as the amount of funds available for plants, seeds, and supplies. In addition, the gardener must consider how much output is desired (e.g., enough to feed a family of four). This can be done without getting into the details of precisely how many tomato plants or cucumber plants there will be.

Decisions of that nature are best left until the broad plans have been worked out.

Now consider how aggregate planning might work in a manufacturing setting. Think of an automobile manufacturer that makes a variety of cars and trucks. For purposes of aggregate planning, a decision on the number of cars and number of trucks to be produced will be made without specifying the breakdown of two-door versus four-door cars, options, etc. Similarly, a decision on four-cylinder and six-cylinder engines will be made, without concern for which engines will go with which cars or trucks. Planners will generally take into account the expected demand for cars, trucks, and engine blocks and the available capacity for making those items. If expected demand and capacity are approximately equal, planners will devote their efforts to meeting demand as efficiently as possible. If capacity exceeds demand, advertising and promotion might be realistic options. If capacity is less than demand, contracting some of the work to outside firms may be an option. In any event planners will be looking at aggregate measures of capacity in making their decisions.

Finally, consider how aggregate planning might work in a large department store. Space allocation is often an aggregate decision. That is, a manager might decide to allocate 20 percent of the available space in the clothing section to women's sportswear, 30 percent to juniors, and so on, without regard to what brand names will be offered, how much of juniors will be slacks, and so on. The aggregate measure might be square feet of space or racks of clothing.

In each of these examples we see that an aggregate approach permits planners to make general decisions about intermediate-range capacity without having to deal with highly specific kinds of details. They can instead concern themselves with overall decisions on levels of output, employment, and inventories. They do this by lumping demand for all products into one or a few categories and planning on that level.

AGGREGATE PLANNING IN PERSPECTIVE

Organizations become involved with capacity decisions on three levels: long term, intermediate term, and short term. Long-term decisions relate to product and service selection (i.e., determining which products or services to offer), facility size and location, equipment decisions, and layout of facilities. These long-term decisions essentially define the capacity constraints within which intermediate, or aggregate, planning must function. Intermediate decisions, as we have said, relate to general levels of employment, output,

TABLE 9–1

Overview of Planning Levels

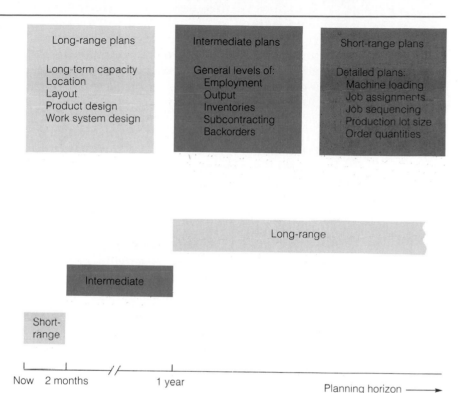

and inventories. These, in turn, define the boundaries, within which short-range capacity decisions must be made. Thus, short-term decisions essentially relate to deciding on the best way to achieve desired results within the constraints resulting from long-term and intermediate term decisions. These involve scheduling jobs, machine loading, job sequencing, and the like. The three levels of capacity decisions are highlighted in Table 9–1.

Long-term capacity decisions were covered in the preceding chapters, and scheduling and related matters are covered in a later chapter, with this chapter covering the intermediate capacity decisions.

AN OVERVIEW OF AGGREGATE PLANNING

Aggregate planning begins with a forecast of expected demand for the intermediate range. This is followed by a general plan to meet demand requirements by setting output, employment, and inventory levels. A series of plans might be considered. Each plan must be

FIGURE 9-1

Overview of Aggregate Planning

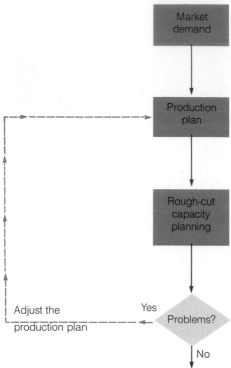

examined in light of feasibility and cost. If a plan is reasonably good but with minor difficulties, in all likelihood it would be reworked. Conversely, a poor plan would undoubtedly be discarded, and alternative plans would be considered until an acceptable one was uncovered. This process is illustrated in Figure 9-1. The production plan is essentially the output of aggregate planning. The process of evaluating various proposed plans in attempting to balance capacity (supply) and demand is known as *rough-cut capacity planning.* That is, the aggregate treatment of capacity prohibits something more than a rough, or approximate, balance of capacity and demand.

THE PURPOSE AND SCOPE OF AGGREGATE PLANNING

In this section we examine the basic problem that aggregate planning addresses—namely, the balancing of supply and demand, along with the purpose of aggregate planning, and the primary decision variables available to planners and associated costs.

FIGURE 9–2

**Projected Demand for
a 12-Period Planning
Horizon**

| **Demand and Capacity** | Aggregate planners are concerned with the *quantity* and the *timing* of expected demand. If total expected demand for the planning period is much different than available capacity over that same period, the major approach of planners will be either to increase demand (if demand is less than capacity) or increase capacity (if demand exceeds capacity). On the other hand, even if total capacity and demand are approximately equal for the planning period, planners are still faced with the problem of dealing with *uneven* demand. The problem of uneven demand is illustrated in Figure 9–2. Notice that in some periods expected demand exceeds average capacity, in others expected demand is less than average capacity, and in some periods the two are roughly equal. The task of aggregate planners is to achieve rough equality of demand and capacity over the entire planning horizon. |

**The Purpose of
Aggregate
Planning**

The purpose of aggregate planning is to develop a feasible production plan on an aggregate level that achieves a balance of expected demand and supply. Moreover, planners are usually concerned with minimizing the cost of the production plan, although cost is not the only consideration.

**Inputs to
Aggregate
Planning**

There are a number of important informational needs for effective aggregate planning. First, the available resources over the planning period must be known, including facilities. Also, a forecast of expected demand must be available. Finally, planners must take into account any policies regarding changes in employment levels (e.g.,

TABLE 9–2

Aggregate Planning Inputs	Resources	Costs
	Work force/production rates	Inventory carrying cost
	Facilities and equipment	Backorders
	Demand forecast	Hiring/firing
		Overtime
	Policy statements on work force changes	Inventory changes
	Subcontracting	Subcontracting
	Overtime	
	Inventory levels/changes	
	Backorders	

some organizations view layoffs as very undesirable, and so they would exclude that option from consideration or perhaps only use it as a last resort).

Table 9–2 lists the major inputs to aggregate planning.

Decision Variables and Costs

Management has a wide range of possible decision options at its disposal for purposes of aggregate planning. These include pricing, promotion, backlogging, using overtime, using part-time workers, subcontracting, adding or deleting extra shifts, stockpiling inventories, and so on. Some of these, such as pricing and promotion, represent options that are intended to alter the pattern of *demand.* Others, such as using part-time workers, overtime, and subcontracting, represent decision options that are intended to alter capacity, or *supply.* Suppose we examine options in more detail.

The basic demand options are the following:

1. *Pricing.* Pricing differentials are commonly used to shift demand from peak periods to off-peak periods. Some airlines, for example, offer lower fares for midweek travel and charge higher fares other times. Many airlines also offer lower fares for night travel. Similarly, movie theaters may offer reduced rates for matinees, and some restaurants offer "early bird specials" in an attempt to shift some of the heavier dinner demand to an earlier time that traditionally has less traffic. Some restaurants may also offer smaller portions at reduced rates, and most have smaller portions and prices for children. The smaller portions act to decrease demand. To the extent that pricing is effective, demand will be shifted so that it more closely corresponds to capacity, albeit for an opportunity cost that represents the lost profit stemming from capacity insufficient to meet demand during certain periods.

An important factor to consider is the degree of price elasticity for the product or service; the more the elasticity, the more effective pricing will be in influencing demand patterns.

2. *Promotion.* Advertising and other forms of promotion, such as displays and direct marketing, can sometimes be very effective in shifting demand so that it conforms more closely to capacity.

Obviously, the timing of these efforts and knowledge of response rates and response patterns will be needed to achieve the desired results. Unlike pricing policy, there is much less control over the timing of demand; there is always the risk that promotion can worsen the condition it was intended to improve.

3. *Backorders.* An organization can shift demand to other periods by allowing backorders. Hence, orders are taken in one period and deliveries promised for a later period. The success of this approach depends on how willing customers are to wait for delivery. Moreover, the cost associated with backorders can be difficult to pin down since it would include lost sales, annoyed or disappointed customers, and perhaps additional paperwork.

4. *New demand.* Many organizations are faced with the problem of having to provide products or services for peak demand in situations where demand is very uneven. For instance, demand for public transportation tends to be very intense during the morning and late afternoon rush hours but much lighter at other times. Creating new demand for the buses at other times (e.g., school trips, clubs, senior citizen groups, and other group trips) would make use of the excess capacity during those slack times. Similarly, many fast-food restaurants are open for breakfast in order to use their capacities more fully, and some landscaping firms in northern climates use their equipment during the winter months for snow plowing. Manufacturing firms that experience seasonal demands for certain products (e.g., snowblowers) are sometimes able to develop a demand for a complementary product (e.g., lawn mowers, garden equipment) that makes use of the same production processes, and they thereby achieve a more consistent use of labor, equipment, and facilities.

The basic options for altering the availability of capacity are the following:

1. *Hire and fire workers.* The extent to which operations are labor intensive determines the impact on capacity that changes in the level of a work force will have on capacity. Beyond that, the resource requirements of each worker can be a factor. For instance, if a supermarket with 14 checkout lines generally has 10 operating, an additional four checkout workers could be added. Hence, the ability to add workers is constrained at some point by other resources needed to support the workers. Conversely, there may be a minimum on the number of workers needed in order to maintain a viable operation (e.g., a skeleton crew).

Union contracts may restrict the amount of hiring and firing a company can do. Moreover, because firing and laying off workers can present serious problems for workers, many firms have policies that either prohibit or limit downward adjustments to a work force. On the other hand, hiring workers presumes an available supply

of workers. This may change from time to time and, at certain times of low supply, have an impact on the ability of an organization to pursue this approach.

Use of hiring and firing entails certain costs. Hiring costs include recruitment, screening, and training to bring new workers "up to speed." Some savings may occur if workers who have recently been laid off are rehired. Firing costs include severance pay, the cost of realigning the remaining work force, and potential bad feelings toward the firm on the part of fired workers as well as some loss of morale for workers who are retained (i.e., in spite of company assurances, some workers will nevertheless believe that they may also be laid off in time).

2. *Overtime/slacktime.* This is a less severe method for changing capacity than hiring and firing workers, and it can be used across the board or selectively where needed. It can also be implemented more quickly than hiring and firing can and allows the firm to maintain a steady base of employees. The use of overtime can be especially attractive in dealing with seasonal demand peaks by reducing the need to hire and train people who will have to be laid off during the "off" season. It also maintains a skilled work force and allows employees a chance to increase earnings. Moreover, in situations that involve crews, it is often necessary to use a full crew rather than to hire one or two additional people. Thus, having the entire crew work overtime would be preferable to hiring some extra people.

On the negative side, some union contracts allow workers to refuse overtime. In those cases it may be difficult to muster a full crew to work overtime or to get an entire production line into operation after regular hours. And although workers often like the additional income overtime can generate, they may not appreciate having to work on short notice or the fluctuations in income that result. Still other considerations relate to the fact that overtime often results in lower productivity, poorer quality, increases in accidents, and increased payroll costs, while idle time results in less efficient use of machines and other fixed assets.

3. *Part-time workers.* In certain instances the use of part-time workers is a viable option. Much depends on the nature of the work, training and skills needed, and union agreements. Seasonal work requiring low to moderate job skills lends itself to part-time workers, who generally cost less than regular workers in both hourly wages and fringe benefits. However, unions may regard such workers unfavorably because they typically do not pay union dues and may lessen the power of unions. Department stores, restaurants, and supermarkets make use of part-time workers. So do parks and recreation departments, resorts, travel agencies, hotels, and other service organizations with seasonal demands. In order to be success-

ful, these organizations must be able to hire part-time employees when they are needed.

4. *Inventories.* The use of inventories allows firms to produce goods in one period and sell or ship them in another period, albeit at a cost of holding or carrying those goods as inventory until they are needed. The cost includes not only storage costs and the cost of money tied up that could be invested elsewhere but also the cost of insurance, obsolescence, deterioration, spoilage, breakage, and so on. In essence, inventories can be built up during periods when production capacity exceeds demand and drawn down in other periods when demand exceeds production capacity. This method is more amenable to manufacturing than services since manufactured goods can be stored whereas services generally cannot. However, an analogous approach used by services is to make efforts to streamline services (e.g., standard forms) or otherwise do a portion of the service during slack periods (e.g., organize the workplace). In spite of these possibilities, services tend to be unable to make much use of inventories to alter capacity requirements.

5. *Subcontracting.* This action enables planners to acquire temporary capacity, although it affords less control over the output and may lead to higher costs as well as quality problems. The question of whether to *make or buy* (in a case that involves manufacturing), or whether to perform a service or hire someone else to do the work generally depends on the following factors:

a. *Available capacity.* If an organization has available capacity, it often makes sense to produce an item or perform a service itself. The additional costs involved would tend to be relatively small compared to those required to buy items or subcontract services.

b. *Expertise.* If a firm lacks the expertise to do a satisfactory job, buying might be a more reasonable alternative.

c. *Quality considerations.* Firms that specialize can usually offer higher quality than an organization can obtain itself. Conversely, special quality requirements or the ability to closely monitor quality may cause a firm to perform the work itself.

d. *The nature of demand.* When demand for an item is high and steady, the organization is usually better off doing the work itself. However, wide fluctuations in demand or small orders can usually be better handled by others. They are often able to combine orders from multiple sources, which results in higher volume and tends to offset individual buyer fluctuations.

e. *Cost.* Any cost savings achieved from buying or making must be weighed against the preceding factors. Cost savings might

come from the item itself or from transportation-cost savings realized by making the item rather than buying it.

In some cases a firm might choose both to perform part of the work itself and let others handle the rest in order to maintain flexibility and as a hedge against loss of a subcontractor. Moreover, this gives the organization a bargaining tool in negotiations with contractors and a head start if it decides at a later date to take over the operation entirely.

BASIC STRATEGIES FOR MEETING UNEVEN DEMAND

Managers have a wide range of decision options they can consider for achieving a balance of demand and capacity in aggregate planning. Since the options that are most suited to influencing demand generally fall more in the realm of marketing than operations (with the exception of backlogging), we shall concentrate on the capacity options, which are in the realm of operations but include the use of backorders.

There are a number of strategies aggregate planners might adopt. Some of the more prominent ones are:

1. Maintain a level work force.
2. Maintain a steady output rate.
3. Match demand period by period.
4. Use a combination of decision variables.

There are other possible strategies that we might consider, but these will suffice to give you a sense of how aggregate planning operates in a vast number of organizations. The first three strategies are "pure" strategies in that each has a single focal point; the last strategy is a "mixed" one in that it lacks the single focus. Under the level work force strategy, variations in demand are met by using some combination of inventories, overtime, part-time workers, subcontracting, and backordering. The main idea is to maintain a steady rate of *regular-time* output, although *total* output could vary. Maintaining a steady rate of output implies absorbing demand variations with inventories, subcontracting, or backlogging. Matching capacity to demand implies a "chase" strategy; the planned output for any period would be the expected demand for that period.

Many organizations find a level work force strategy very appealing. Since work force changes through hiring and firing can have a major impact on the lives and morale of employees and can be disruptive for managers, organizations often prefer to handle uneven demand in other ways. Moreover, changes in work force size can be very costly, and there is always the risk that there will not

be a sufficient pool of workers with the appropriate skills when needed. Aside from these considerations, such changes can involve a significant amount of paperwork. Unions tend to favor a level work force since the freedom to hire and fire workers diminishes union strengths.

In order to maintain a constant level of output and still meet demand requirements, an organization must resort to some combination of subcontracting, backlogging, and use of inventories to absorb fluctuations. Subcontracting requires an investment in evaluating sources of supply as well as possible increased costs, less control over output, and perhaps quality considerations. Backlogs can lead to lost sales, increased record keeping, and lower levels of customer service. Allowing inventories to absorb fluctuations can entail substantial costs by having money tied up in inventories, having to maintain relatively large storage facilities, and incurring other costs related to inventories. Furthermore, inventories are not usually an alternative for service-oriented organizations. However, there are certain advantages, such as minimum costs of recruitment and training, minimum overtime and idle-time costs, fewer morale problems, and stable use of equipment and facilities.

A chase strategy presupposes a great deal of ability and willingness on the part of managers to be flexible in adjusting to demand. A major advantage of this approach is that inventories can be kept relatively low, which can yield substantial savings for an organization. A major disadvantage is the lack of stability in operations; the atmosphere is one of dancing to demand's tune. When forecast and reality differ, morale can suffer since it quickly becomes obvious to all that efforts have been wasted.

Organizations may opt for a strategy that involves some combination of decision variables without a single guiding focus. This allows managers greater flexibility in dealing with uneven demand and perhaps in experimenting with a wide variety of approaches. However, the absence of a clear focus may lead to an erratic approach and confusion on the part of employees.

Choosing a Strategy

Whatever strategy an organization is considering, two important factors are *company policy* and *costs*. Company policy may set constraints on the available options or the extent to which they can be used. For instance, company policy may discourage firing and layoffs except under extreme conditions. Similarly, subcontracting may not be a viable alternative due to the desire to maintain secrecy about some aspect of the manufacturing of a product (e.g., a secret formula or blending process). Often, union agreements impose restrictions. For example, a union contract may specify both minimum and maximum numbers of hours part-time workers can be used.

As a general rule, aggregate planners seek to match supply and demand within the constraints imposed on them by policies or agreements and at a minimum cost. In fact, altenatives are usually evaluated in terms of their overall costs. In the next section a number of different techniques for aggregate planning are described along with some examples of cost evaluation of alternative plans.

TECHNIQUES FOR AGGREGATE PLANNING

There are numerous techniques that can be used to help decision makers with the task of aggregate planning. Generally they fall into one of two categories, informal trial and error techniques and mathematical techniques. In practice, the informal techniques are more commonly used than the mathematical ones. However, a considerable amount of research has been devoted to mathematical techniques, and even though they are not widely used, they often serve as a basis for comparing the effectiveness of alternative techniques for aggregate planning, so it will be instructive to briefly examine them as well as the more informal techniques.

A general procedure for aggregate planning consists of the following steps:

1. Determine demand for each period.
2. Determine capacities (regular time, overtime, subcontracting) for each period.
3. Determine company or departmental policies that are pertinent (e.g., maintain a safety stock of 5 percent of demand, maintain a reasonably stable work force).
4. Determine unit costs for regular time, overtime, subcontracting, holding inventories, backorders, and other relevant costs.
5. Develop alternative plans and compute the cost for each.
6. If satisfactory plans emerge, select the one that best satisfies objectives. Otherwise, return to Step 5.

It can be helpful to use a work sheet that summarizes demand, capacity, and cost for each plan, such as the one illustrated in Table 9–3. In addition, graphs can be used to guide development of alternatives.

Informal Techniques

These approaches consist of developing simple tables or graphs that enable planners to visually compare projected demand requirements with existing capacity, and this provides them with a basis for developing alternative plans for achieving intermediate-range goals. Alternatives are usually evaluated in terms of their overall

TABLE 9–3

Worksheet

Period	1	2	3	4	5			Total
Forecast								
Output								
Regular								
Overtime								
Subcontract								
Output—Forecast								
Inventory								
Beginning								
Ending								
Average								
Backlog								
Costs:								
Output								
Regular								
Overtime								
Subcontract								
Inventory								
Backorders								
Total								

costs. The chief disadvantage of such techniques is that they do not necessarily result in an optimum aggregate plan.

Very often, graphs can be used to guide the development of alternatives. Some planners prefer cumulative graphs, while others prefer to see a period-by-period breakdown of a plan. For instance, Figure 9–3 shows a cumulative graph for a plan with steady output and inventory absorption of demand variations. Figure 9–4 shows a period-by-period breakdown of the same plan. The obvious advantage of a graph is that it provides a visual portrayal of a plan. The choice between these two types of graphs depends on the preference of the planner.

Two examples will be used to illustrate the development and comparison of aggregate plans. In the first example regular output

FIGURE 9–3

**A Cumulative Graph
and Inventory Profile**

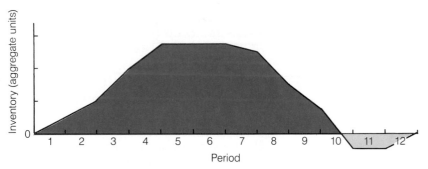

is held steady with inventory absorption of demand variations. This plan is portrayed in Figures 9–3 and 9–4. In the second example a lower rate of regular output is used, supplemented by use of overtime. In both examples some backlogs are allowed to build up.

These examples and the other examples and problems in this chapter are based on the following assumptions:

1. The regular output capacity is the same in all periods. No

FIGURE 9–4

**Level Production and
Fluctuations in
Demand Absorbed by
Inventory**

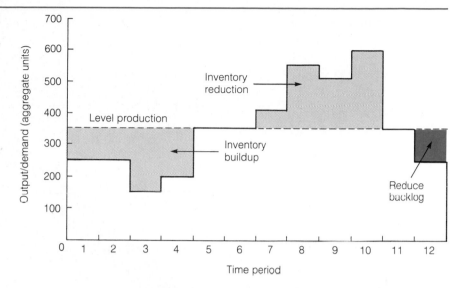

allowance is made for holidays, different numbers of
workdays in different months, and so on. This has been done
for simplicity and ease of computation.

2. Cost (backlog, inventory, subcontracting, etc.) is a linear
    function comprised of unit cost and number of units. This
    is often a reasonable approximation to reality, although
    there may be narrow ranges over which this is true. Cost
    is sometimes more of a step function.

3. Plans are feasible. That is, sufficient inventory capacity
    exists to accommodate a plan, subcontractors with
    appropriate quality and capacity are standing by, and
    changes in output can be made as needed.

4. All costs associated with a decision option can be represented
    by a lump sum or by unit costs that are independent of the
    quantity involved. Again, a step function may be more
    realistic; for purposes of illustration as well as simplicity,
    this assumption is appropriate.

5. Cost figures can be reasonably estimated and are constant
    for the planning horizon.

6. Inventories are built up and drawn down at a uniform rate
    throughout each period, and output occurs at a uniform rate
    throughout each period. However, backlogs are treated as
    if they exist for an entire period, even though in periods
    where they initially appear, they would tend to build up
    toward the end of the period. Hence, this assumption is a
    bit unrealistic for some periods, but it simplifies
    computations.

EXAMPLE 1

Planners are about to prepare the aggregate plan for a company that will cover 12 periods. They have assembled the following information:

Period	1	2	3	4	5	6	7	8	9	10	11	12	Total
Forecast	250	250	150	200	350	350	400	550	500	600	350	250	4,200

Costs:
Output
  Regular time = $2 per unit
  Overtime   = $3 per unit
  Subcontract = $6 per unit
Inventory   = $1 per unit per period on average inventory
Backorders   = $5 per unit per period

They now want to evaluate a plan that calls for a steady rate of regular-time output, mainly using inventory to absorb the uneven demand but allowing some backlog. They intend to start with zero inventory on hand in the first period. Prepare an aggregate plan and determine its cost using the preceding information. Assume a steady output rate of 350 units per period with regular time.

Solution

Period	1	2	3	4	5	6	7	8	9	10	11	12	Total
Forecast	250	250	150	200	350	350	400	550	500	600	350	250	4,200
Output													
Regular	350	350	350	350	350	350	350	350	350	350	350	350	4,200
Overtime	—	—	—	—	—	—	—	—	—	—	—	—	
Subcontract	—	—	—	—	—	—	—	—	—	—	—	—	
Output-Forecast	100	100	200	150	0	0	(50)	(200)	(150)	(250)	0	100	0
Inventory													
Beginning	0	100	200	400	550	550	550	500	300	150	0	0	
Ending	100	200	400	550	550	550	500	300	150	0	0	0	
Average	50	150	300	475	550	550	525	400	225	75	0	0	3,300
Backlog	0	0	0	0	0	0	0	0	0	100	100	0	200
Costs:													
Output													
Regular	$700	700	700	700	700	700	700	700	700	700	700	700	$ 8,400
Overtime	—	—	—	—	—	—	—	—	—	—	—	—	
Subcontract	—	—	—	—	—	—	—	—	—	—	—	—	
Inventory	$ 50	150	300	475	550	550	525	400	225	75	0	0	$ 3,300
Backorders	$ 0	0	0	0	0	0	0	0	0	500	500	0	$ 1,000
Total	$750	850	1000	1175	1250	1250	1225	1100	925	1275	1200	700	$12,700

Note that the total regular-time output of 4,200 units equals the total expected demand. Ending inventory equals beginning inventory plus or minus the quantity Output-Forecast. Average inventory equals

EXAMPLE 1 (concluded)

one half the sum of beginning and ending inventory. If Output-Forecast is negative, inventory is decreased in that period by that amount. If insufficient inventory exists, a backlog that is equal to the shortage amount appears.

The costs were computed as follows. Regular cost in each period equals 350 units × $2 per unit, or $700. Inventory cost equals average inventory × $1 per unit. Backorder cost is $5 per unit. The total cost for this plan is $12,700.

Note that the first two quantities in each column are givens. The remaining quantities in the upper portion of the table were determined working down each column, beginning with the first column. The costs were then computed based on the quantities in the upper part of the table.

EXAMPLE 2

After reviewing the plan developed in the preceding problem, planners have decided to develop an alternative plan. They have learned that one person is about to retire from the company. Rather than replace him, they would like to stay with the smaller work force and use overtime to make up for the lost output. The reduced regular-time output is 330 units per period. The maximum amount of overtime output per period is 40 units. Develop a plan and compare it to the previous one.

Solution

Period	1	2	3	4	5	6	7	8	9	10	11	12	Total
Forecast	250	250	150	200	350	350	400	550	500	600	350	250	4,200
Output													
Regular	330	330	330	330	330	330	330	330	330	330	330	330	3,960
Overtime	0	0	0	0	40	40	40	40	40	40	0	0	240
Subcontract	—	—	—	—	—	—	—	—	—	—	—	—	—
Output-Forecast	80	80	180	130	20	20	(30)	(180)	(130)	(230)	(20)	80	0
Inventory													
Beginning	0	80	160	340	470	490	510	480	300	170	0	0	
Ending	80	160	340	470	490	510	480	300	170	0	0	0	
Average	40	120	250	405	480	500	495	390	235	85	0	0	3,000
Backlog										60	80	0	140
Costs:													
Output													
Regular	$660	660	660	660	660	660	660	660	660	660	660	660	$ 7,920
Overtime	0	0	0	0	120	120	120	120	120	120	0	0	$ 720
Subcontract	—	—	—	—	—	—	—	—	—	—	—	—	
Inventory	$ 40	120	250	405	480	500	495	390	235	85	0	0	$ 3,000
Backorders	$ 0	0	0	0	0	0	0	0	0	300	400	0	$ 700
Total	$700	780	910	1065	1260	1280	1275	1170	1015	1165	1060	660	$12,340

EXAMPLE 2 (concluded)

The amount of overtime that must be scheduled has to make up for the lost output of 20 units per period for 12 periods, which is 240. This is scheduled toward the center of the planning horizon since that is where the bulk of demand occurs. Scheduling it earlier would increase inventory carrying costs; scheduling it later would increase the backlog.

Overall, the total cost for this plan is $12,340, which is $360 less than the previous plan. Regular-time production cost is down, while overtime cost adds $720, making the cost of output $8,640 as compared to a cost of $8,400 in the previous plan. However, this plan achieves savings in both inventory cost and backorder cost, making it somewhat less costly overall than the other plan.

These are only two of many possible options that could be tried. Perhaps some of the others would result in a lower cost. With trial and error, you can never be completely sure you have identified the lowest cost alternative unless every possible alternative is evaluated. Of course, the purpose of these examples was to illustrate the process of developing and evaluating an aggregate plan, rather than to find the lowest cost plan. However, some of the problems at the end of the chapter involve still different alternatives for this situation.

In practice, successful achievement of a good plan depends on the resourcefulness and the persistence of the planner.

Mathematical Techniques

A number of mathematical techniques have been proposed over the last two decades to handle aggregate planning. They range from mathematical programming models to heuristic and computer search models. This section briefly describes some of the better-known techniques.

Linear Programming

Linear programming (LP) models are methods for obtaining optimum solutions to problems involving the allocation of scarce resources in terms of cost minimization or profit maximization. In terms of aggregate planning, the goal would usually be to minimize the sum of costs related to regular labor time, overtime, subcontracting, inventory holding costs, and costs associated with changing the size of the work force. Constraints involve capacities of work force, inventories, and subcontracting.

E. H. Bowman proposed formulating the problem in terms of a transportation-type programming model (described in detail in the supplement to Chapter 5) as a way to obtain aggregate plans that

TABLE 9–4

Transportation Notation for Aggregate Planning

r = Regular production cost per unit
t = Overtime cost per unit
s = Subcontracting cost per unit
h = Holding cost per unit per period
b = Backorder cost per unit per period
n = Number of periods in planning horizon

		Period 1	Period 2	Period 3	...	Ending inventory period n	Unused capacity	Capacity
Period	Beginning inventory	0	h	$2h$	...	nh	0	I_0
1	Regular time	r	$r+h$	$r+2h$	...	$r+nh$	0	R_1
	Overtime	t	$t+h$	$t+2h$	...	$t+nh$	0	O_1
	Subcontract	s	$s+h$	$s+2h$	...	$s+nh$	0	S_1
2	Regular time	$r+b$	r	$r+h$	...	$r+(n-1)h$	0	R_2
	Overtime	$t+b$	t	$t+h$	...	$t+(n-1)h$	0	O_2
	Subcontract	$s+b$	s	$s+h$	...	$s+(n-1)h$	0	S_2
3	Regular time	$r+2b$	$r+b$	r	...	$r+(n-2)h$	0	R_3
	Overtime	$t+2b$	$t+b$	t	...	$t+(n-2)h$	0	O_3
	Subcontract	$s+2b$	$s+b$	s	...	$s+(n-2)h$	0	S_3
	Demand				...			Total

would match capacities with demand requirements and minimize costs.[1] In order to use this approach, planners must identify capacity (supply) of regular time, overtime, subcontracting, and inventory on a period-by-period basis as well as related costs of each variable.

The notation and setup of a transportation table is shown in Table 9–4. Note the systematic way that costs change as you move across a row from left to right. Note that regular cost, overtime cost, and

---

[1] E. H. Bowman, "Production Planning by the Transportation Method of Linear Programming," *Journal of Operations Research Society* 4 (February 1956), pp. 100–103.

subcontracting cost are at their lowest when the output is consumed (delivered, etc.) in the same period it is produced (e.g., at the intersection of Period 1 row and column for regular cost, at the interesection of Period 2 row and column for regular cost, and so on). If goods are made available in one period but carried over to later periods (i.e., moving across a row), holding costs are incurred at the rate of h per period. Thus, holding goods for two periods results in a unit cost of $2h$, irrespective of whether the goods came from regular production, overtime, or subcontracting. Conversely, in the case of backorders, the unit cost increases as you move across a row from right to left, beginning at the intersection of a row and column for the same period (e.g., Period 3). For instance, if some goods are produced in Period 3 to satisfy backorders from Period 2, a unit backorder cost of b is incurred. And if goods in Period 3 are used to satisfy backorders two periods back (i.e., from Period 1) a unit cost of $2b$ is incurred. Unused capacity is generally given a unit cost of 0, although it is certainly possible to insert an actual cost if that seems relevant. Finally, beginning inventory is given a unit cost of 0 if it is used to satisfy demand in Period 0. However, if it is held over for use in later periods, a holding cost of h per unit is added for each period. If the inventory is to be held for the entire planning horizon, a total unit cost of h times the number of periods, n, will be incurred.

Example 3 illustrates the setup and final solution of a transportation model of an aggregate planning problem.

EXAMPLE 3

Given the following information, set up the problem in a transportation format and solve for the minimum cost plan:

	Period		
	1	2	3
Demand	550	700	750
Capacity			
Regular	500	500	500
Overtime.	50	50	50
Subcontract.	120	120	100
Beginning inventory	100		

Costs
Regular time . . . . . $60 per unit
Overtime. . . . . . . 80 per unit
Subcontract. . . . . 90 per unit
Inventory
  carrying cost . . . . $1 per unit per month
Backorder cost . . . . $3 per unit per month

EXAMPLE 3 (continued)

Solution

The transportation solution (see the supplement to Chapter 5) is shown in Table 9–5. Some of the entries require additional explanation:

a. In this example inventory carrying costs are $1 per unit per period (costs are shown in the upper right-hand corner of each cell in the table). Hence, units produced in one period and carried over to a later period will incur a holding cost that is a linear function of the length of time held. (Note the increase of $1 in costs as you move across any row.)

TABLE 9–5

Transportation Solution

	Supply from	Demand for Period 1	Demand for Period 2	Demand for Period 3	Unused capacity (dummy)	Total capacity available (supply)
Period	Beginning inventory	[0] 100	[1]	[2]	[0]	100
1	Regular time	[60] 450	[61]	[62]	[0]	500
	Overtime	[80]	[81] 50	[82]	[0]	50
	Subcontract	[90]	[91] 30	[92]	[0] 90	120
2	Regular time	[63]	[60] 500	[61]	[0]	500
	Overtime	[83]	[80] 50	[81]	[0]	50
	Subcontract	[93]	[90] 20	[91] 100	[0]	120
3	Regular time	[66]	[63]	[60] 500	[0]	500
	Overtime	[86]	[83]	[80] 50	[0]	50
	Subcontract	[96]	[93]	[90] 100	[0]	100
	Demand	550	700	750	90	2,090

EXAMPLE 3 *(concluded)*

b. Linear programming models of this type require that supply (capacity) and demand be equal. A "dummy" column has been added (unused capacity) to satisfy that requirement. Since it does not "cost" anything *extra* to not use capacity in this case, cell costs of $0 have been assigned.

c. No backlogs were needed in this example.

d. The quantities (e.g., 100 and 450 in column 1) are the amounts of output or inventory that will be used to meet demand requirements. Thus, the demand of 550 units in Period 1 will be met using 100 units from inventory and 450 obtained from regular time output.

In a case where backlogs are not permitted, the cell costs for the backlog positions can be made prohibitively high so that no backlogs will appear in the solution.

The main limitations of LP models are the assumptions of linear relationships among variables, the inability to continuously adjust output rates, and the need to specify a single objective (e.g., minimize costs) instead of using multiple objectives (e.g., minimize cost while stabilizing the work force).

Goal Programming

Goal programming is a variation of linear programming that permits the user to specify multiple goals in a priority-based way. The solution represents an attempt to optimize the goals according to priorities. Several applications of goal programming to aggregate planning have been reported in the literature.[2]

Linear Decision Rule

Another optimizing technique, the *linear decision rule,* was developed during the 1950s by Charles Holt, Franco Modigliani, John Muth, and Herbert Simon.[3] It seeks to minimize the combined costs of regular payroll, hiring and layoffs, overtime, and inventory using a set of cost-approximating functions, three of which are *quadratic*

---

[2] See for example, D. A. Goodman, "A New Approach to Scheduling Aggregate Production and Work Force," *AIIE Transactions* 5 (June 1973), pp. 135–41 and S. M. Lee and L. J. Moore, "A Practical Approach to Production Scheduling," *Production and Inventory Management* (1st quarter 1974), pp. 79–92.

[3] Charles C. Holt, Franco Modigliani, John F. Muth, and Herbert A. Simon, *Planning Production, Inventories and Work Force* (Englewood Cliffs, N.J.: Prentice-Hall, 1960).

(contain squared terms), to obtain a single quadratic equation. Using calculus, two *linear* equations (hence, the name "linear decision rule") can be derived from the quadratic equation. One of the equations can be used to plan the output for each period in the planning horizon, and the other can be used to plan the work force size for each period.

Although the model has found some applications, its chief function seems to be as a benchmark against which proposed techniques can be evaluated. In practice the model suffers from three limitations: (1) a specific type of cost function is assumed, (2) considerable effort must usually be expended in obtaining relevant cost data and developing cost functions for each organization, and (3) the method can produce solutions that are not feasible or are impractical.

Management Coefficients

This is a heuristic model proposed by E. H. Bowman that attempts to incorporate previous managerial planning performance into a decision model.[4] The underlying rationale for the model is based on improving performance rather than in trying to develop a "new" optimizing method. The procedure involves the use of multiple-regression analysis to build a decision model.

Parametric Production Planning

This heuristic technique was proposed by C. H. Jones in the late 1960s.[5] The model uses a search routine to develop two decision rules for output and work force size. In several respects it is similar to the linear decision rule: It uses quadratic cost approximating functions and provides two decision rules. Unlike the linear-decision model, it can be used with essentially any cost function.

Simulation Models

A number of simulation models have also been developed for aggregate planning. (Simulation is described in detail in the supplement to Chapter 14.) The essence of these models is to develop computerized models that can be tested under a variety of conditions in an attempt to identify reasonably acceptable (although not always optimum) solutions to problems.

The above models are summarized in Table 9–6.

---

[4] E. H. Bowman, "Consistence and Optimality in Managerial Decision Making," *Management Science* 4 (January 1963), pp. 100–103.

[5] C. H. Jones, "Parametric Production Planning," *Management Science* 13, no. 11 (July 1967), pp. 843–66.

TABLE 9–6

Summary of Planning Techniques

Technique	Solution approach	Characteristics
Graphical/ charting	Trial and error	Intuitively appealing, easy to understand; solution not necessarily optimum
Linear programming	Optimizing	Computerized; linear assumptions not always valid
Goal programming	Optimizing	Allows use of multiple goals
Linear decision rule	Optimizing	Complex, requires considerable effort to obtain pertinent cost information and to construct model; cost assumptions not always valid
Management coefficients	Heuristic	Uses multiple regression to incorporate past managerial performance into a model; attempts to use that as a base to improve performance
Parametric planning	Heuristic	Uses a search routine to develop two decision rules
Simulation	Trial and error	Computerized models allow managers to examine models under a variety of conditions

Aggregate planning techniques aside from trial and error do not appear to be widely used. Instead, in the majority of organizations aggregate planning seems to be done more on the basis of experience along with trial and error methods. It is impossible to say exactly why some of the more mathematical techniques mentioned here, particularly the ones that have the capability to optimize, are not used to any great extent. We can only speculate. Perhaps the level of mathematical sophistication discourages greater use. The fact that the assumptions required in certain models appear unrealistic or that the models may be too narrow in scope are also possibilities. But whatever the reasons, none of the techniques to date have captured the attention of aggregate planners on a broad scale. Goal programming and simulation are two techniques that seem to be gaining in favor. Suffice it to say that research on improved approaches to aggregate planning is continuing.

DISAGGREGATING THE AGGREGATE PLAN

In order to translate the production plan into actual meaningful terms for production, it is necessary to *disaggregate* the aggregate plan. This involves breaking down the aggregate plan into specific

product requirements in order to determine labor requirements (skills, size of work force), materials, and inventory requirements.

This process is discussed in some depth in Chapter 11, Materials Requirements Planning. At this stage, however, it can be useful for you to be aware of the need for disaggregation, as well as some understanding of what the term implies.

Working with aggregation units facilitates intermediate planning. However, in order to operationalize the production plan, those aggregate units have to be converted, or decomposed, into units of actual products or services that are to be produced or offered. For example, a lawn mower manufacturer may have an aggregate plan that calls for 200 lawn mowers in January, 300 in February, and 400 in March. That company may produce push mowers, self-propelled mowers, and riding mowers. Although the mowers probably contain some of the same parts and involve some similar or identical operations to fabricate and assemble, we can easily imagine certain basic differences in the materials, parts, and operations that each type requires. Hence, the 200, 300, and 400 aggregate lawn mowers that are to be produced during those three months must be translated into specific numbers of mowers of each type in order to be able to actually purchase the appropriate materials and parts, schedule operations, and plan inventory requirements.

The result of disaggregating the aggregate plan is a *master schedule,* which simply shows the quantity and timing of *specific* goods or services for a schedule horizon. The master schedule then serves as the basis for *short-range* planning. It should be noted that whereas the aggregate plan covers an interval, say, of 12 months, the master schedule covers only a portion of this. In other words,

FIGURE 9–5

Disaggregating the Aggregate Plan

Aggregate Plan

Month	Jan.	Feb.	Mar.	Apr.	May
*Planned output**	200	300	400	400	350

* Aggregate units

Master Schedule

Month	Jan.	Feb.	Mar.
*Planned output**			
Push	100	100	100
Self-propelling	75	150	200
Riding	25	50	100
Total	200	300	400

* Actual units

the aggregate plan is disaggregated in stages, or phases, that may cover a few weeks to two or three months. Moreover, the master schedule may be updated *monthly,* even though it covers two or three months. For instance, the lawn mower master schedule would probably be updated at the end of January to include any revisions in planned output for February and March as well as new information on planned output for April.

This concept of disaggregating the aggregate plan is illustrated in Figure 9–5. The illustration makes a simple assumption in order to clearly show the concept of disaggregation: the total of the aggregate and the disaggregated units are equal. However, that is not always true. As a consequence, it can require considerable effort to disaggregate the aggregate plan.

SUMMARY

Intermediate-range planning establishes general levels of employment, output, and inventories for periods of two months to one year. In the spectrum of planning, it falls between the broad design decisions of long-range planning and the very specific and detailed short-range planning decisions. It begins with an overall forecast for the planning horizon and ends with preparations for applying the plans to specific products and services.

The essence of intermediate planning is the aggregation of products or services into one "product" or "service." This permits planners to consider overall levels of employment and inventories without having to become involved with specific details that are better left to short-range planning. Planners often use informal graphical and charting techniques to develop plans, although various mathematical techniques have been suggested. It appears that the complexity and the restrictive assumptions of these techniques limit their widespread acceptance in practice.

A manager is attempting to put together an aggregate plan for the coming year. She has obtained a forecast of expected demand for the planning horizon. Basically, the plan must deal with demand that is highly seasonal; demand is relatively high in Periods 3 and 4 and again in Periods 10 and 11, as can be seen from the following forecasts:

Period:	1	2	3	4	5	6	7	8	9	10	11	12	Total
Forecast:	190	230	260	280	210	170	160	160	220	250	260	180	2,570

The department now has 20 full-time people, each of whom can produce 10 units of output per period at a cost of $6 per unit. Inventory carrying cost is $5 per unit per period, and backlog cost is $10 per unit per period. The manager is considering a plan that would involve hiring two people to start working in Period 1, one on a temporary basis who would work only through Period 5. This would cost $500 in addition to unit production costs.

a. What is the rationale for this plan?

b. Determine the total cost of the plan, including production, inventory, and backorder costs.

Solution

a. With the current work force of 20 people each producing 10 units per period, regular capacity is 2,400 units. That is 170 units less than expected demand. Adding one worker would increase regular capacity to 2,400 + 120 = 2,520 units. That would still be 50 units short, or just the amount one temporary worker could produce in five periods. Since one of the two seasonal peaks is quite early, it would make sense to start the temporary right away to avoid some of the backorder cost.

b. The production plan for this strategy is as follows:

Period	1	2	3	4	5	6	7	8	9	10	11	12	Total
Forecast	190	230	260	280	210	170	160	160	220	250	260	180	2,570
Output													
Regular	220	220	220	220	220	210	210	210	210	210	210	210	2,570
Overtime	—	—	—	—	—	—	—	—	—	—	—	—	
Subcontract	—	—	—	—	—	—	—	—	—	—	—	—	—
Output-Forecast	30	(10)	(40)	(60)	10	40	50	50	(10)	(40)	(50)	30	0
Inventory													
Beginning	0	30	20	0	0	0	0	20	70	60	20	0	
Ending	30	20	0	0	0	0	20	70	60	20	0	0	
Average	15	25	10	0	0	0	10	45	65	40	10	0	220
Backlog	0	0	20	80	70	30	0	0	0	0	30	0	230
Costs:													
Output													
Regular @ $6	$1320	1320	1320	1320	1320	1260	1260	1260	1260	1260	1260	1260	$15,420
Overtime													
Subcontract													
Inventory @ $5	$ 75	125	50	0	0	0	50	225	325	200	50	0	$ 1,100
Backorder @ $10	0	0	200	800	700	300	0	0	0	0	300	0	$ 2,300
Total	$1395	1445	1570	2120	2020	1560	1310	1485	1585	1460	1610	1260	$18,820

The total cost for this plan is $18,820, plus the $500 cost for hiring and for the layoff, giving a total of $19,320. This plan may or may not be good. We would need information on other costs and options before settling on one plan.

Although the calculations are relatively straightforward, the backlogs can sometimes seem difficult to obtain. Consider these rules for computing the backlog:

1. Start with the Output-Forecast value. If it is positive and there was a backlog in the preceding period, reduce the backlog by this amount. If the amount exceeds the backlog, the difference becomes the ending inventory for the period. If they are exactly equal, the backlog and the ending inventory will both be equal to zero.

2. If Output-Forecast is negative, subtract it from the beginning inventory. If this produces a negative value, that value becomes the backlog for that period.

DISCUSSION AND REVIEW QUESTIONS

1. What three levels of planning involve operations managers? What kinds of decisions are made at the various levels?
2. What are the three phases of intermediate planning?
3. What is aggregate planning? What is its purpose?
4. Why is there a need for aggregate planning?
5. What are the most common decision variables for aggregate planning in a manufacturing setting? In a service setting?
6. What difficulty can an organization that offers a variety of products and/or services have to deal with in aggregate planning that an organization with one or a few similar products or services would not?
7. Briefly discuss the advantages and disadvantages of each of these planning strategies:

a. Maintain a level rate of output and let inventories absorb fluctuations in demand.
b. Vary the size of the work force to correspond with predicted changes in demand requirements.
c. Maintain a constant work force size but vary hours worked to correspond to predicted demand requirements.

8. What are the primary advantages and limitations of informal graphical and charting techniques for aggregate planning?
9. Briefly describe the planning techniques listed below and give an advantage and disadvantage for each one:
a. Linear programming.
b. Linear decision rule.
c. Management coefficients.
d. Simulation.

PROBLEMS

1. The solved problem illustrated an aggregate plan that involved use of hiring and a layoff as well as inventory absorption of demand variations and some buildup of backlogs. As noted, in order to assess the merits of that plan, certain other infor-

mation would be needed. If you were the manager, what information would you want? Be specific.

2. Prepare two graphs like those in Figure 9–3 for the solved problem at the end of this chapter. Also, prepare a graph like the one in Figure 9–4.

3. (Refer to the solved problem.) Prepare two alternative aggregate plans. Call the original plan A. For plan B, hire one worker at a cost of $200. Make up any shortfall using subcontracting at $8 per unit, with a maximum of 20 units per period. For plan C, do not hire any workers. Use subcontracting as needed. Try to minimize backorders. Compute the total cost of each plan and compare the plans on that basis. Which is best?

4. (Refer to the solved problem.) Suppose another option is to use part-time workers to assist during seasonal peaks. The cost per unit, including hiring and training, is $11, and the output rate is 10 units per worker per period. A maximum of 10 workers can be used, and the same number of part-time workers must be used in all periods that have part-time workers. Compute the total cost for this plan and compare it to the cost of the plan used in the solved problem.

5. (Refer to the solved problem.) Prepare an aggregate plan that uses overtime ($9 per unit, maximum output 25 units per period) and inventory variation. Try to minimize backlogs. Compute the total cost of your plan and compare it to the total cost of the plan used in the solved problem.

6. (Refer to the solved problem.) Prepare an aggregate plan that uses some combination of hiring ($200 per worker), layoff ($100 per worker), subcontracting ($8 per unit, maximum of 20 units per period, must use for a minimum of three consecutive periods), and overtime ($9 per unit, maximum of 25 per period, maximum of 100 for the planning horizon). Compute the total cost and compare it to any of the other plans you have developed. Which plan has the lowest total cost?

7. (Refer to Example 1.) The president of the firm has decided to shut down the plant for vacation and installation of new equipment in Period 4. After installation the cost per unit will remain the same, but the output rate for regular time will be 400.

a. Prepare graphs like those in Figures 9–3 and 9–4 for this revised case.

b. Prepare the aggregate plan and compute its total cost.

8. (Refer to Example 1.) Suppose that the regular output rate will drop to 340 units per period due to an expected change in production requirements. Costs will not change. Prepare an aggregate plan and compute its total cost for each of these alternatives:

a. Use overtime at a rate of 40 units per period as needed. Plan for an ending inventory of zero for Period 12.

b. Use subcontracting at a *maximum* rate of 50 units per period; the usage need not be the same in every period. Have an ending inventory of zero in the last period. Compare these two plans.

9. (Refer to Example 2.) Do each of the following:

a. Prepare graphs like those in Figures 9–3 and 9–4 for the data given in Example 2. Combine regular time and overtime and use those amounts for output in the graphs.

b. If using subcontracting for one or two periods in addition to overtime or in place of overtime is an option, in which period or periods would you use subcontracting, and how much would you use in order to minimize total cost? Assume you can use a maximum of 50 units of subcontracting per period at $6 per unit, but overtime must be either 40 units or zero in any period. Plan for a zero inventory balance at the end of Period 12.

10. (Refer to Example 2.) Determine if a plan to use subcontracting at a maximum rate of 50 units per period as needed with no overtime would achieve a lower total cost than the plan shown in Example 2. Again,

plan for a zero inventory balance at the end of Period 12.

11. Verify the transportation solution shown in Example 3. Use VAM for the initial feasible solution if you are doing this manually.

12. (Refer to Example 3.) Suppose that due to an increase in warehousing costs and other costs, inventory carrying costs are now $2 per unit per month. All other costs and quantities remain the same. Determine a revised solution to this transportation problem.

13. (Refer to Example 3.) Suppose that regular-time capacity will be reduced to 440 units in Period 3 to accomodate a company-wide safety inspection of equipment. What will the additional cost of the optimal plan be as compared to the one shown in Example 3? Assume all costs and quantities are the same as given in Example 3 except for Period 3's regular-time output.

14. Solve the preceding problem using an inventory carrying cost of $2 per unit per period.

SELECTED BIBLIOGRAPHY

Buffa, Elwood S., and Jeffery G. Miller. *Production-Inventory Systems: Planning and Control.* 3d ed. Homewood, Ill.: Richard D. Irwin, 1974.

Fogarty, Donald W., and Thomas R. Hoffmann. *Production and Inventory Management.* Cincinnati: South-Western Publishing, 1983.

Krajewski, L., and L. Ritzman. "Disaggregation in Manufacturing and Service Organizations." *Decision Sciences* 8, no. 1 (1977), pp. 1–18.

Leone, Robert A., and John R. Meyer. "Capacity Strategies for the 1980s." *Harvard Business Review,* November–December 1980, p. 133.

McLain, J. O., and L. J. Thomas. "Horizon Effects in Aggregate Production Planning with Seasonal Demand." *Management Science* 23, no. 7 (March 1977), pp. 728–36.

Posner, M. E., and W. Szwarc. "A Transportation Type Aggregate Production Model with Backordering." *Management Science* 29, no. 2 (February 1983), pp. 188–199.

Vollmann, Thomas E.; William L. Berry; and D. Clay Whybark. *Manufacturing Planning and Control Systems.* Homewood, Ill.: Richard D. Irwin, 1984.

Chapter 10

Inventory Management

After completing this chapter, you should be able to:

1. Define the term *inventory*.
2. Differentiate between independent and dependent demand.
3. List the major reasons for holding inventories.
4. List the main requirements for effective inventory management.
5. Discuss periodic and perpetual review systems.
6. Describe the A-B-C approach and explain how it is useful.
7. Discuss the objectives of inventory management.
8. Describe the basic EOQ model, its assumptions, and solve typical problems.
9. Describe the economic-run-size model and solve typical problems.
10. Describe the quantity-discount model and solve typical problems.
11. Describe reorder-point models and solve typical problems.
12. Describe the single-period model and solve typical problems.

INTRODUCTION 467

    Independent and Dependent Demand 467
    Types of Inventories 468
    Functions of Inventory 468
    Objectives of Inventory Control 469

REQUIREMENTS FOR EFFECTIVE INVENTORY MANAGEMENT 470

    Inventory Accounting Systems 470
    Demand Forecasts and Lead-Time Information 472
    Cost Information 473
    Classification System 474

HOW MUCH TO ORDER: ECONOMIC-ORDER-QUANTITY MODELS 475

    Basic Economic-Order-Quantity (EOQ) Model 476
    Economic Production Run Size 482
    Quantity Discounts 485

WHEN TO REORDER 492

    Constant Demand Rate and Constant Lead Time 493
    Variable Demand Rates and/or Variable Lead Times 493
    Shortages and Service Levels 501

HOW MUCH TO ORDER: FIXED-ORDER-INTERVAL MODEL 505

    Reasons for Using 505
    Determining the Amount to Order 505
    Benefits and Disadvantages 507

HOW MUCH TO ORDER: SINGLE-PERIOD MODEL 508

    Continuous Stocking Levels 509
    Discrete Stocking Levels 511

SUMMARY 513

SOLVED PROBLEMS 516

DISCUSSION AND REVIEW QUESTIONS 522

PROBLEMS 522

SELECTED BIBLIOGRAPHY 526

CASE: THE DEWEY STAPLER COMPANY 527

SUPPLEMENT: PURCHASING 531

> We proceed as follows. First look for five-by-five-by-three-foot bin of gears or parts that looks like it has been there awhile. Pick up a gear and ask, casually. "How much is this worth?" You then ask, "How many of these are in the bin?" followed by, "How long has this bin been here?" and, "What's your cost of money for this company?" I recall one case in a nameless South American country where the unit cost times the number of parts times the time it had been there times the interest rate resulted in a cost-per-day figure that would insure comfortable retirement for the plant manager on the bank of the Rio de la Plata at one of the better resorts to be found there. The plant manager suddenly realized that what he was holding was not just a chunk of high-test steel, but was *real money.* He then pointed out that *he* now understood the value of the inventory but could I suggest a way to drive the point home to upper management? I suggested that he go to the accounting department and borrow enough money to be equal to the bin's value for as long as it had been sitting there, and pile it on the top of the bin. I further suggested that he do that for every bin on the production line. We rapidly figured out that by the time we had the money piled up on the bin, you would not even be able to *see* the bin. My opinion was that if the upper managers were given a tour of the line with the money piled up, they would *never forget it.*[1]

Good inventory management is essential to the successful operation of most organizations. There are a number of reasons for this. One is the amount of money inventory represents, another is the impact that inventories have on the daily operations of an organization. Some organizations have excellent inventory management, and many have satisfactory inventory management. But too many have unsatisfactory inventory management. In some instances that is a sign that management does not recognize the role that inventories play. More often than not, though, the "recognition" is there. What is lacking is an understanding of what needs to be done and how to do it. In this chapter the concepts that underlie good inventory management are explored.

The preceding chapter described *aggregate* inventory planning. This chapter and the next one narrow the focus to *individual items.* The next chapter deals with inventory methods that are best suited for managing inventories of component parts and subassemblies, while this chapter describes methods that are best suited for finished goods, raw materials, purchased parts, and retail items.

---

[1] Gene Woolsey, "On Doing Good Things and Dumb Things in Production and Inventory Control," *Interfaces* 5, no. 3 (May 1975). Copyright 1975, The Institute of Management Science. Reprinted by permission.

The chapter discusses the different functions of inventories, the requirements for effective inventory management, the objectives of inventory control, and techniques for determining *how much* to order and *when* to order.

INTRODUCTION

An *inventory* is a stock or store of goods. Many firms stock hundreds or even thousands of items, ranging from small things like pencils, paperclips, paper, screws, and nuts and bolts to large items like machines, trucks, construction equipment, and airplanes. Naturally, many of the items a firm carries in inventory relate to the kind of business it engages in. Thus, manufacturing firms carry supplies of raw materials, purchased parts, partially completed items, and finished goods as well as spare parts for machines, tools, and other supplies. Department stores carry clothing, furniture, carpeting, stationery, appliances, gifts, cards, and toys. Some also stock sporting goods, paints, and tools. Hospitals stock drugs, surgical supplies, life-monitoring equipment, sheets and pillow cases, and more. Supermarkets stock fresh and canned foods, packaged and frozen foods, household supplies, magazines, baked goods, drug items, and miscellaneous items.

Independent and Dependent Demand

A major distinction in the way inventory planning and control is managed is whether demand for items in inventory is *independent* or *dependent*. *Dependent demand* items are typically subassemblies or component parts that will be used in the production of a *parent* or finished product. In such cases demand (i.e., *usage*) of subassemblies and component parts essentially *depends* on the number of finished units that will be produced. A classic example of this is demand for wheels for new cars. If each car is to have five wheels, then the total number of wheels that would be required for a production run is simply a function of the number of cars that are to be produced in that run. For example, 200 cars would require $200 \times 5 = 1,000$ wheels. *Independent demand* items, on the other hand, are the finished goods or other end items. Generally speaking, these items are sold, or at least shipped out, rather than used in making another product. In such cases there is usually no way to precisely determine how many of these items will be demanded during any given time period because demand typically includes elements of randomness. Therefore, forecasting plays an important role in stocking decisions, whereas for dependent demand items, stock requirements are determined by reference to the production plan. This chapter focuses on management of inde-

pendent demand items, and the next chapter focuses on dependent demand.

Types of Inventories

The inventories most firms hold can be classified into one of the following types:

> Raw materials and purchased parts.
> Partially completed goods (work in process) or goods in transit.
> Finished-goods inventories (manufacturing firms) or merchandise (retail stores).
> Replacement parts, tools, and supplies.

Functions of Inventory

Inventories serve a number of important functions. Among the most salient reasons for holding inventories are the following:

1. To meet anticipated demand.
2. To smooth production requirements.
3. To decouple components of the production-distribution system.
4. To protect against stock-outs.
5. To take advantage of order cycles.
6. To hedge against price increases.
7. To permit operations.

Let's take a look at each of these.

1. *To meet anticipated customer demand.* A customer can be a person who walks in off the street to buy a new stereo system, a mechanic who requests a tool at a tool crib, or a manufacturing operation. These inventories are referred to as *anticipation stocks* because they are held to satisfy planned or expected demand.

2. *To smooth production requirements.* Firms that experience seasonal patterns in demand often build up inventories during off-season periods in order to meet overly high requirements that exist during certain seasonal periods. These inventories are aptly named *seasonal inventories.*

3. *To decouple operations.* Unless successive steps in a production or distribution system have a buffer of inventories between them, they will be so interdependent that an interruption at one point will quickly cause the entire system to grind to a halt as individual steps in the operation have to cease and operations shut down one after the other in domino fashion. Thus, an inventory of raw materials offers a manufacturer some protection from disruption in deliveries caused by the weather or problems with a supplier. Similarly, inventories between successive manufacturing steps act as a buffer that allows other operations to continue temporarily if some operations suffer breakdowns or other problems. And finished goods inventories separate manufacturing and selling op-

erations, enabling income to be generated even though a disruption in manufacturing occurs.

4. *To protect against stock-outs.* Delayed deliveries and unexpected increases in demand increase the risk of shortages. Delays can be due to weather conditions, supplier stock-outs, deliveries of wrong materials, quality problems, and so on. The risk of shortages can be reduced by holding *safety stocks,* which are stocks in excess of anticipated demand.

5. *To take advantage of order cycles.* In order to minimize purchasing and inventory costs, it is often necessary to *buy* quantities that exceed immediate usage requirements. This necessitates storing some or all of the purchased amount for later use. Similarly, it is usually economical to *produce* in large, rather than small, quantities. Again, the excess output must be stored for later use. Hence, inventory storage enables a firm to buy and produce in economic lot sizes without having to try to match purchases or production with demand requirements in the short run. This results in *periodic* orders, or order *cycles.* The resulting stock is known as *cycle stock.* Order cycles are not always due to economic order sizes. In some instances it is more practical or economical to group orders and order at fixed intervals. Nonetheless, cycle stocks still exist.

6. *To hedge against price increases.* Occasionally a firm may suspect that a substantial price increase is about to be made and purchase larger than normal amounts to achieve some savings.

7. *To permit operations.* The fact that production operations take a certain amount of time (i.e., they are not instantaneous) means that there will generally be some *work-in-process* inventory. In addition, intermediate stocking of goods including raw materials, semifinished items, and finished goods at production sites as well as goods stored in warehouses leads to *pipeline* inventories throughout a production-distribution system.

Objectives of Inventory Control

Inadequate control of inventories can result in both understocking and overstocking of items. Understocking results in missed deliveries, lost sales, dissatisfied customers, and production bottlenecks, while overstocking unnecessarily ties up funds that might be more productive elsewhere. Although overstocking would appear to be the lesser of the two evils, the price tag for excessive overstocking can be staggering when inventory holding costs are high, as illustrated by the little story about the bin of gears at the beginning of the chapter. Moreover, matters can easily get out of hand. For example, it is not unheard of for a manager to discover that his or her firm has more than a 100-year supply of some item. (No doubt the firm got a good buy on it!)

There are two main objectives of inventory control. One is to *maximize the level of customer service* (i.e., have the right goods,

in sufficient quantities, in the right place, and at the right time). The other is to *minimize the cost* of providing the high level of customer service.

These two objectives are generally in opposition: High levels of customer service lead to high costs, and low costs usually are accompanied by low levels of customer service. Consequently, most inventory decisions are trade-offs involving a compromise between cost and customer service level. In practice, management may select a certain desired level of customer service, in which case the goal of inventory control is to attain that level at the lowest possible cost. Conversely, management may set cost levels, in which case the goal is usually to attain the highest possible level of customer service under those conditions.

Toward this end, the decision maker's problem is to achieve a *balance* with stocking decisions, avoiding both overstocking as well as understocking. The two fundamental decisions that must be made relate to the *timing* and *size* of orders (i.e., *when* to order and *how much* to order). The majority of material in this chapter is devoted to models that can be applied to assist in making those decisions.

REQUIREMENTS FOR EFFECTIVE INVENTORY MANAGEMENT

Management has two basic functions with respect to inventory. One is to establish a system of accounting for items in inventory, and the other is to make decisions regarding how much to order and when to order. To be effective, it is necessary for management to have the following:

1. A system to *keep track of the inventory* on hand and on order.
2. A reliable *forecast of demand* that includes an indication of possible *forecast error.*
3. Knowledge of *lead times* and *lead-time variability.*
4. Reasonable estimates of inventory *holding costs, ordering costs,* and *shortage costs.*
5. A *classification system* for inventory items.

Let's take a closer look at each of these requirements.

Inventory Accounting Systems

Inventory accounting systems can be periodic or continuous. Under a *periodic system,* a physical count of items in inventory is made at periodic intervals (weekly, monthly) in order to decide how much to order of each type of item. Many small grocers use that approach; a manager periodically checks the shelves and stockroom to determine the quantity on hand. Then the manager estimates how much will be demanded prior to the next review period's delivery and bases the order quantity on that information. An advantage of this

type of system is that orders for many items occur at the same time, and there can be economies in processing and shipping orders. There are also several disadvantages of periodic reviews. One is that there is lack of control between reviews. Another is the need to protect against shortages between review periods by carrying extra stock. A third disadvantage is the need to make a decision on order quantities at each review.

A *continuous inventory system* (also known as a *perpetual* system) keeps track of removals from inventory on a continuous basis, so the system can provide information on the current level of inventory for each item. When the amount on hand reaches a predetermined minimum, a fixed quantity, Q, is ordered. An obvious advantage of this system is the continuous monitoring of inventory withdrawals because of the control it provides. Another advantage is the fixed-order quantity; management can identify an *economic order size* (this concept is discussed in detail later in the chapter). One disadvantage of this approach is the added costs of record keeping. Moreover, a physical count of inventories must still be performed periodically (e.g., annually) to verify records, because of errors, pilferage, spoilage, and other factors that can reduce the effective amount of inventory. Bank transactions such as customer deposits and withdrawals are an example of continuous recording of inventory changes.

Continuous systems range from very simple to very sophisticated. A *two-bin* arrangement is an example of a very elementary system. It involves the use of two containers for inventory. Items are withdrawn from the first bin. When its contents are exhausted, it is time to reorder. Sometimes an order card is placed at the bottom of the first bin. The second bin contains enough stock to satisfy expected demand until the order is filled plus an extra cushion of stock that will reduce the chance of a stock-out if the order is late or if usage is greater than expected. The advantage of this system is that there is no need to record each withdrawal from inventory; the disadvantage is that the reorder card may not be turned in for a variety of reasons (it is misplaced, the person who is supposed to turn it in forgets to, etc.).

Continuous systems can be either *batch* or *online*. In batch systems, inventory records are collected periodically and entered into the system, while in online systems, the transactions are recorded instantaneously. The advantage of online systems is that the system is always up-to-date; with a batch system, a sudden surge in demand could result in reducing the amount of inventory below the reorder point between the periodic read-ins, although frequent batch collections can minimize that problem.

Supermarkets, discount stores, and department stores have always been major users of periodic accounting systems. However, in the last few years many have switched to computerized checkout

systems that use a laser scanning device that reads a *universal product code* (UPC) printed on an item tag or on product packaging. A typical grocery product code is illustrated below.

The zero on the left identifies this as a grocery item, the first five numbers (14800) indicate the manufacturer (MOTT's) and the last five numbers (23208) indicate the specific item (natural style applesauce). Items in small packages, such as candy and gum, use a six-digit number.

UPC scanners represent a major change in the inventory systems of stores that use them. In addition to the increase in speed and accuracy these systems provide, they give managers continuous information on inventories, they reduce the need for periodic inventories and order-size determinations, and they improve the level of customer service by indicating the price and quantity of each item on the customer's receipt, as illustrated below.

```
        BRAVO CAPELLINI        .79
        BUB YUM DBL LIME       .30 T
        2/ LO FAT MILK H G    1.03
        LACTAID MILK           .91
        WEGMAN 2/ MILK QT      .55
        NEWSPAPER              .35
        KR CAS BRICK CHEES    1.59
        GRAPES-GREEN
  .91 LB @ .89 PER LB          .81

        TAX DUE                .02
        TOTAL                 6.35

        CASH                 20.00 *
        CHANGE               13.65

  10/07/85 18:01 21    16     23100  2570
```

Demand Forecasts and Lead-Time Information

Since inventories will be used to satisfy demand requirements, it is essential to have reliable estimates of the amount and timing of demand requirements. Similarly, it is essential to know how long it will take for orders to be delivered. In addition, it is necessary to know the extent to which demand and lead times might vary;

the more potential variability, the greater the need for additional stock to insure against a shortage between deliveries. Thus, there is a crucial link between forecasting and inventory management.

Cost Information   Three basic costs are associated with inventories: holding, transaction (ordering), and shortage costs.

Holding or *carrying costs* relate to physically holding items in storage. They include interest, insurance, taxes,[2] depreciation, obsolescence, deterioration, spoilage, pilferage, breakage, and warehousing costs (heat, light, rent, security). Holding costs also include opportunity costs associated with having funds tied up in inventory that could be used elsewhere.

The significance of the various components of holding cost depends on the type of item involved, although taxes, interest, and insurance are generally based on the dollar value of an inventory. Items that are easily concealed (such as pocket cameras, transistor radios, and calculators) or fairly expensive (cars, TVs) are prone to theft. Fresh seafood, meats and poultry, fresh produce, and baked goods are subject to rapid deterioration and spoilage. Other items such as dairy products, salad dressings, medicines, batteries, and film also have limited shelf lives.

Holding costs are stated in either of two ways. One way is to specify cost as a percentage of unit price, and the other is to specify a dollar amount per unit. In any case typical annual holding costs often range from 20 percent to 40 percent of the value of an item. Thus, to hold a $1 item for one year could cost from 20 cents to 40 cents.

Ordering costs are the costs associated with ordering and receiving inventory. These costs include determining how much is needed, typing up invoices, inspecting goods upon arrival for quality and quantity, and moving the goods to temporary storage. Ordering costs are generally expressed as a fixed-dollar amount per order, regardless of order size.

When a firm produces its own inventory instead of ordering it from a supplier, the costs of machine setup (preparing equipment for the job by adjusting the machine, installing new fixtures, and so on) are analogous to ordering costs (i.e., they are expressed as a fixed charge per run, regardless of the size of the run).

Shortage costs result when demand exceeds the supply of inventory on hand. The costs can include the opportunity cost of not making a sale, loss of customer goodwill, lateness charges, and similar costs. Furthermore, if the shortage occurs in an item carried for internal use (e.g., to supply an assembly line), the cost of lost

---

[2] In some states.

production or downtime is considered a shortage cost. Such costs can easily run into the hundreds of dollars a minute or more.

Shortage costs are usually difficult to measure, and they are often subjectively estimated. Later in the chapter we will see how to evaluate the sensitivity of decisions to these estimates.

Classification System

An important aspect of inventory mangement concerns the fact that items kept in inventory are not of equal importance in terms of dollars invested, profit potential, sales or usage volume, and stockout penalties. For instance, a producer of electrical equipment might have electric generators, coils of wire, and miscellaneous nuts and bolts among the items carried in inventory. It would be unrealistic to devote equal attention to each of these items. Instead, a more reasonable approach would be to allocate control efforts according to relative importance of various items in inventory.

The *A-B-C approach* involves classifying inventory items according to some measure of importance—usually annual dollar usage (i.e., dollar value per unit multiplied by annual usage rate)—and then allocating control efforts accordingly. Typically, three classes of items are used: A (very important), B (moderately important), and C (least important). However, the actual number of categories may vary from organization to organization, depending on the extent to which a firm wants to differentiate control efforts. Generally speaking, with three classes of items, A items often account for about 5 percent to 10 percent of the *number* of items in inventory but about 60 percent to 70 percent of the *dollar usage*. At the other

FIGURE 10–1

A Typical A-B-C Breakdown in Percentage of Dollar Value and Percentage of Items by Category

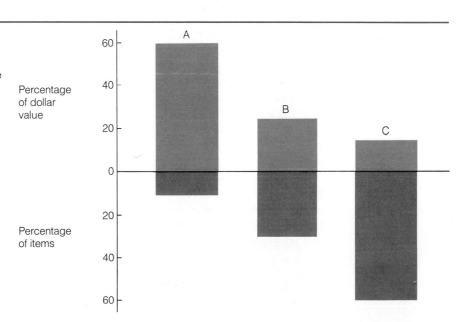

end of the scale, C items might account for about 60 percent of the number of items but only about 15 percent of the dollar usage of an inventory. These percentages may vary from firm to firm, but the point is that in most instances a relatively few items will account for a large share of the value or cost associated with an inventory, and these items should receive a relatively greater share of control efforts. For instance, A items should receive close attention to make sure that customer-service levels are attained, through frequent review of amounts on hand and control over withdrawals, where possible. The C items should receive only loose control (two-bin system, bulk orders), and the B items should have a control effort that lies between these two extremes.

The A-B-C concept is illustrated in Figure 10–1.

EXAMPLE 1

Classify the inventory items as A, B, or C based on annual dollar value, given the information below:

Item	Annual demand	Unit cost	Annual dollar value	
1 . . .	1,000	$4,300	$4,300,000	} A
2 . . .	5,000	720	3,600,000	
3 . . .	1,900	500	950,000	
4 . . .	1,000	710	710,000	} B
5 . . .	2,500	250	625,000	
6 . . .	2,500	192	480,000	
7 . . .	400	200	80,000	
8 . . .	500	100	50,000	
9 . . .	200	210	42,000	} C
10 . . .	1,000	35	35,000	
11 . . .	3,000	10	30,000	
12 . . .	9,000	3	27,000	

Solution

Simply on an intuitive basis, you can see that the first two items have a relatively high annual dollar value. Hence, it would seem reasonable to classify them as A items. The next four items appear to have moderate annual dollar values and should be B items. The remainder should be C items based on their relatively low dollar values.

HOW MUCH TO ORDER: ECONOMIC-ORDER-QUANTITY MODELS

The question of how much to order is frequently determined by using an *economic-order-quantity (EOQ)* model. EOQ models identify the optimum order quantity in terms of minimizing the sum of certain annual costs, which vary with order size.

Three order size models are described in the following sections:

1. The economic-order-quantity model.
2. The economic-run-size model.
3. The quantity-discount model.

Basic Economic-Order-Quantity (EOQ) Model

The basic EOQ model is the simplest of the three models. It is used to identify the order size that will minimize the sum of the annual costs of holding inventory and the annual costs of ordering inventory. The unit purchase price of items in inventory is not generally included in the total cost because the unit cost is unaffected by the order size unless quantity discounts are a factor. The quantity discount version of the basic model will be taken up shortly. If holding costs are specified as a percentage of unit cost, then unit cost is indirectly included in total cost as a part of holding costs.

The basic model involves a number of assumptions—some of which may appear to be idealistic. They are listed in Table 10–1. The implications of some of the assumptions can be seen in the diagram of an inventory cycle depicted in Figure 10–2.

The cycle begins with receipt of an order of Q units. These are withdrawn at a constant rate over time. When the quantity on hand is just sufficient to satisfy demand during lead time (the time between submitting an order and receiving that order), an order for Q units is submitted to the supplier. Because it is assumed that both the usage rate and the lead time do not vary, the order will be received at the precise instant that the inventory on hand falls to zero. Thus, orders are timed to avoid having excess stock on hand and to avoid stock-outs.

The optimum order quantity reflects a trade-off between carrying costs and ordering costs: As order size is varied, one type of cost will increase while the other one decreases. For example, if the order size is relatively small, the average inventory will be low, which will result in low carrying costs. However, a small order size will necessitate frequent orders, and that will drive up annual ordering costs. Conversely, annual ordering costs can be held down by ordering large quantities at infrequent intervals, but that would result in higher average inventory levels and therefore increase carrying costs. These two extremes are illustrated in Figure 10–3.

TABLE 10–1

Assumptions of the Basic EOQ Model

1. There is only one product involved.
2. Annual usage (demand) requirements are known.
3. Usage is spread evenly throughout the year so that the usage rate is reasonably constant.
4. Lead time does not vary.
5. Each order is received in a single delivery.
6. There are no quantity discounts.

FIGURE 10–2

The Inventory Cycle: Profile of Inventory Level Over Time

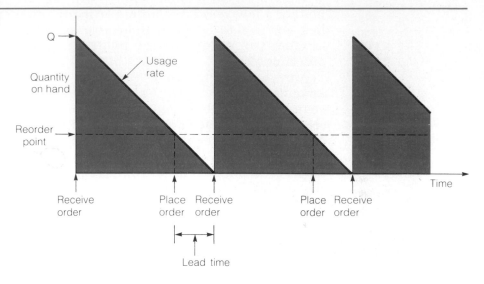

FIGURE 10–3

Average Inventory Level and Number of Orders per Year Are Inversely Related; as One Increases, the Other Decreases

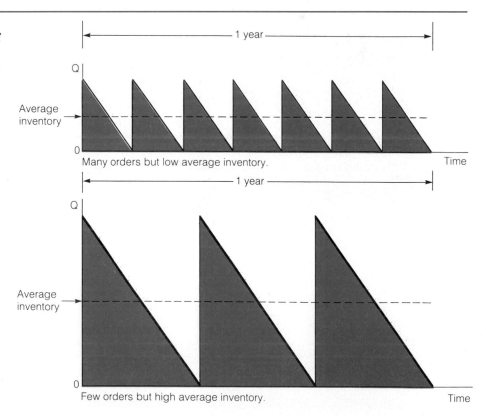

Thus, the ideal solution will typically be an order size that causes neither a few very large orders or many small orders, but one that lies somewhere between those two extremes. The exact amount to order will depend on the relative magnitudes of carrying and ordering costs.

Annual carrying cost is computed by multiplying the average amount of inventory on hand by the cost to carry one unit for a year, even though any given unit would not be held for a year. (Note, though, that 12 units each held for one month is equivalent to holding 1 unit for an entire year.) The average inventory is simply one half of the order quantity: the amount on hand decreases steadily from Q units to 0, for an average of $(Q + 0)/2$, or $Q/2$. Using the symbol H to represent the average annual carrying cost per unit, the total *annual carrying cost* is

$$\text{Annual carrying cost} = \frac{Q}{2} H$$

FIGURE 10–4

A. **Carrying costs are linearly related to order size.**

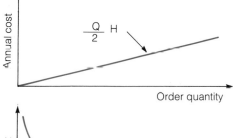

B. **Ordering costs are inversely and nonlinearly related to order size.**

C. **The total-cost curve is U-shaped.**

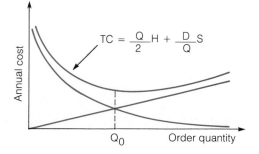

Carrying costs are thus a linear function of Q; carrying costs increase or decrease in direct proportion to changes in the order quantity Q, as illustrated in Figure 10–4A.

On the other hand, annual ordering costs will decrease as order size increases, since for a given annual demand, the larger the order size, the fewer the number of orders needed. For instance, if annual demand is 12,000 units and the order size is 1,000 units per order, there must be 12 orders over the year. But if $Q = 2,000$ units, only six orders will be needed, and if $Q = 3,000$ units, only four orders will be needed. In general, the number of orders per year will be D/Q, where D = Annual demand and Q = Order size. Unlike carrying costs, ordering costs are relatively insensitive to order size, in that regardless of the amount of an order, there are certain activities that must be done, such as determine how much is needed, periodically evaluate sources of supply, and prepare the invoice. Even inspection of the shipment to verify quality and quantity characteristics is not strongly influenced by order size since large shipments are sampled rather than completely inspected. Hence, there is a constant or *fixed* ordering cost. *Annual ordering cost* is a function of the number of orders per year and the ordering cost per order:

$$\text{Annual ordering cost} = \frac{D}{Q} S$$

where

$$S = \text{Ordering cost}$$

Because the number of orders per year, D/Q, decreases as Q increases, annual ordering cost is inversely related to order size, as illustrated in Figure 10–4B.

The total annual cost associated with carrying and ordering inventory when Q units are ordered each time is:

$$
\begin{array}{ccc}
 & \text{Annual} & \text{Annual} \\
TC = & \text{carrying} + & \text{ordering} \\
 & \text{cost} & \text{cost}
\end{array}
$$

$$= \quad \frac{Q}{2} H \quad + \quad \frac{D}{Q} S \tag{10–1}$$

where

D = Demand in units per year
Q = Order quantity in units
S = Order cost in dollars
H = Carrying cost in dollars per unit per year

(Note that D and H must be in the same units, e.g., years.) Figure 10–4C reveals that the total-cost curve is U-shaped and that it reaches its *minimum at the quantity where carrying and ordering costs are equal.* An expression for the optimum order quantity, Q_0, can be obtained using calculus.[3] The result is the formula

$$Q_0 = \sqrt{\frac{2DS}{H}} \qquad (10\text{–}2)$$

Thus, given an annual demand, the ordering cost per order, and the annual carrying cost per unit, the optimum (economic) order quantity can be computed.

The minimum total cost is:

$$TC_{min} = \frac{Q_0}{2}H + \frac{D}{Q_0}S \qquad (10\text{–}3)$$

EXAMPLE 2

A local tire distributor for a national tire company expects to sell approximately 9,600 steel-belted radial tires in a certain size and tread design next year. Annual carrying costs are $16 per tire, and ordering costs are $75. The distributor operates 288 days a year.

a. Determine the EOQ.
b. How many times per year does the store reorder?
c. Determine the length of an order cycle.

Solution

$D = 9,600$ tires per year
$H = \$16$ per unit per year
$S = \$75$

a. $Q_0 = \sqrt{\dfrac{2DS}{H}} = \sqrt{\dfrac{2(9,600)75}{16}} = 300$ tires.

b.   Number of orders per year: $D/Q_0 = \dfrac{9,600 \text{ tires}}{300 \text{ tires}} = 32.$

c.   Length of order cycle: $Q_0/D = \dfrac{300 \text{ tires}}{9,600 \text{ tires}} = \frac{1}{32}$ of a year, which is $\frac{1}{32} \times (288)$ or nine workdays.

---

[3] The minimum point of the total-cost curve can be found by differentiating TC with respect to Q, setting the result equal to zero, and solving for Q. Thus,

1. $\dfrac{dTC}{dQ} = \dfrac{dQ}{2}H + d(D/Q)S = H/2 - DS/Q^2$

2. $0 = H/2 - DS/Q^2$, so $Q^2 = \dfrac{2DS}{H}$ or $Q = \sqrt{\dfrac{2DS}{H}}.$

Note, too, that the second derivative is positive, which indicates a minimum has been obtained.

Carrying costs are sometimes stated as a percentage of the purchase price of an item rather than as a dollar amount per unit. However, as long as the percentage is converted into a dollar amount, the EOQ formula is still appropriate.

EXAMPLE 3

Piddling Manufacturing assembles television sets. It purchases 3,600 black-and-white picture tubes a year at $65 each. Ordering costs are $31, and annual carrying costs are 20 percent of the purchase price. Compute the optimum quantity and the total annual cost of ordering and carrying the inventory.

Solution

$D = 3,600$ picture tubes per year
$S = \$31$
$H = 20\%(\$65) = \$13$

$$Q_0 = \sqrt{\frac{2DS}{H}} = \sqrt{\frac{2(3,600)(31)}{13}} = 131 \text{ picture tubes}$$

$$
\begin{aligned}
TC &= \text{Carrying costs} + \text{Ordering costs} \\
&= \quad (Q_0/2)H \quad + \quad (D/Q_0)S \\
&= \quad (131/2)13 \quad + \quad (3,600/131)31 \\
&= \quad\quad \$852 \quad\quad + \quad\quad \$852 \quad\quad = \$1,704
\end{aligned}
$$

Note that the ordering and carrying costs are equal at the EOQ, as illustrated in Figure 10–4C.

Comment. Holding and ordering costs are typically estimated values rather than values that can be precisely determined, say, from accounting records. In fact, holding costs are sometimes *designated* by managers instead of *computed.* Consequently, the EOQ should be regarded as an approximate quantity rather than an exact quantity. Thus, rounding the calculated value is perfectly acceptable; stating a value to several decimal places would tend to give an unrealistic impression of the precision involved. An obvious question, then, is this: How good is this "approximate" EOQ in terms of minimizing cost? The answer is that the EOQ is fairly robust; even if it is off by a large margin, the total cost suffers relatively little. For instance, an EOQ that varies by less than −20 percent to +30 percent from the true value will yield a total cost that is within ±5 percent of the minimum. This is due to the way the EOQ is calculated: Errors may cancel each other out, and taking the square root reduces the effect of errors. Hence, there is actually a range or "zone" of workable values for the EOQ, as depicted in Figure 10–5.

FIGURE 10–5

The Total-Cost Curve
Is Relatively Flat Near
the EOQ

Economic
Production
Run Size

In the basic EOQ model it is assumed that orders are delivered as whole units at a single point in time (instantaneous replenishment) as opposed to multiple deliveries spread over a period of time. However, in some instances, particularly those in which a firm is both a producer and user, inventories tend to build up gradually over time instead of instantaneously, because the firm is producing and using the item simultaneously. The objective of an EOQ analysis in such cases is to identify an optimum *run* size.

If usage and production are equal, there will not be an inventory buildup since all output will be used immediately, and the question of run size doesn't come up. In the more typical case the production rate *exceeds* the usage rate, creating a situation depicted in Figure 10–6. Because the production rate is greater than the usage rate, production occurs over only a portion of each cycle, while usage occurs over the entire cycle. During the production phase of the cycle, inventory builds up at a rate equal to the difference between production and usage rates. For example, if the daily production rate is 20 units and the daily usage rate is 5 units, inventory will build up at the rate of $20 - 5 = 15$ units per day. As long as production occurs, the inventory level will continue to build; when production ceases, the inventory level will begin to decrease. Hence, the inventory level will be a maximum at the point where production ceases. When the amount of inventory on hand is exhausted, production is resumed and the cycle repeats itself.

Since the firm makes the product itself, there are no ordering costs as such. Nonetheless, with every run there are setup costs, which are analogous to ordering costs. Like ordering costs, setup costs are also independent of the lot (run) size, and they are treated in the formula in exactly the same way ordering costs are. Hence, the larger the run size, the fewer the number of runs needed and, hence, the lower the annual setup cost. The number of runs is D/Q, and the annual setup cost is equal to the number of runs per year times the setup cost per run: $(D/Q)S$.

FIGURE 10–6

EOQ with Noninstantaneous Replenishment

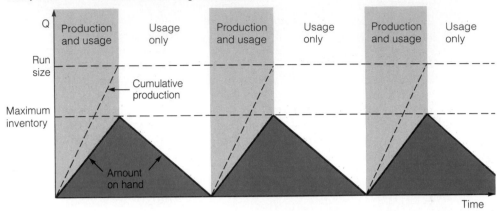

The objective of this model, then, is to minimize the sum of setup and carrying costs. Total cost is:

$$TC_{min} = \text{Carrying cost} + \text{Setup cost}$$

$$= \left(\frac{I_{max}}{2}\right)H + (D/Q_0)S \qquad \textbf{(10–4)}$$

where

I_{max} = Maximum inventory

The economic run quantity is:

$$Q_0 = \sqrt{\frac{2DS}{H}}\,\sqrt{\frac{p}{p-u}} \qquad \textbf{(10–5)}$$

where

p = Production rate
u = Usage or demand rate

The maximum and average inventory levels are:

$$I_{max} = \sqrt{\frac{2DS}{H}}\,\sqrt{\frac{p-u}{p}} \quad \text{and} \quad I_{average} = \frac{I_{max}}{2} \qquad \textbf{(10–6)}$$

The cycle time for the economic run size is a function of the run size and the usage (demand) rate:

$$\text{Cycle time} = \frac{Q_0}{u} \qquad \textbf{(10–7)}$$

Similarly, the run time is a function of the run size and the production rate:

$$\text{Run time} = \frac{Q_0}{p} \qquad \textbf{(10–8)}$$

EXAMPLE 4

A toy manufacturer uses 48,000 rubber wheels per year for its popular dump trunk series. The firm makes its own wheels, which it can produce at a rate of 800 per day. The toy trucks are assembled uniformly over the entire year. Carrying cost is $1 per wheel a year. Setup costs for a production run of wheels is $45. The firm operates 240 days per year. Determine each of the following:

a. The optimum run size.
b. The minimum total annual cost for carrying and setup.
c. The cycle time for the optimum run size.
d. The run time.

Solution

$D = 48,000$ wheels per year
$S = \$45$
$H = \$1$ per wheel per year
$p = 800$ wheels per day
$u = 48,000$ wheels per 240 days or 200 wheels per day

a. $Q_0 = \sqrt{\dfrac{2DS}{H}} \sqrt{\dfrac{p}{p-u}}$

$= \sqrt{\dfrac{2(48,000)45}{1}} \sqrt{\dfrac{800}{800-200}}$

$= 2,400$ wheels

b. $TC_{min} = $ Carrying cost $+$ Setup cost

$= \left(\dfrac{I_{max}}{2}\right) H \qquad + (D/Q_0)S$

Thus, we must first compute I_{max}:

$I_{max} = \sqrt{\dfrac{2DS}{H}} \sqrt{\dfrac{p-u}{p}} = \sqrt{\dfrac{2(48,000)45}{1}} \sqrt{\dfrac{800-200}{800}} = 1,800$ wheels

$TC = \dfrac{1,800}{2} \times \$1 + \dfrac{48,000}{2,400} \times \$45$

$= 900 + 900 = \$1,800$

Note, again, the equality of costs (in this instance, setup and carrying costs) at the EOQ.

c. Cycle time $= \dfrac{Q_0}{u} = \dfrac{2,400 \text{ wheels}}{200 \text{ wheels per day}} = 12$ days

d. Run time $= \dfrac{Q_0}{p} = \dfrac{2,400 \text{ wheels}}{800 \text{ wheels per day}} = 3$ days

Quantity Discounts

Quantity discounts are price reductions for large orders offered to customers to induce them to buy in large quantities. For example, a Chicago surgical supply company publishes the price list shown in Table 10–2 for boxes of gauze strips. Note that the price per box decreases as order quantity increases.

If quantity discounts are offered, the customer must weigh the potential benefits of reduced purchase price and fewer orders that will result from buying in large quantities against the increase in carrying costs caused by higher average inventories. Hence, the buyer's goal in the case of quantity discounts is to select the order quantity that will minimize total costs, where total cost is the sum of carrying cost, ordering cost, *and* purchasing cost:

$$TC = \text{Carrying cost} + \text{Ordering cost} + \text{Purchasing cost}$$

$$= \left(\frac{Q}{2}\right)H \quad + \quad \left(\frac{D}{Q}\right)S \quad + \quad PD \tag{10–9}$$

where P = Unit price

Recall that in the basic EOQ model, determination of order size did not involve the purchasing cost. The rationale for not including unit price is that under the assumption of no quantity discounts, price per unit is the same for all order sizes. Inclusion of unit price in the total cost computation in that case would merely increase the total cost by the amount P times D. A graph of total annual purchase cost versus quantity would be a horizontal line. Hence, including purchasing costs would merely raise the total-cost curve by the same amount *(PD)* at every point. That would not change the minimum, however. This is illustrated in Figure 10–7.

When quantity discounts are present, there is a separate U-shaped total-cost curve for each unit price. Again, including unit prices merely raises each curve by a constant amount. However, because the unit prices are all different, each curve is raised by a different amount: Smaller unit prices will raise a total-cost curve by less than larger unit prices. In addition, no one curve applies

TABLE 10–2

Price List for Extra-Wide Gauze Strips	*Order quantity*	*Price per box*
	1 to 44	$2.00
	45 to 69	1.70
	70 or more	1.40

FIGURE 10–7

Adding *PD* Doesn't Change the EOQ

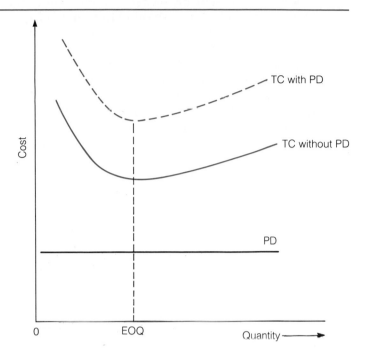

FIGURE 10–8

The Total-Cost Curve with Quantity Discounts Is Composed of a Portion of the Total-Cost Curve for Each Price

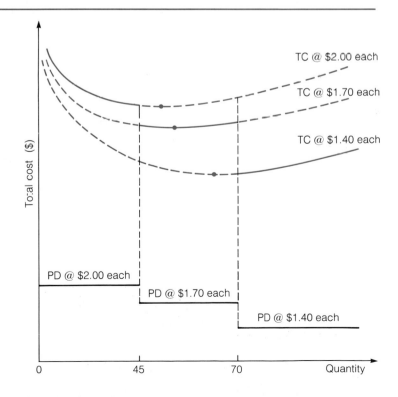

to the entire range of quantities; each curve applies to only a *portion* of the range. This is illustrated in Figure 10–8. Hence, the applicable or *feasible* total cost is initially on the curve with the highest unit price, then drops down, curve by curve, at the *pricebreaks,* which are the minimum quantities needed to obtain the discounts. Thus, the pricebreaks for gauze strips are at 45 and 70 boxes. The result is a total-cost curve with *steps* at the pricebreaks.

Note that even though each curve has a minimum, those points are not necessarily feasible. For example, the minimum point for the $1.40 curve in Figure 10–8 appears to be about 65 units. However, the price list shown in Table 10–2 indicates that an order size of 65 boxes will involve a unit price of $1.70. The actual total-cost curve is denoted by the solid lines; only those price/quantity combinations are feasible. The objective of the quantity-discount model is to identify an order quantity that will represent the lowest total cost for the entire set of curves.

There are two general cases: one in which carrying costs are constant (e.g., $2 per unit) and the other in which carrying costs are stated as a percentage of purchase price (e.g., 20 percent of unit price). When carrying costs are constant, there will be a single EOQ that is the same for all of the cost curves. Consequently, the total-cost curves line up vertically, with the only differing feature among the curves being that lower unit prices are reflected by lower total-cost curves. This is illustrated in Figure 10–9A. For purposes of illustration, the horizontal purchasing cost lines have been omitted.

When carrying costs are specified as a percentage of unit price, each curve will have a different EOQ. Since carrying costs are a percentage of price, lower prices will mean lower carrying costs and larger EOQs. Thus, as price decreases, each curve's EOQ will be to the right of the next higher curve's EOQ, as illustrated in Figure 10–9B.

The procedure for determining the overall EOQ differs slightly, depending on which of these two cases is relevant. For carrying costs that are constant, the procedure is:

1. Compute the common EOQ.
2. Only one of the curves will have the EOQ in its feasible range since the ranges do not overlap. Identify that curve.
   a. If the feasible EOQ is on the lowest price curve, that is the optimum order quantity.
   b. If the EOQ is on any other curve, compute the total cost for the EOQ and for the pricebreaks of all *lower* cost curves. Compare the total costs; the quantity (EOQ or pricebreak) that yields the lowest total cost is the optimum order quantity.

FIGURE 10–9

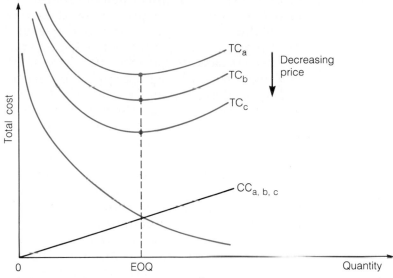

A. When carrying costs are constant, all curves
    have the same EOQ.

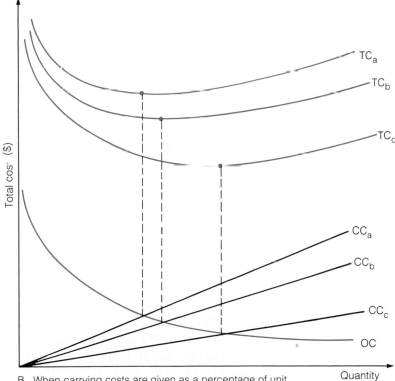

B. When carrying costs are given as a percentage of unit
    price, price decreases decrease carrying costs and
    that causes an increase in the EOQ.

EXAMPLE 5

The maintenance department of a large hospital uses 816 cases of liquid cleanser annually. Ordering costs are $12, carrying costs are $4 per case a year, and the new price schedule indicates that orders of less than 50 cases will cost $20 per case, 50 to 79 cases will cost $18 per case, 80 to 99 cases will cost $17 per case, and larger orders will cost $16 per case. Determine the optimum order quantity and the total cost.

Solution

(See Figure 10–10.)

FIGURE 10–10

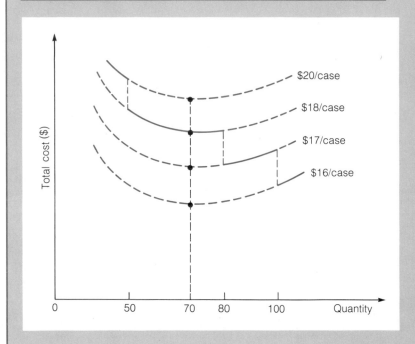

$D = 816$ cases per year
$S = \$12$
$H = \$4$ per case per year

Range	Price
0 to 49	$20
50 to 79	18
80 to 99	17
100 or more	16

a. Compute common EOQ: $Q_0 = \sqrt{\dfrac{2DS}{H}} = \sqrt{\dfrac{2(816)12}{4}} = 70$ cases.

EXAMPLE 5 *(concluded)*

b. The 70 cases can be bought at $18 per case since 70 falls in the range of 50 to 79 cases. The total cost to purchase 816 cases a year, at the rate of 70 cases per order, will be:

$$TC_{70} = \text{Carrying cost} + \text{Order cost} + \text{Purchase cost}$$
$$= (Q/2)H \qquad + (D/Q_0)S \quad + PD$$
$$= (70/2)4 \qquad + (816/70)12 + 18(816) = \$14{,}968$$

Since lower cost curves exist, each must be checked against the minimum cost generated by 70 cases at $18 each. In order to buy at $17 per case, at least 80 cases must be purchased. (Because the *TC* curve is rising, 80 cases will have the lowest *TC* for that curve's feasible region.) The total cost at 80 cases will be:

$$TC_{80} = (80/2)4 + (816/80)12 + 17(816) = \$14{,}154$$

To obtain a cost of $16 per case, at least 100 cases per order are required, and the total cost will be:

$$TC_{100} = (100/2)4 + (816/100)12 + 16(816) = \$13{,}354$$

Therefore, since 100 cases per order yields the lowest total cost, 100 cases is the overall optimum order quantity.

When carrying costs are expressed as a percentage of price, the procedure for determining the best purchase quantity is:

1. Beginning with the lowest price, compute the EOQs for each price range until a feasible EOQ is found (i.e., until an EOQ is found that falls in the quantity range for its price).
2. If the EOQ for the lowest price is feasible, it is the optimum order quantity. If the EOQ is not the lowest price range, compare the total cost at the pricebreak for all *lower* prices with the total cost of the feasible EOQ. The quantity that yields the lowest total cost is the optimum.

EXAMPLE 6

Surge Electric uses 4,000 toggle switches a year. Switches are priced as follows: 1 to 499, 90 cents each; 500 to 999, 85 cents each; and 1,000 or more are 82 cents each. It costs approximately $18 to prepare an order and receive it, and carrying costs are 18 percent of purchase price per unit on an annual basis. Determine the optimum order quantity and the total annual cost.

Solution

(See Figure 10–11.)

EXAMPLE 6 *(continued)*
FIGURE 10–11

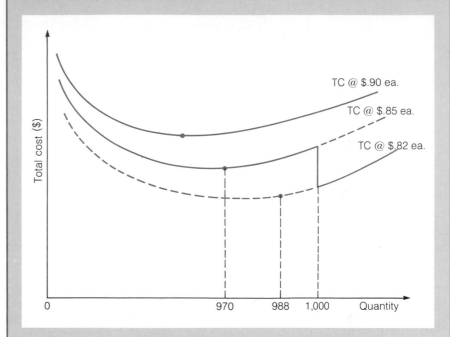

$D = 4,000$ switches per year
$S = \$18$
$H = 0.18P$

Range	Unit price	H
0 to 499	$0.90	0.18(0.90) = 0.1620
500 to 999	$0.85	0.18(0.85) = 0.1530
1,000 or more . . .	$0.82	0.18(0.82) = 0.1476

a. Find the EOQ for each price, starting with the lowest price, until a feasible EOQ is located.

$$EOQ_{0.82} = \sqrt{\frac{2DS}{H}} = \sqrt{\frac{2(4,000)18}{0.1476}} = 988 \text{ switches}$$

Since 988 switches will cost $0.85 each rather than $0.82 each, 988 is not a feasible EOQ. Next, try $0.85 per unit:

$$EOQ_{0.85} = \sqrt{\frac{2(4,000)18}{0.153}} = 970 \text{ switches}$$

This is feasible; 970 switches fall in the $0.85 range of 500 to 999.

EXAMPLE 6 *(concluded)*

b. Compute the TC for 970 and compare it to the total cost of the minimum quantity necessary to obtain a price of $0.82 per switch:

$$TC = \text{Carrying costs} \quad + \text{Ordering costs} + \text{Purchasing costs}$$

$$= \quad \left(\frac{Q}{2}\right)H \quad + \quad \left(\frac{D}{Q}\right)S \quad + \quad PD$$

$$TC_{970} = (970/2)(0.153) \quad + (4{,}000/970)18 \; + 0.85(4{,}000) = \$3{,}548$$

$$TC_{1{,}000} = (1{,}000/2)(0.1476) \; + (4{,}000/1{,}000)18 + 0.82(4{,}000) = \$3{,}426$$

Thus, the minimum-cost order size is 1,000 switches.

This completes our discussion of EOQ models.

WHEN TO REORDER

EOQ models answer the question of how much to order, but they do not address the question of when to order. The latter is the function of reorder-point models, which identify the *reorder point (ROP)* in terms of a *quantity:* the reorder point occurs when the quantity on hand drops to a prespecified amount. That amount generally includes expected demand during lead time and perhaps an extra cushion of stock, which serves to reduce the probability of experiencing a stock-out during lead time.

There are four determinants of the reorder point quantity:

1. The rate of demand.
2. The length of lead time.
3. The extent of demand and lead time variability.
4. The degree of stock-out risk acceptable to management.

We will consider reorder point models for these cases.

1. Constant demand rate, constant lead time.
2. Variable demand rate, constant lead time.
3. Constant demand rate, variable lead time.
4. Variable demand rate and variable lead time.

The following symbols are used in the various models:

Demand	*Lead time*
d = Constant demand rate	LT = Constant lead time
$\bar{d}$ = Average demand rate	$\overline{LT}$ = Average lead time
σ_d = Standard deviation of demand rate	σ_{LT} = Standard deviation of lead time

The models generally assume that any variability in either demand rate or lead time can be adequately described by a normal distribution. However, this is not a strict requirement—the models provide approximate reorder points even in cases where actual distributions depart substantially from normal.

The discussion begins with the simplest case (demand and lead time both constant) and proceeds to models that can be used when either demand or lead time, or both, are variable.

Constant Demand Rate and Constant Lead Time

When both the demand (usage) rate and lead time are constant, there is no risk of a stock-out created by increased demand or lead times longer than expected. In such a case the ROP is equal to the product of usage rate and lead time; no extra cushion of stock is needed.

EXAMPLE 7

Tingly takes Two-a-Day vitamins, which are delivered to his home by a routeman seven days after an order is called in. At what point should Tingly telephone his order in?

Solution

Usage = 2 vitamins per day
Lead time = 7 days

ROP = Usage × Lead time
= 2 Vitamins per day × 7 days = 14 vitamins

Thus, Tingly should reorder when 14 vitamin tablets are left.

Variable Demand Rates and/or Variable Lead Times

The concept of reorder points is easy to grasp when both demand rate and lead time are constant. In fact, this is the main reason for discussing that case, since under normal circumstances, one or the other of these, or both, tend to exhibit some variability. In order to discuss these more realistic cases, two additional concepts must be introduced: *safety stock* and *service level.*

Safety Stock

When there are variations in either the demand rate or the lead time, the possibility of stock-outs must be dealt with. Unlike the

case of constant demand and lead time, it is no longer completely certain how much stock will be needed to satisfy demand during lead time. Variations in the demand rate can result in a temporary surge in demand, which will drain inventory more quickly than expected, and variations in delivery times can lengthen the time a given supply must cover. In order to compensate for uncertainties in either demand rate or lead time, additional stock must be carried to reduce the risk of a stock-out during the lead-time interval. This buffer or *safety stock* is stock that is held in excess of expected demand. In essence, it is a form of insurance.

Figure 10–12 illustrates how safety stock can reduce the risk of a stock-out during lead time (LT). Note that stock-out protection is needed only during lead time. If there is a sudden surge at any point during the cycle, this will trigger another order, and once that order is received, the danger of an imminent stock-out is practically negligible.

In general, the ROP when variations exist in either usage or lead time is:

$$ROP = \frac{\text{Expected demand}}{\text{during lead time}} + \text{Safety stock} \qquad \textbf{(10–10)}$$

FIGURE 10–12

Safety Stock Reduces the Risk of a Stock-Out while Waiting for an Order to Be Delivered

---

EXAMPLE 8

Paul's Plant Place uses an average of 200 plastic bags per day, and lead time averages four days. Because both usage rate and lead time are variable, Paul carries a safety stock of 100 bags to lessen the chance of a stock-out. Determine the ROP.

Solution

$$ROP = \frac{\text{Expected demand}}{\text{during lead time}} + \text{Safety stock}$$
$$= 200 \text{ bags per day} \times 4 \text{ days} + 100 \text{ bags} = 900 \text{ bags}$$

Thus, reorder when existing stock equals 900 bags.[4]

Service Level

Because it costs money to hold safety stock, a manager must carefully weigh the cost of carrying safety stock against the reduction in stock-out risk it provides, since the service level increases as the risk of stock-out decreases. Order cycle *service level* can be defined as the probability that demand will not exceed supply during lead time (i.e., that the amount of stock on hand will be sufficient to meet demand). Hence, a service level of 95 percent implies a probability of 95 percent that demand will not exceed supply during lead time. An equivalent statement is that demand will be satisfied in 95 percent of such instances. It does *not* mean that 95 percent of demand will be satisfied. The risk of a stock-out is the complement of service level; a customer service level of 95 percent implies a stock-out risk of 5 percent. In general,

Service level = 100 percent − Stock-out risk

A bit later we will see how the order cycle service level relates to the *annual* service level.

The amount of safety stock that is appropriate for a given situation will depend on the following factors:

1. The average demand rate and average lead time.
2. Demand and lead time variabilities.
3. The desired service level.

For a given order cycle service level, the greater the variability in either demand rate or lead time, the greater the amount of safety stock that will be needed to achieve that service level. Similarly, for a given amount of variation in demand rate or lead time, achiev-

---

[4] This answer assumes that demand rates and lead times are independent. The same assumption underlies all of the ROP models described in this chapter.

ing an increase in the service level will require increasing the amount of safety stock. Selection of a service level may reflect stock-out costs (e.g., lost sales, customer dissatisfaction), or it might simply be a policy variable (e.g., the manager wants to achieve a specified service level for a certain item).

Variable Demand Rate, Constant Lead Time

This model assumes that demand during lead time is composed of a series of *independent* daily demands that can be described by a normal distribution. In order to use the model, it is necessary to know the average daily demand rate and its standard deviation. That information is then used to determine the expected demand and standard deviation of demand for the lead-time period.

Figure 10–13 illustrates daily rates that are normally distributed. In effect, each day's demand is analogous to a random draw from a normal distribution, and we want to estimate demand for the entire lead-time interval.

Expected demand is nothing more than the sum of average daily demand during lead time. Thus, if average daily demand is seven units per day, and if lead time is 10 days, then expected total demand during lead time is seven units per day times 10 days, or 70 units. This quantity will tend to be normally distributed and have a variance that is equal to the sum of the individual (daily) variances.[5] If the daily variance equals four (i.e., the daily standard deviation equals two), the sum of variances for lead time is $4 \times 10 = 40$. Then the standard deviation of the total demand is the square root of 40, which is 6.32. Note: this assumes that daily demands are independent.

For variable demand with constant lead time, the reorder point is:

$$ROP = \frac{\text{Expected demand}}{\text{during lead time}} + \frac{\text{Safety}}{\text{stock}} \qquad \text{(10–11)}$$
$$= \bar{d}LT + z\sqrt{LT}\,(\sigma_d)$$

where

$\bar{d}$ = Average demand rate
LT = Lead time
σ_d = Standard deviation of demand rate

Note that the standard deviation of *lead time* demand is $\sqrt{LT}\,(\sigma_d)$. Service level is equivalent to the probability that demand will not exceed the quantity on hand at the reorder point. For a normal distribution, this amounts to the area under the curve to the left of ROP, as shown in Figure 10–14.

---

[5] Variance = (Standard deviation)^2.

FIGURE 10–13

Total Demand during Lead Time Is Normally Distributed with a Mean Equal to the Sum of Daily Means and a Variance Equal to the Sum of Daily Variance

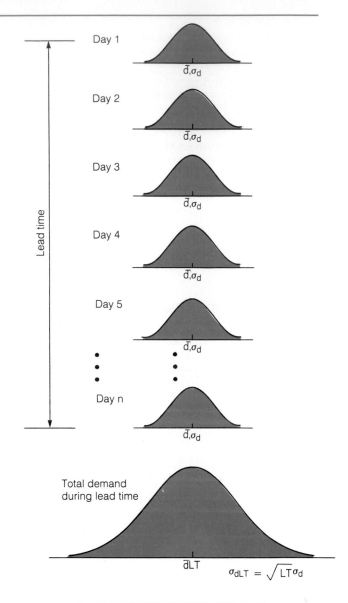

FIGURE 10–14

Service Level Is the Probability that Demand Will Not Exceed the ROP Amount

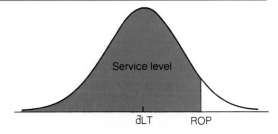

EXAMPLE 9

A pharmacy dispenses a generic drug at an average rate of 50 milligrams per day. An examination of pharmacy records suggest that daily demand is approximately normal and has a standard deviation of five milligrams per day. Lead time is four days, and the pharmacist wants a stock-out risk that does not exceed 1 percent.

1. Determine the ROP.
2. How much safety stock should be carried?
3. What service level would a reorder point of 215 mg provide?

Solution

$$\bar{d} = 50 \text{ mg per day}$$
$$\sigma_d = 5 \text{ mg per day}$$
$$LT = 4 \text{ days}$$

a. Service level = $100\% - \text{Risk} = 99\%$; $z = 2.33$ (Appendix Table B)

$$ROP = \bar{d}LT + z\sqrt{LT}\,(\sigma_d)$$
$$= 50(4) + 2.33\sqrt{4}(5) = 223.3 \text{ mg}$$

b. $SS = z\sqrt{LT}\,(\sigma_d) = 2.33\sqrt{4}(5) = 23.3 \text{ mg}$

c. $z = \dfrac{ROP - \text{Expected demand}}{\sqrt{LT}\,(\sigma_d)} = \dfrac{215 - 200}{\sqrt{4}(5)} = 1.5$

This equates to a service level of .9332 (from Appendix Table B).

EXAMPLE 10

Jack's Pizza Parlor uses 1,000 large cans of tomatoes a month at an average rate of 40 per day for each of the 25 days per month the parlor is open. Usage can be approximated by a normal distribution with a standard deviation of three cans per day. Lead time is constant

---

EXAMPLE 10 (concluded)

at four days. Monthly carrying costs are two cents per can, and ordering costs are $2.

1. Determine the economic order quantity.
2. For a service level of 99 percent, how many cans of tomatoes should Jack have on hand when he reorders?

Solution

a. (Ordinarily, demand and carrying costs will be in annual amounts. However, the fact that they are *both* expressed in monthly amounts is acceptable and will not affect the answer if left in those units.)

$$D = 1{,}000 \text{ cans per month} \quad S = \$2, \ H = \$0.02 \text{ per can per month}$$

$$Q_o = \sqrt{\frac{2DS}{H}} = \sqrt{\frac{2(1{,}000)2}{.02}} = 447 \text{ cans}$$

b. $\bar{d} = 40$ cans per day, $\sigma_d = 3$ cans per day, $LT = 4$ days

$$ROP = \bar{d}LT + z\sqrt{LT}\,(\sigma_d) = 40(4) + 2.33\sqrt{4}(3) = 174 \text{ cans}$$

Constant Demand Rate, Variable Lead Time

A variable lead time might assume any of a variety of patterns. For purposes of illustration, let's assume it can be described by a normal distribution. When lead time is normally distributed, the expected demand during lead time is normally distributed, but its variance does not encompass any summing of variances, as it did in the preceding model. The reason is that the actual lead time

FIGURE 10–15

With Constant Demand and Normally Distributed Lead Time, Total Usage during Lead Time Will Be Normally Distributed

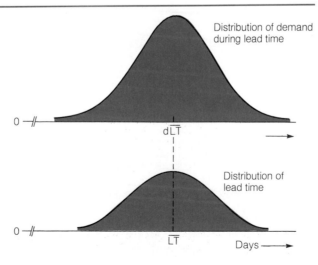

in any given cycle will be *one* number (e.g., two weeks) rather than a series of numbers (i.e., lead time demands).

In this case the expected demand during lead time is equal to $d\overline{LT}$, and the standard deviation of demand during lead time is equal to $d\sigma_{LT}$ (see Figure 10–15). The reorder point is:

$$ROP = d\overline{LT} + zd\,\sigma_{LT}, \qquad (10\text{–}12)$$

where

d = The (constant) demand rate
$\overline{LT}$ = Average lead time
σ_{LT} = Standard deviation of lead time

EXAMPLE 11

An automatic burner uses 2.1 gallons of oil per day. Lead time is normally distributed with a mean of six days and a standard deviation of two days. Determine the ROP to have a service level of 98 percent. How much of that quantity is safety stock?

Solution

$d = 2.1$ gallons per day, $\overline{LT} = 6$ days, $\sigma_{LT} = 2$ days

$$
\begin{aligned}
ROP &= d\overline{LT} + zd\,\sigma_{LT} \\
&= 2.1(6) + 2.055(2.1)2 \\
&= 12.6 + 8.63 = 21.23 \text{ gallons} \qquad \text{Safety stock} = 8.63 \text{ gallons}
\end{aligned}
$$

Variable Demand Rate and Variable Lead Time

When both the demand rate and lead time are variable, it seems reasonable that safety stock would be larger than if one of these were constant, in order to compensate for the increased variability.

In this case, expected demand during lead time is average daily demand multiplied by average lead time (in days).

If daily demand is normally distributed and if lead time is also normally distributed, then total demand during lead time will be normally distributed with a mean equal to $\bar{d}(\overline{LT})$. Its variance is actually the sum of the variances of demand and lead time, and the standard deviation is the square root of that sum:

$$\begin{array}{l}\text{Standard deviation of total} \\ \text{demand during lead time}\end{array} = \sqrt{\sigma^2_{demand} + \sigma^2_{lead\ time}} \qquad (10\text{--}13)$$

where

$$\sigma_{demand} = \sqrt{\overline{LT}}\ \sigma_d \quad \text{and} \quad \sigma_{lead\ time} = \bar{d}\,\sigma_{LT}$$

Hence,

$$\sigma_{dLT} = \sqrt{(\sqrt{\overline{LT}}\ \sigma_d)^2 + (\bar{d}\,\sigma_{LT})^2} = \sqrt{\overline{LT}\sigma^2_d + \bar{d}^2\sigma^2_{LT}}, \quad \text{and} \qquad (10\text{--}14)$$

$$ROP = \bar{d}(\overline{LT}) + z\sqrt{\overline{LT}\sigma^2_d + \bar{d}^2\sigma^2_{LT}} \qquad (10\text{--}15)$$

(Note that every variable under the square root sign is squared *except* $\overline{LT}$.)

EXAMPLE 12

Consumption of Mug Beer at a local tavern is known to be normally distributed with a mean of 150 bottles per day and a standard deviation of 10 bottles per day. Delivery time is also normally distributed with a mean of six days and a standard deviation of one day. How many bottles of Mug should be on hand at reorder time in order to be 90 percent sure of not running out before the delivery arrives?

Solution
$\bar{d} = 150$ bottles per day, $\quad \overline{LT} = 6$ days
$\sigma_d = 10$ bottles per day, $\quad \sigma_{LT} = 1$ day

$$ROP = \bar{d}(\overline{LT}) + z\sqrt{\overline{LT}\sigma^2_d + \bar{d}^2\sigma^2_{LT}}$$

$$= 150(6) + 1.28\sqrt{6(10)^2 + 150^2(1)^2}$$

$$= 900 \quad + 1.28\sqrt{23{,}100} = 1{,}095 \text{ bottles}$$

Shortages and Service Levels

The ROP computation does not reveal the expected *amount* of shortage for a given lead-time service level. The expected number of units short can, though, be very useful to a manager, sometimes even more useful than the service level figure. This quantity can easily be determined from the same information that is used to compute the ROP with one additional piece of information, which is contained in Table 10–3. Use of the table assumes that the distribution of lead-time demand can be adequately represented by a

TABLE 10–3

Normal Distribution Service Levels and Unit Normal Loss Function

z	Lead-time service level	$E(z)$	z	Lead-time service level	$E(z)$	z	Lead-time service level	$E(z)$	z	Lead-time service level	$E(z)$
−2.40	.0082	2.403	−0.80	.2119	.920	0.80	.7881	.120	2.40	.9918	.003
−2.36	.0091	2.363	−0.76	.2236	.889	0.84	.7995	.112	2.44	.9927	.002
−2.32	.0102	2.323	−0.72	.2358	.858	0.88	.8106	.104	2.48	.9934	.002
−2.28	.0113	2.284	−0.68	.2483	.828	0.92	.8212	.097	2.52	.9941	.002
−2.24	.0125	2.244	−0.64	.2611	.798	0.96	.8315	.089	2.56	.9948	.002
−2.20	.0139	2.205	−0.60	.2743	.769	1.00	.8413	.083	2.60	.9953	.001
−2.16	.0154	2.165	−0.56	.2877	.740	1.04	.8508	.077	2.64	.9959	.001
−2.12	.0170	2.126	−0.52	.3015	.712	1.08	.8599	.071	2.68	.9963	.001
−2.08	.0188	2.087	−0.48	.3156	.684	1.12	.8686	.066	2.72	.9967	.001
−2.04	.0207	2.048	−0.44	.3300	.657	1.16	.8770	.061	2.76	.9971	.001
−2.00	.0228	2.008	−0.40	.3446	.630	1.20	.8849	.056	2.80	.9974	.0008
−1.96	.0250	1.969	−0.36	.3594	.597	1.24	.8925	.052	2.84	.9977	.0007
−1.92	.0274	1.930	−0.32	.3745	.576	1.28	.8997	.048	2.88	.9980	.0006
−1.88	.0301	1.892	−0.28	.3897	.555	1.32	.9066	.044	2.92	.9982	.0005
−1.84	.0329	1.853	−0.24	.4052	.530	1.36	.9131	.040	2.96	.9985	.0004
−1.80	.0359	1.814	−0.20	.4207	.507	1.40	.9192	.037	3.00	.9987	.0004
−1.76	.0392	1.776	−0.16	.4364	.484	1.44	.9251	.034	3.04	.9988	.0003
−1.72	.0427	1.737	−0.12	.4522	.462	1.48	.9306	.031	3.08	.9990	.0003
−1.68	.0465	1.699	−0.08	.4681	.440	1.52	.9357	.028	3.12	.9991	.0002
−1.64	.0505	1.661	−0.04	.4840	.419	1.56	.9406	.026	3.16	.9992	.0002
−1.60	.0548	1.623	0.00	.5000	.399	1.60	.9452	.023	3.20	.9993	.0002
−1.56	.0594	1.586	0.04	.5160	.379	1.64	.9495	.021	3.24	.9994	.0001
−1.52	.0643	1.548	0.08	.5319	.360	1.68	.9535	.019	3.28	.9995	.0001
−1.48	.0694	1.511	0.12	.5478	.342	1.72	.9573	.017	3.32	.9995	.0001
−1.44	.0749	1.474	0.16	.5636	.324	1.76	.9608	.016	3.36	.9996	.0001
−1.40	.0808	1.437	0.20	.5793	.307	1.80	.9641	.014	3.40	.9997	.0001
−1.36	.0869	1.400	0.24	.5948	.290	1.84	.9671	.013			
−1.32	.0934	1.364	0.28	.6103	.275	1.88	.9699	.012			
−1.28	.1003	1.328	0.32	.6255	.256	1.92	.9726	.010			
−1.24	.1075	1.292	0.36	.6406	.237	1.96	.9750	.009			
−1.20	.1151	1.256	0.40	.6554	.230	2.00	.9772	.008			
−1.16	.1230	1.221	0.44	.6700	.217	2.04	.9793	.008			
−1.12	.1314	1.186	0.48	.6844	.204	2.08	.9812	.007			
−1.08	.1401	1.151	0.52	.6985	.192	2.12	.9830	.006			
−1.04	.1492	1.117	0.56	.7123	.180	2.16	.9846	.005			
−1.00	.1587	1.083	0.60	.7257	.169	2.20	.9861	.005			
−0.96	.1685	1.049	0.64	.7389	.158	2.24	.9875	.004			
−0.92	.1788	1.017	0.68	.7517	.148	2.28	.9887	.004			
−0.88	.1894	.984	0.72	.7642	.138	2.32	.9898	.003			
−0.84	.2005	.952	0.76	.7764	.129	2.36	.9909	.003			

normal distribution. If it can, the expected number of units short in each order cycle is given by this formula:

$$E(n) = E(z)\,\sigma_{dLT} \tag{10–16}$$

where $E(n)$ = the expected number of units short per order cycle
$E(z)$ = the standardized number of units short listed in Table 10–3
σ_{dLT} = the standard deviation of lead-time demand

EXAMPLE 13

The standard deviation of lead-time demand is known to be 16 units. Lead-time demand is approximately normal.

a. For a lead-time service level of 90 percent, determine the expected number of units short for any order cycle.
b. What lead-time service level would an expected shortage of 2 units imply?

Solution

$\sigma_{dLT} = 16$ units

a. Lead-time (cycle) service level = .90. From Table 10–3, E(z) = .048. Using formula 10–16, E(n) = .048 (16 units) = .768 unit.
b. For the case where E(n) = 2, we must solve for E(z) and then use Table 10–3 to determine the lead-time service level that implies. Thus, E(n) = E(z) σ_{dLT}, so E(z) = E(n)/σ_{dLT} = 2/16 = .125. From Table 10–3, this implies a service level of approximately 78 percent (interpolating).

The expected number of units short is just that—an expected or *average* amount; the exact number of units short in any given cycle will be an amount close to that. Moreover, if discrete items are involved, the number of units short in any cycle must be an integer.

Having determined the expected number of units short for an order cycle, we can now determine the expected number of units short per year. It is simply the product of the expected number of units short per cycle and the number of cycles (orders) per year. Thus,

$$E(N) = E(n)\frac{D}{Q} \tag{10–17}$$

where E(N) = the expected number of units short per year.

EXAMPLE 14

Given the following information:
$D = 1,000$, $Q = 250$, and $E(n) = 2.5$, determine the expected number of units short per year.

Solution

using the formula $E(N) = E(n)\dfrac{D}{Q}$

$$E(N) = 2.5\left(\frac{1000}{250}\right) = 10.0 \text{ units per year.}$$

It is sometimes convenient to think of service level in annual terms. For instance, one definition of annual service level is the percentage of demand filled directly from inventory. Thus, if $D = 1,000$ and 990 units were filled directly from inventory (shortages totaling 10 units over the year were recorded), the annual service level would be $990/1,000 = 99$ percent. Annual service level is related to, but generally more than, lead-time service level. The two service levels can be related using the following formula:

$$E(N) = (1 - SL_{annual})D \qquad\qquad (10\text{--}18)$$

Using formulas 10–17 and 10–16, $E(N) = E(n)\dfrac{D}{Q} = E(z)\ \sigma_{dLT}\dfrac{D}{Q}$. Thus,

$$(1 - SL_{annual})D = E(z)\,\sigma_{dLT}\frac{D}{Q}. \qquad\qquad (10\text{--}19)$$

EXAMPLE 15

Given a lead-time service level of .90, $D = 1,000$, $Q = 250$, and $\sigma_{dLT} = 16$, determine the annual service level.

Solution

From Table 10–3, $E(z) = .048$ for a 90 percent lead-time service level. Using Formula 10–19 we find:

$$(1 - SL_{annual})(1,000) = .048(16)\left(\frac{1,000}{250}\right)$$

$$= 3.072.$$

Solving for the annual service level yields

$$SL_{annual} = 1 - \frac{3.072}{1,000} = .997.$$

Note that in the preceding example a lead-time service level of 90 percent provided an annual service level of 99.7 percent. Naturally, different values of D, Q, and σ_{dLT} will tend to produce different results for a cycle service level of 90 percent. Nonetheless, in general the annual service level will be greater than the cycle service level. In addition, since the annual service level as we have defined it relates to the percentage of units short per year, it may make sense to base cycle service levels on a specified annual service level. This would mean setting the annual level and then using Formula 10–19 to solve for $E(z)$ and then using that value to obtain the service level for the order cycles.

HOW MUCH TO ORDER: FIXED-ORDER-INTERVAL MODEL

When inventory replenishment is based on EOQ/ROP models, *fixed quantities* of items are ordered at varying time intervals. Just the opposite occurs under the *fixed-order-interval (FOI)* model: Orders for *varying quantities* are placed at fixed time intervals (weekly, every 20 days, etc.).

There are a number of differences between these two approaches to reordering. For instance, both are sensitive to demand experience just prior to reordering, but in somewhat different ways. In the fixed-quantity model, a higher than normal demand causes a *shorter time* between orders, while in the fixed-interval model, the result would be a *larger order size*. Another difference is that the fixed-quantity model requires close monitoring of inventory levels in order to know *when* the amount on hand has reached the reorder point, while the fixed-interval model requires only a periodic review (i.e., physical inspection) of inventory levels just prior to placing an order to determine *how much* is needed.

Reasons for Using   Under certain conditions, the use of fixed-order intervals is quite practical. In some cases a supplier's policy might encourage orders at fixed intervals. Even if that is not the case, grouping orders for items from the same supplier can produce savings in shipping costs. Furthermore, some situations do not readily lend themselves to continuous monitoring of inventory levels. Many retail operations (e.g., drugstores, small grocery stores) fall into this category. The alternative for them is to use fixed-order intervals, which require only periodic checks of inventory levels.

Determining the Amount to Order   If the demand rate and lead time are both constant, the fixed-interval model and the fixed-order-quantity model function identically. The differences in the two models become apparent only when examined under conditions of variability. As in the ROP model, there can be variations in demand only, lead time only, or variations in both demand and lead time. However, for the sake of simplicity, and because it is perhaps the most frequently encountered situation, the discussion here will *focus on only variable demand and constant lead time.*

Figure 10–16 provides a comparison of the fixed-quantity and fixed-interval systems. Notice that in the fixed-quantity arrangement orders are triggered by a *quantity* (ROP), while in the fixed-interval arrangement, orders are triggered by a *time*. Because of this, the fixed-interval system must have stock-out protection for lead time plus the next order cycle, but the fixed-quantity system needs protection only during lead time since additional orders can be placed at any time and will be received shortly (lead time) there-

FIGURE 10–16

Comparison of Fixed-Quantity and Fixed-Interval Ordering

A. Reordering fixed quantities

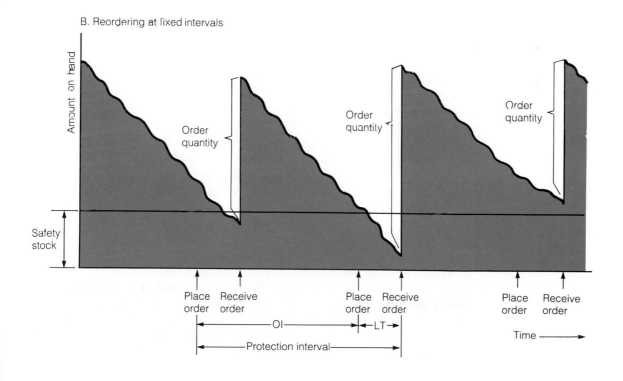

B. Reordering at fixed intervals

after. Consequently, there is a greater need for safety stock in the fixed-interval model than there is in the fixed-quantity model. Note, for example, the large dip into safety stock during the second order cycle with the fixed-interval model.

Order size in the fixed-interval model is determined by the following computation:

$$(10\text{--}20)$$

$$\begin{array}{ccccc} \text{Amount} \\ \text{to order} \end{array} = \begin{array}{c} \text{Expected demand} \\ \text{during protection} \\ \text{interval} \end{array} + \begin{array}{c} \text{Safety} \\ \text{stock} \end{array} - \begin{array}{c} \text{Amount on hand} \\ \text{at reorder time} \end{array}$$

$$= \quad \bar{d}(OI + LT) \quad + z\,\sigma_d\sqrt{OI + LT} \; - \qquad A$$

where

$OI =$ Length of time between orders
$A =$ Amount on hand at reorder time

(As in previous models, it is assumed that demand during the protection interval is normally distributed.)

EXAMPLE 16

Given the following information, determine the amount to order:

$\bar{d} = 30$ units per day,   Desired service level $= 99\%$
$\sigma_d = \;3$ units per day,   Amount on hand at reorder time $= 71$ units
$LT = \;2$ days, $OI = 7$ days between orders.

Solution

$z = 2.33$ for 99 percent service level

$$\begin{array}{c} \text{Amount} \\ \text{to order} \end{array} = \bar{d}(OI + LT) + z\,\sigma_d\sqrt{OI + LT} - A$$

$$= \;\; 30(7 + 2) \;\; + 2.33(3)\sqrt{7 + 2} - 71 = 220 \text{ units.}$$

Benefits and Disadvantages

The fixed-interval system results in the tight control needed for A items in an A–B–C classification due to the periodic reviews it requires. In addition, when two or more items come from the same supplier, grouping orders can yield savings in ordering, packing, and shipping costs. Moreover, it may be the only practical approach if inventory withdrawals cannot be closely monitored.

On the negative side, the fixed-interval system necessitates a larger amount of safety stock for a given risk of stock-out due to the need to protect against shortages during an entire order interval plus lead time (instead of lead time only), and this increases the carrying cost. Also, there are the costs of the periodic reviews.

HOW MUCH TO ORDER: SINGLE-PERIOD MODEL

This model is used to handle ordering of perishables (such things as fresh fruits and vegetables, seafood, and cut flowers) as well as items that have a limited useful life (such as newspapers and magazines). The thing that sets these items apart from those previously discussed is that unsold or unused items are not typically carried over from one period to the next, at least not without penalty. Day-old baked goods, for instance, are often sold at reduced prices, leftover seafood may be discarded, and out-of-date magazines may be offered to used book stores at bargain rates. At times there may even be some cost associated with disposal of leftover goods. We can also include in the single-period category spare parts for specialized equipment. The *period* in such cases is the life of the equipment, assuming that the parts cannot be used for other equipment.

Analysis of single-period situations generally focuses on two costs: shortage and excess. Shortage cost may include a charge for loss of customer goodwill as well as the opportunity cost of lost sales. Generally, *shortage cost* is unrealized profit per unit. That is,

$$C_{shortage} = C_s = \text{Revenue per unit} - \text{Cost per unit}$$

If a shortage or stock-out relates to an item used in production or a spare part for a machine, then *shortage cost refers to the actual cost of lost production.*

Excess cost pertains to items left over at the end of the period. In effect, excess cost is the difference between purchase cost and salvage value. That is,

$$C_{excess} = C_e = \text{Original cost per unit} - \text{Salvage value per unit}$$

Note that if there is cost associated with disposing of excess items, the salvage will be negative and therefore increase the excess cost per unit.

The goal of the single-period model is to identify the order quantity, or stocking level, that will minimize the long-run excess and shortage costs.

There are two general categories of problems that we will consider: those for which demand can be approximated using a continuous distribution (perhaps a theoretical one such as a uniform or normal distribution) and those for which demand can be approximated using a discrete distribution (say, historical frequencies, or else a theoretical distribution such as the Poisson). The kind of

inventory in question can give an indication of which type of model might be appropriate. For example, demand for petroleum, liquids, and gases would tend to vary over some *continuous scale,* thus lending itself to description by a continuous distribution. Demand for houses, cars, and typewriters is expressed in terms of *number of units* demanded and lends itself to description by a discrete distribution.

Continuous Stocking Levels

The concept of identifying an optimum stocking level is perhaps easiest to visualize when demand is *uniform.* Choosing the stocking level is quite similar to balancing a seesaw, but instead of having a person on each end of the seesaw, we have excess cost per unit, C_e, on one end of the distribution and shortage cost per unit, C_s, on the other. The optimum stocking level is analogous to the fulcrum of the seesaw; the stocking level equalizes the cost weights, as illustrated in Figure 10–17.

The *service level* is the *probability* that demand will not exceed the stocking level, and computation of the service level is the key to determining the optimum stocking level. Service level is:

$$\text{Service level} = \frac{C_s}{C_s + C_e} \tag{10-21}$$

where

C_s = Shortage cost per unit
C_e = Excess cost per unit

If actual demand exceeds S_o, there is a shortage; hence, C_s is on the right end of the distribution. Similarly, if demand is less than S_o, there is an excess, so C_e is on the left end of the distribution. When $C_e = C_s$, the optimum stocking level is halfway between the end points of the distribution. If one cost is greater than the other, S_o tends to be closer to the *larger* cost.

FIGURE 10–17

The Optimum Stocking Level Balances Unit Shortage and Excess Costs

EXAMPLE 17

Sweet cider is delivered weekly to Pappy's Produce Stand. Demand varies uniformly between 300 liters per week and 500 liters per week. Pappy says 20 cents per liter for the cider and charges 80 cents per liter for it. Unsold cider has no salvage value and cannot be carried over into the next week due to spoilage. Find the optimum stocking level and its stock-out risk for that quantity.

Solution

$$C_e = \text{Cost per unit} - \text{Salvage value per unit}$$
$$= \$0.20 \qquad\qquad - \$0$$
$$= \$0.20 \text{ per unit}$$

$$C_s = \text{revenue per unit} - \text{cost per unit}$$
$$= \$0.80 \qquad\qquad - \$0.20$$
$$= \$0.60 \text{ per unit}$$

$$SL = \frac{C_s}{C_s + C_e} = \frac{\$0.60}{\$0.60 + \$0.20} = 0.75$$

Thus, the optimum stocking level must satisfy demand 75 percent of the time. For the uniform distribution, this will be at a point equal to the minimum demand plus 75 percent of the difference between maximum and minimum demand:

$$S_o = 300 + 0.75(500 - 300) = 450 \text{ liters}$$

The stock-out risk is $1.00 - SL = 1.00 - .75 = .25$.

A similar approach applies if demand is normally distributed.

EXAMPLE 18

Pappy's Stand also sells a blend of cherry juice and apple cider. Demand for the blend is approximately normal with a mean of 200 liters per week and a standard deviation of 10 liters per week. $C_s =$ 60 cents per liter and $C_e = 20$ cents per liter. Find the optimum stocking level for the apple-cherry blend.

Solution

$$SL = \frac{C_s}{C_s + C_e} = \frac{\$0.60}{\$0.60 + \$0.20} = 0.75$$

EXAMPLE 18 (concluded)

This indicates that 75 percent of the area under the normal curve must be to the left of the stocking level. From Appendix, Table B we see that a value of z between +.67 and +.68, say +.675, will satisfy this. Thus,

$$S_o = 200 \text{ liters} + .675 \ (10 \text{ liters}) = 206.75 \text{ liters}$$

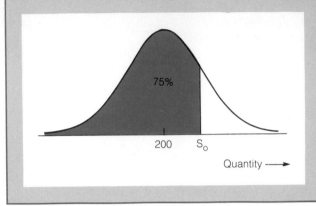

Discrete Stocking Levels

When stocking levels are discrete rather than continuous, the service level computed using the ratio $C_s/(C_s + C_e)$ usually does not coincide with a feasible stocking level (e.g., the optimum amount may be between, say, five and six units). The solution is to stock at the next highest level (e.g., six units). In other words, choose

FIGURE 10–18

The Service Level Achieved Must Equal or Exceed the Ratio
$$\frac{C_s}{C_s + C_e}$$

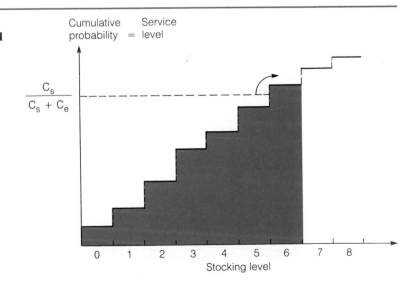

the stocking level so that the desired service level is equaled or *exceeded.* This concept is illustrated in Figure 10–18.

EXAMPLE 19

Historical records on the usage of spare parts for several large hyraulic presses are to be used as an estimate of usage for spares of a newly installed press. Stock-out costs involve downtime expenses and special ordering costs. These average $4,200 per unit short. Spares cost $800 each, and unused parts have zero salvage. Determine the optimum stocking level.

Number of spares used	Relative frequency	Cumulative frequency
0	0.20	0.20
1	0.40	0.60
2	0.30	0.90
3	0.10	1.00
4 or more	0.00	
	1.00	

Solution

$C_s = \$4,200$, $C_e = \$800$

$$SL = \frac{C_s}{C_e + C_s} = \frac{\$4,200}{\$800 + \$4,200} = 0.84$$

The cumulative frequency column indicates the percentage of time that demand did not exceed (was equal to or less than) some amount. For example, demand does not exceed one spare 60 percent of the time, or two spares 90 percent of the time. Thus, in order to achieve a service level of *at least* 84 percent, it is necessary to stock two spares (i.e., to go to the next highest stocking level).

EXAMPLE 20

Demand for long-stemmed red roses at a small flower shop can be approximated using a Poisson distribution that has a mean of four dozen per day. Profit on the roses is $3 per dozen. Leftover flowers are marked down and sold the next day at a loss of $2 per dozen. Assume that all marked-down flowers are sold. What is the optimum stocking level?

Solution

$$C_s = \$3, \ C_e = \$2, \quad SL = \frac{C_s}{C_s + C_e} = \frac{\$3}{\$3 + \$2} = 0.60$$

Obtain the cumulative frequencies from the Poisson table (Table C in the Appendix) for a mean of 4.0:

> ### EXAMPLE 20 *(concluded)*
>
> | Demand *(dozen per day)* | Cumulative *frequency* |
> |---|---|
> | 0 | .018 |
> | 1 | .092 |
> | 2 | .238 |
> | 3 | .434 |
> | 4 | .629 |
> | 5 | .785 |
> | ⋮ | ⋮ |
>
> Compare the service level to the cumulative frequencies. Stock four dozen in order to attain a service level that exceeds 0.60.

One final point about discrete stocking levels: If the computed service level *exactly* equal to the cumulative probability associated with one of the stocking levels, there are two equivalent stocking levels in terms of minimizing long-run cost, the one with equal probability and the next higher one. For instance, in the preceding example, if the ratio had been equal to .629, we would be indifferent between stocking four and stocking five dozen roses each day.

SUMMARY

Good inventory management is often the mark of a well-run organization. Inventory levels must be planned carefully in order to balance the cost of holding inventory and the cost of providing reasonable levels of customer service. Successful inventory management requires a system to keep track of inventory transactions, accurate information about demand and lead times, realistic estimates of certain inventory-related costs, and a priority system for classifying the items in inventory and allocating control efforts.

The models described in this chapter are relevant for instances where demand for inventory items is *independent*. Four classes of models are described: EOQ, ROP, fixed interval, and single-period. The first three types are appropriate if unused items can be carried over into subsequent periods, and the single-period model is appropriate when items cannot be carried over. EOQ models address the question of *how much* to order. The ROP models address the question of *when to order* and are particularly helpful in dealing with situations that include variations in either usage rates or lead times. ROP models involve service-level and safety-stock

TABLE 10–4

Summary of Inventory Formulas

Model	Formula	Symbols
1. *Basic EOQ*	$Q_o = \sqrt{\dfrac{2DS}{H}}$ (10–2) $TC = \dfrac{Q}{2}H + \dfrac{D}{Q}S$ (10–1)	Q_o = Economic order quantity D = Annual demand S = Order cost H = Annual carrying cost per unit
2. Economic run size	$Q_o = \sqrt{\dfrac{2DS}{H}}\sqrt{\dfrac{p}{p-u}}$ (10–5) $I_m = \sqrt{\dfrac{2DS}{H}}\sqrt{\dfrac{p-u}{p}}$ (10–6) $TC = \dfrac{I_m}{2}H + \dfrac{D}{Q}S$ (10–4)	Q_o = Optimum run size p = Production or delivery rate u = Usage or demand rate I_m = Maximum inventory level

3. Reorder point under
   a. Constant demand and lead time
 	
   b. Variable demand rate
 	
   c. Variable lead time
 	
   d. Variable lead time and demand
	$ROP = d(LT)$
	
	 $ROP = \bar{d}LT + z\sqrt{LT}(\sigma_d)$ (10–11)
	
	 $ROP = d\overline{LT} + zd(\sigma_{LT})$ (10–12)
	
	 $ROP = \bar{d}\overline{LT} + z\sqrt{\overline{LT}\sigma_d^2 + \bar{d}^2\sigma_{LT}^2}$ (10–15)
		ROP = Quantity on hand at reorder point
		 d = Demand rate
		 LT = Lead time
		 $\bar{d}$ = Average usage rate
		 σ_d = Standard deviation of demand rate
		 z = Standard normal deviation
		 $\overline{LT}$ = Average lead time
		 σ_{LT} = Standard deviation of lead time

4. ROP shortages
   a. Units short per cycle
 	
   b. Units short per year
 	
   c. Annual service level
	$E(n) = E(z)\sigma_{dLT}$ (10–16)
	
	 $E(N) = E(n)\dfrac{D}{Q}$ (10–17)
	
	 $(1 - SL_{annual})D = E(z)\sigma_{dLT}\dfrac{D}{Q}$ (10–19)
		$E(n)$ = Expected no. short per cycle
		 $E(z)$ = Standardized number short
		 σ_{dLT} = Std. deviation of lead-time demand
		 $E(N)$ = Expected no. short per year
		 SL_{annual} = Annual service level

5. Fixed interval	$Q = \bar{d}(OI + LT) + z\sigma_d\sqrt{OI + LT} - A$ (10–20)	OI = Time between orders A = Amount on hand at order time
6. Single period	$SL = \dfrac{C_s}{C_s + C_e}$ (10–21)	C_s = Cost of shortage per unit C_e = Cost of excess per unit SL = Service level

considerations. When the time between orders is fixed, the order-interval model is useful. The single-period model identifies a period stocking level that will balance the expected costs of shortage and excess resulting from variations in demand. The models presented in this chapter are summarized in Table 10–4.

SOLVED PROBLEMS

1. *Basic EOQ.* A toy manufacturer uses approximately 32,000 silicon chips annually. The chips are used at a steady rate during the 240 days the plant operates. Annual holding cost is 60 cents per chip, and ordering cost is $24. Determine:
   a. The optimum order size.
   b. The number of workdays in an order cycle.

   ## Solution

   $D = 32,000$ chips per year
   $S = \$24$
   $H = \$.60$ per unit per year

   a. $Q_o = \sqrt{\dfrac{2DS}{H}} = \sqrt{\dfrac{2(32,000)\$24}{\$.60}} = 1,600$ chips.

   b. $\dfrac{Q_o}{D} = \dfrac{1,600 \text{ chips}}{32,000 \text{ chips/yr}} = \dfrac{1}{20}$ year (i.e., $\dfrac{1}{20} \times 240$ days) or 12 days.

2. *Economic production run size.* The Dine Corporation is both a producer and user of brass couplings. The firm operates 220 days a year and uses the couplings at a steady rate of 50 per day. Couplings can be produced at a rate of 200 per day. Annual storage costs are $1 per coupling, and machine setup costs are $35 per run.
   a. Determine the economic run size.
   b. Approximately how many runs per year will there be?
   c. Compute the maximum inventory level.
   d. Determine the length of the *pure consumption* portion of the cycle.

   ## Solution

   $D = 50$ units per day $\times 220$ days per year $= 11,000$ units per year
   $S = \$35$
   $H = \$1$ per unit per year
   $p = 200$ units per day
   $u = 50$ units per day

   a. $Q_o = \sqrt{\dfrac{2DS}{H}} \sqrt{\dfrac{p}{p-u}} = \sqrt{\dfrac{2(11,000)35}{1}} \sqrt{\dfrac{200}{200-50}} = 1,013$ units.

   b. Number of runs per year: $D/Q_o = 11,000/1,013 = 10.86$, or 11.

   c. $I_{max} = \sqrt{\dfrac{2DS}{H}} \sqrt{\dfrac{p-u}{p}} = \sqrt{\dfrac{2(11,000)35}{1}} \sqrt{\dfrac{200-50}{200}}$
   $= 759.93$ or 760 units.

   d. Length of cycle $= \dfrac{Q_o}{u} = \dfrac{1,013 \text{ units}}{50 \text{ units per day}} = 20.26$ days.

$$\text{Length of run} = \frac{Q_o}{p} = \frac{1,013 \text{ units}}{200 \text{ units per day}} = 5.065 \text{ days.}$$

$$\begin{array}{c}\text{Length of pure} \\ \text{consumption portion}\end{array} = \text{Length of cycle} - \text{Length of run}$$

$$= 20.26 - 5.065 = 15.20 \text{ days.}$$

3. *Quantity discounts.* A small manufacturing firm uses roughly 3,400 pounds of a chemical dye a year. Currently the firm purchases 300 pounds per order and pays $3 per pound. The supplier has just announced that orders of 1,000 pounds or more will be filled at a price of $2 per pound. The manufacturing firm incurs a cost of $100 each time it submits an order and assigns an annual holding cost of 17 percent of the purchase price per pound.
    a. Determine the order size that will minimize total cost.
    b. If the supplier offered the discount at 1,500 pounds instead of at 1,000 pounds, what order size would minimize total cost?

Solution

$D = 3,400$ pounds per year
$S = \$100$
$H = 17\% P$

a. Compute the EOQ for $2 per pound:

$$Q_{\$2 \text{ per pound}} = \sqrt{\frac{2DS}{H}} = \sqrt{\frac{2(3,400)100}{0.17(2)}} = 1,414 \text{ lb.}$$

Since this quantity is feasible at $2 per pound, it is the optimum.

b. When the discount is offered at 1,500 lb., the EOQ for the $2-per-pound curve is no longer feasible. Consequently, it becomes necessary to compute the EOQ for $3 per pound and compare the total cost for that order size with the total cost using the pricebreak quantity (i.e., 1,500).

$$Q_{\$3 \text{ per pound}} = \sqrt{\frac{2DH}{H}} = \sqrt{\frac{2(3,400)100}{0.17(3)}} = 1,155 \text{ lb.}$$

$$TC = \left(\frac{Q}{2}\right)H \quad + \quad \left(\frac{D}{Q}\right)S \quad + \quad PD$$

$$TC_{1,155} = \left(\frac{1,155}{2}\right)0.17(3) + \left(\frac{3,400}{1,155}\right)100 + 3(3,400)$$

$$= \quad \$294.53 \quad + \quad \$294.37 \quad + \$10,200 = \$10,789$$

$$TC_{1,500} = \left(\frac{1,500}{2}\right)0.17(2) + \left(\frac{3,400}{1,500}\right)100 + 2(3,400)$$

$$= \quad \$255 \quad + \quad \$226.67 \quad + \$6,800 = \$7,282$$

Hence, because it would result in a lower total cost, 1,500 is the optimum order size.

4. *ROP for variable demand and constant lead time.* The housekeeping department of a motel uses approximately 400 washcloths per day. The actual amount tends to vary with the number of customers who stay on any given night. Usage can be approximated by a normal distribution that has a mean of 400 and a standard deviation of nine washcloths per day. A linen supply company delivers towels and washcloths every third day. If the motel policy is to maintain a stock-out risk of 2 percent, what is the minimum number of washcloths that must be on hand at reorder time, and how much of that amount can be considered safety stock?

Solution

$$\bar{d} = 400 \text{ washcloths per day} \qquad LT = 3 \text{ days}$$
$$\sigma_d = \quad 9 \text{ washcloths per day} \qquad \text{Risk} = 2\%, \text{ so service level} = 98\%$$

From Appendix Table B, the z value that corresponds to an area under the normal curve to the left of z for 98 percent is about $+2.055$.

$$ROP = \bar{d}LT + z\sqrt{LT}\,\sigma_d = 400(3) + 2.055\sqrt{3}\,(9)$$
$$= 1,200 + 32.03, \text{ or approximately } 1,232$$

Safety stock is approximately 32 washcloths.

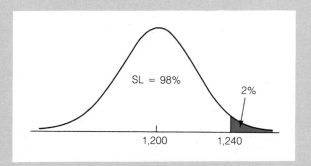

5. *ROP for constant demand and variable lead time.* The motel in the preceding example uses approximately 600 bars of soap each day, and this tends not to vary by more than a few bars either way. Lead time for soap delivery is normally distributed with a mean of six days and a standard deviation of two days. A service level of 90 percent is desired. Find the ROP.

    Solution

    $$d = 600 \text{ bars per day}$$
    $$SL = 90\%, \text{ so } z = +1.28 \text{ (from Appendix Table B)}$$
    $$\overline{LT} = 6 \text{ days}$$
    $$\sigma_{LT} = 2 \text{ days}$$

    $$ROP = d\overline{LT} + z\,d\,(\sigma_{LT})$$
    $$= 600(6) + 1.28(600)2$$
    $$= 5{,}136 \text{ bars of soap}$$

6. *ROP for variable demand rate and variable lead time.* The motel replaces broken glasses at the rate of 25 per day. In the past this quantity has tended to vary normally and have a standard deviation of three glasses per day. Glasses are ordered from a Cleveland supplier. Lead time is normally distributed with an average of 10 days and a standard deviation of two days. What ROP should be used to achieve a service level of 95 percent?

    Solution

    $$\overline{d} = 25 \text{ glasses per day} \qquad \overline{LT} = 10 \text{ days}$$
    $$\sigma_d = 3 \text{ glasses per day} \qquad \sigma_{LT} = 2 \text{ days}$$
    $$SL = 95\%, \text{ so } z = +1.65 \text{ (Appendix Table B)}$$
    $$ROP = \overline{d}\,\overline{LT} + z\sqrt{\overline{LT}\sigma_d^2 + \overline{d}\,\sigma_{LT}^2}$$
    $$= 25(10) + 1.65\sqrt{10(3)^2 + (25)^2(2)^2}$$
    $$= 334 \text{ glasses}$$

7. *Shortages and service levels.* The manager of a store that sells office supplies has decided to set an annual service level of 96 percent for a certain model of telephone answering equipment. The store sells approximately 300 of this model a year. Holding cost is $5 per unit annually, ordering cost is $25, and $\sigma_{dLT} = 7$.

   a. What average number of units short per year will be consistent with the specified annual service level?

   b. What average number of units short per order cycle will provide the desired annual service level?

   c. What lead-time service level is necessary for the 96 percent annual service level?

Solution

$$SL_{annual} = 96\%, D = 300 \text{ units}, H = \$5, S = \$25, \sigma_{dLT} = 7$$

a. $E(N) = (1 - SL_{annual})D = (1 - .96)(300) = 12 \text{ units.}$

b. $E(N) = E(n)\dfrac{D}{Q}.$ Solving for $E(n)$ we have

$$E(n) = E(N)/\left(\frac{D}{Q}\right) = 12/\left(\frac{300}{Q}\right).$$

$$Q = \sqrt{\frac{2DS}{H}} = \sqrt{\frac{2(300)(25)}{5}} = 54.77 \text{ (round to 55).}$$

Then $E(n) = 12/\left(\dfrac{300}{55}\right) = 2.2.$

c. In order to find the lead-time service level, the value of $E(z)$ is needed. Since we know the value of $E(n)$ is 2.2 and that $E(n) = E(z)\sigma_{dLT}$, we have $2.2 = E(z)(7)$. Solving for $E(z)$ gives us $E(z) = 2.2/7 = .314$. Interpolating in Table 10–3 gives us the approximate lead-time service level. Thus, $\dfrac{.307 - .314}{.307 \quad .324} = \dfrac{.5793 - x}{.5793 - .5636}.$ Solving, $x = .5728.$

   [To interpolate, find the two values in the $E(z)$ column the computed number falls between. Then find the difference between the computed value and one end of the range, and divide the difference between the two ends of the range. Perform the corresponding calculation on the two service levels using x for the unknown value and solve for x.] Often, simply "eyeballing" the unknown value will suffice.

8. *Fixed-order-interval model.* A lab orders a number of chemicals from the same supplier every 30 days. Lead time is five days. The assistant manager of the lab must determine how much of one of these chemicals to order. A check of stock revealed that 11 25-milliliter jars are on hand. Daily usage of the chemical is approximately normal with a mean of 15.2 ml per day and a standard deviation of 1.6 ml per day. The desired service level for this chemical is 95 percent.

    a. How many bottles of the chemical should be ordered?

    b. What is the average amount of safety stock of the chemical?

Solution

$$\bar{d} = 15.2 \text{ ml per day} \quad OI = 30 \text{ days} \quad SL = 95\% \text{ requires } z = 1.65$$
$$\sigma_d = 1.6 \text{ ml per day} \quad LT = 5 \text{ days} \quad A = 11 \text{ jars} \times 25 \text{ ml per jar}$$
$$= 275 \text{ ml}$$

a. $\dfrac{\text{Amount}}{\text{to order}} = \bar{d}(OI + LT) + z\sigma_d \sqrt{OI + LT} - A$

$$= 15.2(30 + 5) + 1.65(1.6)\sqrt{30 + 5} - 275$$

$$= 272.62 \text{ ml}$$

Convert this to number of jars: $\dfrac{272.65 \text{ ml}}{25 \text{ ml per jar}} = 10.90$ or 11 jars.

b. Safety stock $= z\sigma_d \sqrt{OI + LT}$

$$= 1.65(1.6)\sqrt{30 + 5} = 15.62 \text{ ml}$$

9. *Single-period model.* A firm that installs cable TV systems has a certain piece of equipment that it carries two spare parts for. The parts cost $500 each and have no salvage value. Part failures can be modeled by a Poisson distribution with a mean of two failures during the useful life of the equipment. Holding and disposal costs are negligible. Estimate the apparent range of shortage cost.

Solution

$$C_s \text{ is unknown,} \quad C_e = \$500$$

Using the Poisson table, Appendix Table C, for a mean of two we obtain these values:

Number of failures	Cumulative probability
0	.135
1	.406
2	.677
3	.857
4	.947
5	.983
⋮	⋮

We know that for the optimum stocking level, the service level must usually be rounded up to a feasible stocking level. Hence, we know that the service level must have been between .406 and .677 in order to make two units the optimum level. By setting the service level equal first to .406 and then to .677, we can establish bounds on the possible range of shortage costs.

$$\frac{C_s}{C_s + \$500} = .406, \text{ so } C_s = .406(\$500 + C_s)$$

Solving, we find $C_s = \$341.75$. Similarly,

$$\frac{C_s}{C_s + \$500} = .677, \text{ so } C_s = .677(\$500 + C_s)$$

Solving for C_s we find $C_s = \$1,047.99$. Hence, the apparent range of failure or shortage cost is $341.75 to $1,047.99.

DISCUSSION AND REVIEW QUESTIONS

1. What are the primary reasons for holding inventory?
2. What are the requirements for effective inventory management?
3. Briefly describe each of the costs associated with inventory.
4. Contrast independent and dependent demand with respect to inventories.
5. List the major assumptions of the EOQ model.
6. Why isn't price considered explicitly in the basic EOQ model? How is it sometimes indirectly included?
7. Why is the economic run size greater than the order size under the basic EOQ model? What would happen to the difference between the two quantities if the production rate was, say, 20 times the usage rate? What would happen if production and usage rates were equal?
8. What are quantity discounts? What three costs enter into the order-quantity decision when discounts are available?
9. What is safety stock and why is it held?
10. Under what circumstances would the amount of safety stock held be (a) large? (b) small? (c) zero?

11. What is the single-period model and when is it appropriate?
12. What is meant by the term *service level*? Generally speaking, how is service level related to the amount of safety stock held?
13. Can the optimum stocking level in a single-period model ever be less than expected demand? Explain briefly.
14. Describe briefly the A–B–C approach to inventory control.
15. The purchasing agent for a company that assembles and sells air-conditioning equipment in a Latin American country has noted that the cost of compressors has increased significantly each time they have been reordered. The company uses an EOQ model to determine order size. What are the implications of this price escalation with respect to order size? What factors other than price must be taken into consideration?
16. Explain how a decrease in setup time can lead to a decrease in the average amount of inventory a firm holds, and why that would be beneficial.

PROBLEMS

1. A large bakery buys sugar in 100-pound bags. The bakery uses an average of 1,344 bags a year. Preparing an order and receiving a shipment of sugar involves a cost of $3 per order. Annual carrying costs are $14 per bag.

   a. Determine the economic order quantity.
   b. What is the average number of bags on hand?
   c. How many orders per year will there be?

d. Compute the total cost of ordering and carrying sugar.

2. A gasoline pump is used to remove water from construction sites 300 days a year. The generator consumes 80 liters of fuel each day. Storage and handling costs are $4 per liter a year, and ordering and receiving the shipments of fuel involves a cost of $12 each.
   a. Find the optimum order size.
   b. If storage and handling costs increase to $5 per year, by how much will the total cost change?

3. Garden Variety Flower Shop uses 900 clay pots annually. The pots are purchased at 60 cents each. Carrying costs are assumed to be 15 percent of purchase price, and ordering costs are $7 per order.
   a. Determine the EOQ.
   b. Compute the annual ordering cost and the annual carrying cost.
   c. Are the annual ordering and carrying costs always equal at the EOQ?

4. A produce distributor uses 800 packing crates a month, which it purchases at a cost of $10 each. The manager has assigned an annual carrying cost of 25 percent of the purchase price per crate. Ordering costs are $28. Currently the manager orders once a month. How much could the firm save annually in ordering and carrying costs by using the EOQ?

5. Bull Construction mines and supplies gravel to local road construction projects. Demand for gravel is 40 tons per day. Bull can mine the gravel at a rate of 100 tons per day. Preparation for mining costs $50, and storage and handling costs are $5 per ton on an annual basis. The firm operates 200 days per year.
   a. What run size is most economical?
   b. Compute the maximum inventory.
   c. Determine the approximate length of a production run in days.
   d. Approximately how many workdays are there in a cycle?

6. Given the information below, compute and plot the annual carrying cost, ordering cost, and total cost for order quantities of 100 units to 800 units in steps of 100 units:

   > Annual usage = 14,400 units
   > Carrying cost = $5 per unit
   > Ordering cost = $40

7. The Friendly Sausage Factory (FSF) can produce hotdogs at a rate of 5,000 per day. FSF supplies hotdogs to local stores and restaurants at a steady rate of 250 per day. The cost to prepare the equipment for producing hotdogs is $22. Annual holding costs are 15 cents per hotdog. The factory operates 300 days a year. Find:
   a. The optimum run size.
   b. The number of runs per year.
   c. The length (in days) of a run.

8. A firm that trains crane operators guarantees its graduates an annual salary of at least $10,000, which it pays from the time of graduation until the student is employed. Demand for graduates is steady throughout the year and averages 100 per year. The cost per class for the firm is $4,100, regardless of class size.
   a. What is the optimum class size?
   b. How often should the course be offered?

9. A jewelry firm buys semiprecious stones that it uses in making bracelets and rings. The supplier quotes a price of $8 per stone for quantities of 600 stones or more, $9 per stone for orders of 400 to 599 stones, and $10 per stone for lesser quantities. The jewelry firm operates 200 days per year. Usage rate is 25 stones per day, and ordering costs are $48.
   a. If carrying costs are $1 per year for each stone, find the order quantity that will minimize total annual cost.
   b. If annual carrying costs are 17 percent of unit cost, what will the optimum order size be?
   c. If lead time is six working days, at what point should the company reorder?

10. A mail-order house buys gummed labels in boxes of 8,000 labels. The firm uses 18,000 boxes a year. Carrying costs are 20 cents per box a year, and ordering costs

are $32. The price schedule below applies. Determine:

   a. Optimum order quantity.

   b. The number of orders per year.

Number of boxes	Price per box
1,000 to 1,999	$1.25
2,000 to 4,999	1.20
5,000 to 9,999	1.18
10,000 or more	1.15

11. A charitable organization assembles and sells novelty items. Annual demand is 80,000 units, ordering and preparation costs run $60, and carrying costs are 30 percent of unit price per year. For quantities of 5,000 units or less, the cost is 12 cents per unit, for 5,001 to 9,800 units the cost is 10 cents per unit, and for larger orders the cost is 8 cents per unit. Find the optimum order size.

12. A manufacturer of baby strollers purchases the seat portion of the stroller from a supplier who lists these prices: less than 1,000 seats, $5 each; 1,000 to 3,999, $4.95 each; 4,000 to 5,999, $4.90 each; and 6,000 or more, $4.85 each. Ordering costs are $50, annual carrying costs are 20 percent of purchase cost, and annual usage is 4,900 seats. Determine an order quantity that will minimize total cost.

13. A newspaper publisher uses roughly 800 feet of baling wire each day to secure bundles of newspapers while they are being distributed to carriers. The paper is published Monday through Saturday. Ordering lead time is six workdays. What is the appropriate reorder point quantity given that the company desires a service level of 95 percent, assuming that stock-out risk for various levels of safety stock are as follows: 1,500 ft, 0.10; 1,800 feet, 0.05; 2,100 feet, 0.02; and 2,400 feet, 0.01.

14. Demand for walnut-fudge ice cream at the Sweet Cream Dairy can be approximated by a normal distribution with a mean of 21 gallons per week and a standard deviation of 3.5 gallons per week. The new manager desires a service level of 90 percent. Lead time is two days, and the dairy is open seven days a week. (Hint: work in terms of weeks.)

   a. If an ROP model is used, what ROP would be consistent with the desired service level?

   b. If a fixed-interval model is used instead of an ROP model, what order size would be needed for the 90 percent service level with an order interval of 10 days and a supply of 2 gallons on hand at the order time?

15. A large accounting firm uses five 100-sheet boxes of letterhead stationery a week. Experience suggests that usage can be well approximated by a normal distribution with a mean of five boxes per week and a standard deviation of one half box per week. Two weeks are required to fill an order for letterhead stationery. Ordering cost is $2, and annual holding cost is 20 cents per box.

   a. Determine the economic order quantity for minimizing ordering and carrying costs assuming a 52-week year.

   b. If the firm reorders when the supply on hand is 12 boxes, compute the risk of a stock-out.

   c. If instead of an ROP, a fixed interval of seven weeks is used for reordering, what risk of stock-out does the firm incur if it orders 36 boxes when the amount on hand is 12 boxes?

16. Assume you must determine the maximum number of riders that will be permitted to ride in an elevator at any given time. It is known that rider weights are normally distributed with a mean of 160 pounds and a standard deviation of 25 pounds. Find the elevator capacity such that the weight limit of 2,400 pounds will not be exceeded 95 percent of the time. (Hint: The "inventory" is 2,400 pounds, and "lead time" is analogous to the number of riders; determine the lead time.)

17. The manager of a furniture manufacturing plant hopes to achieve a better allocation of inventory control efforts by adopting an A–B–C approach to inventory control. Given the monthly usages listed below, classify the items in A, B, and C categories according to dollar usage.

Item		Usage	Unit cost
4021	. . .	50	$1,400
9402	. . .	300	12
4066	. . .	40	700
6500	. . .	150	20
9280	. . .	10	1,020
4050	. . .	80	140
6850	. . .	2,000	15
3010	. . .	400	20
4400	. . .	7,000	5

18. Ned's Natural Foods sells unshelled peanuts by the pound. Historically, Ned has observed that daily demand is normally distributed with a mean of 80 pounds and a standard deviation of 10 pounds. Lead time also appears normally distributed with a mean of eight days and a standard deviation of one day. What ROP would provide a 90 percent lead-time service level? What is the expected number of units (pounds) short per cycle? (Hint: Use formula 10–14 for σ_{dLT}.)

19. Regional Supermarket is open 360 days per year. Daily use of cash register tape averages 10 rolls. Usage appears normally distributed with a standard deviation of two rolls per day. Ordering tape involves a cost of $1, and carrying costs are 40 cents per roll a year. Lead time is three days.
    a. What is the EOQ?
    b. What ROP will provide a lead-time service level of 96 percent?
    c. What is the expected number of units short per cycle with 96%? Per year?
    d. What is the annual service level?

20. An automatic machine produces rivets from bar stock at a rate of 1,200 per day, 250 days a year. The order size is 2,000 feet. Fifteen rivets can be cut from one foot of stock. Delivery lead time on stock is known to be normally distributed with a mean of nine days and a standard deviation of two days.
    a. How much bar stock is used per day?
    b. How much safety stock is needed for a stockout risk of 3 percent for each order cycle? Use $\sigma_{dLT} = d\,\sigma_{LT}$.
    c. What is the annual service level?

21. A service station uses 1,200 cases of oil a year. Ordering cost is $40, and annual carrying cost is $3 per case. The station owner has specified an *annual* service level of 98 percent. What ROP is appropriate if lead-time demand is normally distributed with a mean of 80 cases and a standard deviation of 4 cases? What is the lead-time service level?

22. A drugstore uses fixed order cycles for many of the items it stocks. The manager likes a service level of .98. Determine the order size that will be consistent with this service level for these items for an order interval of 14 days and a lead time of 2 days:

Item	Average daily demand	Standard deviation	Quantity on hand
K033	60	5	420
K144	50	4	375
L700	8	2	160

23. Demand for jelly doughnuts on Saturday mornings at Don's Doughnut Shoppe is shown below. Determine the optimum number of doughnuts in dozens to stock if labor, materials, and overhead are estimated to be 80 cents per dozen, doughnuts are sold for $1.20 per dozen, and leftover doughnuts at the end of each day are sold the next day for one half off. What is the resulting service level?

Demand (dozens)	Relative frequency
19	.01
20	.05
21	.12
22	.18
23	.13
24	.14
25	.10
26	.11
27	.10
28	.04
29	.02

24. A public utility intends to buy a turbine as part of an expansion plan and must now decide on the number of spare parts to order. One part, No. X145, can be purchased for $100 each. Carrying and disposal costs are estimated to be 145 percent of the purchase price over the life of the turbine. A stock-out would cost roughly $88,000 due to downtime, ordering, and "special purchase" factors. Historical records based on

the performance of similar equipment operating under similar conditions suggests that demand for spares will tend to approximate a Poisson distribution with a mean of 3.2 parts for the useful life of the turbine. Find the optimum number of spares to order.

25. Skinner's Fish Market buys fresh Boston bluefish daily for $1.40 per pound and sells it for $1.90 per pound. At the end of each business day, any remaining bluefish is sold to a producer of catfood for 80 cents per pound. Daily demand can be approximated by a normal distribution with a mean of 80 pounds and a standard deviation of 10 pounds. Determine the optimum stocking level.

26. A small grocery store sells fresh produce, which it obtains from a local farmer. During the strawberry season, demand for fresh strawberries can reasonably be approximated using a normal distribution with a mean of 40 quarts per day and a standard deviation of 6 quarts per day. Excess costs run 35 cents per quart. The grocer orders 49 quarts per day. What is the implied cost of shortage per quart? Why might this be a reasonable figure?

27. Demand for devils-food whipped-cream layer cakes at a local pastry shop can be approximated using a Poisson distribution with a mean of six per day. The manager estimates it costs $3 to prepare each cake. Fresh cakes sell for $4 and day-old cakes sell for $3 each. What stocking level is appropriate if one half of the day-old cakes are sold and the rest thrown out?

28. Burger Prince buys top-grade ground beef for $1.00 per pound. A large sign over the entranceway guarantees that the meat is fresh daily. Any leftover meat is sold to the local high school cafeteria for 80 cents per pound. Four hamburgers can be prepared from each pound of meat. Burgers sell for 60 cents each. Labor, overhead, meat, buns, and condiments cost 50 cents per burger. Demand is normally distributed with a mean of 400 pounds per day and a standard deviation of 50 pounds per day. What daily order quantity is optimum? (Hint: Shortage cost must be in dollars per pound.)

29. Demand for rug cleaning machines at Clyde's U-Rent-It is shown below. Machines are rented by the day only. Profit on the rug cleaners is $10 per day. Clyde has four rug cleaning machines.

Demand	Frequency
0	0.30
1	0.20
2	0.20
3	0.15
4	0.10
5	0.05
	1.00

a. Assuming that Clyde's stocking decision is optimal, what is the implied range of excess cost per machine?

b. Your answer from part a has been presented to Clyde, and he protests that the amount is too *low*. Would this suggest an increase or a decrease in the number of machines he stocks? Explain.

c. Suppose now that the $10 mentioned as profit is instead the excess cost per day for each machine and that the shortage cost is unknown. Based on the assumption that four machines is optimal, what is the implied range of shortage cost per machine?

30. Refer to Solved Problem 9. For what range of shortage cost would not carrying any spare parts be the best strategy?

SELECTED BIBLIOGRAPHY

Buffa, Elwood, and James S. Dryer. *Essentials of Management Science/Operations Research.* New York: John Wiley & Sons, 1978.

Chase, Richard B., and Nicholas J. Aquilano. *Production and Operations Management.* 4th ed. Homewood, Ill.: Richard D. Irwin, 1985.

Eppen, F. J., and G. D. Gould. *Introductory Management Science.* Englewood Cliffs, N.J.: Prentice-Hall, 1984.

Fogarty, Donald W., and Thomas R. Hoffmann. *Production and Inventory Management,* Cincinnati, Ohio: South-Western Publishing Co., 1983.

Levin, Richard I.; Charles A. Kirkpatrick; and David S. Rubin. *Quantitative Approaches to Management.* 5th ed. New York: McGraw-Hill, 1982.

Love, Stephen F. *Inventory Control.* New York: McGraw-Hill, 1979.

Peterson, R., and E. A. Silver. *Decision Systems for Inventory Management and Production Planning.* 2d ed. New York: John Wiley & Sons, 1984.

Tersine, Richard J. *Principles of Inventory and Materials Management.* 2d ed. New York: Elsevier North-Holland, 1982.

Vollmann, Thomas E.; William L. Berry; and D. Clay Whybark. *Manufacturing Planning and Control Systems.* Homewood, Ill.: Richard D. Irwin, 1984.

Case

*The Dewey Stapler Company**

From: Martin Crane, Sales Manager

To: Allen Grace, President

Dear Allen:

Well, it has been a very disappointing year. We've missed our quota by 10 or 15 percent in virtually every district and this is the year I had such high hopes for. When we decided to open up four branch warehouses rather than shipping from our central location only, I was convinced that this would give us better customer service. The last of the warehouses was opened up last May, just before our peak summer season, so perhaps some of the problem is just not having enough experience with branch warehouses. But I think it goes deeper than that.

Our warehouse men are authorized to keep a one-month supply of inventory on hand. While I know you feel strongly that the substantial increase in inventory we had during the year was due to the warehouse program, I can't see why it requires any more inventory to keep a month's supply on hand in four branches and a main location than it did to keep a month's supply on hand back at the main location. A month's supply is a month's supply no matter how you look at it.

* Reprinted by permission from Oliver W. Wright, *Production and Inventory Management in the Computer Age* (Boston: Cahners, 1974).

To my way of thinking, the real problem is customer service. Our salesmen are demoralized. They simply can't get the stock shipped out of the warehouses because the warehouses don't have it on hand. Forty percent of our customer orders, of course, are still being shipped out of the main location. Our warehouse people tell me that these customer orders get preference and their stock replenishment orders are pushed aside.

Allen, we've got to solve this problem. There's no sense in having a sales force if we can't have the stock to back them up. I propose the plant location be required to ship warehouse stocking orders just the same as they ship customer orders. They should treat the warehouses like a customer. In fact, the warehouses are their *biggest* customer and should be serviced accordingly. I propose also that the one-month inventory guideline be removed. Let the warehouse men stock whatever they think they need to support the salesmen. I would volunteer to have my district managers sit with the branch warehouse people to give them some idea of what they should really be ordering.

Allen, this branch warehouse program has been as big a disappointment to me as it has to you. I know you're concerned about the fact that inventories have been going up, but I frankly attribute that to poor management back at the plant. And, quite honestly, Allen, I don't think that people at the plant realize our problems out here in the field and are giving us the kind of support we need. Without it, we have no chance of making the sales quota. Instead of selling, I'm spending most of my time playing chaplain to a bunch of demoralized salesmen.

Sincerely,

Martin

From: Robert Ellers, Inventory Manager
To: Allen Grace, President

Dear Mr. Grace:

You asked me what my plans were to respond to Martin Crane's letter of January 5. I don't know where to start. This warehouse program has really torn us apart.

We thought that when branch warehouses were added, we would simply have to split some of the stock we had among the warehouses. Instead, we've had to build up the inventory very substantially. We don't get any plans from the warehouses at all. All we see is orders. We have no idea what their inventory position is when we get the orders and we only get them two to three weeks before we have to ship them. Then comes the moment of truth. We have a shortage on a particular item. Here's a customer order and also a warehouse stock replenishment order. Does the warehouse really need it? We know the customer does. In practice, I must admit we wind up waiting until the warehouse screams although we know we may very well be hurting customer service at the branch warehouses.

Mr. Grace, I'm more worried about *this* year than I was about last. Some of the warehouses that had been on the air since year before last showed a disturbing tendency to keep their inventories low during the off-season so that they could boast about their inventory turnover. Then during the peak season, they expect me to turn the faucet on back at the plant. We don't have enough storage space at the plant to build up the inventory required during the off-season in order to keep people working at a steady rate. We need this inventory buildup in order to give good service during the peak season. I've been told repeatedly by plant management that we must keep people working at a steady rate.

All this squabbling about inventory levels prompts me to suggest an approach. We normally would manufacture in a lot size that would be equivalent to about a three-month's supply. When we do that, why don't I just ship a three-month's supply out to each branch warehouse, and then we won't have to bother worrying about them until the next lot is manufactured. Then they can't complain that they're not getting their fair share.

One of the disturbing elements that you may not have heard about is that Frank, our traffic manager, has now suggested that we ship to the West Coast warehouses by sea. This would mean going through the Panama Canal and would substantially increase our lead time and reduce our flexibility. He says, "Flexibility is like motherhood. I'm talking a $50,000 savings in transportation costs, and if you guys have to work a little harder to make that happen, so be it."

Mr. Grace, I really am almost at my wit's end. Perhaps one of the things we ought to consider would be a computer system for tying all of the warehouses together so we could cover a shortage at one warehouse by shipping from another warehouse. Last September, I checked on items that were out of stock in the Atlanta warehouse and I found that virtually everyone of them was in adequate supply throughout the system; i.e., we either had them in

Dallas, Los Angeles, Chicago, or back at the main plant. This type of computer system would be expensive, but perhaps this is the answer to our service problems.

Sincerely,

Robert Ellers

Question

The Dewey Stapler Company has some very serious problems. There are a number of misconceptions about inventory management in the company that need to be corrected. Take the position of a consultant being called in by Allen Grace, the president. You have enough information in these letters to give him some very helpful recommendations. Write a memo outlining your thoughts. Include a discussion of what will happen to service levels if total inventory investment remains constant.

Purchasing

PURCHASING INTERFACES, 532

PURCHASING OBJECTIVES, 533

THE PURCHASING CYCLE, 534

VALUE ANALYSIS, 535

EVALUATING SOURCES OF SUPPLY (VENDOR ANALYSIS), 535

DETERMINING PRICES, 537

CENTRALIZED VERSUS DECENTRALIZED PURCHASING, 537

VENDOR RELATIONS, 538

SUMMARY, 539
DISCUSSION AND REVIEW QUESTIONS, 539
SELECTED BIBLIOGRAPHY, 539

After completing this supplement, you should be able to:

1. Describe how purchasing interfaces with other areas of the organization and with suppliers.
2. Outline the objectives of purchasing.
3. Describe the purchasing cycle, especially determination of price and sources of supply.
4. Discuss the issue of centralized purchasing versus decentralized purchasing.
5. Describe and discuss value analysis.
6. Discuss the importance of good vendor relations.

Purchasing is responsible for obtaining material inputs for the operating system. This supplement describes the purchasing function as it operates in most organizations. It begins by discussing how purchasing interacts with other functional areas of the organization and with outside suppliers. Determination of sources of supply and price are examined along with the concept of value analysis.

PURCHASING INTERFACES

As a service function, purchasing has interfaces with a number of other functional areas, as well as with outside suppliers. Purchasing is the connecting link between the organization and its suppliers. In this capacity, it exchanges information with suppliers and functional areas. The interactions between purchasing and these other areas are briefly summarized in the following paragraphs.

Operating units comprise the main source of requests for purchased materials, and close cooperation between these units and the purchasing people is mandatory if quality, quantity, and delivery goals are to be met. Changes in specifications, cancellations, or changes in quantity or delivery times must be communicated immediately in order for purchasing to be effective.

The purchasing department may require the assistance of the *legal* department in contract negotiations as well as in drawing up bid specifications for nonroutine purchases. In addition, the legal department may be called upon to help interpret legislation on pricing, product liability, and contracts with suppliers.

Accounting is responsible for handling payments to suppliers and must be notified promptly when goods are received in order to be able to take advantage of possible discounts. In many firms *data processing* is handled by the accounting department, which involves inventory records, checking invoices, and monitoring vendor performance.

Design or *engineering* usually prepares material specifications, which must be communicated to purchasing. Because of its contacts with suppliers, purchasing is often in a position to pass information about new products and materials improvements on to design personnel. Also, design and purchasing people may work closely in determining if changes in specifications, design, or materials can reduce the cost of purchased items (see value analysis, below).

Receiving checks incoming shipments of purchased items to determine if quality, quantity, and timing objectives have been met, and moves the goods to temporary storage. Purchasing must be notified when shipments are late; accounting must be notified when shipments are received so that payments can be made; and both

FIGURE 10S–1

**Purchasing Interfaces
with Functional Areas
of the Firm and with
Suppliers**

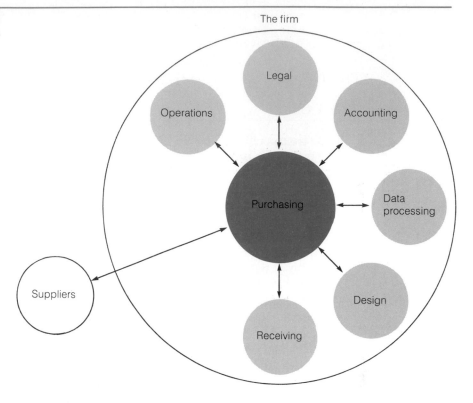

purchasing and accounting must be apprised of current information on continuing vendor evaluation.

Suppliers or vendors work closely with purchasing to learn what materials will be purchased and what kinds of specifications will be required in terms of quality, quantity, and deliveries. Purchasing must rate vendors on cost, reliability, and so on (see vendor analysis below). Good supplier relations can pay dividends on rush orders and changes, and vendors provide a good source of information on product and material improvements.

Figure 10S–1 summarizes the purchasing interfaces.

PURCHASING OBJECTIVES

The basic objectives of purchasing can be summarized as follows:

1. To determine the quality and quantity needed and when an item is needed.

2. To obtain the best possible price.
3. To maintain good relations with suppliers.
4. To maintain sources of supply.
5. To be knowledgeable on prices, new products, and new services that become available.

THE PURCHASING CYCLE

The purchasing cycle begins with a request from within the organization to purchase material, equipment, supplies, or other items from outside the organization, and the cycle ends when the purchasing department is notified that a shipment has been received in satisfactory condition. The main steps in the cycle are:

1. *The requisition is received by purchasing.* The requisitions include *(a)* a description of the item or material desired, *(b)* the quantity and quality necessary, *(c)* desired delivery dates, and *(d)* who is requesting the purchase.

2. *A supplier is selected.* The purchasing department must identify suppliers who have the capability of supplying the desired goods. If no suppliers are currently listed in the files, new ones must be sought. If one or more suppliers are available, vendor ratings may be referred to in choosing among vendors, or perhaps rating information can be relayed to the vendor with the thought of upgrading future performance.

3. *The order is placed with a vendor.* If the order involves a large expenditure, particularly for a one-time purchase, say of equipment, vendors will usually be asked to bid on the job, and operating and design personnel may be asked to assist in negotiations with a vendor. Large volume, continuous usage items are often covered by blanket purchase orders, which often involve annual negotiation of prices with deliveries subject to request throughout the year. Moderate volume items may also have blanket purchase orders, or they may be handled on an individual basis. Small purchases may be handled directly between the operating unit requesting the item and the supplier, although care must be taken so that some control is exercised over those purchases. Otherwise, they tend to get out of hand.

4. *Monitoring orders.* Routine follow-up on orders, particularly large orders or those with lengthy delivery schedules, allows the purchasing department to foresee delays and relay this information to the appropriate operating units. Likewise, changes in quantity and delivery needs of the operating units must be relayed to suppliers so that they can have time to adjust their plans.

5. *Receiving orders.* Incoming shipments from vendors must be checked for quality and quantity. Purchasing must be notified, as

must accounting and the operating unit that requested the goods. If the goods are not received in satisfactory condition, they may have to be returned to the supplier for credit or replacement or subjected to detailed inspection. Again, purchasing, accounting, and the operating unit must be notified. In either case, vendor evaluation records must be updated.

VALUE ANALYSIS

Value analysis involves an examination of the *function* of purchased parts and materials in an effort to reduce the cost and/or to improve the performance of those items. Typical questions that would be asked as part of the analysis include such things as: Could a cheaper part or material be used? Is the function necessary? Can the function of two or more parts or components be performed by a single part for a lower cost? Can a part be simplified? Could product specifications be relaxed, and would this result in a lower price? Could standard parts be substituted for nonstandard parts?

Naturally, such an investigation cannot be performed each time materials are ordered. However, value analysis should be conducted periodically on large cost-volume items because of the potential savings.

Although purchasing does not ordinarily have the authority to implement changes on the basis of a value analysis, it can make suggestions to operating units, to designers, and to suppliers, which may lead to improved performance of purchased goods and/or reduce the cost of those goods. Purchasing people can offer a different perspective to the analysis than those in either design or operations, and purchasing people, because of their association with suppliers, possess information not known to others within the organization. If a fair amount of technical knowledge is required to review a part or product, a team can be formed with representatives from design and/or operations to work with purchasing in conducting the analysis.

EVALUATING SOURCES OF SUPPLY (VENDOR ANALYSIS)

In many respects, choosing a vendor involves taking into account many of the same factors that you or I would if we were about to make a major purchase (e.g., a car or a stereo system). A company considers price, quality, the supplier's reputation, past experience with the supplier, and service after the sale. The main difference is that a company, because of the quantities it orders and because of production requirements, often provides suppliers with detailed

specifications of the materials or parts it wants instead of buying items off the shelf, although even large companies buy standard items that way.

The main factors firms look at when they select vendors are:

1. *Price.* This is the most obvious factor, along with any discounts offered, although it may not be the most important factor.
2. *Quality.* A company may be willing to spend more money to obtain desired-quality parts.
3. *Services.* Special services can sometimes be very important in choosing a supplier. Replacement of defective items, instruction in the use of equipment, repair of equipment, and similar services can be instrumental in selecting one supplier over another.

"The instructions are pasted on the back."

Reprinted from *The Wall Street Journal;* permission Cartoon Features Syndicate.

4. *Location.* Location of a supplier can have impact on shipping time, transportation costs, and response time for rush orders or emergency service. Local buying can create goodwill in the community by helping the local economy.
5. *Inventory policy of supplier.* If a supplier maintains an inventory policy of keeping spare parts on hand, this could be helpful in the case of an emergency breakdown of equipment.
6. *Flexibility.* The willingness and ability of a supplier to respond to changes in demand, as well as a willingness to accept design changes could be important considerations.

DETERMINING PRICES

There are essentially three ways that prices are determined: published price lists, competitive bidding, and negotiation.

In many instances organizations buy products and services that have fixed or *predetermined prices.* This is generally the case for standard items that are bought infrequently and/or in small quantities.

For large orders of standard products and services, *competitive bidding* is often used. This involves sending requests for bids to potential suppliers, which ask vendors to quote a price for a specified quantity and quality of items or for a specified service to be performed. Government purchases are usually made using competitive bidding.

Negotiated purchasing is used for special purchasing situations, such as in cases where specifications are vague, when one or a few customized products or services are involved (e.g., space exploration), and when few potential sources exist. There are several myths concerning negotiated purchasing that should be recognized:

1. Negotiation is a win-lose confrontation.
2. The main goal is to obtain the lowest possible price.
3. Each negotiation is an isolated transaction.[1]

Realistically speaking, no one likes to be taken advantage of. Furthermore, contractors and suppliers need a reasonable profit in order to survive. Therefore, a take-it-or-leave-it approach or one that capitalizes extensively on the weaknesses of the other party will serve no useful purpose and may have detrimental effects that surface at a later time. The most reasonable approach is one of give and take, with each side giving and receiving some concessions.

CENTRALIZED VERSUS DECENTRALIZED PURCHASING

Centralized purchasing means that purchasing is handled by one special department. Decentralized purchasing means that individual departments or separate locations handle their own purchasing requirements.

Centralized purchasing may be able to obtain lower prices than decentralized units if the higher volume created by combining orders enables it to take advantage of quantity discounts offered on large orders, as well as obtain better service and closer attention

---

[1] Richard J. Tersine, *Production/Operations Management: Concepts, Structure, and Analysis,* 2d ed. (New York: Elsevier North-Holland Publishing, 1985), p. 598.

from suppliers. In addition, centralized purchasing often enables companies to assign certain categories of items to specialists, who tend to be more efficient because they are able to concentrate their efforts on relatively few items instead of spreading themselves across many items.

Decentralized purchasing has the advantage of being aware of differing "local" needs and being more able to respond to those needs. Decentralized purchasing usually can offer quicker response than centralized purchasing can. In the case of widely scattered locations, decentralized purchasing may be able to save on transportation costs by buying locally, which has the added attraction of creating goodwill in the community.

Some organizations manage to take advantage of both centralization and decentralization by permitting individual units to handle certain items while centralizing purchases of other items. For example, small orders and rush orders may be handled locally, or by departments, while centralized purchases would be used for high volume, high value items for which discounts would be applicable or for which specialists could provide better service than local buyers or departments could.

VENDOR RELATIONS

American firms are becoming increasingly aware of the importance of building good relations with their vendors. In the past too many firms regarded their vendors as adversaries and dealt with them on that basis. One lesson many have learned from the Japanese is that there can be numerous benefits from having good vendor relations. Among them are vendor flexibility in terms of accepting changes in delivery schedules, quality, and quantities. Moreover, vendors can often help in identifying problems and offer suggestions for solving them. Thus, simply choosing and switching vendors on the basis of price is a very shortsighted approach for handling an ongoing need.

Many Japanese firms rely on one or a few vendors to handle their needs. In contrast, many U.S. firms deal with numerous vendors. Perhaps they want to remain flexible, and possibly there are some advantages in playing one off against the others. However, it would appear that in many instances firms have too many vendors to deal with, although reducing that number to one or a few, as the Japanese have done, may be too extreme. A more realistic approach would be to move in the direction of a reduction (i.e., a middle ground).

SUMMARY

Purchasing is responsible for obtaining material inputs for the organization. This includes the actual purchasing of materials as well as vendor selection and conducting value analyses on purchased items. The basic design question in purchasing is whether to centralize or decentralize it. Centralization provides for closer control and may produce certain economies, while decentralized purchasing tends to have quick response and may better serve local needs. Value analysis may be performed periodically to assure that purchased item cost benefit is being optimized. Vendors are evaluated for cost, service after the sale, reliability, and quality.

DISCUSSION AND REVIEW QUESTIONS

1. Briefly describe how purchasing interacts with other functional areas of the firm such as accounting and design.
2. Describe value analysis. Why is purchasing a good location for this task?
3. Should the supplier with the highest quality/lowest price combination always be selected over others?
4. Discuss the issue of centralization versus decentralization as it applies to the purchasing function.
5. Discuss the determination of prices.
6. Discuss the importance of good vendor relations.

SELECTED BIBLIOGRAPHY

Ammer, Dean S. *Material Management and Purchasing.* Homewood, Ill.: Richard D. Irwin, 1980.

Heinritz, Stuart F., and Paul V. Farrell. *Purchasing: Principles and Practices.* 5th ed. Englewood Cliffs, N.J.: Prentice-Hall, 1971.

Hopeman, Richard J. *Production and Operations Management.* 4th ed. Columbus, Ohio: Charles E. Merrill Publishing, 1980.

Kraljic, Peter. "Purchasing Must Become Supply Management." *Harvard Business Review,* September–October 1983, p. 109.

Leenders, M. R. et al. Purchasing and Materials Management. 7th ed. Homewood, Ill.: Richard D. Irwin, 1980.

Riggs, James L. *Production Systems: Planning, Analysis and Control.* 3d ed. Santa Barbara, Calif.: Wiley/Hamilton, 1981.

Tersine, Richard J. *Materials Management and Inventory Systems.* New York: Elsevier North-Holland Publishing, 1976.

Material Requirements Planning

After completing this chapter, you should be able to:

1. Describe the conditions under which MRP is most appropriate.
2. Describe the inputs, outputs, and nature of MRP processing.
3. Contrast regenerative and net-change updating.
4. Explain how requirements in the master schedule are translated into material requirements for lower-level items.
5. Discuss possible uses of safety stock and safety time.
6. Explain how an MRP system is useful in capacity requirements planning.
7. Outline the potential benefits as well as some of the difficulties users have encountered with MRP.
8. Describe MRP II and how it relates to MRP.
9. Discuss the Japanese approach to manufacturing planning and control, and contrast it with the typical U.S. approach.

Dependent versus Independent Demand, 542

AN OVERVIEW OF MRP, 543

MRP INPUTS, 545
  The Master Schedule, 545
  The Bill-of-Materials File, 547
  The Inventory-Records File, 550

MRP PROCESSING, 550
  Updating the System, 559

MRP OUTPUTS, 560

OTHER CONSIDERATIONS, 560
  Safety Stock, 560
  Lot Sizing, 561

CAPACITY REQUIREMENTS PLANNING, 565

BENEFITS AND LIMITATIONS OF MRP, 567

MRP II, 568

THE JAPANESE APPROACH, 570
  Will it Work Here? 576

MRP II VERSUS KANBAN, 579

SUMMARY, 581
SOLVED PROBLEMS, 582
DISCUSSION AND REVIEW QUESTIONS, 585
PROBLEMS, 586
SELECTED BIBLIOGRAPHY, 588

Here are the views of managers in two companies that have tried material requirements planning (MRP):

"I don't know how we managed to get along without MRP for as long as we did. Our scheduling has gone from a state of turmoil to relative calm. We have achieved a substantial reduction in inventory size and cost, and yet our customer-service levels have actually improved quite a bit. We are more than satisfied with MRP; it allows us to *plan* instead of having to spend all of our time trying to *react* to one crisis after another. I would strongly recommend that all manufacturing firms adopt MRP or some similar approach."

"We had heard so many good things about MRP that we couldn't wait to get started, but so far, it seems like we've just been spinning our wheels. We're not even close to going online with it, and yet we've already exceeded our original time estimates and our costs are out of sight. Everyone is discouraged at this point, especially the brass. There is even some talk now of just scrapping the whole darn idea."

These two views reflect the range of reactions that typifies efforts of manufacturing firms to implement and use material requirements planning. This chapter examines the major issues of this very current topic, including the need for this approach, the basic concepts of planning requirements, the benefits and limitations, and some of the reasons for the difficulties some firms have encountered in attempting to implement material requirements planning. It then goes on to describe two other approaches to production control for dependent demand items: MRP II and the so-called Japanese approach. MRP II is an expanded approach to resource planning that incorporates MRP; the Japanese approach is similar in purpose to MRP II but markedly different in the way it functions.

The preceding chapter focused on inventory management under conditions of *independent* demand. In this chapter the focus is on managing inventories that have *dependent* or *derived* demand.

Dependent versus Independent Demand

As noted in the previous chapter, a major distinction in the way inventories are managed relates to the nature of demand for those items. When demand for items is *derived* from plans to make certain products, as it is in the case of raw materials, parts, and subassemblies, which are used in producing a finished product, those items are said to have *dependent* demand. Hence, the parts and materials that go into the production of an automobile are examples of dependent demand since the total amount of parts and raw materials that will be needed during any time period is a function of the number of cars that will be produced. Conversely, demand for the finished cars is independent in the sense that it cannot be based on demand for some higher-level item.

FIGURE 11–1

**Comparison of
Independent and
Dependent Demand**

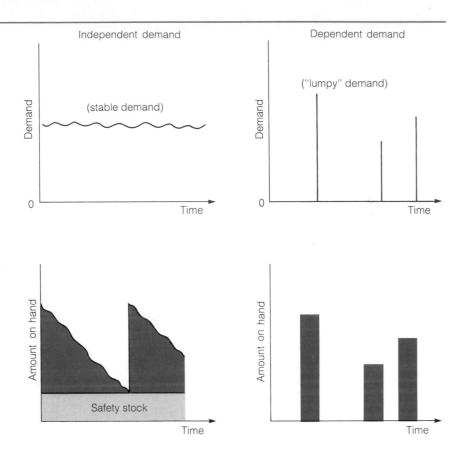

Independent demand is fairly stable, once allowances are made for seasonal variations, but dependent demand tends to be sporadic or "lumpy": large quantities are used at specific points in time with little or no usage at other times. Because of these tendencies, independent-demand items must be carried on a continual basis, but dependent-demand items only need to be stocked just prior to the time they will be needed in the production process. Moreover, the predictability of usage of dependent-demand items means that there is little or no need for safety stock. Figure 11–1 illustrates the contrasts in independent- and dependent-demand inventories.

AN OVERVIEW OF MRP

Materials Requirements Planning (MRP) is a computer-based information system designed to handle ordering and scheduling of dependent-demand inventories (e.g., raw materials, component parts,

and subassemblies). A production plan for a specified number of finished products is translated into requirements for component parts (raw materials, etc.) working backward, using lead-time information to determine when and how much to order. Hence, requirements for end items generate requirements for lower-level components, which are broken down by planning periods (e.g., weeks) so that ordering, production, and assembly can be scheduled for timely completion of end items while keeping inventory levels reasonably low.

Material requirements planning is as much a philosophy as it is a technique, and as much an approach to scheduling as it is to inventory control.

Historically, ordering and scheduling of assembled products suffered from two things. One was the enormous task of setting up schedules, keeping track of large numbers of parts and components, and coping with schedule and order changes. The other was that little effort was made to differentiate between independent demand and dependent demand; all too often, techniques that were designed for independent-demand items were being used to handle assembled items, which resulted in excessive inventories. Consequently, inventory planning and scheduling presented major problems for manufacturers.

In the last decade or so, manufacturers began to recognize the importance of the distinction between independent- and dependent-demand items and to approach these two categories of items in different ways. Much of the burden of record keeping and determining material requirements in many firms has now been transferred to computers, using techniques such as MRP. Much of the credit for publicizing MRP and educating potential users about MRP goes to Joseph Orlicky, author of the book *Material Requirements Planning* (New York: McGraw-Hill, 1975) and George Plossl, Oliver Wight, and the American Production and Inventory Control Society (APICS).

MRP begins with a schedule for finished goods that is converted into a schedule of requirements for the subassemblies, component parts, and raw materials that will be needed to produce the finished items in the specified time frame. Thus, MRP is designed to answer three questions: *what* is needed, *how much* is needed, and *when* is it needed.

The primary inputs of MRP are a bill of materials, which tells what a finished product is composed of, a master schedule, which tells how much finished product is desired and when, and an inventory-records file, which indicates how much inventory is on hand or on order.

This information is processed using various computer programs

FIGURE 11–2

Overview of MRP

to determine the *net* requirements for each period of the planning horizon.

Outputs from the process include planned-order schedules, order releases, changes, performance-control reports, planning reports, and exception reports.

These topics are discussed in more detail in subsequent sections. An overview of an MRP system is provided in Figure 11–2.

MRP INPUTS

As illustrated in Figure 11–2, there are three major sources of information in an MRP system: a master schedule, a bill-of-materials file, and an inventory-records file. Each of these inputs is described in this section, beginning with the master schedule.

The Master Schedule

The *master schedule* states which *end items* are to be produced, when these end items are needed, and what quantities are needed. Figure 11–3 illustrates a portion of a master schedule that shows

FIGURE 11–3

Item: X	1	2	3	4	5	6	7	8
Quantity				100				150

A Master Schedule for End-Item X

Week number

planned output for end-item X for the planning horizon. Hence, the schedule indicates that 100 units of X will be needed (e.g., for shipment to customers) at the start of week 4 and that another 150 units will be needed at the start of week 8.

The quantities in a master schedule can come from a number of different sources, including customer orders, forecasts, orders from warehouses to build up seasonal inventories, and external demand.

The master schedule separates the planning horizon into a series of time periods or time *buckets.* These are often in weeks. However, the time buckets need not be of equal length. In fact, the near-term portion of a master schedule may be in weeks, while later portions may be in months or quarters. Usually, plans for those more-distant time periods are more tentative than near-term requirements.

While there is no set period of time that a master schedule must cover, most managers like to plan well enough into the future that they have some general idea of probable upcoming demands for the near future. It is important, though, that the master schedule cover the *stacked* or *cumulative lead time* necessary to produce the end items. This amounts to the sum of the lead times that sequential phases of the production or assembly process require, as illustrated in Figure 11–4, where a total of nine weeks of lead time is needed from ordering parts and raw materials until final assembly is completed.

FIGURE 11–4

The Planning Horizon Must Cover the Cumulative Lead Time

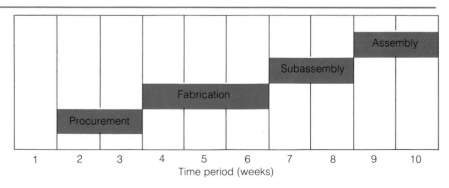

Time period (weeks)

Generally speaking, a master schedule is generated initially in terms of what is *needed* and not what is *possible,* so the initial schedule may or may not be feasible given the limits of the production system. Moreover, what appears on the surface to be a feasible master schedule may not be so when end items are translated into requirements for procurement, fabrication, and assembly. Unfortunately, the MRP system cannot distinguish between a feasible master schedule and a nonfeasible one. Consequently, it is often necessary to run a proposed master schedule through MRP processing in order to obtain a clearer picture of actual requirements, which can then be compared to available capacity. If it turns out that the current master schedule is not feasible, a decision may be made to increase capacity (e.g., through overtime or subcontracting) or to revise the master schedule. In the latter case this may entail several revisions, each of which is run through the system until a feasible plan is obtained. At that point, the master schedule is *frozen,* at least for the near-term time periods, thus establishing a firm schedule from which to plan requirements.

The Bill-of-Materials File

A *bill of materials* (BOM) contains a listing of all of the assemblies, subassemblies, parts, and raw materials that are needed to produce *one* unit of a finished product. Thus, each finished product has its own bill of materials.

The listing in the bill-of-materials file is hierarchical; it shows the quantity of each item (in parentheses) needed to complete one unit of the next-highest level of assembly. The nature of this aspect

FIGURE 11–5

A Product-Structure Tree for End-Item X

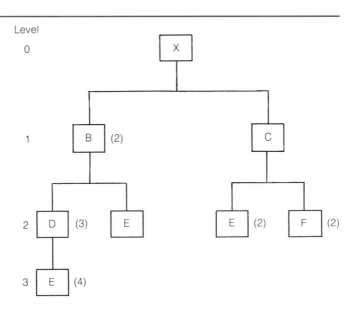

of a bill of materials is perhaps most readily grasped by considering a *product-structure tree,* such as the one illustrated in Figure 11–5. We see that end-item X is composed of two Bs and one C. Moreover, each B requires three Ds and one E, and each D requires four Es. Similarly, each C is made up of two Es and two Fs. These *requirements* are listed by *level,* beginning with level 0 for the end item, then level 1 for the next-lowest level, and so on. The items at each level are *components* in terms of the next-highest level and at the same time *parents* of their respective components. Note that the quantities of each item in the product-structure tree refer only to the amounts needed to complete the next-highest assembly.

A product-structure tree is useful in illustrating how the bill of materials is used to determine the quantities of each of the *ingredients* (requirements) needed to obtain a desired number of end items.

EXAMPLE 1

Using the information presented in Figure 11–5, do the following:

1. Determine the quantities of B, C, D, E, and F needed to assemble one X.
2. Determine the quantities of these components that will be required to assemble 200Xs.

Solution

a.

Component		Quantity
B	2 Bs per X	= 2
D	3 Ds per B $\times$ 2 Bs per X	= 6
E	4 Es per D $\times$ 3 Ds per B $\times$ 2 Bs per X	= 24
E	1 E per B $\times$ 2 Bs per X	= 2
C	1 C per X	= 1
E	2 Es per C $\times$ 1 C per X	= 2
F	2 Fs per C $\times$ 1 C per X	= 2

Note that E appears in three separate places; its total requirements can be determined by summing the separate amounts, which is 28.

b. In order to assemble 200 units of X, the quantities of each component determined in part **a** must be multiplied by 200. Hence, there must be 200(2) = 400 Bs, 200(6) = 1,200 Ds, 200(28) = 5,600 Es, and so on.

When requirements are calculated in an MRP system, the computer in effect scans the product-structure *level by level,* starting

FIGURE 11–6

Low-Level Coding for Component E

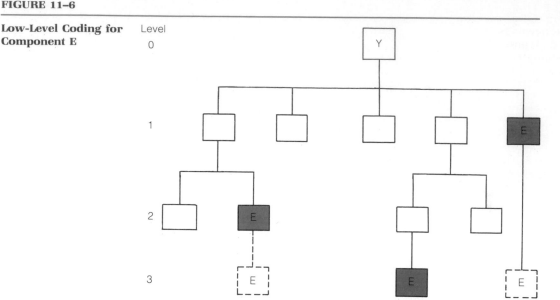

at the top. When a component (such as E in Figure 11–5) appears on more than one level, its total requirements cannot be determined until all levels have been scanned. From a computational standpoint, this is somewhat inefficient. A simplification that is sometimes used to increase efficiency is *low-level coding,* which involves restructuring the BOM so that all occurrences of an item are made to coincide with the lowest level that the item appears. Figure 11–6 illustrates how component E, which appears in three different levels of product Y, can be rearranged so that it appears at only one level.

Comment.   When the concept of low-level coding comes up, students are often puzzled by the following question: What happens if a component that appears at different levels is "buried" at an upper level and can't be lowered, like G seems to be in Figure 11–7? The answer, in terms of Figure 11–7, has two parts. One is that low-level coding is not limited to items at the end of "branches." The parent (G) and its components (and theirs, if necessary) can all be lowered, if need be, to achieve low-level coincidence. The other part of the answer lies in the fact that parent G should have the same components anywhere it appears in the product-structure. In other words, the components H and I would always be required to assemble one G. If for some reason there is an exception to this, then one of the Gs should be given a different name; each name should carry a unique set of component requirements irrespective of where it appears in the product-structure.

FIGURE 11–7

One G Seems to Be Buried, Apparently Preventing Low-Level Coding

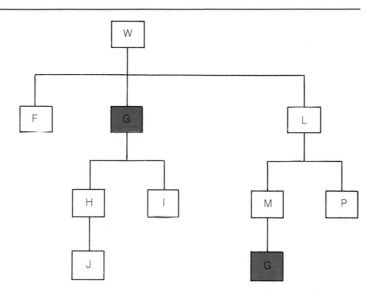

The Inventory-Records File

The *inventory-records file* is used to store information on the status of each item by time period. This includes gross requirements, scheduled receipts, and expected amount on hand. It also includes other details for each item, such as supplier, lead time, and lot size. In addition, changes due to stock receipts and withdrawals, canceled orders, and similar events are recorded in this file.

MRP PROCESSING

MRP processing involves taking the end-item requirements that are specified by the master schedule and "exploding" them into *time-phased* requirements for assemblies, parts, and raw materials using the bill of materials offset by lead times. The time-phasing of requirements can be readily seen in the assembly-time chart in Figure 11–8. For example, raw materials D, F, and I must be ordered at the start of week 2, part D must be ordered at the start of week 4, and part H at the start of week 5 in order to be available for delivery as planned.

The quantities that are generated by exploding the bill of materials are *gross requirements:* they do not take into account any inventory that is currently on hand or due to be received. The materials that must actually be acquired in order to meet the demand generated by the master schedule are the *net material requirements.*

FIGURE 11–8

Assembly-Time Chart Showing Material-Order Points Needed to Meet Scheduled Availability of the End Item

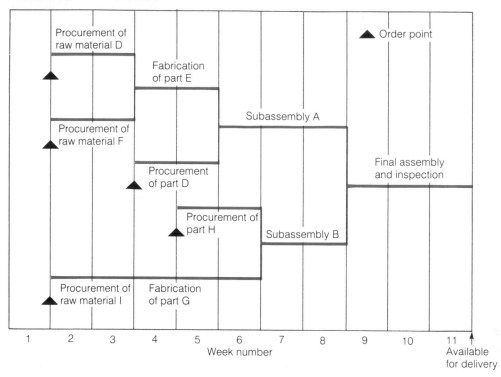

The determination of the net requirements *(netting)* is the core of MRP processing. It is accomplished by subtracting from gross requirements the sum of inventory on hand and any scheduled receipts and then adding in safety stock requirements, if applicable:

$$\begin{matrix} \text{Net} \\ \text{Requirements} \\ \text{in period } t \end{matrix} = \begin{matrix} \text{Gross} \\ \text{Requirements} \\ \text{in period } t \end{matrix} - \left(\begin{matrix} \text{Inventory} \\ \text{Available} \\ \text{in period } t-1 \end{matrix} + \begin{matrix} \text{Scheduled} \\ \text{Receipts} \\ \text{in period } t \end{matrix} \right) + \begin{matrix} \text{Safety} \\ \text{stock} \end{matrix} \tag{11-1}$$

(For simplicity, safety stock is omitted from computations in examples and problems.)

The *timing* and *sizes* of orders (i.e., materials ordered from suppliers or work *started* within the firm) are determined by *planned-order releases.* The timing of the receipts of these quantities is indicated by *planned-order receipts.* Depending on ordering policy, the planned-order releases may be in predetermined lot sizes (i.e., the

same quantity ordered each time), or they may be equal to the quantity needed at that time. There are other possibilities, but these two seem to be the most widely used. The following example illustrates the contrast between these two ordering policies as well as the general concepts of time-phasing material requirements in MRP. As you work through the example, you may find it useful to refer to the list of terms described below.

Gross requirements: The total expected demand for an item or raw material during each time period. For end items, these quantites are shown in the master schedule; for components, these quantities equal the planned-order relcases of their respective parents.

Scheduled receipts: Open orders scheduled to arrive from vendors or elsewhere in the pipeline.

Inventory available: The expected amount of inventory that will be on hand at the *beginning* of each time period: Scheduled receipts & last period's Available − Gross requirements. (0 if negative.)

Net requirements: The actual amount needed in each time period.

Planned-order receipts: The quantity expected to be received by the *beginning* of the period in which it is shown. Under lot-for-lot ordering, this quantity will equal net requirements. Under lot-size ordering, this quantity may exceed net requirements. Any excess is addcd to available inventory in the same time period.

Planncd-ordcr releases: Indicates a planned amount to order in each time period. Equals "planned-order receipts" offset by lead time. This amount generates gross requirements at the next-lower level in the assembly or production chain. When an order is executed, it is removed from the "planned-order receipts" and "planned-order release" rows and entered in the "scheduled receipts" row.

These quantities are used in a time-phased plan in this format:

Week number:	1	2	3	4	5	6	7	8
Item:								
Gross requirements								
Scheduled receipts								
Available								
Net requirements								
Planned-order receipt								
Planned-order release								

EXAMPLE 2

A firm that produces wood shutters and bookcases has received two orders for shutters: one for 100 shutters and one for 150 shutters. The 100-unit order is due at the start of week 4 of the current schedule, and the 150-unit order is due for delivery at the start of week 8. Each shutter consists of four slatted wood sections and two frames. The wood sections are made by the firm, and fabrication takes one week. The frames are ordered, and lead time is two weeks. Assembly of the shutters requires one week. There is a scheduled receipt of 70 wood sections in week 1. Determine the size and timing of planned-order releases necessary to meet delivery requirements under each of these conditions:

1. Lot-for-lot ordering (i.e., order size equal net requirements).
2. Lot-size ordering with a lot size of 320 units for frames and 470 units for wood sections.

Solution

a. Develop a master schedule.

Week number:	1	2	3	4	5	6	7	8
Quantity:				100				150

b. Develop a product-structure tree.

Shutter

Frames(2)   Wood
                                 sections(4)

c. Develop an assembly-time chart.

EXAMPLE 2 *(continued)*

    d. Using the master schedule, determine gross requirements for shutters. Next, compute net requirements. Assuming lot-for-lot ordering, determine planned-order receipt quantities and the planned-order release timing to satisfy the master schedule (see Figure 11–9).

FIGURE 11–9

MRP Schedule with Lot-for-Lot Ordering

Master schedule for shutters

Week number	1	2	3	4	5	6	7	8
Quantity				100				150

Shutters:
LT = 1 wk

	1	2	3	4	5	6	7	8
Gross requirements				100				150
Scheduled receipts								
Available								
Net requirements				100				150
Planned-order receipts				(100)				(150)
Planned-order releases			(100)				(150)	

times 2   times 2

Frames:
LT = 2 wk

	1	2	3	4	5	6	7	8
Gross requirements			200				300	
Scheduled receipts								
Available								
Net requirements			200				300	
Planned-order receipts			(200)				(300)	
Planned-order releases	(200)				(300)			

times 4   times 4

Wood sections:
LT = 1 wk

	1	2	3	4	5	6	7	8
Gross requirements			400				600	
Scheduled receipts	70							
Available	70	70	0					
Net requirements			330				600	
Planned-order receipts			(330)				(600)	
Planned-order releases		(330)				(600)		

EXAMPLE 2 *(continued)*

Since the master schedule calls for 100 shutters to be ready for delivery at the start of the fourth week, and since no shutters are projected to be on hand at that time, the net requirements are also 100 shutters. Therefore, planned receipts for the fourth week equal 100 shutters. Since shutter assembly requires one week, this means a planned-order release at the start of the third week.

Using the same logic, 150 shutters must be assembled during the seventh week in order to be available for delivery at the start of the eighth week.

e. The planned-order release of 100 shutters at the start of the third week means that 200 frames (gross requirements) must be available at that time. Since none are expected to be on hand, this generates net requirements of 200 frames and necessitates planned receipts of 200 frames by the start of the third week. With a two-week lead time, this means that 200 frames must be ordered at the start of the first week.

Similarly, the planned-order release of 150 shutters at week 7 generates gross and net requirements of 300 frames for week 7 as well as planned receipts for that time. The two-week lead time means frames must be ordered at the start of week 5.

f. The planned-order release of 100 shutters at the start of the third week also generates gross requirements of 400 wood sections at that same time. However, because 70 wood sections are expected to be on hand, net requirements are $400 - 70 = 330$. This means planned receipt of 330 by the start of the third week. Since fabrication time is one week, the fabrication must start (planned-order release) at the beginning of week 1.

Similarly, the planned-order release of 150 shutters at week 7 generates gross requirements of 600 wood sections at that point. Since no on-hand inventory of wood sections is projected, net requirements are also 600, and planned-order receipt is 600 units. Again, the one-week lead time means 600 sections are scheduled for fabrication at the start of the sixth week.

g. Under *lot-size ordering,* the only difference is the possibility that planned receipts will exceed net requirements. The excess is added to on-hand inventory. For example, in Figure 11–10, the order size for frames is 320 units. Net requirements for week 3 are 200, thus there is an excess of $320 - 200 = 120$ units, which become on-hand inventory in the same week. Similarly, net frame requirements of 180 units are 140 less than the 320 order size, and again the excess becomes on-hand inventory in week 8. The same thing happens with wood sections: an excess of planned receipts in periods 3 and 7 that is added to available inventory in periods 3 and 7.

EXAMPLE 2 *(concluded)*
FIGURE 11–10

MRP Schedule with Lot Sizes for Components

Master schedule for shutters

Week number	1	2	3	4	5	6	7	8
Quantity				100				150

Shutters:
LT = 1 week
Lot size = None

	1	2	3	4	5	6	7	8
Gross requirements				100				150
Scheduled receipts								
Available								
Net requirements				100				150
Planned-order receipts				(100)				(150)
Planned-order releases			(100)				(150)	

times 2   times 2

Frames:
LT = 2 week
Lot size = 320

	1	2	3	4	5	6	7	8
Gross requirements			200				300	
Scheduled receipts								
Available			120	120	120	120	140	140
Net requirements			200				180	
Planned-order receipts			(320)				(320)	
Planned-order releases	(320)				(320)			

times 4   times 4

Wood sections:
LT = 1 week
Lot size = 470

	1	2	3	4	5	6	7	8
Gross requirements			400				600	
Scheduled receipts	70							
Available	70	70	140	140	140	140	10	10
Net requirements			330				460	
Planned-order receipts			(470)				(470)	
Planned-order releases		(470)			(470)			

Another perspective on the process of determining material requirements for subassemblies components is given in Figure 11–11.

Example 2 is useful for describing some of the main features of MRP processing, but it understates the enormity of the task of keeping track of material requirements, especially in situations where the same subassemblies, parts, or raw materials are used

FIGURE 11–11

Net Requirements at Each Level Determine Gross Requirements at the Next

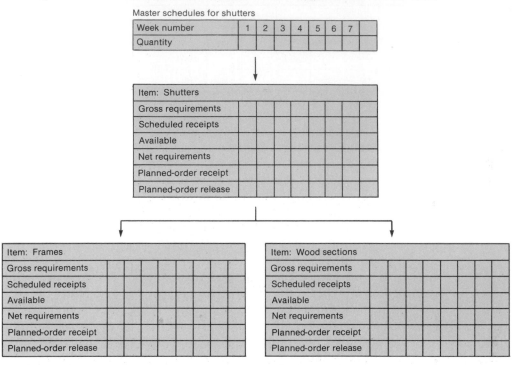

in a number of different products. Differences in timing of demands and quantities needed as well as revisions caused by late deliveries, high scrap rates, and canceled orders all impact on processing.

Consider, for example, bracket G, which is used for end items W, X, and Y as shown by their product trees in Figure 11–12. For

FIGURE 11–12

Bracket G Is Used in Three Different Products

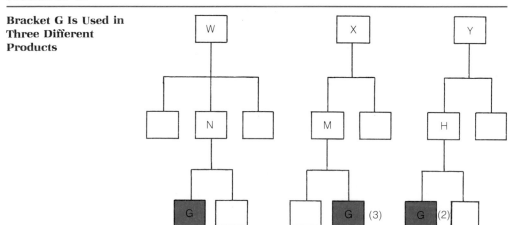

FIGURE 11–13

**Master Schedule for
End Items That Use
Bracket G**

Week number

End item	1	2	3	4	5	6	7
W			50		70		60
X			200			100	
Y		30			80	90	

the sake of simplicity, assume that all lead times are one week. Suppose that the master schedule for these products is as shown in Figure 11–13. Note that these are the *gross requirements* for these end items; *net requirements* will be less by the amount of any on-hand inventories. The same holds true for net requirements for subassemblies N, M, and H. Each of these factors must be taken into account in calculating net material requirements for G. The gross requirements for G by parent might look something like the schedule shown in Figure 11–14, with the net requirements for G equal to the sum of these amounts minus any projected on-hand inventory of G, which is also shown in Figure 11–14. Note: the on-hand quantities of the end items are not given, nor are those quantities given for parents N, M, and H. However, the point here is not the computations, but that gross requirements for bracket G are generated by the net requirements of all of its "parents."

The term *pegging* is used to denote working this process in reverse; that is, identifying the parent items that have generated a given set of material requirements for some item such as G. While

FIGURE 11–14

**Net Requirements for
Bracket G**

Week number

Net requirements for G due to:	1	2	3	4	5	6	7
N	40		50		40		
M	120			240			
H				160	120		
Total	160		50	400	160		

	1	2	3	4	5	6	7
Gross requirements	160		50	400	160		
Available	200	40	40	0	0		
Net requirements			10	400	160		

the process might appear simple enough, given the product trees and schedules shown here, when this information is computerized, special efforts must be made so that requirements can be traced to specific parents.

The importance of the computer becomes quite evident when you stop to realize that a typical firm would tend to have not one but many end items for which it needs to develop material-requirements plans, each with its own set of components. Inventories on-hand and on order, schedules, order releases, and so on must all be updated as changes and rescheduling occur. Without the aid of a computer, the task would be quite hopeless; with the aid of a computer, all of these things can be accomplished with a lot less difficulty.

Updating the System

There are two basic approaches to updating MRP records; regenerative and net change. A *regenerative system* is one that is updated periodically; a *net-change system* is one that is continuously updated.

A regenerative system is essentially a batch-type system that compiles all changes (e.g., new orders, receipts) that occur within the time interval (e.g., week) and periodically updates the system. Using that information, a revised production plan is developed (if needed), in the same way that the original plan was developed (i.e., exploding the bill of materials, level by level, etc.).

In a net-change system, the basic production plan is modified to reflect changes as they occur. Hence, if some purchased parts had to be returned to a vendor because they were defective, this information is entered into the system as soon as it becomes known. Only the *changes* would be exploded through the system, level by level, but the basic plan would not be regenerated.

The regenerative system is best suited to systems that are fairly stable, while the net-change system lends itself more to systems that tend to have frequent changes. The obvious disadvantage of a regenerative system is the potential amount of lag between the time information becomes available and the time it can be incorporated into the material-requirements plan. On the other hand, processing costs are typically less using regenerative systems, and there is the possibility that changes that occur in a given time period will end up canceling each other, thereby avoiding the need to modify the plan and then remodify it. The disadvantages of the net-change system relate to the computer-processing costs involved in continuously updating the system and the fact that many small changes can keep the system in a constant state of flux. One way around that is to enter minor changes periodically, but enter major changes immediately. The primary advantage of the net-change system is that management can have up-to-date information for planning and control purposes.

MRP OUTPUTS

MRP systems have the ability to provide management with a fairly broad range of outputs. These are often classified as *primary reports,* which are the main reports, and *secondary reports,* which are optional outputs.

Primary reports concern production and inventory planning and control. These reports normally include the following:

1. A schedule of *planned orders,* which indicates the amount and timing of future orders.
2. *Order releases,* which authorize the execution of planned orders.
3. *Changes* to planned orders, which can include revisions of due dates or order quantities as well as cancellations of orders.

Secondary reports concern such things as performance control, planning, and exceptions:

1. *Performance-control reports* are used to evaluate system operation. They aid managers by measuring deviations from plans, including missed deliveries and stock-outs, and by providing information that can be used to assess cost performance.
2. *Planning reports* are useful in forecasting future inventory requirements. They include purchase commitments and other data that can be used to assess future material requirements.
3. *Exception reports* call attention to major discrepancies such as late and overdue orders, excessive scrap rates, reporting errors, and requirements for nonexistent parts.

The wide range of outputs generally permits users to adapt MRP to their particular needs.

OTHER CONSIDERATIONS

Aside from the main details of inputs, outputs, and processing, there are a number of other aspects of MRP that the manager must be knowledgeable about. These include the question of whether to hold safety stock, lot-sizing choices, and the possible use of MRP for items that are not finished products.

Safety Stock

Theoretically, inventory systems with dependent demand should not require safety stock below the end-item level. In fact, this is

one of the main advantages of an MRP approach. Supposedly, safety stock is not needed because usage quantities can be projected once the master schedule has been established. Practically speaking, however, there may be exceptions to this. For example, a bottleneck process or one with varying scrap rates can cause shortages in downstream operations. Furthermore, shortages can occur if orders are late or fabrication or assembly times are longer than expected. On the surface, these are the kinds of conditions that lend themselves to the use of safety stock to maintain smooth operations. However, the problem is somewhat complicated when dealing with multiechelon items (i.e., multiple-level items such as assembled products) by the fact that a shortage of *any* component will prevent finishing the final assembly. Thus, a major advantage of MRP would be lost by holding safety stock for all lower-level items.

MRP systems deal with these problems in several ways. The first step is for a manager to identify those activities or operations that are subject to variability and then to determine the extent of that variability. When lead times are variable, the concept of safety *time* is often used instead of safety *stock.* This results in scheduling orders for arrival or completion enough ahead of the time they are needed to eliminate or substantially reduce the chance of having to wait for those items. When quantities tend to vary, some safety stock may be called for. However, the manager must carefully weigh the need and cost of carrying the extra stock. Frequently, managers elect to carry safety stock for *end* items because these are subject to random demand and for *selected* lower-level operations when safety time is not feasible, say because of capacity limitations.

Lot Sizing

An important issue in inventory management, whether for independent- or dependent-demand items, is choosing a lot size to order or for production. This is called *lot sizing.* For independent-demand items, economic order sizes and economic run sizes are widely used. However, for dependent-demand systems, there is a much wider variety of plans used for determining lot sizes, mainly because no one plan has a clear advantage over the others. Some of the most popular of these plans for lot sizing are described in this section.

Whether we are dealing with independent- or dependent-demand systems, a primary goal of inventory management is to minimize the sum of ordering cost (or setup cost) and holding cost. It is often the case with independent demand that demand is uniformly distributed throughout the planning horizon (e.g., six months, year). Demand tends to be much more lumpy for dependent demand, and the planning horizon shorter (say, three months), so that economic lot sizes are usually much more difficult to identify. Consider the situation depicted in Figure 11–15. Period demands vary from one

FIGURE 11–15

Demand for Part K

	Period				
	1	*2*	*3*	*4*	*5*
Demand	70	50	1	80	4
Cumulative demand	70	120	121	201	205

to 80 units, and no demand size repeats, at least over the horizon shown.

There can be economies realized by grouping order or run sizes. This would be the case if the additional cost incurred by holding the extra units until they were used led to a savings in setup or ordering cost. This determination can be very complex at times, for several reasons. One is that combining period demands into a single order, particularly for middle-level or end items, has a cascading effect down through the product tree. That is, in order to achieve this grouping, items at lower levels in the tree must also be grouped. Hence, their setup and holding costs must also be incorporated into the decision. Another reason is the uneven period demands and the relatively short planning horizon. These factors require a continual recalculation and updating of lot sizes. Not surprisingly, the methods used to handle the lot sizing question range from complex ones, which attempt to include all relevant costs, to very simple ones, which are easy to use and understand. And in certain cases, the simple models seem to approach cost minimization, although generalizations are difficult. Let's consider some of these models.

Lot-for-lot ordering. This is perhaps the simplest of all the approaches used. The order or run size for each period is set equal to demand for that period. This method was demonstrated in Example 2. Not only is the order size obvious, but it also virtually eliminates holding costs for parts carried over to other periods. Its two chief drawbacks are that it usually involves many different order sizes and so cannot take advantage of economies associated with a fixed order size (e.g., standard containers and other standardized procedures), and it involves a new setup for each run. If setup costs can be significantly reduced, this approach may approximate a minimum cost result.

Economic-order-quantity models (covered in Chapter 10) are sometimes used. They can lead to minimum costs if usage is fairly uniform. This is sometimes the case for lower-level items that are common to different parents and for raw materials. However, the more lumpy demand is, the less appropriate such an approach is.

Since demand tends to be most lumpy at the end-item level, EOQ models tend to be less useful for end items than for items and materials at the lowest levels.

Fixed period ordering provides coverage for some predetermined number of periods (e.g., two or three). In some instances the span is simply arbitrary, while in other cases a review of historical demand patterns may lead to a more rational designation of a fixed period length. A simple rule would be: Order to cover a two-period interval. A variation of the rule is to modify it when common sense suggests a better way. For example, take a look at the demands shown in Figure 11–15. Using a two-period rule, an order size of 120 units would cover the first two periods. The next two periods would be covered by an order size of 81 units. However, the demands in periods 3 and 5 are so small, it would make sense to combine them both with the 80 units, and order 85 units.

The *part-period* model represents another attempt to balance setup and holding costs. The term *part-period* refers to holding a part or parts over a number of periods. For instance, if 10 parts were held for 2 periods, this would be $10 \times 2 = 20$ part-periods. The economic part-period (EPP) can be computed as the ratio of setup costs to the cost to hold a unit for one period. Thus, the formula for computing the EPP is:

$$\text{EPP} = \frac{\text{Setup cost}}{\begin{array}{c}\text{Unit holding cost} \\ \text{per period}\end{array}} \tag{11–2}$$

In order to determine an order size that is consistent with the EPP, various order sizes are examined for a planning horizon, and each one's part-periods is determined. The one that comes closest to the EPP is selected as the best lot size. The order sizes that are examined are based on cumulative demand. The following example illustrates this approach.

EXAMPLE 3

Use the part-period method to determine order sizes for this demand schedule:

				Period				
	1	*2*	*3*	*4*	*5*	*6*	*7*	*8*
Demand	60	40	20	2	30	—	70	50
Cumulative demand	60	100	120	122	152	152	222	272

EXAMPLE 3 *(concluded)*

Setup cost is $47 per run for this item, and unit holding cost is $.56 per period.

Solution

1. First compute the EPP: EPP $= \dfrac{\$47}{\$.56} = 83.93$, which rounds to 84 part-periods.
2. Next, try the cumulative lot sizes, beginning with 60, until the part-periods approximate the EPP. Continue this process for the planning horizon. This leads to the following:

Period	Lot size	Extra inventory carried	Periods carried	Part-periods	Cumulative part-periods	
1	60	0	0	0	0	
	100	40	1	40	40	
	120	20	2	40	80	
	122	2	3	6	86*	[closest to 84]
5	30	0	0	0	0	
	100	70	2	140	140*	[closest to 84]
8	50	0	0	0	0	

The computations of part-periods indicate that 122 units should be ordered to be available at period 1, and 100 units should be ordered to be available at period 5. The next lot will be ordered for period 8, but we do not have enough information now to determine its size.

The lot sizes considered for period 1 correspond to cumulative demand. Once the best lot size has been identified, the cumulative demand is set equal to zero and then summed beginning for the next period. In this case the lot size of 122 covers the first four periods, so cumulative demand is started next for period 5. That next lot size covers through period 7, and the count begins again at period 8.

The process works quite well for the first lot size since the cumulative part-periods is quite close to the EPP, but the effect of lumpy demand is very apparent for the second lot size of 100 (140 part-periods is not very close to 84 part-periods).

The *Wagner-Whitin algorithm* attempts to minimize the sum of ordering and carrying costs using dynamic programming to select the ordering strategy to cover net requirements in each period for the complete net-requirements schedule. The advantage of this approach is that the algorithm identifies a relatively few strategies, which it then compares, selecting the one that minimizes total costs.

The disadvantage of the technique is that its complexity makes it highly unlikely that the average user will be able to understand it, which not only decreases the chance of having the technique selected for use in the first place, but also increases the risk of misusing it or misinterpreting the results.

The choice of a lot-sizing technique must take into account the nature of demand (degree of uniformity), the relative importance of carrying costs versus ordering costs, and any other considerations that affect ordering. It appears that no one technique is suited to all conditions.

Regardless of the lot-sizing technique in use, there is always the possibility of adjustments in order sizes due to allowance for shrinkage or scrap, minimum and maximum order quantities established by management (e.g., do not order more than five months' supply), operating or shipping constraints (e.g., 200 pieces per run or 12 dozen per shipment) that require rounding of order sizes (usually up) to these amounts, and similar factors.

CAPACITY REQUIREMENTS PLANNING

One of the most important features of MRP is its ability to aid managers in capacity planning. As noted previously, a master schedule that appears feasible on the surface may turn out to be far from feasible in terms of resource requirements needed for fabrication and/or subassembly operations of lower-level items.

An overview of the capacity-planning process is presented in Figure 11–16. The process begins with a proposed or tentative master schedule that must be tested for feasibility and possibly adjusted before it becomes permanent. The proposed schedule is processed using MRP to ascertain the material requirements that such a schedule would generate. These are then translated into resource (i.e., capacity) requirements, often in the form of a series of *load reports* for each department or work center that compare known and expected future capacity requirements with projected capacity availability. The nature of a load report is illustrated in Figure 11–17. It shows expected resource requirements (i.e., usage) for jobs currently being worked on, for planned orders, and for expected orders for the planning horizon. Given this sort of information, the manager can more easily determine whether there is sufficient capacity to satisfy these requirements. If there is enough capacity, the portion of the master schedule that generates these requirements can be frozen. In the load report illustrated in Figure 11–17, planned-order releases in the fourth time period will cause an overload. However, it appears possible to accomodate demand by

FIGURE 11–16

**Using MRP to Assist in
Planning Capacity
Requirements**

Source: Stephen Love, *Inventory Control* (New York: McGraw-Hill, 1979), p. 164. Reprinted by permission.

FIGURE 11–17

**A Hypothetical
Department Load
Report**

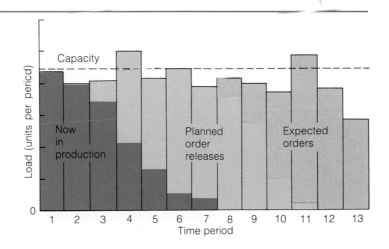

slightly shifting some orders to adjacent periods. Similarly, an over-load appears likely in period 11, but that too can be handled by shifting some jobs to adjacent time periods. In cases where capacity is insufficient, a manager may be able to increase capacity (by scheduling overtime, transferring personnel from other areas, or subcontracting some of the work) if this is possible and economical or else revise the master schedule and repeat the process until an acceptable master schedule is obtained.

If the master schedule must be revised, this generally means that the manager must assign *priorities* to orders, since some orders will be finished later than originally planned.

BENEFITS AND LIMITATIONS OF MRP

MRP offers a number of benefits to the typical manufacturing or assembly type of operation. These generally include:

1. Low levels of in-process inventories.
2. The ability to keep track of material requirements.
3. The ability to evaluate capacity requirements generated by a given master schedule.
4. A means of allocating production time.

The benefits of MRP depend in large measure on the use of a computer to maintain up-to-date information on material requirements.

In order to implement and operate an effective MRP system, it is necessary to have:

1. A computer and the necessary software programs to handle computations and maintain records.
2. Accurate and up-to-date:
   a. Master schedule.
   b. Bills of materials.
   c. Inventory records.
3. Integrity of file data.

Unfortunately, some of the firms that have attempted to install an MRP system have seriously underestimated the importance of these items. In many cases bills of materials have been outdated because design changes were not incorporated into the records, leading to parts lists that do not correspond to what is actually required to assemble the finished product. In addition, it is not un-usual for a firm to discover that the same part is being carried under different part numbers, making it difficult to develop mean-

ingful records. Moreover, some firms have encountered resistance from foremen and others, often along the line of: "We've managed for 30 years without this blankety-blank stuff, so why bother with it now?"

Because of these obstacles, it can take a year or more to implement MRP, taking into account employee education, training, and *convincing,* and correction of record-keeping deficiencies.

On the whole, the introduction of MRP has led to major improvements in scheduling and inventory management. Nonetheless, it has not proved to be the cure-all that many hoped it would be. Consequently, manufacturers are beginning to take a much broader view of resource planning. One such approach is referred to as MRP II.

MRP II

In the early 80s, materials requirements planning was expanded into a much broader approach for planning and scheduling the resources of manufacturing firms. This expanded approach has been dubbed MRP II, which refers to Manufacturing Resources Planning. It has not replaced MRP, nor is it an improved version of MRP. Rather, it represents an effort to expand the scope of production resource planning and to involve other functional areas of the firm in the planning process. Marketing and finance are the two most notable areas that are impacted by—and have an impact on—the manufacturing plan.

In too many instances, production, marketing, and finance operate without complete knowledge or seeming regard for what the other areas of the firm are doing. Obviously, to be most effective, all areas of the firm need to focus on a common set of goals. A major purpose of MRP II is to integrate these primary functions as well as other functions such as personnel, engineering, and purchasing in the planning process.

Materials requirements planning is at the heart of the process, which is illustrated in Figure 11–18. The process begins with an aggregation of demand from all sources (e.g., firm orders, forecasts, safety stock requirements). Production, marketing, and finance personnel work toward developing a master schedule. Although manufacturing people will have a major input in determining that schedule and a major responsibility for making it work, marketing and finance will also have important inputs and responsibilities. The rationale of having these functional areas work together is the increased likelihood of developing a plan that will work and one that

FIGURE 11–18

**An Overview
of MRP II**

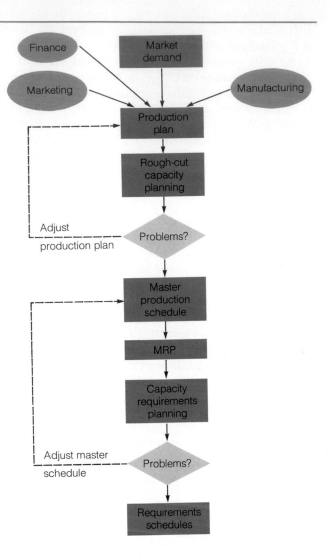

everyone can live with. Moreover, because each of these functional areas has been involved in formulating the plan, they will have reasonably good knowledge of the plan and work toward achieving it.

In addition to the obvious manufacturing resources needed to support the plan, financing resources will be needed and must be planned for, both in amount and timing. Similarly, marketing resources will also be needed in varying degrees throughout the process. In order for the plan to work, it must be determined that all of these necessary resources will be available as needed. Often,

an initial plan must be revised based on an assessment of the availability of various resources. Once these have been decided, the master schedule can be firmed up.

At this point material requirements planning comes into play, generating material and schedule requirements. Then, more detailed capacity requirements planning must be done to determine if these more specific capacity requirements can be met. Again, some adjustments in the master schedule may be required.

As the schedule unfolds and actual work begins, a variety of reports are generated that help managers to keep a pulse on how well actual experience complies with plans and to make any necessary adjustments to keep operations on track.

In effect, this is a continuing process, with the master schedule being updated and revised as necessary to achieve corporate goals. The business plan that governs the entire process also usually undergoes changes, although these tend to be less frequent than the changes made at lower levels (i.e., the master schedule).

Finally, it should be noted that most MRP II systems have the capability to do simulation. This enables managers to answer a variety of "what if . . ." questions, thereby gaining a better appreciation of available options and their consequences.

Since MRP is at the heart of MRP II, the computer is an important tool in MRP II, one that is heavily relied upon for information processing.

THE JAPANESE APPROACH

Japanese manufacturers are becoming increasingly well-known for their success in productivity and quality improvements, particularly in the area of repetitive manufacturing (e.g., automobiles, appliances, electronic equipment, and cameras). This is especially interesting since the Japanese approach to production planning and control in repetitive manufacturing tends to differ quite a bit from the approach used by many American manufacturers. Hence, it will be useful to examine the Japanese approach and to consider the lessons they provide for American manufacturing.

A major innovator of the Japanese approach has been Toyota Motor Company. In fact, we can learn a good deal about Japanese methods by taking a look at Toyota's methods. The following article, reprinted from *The Wall Street Journal*, presents an overview of those methods.

The Nuts and Bolts of Japan's Factories

Urban C. Lehner

"If American automobile king Henry Ford I were alive today, I am positive he would have done what we did with our Toyota production system."

—Taiichi Oono in his 1978 book
The Toyota Production System

TOYOTA CITY, Japan—Groping to explain "how Japan does it," experts have made much of the close ties between business and government and of the loyalty of Japan's highly skilled workers to their employers. They've noted the fierce competitiveness of Japanese companies in their home market, the nation's high savings rate, even the relative scarcity of lawyers.

Doubtless these are among the pieces needed to solve the puzzle. But some management consultants who've studied how Japan makes such high-quality, competitively priced products say there's another piece often overlooked. The Japanese, they say, have proved themselves increasingly adroit at organizing and running manufacturing operations. Japanese managers may lack the MBAs or the ability to plot big-picture business strategy of their American counterparts. But they know how to run factories.

"There's a growing acceptance that Japanese success is based at least in part on the development of manufacturing techniques that often tend to outrun our own," says management consultant Rex Reid, head of A. T. Kearney's Toyota office.

One of the most interesting examples of Japanese production-management skills is a concern quite familiar to Americans: Toyota

Motor Co., the largest-selling foreign auto maker in the U.S.

Believe in their system

Toyota officials resist claiming that their way of building autos is better than anyone else's. They're somewhat embarrassed by the exuberant projections of Henry Ford's behavior essayed by their former chief production executive, Taiichi Oono, in his 1978 book. But Toyota men clearly remain believers in what Mr. Oono called "the Toyota production system."

For a first-hand look at the system, take a walk through the Tsutsumi plant here in Toyota City, a town of 280,000 in central Japan that's the site of eight of Toyota's 10 factories. Over here, Muneo Nakahara, 26 years old and an eight-year Toyota veteran, is doing his job. With the help of an overhead crain that Mr. Nakahara controls from a hand-held device, he hoists auto engines onto a conveyor belt that will take them to be matched up with auto bodies.

Mr. Nakahara is lifting the engines onto the conveyor from a small flat-bed truck that has brought them from the engine plant. Only two trucks carrying only 12 engines apiece park at Mr. Nakahara's post at any given time, so every few minutes an empty truck drives back to the engine plant and a new one takes its place.

That's the first feature of the Toyota system: no inventories. Toyota's factories keep on hand only that amount of parts needed for immediate production, from a few minutes' worth up to a few hours' worth depending on the part. When fresh parts are needed— and only when they're needed—they're delivered from other Toyota plants or from outside suppliers directly to the production line.

Outsiders who've seen Toyota in action of-

ten call this the "kanban system," kanban being the Japanese word for the piece of paper enclosed in clear plastic that accompanies each bin of parts. (When a worker on the line begins drawing from a new bin, he removes the kanban and routes it back to the supplier, for whom it serves as an order for a new bin of parts.) But Toyota officials say the pieces of paper are just tools. They call this inventory-control aspect of their broader system the "just-in-time" system.

The same philosophy guides the meshing of operations within each plant. An assembly line that is building subcomponents makes just that number of subcomponents immediately needed at the next stage of production. When it's made enough, it's changed over to build some other kind of subcomponent for awhile. Likewise, the final assembly line builds first one kind of car, then another, in small lots—only as much as called for in actual orders from Toyota's sales unit. Toyota engineers "average" and "level" production among the lines to coordinate output without building inventories. They compare auto assembly to rowing a boat: Everybody has to be pulling on the oars at the same rate.

"They concentrate very heavily on avoiding end-item and intermediate-item storage," says a Ford official in Detroit who's seen the system at work. "They throw out the whole concept of mass production."

The benefits are substantial. Toyota doesn't need space for inventory, people to handle and control inventory, or borrowed money to finance inventory. "It cuts costs in a lot of ways," says an official of Nissan Motor Co., Japan's second-largest automaker, which has adopted an inventory-control system similar to its rival's in some plants.

Then there are the side benefits. Because Toyota is constantly changing over its machines to make new things, its workers have become fast at repair and changeover. In his book, Mr. Oono cites a mold on a press that took two to three hours to change in the 1940s. Today "it takes only three minutes to change the mold," Mr. Oono says.

Aside from its emphasis on holding down inventories, Toyota's system stresses quality controls. Throughout the Tsutsumi plant are boards with electric lights to indicate conditions on each assembly line. A red light means a line has been stopped because of a problem. Every worker has a button or cord with which he can stop the line, and he's told to use it whenever he thinks something's wrong with the operation of the line or when he spots defects in the product.

"We lose production temporarily this way," concedes Fujio Cho, manager of the production control department at Toyota's headquarters. "But in our experience stopping lines helps us detect problems early and avoid bad practices."

Another feature that becomes clear is the company's penchant for training workers to do more than one job. The man who runs one machine switches off every few moments to run another. The man who feeds rear windows to a robot also "tags" car shells with instructions telling workers farther down the line what to install in them. This versatility allows Toyota to realign its work force more efficiently when business is bad.

Indeed, "recession" thinking underlies a big part of Toyota's system. Much of the system originated in the late 1940s and early 1950s, when Toyota was producing exclusively for a domestic market that wasn't very strong. The company has been operating on the conventional assumption that it's most efficient to produce in large lots, "but that kind of thinking has pushed us close to bankruptcy, because the large lots we were producing couldn't be sold," says Mr. Cho. Toyota couldn't lay off workers—Japan's a "lifetime" employment system—so Toyota executives hit upon the simple yet radical idea that still pervades its operations: Overproduction is waste.

Special relationship

It is, of course, open to question whether Toyota's is the best way to make cars, and Toyota officials themselves doubt whether

other auto makers could adopt it readily. They note among other problems that it takes a special kind of relationship with suppliers to make the system work.

Fully 50 of Toyota's 250 suppliers are headquartered in Toyota City, and almost all have plants here. They have to be close to make all those deliveries every day. It still shocks Toyota officials to be told that American auto makers buy parts from suppliers all over the U.S. and even from suppliers in Europe and Japan. Toyota's most distant supplier is a five-hour drive away.

Then, too, suppliers must have close working relations with Toyota to adjust to Toyota's peculiar needs. It isn't surprising that many of Toyota's suppliers do all or most of their business with Toyota, and that Toyota owns large blocks of the stock of some of its most important suppliers. Many suppliers, even those Toyota doesn't own, have adopted Toyota's production system for their own operations. It improves coordination with Toyota, and helps them avoid getting stuck with the inventory buildup that Toyota refuses to get stuck with.

The point isn't whether Toyota's system is best. The point is that it's very good, and that Toyota is in many ways typical of Japanese manufacturers in its continual striving to improve production techniques. When experts talk about the competitiveness of Japanese products in international markets, that's something that shouldn't be forgotten.

This article provides a number of very important insights on the *just-in-time* (JIT) approach to manufacturing along with some reasons for the successes the Japanese manufacturers have achieved. Let's take a closer look at the important points of the article.

The just-in-time approach attempts to minimize inventories. It accomplishes this by ordering and producing very small batches. Ideally, as each order of raw material arrives from a vendor, it goes directly into production, and as each batch is finished at one work center, it is moved to the following work center where the previous order has just been completed, and work is begun on the new order. Hence, inventories of raw materials and purchased parts are purposely kept as small as possible, as are inventories of partially completed goods between operations. Naturally, this means that a disruption anywhere in the system can easily cause the entire system to come to a halt since there is little slack between operations. However, the Japanese see this as an opportunity to learn where the weak points are in the system *and to correct those problems* so they do not recur. By way of contrast, most U.S. manufacturers carry safety stock "just in case. . . ." According to the JIT philosophy, buffers of inventory tend to cover up or hide problems that keep recurring and are never resolved, partly because they aren't always obvious and partly because the presence of inventory seems to make the problems less serious. Needless to say, the additional inventory carries a burden in terms of holding costs.

In order to maintain a JIT system with little inventory and small run sizes, it is necessary to have quick, low-cost changeovers and setups. That is, the basic concept of an economic run size is not refuted by the JIT approach. Rather, by driving down setup costs, the run size that minimizes total cost is decreased. Setup costs are driven down through research that leads to improved methods and equipment and through such approaches as group technology, where families of similar items are processed in sequence. The similarities result in the need for only partial teardowns and setups between runs of different items within the family.

Another factor that enables JIT users to keep in-process inventories low is small run sizes. Unlike most U.S. manufacturers, who use large run sizes to reduce the setup cost per unit, the Japanese produce a small number of one item, then a small number of another, and so on. The ability to quickly change over equipment and have relatively low-cost setups permits them to do this and keep inventories low in the process. This contrast between large and small run sizes is illustrated in Figure 11–19.

One potential source of disruptions in a JIT system is problems with quality. When these sorts of problems appear, they must be investigated and corrected in order to eliminate recurrences. Again, the willingness to commit the time, effort, and money to correct problems at the source is essential to the success of the system.

Toyota uses a "kanban" system for production control. Kanbans are manually prepared cards that authorize either the movement of parts or materials (conveyance kanbans) or production operations (production kanbans). There are also vendor kanbans, which authorize shipments of materials or parts from suppliers. Each kanban is a card roughly 4 inches by 8 inches that contains all the information pertinent to a batch or lot of parts. This includes the origin and destination of the lot, part name and number, the kind of part, a kanban number, the quantity of parts or material per

FIGURE 11–19

JIT versus Large Lot Run Sizes

JIT approach

AAA   BBBBBBB   CC   AAA   BBBBBBB   CC   AAA   BBBBBBB   CC   AAA   BBBBBBB   CC

time —→

Large lot approach

AAAAAAAAAAAAAAAA   BBBBBBBBBBBBBBBBBBBBBBBBBBBBBBBBB   CCCCCCCCC   AAAAAAAAAAAA

time —→

parent item, and a work station number if applicable. The kanbans function as an integral part of the control system. No part or lot can be moved or worked on without one of these authorization cards. Roughly, the system works as follows. A kanban card is affixed to each container. When a work station needs to replenish its supply of parts, a worker goes to the area where these parts are stored and withdraws one container of parts. Each container holds a predetermined quantity (i.e., the economic lot size). The worker removes the kanban card from that container and posts it in a designated spot where it will be clearly visible, and the worker then moves the lot to the work station. The posted kanban is then picked up by a stock person who replenishes the stock with another container, and so on down the line. In effect, then, the kanban system is a "pull" system: demand for parts triggers a replenishment, and parts are supplied only as usage dictates. Similar withdrawals and replenishments occur all up and down the line from finished-goods inventory to vendors, all controlled by kanbans. In fact, if supervisors decide the system is too loose because inventories are building up, they may decide to withdraw some kanbans, thereby tightening the system. Conversely, if the system seems too tight, additional kanbans may be introduced to bring the system into balance.

The just-in-time system has yet another mechanism for maintaining balance: it is designed to identify bottlenecks and potential bottlenecks. In addition to carefully balancing the system prior to production, each work station is equipped with a light system (andon) that is used to signal problems. A green light means no problem; an amber light indicates a worker is falling a bit behind; and a red light indicates the worker has a problem (e.g., an equipment breakdown or a quality problem). Workers are cross-trained, so that if one falls behind, others are able to assist until the system is back on track. Moreover, workers are also trained to handle many equipment repairs, thereby reducing the impact of equipment failures on the length of a disruption. In addition, because of the cross-training, workers can fill in for others in the case of illness or other problems. Hence, teamwork is an important part of the JIT approach.

Close vendor relationships are also important. Typically, manufacturers use only one or a few vendors, who are often located nearby. Vendors generally also use a JIT system. That, plus their nearby locations, enables them to frequently ship small lot sizes to the producing firm, which fits into the producer's JIT system.

An overview of the differences between the kanban philosophy and typical U.S. philosophy is presented in Table 11–1. It implies that key reasons for the Japanese success lie in how they treat inventories, lot sizes, setups, vendors, quality, and their workers.

TABLE 11-1

Comparison of Kanban and Typical U.S. Manufacturing Philosophies

Factors	Toyota's kanban	American philosophy
Inventory	A liability. Every effort must be extended to do away with it.	An asset. It protects against forecast errors, machine problems, late vendor deliveries. More inventory is "safer."
Lot sizes	Immediate needs only. A minimum replenishment quantity is desired for both manufactured and purchased parts.	Formulas. We're always revising the optimum lot size with some formula based on the trade-off between the cost of inventories and the cost of set up.
Set ups	Make them insignificant. This requires either extremely rapid changeover to minimize the impact on production, or the availability of extra machines already set up. Fast changeover permits small lot sizes to be practical, and allows a wide variety of parts to be made frequently.	Low priority. Maximum output is the usual goal. Rarely does similar thought and effort go into achieving quick changeover.
Queues	Eliminate them. When problems occur, identify the causes and correct them. The correction process is aided when queues are small. If the queues are small, it surfaces the need to identify and fix the cause.	Necessary investment. Queues permit succeeding operations to continue in the event of a problem with the feeding operation. Also, by providing a selection of jobs, the factory management has a greater opportunity to match up varying operator skills and machine capabilities, combine set ups and thus contribute to the efficiency of the operation.
Vendors	Co-workers. They're part of the team. Multiple deliveries for all active items are expected daily. The vendor takes care of the needs of the customer, and the customer treats the vendor as an extension of his factory.	Adversaries. Multiple sources are the rule, and it's typical to play them off against each other.
Quality	Zero defects. If quality is not 100%, production is in jeopardy.	Tolerate some scrap. We usually track what the actual scrap has been and develop formulas for predicting it.
Equipment maintenance	Constant and effective. Machine breakdowns must be minimal.	As required. But not critical because we have queues available.
Lead times	Keep them short. This simplifies the job of marketing, purchasing, and manufacturing as it reduces the need for expediting.	The longer the better. Most foremen and purchasing agents want more lead time, not less.
Workers	Management by consensus. Changes are not made until consensus is reached, whether or not a bit of arm twisting is involved. The vital ingredient of "ownership" is achieved.	Management by edict. New systems are installed in spite of the workers, not thanks to the workers. Then we concentrate on measurements to determine whether or not they're doing it.

Source: Modern Materials Handling, Copyright 1982 in article by Walter E. Goddard, Oliver Wight Education Associates, by Cahners Publishing Company, Division of Reed Holdings, Inc.

Will It Work Here?   The Japanese seem to be quite successful in achieving a high-quality, very productive manufacturing system, one in which inventory costs are relatively low by conventional standards. The obvious question is: Will it work here?

The answer is as of yet uncertain. A few U.S. manufacturers have tried to adopt the Japanese methods, and many others are studying them very carefully. For those who have tried them, the results have been varied. Kawasaki, U.S.A. is reported to have successfully implemented a JIT system. On the other hand, for U.S. automakers, the results have been mixed, as noted in the following article.

Auto Makers Have Trouble with "Kanban"

DETROIT—Sushi may be sweeping the West Coast, but here in Motor City the latest craze is *Kanban*.

Kanban is the word for Japanese auto manufacturers' precise methods of controlling inventories so that suppliers deliver needed parts to the assembly line "just in time." Holding inventories of engines, axles, and other parts to an absolute minimum saves Japanese auto makers hundreds of dollars per car in storage and carrying costs.

American car makers would dearly love such savings, but, like raw fish, Kanban may be difficult to swallow. As they get deeper into it, the domestic auto companies are finding that their system of manufacturing cars favors large stockpiles of parts. Changing that system is going to be a difficult and expensive process.

Over the long haul, altering the inventory system probably will be worth the effort. Robert Burrows, a specialist in inventory management at Booz, Allen & Hamilton Inc., estimates that it costs General Motors well over $3 billion a year to carry its approximately $9 billion in worldwide inventories. The costs include storage, handling, staffing, freight charges, and losses due to obsolescence, defects, and tying up of inventory funds that otherwise could be earning a profitable re-

turn. GM, Mr. Burrows says, could cut those expenses by more than two thirds.

Some success

Progress comes easy at first. Anthony E. Ewert, director of materials management at GM's Buick Motor division, found he could reduce stocks of metal body stampings at Buick's Flint assembly plant merely by switching to truck delivery from rail delivery. Trucks now make three deliveries of stampings a day, usually keeping the plant's inventory under 700. For years, stampings had been delivered every two days on rail cars, and the plant's inventory often totaled more than 4,000.

Other auto makers have had some success, too. Ford Motor Co. says it has reduced its stock by $750 million in the past two years, slashing its carrying costs by more than $250 million. Chrysler claims a $200 million reduction in inventories in the past six months.

But as they solve the easy problems, auto executives in charge of installing the new system are encountering other obstacles, including the different geographic distribution of U.S. factories and widespread resistance to change within their companies.

In Japan, most suppliers are clustered around auto makers' assembly plants, making timely delivery cheaper and more reliable. U.S. assembly plants and suppliers are scattered around the country. Some parts take weeks to be shipped, which increases both the amount of inventory in transit and the sup-

plies needed to guard against interrupted deliveries. A GM executive estimates that at any time more than half of the company's inventory is on trucks and trains.

Demand and supplies

Another difficulty for domestic auto makers has been to set accurate production forecasts. Faced with sputtering demand, the car companies have had trouble judging how many parts to order. "You need about 20 days of orders in hand to set a smooth schedule," says William J. Harahan, Ford's manager of manufacturing planning. "But lately we've been lucky to get 10 days."

The Japanese, on the other hand, have been able to run their plants at near full capacity, allowing them to schedule production weeks in advance and to send exact instructions to their suppliers. "They've got it down to where they can tell a vendor they want a certain number of parts delivered next week at a specified hour," says GM's Mr. Ewert. "We can't do that."

The Japanese system also is simpler to manage because the companies rely on fewer suppliers. Toyota Motor Co. has less than 250. By comparison GM has more than 3,500 suppliers just for its assembly operations, an amount it hopes to reduce.

Stocking for options

The drive to trim inventories at U.S. plants goes against long-standing practices. For years, marketing departments in auto companies have demanded numerous options and different trim packages so that customers can practically design their own cars. Manufacturing executives usually agreed to the idea of options because it didn't add much to the amount of labor that went into a car.

But the effect on inventories has been enormous. A buyer of one of Chrysler's Omni subcompacts can choose among several different chrome strips to go on the car doors. Because the strips require different mountings, the assembly plant has to stock several kinds of chrome strips as well as several kinds of doors.

Incentive systems in manufacturing also don't support inventory control. Robert Stone, a GM vice president, says a program to reduce stock at one plant ran into trouble because the production superintendent refused to turn off his equipment when the factory was building too many parts. The reason: His salary was based on the efficiency of his output.

Even the layout of their plants is an obstacle for U.S. auto makers. The Buick assembly plant in Flint, for example, was built in 1946 to accommodate mostly rail deliveries. Now that Mr. Ewert is trying to switch more deliveries to trucks, one of his biggest headaches is moving trucks in and out of the plant's small loading docks. If sales pick up, the loading docks could be swamped.

So far, most of the steps U.S. auto makers have taken involve their costliest parts: engines, transmissions, and axles. "That's the area to begin," says Buick's Mr. Ewert. "You can affect about 90 percent of the dollars you have tied up by tightening down on 10 percent of the parts."

GM claims success at some of its Midwestern assembly plants with a new procedure to control the supply of major components by ordering each morning only the parts needed that day. Previously, the parts were shipped based on an average daily requirement, which often varied significantly from the actual production.

Ford, however, recently had to abandon a similar system for shipping engines from a factory in Dearborn, Michigan, to a nearby assembly plant. A Ford official says sporadic production at the car plant was hurting the engine factory's ability to produce at a smooth, efficient rate.

Auto makers are confident that the new procedures will work better when car sales pick up. But they still see a long fight in the battle against inventories. "It took Toyota 10 years to implement their system," says Ford's Mr. Harahan. "We've really just begun."

One very real issue facing manufacturers who want to adopt a JIT approach is that a considerable amount of time, effort, and dollars must go into *pre*-JIT preparations. For instance, major quality problems must be ironed out before converting to JIT or else the system will continually be stopping for corrective action. The good news is that this would force domestic producers to face their problems squarely; the bad news is that many are already under the gun to improve their income statements, and this would strain those statements even more. It may be that sooner or later manufacturers and stockholders will have to bite the bullet and recognize that Band-Aid solutions are temporary at best, but they can't provide long-term relief from the problems manufacturers are now facing.

MRP II VERSUS KANBAN[1]

While the goals of MRP II and kanban are essentially the same (i.e., to improve customer service, reduce inventories, and increase productivity), their approaches are quite different. Neither MRP nor kanban is a stand-alone system—each exists within a larger framework. MRP II is basically a computerized system; kanban is a manual system.

Kanban systems generally involve very small lot sizes, short lead times, and high-quality output, and they exemplify teamwork. Kanban is essentially a two-bin type of inventory; supplies are replenished semiautomatically when they reach a predetermined level. MRP II is more concerned with projecting requirements and planning and leveling capacity via the computer.

A major benefit of the kanban system is its simplicity; a major benefit of MRP II is its ability to handle complex planning and scheduling quickly and efficiently. It also handles changes fairly easily. In addition, MRP II is capable of simulation (i.e., it enables management to answer "what if . . ." questions) for capacity planning.

A comparison of how eight manufacturing functions are controlled by kanban and MRP II is presented in Table 11–2. Note that the two are the same in terms of employing a master schedule (products to be built) but different in terms of every other function. Note, too, that the kanban approach is considerably less formal than MRP II.

Another difficulty is that the philosophies that underlie JIT systems are quite different from the philosophies that manufacturers have traditionally held. Hence, a major effort to change will be

---

[1] Based on an article by Walt Goddard, "Kanban versus MRP II—Which Is Best for You?" *Modern Materials Handling,* November 5, 1982.

TABLE 11–2

Comparison of Kanban and MRP II

Functions	Categories	Kanban system	MRP II
Rates of output	Families of products	Leveling	Production plan
Products to be built	Finished goods for make-to-stock, customer orders for make-to-order	Master production schedule	Master production schedule
Materials required	Components—both manufactured and purchased	Kanban cards	Material requirements planning (MRP)
Capacity required	Output for key work centers and vendors	Visual	Capacity requirements planning (CRP)
Executing capacity plans	Producing enough output to satisfy plans	Visual	Input/output controls (I/O)
Executing material plans—manufactured items	Working on right priorities in factory	Kanban cards	Dispatching reports
Executing material plans—purchased items	Bringing in right items from vendors	Kanban cards and unofficial orders	Purchasing reports
Feedback information	What cannot be executed due to problems	Andon	Anticipated delay reports

Note: The same functions are performed by every manufacturing company; however, the tools used by Kanban differ greatly from the MRP II tools. Under Kanban, the tools are manual—Kanban cards, Andon lights, visual checks, and oral orders. Under MRP II, the most important tool is the computer.

Source: Reprinted from Walt Goddard, "Kanban versus MRP II—Which Is Best for You?" *Modern Materials Handling*, November 5, 1982.

required. That will not occur without the support of top management, and even then, it will undoubtedly require much effort on all levels to overcome the ingrained resistance to these kinds of changes. Chief among these philosophies is that inventories of safety stocks should be maintained "just in case" something goes wrong. Realistically speaking, the focus has to shift from "who's to blame?" to "let's fix this so it won't happen again."

Whether manufacturers should adopt the kanban method is debatable. Some form of it may be useful, but kanban is merely an information system; by itself it offers little in terms of helping manufacturers to become more competitive and/or productive. By the same token, MRP by itself will not achieve those results either. Instead, it is the overall approach to manufacturing that is crucial; it is the commitment and support of top management and the continuing efforts of all levels of management to find new ways to improve their manufacturing planning and control techniques and then to adapt those techniques to fit their own particular set of circumstances that will determine the degree of success. What can be said is that problems must be identified and eliminated in the

manufacturing cycle and that improved methods of production planning and control are needed—improvements that will only come about through effort and determination.

SUMMARY

Material requirements planning (MRP) is an information system used to handle ordering of dependent-demand items (i.e., components of assembled products). The planning process begins with customer orders, which are used along with any back orders to develop a master schedule that indicates the timing and quantity of finished items. The end items are exploded using the bill of materials, and a gross-requirements plan is developed, which shows quantity and timing for ordering or producing components. Comparing gross requirements to stock on hand produces a net-requirements plan, which shows the quantity and timing actually needed to obtain the finished products desired. The main features of MRP are the time-phasing of requirements, the identification of components, and planned-order releases. In order to be successful, MRP requires a computer program and accurate master schedules, bills of materials, and inventory data. Firms that have not had reasonably accurate records or schedules have experienced major difficulties in trying to implement MRP.

MRP II is a second-generation approach to planning that incorporates MRP; it has a broader scope to manufacturing resource planning in that it links business planning, production planning, and the master schedule.

The Japanese approach to repetitive manufacturing involves a just-in-time philosophy with high quality, low inventories, short lead times, and few vendors. Unlike MRP, it does not involve use of a computer. The success of the Japanese manufacturers suggests that domestic manufacturers might gain some valuable insights by studying the Japanese methods, although it is not clear that those methods should be adopted. Instead, it seems that U.S. managers might concern themselves with *why* those methods work and how they could use the tools available to them to make their systems perform more competitively.

1. The product-structure tree shown below indicates the components needed to assemble one unit of product **W**. Redraw the tree so that it conforms to low-level coding and determine the quantities of each component that will be needed to assemble 100 units of **W**.

Solution

An easy way to compute and keep track of component requirements is to do it right on the tree, as illustrated below. Using low-level coding, it is then relatively simple to group like items in order to determine overall requirements.

Summary:

Level	Item	(1 W) Quantity	(100 W) Quantity
0 . . .	W	1	100
1 . . .	A	1	100
	B	2	200
	C	4	400
2 . . .	E	5	500
	F	2	200
	G	8	800
3 . . .	D	22	2,200

2. The product-structure tree for end-item E is shown below. The manager wants to know the material requirements for ordered-part R that will be needed to complete 120 units of E by the start of week 5. Lead times for items are: one week for level 0 items, one week for level 1 items, and two weeks for level 2 items. There is a scheduled receipt of 60 units of M in week 2 and 100 units of R in week 1. Lot-for-lot ordering is used.

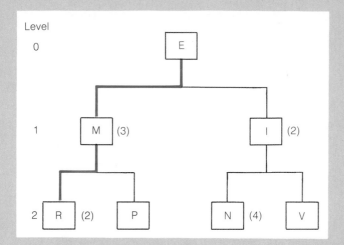

Solution

A *partial* assembly-time chart that includes R and leads to completion of E by the start of week 5 looks like this:

The master schedule for E and requirements plans for E, M, and R are shown below.

Master schedule for E

Week number	1	2	3	4	5
Quantity:					(120)

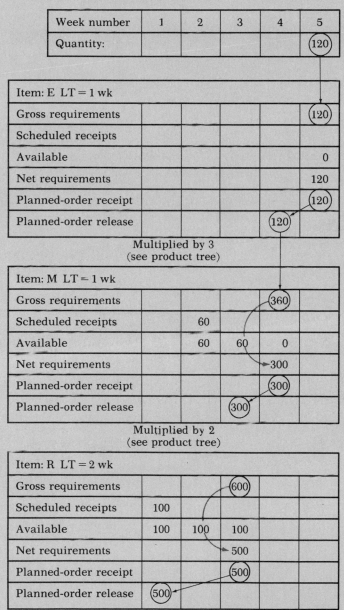

Item: E LT = 1 wk	1	2	3	4	5
Gross requirements					(120)
Scheduled receipts					
Available					0
Net requirements					120
Planned-order receipt					(120)
Planned-order release				(120)	

Multiplied by 3
(see product tree)

Item: M LT = 1 wk	1	2	3	4	5
Gross requirements				(360)	
Scheduled receipts		60			
Available		60	60	0	
Net requirements				300	
Planned-order receipt				(300)	
Planned-order release			(300)		

Multiplied by 2
(see product tree)

Item: R LT = 2 wk	1	2	3	4	5
Gross requirements			(600)		
Scheduled receipts	100				
Available	100	100	100		
Net requirements			500		
Planned-order receipt			(500)		
Planned-order release	(500)				

The table entries are arrived at as follows:

Master schedule: 120 units of E to be available at the start of week 5.

Item E: Gross requirements equal quantity specified in master schedule. Since there is no on-hand inventory, net requirements also equal 120 units. Using lot-for-lot ordering, 120 units must be scheduled to be available at the start of week 5. Since there is a one week lead time for assembly of Es, an order will need to be released (i.e., work started) at the beginning of week 4.

Item M: The *gross* requirements for M are three times E's *net* requirements since each E requires three Ms. These must be available at the start of week 4. The net requirements are 60 units less due to the 60 units expected to be on hand at that time. Hence, 300 additional units of M must be available at the start of week 4. With the one week lead time, there must be an order release at the start of week 3.

Item R: Since each M requires two units of R, 600 Rs will be needed to assemble 300 units of M. However, 100 units will be on hand, so only 500 need to be ordered. Since there is a lead time of two weeks, the 500 Rs must be ordered at the start of week 1.

DISCUSSION AND REVIEW QUESTIONS

1. Contrast independent and dependent demand.
2. When is MRP appropriate?
3. Briefly define or explain each of these terms:
   a. Master schedule.
   b. Bill of materials.
   c. Inventory records file.
   d. Gross requirements.
   e. Net requirements.
   f. Time-phased plan.
   g. Low-level coding.
4. What is meant by the term *level-by-level processing*? Why does it require low-level coding?
5. What factors can create safety stock requirements in an MRP system?
6. What is meant by the term *safety time*?
7. Contrast *net change* systems and *regenerative* systems for MRP.
8. Briefly discuss the requirements for effective MRP.
9. What are some of the main advantages and limitations of MRP?
10. How can the use of MRP contribute to productivity?
11. Briefly describe MRP II and indicate how it relates to MRP.
12. Describe the just-in-time approach.
13. Contrast the just-in-time, kanban philosophy with that of a typical U.S. manufacturing company.
14. List the main factors that have contributed to the success of Japanese manufacturers in repetitive manufacturing.
15. What difficulties did U.S. automobile manufacturers encounter when they tried to use a kanban approach? Why?
16. Compare MRP II and kanban.
17. What is lot sizing, and why is it an issue with lumpy demand?
18. What is the goal of lot sizing? What are some of the methods used for lot sizing in MRP systems? At what level is an economic lot size usually most relevant? Why?
19. Explain what is meant by this statement: "JIT tends to be more a 'pull' system while MRP tends to be more of a 'push' system."
20. Contrast "planned-order receipts" and "scheduled receipts."

PROBLEMS

1. Given the product-structure tree below, do the following:
   a. Redraw the tree so that it conforms to low-level coding.
   b. Determine the quantities of each of the components that will be required to assemble 60 units of P.

2. Given the following listing of parents and components, construct two product-structure trees using low-level coding and then determine what quantity of each item will be required to make 125 units of end-item W and 50 units of end-item Y.

W	Y
A(2)	A
B(4)	B(2)
C(4)	K(3)

A	*A*
D(2)	D(2)
E	E

B	*B*
F(2)	F(2)

D	*D*
F(4)	F(4)
E(2)	E(2)
G(4)	G(4)

C	*K*
H	L
G(2)	C(4)

	C
	H
	G(2)

3. Determine material requirements plans for parts N and V and subassembly I as described in Solved Problem 2.
   a. Assume that there are currently 100 Ns on hand and scheduled receipts of 40 Is and 10 Vs in week 3. No Es are

Tree for Problem 1

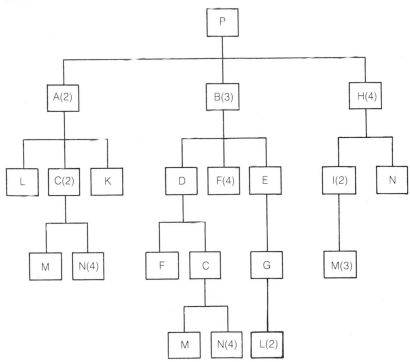

on hand; 120 Es are needed at the start of week 5.

b. Assume on hand and scheduled receipts as in part **a.** But now suppose that 100 Es are needed at the start of week 5 and 50 at the start of week 7. Also, use these *fixed* order sizes: N, 800; and V, 200. Use lot-for-lot ordering for I.

4. A firm that produces electric golf carts has just received an order for 200 carts, which are to be ready for delivery at the start of week 8. Information concerning the product structure, lead times, and quantities on hand are shown below. Using this information, do each of the following:

a. Construct a product tree.

b. Construct an assembly-time chart.

c. Develop a material requirements plan that will provide 200 golf carts by week 8 assuming lot-for-lot ordering.

Parts list for electric golf cart	Lead time	Quantity on hand
Electric golf cart.	1	0
Top	1	40
Base.	1	20
Top		
Supports (4).	1	200
Cover	1	0
Base		
Motor	2	300
Body.	3	50
Seats (2)	2	120
Body		
Frame	1	35
Controls	1	0
Wheel assemblies (4) . .	1	240

5. (Refer to the previous problem.) Assume there has been a change in the quantity and timing of orders for golf carts, which is apparently due to unusually mild weather. The revised plan calls for 100 golf carts at the start of week 6, 100 at the start of week 8, and 100 at the start of week 9.

a. Develop a master schedule for this revised plan.

b. Determine the timing and quantities for orders for tops and bases.

c. Assume now that due to equipment problems, capacity for assembling

bases is 50 units per week. Revise your material plan for bases to reflect this but still meet delivery dates.

6. Assume that you are the manager of Assembly, Inc., and that you have just received an order for 40 units of an industrial robot, which are to be delivered at the start of week 7 of your schedule. Using the information below, determine how many units of subassembly G should be ordered and the timing of those orders, given that subassembly G must be ordered in multiples of 80 units. Assume also that there is no other use for the components of this particular robot.

Item	Lead time (weeks)	On hand	Components
Robot . . .	2	10	B,G,C(3)
B	1	5	E,F
C	1	20	G(2),H
E	2	4	—
F	3	8	—
G	2	15	—
H	1	10	—

7. A manufacturing firm buys a certain part in varying quantities throughout the year. Ordering cost is $11 per order, and carrying cost is $.14 per piece per month. Given the following demand schedule for the part for the next eight months, what order sizes would be indicated using an economic part-period approach, and when should each order be received?

Period	Demand
1	—
2	80
3	10
4	30
5	—
6	30
7	—
8	30

8. A firm periodically produces a part that is a basic component of an assembled product it makes. Each time the part is run, a fixed cost of $125 is incurred. The cost to carry one unit for a month has been estimated to be $1.65. For the demand schedule shown, determine the quantity and timing of runs that would be consistent with an economic part-period ap-

proach. Assume a one-week lead time for each run.

Period	Demand
1	40
2	20
3	100
4	20
5	—
6	20
7	80

9. Assume that you are the manager of a shop that assembles power tools. An order has just been received for 50 chain saws, which are to be shipped at the start of week 8. Pertinent information on the saws is:

Item	LT (wk)	On hand	Components
Saw	2	15	A(2),B(1) C(3)
A	1	10	E(3),D(1)
B	2	5	D(2),F(3)
C	2	30	E(2),D(2)
D	1	20	
E	1	10	
F	2	30	

Develop a product-structure tree, an assembly-time chart, and a master schedule. Also, develop the material requirements plan for component E.

10. End-item P is composed of three subassemblies, K, L, and W. K is assembled using 3 Gs and 4 Hs; L is made of 2 Ms and 2 Ns; and W is made using 3 Zs. On-hand inventories are 20 Ls, 40 Gs, and 200 Zs. Scheduled receipts are 10 Ks at the start of week 3 and 30 Ks at the start of week 6.

One hundred Ps are to be shipped at the start of week 7. Lead times are two weeks for subassemblies and one week for components G, H, and M. Final assembly of P requires two weeks. Develop each of the following:

a. A product-structure tree.
b. An assembly-time chart.
c. A master schedule for P.
d. A material requirements plan for K, G, and H.

SELECTED BIBLIOGRAPHY

Blumberg, D. F. "Factors Affecting the Design of a Successful MRP System." *Production and Inventory Management* 21, no. 4, 4th quarter 1980, pp. 50–62.

Fox, Robert E. "OPT vs. MRP: Thoughtware versus Software." *Inventories & Production Magazine* 3, no. 6 (November–December 1983).

————. "MRP, Kanban, or OPT: What's Best?" *Inventories & Production Magazine* 2, no. 4 (July–August 1982).

Goddard, Walt. "Kanban versus MRP II—Which Is Best for You?" *Modern Materials Handling,* November 5, 1982, pp. 40–48.

LaForge, R. C. "MRP and the Part-Period Algorithm." *Journal of Purchasing Management,* Winter 1982, pp. 21–26.

Love, Stephen. *Inventory Control.* New York: McGraw-Hill, 1979.

Monden, Yasuhiro. "Adaptable Kanban System Helps Toyota Maintain Just-in-Time Production." *Industrial Engineering,* May 1981, pp. 29–46.

————. "How Toyota Shortened Supply Lot Production Waiting Time, and Conveyance Time." *Industrial Engineering,* September 1981, pp. 22–30.

————. "What Makes the Toyota Production System Really Tick?" *Industrial Engineering* 13, no. 1 (January 1981), pp. 38–46.

Orlicky, Joseph. *Material Requirements Planning.* New York: McGraw-Hill, 1975.

Schonberger, Richard J. "Applications of Single-Card and Dual-Card Kanban." *Interfaces* 13, no. 4 (August 1983), pp. 56–67.

Schulz, T. "MRP to BRP: The Journey of the 80's." *Production and Inventory Manage-*

ment Review and APICS News 1 (October 1981), p. 29.

Theisen, E. C., Jr.   "New Game in Town—The MRP Lot Size." *Production and Inventory Management,* 2d quarter 1974, pp. 1–13.

Weiss, Andrew.   "Simple Truths of Japanese Manufacturing." *Harvard Business Review* 62, no. 4 (July–August 1984), pp. 119–25.

Wight, Oliver W.   *The Executive's Guide to Successful MRP II.* Williston, Vt.: Oliver Wight Limited Publications, 1982.

Chapter 12

Scheduling

After completing this chapter, you should be able to:

1. Explain what scheduling involves and the importance of good scheduling.
2. Discuss scheduling needs in high-volume systems.
3. Discuss scheduling needs in job shops.
4. Use and interpret Gantt charts, and use the assignment method for loading.
5. Discuss and give examples of commonly used priority rules.
6. Describe some of the unique problems encountered in service systems and describe some of the approaches used for scheduling service systems.

SCHEDULING IN HIGH-VOLUME SYSTEMS, 593

SCHEDULING IN INTERMEDIATE-VOLUME SYSTEMS, 595

SCHEDULING IN JOB SHOPS, 596

   Loading, 596
   Sequencing, 603
   Sequencing Jobs through Two Work Centers, 608
   Optimized Production Technology, 610

SCHEDULING IN SERVICE SYSTEMS, 611

   Appointment Systems, 612
   Reservation Systems, 613
   Scheduling Multiple Resources, 613

SUMMARY, 614
SOLVED PROBLEMS, 615
DISCUSSION AND REVIEW QUESTIONS, 619
PROBLEMS, 619
SELECTED BIBLIOGRAPHY, 621

Scheduling involves the *timing* of specific operations. It includes the use of equipment and facilities as well as human activities. Regardless of the nature of an organization's activities, scheduling is generally an important task. For example, manufacturers must schedule workers, purchases, production, and so on. Hospitals must schedule admissions, surgery, nursing staff, and support functions such as meal preparation and service, cleaning, building maintenance, grounds crews, office personnel, and security staff. Doctors, dentists, lawyers, hair dressers, and the like must schedule appointments as well as other duties. Educational institutions must schedule classrooms, instructors, and students.

In the decision-making hierarchy, scheduling decisions are the final step before actual output is achieved. The process essentially begins as capacity planning, when many decisions regarding facilities and equipment acquisition are made. These are often long-term decisions. In the aggregate-planning stage, decisions regarding the general use of facilities, personnel, and subcontracting are made. It still remains, however, to develop *specific* work assignments and other decisions related more precisely to the actual work itself. This sequence of planning is outlined in Figure 12–1. The transition from aggregate planning to scheduling can perhaps be clarified in terms of a master schedule, which was discussed in the preceding chapter in the context of MRP. Note, however, that a master schedule is simply a mechanism for stating planned output, and that it serves a useful function that is not limited to MRP systems. Thus, both manufacturing and services generally rely on master schedules for planning purposes. In effect, the master schedule is a *disaggregation* of the aggregate plan; it converts those more general plans into specific plans for final output of goods or services. Recognize, though, that the master schedule does not complete the job of scheduling: the overall schedule must itself be translated into require-

FIGURE 12–1

Overview of the Capacity/Scheduling Chain

ments for the individual goods and services that will be needed in the transformation process.

At each level in the process from capacity planning to scheduling, the contraints become narrower and more defined. In part this is due to the lead time needed to achieve changes. Consequently, scheduling decisions are usually made in a highly constrained environment.

Generally speaking, the objectives of scheduling are to achieve trade-offs among conflicting goals, which include efficient utilization of staff, equipment, and facilities, and minimization of customer waiting time, inventories, and process times.

Scheduling tasks are largely a function of the volume of system output. High-volume systems require substantially different approaches than job shops, and project scheduling requires still different approaches than either of those systems. In this chapter we shall consider scheduling for high-volume systems, intermediate-volume systems, and job-shop scheduling, and leave until the next chapter the subject of project scheduling.

SCHEDULING IN HIGH-VOLUME SYSTEMS

Scheduling encompasses allocating workloads to specific work centers and determining the sequence in which operations are to be performed. High-volume systems are characterized by standardized equipment and activities that provide identical or highly similar operations on customers or products as they pass through the system. Examples of high-volume products include autos, typewriters, radios and televisions, stereo equipment, toys, and appliances. Examples of services include cafeteria lines, news broadcasts, and mass inoculations. Because of the highly repetitive nature of these systems, many of the loading and sequencing decisions are determined during the design of the system. The use of highly specialized tools and equipment, the arrangement of equipment, the use of specialized material-handling equipment, and the division of labor are all designed to enhance the flow of work through the system, since all items follow virtually the same sequence of operations.

A major aspect in design of flow systems is *line balancing,* which concerns allocating the required tasks to work stations so that they satisfy technical (sequencing) constraints and are balanced with respect to equal work times among stations. Highly balanced systems result in the maximum utilization of equipment and personnel as well as the highest possible rate of output. Line balancing is discussed in Chapter 7.

In setting up flow systems, designers must consider the potential discontent of workers related to the specialization of job tasks these systems entail: high work rates are often achieved by dividing the work into a series of relatively simple tasks that are assigned to different workers. The resulting jobs tend to be boring and monotonous and may give rise to fatigue, absenteeism, turnover, and other problems, all of which have a tendency to reduce productivity and disrupt the smooth flow of work through the system. These problems and potential solutions are elaborated on in Chapter 8, which deals with the design of work systems.

In spite of the built-in attributes of flow systems related to scheduling, there remain a number of problems with respect to scheduling. One stems from the fact that few flow systems are *completely* devoted to a single product or service. Most must handle a variety of sizes and models. Thus, an automobile manufacturer will assemble many different combinations of cars—two-door and four-door models, some with air conditioning and some not, some with deluxe trim and others with standard trim, some with tape decks, some with tinted glass, and so on. The same can be said for producers of appliances, electronic equipment, toys and so on. Each change involves slightly different inputs that must be scheduled into the line, such as different parts and materials and different processing requirements. If the line is to operate smoothly, the flow of materials and the work must be coordinated. This amounts to scheduling the inputs, the processing, and the outputs, as well as scheduling purchases. In addition to achieving a smooth flow, it is important to avoid excessive buildups of inventories. Again, each variation in size or model will tend to have somewhat different inventory requirements, so that additional scheduling efforts will be needed.

Another source of scheduling requirements are disruptions to the system that generate less than the desired amount of output. These can be caused by equipment failures, material shortages, accidents, and absences. Practically speaking, usually it is not possible to increase the rate of output to compensate for these factors, mainly due to the fact that flow systems are designed to operate at a given rate. Instead, strategies involving subcontracting or overtime are often required, although subcontracting on short notice is not always feasible. Sometimes work that is partly completed can be made up off the line.

The reverse situation can also impose scheduling problems, although less severe. This happens when the desired amount of output is less than the usual rate. However, instead of slowing the rate of output, it is usually necessary to operate the system at the usual rate, but for fewer hours. For instance, a production line might operate for seven hours a day instead of eight for a while.

SCHEDULING IN INTERMEDIATE-VOLUME SYSTEMS

Intermediate-volume system outputs fall between the standardized type of output of the high-volume systems and the made-to-order output of job shops. Like the high-volume systems, intermediate-volume systems typically produce standard outputs. And if manufacturing is involved, the products may be made for stock rather than for special order. However, the volume of output in such cases is not large enough to justify devoting continual production. Instead, it is more economical to process these items *intermittently.* Thus, intermediate-volume work centers periodically shift from one job to another. In contrast to a job shop, though, the run sizes are relatively large.

The two basic questions in these systems are what *run size* to use and in what *sequence* jobs should be processed.

In part, the question of run size can be answered using a model such as the economic run size one discussed in the chapter on inventory management. The run size that would minimize setup and inventory costs was

$$Q_o = \sqrt{\frac{2DS}{H}} \sqrt{\frac{p}{p-u}} \qquad (12\text{--}1)$$

Now this approach works well in the context of a single product but must be modified somewhat when multiple products are involved. One reason is that setup costs can be dependent on the order of processing: some products will have similar setups so it can be less expensive to process them in sequence to take advantage of that. Another difficulty arises because usage is not always as smooth as assumed in this model. Consequently, some products will tend to be used up faster than expected and have to be replenished sooner. Also, because multiple products are to be processed, it is not always possible to schedule production to correspond with optimum run intervals.

Therefore, a second approach, called *runout time,* is often used. It may be used in conjunction with the economic-run-size model or without it. The concept of that approach is expressed by the following equation:

$$\text{Runout time} = \frac{\text{Production available} + \text{Current inventory}}{\text{Demand rate}}$$

The runout time is computed for each product, and the products are ranked according to this measure. The lower the runout time, the more crucial it is to replenish the supply of an item. Thus, if product A has a runout time of 4.0 weeks, product B has a runout

time of 1.2 weeks, and product C has a runout time of 2.5 weeks, the processing order would be B–C–A.

Modifications to the economic-run-size formula to allow for multiple products and dependent setups, and elaboration of the runout-time approach are somewhat beyond the scope of this text. However, both topics are covered in more detail in the references found at the end of this chapter if you are interested.

SCHEDULING IN JOB SHOPS

The characteristics of job shops are quite different than high- and intermediate-volume systems. Products are made to order, and orders usually differ considerably in terms of processing requirements, materials needed, processing time, and processing sequence and setups. Because of these circumstances, scheduling and controlling in job shops is usually fairly complex. This is compounded by the fact that it is impossible to establish firm schedules prior to receiving the actual job orders.

Job-shop processing gives rise to two basic issues for schedulers: how to distribute the workload among work centers and what job processing sequence to use.

Loading

Loading refers to the assignment of jobs to processing (work) centers. In cases where a job can only be processed by a *specific* center, loading presents little difficulty. However, problems arise when two or more jobs are to be processed and there are a number of work centers capable of performing the required work. In such cases the operations manager needs some way of assigning jobs to the centers.

In making assignments, managers often seek an arrangement that will either minimize processing and setup costs, minimize idle time among work centers, or minimize job completion time, depending on the situation.

A number of approaches are used for loading, ranging from purely intuitive to using linear programming. Two of these approaches are described in the following sections: The use of Gantt charts and the assignment method of linear programming.

Gantt charts are visual aids used for a variety of purposes related to loading and scheduling. They derive their name from Henry Gantt, who pioneered the use of charts for industrial scheduling in the early 1900s. Gantt charts can be used in a number of different ways, two of which are illustrated in Figure 12–2, which shows

FIGURE 12–2

Examples of Charts Used for Scheduling

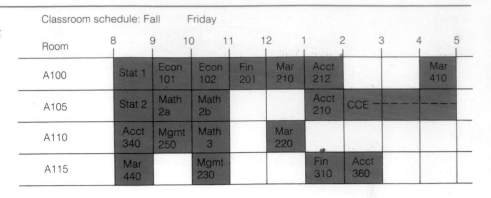

Classroom schedule: Fall   Friday

Room	8	9	10	11	12	1	2	3	4	5
A100	Stat 1	Econ 101	Econ 102	Fin 201	Mar 210	Acct 212				Mar 410
A105	Stat 2	Math 2a	Math 2b			Acct 210	CCE - - - -			
A110	Acct 340	Mgmt 250	Math 3		Mar 220					
A115	Mar 440		Mgmt 230			Fin 310	Acct 360			

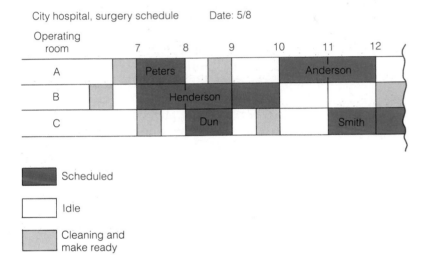

City hospital, surgery schedule   Date: 5/8

Operating room	7	8	9	10	11	12
A		Peters			Anderson	
B		Henderson				
C		Dun			Smith	

▮ Scheduled

▢ Idle

▨ Cleaning and make ready

scheduling classrooms for a semester and scheduling hospital operating rooms for a day.

The purpose of Gantt charts is to organize and clarify the actual or intended use of resources in a *time framework.* In most cases a time scale is represented horizontally, and resources to be scheduled are listed vertically. The use of the resources is reflected in the body of the chart.

Managers may use the charts for trial-and-error schedule development to get an idea of what different arrangements would involve. Thus, a tentative surgery schedule might reveal insufficient allowance for surgery that extends beyond its expected duration, and be revised accordingly. Use of the chart for classroom schedul-

FIGURE 12–3

A Gantt Load Chart

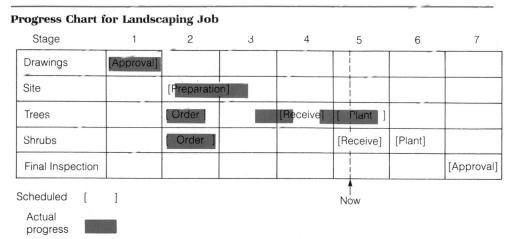

ing would help avoid assigning two different classes to the same room at the same time.

There are a number of different types of Gantt charts. Two of the most commonly used are the *load* chart and the *schedule* chart.

A load chart depicts the loading and idle times of a group of machines or a list of departments. A typical load chart is illustrated in Figure 12–3. This particular chart indicates that work center 3 is completely loaded for the entire week, center 4 will be available after noon on Tuesday, and the other two centers have idle time scattered throughout the week. This information can help a manager in reworking loading assignments to better utilize the centers. For instance, if all centers perform the same kind of work, the manager might want to free one center for a long job or for a rush

FIGURE 12–4

Progress Chart for Landscaping Job

order. It also shows when certain jobs are scheduled to start and finish and where idle time is expected.

A schedule chart is often used to monitor the progress of jobs. The vertical axis on this type of Gantt chart shows the orders or jobs in progress, and the horizontal axis shows time. The charts indicate which jobs are on schedule and which are behind or ahead.

A typical schedule chart is illustrated in Figure 12–4. It shows the current status of a landscaping job along with planned and actual starting and finishing times for the five stages of the job. We can see from the chart that approval was on schedule, as was ordering of trees and shrubs. The site preparation was a bit behind schedule. The trees were received earlier than expected, and planting is ahead of schedule. However, the shrubs have not been received as of yet. The chart indicates some slack between scheduled receipt of shrubs and shrub planting, so if the shrubs arrive by the end of the week, it appears the schedule can still be met.

In spite of the obvious benefits of these charts, they also possess certain limitations, the chief one being the need to repeatedly update the chart to keep it current. In addition, a chart does not directly reveal costs associated with alternative loadings. Finally, a job's processing time may vary depending on the work center involved: certain stations or work centers may be capable of processing some jobs faster than other stations. Again, that situation would increase the complexity of evaluating alternative schedules. Nonetheless, Gantt charts are the most widely used devices for scheduling.

The *assignment method* is a special-purpose linear programming model that is useful in situations that call for assigning tasks or other work requirements to resources. Typical examples include assigning jobs to machines or workers, territories to salespeople, and emergency calls to telephone repair crews. The idea is to obtain an optimum *matching* of tasks and resources. Commonly used criteria include costs, profits, efficiency, and performance.

A typical problem is illustrated in Table 12–1, where four jobs are to be assigned to four machines. The problem is arranged in a format that will facilitate evaluation of assignments. The numbers in the body of the table represent the value or cost associated

TABLE 12–1

A Typical Assignment Problem

		Machine			
		A	*B*	*C*	*D*
	1	8	6	2	4
Job	*2*	6	7	11	10
	3	3	5	7	6
	4	5	10	12	9

with each job-machine combination. In this case the numbers represent costs. Thus, it would cost $8 to do job 1 on machine A, $6 to do job 1 on machine B, and so on. If the problem involved minimizing the cost for job 1 alone, it is apparent that it would be assigned to machine C since that combination has the lowest cost. However, that assignment does not take into account the other jobs and their potential costs, which is important since the lowest cost assignment for any one job may not be consistent with a minimum cost assignment when all jobs are considered.

If there are to be n matches, there are $n!$ different possibilities. In this case there are $4! = 24$ different matches. One approach would be to investigate each match and select the one with the lowest cost. However, even for a problem of this small size, considerable time and effort would be called for. Instead, a much simpler approach is to use the *assignment method* to identify the lowest cost solution.

To be able to use the assignment method, a one-for-one matching is required. Each job, for example, must be assigned to only one machine. It is also assumed that every machine is capable of handling every job, and that the costs or values associated with each assignment combination are known and *fixed* (i.e., not subject to variation).

Once the relevant cost information has been acquired and arranged in tabular form, the basic procedure of the assignment method is:

1. Subtract the smallest number in each row from *every* number in the row. Enter the results in a new table.
2. Subtract the smallest number in each column of the new table from *every* number in the column. Enter the results in another table.
3. Test to see if an optimum assignment can be made. This is accomplished by determining the *minimum* number of lines that are needed to cover all zeros. If the number of lines equals the number of rows, an optimum assignment is possible. In that case go to step 6. Otherwise, go on to step 4.
4. If the number of lines is less than the number of rows, modify the table in this way:
    a. Subtract the smallest uncovered number from every *uncovered* number in the table.
    b. Add the smallest uncovered number to the numbers at *intersections* of covering lines.
5. Repeat steps 3 and 4 until an optimal table is obtained.
6. Make the assignments. Begin with rows or columns with only one zero. Match items that have zeros, using only one match for each row and each column: Cross out both the row and column after the match.

EXAMPLE 1

Determine the optimum assignment of jobs to machines for the data below (from Table 12–1).

	Machine			
Job	A	B	C	D
1	8	6	2	4
2	6	7	11	10
3	3	5	7	6
4	5	10	12	9

Solution

a. Subtract the smallest number in each row from every number in the row and enter the results in a new table. The result of this *row reduction* is:

	Machine			
Job	A	B	C	D
1	6	4	0	2
2	0	1	5	4
3	0	2	4	3
4	0	5	7	4

b. Subtract the smallest number in each column from every number in the column and enter the results in a new table. The result of this *column reduction* is:

	Machine			
Job	A	B	C	D
1	6	3	0	0
2	0	0	5	2
3	0	1	4	1
4	0	4	7	2

c. Determine the minimum number of lines needed to cover all zeros. (Try to cover as many zeros as possible when drawing lines.)

EXAMPLE 1 (concluded)

d. Since only three lines are needed to cover all zeros, this is not the optimum.

e. Subtract the smallest uncovered value (in this case, 1) from every uncovered number and add it to numbers that are at the intersections of covering lines. The results are:

Machine

Job	A	B	C	D
1	7	3	0	0
2	1	0	5	2
3	0	0	3	0
4	0	3	6	1

f. Determine the minimum number of lines needed to cover all zeros (four). Since this equals the number of rows, the optimum assignment can be made.

Machine

Job	A	B	C	D
1	7	3	0	0
2	1	0	5	2
3	0	0	3	0
4	0	3	6	1

g. Make assignments: Start with rows and columns with only one zero. Match jobs with machines that have a zero cost:

Machine

Job	A	B	C	D
1	7	3	[0]	0
2	1	[0]	5	2
3	0	0	3	[0]
4	[0]	3	6	1

As you can see, the process is relatively simple compared to some of the other linear programming techniques. One extension of this technique that is worth knowing is the ability to prevent undesirable assignments. For example, union rules may prohibit one per-

son's assignment to a particular job, or a manager might wish to avoid assigning an unpleasant job to the person who did it last. Whatever the reason, specific combinations can be avoided by assigning a relatively high cost to that combination. For instance, in the previous example, if combination 1–A is to be avoided, assigning a cost of $50 to that combination will achieve the desired effect because $50 is much greater than the other costs. In a situation involving profits instead of costs, the profits can be converted to *relative costs* by subtracting *every* number in the table from the largest number and then proceeding as in a minimization problem.

The simplicity of the assignment method belies its usefulness when the assumptions are met. Not only does it provide a rational method for making assignments, it guarantees an optimal solution, often without the use of a computer. In fact, computers are necessary only for fairly large problems.

Sequencing

While loading decisions determine the machines or work centers that will be used to process specific jobs, they do not indicate the *order* in which the jobs waiting at a given work center are to be processed.

If work centers are lightly loaded and if jobs all require the same amount of processing time, sequencing presents no particular difficulties. However, for heavily loaded work centers, especially in situations where relatively lengthy jobs are involved, processing order can be very important in terms of costs associated with jobs waiting for processing and in terms of idle time at the work centers. In this section we shall examine some of the ways in which jobs are sequenced.

Typically, a number of jobs will be waiting for processing. *Priority rules* are simple heuristics used to select the order in which the jobs will be processed. Some of the most common are listed in Table 12–2.

The rules generally involve the assumption that job setup cost and time are *independent* of processing sequence. In cases where

TABLE 12–2

Possible Priority Rules	FCFS (first come, first served). Jobs are processed in the order that they arive at a machine or work center.
	SPT (shortest processing time). Jobs are processed according to processing time at a machine or work center: shortest job first.
	DD (due date). Jobs are selected according to due date: earliest due date first.
	S/O (slack per operation). Jobs are processed according to average slack time (time until due date minus remaining time to process). Compute by dividing slack time by number of remaining operations including the current one.
	RUSH. Emergency or preferred customers first.

this assumption is not reasonably satisfied, simulation can provide a method for evaluating sequencing alternatives.

The effectiveness of any given sequence is often judged in terms of one of three measures: average completion time, average job lateness, or average number of jobs at a work center. Two of these measures, average completion time and average number of jobs at a work center, are directly correlated. Hence, to use both for a given case would be redundant. In the examples and problems both are employed simply for purposes of illustration.

Of these five rules, RUSH scheduling is quite simple and needs no explanation. The other four rules are illustrated in the following two examples.

EXAMPLE 2

Processing times and due dates for six jobs waiting to be processed at a work center are given in the table below. Determine the sequence of processing according to each of these rules: (a) FCFS, (b) SPT, (c) DD.

Job	Processing time (days)	Due date (days)
A	2	7
B	8	16
C	4	4
D	10	17
E	5	15
F	12	18

Assume jobs arrived in the order shown.

Solution

a. The FCFS sequence is simply A–B–C–D–E–F. The measures of effectiveness are:
   (1) *Average completion time:* $120/6 = 20.0$ days.
   (2) *Average job lateness:* $54/6 = 9.0$ days.
   (3) *Average number of jobs at the work center:* $120/41 = 2.93$.

Job sequence	(1) Processing time	(2) Flow time	(3) Due date	(3) − (2) Days late
A	2	2	7	0
B	8	10	16	0
C	4	14	4	10
D	10	24	17	7
E	5	29	15	14
F	12	41	18	23
	41	120		54

The flow time column indicates *cumulative* processing time, so summing these times and dividing by the total number of jobs processed indicates the average *time* each job spends at the work

EXAMPLE 2 (concluded)

center. Similarly, the average *number* of jobs at the center is found by summing the flow times and dividing by the total processing time.

b. Using the SPT rule, the job sequence is A–C–E–B–D–F (see the table below). The resulting values for the three measures of effectiveness are:

(1) *Average completion time:* 108/6 = 18 days.

(2) *Average job lateness:* 40/6 = 6.67 days.

(3) *Average number of jobs at the work center:* 108/41 = 2.63.

Sequence	(1) Job time	(2) Flow time	(3) Due date	(3) − (2) Days late
A	2	2	7	0
C	4	6	4	2
E	5	11	15	0
B	8	19	16	3
D	10	29	17	12
F	12	41	18	23
	41	108		40

c. Using earliest due date as the selection criterion, the job sequence is C–A–E–B–D–F. The measures of effectiveness are (see table below):

(1) *Average completion time:* 110/6 = 18.33 days.

(2) *Average job lateness:* 38/6 = 6.33 days.

(3) *Average number of jobs at the work center:* 110/41 = 2.68.

Sequence	(1) Job time	(2) Flow time	(3) Due date	(3) − (2) Days late
C	4	4	4	0
A	2	6	7	0
E	5	11	15	0
B	8	19	16	3
D	10	29	17	12
F	12	41	18	23
	41	110		38

The results of these three rules are summarized in Table 12–3.

TABLE 12–3

Comparison of the Three Rules

Rule	Average completion time (days)	Average lateness (days)	Average number of jobs at the work center
FCFS	20.00	9.00	2.93
SPT	18.00	6.67	2.63
DD	18.33	6.33	2.68

In this example the SPT rule was the best according to two of the measures of effectiveness, and tied the DD rule on one (average lateness). The FCFS rule was the worst in every case. For a different set of numbers, the DD rule (or perhaps another rule not mentioned here) might prove superior to SPT in terms of average job lateness or some other measure of effectiveness. However, SPT is always superior in terms of minimizing flow time and, hence, in minimizing the average number of jobs at the work center and completion time. It is best for each shop or organization to consider carefully its own circumstances and the measures of effectiveness it feels are important in selecting a rule to use.

Generally speaking, the FCFS rule turns out to be the least effective rule.

The primary limitation of the FCFS rule is that long jobs will tend to delay other jobs. If a process consists of work on a number of machines, machine idle time for downstream work stations will be increased. However, in service systems in which customers are directly involved, the FCFS rule is by far the dominant priority rule, mainly because of its inherent "fairness" but also perhaps because of the inability to obtain realistic estimates of processing times for individual jobs. The FCFS rule also has the advantage of simplicity.

Because the SPT rule always results in the lowest average completion time, it can result in lower in-process inventories. And because it usually provides the lowest average lateness, it provides better customer-service levels. Finally, since it always involves a lower average number of jobs at the work center, there tends to be less congestion in the work area. SPT also minimizes downstream idle time.

The major disadvantage of the SPT rule is that it tends to make long jobs wait, perhaps for rather long times (especially if new, shorter jobs are continually added to the system). Various modifications may be used in an effort to avoid this (e.g., after waiting for a given time period, any remaining jobs are automatically moved to the head of the line). This is known as the *truncated* SPT rule.

The DD rule directly addresses due dates and usually minimizes lateness. Although it has intuitive appeal, its main limitation is that it does not take processing time into account. One possible consequence is that it can result in some jobs waiting a long time, which adds both to in-process inventories and to shop congestion.

Let's take a look now at the S/O (slack per operation) rule.

EXAMPLE 3

Use the S/O rule to schedule the jobs shown below. Note that processing time includes the time remaining for the current and subsequent operations. In addition, we will need to know the number of operations remaining, including the current one. This information is presented below:

Job	Remaining processing time	Due date	Remaining number of operations
A	4	14	3
B	16	32	6
C	8	8	5
D	20	34	2
E	10	30	4
F	18	36	2

Solution

Determine the difference between the due date and the processing time for each operation. Divide that amount by the number of remaining operations and rank them from low to high. This yields the sequence of jobs:

Job	(1) Remaining processing time	(2) Due date	(3) (2) − (1) Slack	(4) Remaining number of operations	(5) (3) ÷ (4) Ratio	(6) Rank
A	4	14	10	3	3.33	3
B	16	32	16	6	2.67	2
C	8	8	0	5	0	1
D	20	34	14	2	7.00	6
E	10	30	20	4	5.00	4
F	18	36	12	2	6.00	5

The indicated sequence (see column 6) is: C–B–A–E–F–D.

Using the S/O rule, the designated job sequence may change after any given operation, so it is wise to reevaluate the sequence after each operation. Note that any of the previously mentioned priority rules could be used on a station-by-station basis for this situation; the only difference is that the S/O approach incorporates downstream information in arriving at a job sequence.

In actuality, there are many priority rules available to sequence jobs, and some other rule might provide superior results for a given set of circumstances. The purpose of examining these few rules was to provide insight into the nature of sequencing rules.

In the following section a special-purpose algorithm that can be used to sequence a set of jobs that must all be processed at the same two machines or work centers is described.

Sequencing Jobs through Two Work Centers

Johnson's rule is a technique that can be used to minimize the throughput (completion) time for a group of jobs that are to be processed on two machines or at two successive work centers.[1] It also minimizes the total idle time at the work centers. In order to use the technique, several conditions must be satisfied:

1. Job time (including setup and processing) must be known and constant for each job at each work center.
2. Job times must be independent of the job sequence.
3. All jobs must follow the same two-step work sequence.
4. Job priorities cannot be used.

Determination of the optimum sequence involves these steps:

1. List the jobs and their times at each work center.
2. Select the job with the shortest time. If the shortest time is at the first work center, schedule that job first; if the time is at the second center, schedule the job last. Break ties arbitrarily.
3. Eliminate the job and its times from further consideration.
4. Repeat steps 2 and 3, working toward the center of the sequence, until all jobs have been scheduled.

EXAMPLE 4

A group of six jobs are to be processed through a two-step operation. The first operation involves degreasing, and the second involves painting. Processing times are shown below. Determine a sequence that will minimize the total completion time for this group of jobs.

Processing time (hours)

Job	Work Center 1	Work Center 2
A	5	5
B	4	3
C	8	9
D	2	7
E	6	8
F	12	15

Solution

a. Select the job with the shortest processing time. It is job D with a time of two hours.

---

[1] S. M. Johnson, "Optimal Two- and Three-Stage Production Schedules with Setup Times Included," *Naval Research Quarterly* 1 (March 1954), pp. 61–68.

EXAMPLE 4 (continued)

b. Since the time is at the first center, schedule job D first. Eliminate job D from further consideration.

c. Job B has the next shortest time. Since it is at the second work center, schedule it last and eliminate job B from further consideration. We now have:

1st	2d	3d	4th	5th	6th
D					B

d. The remaining jobs and their times are:

Job	1	2
A . .	5	5
C . .	8	9
E . .	6	8
F . .	12	15

Note that there is a tie for the shortest remaining time: Job A has the same time at each work center. It makes no difference, then, whether we place it toward the beginning or end of the sequence. Suppose we place it toward the end arbitrarily. We now have:

1st	2d	3d	4th	5th	6th
D				A	B

e. The shortest remaining time is six hours for job E at work center 1. Thus, schedule that job toward the beginning of the sequence (after job D). Thus,

1st	2d	3d	4th	5th	6th
D	E			A	B

f. Job C has the shortest time for the remaining two jobs. Since it is for the first work center, it is placed third in the sequence. Finally, the remaining job (F) is assigned to the fourth position, and the result is:

1st	2d	3d	4th	5th	6th
D	E	C	F	A	B

EXAMPLE 4 (concluded)

g. The easiest way to determine the throughput time and idle times at the work centers is to construct a chart:

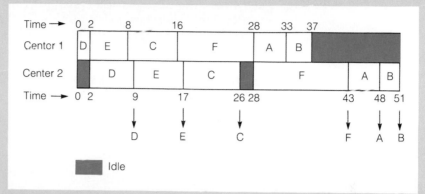

Thus, the group of jobs will take 51 hours to complete. The second work center will wait two hours for its first job and also wait two hours after finishing job C. Center 1 will be finished in 37 hours. Of course, idle periods at the beginning or end of the sequence could be used to do other jobs or for maintenance or setup/tear-down activities.

When significant idle time at the second work center occurs, job splitting at the first center just prior to the occurrence of idle time may alleviate some of it and also shorten throughput time. In the preceding example this was not a problem. The last solved problem at the end of this chapter illustrates the use of job splitting.

Optimized Production Technology

Optimized Production Technology (OPT) is a proprietary software package owned by Creative Output, Inc., of Milford, Connecticut. Information on the package is somewhat limited due to the proprietary nature of the technique. However, it is said to involve the use of mathematical programming, networking, and simulation.

A basic feature of OPT is the special attention it directs to *bottleneck operations.* The rationale of OPT is that bottleneck operations have an impact on an entire plant, and the best way to schedule a plant is to identify the bottleneck operations and try to optimize their use. The nonbottleneck operations are not critical and can therefore be treated differently. The OPT philosophy contends that the standard costs of bottleneck operations are understated because they don't take into account the fact that these operations constrain the entire system. Hence, OPT begins its scheduling procedure with the bottleneck operations and attempts to maximize their output. In essence, OPT is a finite loading procedure.

OPT consists of four basic modules:

1. *Buildnet.* This contains data on a plant's raw materials, purchased parts, products, work center capabilities, and customer orders.
2. *Serve.* This module identifies the bottleneck operations by running load profiles for each operation or work center.
3. *Split.* This module divides the system into two categories: critical operations (i.e., bottlenecks) and noncritical.
4. *Brain.* This module contains a set of algorithms that actually perform the scheduling.

OPT simulates different schedules and then selects a schedule based on the simulations.

There are two lot sizes in the OPT approach, a *process batch* and a *transfer batch.* The process batch is a lot size released to the shop. In order to optimize the output of bottlenecks, large batches (few setups) are run. However, since nonbottleneck operations have idle time, it does not make sense to attempt to maximize their output; There is nothing to gain by increasing idle time. Consequently, smaller lot sizes and more frequent setups can be used on such operations. The small batch sizes are the transfer lots. Hence, OPT deliberately schedules a variety of lot sizes, unlike more conventional approaches that use a single lot size throughout a shop for a job. You might think of this as lot splitting with multiple split sizes. An important feature of the software is to select the appropriate lot size for each operation.

As you might expect, OPT directs its use of both safety stock and safety time to facilitate flow through bottleneck operations. By concentrating these resources, it seeks to gain the maximum benefit from them and generally minimize inventories otherwise devoted to this purpose.

Since OPT is still relatively new, widespread experience on its use is not yet available. Nonetheless, users have reported a number of benefits. One is that OPT appears to be quicker and less costly to implement than a system such as MRP. Like MRP, OPT requires extensive preliminary effort to obtain accurate, up-to-date information in data files on work standards, machine capabilities, product structures, and so on. OPT seems to require more detail than MRP, and many view the process of going through this effort as an important benefit because of the improved data base it produces.

SCHEDULING IN SERVICE SYSTEMS

Scheduling service systems presents certain problems not generally encountered in manufacturing systems. This is due primarily to (1) the inability to store or inventory services and (2) the random

nature of customer requests for service. In some situations the second difficulty can be moderated by using appointment or reservation systems, but the inability to store services in most cases is a fact of life that managers must contend with.

An important goal in service systems is to match the flow of customers and service capabilities. An ideal situation is one in which there is a smooth flow of customers through the system. This would occur if each new customer arrived at the precise instant that the preceding customer's service was completed, in a case such as a physician's office, or where the demand for a service such as air travel just equaled the number of available seats. In each of these situations customer waiting time would be minimized, and there would be full utilization of the service system staff and equipment. Unfortunately, because of the random nature of customer requests for service that generally prevails in service systems, it is nearly impossible to provide service capacity that will match demand. Moreover, if service times are subject to variability—say, because of differing processing requirements—the inefficiency of the system is compounded. The inefficiencies can be reduced if arrivals can be scheduled (e.g., appointments), as in the case of doctors and dentists. However, there are many situations in which appointments are not practical (supermarkets, gas stations, theaters, hospital emergency rooms, repair of equipment breakdowns). Chapter 14 on queuing analysis focuses on those kinds of situations. There, the emphasis is on intermediate-term decisions related to service capacity. In this section we shall concern ourselves with short-term *scheduling* in which much of the capacity of a system is essentially fixed, and the goal is to achieve a certain degree of customer service by efficient utilization of that capacity.

Appointment Systems

Appointment systems are intended to control the timing of customer arrivals in order to minimize customer waiting while at the same time achieving a high degree of capacity utilization. A doctor can use an appointment system to schedule office patients during the afternoon while leaving the mornings free for hospital duties. Similarly, an attorney can schedule clients around court appearances. Even with appointments, however, problems can still arise due to lack of punctuality on the part of patients or clients, no-shows, and the inability to completely control the length of contact time (e.g., a dentist might run into complications in filling a tooth and have to spend additional time with a patient, thus backing up later appointments). Some of this can be avoided—say, by trying to match the time reserved for a patient or client with the specific needs of that case rather than setting appointments at regular intervals. Even with the problems of late arrivals and no-shows, the appoint-

ment system is a tremendous improvement over allowing random arrivals.

Reservation Systems

Reservation systems are designed to enable service systems to formulate a fairly accurate estimate of the demand on the system for a given time period and to minimize customer disappointment generated by excessive waiting or inability to obtain service. Reservation systems are widely used by resorts, hotels and motels, and restaurants as well as in some modes of transportation (airlines, car rentals). In the case of restaurants, reservations enable management to spread out or group customers so that demand matches service capabilities. As with appointment systems, late arrivals and no-shows can disrupt the system. An approach to the no-show problem is illustrated in Chapter 4, using a decision matrix. The problem can also be viewed as a single-period inventory problem, as described in Chapter 10.

Scheduling Multiple Resources

In some situations it is necessary to coordinate the use of more than one resource. For example, hospitals must schedule surgeons, operating rooms, operating room staffs, recovery room staffs, admissions, special equipment, nursing staffs, and so on. Similarly, educational institutions must schedule faculty, classrooms, audiovisual equipment, and students. As you might guess, the greater the number of resources that must be scheduled, the greater the complexity of the problem, and the less likely it becomes that an optimum schedule can be achieved. The problem is further complicated by the variable nature of such systems. For example, educational institutions frequently change their course offerings, student enrollments change, and students exhibit different course-selection patterns.

Some schools and hospitals are using computer programs to assist them in devising acceptable schedules, although many appear to be using intuitive-based approaches, with varying degrees of success.

Airlines are another example of service systems that require the scheduling of multiple resources. Flight crews, aircraft, baggage handling equipment, ticket counters, gate personnel, boarding ramps, and maintenance personnel all have to be coordinated. Furthermore, government regulations on the number of hours a pilot can spend flying place an additional restriction on the system. Another interesting variable is the fact that, unlike most systems, the flight crews and the equipment do not remain in one location. Moreover, the crew and the equipment are not usually scheduled as a single unit. Flight crews are often scheduled so that they return to their base city every two days or more often, and rest breaks must be considered. On the other hand, the aircraft may be in almost

continuous use except for periodic maintenance and repairs. Consequently, flight crews commonly follow different trip patterns than the aircraft.

SUMMARY

Scheduling involves the timing and coordination of operations. Such activities are fundamental to virtually every organization. Scheduling problems differ according to whether a system is designed for high volume, intermediate volume, or as a job shop. Scheduling problems are particularly complex for job shops because of the variety of jobs these systems are required to process.

The two major problems in scheduling job shops are assigning jobs to machines or work centers and designating the sequence of job processing at a given machine or work center. Gantt load charts are frequently employed to help managers visualize workloads, and they are useful for describing and analyzing sequencing alternatives. In addition, both heuristic and optimizing methods are used to develop loading and sequencing plans. For the most part, the optimization techniques can be used only if certain assumptions can be made.

Customer requirements in service systems generally present very different circumstances than those encountered in manufacturing systems. Appointment and reservation systems can sometimes be used for scheduling purposes, although not all systems are amenable to this. When multiple resources are involved, the task of balancing the system can be fairly complex.

1. *The assignment method.* The table below contains information on the cost to run three jobs on four available machines. Determine an assignment plan that will minimize opportunity costs.

		Machine			
		A	B	C	D
Job	1	12	16	14	10
	2	9	8	13	7
	3	15	12	9	11

Solution

In order to be able to use the assignment method, the number of jobs and machines must be equal. To remedy this situation, add a *dummy* job with costs of 0 and then solve as usual:

		Machine			
		A	B	C	D
Job	1	12	16	14	10
	2	9	8	13	7
	3	15	12	9	11
(dummy)	4	0	0	0	0

a. Subtract the smallest number from each row. The results are:

		Machine			
		A	B	C	D
Job	1	2	6	4	0
	2	2	1	6	0
	3	6	3	0	2
	4	0	0	0	0

b. Subtract the smallest number in each column. (Because of the dummy zeros in each column, the resulting table will be unchanged.)

c. Determine the minimum number of lines needed to cover the zeros. One possible way is:

		Machine			
		A	B	C	D
Job	1	2	6	4	0
	2	2	1	6	0
	3	6	3	0	2
	4	0	0	0	0

(Lines cover column C, column D, and row 4.)

d. Since the number of lines is less than the number of rows, modify the numbers.

    (1) Subtract the smallest uncovered number (1) from each uncovered number.

    (2) Add the smallest uncovered number to numbers at line intersections.

The result is:

		Machine			
		A	B	C	D
Job	1	1	5	4	0
	2	1	0	6	0
	3	5	2	0	2
	4	0	0	1	1

e. Test for optimality:

		Machine			
		A	B	C	D
Job	1	1	5	4	0
	2	— 1 — 0 — 6 — 0 —			
	3	5	2	0	2
	4	— 0 — 0 — 1 — 1 —			

Since the minimum number of lines equals the number of rows, an optimum assignment can be made.

f. Assign jobs to machines. Start with rows 1 and 3 since they each have one zero, and columns A and C, also with one zero each. The result is:

		Machine			
		A	B	C	D
Job	1	1	5	4	[0]
	2	1	[0]	6	0
	3	5	3	[0]	2
	4	[0]	0	1	1

g. Compute total costs, referring back to the original table for costs:

```
1–D . . . . $10
2–B . . . .   8
3–C . . . .   9
4–A . . . .   0
             ───
            $27
```

h. The implication of assignment 4–A is that machine A will not be assigned one of these jobs. It may remain idle or be used for another job.

2. *Priority rules.* Job times (including processing and setup) are shown in the table below for five jobs waiting to be processed at a work center:

Job	Job time (days)	Due date (days)
a . . .	12	15
b . . .	6	24
c . . .	14	20
d . . .	3	8
e . . .	7	6

Determine the processing sequence that would result from each of these priority rules:

a. FCFS   **b.** SPT   **c.** DD

Solution

(Assume job times are independent of processing sequence.)

a. FCFS			**b.** SPT			**c.** DD		
Job	Order		Job	Job time	Order	Job	Due date	Order
a . . .	1		a . .	12	4	a . .	15	3
b . . .	2		b . .	6	2	b . .	24	5
c . . .	3		c . .	14	5	c . .	20	4
d . . .	4		d . .	3	1	d . .	8	2
e . . .	5		e . .	7	3	e . .	6	1

3. Using the information given below, determine an order-processing sequence using the S/O priority rule.

Order	Processing time remaining (days)	Due date (days)	Number of operations remaining
A	20	30	2
B	11	18	5
C	10	6	2
D	16	23	4

Solution

(Assume times are independent of processing sequence.)

	(1) Remaining processing time	(2) Due date	(3) (2)–(1) Slack	(4) Number of operations	(5) Ratio	(6) Rank (sequence)
Order						
A	20	30	10	2	5.00	4
B	11	18	7	5	1.40	2
C	10	6	−4	2	−2.00	1
D	16	23	7	4	1.75	3

(Note that one ratio is negative. When negatives occur, assign the *lowest* rank to the *most negative* number.)

4. *Sequencing jobs through two work centers.* Use Johnson's rule to obtain the optimum sequence for processing the jobs shown through work centers A and B.

| Job | *Job times in hours* | |
	Work center A	Work center B
a	2.50	4.20
b	3.80	1.50
c	2.20	3.00
d	5.80	4.00
e	4.50	2.00

Solution

    a. Identify the smallest time: job *b* (1.50 hours at work center B). Since the time is for B, schedule this job last.

    b. The next smallest time is for job *e* (2.00 hours at B). Schedule job *e* next-to-last.

    c. Identify the smallest remaining job time: job *c* (2.20 hours at center A). Since the time is in the A column, schedule job *c* first. At this point we have:

$$c, \_\_, \_\_, e, b$$

    d. The smallest time for remaining jobs is the 2.50 hours for job *a* at center A. Schedule this job after job *c*. The one remaining job (job *d*) fills the remaining slot. Thus, we have:

$$c\text{--}a\text{--}d\text{--}e\text{--}b$$

5.   For the previous problem, determine what effect splitting jobs *c, d, e,* and *b* in work center A would have on the idle time of work center B and on the throughput time. Assume that each job can be split into two equal parts.

Solution

We assume that the processing sequence remains unchanged, and proceed on that basis. The solution from the previous problem is shown in the following chart. The next chart shows job processing at center B when splitting is used.

An inspection of these two figures will reveal that throughput time has decreased from 20.30 hours to 19.55 hours. In addition, the original idle time was 5.6 hours, while after splitting certain jobs it was reduced to 4.85 hours. Hence, some improvement was achieved. Note, though, that for jobs toward the end of the sequence, processing times at B are generally less than at A. As a result, jobs such as *e* and *b* at B were scheduled so that they were *centered* around the finishing times of *e* and *b* respectively at A in order to avoid having to break the jobs due to waiting for the remainder of the split job from A. Thus, generally the greatest advantage from job splitting comes from splitting earlier jobs when using Johnson's rule for sequencing.

DISCUSSION AND REVIEW QUESTIONS

1. Why is scheduling fairly simple for continuous systems but fairly complex for job shops?
2. What are the main decision areas of job shop scheduling?
3. What are Gantt charts? How are they used in scheduling? What advantages and limitations are associated with Gantt charts?
4. What are the basic assumptions of the assignment method of linear programming?
5. Briefly describe each of these priority rules: (**a**) FCFS, (**b**) SPT, (**c**) DD, (**d**) S/O, (**e**) RUSH.
6. Why are priority rules needed?
7. What problems do service systems present for scheduling the use of resources that are not generally found in manufacturing systems?
8. Doctors' and dentists' offices frequently schedule patients at regularly spaced intervals. What problems can this create? Can you suggest an alternative approach that might reduce these problems? Under what circumstances would regularly spaced appointments constitute a reasonable approach to patient scheduling?
9. How are scheduling and productivity related?
10. What factors would you take into account in deciding whether to split a job?

PROBLEMS

1. Use the assignment method to determine the best way to assign workers to jobs, given the cost information below. Compute total cost for your assignment plan.

| | | Job | | |
		A	B	C
Worker	1	5	8	6
	2	6	7	9
	3	4	5	3

2. Rework the previous problem treating the numbers in the table as profits instead of costs. Compute the total profit.

3. Assign trucks to delivery routes so that total costs are minimized, given the cost data shown below. What are total costs?

| | | Route | | | | |
		A	B	C	D	E
Truck	1	4	5	9	8	7
	2	6	4	8	3	5
	3	7	3	10	4	6
	4	5	2	5	5	8
	5	6	5	3	4	9

4. Develop an assignment plan that will minimize processing costs, given the information shown, and interpret your answer.

	Machine		
Job	*A*	*B*	*C*
1	12	8	11
2	13	10	8
3	14	9	14
4	10	7	12

5. Use the assignment method to obtain a plan that will minimize the processing costs in the table below under these conditions:

   a. The combination 2–D is undesirable.

   b. The combinations 1–A and 2–D are undesirable.

	Machine				
	A	*B*	*C*	*D*	*E*
1	14	18	20	17	18
2	14	15	19	16	17
Job 3	12	16	15	14	17
4	11	13	14	12	14
5	10	16	15	14	13

6. The table below contains information concerning four jobs that are awaiting processing at a work center:

Job	Job time (days)	Due date (days)
A	14	20
B	10	16
C	7	15
D	6	17

   a. Sequence the jobs using (1) FCFS, (2) SPT, and (3) DD. Assume the list is by order of arrival.

   b. For each of the methods in part **a** determine (1) the average completion time, (2) the average lateness, and (3) the average number of jobs at the work center.

   c. Is one method superior to the others? Explain.

7. Using the information presented in the table shown, identify the processing sequence that would result using (1) FCFS, (2) SPT, and (3) DD. For each method, determine (1) average job completion time, (2) average job lateness, and (3) average number of jobs in the system.

Job	Operation time (hours)	Due date (hours)
a	7	4
b	4	10
c	2	12
d	11	20
e	8	15

8. The table below shows orders to be processed at a machine shop as of 8 A.M. Monday. The jobs have different operations they must go through. Processing times are in days. Jobs are listed in order of arrival.

   a. Determine the processing sequence at the first work center using each of these rules: (1) FCFS, and (2) S/O.

   b. Compute the effectiveness of each rule using each of these measures: (1) average completion time, (2) average job lateness, and (3) average number of jobs at the work center.

Job	Processing time (days)	Due date (days)	Remaining number of operations
A	8	20	2
B	10	18	4
C	5	25	5
D	11	17	3
E	9	35	4

9. A wholesale grocery distribution center uses a two-step process to fill orders. Tomorrow's work will consist of filling the seven orders shown below. Determine a job sequence that will minimize the time required to fill the orders.

Order	Time (hours) Step 1	Step 2
A	1.20	1.40
B	0.90	1.30
C	2.00	0.80
D	1.70	1.50
E	1.60	1.80
F	2.20	1.75
G	1.30	1.40

10. The times required to complete each of eight jobs on two machines are given below. Each job must follow the same sequence, beginning with machine A and moving to machine B.

a. Determine a sequence that will minimize throughput time.

b. Construct a chart of the resulting sequence and find B's idle time.

c. For the sequence determined in **a**, how much could B's idle time be reduced by splitting the last two jobs in half?

Time (hours)

Job	Machine A	Machine B
a . . .	16	5
b . . .	3	13
c . . .	9	6
d . . .	8	7
e . . .	2	14
f . . .	12	4
g . . .	18	14
h . . .	20	11

11. Given the operation times below,

a. Develop a job sequence that minimizes idle time at the two work centers.

b. Construct a chart of the activities at the two centers and determine each one's idle time assuming no other activities are involved.

Job (times in minutes)

	A	B	C	D	E	F
Center 1. .	20	16	43	60	35	42
Center 2. .	27	30	51	12	28	24

12. A shoe repair operation uses a two-step sequence that all jobs in a certain category follow. For the group of jobs listed,

a. Find the sequence that will minimize total completion time.

b. Determine the amount of idle time for work station B.

c. What jobs are candidates for splitting? Why? If they were split how much of a reduction in idle time and throughput time would there be?

Job (times in minutes)

	a	b	c	d	e
Station A. . .	27	18	70	26	15
Station B. . .	45	33	30	24	10

13. A foreman has determined processing times at a work center for a set of jobs and now wants to sequence them. Given the information shown, do the following:

a. Determine the processing sequence using (1) FCFS, (2) SPT, and (3) DD. For each sequence, compute the average job lateness, the average completion time, and the average number of jobs at the work center. The list is FCFS order.

b. Using the results of your calculations in part **a**, show that the average completion time and the average number of jobs measures are equivalent for all three sequencing rules.

Job	Job time (days)	Due date	Operations remaining
a . . .	4.5	10	2
b . . .	6.0	17	4
c . . .	5.2	12	3
d . . .	1.6	27	5
e . . .	2.8	18	3
f . . .	3.3	19	1

14. Given the information in the following table, determine the processing sequence that would result using the S/O rule.

Job	Remaining processing time (days)	Due date	Remaining number of operations
a	5	8	2
b	6	5	4
c	9	10	4
d	7	12	3
e	8	10	2

SELECTED BIBLIOGRAPHY

Baker, K. R. *Introduction to Sequencing and Scheduling.* New York: John Wiley, 1974.

Buffa, Elwood S., and Jeffery G. Miller. *Production-Inventory Systems: Planning and Control.* 3d ed. Homewood, Ill.: Richard D. Irwin, 1979.

Chase, Richard, and Nicholas Aquilano. *Production and Operations Management.*

4th ed. Homewood, Ill.: Richard D. Irwin, 1985.

Fogarty, Donald W., and Thomas R. Hoffmann. *Production and Inventory Management.* Cincinnati, Ohio: South-Western Publishing, 1983.

McClain, John O., and L. Joseph Thomas. *Operations Management: Production of Goods and Services.* 2d ed. Englewood Cliffs, N.J.: Prentice-Hall, 1985.

Schonberger, Richard J. *Operations Management: Planning and Control of Operations and Operating Resources.* Plano, Tex.: Business Publications, 1981.

Tersine, Richard J. *Production/Operations Management: Concepts, Structure, and Analysis.* New York: Elsevier-North Holland Publishing, 1980.

Vollmann, Thomas E.; William L. Berry; and D. Clay Whybark. *Manufacturing Planning and Control Systems.* Homewood, Ill.: Richard D. Irwin, 1984.